Capital Cities at War
A Cultural History

Second volume of a two-volume pioneering comparative history of the capital cities of Britain, France, and Germany during the Great War. Leading historians explore these wartime cities, from the railway stations where newcomers took on new identities to the streets they surveyed and the pubs, cafes, and theatres they frequented, and examine notions of identity, the sites and the rituals of city life, and wartime civic and popular culture. The volume offers the first comparative cultural history of London, Paris, and Berlin and reveals the great affinities and similarities between cities on both sides of the line. It shows the transnational character of metropolitan life and the different cultural resources which the men and women of these cities drew upon during 1,500 days of war. The practices of metropolitan life go well beyond national histories and this volume suggests the outlines of a fully European history of the Great War.

JAY WINTER is Charles J. Stille Professor of History at Yale University. He is a specialist on the First World War and its impact on the twentieth century. His numerous publications include *1914–1918. The Great War and the Shaping of the Twentieth Century* (1998), and, with Antoine Prost, *The Great War in History: Debates and Controversies, 1914 to the Present* (2006).

JEAN-LOUIS ROBERT is Emeritus Professor of History at Université Paris I Panthéon-Sorbonne. He has edited, with Jay Winter, *Capital Cities at War: Paris, London, Berlin 1914–1919* (1997) and, with Antoine Prost and Chris Wrigley, *The Emergence of European Trade Unionism* (2004).

Studies in the Social and Cultural History of Modern Warfare

General Editor

Jay Winter, *Yale University*

Advisory Editors

Omer Bartov, *Brown University*
Carol Gluck, *Columbia University*
David M. Kennedy, *Stanford University*
Paul Kennedy, *Yale University*
Antoine Prost, *Université de Paris-Sorbonne*
Emmanuel Sivan, *Hebrew University of Jerusalem*
Robert Wohl, *University of California, Los Angeles*

In recent years the field of modern history has been enriched by the exploration of two parallel histories. These are the social and cultural history of armed conflict, and the impact of military events on social and cultural history.

Studies in the Social and Cultural History of Modern Warfare presents the fruits of this growing area of research, reflecting both the colonization of military history by cultural historians and the reciprocal interest of military historians in social and cultural history, to the benefit of both. The series offers the latest scholarship in European and non-European events from the 1850s to the present day.

For a list of titles in the series, please see end of book.

Capital Cities at War

Paris, London, Berlin 1914–1919

Volume 2

A Cultural History

Edited by

Jay Winter
and
Jean-Louis Robert

CAMBRIDGE
UNIVERSITY PRESS

CAMBRIDGE UNIVERSITY PRESS
Cambridge, New York, Melbourne, Madrid, Cape Town, Singapore, São Paulo

Cambridge University Press
The Edinburgh Building, Cambridge CB2 8RU, UK

Published in the United States of America by Cambridge University Press,
New York

www.cambridge.org
Information on this title: www.cambridge.org/9780521870436

First published 2007

Printed in the United Kingdom at the University Press, Cambridge

A catalogue record for this publication is available from the British Library

ISBN 978-0-521-87043-6 hardback

Contents

Figures

Acknowledgements

This, the second volume of our study of capital cities in wartime, took eight years to complete. There are many people and institutions to which we owe thanks for encouragement, assistance, and support in a task that seemed, like Tennyson's brook, to be in danger of running on forever.

Among those who provided assistance, we must first thank the Centre nationale de la recherche scientifique in Paris, which supported the project by enabling us to conduct collective meetings in the congenial environment of the Centre d'histoire sociale du vingtième siècle in Paris, at a time when it was still known as the Centre d'histoire des mouvements ouvriers et du syndicalisme. The name changed but the hospitality did not. The Master and Fellows of Pembroke College, Cambridge, graciously welcomed us to my old college, the tranquillity of which contrasted so sharply with the subject of this book. Hew Strachan of All Souls College, Oxford and Pierre Purseigle, through the Maison Française in Oxford, enabled us to meet in Oxford. The late Wolfgang Mommsen kindly brought our working group together at the Wissenschaftskolleg in Berlin. Yale University's Center for International and Area Studies, and Gus Ranis in particular, as well as Yale's Provost's Office, were generous in support, in particular in providing a subvention for the help provided by Helen McPhail in turning French chapters into English. It was always a pleasure working with her as a fellow scholar and explorer of the mysteries of French historical writing.

Finally I would like to thank Jean Field, the finest copy editor an author or editor could wish for. What she did not catch and correct was not worth catching. To be sure, any errors that remain are the responsibility of the collective.

JAY WINTER
Florence
May 2006

Foreword: a note on authorship

In the first volume of this project, we described the method we have adopted for collective work. It may be helpful to review these remarks here. Each chapter in both volumes is the product of work of three kinds:
1. research in the three capital cities;
2. the initial writing of drafts dealing with each topic in all three cities. These drafts were discussed and revised in light of a series of meetings held by the collective; and
3. the writing of a synthesis of each chapter by one or two people we term 'convenors'.

The convenors' names are listed in bold type below. Names not in bold type are those of people who wrote parts of chapters subsequently synthesized by the convenors. Thus each chapter is the product of collective labour. In addition, the first reference to each chapter acknowledges the work of other members of the working group in individual parts of the book. All of us did research for parts of this study not acknowledged on the title page of this book. That is built into collective historical writing. The authorial voice is that of the group, rather than of any one individual. We take collective responsibility for the interpretations offered and for any errors that may remain.

Jay Winter
Yale University
May 2006

A list of convenors (bold type) and co-authors of individual chapters

1. **Introduction: The practices of metropolitan life in wartime Jay Winter, Yale University**
2. **Railway stations: gateways and termini Adrian Gregory, Pembroke College, Oxford**
   Emmanuelle Cronier, University of Paris – I
   Pierre Purseigle, University of Toulouse
   Jeffrey Verhey, Humboldt University
3. **The street Emmanuelle Cronier, University of Paris – I**
   Belinda Davis, Rutgers University
   Jan Rüger, Birkbeck College, London
   Armin Triebel, Potsdam University
4. **Entertainments Jan Rüger, Birkbeck College, University of London**
   Martin Baumeister, University of Munich
   Emmanuelle Cronier, University of Paris – I
5. **Exhibitions Stefan Goebel, University of Kent, Canterbury and Institute of Historical Research, London**
   Kevin Repp, Yale University
   Jay Winter, Yale University
6. **Schools Stefan Goebel, University of Kent, Canterbury and Institute of Historical Research, London**
   Dina Copelman, George Mason University
   Eberhard Demm, University of Lyon III (emeritus) / Technical University of Koszalin, Poland
   Elise Julien, University of Paris – I / Free University of Berlin
7. **Universities Elizabeth Fordham, Ecole des hautes études en sciences sociales, Paris,**
   Nicolas Beaupré, University Blaise Pascal, Clermont-Ferrand
   Eberhard Demm, University of Lyon III (emeritus) / Technical University of Koszalin, Poland
8. **Public space, political space Jon Lawrence, Emmanuel College, Cambridge**
   Elizabeth Fordham, Ecole des hautes études en sciences sociales, Paris
   Adrian Gregory, Pembroke College, Oxford

Jon Lawrence, Emmanuel College, Cambridge
Danielle Tartakowsky, University of Paris – VII
Jeffrey Verhey, Humboldt University

9. **The home and family life**
   Catherine Rollet, University of Versailles–
   Saint-Quentin-en-Yvelines
   Emmanuelle Cronier, University of Paris – I
   Eberhard Demm, University of Lyon III (emeritus) / Technical
   University of Koszalin, Poland
   Adrian Gregory, Pembroke College, Oxford

10. **Hospitals**
    Jay Winter, Yale University
    Sophie Delaporte, University of Picardie
    Peter Leese, Jagiellonian University, Cracow
    Paul Lerner, University of Southern California
    Jeffrey Reznick, National Museum of Health and Medicine,
    Armed Forces Institute of Pathology, Washington, D.C.

11. **Religious sites and practices**
    Adrian Gregory, Pembroke College, Oxford
    Annette Becker, University of Paris – X
    John Moses, University of New South Wales, Armidale
    Patrick Porter, King's College London
    Jeffrey Verhey, Humboldt University

12. **Cemeteries**
    Carine Trevisan, University of Paris – VII
    Elise Julien, University of Paris – I / Free University
    of Berlin
    Jay Winter, Yale University

13. **Conclusion**
    Jean-Louis Robert, University of Paris – I
    Jay Winter, Yale University

1   The practices of metropolitan life in wartime

Jay Winter

When we survey the practices of metropolitan life in wartime, we confront an overwhelmingly complex story. In volume I of this study, we interpreted the evidence we compiled on the social and economic history of the war by using the theories of Amartya Sen on entitlements, capabilities, and functionings.[1] In this, our second volume devoted to the cultural history of the war, we adopt a more eclectic approach.

No one interpretive framework can possibly accommodate the richness of cultural expression and activity in Paris, London, and Berlin in the war years 1914 to 1919. Instead, we explore a series of different approaches, some more useful than others in particular chapters. It may be helpful to survey these interpretive approaches, and then to point to their particular utility in the construction of this book.

War, metropolitan life, and identities in wartime

The first interpretive tool we employ here is the notion of identity. This concept has a huge literature surrounding it, drawn from a number of different disciplines, encompassing identity crises, identity politics, gendered identities, regional identities, ethnic identities, and national identities, among other categories.[2] We have drawn on this literature in a restricted sense, exploring notions of 'identity' in three ways.

The first is the sense of identity as the apparel of individuality. Here identities are constructed; they are self-fashioned, and once fashioned,

---

[1] Amartya Sen, *Poverty and famines: an essay on entitlement and deprivation* (Oxford, 1981); Sen, *Development as freedom* (New York, 1999).

[2] Erik H. Erikson, *Young man Luther: a study in psychoanalysis and history* (New York, 1962); Erikson, *Identity and the life cycle* (New York, 1980); Stephen Greenblatt, *Renaissance self-fashioning: from More to Shakespeare* (Chicago, 1980); Natalie Zemon Davis, *The return of Martin Guerre* (Cambridge, Mass., 1983); Gábor Gyáni, *Identity and the urban experience: fin-de-siècle Budapest*, trans. Thomas J. DeKornfeld (New York, 2004); Odo Marquard and Karlheinz Stierle (eds.), *Identität* (Munich, 1996, 2 vols.).

they can be tailored and retailored to suit different purposes.[3] For instance, the figure of Charlie Chaplin was iconic during the war. He was a symbol, to be sure, but he was also a very individual figure, someone who did things no one else could do with his body, his gestures, his face. Songs celebrated him; the cinema popularized him as a Londoner, a Cockney, a veteran of the London stage. Chaplin's identity on stage or screen was unique. To be sure, individual identity is both personal and collective. As Halbwachs put it, we are never the first people who know who we are. Others tell us. But what we do with that knowledge is a matter of temperament and opportunity.

The same can be said of the millions of British men who put on a uniform voluntarily in 1914 and 1915. When they did so, they took on a new identity, that of a soldier, but they did not do so alone. There were as many reasons for volunteering as there were volunteers, but many joined up in groups, with their 'pals' from work, from school, from football teams, and the like.[4] Their identities were both individually fashioned, a matter of choice, and a matter of group loyalty.

There is no need to separate individual and social identities. What is important is that a war of massive mechanical destruction made individuality even more precious than ever before. That is why letter-writing and photograph-taking were so important; they reminded soldiers who they had been before and who (God willing) they would be after the war. When a soldier was discharged, he left his wartime uniform and gear behind, and became a civilian again. Some were not so fortunate; they never escaped from their wartime identity.[5] They were the unlucky ones. The majority found a way back home again back to their civilian identities.

The second sense of the term we use in this study is more strictly collective. It is national and about belonging to one side in a conflict. An identity in wartime is a passport to inclusion in one warring side, defined in large part by its exclusion of the 'other', a term reserved (though never exclusively) for the enemy. When the Academy of Medicine in Paris erased from its ledgers those of its members who were German, they were defining their own identity by negative reference.

Identities described opposites on the home front too. Here we touch on the critical separation of the identity of the soldiers from that of the people whose lives and homes they joined up to defend. In this sense, identities were braided together too; once again they entail pairs or opposites informing the moral economy of metropolitan life in wartime. Most of

---

[3] Greenblatt, *Renaissance self-fashioning*.
[4] Jay Winter, *The Great War and the British people* (London, 2002), ch. 2.
[5] Eric Leed, *No man's land. Combat and identity in the First World War* (Cambridge, 1979).

the time these two collectives – soldiers and civilians – eyed each other with abiding respect, solidarity, and affection, but at other times, with uneasiness and anxiety. This distinction informed the moral code of austerity and sobriety through which the shirker, the black marketeer, and the profiteer became the internal enemy, enjoying the spoils of war while soldiers faced unimaginable hardship.

A third way in which we use the term 'identity' lies between the individual and the national. It is local in character. Metropolitan identities rested on a sense of place. What did it mean to say that one was a Londoner or a Berliner in wartime? What characteristics did the class of people share who claimed to be Parisian? To be sure, some simply meant by claiming to be Londoners that that city was their place of birth or residence. But there was another dimension to this metropolitan identity, one related to a sense of a shared landscape and a shared set of cultural references located in that particular place. Berliners were people strolling around the Tiergarten, just as Londoners were those meandering through Regent's Park. Other notions of metropolitan identity arose out of proximity or access to public sites, like Piccadilly Circus, Potsdamer Platz, or Place de la Concorde. And within these cities, inhabitants identified themselves with those living in smaller *quartiers*, such as Cockneys in east London or Parisian workers in Belleville.

We all live with multiple identities, rarely troubling over the contradictions between them. But in wartime, identities became both clearer and more significant than ever before. Just consider the distinction between combatants and non-combatants; not wearing a uniform was supposed to confer a privilege – immunity from fire – when an invading army crossed a populated region. It did not always do so, but the norms were clear.

In wartime, identities on all levels – that of the individual, the *quartier*, the city, the nation – always overlapped. Some forms became essentialized in wartime. That is, the inherent character of one group of people was read into their behaviour. Stereotypes proliferated, and hatreds drew on them with gusto. For these reasons, everyone needed a cultural passport in wartime. Without it, without visible or audible signs of commonality with the neighbours on your side, ordinary people risked being identified as the enemy.

In wartime, individuals changed the clothes of their lives; they put on uniforms; they accepted, however reluctantly, the division between 'us' and 'them', and knew how to distinguish between the two; and they expressed their solidarities in terms of their attachment to particular places and sites. The outbreak of war brought into focus or clarified individual, national, urban, and local identities in these three capital cities. How this happened is one of the themes of this book.

In this study, we take identities to be performative. They are expressed and reiterated in public at particular sites and times. Once again, we historians have benefited from the work of our colleagues in neighbouring disciplines who have highlighted the significance of performativity in speech acts, in gendered dress and behaviour, and in ritual life.[6] Our working definition of the term 'identity' is, therefore, active, dynamic, and unstable. Identities emerge and are reaffirmed through the cultural performance of social bonds. Those bonds can be intimate, confined to the family or a few friends. Or they can be broader than that.

During the Great War the cultural performance of the social bonds of nationhood, of solidarity and determination, as well as of protest and opposition, were expressed time and again in Paris, London, and Berlin. By undertaking a scholarly perambulation through these three cities, we see not only the sites that everyone in the cities recognized as iconic or symbolic – Unter den Linden, Piccadilly, the Champs Elysées – but we also consider the reconfiguration of these sites and others much less prominent as locations where the social bonds of citizenship and solidarity were performed.

One example is the railway station. Ports of entry to the city, sites of commerce and commuting for generations, these vast buildings became places where identities were exchanged: from civilian to soldier, and with luck, back again from soldier to civilian. Street life expressed solidarities too, as millions of soldiers from all parts of the world strode through the boulevards and alleys of these towns. Clubs, pubs, bars, theatres, and cabarets – vital elements in metropolitan life – were also places where solidarities were formed and displayed, for cash, to be sure. In London's theatre district, civilians played soldiers on stage, in front of audiences made up largely of soldiers playing civilians while on leave. In metropolitan hospitals, soldiers under treatment who were ambulatory and itching to wander around the streets of London were required to wear blue uniforms. This dress told everyone they saw or met who they were: they were soldiers recuperating from war wounds, rather than shirkers, wriggling out of their military responsibilities.

---

[6] Judith Butler, *Excitable speech: a politics of the performative* (London, 1997); Butler, 'Giving an account of oneself', *Diacritics*, vol. 31, no. 4 (Winter, 2001), pp. 22–40; Jonathan D. Culler, 'Philosophy and literature: the fortunes of the performative', *Poetics Today*, vol. 21, no. 3 (Autumn, 2000), pp. 503–19; Judith Butler, Stanley Aronowitz, Ernesto Laclau, Joan Scott, Chantal Mouffe, and Cornel West, 'The identity in question', *October*, vol. 61 (Summer, 1992), pp. 108–20.

Other identities were on display in the great exhibition halls of these cities, which highlighted the nature of civilization on one side or the other. The same effort to express the cultural achievements of the nation at war is evident in schools, where the next generation of recruits was educated and instructed in their civic and national duties. Hospitals were an essential part of the metropolitan landscape; they were places where identities were confirmed or reaffirmed: able-bodied or disabled; sane or insane. They were sites of hope and anxiety in equal part. So were churches.

In this book, we see what were the practices of metropolitan life by moving through these cities. The structure of this book follows a series of trajectories which were well known and well established long before the outbreak of war in 1914. But considering each of these sites shows how the exigencies of war provided a framework for their re-appropriation and their reconfiguration as places where the social bonds of wartime were performed in public.

As in every other facet of the history of the war, including the economic and social themes examined in volume I, the boundaries between the private and public realms were weakened or at times erased in wartime. That is why we have included a chapter on the *foyer*, the household, and the ways in which it became a centre of activity linking those at home and those at the front.

Were these capital cities simply larger versions of every small town and village in these three combatant countries? In a way, the answer is yes, since mobilization happened everywhere, and no town was spared the news that someone had died at the front. Identities were performed in village squares and churches as vividly as in the streets of the great cities. But in another sense, these metropolitan centres were both unique and representative. Their status as the political centres of the three major warring nations separated them from other cities and towns. Here is where the President of the French Republic resided, though like everyone else in positions of power, he left the city between September and December 1914 when Paris risked encirclement. Here is where the British Parliament met throughout the war, as did the Reichstag. Here is where the great ministries of state had their offices, and where the general staffs met the politicians to coordinate their war plans.

There were other ways in which Paris, London, and Berlin were unique. Without them, this industrialized war simply could not have been waged. They were sites of transit on a scale which dwarfed virtually all provincial cities. Without Paris, the French army simply could not have moved east or north depending on where the German threat was heaviest at the time. Without London, the Allied armies would have been stripped of all their essential supplies. Berlin was different. It was both the youngest and the most dynamic of the three, having quadrupled in population between 1870 and 1914. But its location at the core of the German empire put it at a greater distance from the Western front, where the war was won and lost. Paris and London were closer to the fighting, and absolutely critical centres of supply and communication. But Berlin mattered too. When potatoes sent to Berlin for the home population did not reach their destination, but were somehow pilfered en route and sold at a vast premium, a social crisis emerged. To be sure, the German army was defeated in the field in the summer of 1918, but by then thousands of men in uniform knew that their families living in the capital city were going hungry. Why carry on when victory was out of sight and further suffering at the front and at home appeared to be absolutely pointless? What happened in Berlin, just as much as in Paris and London, mattered crucially to the men at the front.

Metropolitan space, place, and site

Here, as throughout this study, the boundaries between economic and social history, on the one hand, and cultural history, on the other, crumble. In this volume the sites we choose to investigate are very material ones. They are stable physically, and take a lot of cash to maintain, but they are unstable culturally. As Michel de Certeau put it, 'spatial practices in fact secretly structure the determining conditions of social life'.[7] He went on further to define cities spatially, and we follow his lead in viewing metropolitan life as 'a way of conceiving and constructing space on the basis of a finite number of stable, isolatable, and interconnected properties'.[8] It is the transformation of what de Certeau terms 'the operations, the urban practices' surrounding particular urban sites which constitutes one of the central themes of this book.

De Certeau famously began a disquisition on what constitutes a city by viewing it from the 110th floor of the World Trade Centre in Manhattan. But this panoptical view is not the one he believed could tease out the secrets of city life. To this end, he urged us to concentrate on walking, on wandering, on moving through the city in the ways city-dwellers do. The story of urban practices, he insisted,

begins on ground level, with footsteps. They are myriad, but do not compose a series. They cannot be counted because each unit has a qualitative character: a

---

[7] Michel de Certeau, *The practice of everyday life*, trans. by Steven F. Rendall (Berkeley, 1984), p. 96.
[8] Ibid., p. 94.

style of tactile apprehension and kinesthetic appropriation. Their swarming mass is an innumerable collection of singularities. Their intertwined paths give their shape to spaces. They weave places together. In that respect, pedestrian movements form one of those 'real systems whose existence in fact makes up the city'. They are not localized; it is rather they that spatialize.[9]

We adopt de Certeau's vision in this book, and invite the reader to join us in a perambulation through these three cities. The map that we describe is one that city-dwellers drew for us by describing different trajectories in the course of their daily lives. 'Walking', de Certeau observed, 'is to the urban system what the speech act is to language or to the statement uttered.' To walk through a city is to appropriate it; moving through the metropolis at ground level 'is a spatial acting out of the place; and it implies *relations* among differentiated positions',[10] horizontally as between *quartiers* adjacent to each other, and vertically as between social and political classes. In effect, city-dwellers 'spoke' the city by traversing it. And so do we.

First we start at the railway stations; then move on to the city streets themselves, seeking out points of entertainment, and evading those charged with enforcing public order. We enter the music halls and pubs, and then turn to more elevated, more refined environments – the exhibition halls, the great museums, the schools and universities. Inevitably we come to the great squares, the public places in which and on which so much history had been written, and watch the battle between those groups which wanted to seize them to make urban political statements and the police who preferred silence to uncontrolled speech and demonstrations.

These destinations were prominent and essential metropolitan sites, and urban trajectories inevitably crossed them. But there were many other trajectories which both paralleled and diverged from them. These embraced the sites and rites of passage of individual and family life. We enter the *foyers*, the hospitals, and churches, which were where families lived, sought help, worshipped, and died. And finally we arrive at metropolitan cemeteries, the end of the line. In this network of urban sites, we depart from de Certeau, who referred to them as administrative units for the broken down, the 'waste products' of metropolitan life.[11] We concentrate on how the appropriation of these spaces by city-dwellers themselves transformed their functional operations into culturally significant ones.

Each of these sites was radically transformed by the war. In Paris and London the threat of aerial or artillery bombardment loomed large. The

---

[9] Ibid., p. 97.   [10] Ibid., pp. 97–8.   [11] Ibid., p. 94.

cities were darker places than they had been for a century; enemies were watching from the air. The fact that death could and did come from above set a new and still vivid precedent for the century of total war which followed. This new sense of danger in metropolitan life makes it difficult to adopt an entirely street-level perspective in this study. Those who traversed these cities certainly looked up, and hoped that what they saw would not kill them. Such a sense of death and danger must be added to our understanding of metropolitan cities at war.

What is most striking, and most remarkable, is the stoicism of many city-dwellers, the way they bore their anxieties over the fate of loved ones in uniform, and accepted these new and alarming facts of urban life. Metropolitan populations continued to 'write' and to 'speak' their cities through their mundane cultural practices, but in wartime they did so in a multitude of ways, some pointing towards a familiar past, others towards an uncharted future.

In the following chapters, we explore many forms of cultural adaptation to war through what we term sites of cultural expression. They are in no way exhaustive; other sites could have been chosen. In each of them, representations were fashioned, adapted, and consumed. Cultural artefacts – letters, diaries, parcels, posters, plays, sculptures, street shrines, banners, wreaths, and so on – were produced and displayed or sold or sent on their way. An analysis of each of these sites in the three capital cities can teach us much about the way the structural effects of the conflict, explored in volume I of this project, were configured, imagined, and endured in wartime and after.

Comparisons

In volume I, the agenda of comparative history was explored in straightforward ways. Thus, wherever possible, similar statistical time series were constructed or reproduced enabling us to explore variations in military mobilization, work, wages, consumption, and public health in these three cities. In the field of cultural history, the issue of comparison is more difficult and more complex, and thus we offer two kinds of comparison in this volume. The first is fully comparative. It treats the three cities as equals, enabling us to see how, in various sites in all three cities, different representations emerged.

The second approach may be termed 'relational' in that in certain chapters we focus primarily on one metropolitan centre, highlighting its special cultural forms and expressions by reference to the other two cases. The choice of this second option – the relational mode of comparison – is dictated by the sources: there are areas where the cases are so different, and the archival traces so uneven, that it is wise to use what we might term a 'geometrical approach', in placing one case at the centre, and using evidence of the other two cities to make a particular point about that particular case. Thus the politics of public space was a deeply important matter in London; in Paris and Berlin, the army hierarchy stood in the way of such debates. Similarly, the river dominated parts of the urban landscape in Paris and London; not so in Berlin. The chapters in this book adopt a pragmatic approach here, and explore comparison in whatever way helps to make sense of the particular cultural practices under review.

At the same time, we are well aware of the limits of all comparisons in this field. One reason for diffidence is linguistic. The nuances of particular historical notation make comparison both essential (to enable us to grasp particularity) and maddeningly difficult. Think of the difficulty of translating the phrase 'shell shock', or in rendering the shades of meaning in the English phrase 'war memorial' into other European languages. 'Shell shock' is not 'choc traumatique', and war memorials are not 'monuments aux morts'.[12] Poetry is fundamentally untranslatable, which is one reason why the works of Wilfred Owen, for example, iconic in Britain, were not translated into French for eighty years. The receptors are different; what James Joll called the 'unspoken assumptions' are different.[13]

In volume I, we highlighted both affinities and clear differences among the three cities' wartime histories. Here, we also use comparison to show similarities as well as to disclose the ineluctable, irreducible differences and particularities of national and urban cultures. One function of comparative history, therefore, is to help frame in a more informed way questions of particular national experience. From this angle, comparative history is a partner – perhaps an essential partner – of national history, a way of deepening our understanding of individual cases, and not a different or alternative field of study at all.

One of the attractions of metropolitan history is the way it enables us to escape from the mistaken view that a nation's cultural history is homogenous. At times, comparisons disclose commonalities among these cities. Popular theatres, hospitals, and cemeteries, for instance, were familiar and integral parts of the urban landscape. In each case, people of very different social origins came together to these places for roughly similar reasons. But in other cases, particularities, even singularities, in the way these cities were organized, must be recognized. Comparisons of different kinds tell us what these differences were, and help us see even

---

[12] Special issue, *Journal of contemporary history* (January 2000).
[13] *1914: the unspoken assumptions; an inaugural lecture 25 April 1968* (London, 1968).

during the dark years of the Great War what made these cities unique and vibrant spaces to those who lived in them.

Metropolitan nostalgia and metropolitan iconoclasm

At this juncture, it is apparent that we must vary the conceptual tools we use in order to understand the complexity of metropolitan life in this period. To privilege the subject of identities and sites is important, but it should not be done to the exclusion of other themes and other cultural practices. To this end, we have employed a binary distinction between 'nostalgia' and 'iconoclasm' as poles between which the cultural life of these three cities unfolded.

This distinction enables us to see more clearly a theme running through the cultural history of the Great War which has a distinctively metropolitan facet. That theme is the extent to which the first fully industrialized war in history precipitated a deluge of traditional forms of language, perception, and signifying practices. In Paris, London, and Berlin, as elsewhere, the terms and images used to shape these discursive forms arose out of and shaped a partly mythical construction of a pre-war metropolitan world of pub, café, music hall, and theatre. These sites of sociability and entertainment presented a highly sentimentalized set of images and sounds, which flourished during a war which introduced very un-sentimental forms of destruction and bloodshed. Other sites of cultural work similarly partook of this cultural move. The *foyer* was mythologized, and gender roles deepened, at a time when households and the sexual division of labour were being turned upside down. The nostalgic turn in metropolitan cultural life is one of the key subjects of this book.

At times parallel to it, at other times intersecting it, was a very different cultural vector. What might be termed cultural iconoclasm was a perennial phenomenon in these three cities, and though the war set limits on what could be thought or at least what could be said or written, there remained pockets of resistance which flourished, particularly in the latter part of the conflict and in its aftermath. Metropolitan cultural life was in one sense the product of these two vectors: one moving back in time, another moving ahead. Together they met in particular places on particular streets and at particular times in these three capital cities.

Metropolitan nostalgia

One way of framing these comparisons is in terms of a certain kind of cultural activity loosely gathered under the heading of 'metropolitan nostalgia'. First it may be helpful to consider what the term 'nostalgia' means, and then turn to the question as to how it can help shape a study of comparative metropolitan life in Paris, London, and Berlin during and after the Great War.[14]

Nostalgia, writes Svetlana Boym, is a term originating in warfare. It was coined by physicians in the seventeenth century to capture the sadness of Swiss mercenaries remote from their Alpine pastures and homes. At times, it is pathological; at other times, it is a style of thought, a way of remembering. It is 'a yearning for a different time – the time of our childhood, the slower rhythms of our dreams'.[15] It is not the same as melancholia, which is an individual affliction, but dwells rather on 'the relationship between individual biography and the biography of groups or nations, between personal and collective memory'.[16] Wartime is an extended period when nostalgia flourishes and leaves its unmistakable marks on many facets of cultural life.

Nostalgia takes many forms, and most of them reside outside the centralizing tendencies of the modern nation state, which did not yet exist when the term came into use in the 1680s. To be sure, though, in the nineteenth and twentieth centuries political groups and national leaders turned to nostalgia time and again as a powerful mobilizing force. It is full of affect and easily can be sentimentalized and marketed in visual or physical forms. No national movement is without its kitsch, its badges and plastic flags, its statues and symbols, and in wartime these objects appeared by the thousand. Their production was a form of patriotic work, and such representations were never independent of the needs of ruling elites, who liked to use the term 'tradition' to signify their place in the long vista of the national or imperial narrative. From the late nineteenth century, to look back on the past nostalgically was for them to justify their power and their policies.[17]

I have spoken of wartime producing an outpouring of 'traditional' modes of expression. We can go beyond the general term 'tradition' – itself fraught with difficulties,[18] by discussing the different ways in which contemporaries expressed their longing for a past slipping through their

---

[14] Malcolm Shaw and Christopher Chase, 'The dimensions of nostalgia' and David Lowenthal, 'Nostalgia tells it like it wasn't', in Shaw and Chase (eds.), *The imagined past: history and nostalgia* (Manchester, 1989), pp. 1–17, and 18–32; Susan Stewart, *On longing* (Baltimore, 1985); Vladimir Yankelévitch, *L'irréversible et la nostalgie* (Paris, 1974); George Stauth and Brian Turner, 'The moral sociology of nostalgia', in Stauth and Turner (eds.), *Nietzsche's dance* (Oxford, 1988), pp. 10–22.

[15] Svetlana Boym, *The future of nostalgia* (New York, 2001), p. xv.

[16] Boym, *Nostalgia*, p. xvi.

[17] Eric Hobsbawm and Terence Ranger (eds.), *The invention of tradition* (Cambridge, 1980).

[18] Edward Shils, *Tradition* (Chicago, 1981).

fingers, a past for which they felt increasingly nostalgic. Nostalgia is not simply a tool elites used to manipulate the masses. The space in which nostalgia flourished was (and still is) much wider than that. The sentiments it encodes are too ambiguous and complex to be so easily corralled into the way political leaders manufactured consent. We need to go beyond the purely functional to understand the multiform character of nostalgia.

Alongside the 'restorative nostalgia' of political leaders who want to return to a pre-lapsarian past, Boym posits another kind of nostalgia, which she terms 'reflective nostalgia'. It is a critical state of mind, remote from particular political or nationalist projects, in which groups of individuals express their longing for 'shared everyday frameworks of collective or cultural memory', stories they tell each other about the 'potential space' they once inhabited in their daily lives.[19] Why 'potential'? Because this kind of nostalgia has an element of playfulness in it, a kind of shared reverie with people in their neighbourhoods, who traversed the same streets they inhabited in their earlier lives. And because 'reflective nostalgia' is marked by a clear understanding that Heraclitus was right – we cannot enter the same stream twice. Reflective nostalgia admits to the loss of collective memories, to 'the impossibility of homecoming',[20] and abjures any faith in the material reconstruction of a lost world. Such nostalgia expresses liminality – being stranded on an island remote from the past but with an uncertain future on the other shore as well.

Boym borrows from the work of Reinhard Koselleck to deepen our understanding of how nostalgia operates.[21] When what Koselleck termed our 'horizon of expectations' – how in the present we imagine the future – is disturbed, because of an upheaval like war, then the link between the present and the past – which he terms the 'space of experience' – is weakened or severed. If, metaphorically or physically, we cannot go home again, then the line of a lifetime becomes discontinuous, fractured, uncertain. Nostalgia expresses that troubling uncertainty.

There is as well a palpable difference in style between those who adopt the two forms of nostalgia described by Boym. Restorative nostalgics are solemn and hortatory; reflective nostalgics are ironic and have a wistful smile on their faces, aware of the absurdity or impossibility of their dreams. The first build or try to build real cathedrals on the ground; the second build imaginary cathedrals in the air, cathedrals which may never have existed in the first place.

There is much to be gained in a cultural history of capital cities of war by drawing on this critical distinction between 'restorative nostalgia' with

---

[19] Boym, *Nostalgia*, pp. 52–3.   [20] Ibid., p. xvii.   [21] Ibid., pp. 9–10.

its grandiose projects of national reconstruction and 'reflective nostalgia' with its sense of smaller-scale affinities and the impossibilities of a full return to an imagined past. Urban history in wartime has marks of both kinds of nostalgia in abundance, and neither fully eclipsed the other. Together they help us to understand how contemporaries configured 'tradition' – understood as the past in the present – and how they feared and framed the disappearance during and after the war of what they took to be traditional ways of life.

There is another aspect of these two facets of nostalgia of particular relevance to urban history in wartime. What both forms of nostalgia share is a sense of mourning for a past either partially or totally out of reach. Restorative nostalgia is closer to what Freud called 'melancholy' – a fixation on a past which we cannot let go. 'Reflective nostalgia', Boym notes, 'is a form of deep mourning that performs a labor of grief both through pondering pain and through play that points to the future.'[22] Restorative nostalgia does not let go of the past, but posits its resurrection; reflective nostalgia dwells more on what cannot be regained, and perhaps what is best laid to rest.

In wartime cities, street shrines alerted those who passed to the sadness which descended on families throughout the war; the hospitals and garrisons and cemeteries were there too, and each brought city-dwellers back abruptly to the cruelties of war. Here was a world in which total restoration was not going to happen. '[T]he stronger the loss', writes Boym, 'the more it is overcompensated with commemorations, the starker the distance from the past, ... the more it is prone to idealization.'[23] The history of metropolitan cultural life, in music hall, in theatre, in song, is marked by this tendency towards constructing such an idealized past.

Many aspects of urban cultural life bear the marks of the effort to dream about and conjure up the world before the deluge. What is striking is the way such dreams were inscribed on the landscape of these three capital cities. This is hardly surprising. Nostalgia is triggered by sites, especially but not only by urban ones.[24] One reason that Paris, London, and Berlin are fertile fields for nostalgia is that they are palimpsests of the richest sort. Narratives about the past jostle with each other in bricks and mortar, on the spires of churches, or the façades of public buildings, or in the sweep of public spaces and parks.

A 'Topos', Boym reminds us, 'refers both to a place in discourse and a place in the world.' Stories about the past form the 'architecture of our

---

[22] Ibid., p. 55.   [23] Ibid., p. 17.
[24] M. Christine Boyer, *The city of collective memory: its historical imagery and architectural entertainments* (Cambridge, Mass., 1994).

memory', stimulated and shared by those who see the same places we do, and understand how powerfully emotive they are as '*contexts* for remembrances'. Many such 'contexts' were built to evoke memories, especially in imperial settings, but others are what Alois Reigl calls 'unintentional memorials', pieces of the past, ruins that suggest a vanished world. 'The memorable', Michel de Certeau observed, 'is that which can be dreamed about a [specific] place.'[25]

One way of sensing the way nostalgia was a central facet of metropolitan life is to trace the pathways used by contemporaries to traverse them. As we have noted, walking is a way of retrospectively mapping a city, of reiterating itineraries of a mundane kind which evoke the rhythms and colours of past life. That is one reason why we include 'the street' in our perambulation of these cities in wartime. For these arteries of daily life were (and are still) powerful triggers of remembrance.

In light of this discussion, it may become apparent why a central issue in this volume is the ambiguous relationship between facets of material and military realities which made these cities distinctively 'modern' and the impulses to return nostalgically to an imagined past of urban sociability, the defence of which was one of the reasons why the war was fought in the first place. Material and human mobilization of dizzying force and rapidity kindled the fires of nostalgia for an earlier, a simpler, a more predictable, way of life. Herein lies a deep irony. The more the war modified urban life, the greater the urge to return imaginatively to its pre-war contours through a multitude of cultural forms. The more modern the war, the more nostalgic the re-presentation of what the war was supposed to preserve, but what instead it transformed forever.

This contradictory rhetoric of remembrance was captured in literary form time and again in the inter-war years and after. 'Never such innocence again', Philip Larkin wrote in 1964, in the quintessential pre-lapsarian register of reflective nostalgia. Similarly inclined was the American writer F. Scott Fitzgerald. *Tender is the night* was published in 1934, two years after Lutyens's great arch at Thiepval was inaugurated. It is there, to the battlefields of the Somme that Fitzgerald brings his two central figures, Dick Diver and his lover Rosemary Hoyt. Dick looks out over the landscape, and tells Rosemary:

See that little stream – we could walk to it in two minutes. It took the British a month to walk to it – a whole empire walking very slowly, dying in front and pushing forward behind. And another empire walked very slowly backward a few inches a day, leaving the dead like a million bloody rugs. No European will ever do

---

[25] Certeau, *Practice*, p. 109. Alois Reigl, 'The modern cult of monuments: its character and its origin', *Oppositions*, 25 (1982), pp. 21–51.

that again in this generation ... This western-front business couldn't be done again, not for a long time. The young men think they could do it, but they couldn't. They could fight the first Marne again but not this. This took religion and years of plenty and tremendous sureties and the exact relation that existed between the classes. The Russians and Italians weren't any good on this front. You had to have a whole-souled sentimental equipment going back farther than you could remember. You had to remember Christmas, and postcards of the Crown Prince and his fiancée, and little cafés in Valence and beer gardens in Unter den Linden and weddings at the mairie, and going to the Derby, and your grandfather's whiskers ... This kind of battle was invented by Lewis Carroll and Jules Verne and whoever wrote *Undine*, and country deacons bowling and mar-raines in Marseilles and girls seduced in the back lanes of Württemberg and Westphalia. Why this was a love battle – there was a century of middle-class love spent here.

'All my beautiful lovely safe world blew itself up here with a great gust of high explosive love', Dick mourned persistently. 'Isn't that true, Rosemary?'[26] One of the challenges of this volume is to see in what ways, in which sites, and to what extent while the war was going on, contemporaries shared these re-presentations of an idealized past and their bitter-sweet elegiac mode of reflection on the necessities and impossibilities of return to the pre-war world.

From nostalgia to iconoclasm

The metropolitan construction of a nostalgic vision tells us much about the ways city-dwellers tried to understand the wartime world in which they lived. Nostalgia was not simply a profitable mainstay of popular culture; it was imbedded in high culture as well, and indeed its ubiquity helps us to see the futility of separating the two. There was a return to order in painting and sculpture, leading to a greater emphasis on the human figure and profile.[27] And experimentation in cinema brought the centrepiece of mass entertainment into the workshops and clubs of the avant-garde.

Both the very old and the very new were on display in these cities on the eve of the war. This is hardly surprising, since part of their appeal was that they were the location of a host of outlets for the production, dissemination, and exchange of cultural products. The press spanned the gamut between mass circulation dailies and ephemeral reviews. Advertising was everywhere. Salons, clubs, and universities provided limitless horizons for those who wanted to hear the latest news in science and the arts. Little

[26] F. Scott Fitzgerald, *Tender is the night: a romance* (New York, 1934), pp. 117–18.
[27] Ken Silver, *Esprit de corps. The art of the Parisian avant-garde and the First World War, 1914–1925* (Princeton, 1989).

theatres and massive picture palaces and music halls offered just about every kind of performance.

When we enter this rich and varied world in wartime, we find conflicting signals and movements. While cultural conservatism was one metropolitan response to war, cultural iconoclasm existed alongside it. One way to configure the cultural history of the war is in terms of the dialectical clash of the two. Paris, London, and Berlin were nodal points of cultural experimentation in the pre-war years. The presence of rebels – painters, writers, sculptors, and assorted troublemakers – in these cities gave them their particular flavour and appeal. These iconoclasts were cosmopolitan. Picasso was hardly French, and it was in an exchange with his Berlin colleagues that the French poet of Polish origin, Guillaume Apollinaire, invented the term 'surrealism'. Artistic movements were emphatically international in the pre-war period.

Initially, the war disrupted this cosmopolitan environment, forcing artists in all combatant countries to reconfigure cultural life in predominantly national (and later in nationalist) terms. This set of pressures leading to the nationalization of cultural life set severe constraints on what could be said and on what could be done in wartime. And yet capital cities remained places where shibboleths were exposed and limits explored or transgressed. Their dreams survived the thought police at work during the war. It took time, but slowly the notion of art as imagination without a passport began to resurface. And when it did, it brought together in Paris, London, or Berlin those small groups of artists and intellectuals who were prepared to defy convention and speak their minds without fear or favour.

Three brief examples will gesture towards a much broader world of cultural iconoclasm in these cities in the period 1914 to 1920. The first is an attempt at wartime propaganda on behalf of the Allied cause that went badly wrong in Paris in 1917. Pablo Picasso joined Jean Cocteau and Erik Satie in the creation of a ballet entitled 'Parade', first performed by Diaghilev and the Ballet Russe at the Théâtre du Champs-Élysées on 18 May 1917. When the curtain rose, the audience of well-to-do Parisians was shocked. Their reaction to seeing dancers wearing massive cubist frames was puzzlement; hearing Erik Satie's music and following Léonide Massine's choreography were even more bewildering. The result was uproar and scandal.[28]

Why did it all go wrong? Because the conservative atmosphere of wartime cultural life pushed the limits of artistic experimentation back

[28] R. H. Axsom, *Parade. Cubism as theatre* (New York, 1979).

at the same time as many artists were intent, as was their wont, to push the limits forward. The story of 'Parade' was framed in the form of a traditional *forain*, or a come-on for customers being invited to enter a fairground show; but the way it was done was so unfamiliar that the audience was literally aghast. Iconoclasm in the interests of promoting Allied solidarity had simply gone too far.

The second instance of the collision between the nationalization of cultural forms and the persistence of experimentation in the arts occurred in London. There an American-born Jew of Polish ancestry, Jacob Epstein, created sculpture of a kind which brought down on his head the outrage of self-appointed spokesmen for 'British' art.[29] When conscripted, Epstein had hoped to become an official war artist, but this idea was vetoed by a more conservative British sculptor, Sir George Frampton. Epstein's origins and his outlook were simply too iconoclastic for officialdom.[30] He continued to serve as a regular soldier, had a nervous breakdown, and was invalided out of the army. He went back to his work in London and continued to produce sculpture that outraged the conventional art world.

The third example of the way the war turned up the heat on metropolitan artists, who responded in kind, occurred in Berlin. There a group of artists and anti-war activists followed earlier developments in Switzerland to craft an art of defiance they called 'Dada'.

Richard Huelsenbeck was one of the high priests of this movement of protest against the whole world of 'reason' underlying the butchery of the Great War. He was a German poet who had failed his physical examination for military service in 1914. A pacifist, he moved to Switzerland, where he joined an international group of bohemians who met at the Cabaret Voltaire in Zurich. Pointing to a dictionary held by a fellow iconoclast, Hugo Ball, Huelsenbeck found the word 'Dada', a children's word connoting a hobby horse. To him, this was a perfect sign of the newness of their art, its primitiveness, its ground-zero location, emerging from the rubble of the world intent on committing collective suicide during the war. To Huelsenbeck, Dada had to be a 'volcanic eruption', burning away the rotten wartime world in its path.[31] Returning to Berlin in 1917, he helped form another Dada cell with like-minded artists and writers; among them were George Grosz, Raoul Hausmann, and John Heartfield. To these people, absolutely nothing was sacred about the old

[29] Elizabeth Barker, 'The primitive within: the question of race in Epstein's career 1917–1929', in Terry Friedman and Evelyn Silber (eds.), *Jacob Epstein. Sculpture and drawings* (London, 1987).

[30] Richard Cork, *Jacob Epstein* (London, 1999), pp. 40ff.

[31] Richard Huelsenbeck, 'Dada lives!', in Robert Motherwell and Jack D. Flam (eds.), *The Dada painters and poets* (Boston, 1981), p. 280.

order. Most public monuments, Huelsenbeck affirmed, should be smashed. Offending convention was their trademark and their delight.

Never shy about causing offence, they organized the first International Dada Fair at the Borchard Gallery in Berlin on 5 June 1920. The walls were decorated by collages by Heartfield and spoofs of classical art. But the *pièce de résistance* was suspended from the ceiling. There visitors who looked up confronted a lifesize mannequin of a German soldier with a hog's head. This creature was dubbed by Heartfield the 'Prussian Archangel'. Around the neck of this floating soldier was a note saying that he had been 'hanged by the revolution'. Charges were brought against Grosz and Heartfield, and they were duly fined for defaming the military.

While much of Berlin Dada was profoundly German in outlook and content, its international spirit was unmistakable. These were artists dedicated to resisting cultural conformity and to defying any construction of art in purely national terms. National cultural frontiers were meaningless to Dada, and in their ferocious and deliberately outrageous behaviour, they embodied a long-standing metropolitan tradition which had been shaken by the war, but not broken by it.

We are dealing here with very small groups, unknown to the vast majority of inhabitants of these three cities. Yet any cultural history which ignored them would miss much about what made Paris, London, and Berlin magnets for those thirsting for experimentation, even while the war was going on.

Part of what attracted them was the sense of the metropolis as theatre. That is, conflicts of a social or political kind were performed in these cities. The war of representations was carried out in public. Galleries were sites of contestations, so was the stage. These collisions of norms and beliefs happened in the open, in the light of day, or at night, in particular urban sites. They disclosed much about the limits of public taste and the irresistible temptation some men and women felt to try at all times to supersede such boundaries. At one and the same time disturbing and exhilarating, the cultural life of capital cities in wartime followed varied trajectories, multiple pressures to conform to a national model, and persistent efforts to defy them.

In sum, it is evident that no one interpretation of the comparative cultural history of these three cities in wartime will suffice. Metropolitan nostalgia and metropolitan iconoclasm lived together in vigorous incompatibility. Some of the following chapters disclose a search for a vanishing world, the defence of which was what the war was about. Some chapters highlight rupture and new ways of thinking about the past in the present – Koselleck's 'sphere of experience' – as well as breaks in the way contemporaries configured the future in the present – the 'horizon of expectations'. The Russian Revolution, the German revolution, the fall of empires and dynasties, the transformation of the character and prominence of labour movements were discontinuities of a kind which made it hard to dwell solely or primarily on the rhetoric of return. In many respects, a sense of new possibilities and a sense of longing for what were configured as older 'certainties' occupied the same space in wartime and post-war cultural life. These opposed cultural vectors came together in a myriad of ways in this period, creating a complex field of force which is central to this, the second, volume of our history of Paris, London, and Berlin in the Great War.

Part I

Cityscapes

2 Railway stations: gateways and termini

Adrian Gregory

> The father reaches down from the window,
> And grips the boy's hand,
> And does not speak at all.
> Will the train never start?
>
> He takes the boy's chin in his hand
> Leaning out through the window
> And lifts the face that is so young, to his,
> They look and look,
> And know they may never look again.
>
> Will the train never start?
> God, make the train start!
>
> Helen Mackay, 'Train', *London, one November* (London, 1915)

The city gates

The railway station was pre-eminently the site where the war and the metropolis met. It was also central to the existence of both. Neither the First World War nor the capital cities of 1914–1918 would have been recognizable or even conceivable without the railway.[1]

The railways shaped the war as they had already shaped the cities. They had transformed London, Paris, and Berlin from 'metropoli' to 'megalopoli'. By 1914 London had reached the point where it was impractical to walk in a day from one urban boundary to another. Paris and Berlin remained more viable for pedestrians, but each had a degree of sprawl. In addition, the railway had linked the urban cores with satellite towns and dormitory communities thus extending the significance of the capitals as places of work and leisure over much larger areas. Railways and subways, assisted by tramways and horse transport, were the key to this

---

[1] This chapter was written by Adrian Gregory. Emmanuelle Cronier provided material for Paris; Pierre Purseigle contributed material on refugees in Paris and London; Jeff Verhey and Stefan Goebel provided material on Berlin.

development. The age of the automobile was barely dawning in 1914. The development of railways turned London in particular into the archetypal commuter city, but all three cities were reshaped in the same way. There was a good deal of cultural commentary in Paris about the new suburbs; more working-class than London's. In all three cases, the old city gates were no longer relevant. The railway stations were the new gateways.

Railways fed the cities, literally and figuratively. They brought in the migrants who swelled the urban masses and played an increasingly important role in allowing their provisioning. London, as a major port city, was a partial exception to both these points, but even so human and consumable resources for the city were brought by rail from other British ports, a situation intensified in wartime. For Paris and Berlin, each with limited port facilities, the significance of railway termini was all the greater.

The great stations were the very symbols of modernity, 'the locomotive was the hearse of the old order of things'. Railway time became national time, extending the control of the capitals over the provinces. The stations were frequently works of art, the cathedrals of the nineteenth century, show-pieces of innovative architectural style.

Stations always mattered, as frontiers and liminal zones, places of transition, arrival, and departure, for shedding social roles and adopting new ones. Wartime multiplied this function in manifold ways. This chapter will explore the urban frontier. Here was the interface with the war itself: mobilization and demobilization, the arrival and departure of refugees, soldiers on leave and the wounded and also the more subtle questions of re-definitions of boundaries, artistic and political, which centred on the stations. As a poem in *Le petit Parisien* put it as early as 8 September 1914:

> What you see is what you hear.
> Around the stations.
> A spectacle evoking both tragic and comforting visions.
> There, In front of the Gare du Nord, among the massive buildings whose
>   Glass façades reflect the gas lights, a mass of people, each night,
>   Gathers.
> Muted groups of people, animated by an attentive curiosity.
> People who do not know each other, who will never meet again, talk
>   familiarly among one another.
> Questions are put; the latest official announcements are discussed;
>   people try to interpret the latest military communiqué.
> Where is our side?
> Where is the enemy?
> Almost everyone there has someone in uniform, someone called to
>   make the effort and the sacrifice!

And a thousand cares, sternly repressed, surround these railway
    stations,
where at this moment of supreme crisis, the life of the nation is
    concentrated.
It is from here that the troop trains depart.
It is here that troops from the rear arrive,
and become the men of the front line.[2]

The station as a site of lived experience in wartime is appropriately our starting point in this perambulation through Paris, London, and Berlin between 1914 and 1919.

The stations

The main railway termini were products of the mid-nineteenth-century railway boom. In 1914 London had seven major stations: Euston, King's Cross/St Pancras (two adjacent stations), Liverpool Street, Victoria (in reality two adjacent stations run by different companies), Charing Cross, Waterloo, and Paddington. They were built between 1837 (Euston) and 1874 (Liverpool Street). Five were north of the Thames and two (Victoria and Waterloo) were south of the river and orientated towards the south coast. Victoria would be the station where the influence of the war would be most pervasive and persistent. Central London was additionally served by numerous smaller stations which were significant destinations for commuters, for example London Bridge, Cannon Street, and Holborn Viaduct.

The main London stations were very central. Liverpool Street was adjacent to the City of London and Charing Cross was in the heart of Westminster opening on to Trafalgar Square, with Waterloo a short walk over Westminster Bridge. Intra-city communications were increasingly reliant on the metropolitan and district underground (the tube) and above-ground railways which linked the main stations with each other and with intermediate points. The trans-London system was put under substantial strain by the war; new routes had to be opened or dedicated to ease increased traffic and superfluous routes closed. Remarkably, the electrification programme for some South Coast routes was continued and actually completed in 1915. Evidently the value of the system in saving coal and manpower was recognized.

In 1914 Berlin had five major train stations: Anhalter Bahnhof, Potsdamer Bahnhof, Görlitzer Bahnhof, Ostbahnhof, Stettiner Bahnhof. These stations, on the outskirts of the city as it existed when they were

---

[2] *Le petit Parisien*, 8 September 1914.

built, became inner-city train stations, as the city grew, quite extensively, in the late nineteenth and early twentieth century. Berlin was the most important focus for trains from the north, the east, and the south-east. The city also had a very good internal public transportation system. The origins of this system lie in the so-called S-Bahn, which was built in part in order to speed up the mobilization. Previously the troops had to be unloaded and march through the city; this had taken a day. The U-Bahn was begun in 1892, and a number of lines already existed in 1914. German railways had had a strong strategic purpose from the outset and because of the two-front nature of Germany's war, the war's impact was more evenly spread for Berlin's stations than in the other two cities.

Strategic concerns had also played an important role in the railway development of Paris. More than either London or Berlin, Paris was the absolute hub of the French railway system and the essential point of transfer during mobilization. In turn this played a role in making Paris a critical strategic target for the German armies. The capture or even encirclement of Paris would paralyse the French railways. French soldiers who believed that the war was being fought 'in defence of Paris' were correct in a fundamental sense.

The centrality of Paris meant that the impact of the outbreak of war would be felt at all the stations. Troops poured in from the south and west, to the Gare d'Austerlitz and the Gare de Lyon. Likewise in August 1914 and March 1918, these stations were filled with well-heeled refugees from the city fleeing the approaching German armies. But it was the stations that served the North and East that were most profoundly affected: the Gare du Nord and Gare de l'Est. These stations received the mass of refugees from northern and eastern France and were the arrival and departure points for the military traffic to and from the front. These stations were brought under complete military control and along with their surrounding area became to some degree a separate militarized sector in wartime, adjacent to but distinct from the city as a whole.

The main railways in Germany were state-controlled even before the war; those in France were private, but limited in number. Britain by contrast had dozens of competing commercial companies, the biggest of which centred on London. On 2 August 1914 the largest British railways were brought under 'state control' although the actual mechanism was a Railway Executive Committee formed of the chairmen of the largest companies (and, of course, based in London).

In principle one would imagine that the greater level of strategic planning and state control in the German and French systems would allow better adaptation to wartime conditions. In fact, the opposite was the case. A diversity of ownership meant that, in important respects, the British railways were over-resourced and over-manned, with substantially more locomotives and twice the carriages per mile of Germany and three times that of France. This surplus capacity became invaluable in war-time.[3] As the heaviest capacity in all three nations was around the capitals, it is likely that rolling-stock reserves were greater in London than in Paris and Berlin.

In a sense, the war began at the stations well before the first shots were fired. During the last days of July and the first days of August, stations were filled with desperate tourists trying to get home, to escape from enemy countries before war broke out or, in the case of neutrals, particularly Americans trying to escape the impending cataclysm. London saw both French and German reservists marching off to the stations to join their units. The French were apparently cheered, the Germans usually treated with icy respect, but occasionally jeered.

1914: Mobilization

The process of mobilization straddled the outbreak of war in all three cities. In Berlin, the 'curious' crowds turned their attention away from the news and towards the history unfolding around them in the German capital.[4] What better place to watch history unfold than at the train stations? The trains and the train stations became the focus of public attention, although mobilization began at the army barracks dotted around the city. The troops came, for example, to the barracks on General Pape Straße, via trains which brought them to Berlin, including the U-Bahn and the Metro. Mobilization went off like clockwork.

The public interest was drawn to 'novelty ... something unexpected'.[5] On Sunday, 2 August, thousands gathered at the train stations on the first day of mobilization, to watch those drafted leave for barracks in other towns or cities. The social composition of these 'spectator crowds', those who came to watch 'history', resembled the 'curious' crowds of July: they were largely middle- and upper-middle-class. Observers saw little enthusiasm among the people; rather 'the bitter necessity of the moment can be

---

[3] J. A. B. Hamilton, *Britain's railways in World War I* (London, 1967), p. 29.

[4] Jeffrey Verhey, *The spirit of 1914: militarism, myth, and mobilization in Germany* (Cambridge, 2000), pp. 22–57.

[5] 'Der erste Sieg', *Deutsche Zeitung*, 8 August 1914 (Morgen), no. 348, p. 1.

seen in the expressions of all, although more so among those accompanying the soldiers than among the soldiers themselves'.[6] Tears flowed freely on the 'crying faces of women and young girls who had brought their loved ones to the train station'.[7] Curious crowds gathered on the sidewalks to watch troops march from their barracks to the train stations on their way to the front. In the first weeks of the war these were usually sombre audiences. The Danish member of the Reichstag, Hans Peter Hanssen, wrote in his diary that the cavalry leaving Berlin on 4 August were well groomed, the lances were decorated with flowers, 'but there is no enthusiasm'.[8] The *Tägliche Rundschau* described the parade of one regiment marching down Unter den Linden on 8 August 1914, 'there the Alexander [regiment] comes with a clanging sound. A couple of hurrahs accompany them; otherwise one quietly takes off one's hat.'[9]

Towards the end of the month the curious people turned their attention to the wounded. Around 15 August the first trains with wounded pulled into Berlin. As one *Tägliche Rundschau* journalist noted, 'that pulls. One wants to see that. Chocolate and books are packed, roses are bought, bottles of wine put in paper bags.'[10] Crowds of thousands showed up at the train stations. Many journalists and contemporaries complained about this, and eventually the government took measures to shield the wounded from the public gaze, to keep the public out of the train stations where there were wounded. Other sorts of curious crowds gathered at the train stations. Prisoners of war were the next main attraction. In late August and September thousands of curious people, mostly bourgeois women, came to the train stations to catch a glimpse of the incoming prisoners of war. These crowds of curiosity were not the only type; there were other crowds, for example, crowds of exhaustion and panic.

The most striking examples of crowds of exhaustion and panic were the refugees fleeing the war in the east. Already before the declaration of war some 'mostly well-to-do residents' in the areas bordering Russia fled their homes and moved west. With the declaration of war, the number of

---

[6] 'Die Weltstadt rüstet. Berlin am ersten Mobilmachungstag', *Berliner Morgenpost*, 3 August 1914, no. 210, pp. 3–4. Described for Berlin in 'Die Stimmung in Berlin', *Norddeutsche Allgemeine Zeitung*, 5 August 1914, 181.

[7] 'Die Stimmung in Berlin', *Leipziger Neueste Nachrichten*, 3 August 1914, 213.

[8] Hans Peter Hannsen, *Diary of a dying empire* (Bloomington, Ind., 1955), p. 25.

[9] 'Der zweite Kriegssonntag', *Tägliche Rundschau*, 10 August 1914, 372 (Sonderausgabe), p. 4. 'Der Geist der Berliner Volksmassen', *Kreuz-Zeitung*, 3 August 1914, no. 360, p. 3, however, describes a parade with cheering crowds on 2 August 1914. I have found no corroboration of this report.

[10] 'Sonntag auf dem Kreuzberg', *Tägliche Rundschau*, 17 August 1914, no. 385 (Sonderausgabe), p. 4.

people leaving the border areas increased.[11] In the middle of August, after the Russian troops began their invasion of East Prussia, more people left, often literally with their possessions on their backs. One government official estimated that all told over 870,000 people left their homes in August.[12] That figure represents upwards of 20 to 30 per cent of the population in the eastern provinces. Many of them went through the Berlin train stations and had a strong impact upon public morale. On 23 August several thousand refugees arrived in Berlin. They brought with them stories of Russian barbarism, of 'heads being cut off, children being burned, women raped'. Yet, as one journalist noted, these stories had been passed on; no one had first-hand experience of Russian atrocities. The power of wartime rumour in an atmosphere of limited and uncertain information was already manifest.[13]

And alongside them, there were the 'enthusiastic' crowds. Key evidence cited for a Germany united in enthusiasm was drawn from images of crowds accompanying the departing troops. But as we have already noted, the departure of the troops was at *first* a solemn affair. Only towards the middle of the month did the departure become a festive event. Then, thousands of men, women, and children turned out to watch the regimental parade, to give the soldiers *Liebesgaben* such as chocolate, food, flowers, and cigars.[14] Yet even before this sort of cheering audience became institutionalized, there were examples of charity and support which many contemporaries viewed as evidence of 'enthusiasm'. This enthusiasm, too, had little to do with a real war. The troops clearly enjoyed being waved at, and taken care of at the train stations, especially by the young women. As one *Berliner Morgenpost* journalist noted, 'the taking care of the troops has taken on the character of a party ... young women dressed in their prettiest clothes', who were 'living out their instincts'.[15]

---

[11] A. Brackmann, 'Aus der Fluchtbewegung', in A. Brackmann (ed.), *Ostpreussische Kriegshefte auf Grund amtlicher und privater Berichte: zweites Heft: Fluchtbewegung und Flüchtlingsfürsorge* (Berlin, 1915), p. 7.

[12] Ibid., p. 28. See, too, Dieter Stüttgen, *Die Preussische Verwaltung des Regierungsbezirks Gumbinnen 1871–1920* (Cologne and Berlin, 1980), p. 352.

[13] 'Warnung vor der Kriegsangst', *Heimsdorff-Weidmannsluster Zeitung*, 27 August 1914, no. 101. Eberhard Buchner (ed.), *Kriegsdokumente; der Weltkrieg 1914 ... in der Dargtellung der Zeitgenössischen Presse* (Munich, 1914–18) volume II, pp. 69ff.; and the report of the local government official (signed Regierungspräsident Graf Keyserlick) in GhStAPK, Rep. 77, Titel 1310, no. 1, Bd 1, no p.

[14] 'Liebesgaben auf dem Bahnhof', *Kieler Zeitung*, 8 August 1914 (Abend), 2. Blatt, describes how over 1,000 cigars, a gift from a citizen of Kiel, were passed out at the train station by the Red Cross to the members of the 85th division, stationed in Kiel.

[15] 'An eine kleine, aber lästig bemerkbar werdende Minderheit unseren Mitbürgern', *Berliner Morgenpost*, 10 August, p. 3.

The train stations were also watched and guarded at the beginning of the war because of an outbreak of 'spy fever'. This meant all of the train stations, including the metros, attracted men of advanced years engaged in civil defence. This was a part of the 'playing at war', with the local baker, butcher, and candle-stick maker dressed in uniform and trying to stand at attention, at least as much as belly and years would allow. As there were hundreds of train stations, there were hundreds of guards in Berlin. This only lasted a couple of weeks, but it seems to have been great fun, and afterwards there were all sorts of commemorative photos and medals, and speeches, to remember it.

Troops departing accompanied by tears and cheers, spy scares and rumours and the arrival of the first wounded: these were common features at the stations in all three cities. But there were variants. There were no early victories to celebrate in London and Paris and no mass arrival of prisoners. The scale of mobilization in London was both voluntary and significantly smaller, and the disruption to normal civilian transport significantly less. But London had its rumours too. One related the transit of several divisions of Russian troops from Scotland to the south coast, rightly described as the 'biggest non-event' in the history of wartime transport, but a reflection of the real novelty of any mass movement of troops by train. This rumour was not London-specific, but Londoners repeated the story with as much gusto as everyone else, always attributed to a 'friend of a friend', rarely genuinely believed, but often retold.

Refugees: London and Paris

Berlin had its refugees in August 1914, but by the end of the month the German victory at Tannenberg had secured the position in East Prussia. By contrast the story of refugees in London and Paris was greater in scale and duration. The mass arrival of refugees occurred earlier in Paris and Berlin than in London; on the other hand, the arrival of Belgian refugees in London lasted longer, climaxing with the panic evacuation of Antwerp in the middle of September.

Paris, and Paris alone, also saw a mass exodus of its own population. This extended as far as the Chamber of Deputies which relocated to Bordeaux in early September as the German armies approached. The experience of siege in 1870–1 was ingrained in the Parisian consciousness: in the memory of those who had survived it, in the stories they had told their children, and in the folklore of the city. It was perfectly understandable that many of those with the resources to escape crowded the southbound trains rather than face the prospect of eating rats. This panic evacuation would be mirrored in March and April 1918 when the German army once again lunged for Paris. In both cases it was the middle classes who appear to have crowded the trains.

Those fleeing the city caused much contemptuous comment amongst those staying behind, but it was those fleeing *into* the city who would attract the most public notice. The idea of the refugee, so powerful in metropolitan wartime culture, was imminently connected with the arrival of the refugee in the metropolis. The Parisian newspapers gave an account of the arrival of the invasion's victims who, as soon as they had set foot on the railway stations' platforms of Paris, were born as 'refugees' in the eyes of the other civilians who were deeply affected by the 'painful sight' they offered.[16]

In the case of Paris, there were many Belgian refugees, but the predominant group were fellow countrymen, fleeing from northern France. In London, the influx was clearly foreign, the very Belgians for whom the British, officially at least, were fighting. During the first weeks of the conflict, when the restriction of information prevented the populations from knowing what was going on at the front, the arrival of Belgian refugees constituted one of the first public exposures to what the war meant. In those stations, from which husbands, brothers, and fathers had left, where the tragedy of separation had been played out, the misfortune of the refugees was now unfolding.

In London, the reception and distribution of refugees was organized at Victoria, Charing Cross, and Liverpool Street stations. Here is one woman's account of it:

One evening another man and myself were sent to Charing Cross to meet a late train, after waiting an hour in the very dimly lighted station we went to the trains to be told, at the last moment, they were all being sent into Victoria & we were hurrying out when a young man came up to us seeing our sashes and asked if we spoke French & then told us his pathetic story – he was trying to meet all the refugee trains to find his mother & sisters – refugees from Brussels – & apparently had been doing this for nights.[17]

In leaving the combat zones, the refugees literally gave shape to a set of representations of enemy brutality and allied gallantry. Observers commented: 'you should live in it to realize it – the sad, weary faces of those poor homeless, penniless people some having lost their children'[18] or, in Paris, 'The excitement was always greatest near the Gare de l'Est. The exodus from the invaded departments goes on and on. It is a lamentable

---

[16] *Le petit Parisien*, 29 August 1914.
[17] Imperial War Museum, London (IWM), Essington-Nelson, Miss A. 86/48/1.
[18] Ibid.

procession of poor wretches carrying all the possessions that they still have. It is hard to imagine a sadder spectacle.'[19]

Just arrived at the Gare du Nord in Paris, refugees were telling stories that newspapers would instantly pass on and reformulate. According to *The Times* of London:

as they sit there they are talking about one thing – of what the 'Boches' have done to the villages they have passed through already. 'They cut the hands off the little boys, so that there shall be no more soldiers for France. They kill the women, and the things they do to the young girls, monsieur, are too terrible to be told. They burn everything and steal and destroy.'[20]

Likewise, refugees' tales prominently figured in the Parisian press:

Refugees from Belgium and the North of France tell terrible stories. One man said this: 'Sir, a horrible vision. The Germans arrived Sunday. First they blocked all the mine shafts, even though some workers were still underground. These unfortunate men were buried alive in their galleries. Most inhabitants of the town fled into their cellars, where they thought they would be safe. The soldiers found them with their lances and their sabres; they were massacred.'

Just as in the Berlin case, the press magnified the atrocity stories and panic rumours brought to the stations by refugees. Deliberate invention was probably rare, for there were enough horror stories without resort to that. Both those recounting the stories and the journalists who publicized them probably believed them to be true. What better instance is there of the overheated atmosphere of the first months of the war?

For the urban populations such tales had a double significance. These stories served to represent the potential fate of their homes and loved ones should the German armies arrive, a possibility which could spur either resolution, such as the boom in voluntary recruiting in London, or panic, the flight of the wealthy from Paris. But they also spurred voluntary action on behalf of the victims, an important early stage in culturally mobilizing the metropolis for war.

In Paris, the Gare du Nord and Gare de l'Est witnessed the largest arrivals of refugees while their premises and surroundings were the setting of numerous local charitable initiatives.

Many, many French refugees have arrived last night and this morning at the Gare de l'Est. Just like their brothers in misfortune, the Belgians, they are being sent to Brittany and to Normandy. The Blue Cross, a society from the 10th arrondissement had the happy and touching idea to create a free canteen in the station, where these poor people are immediately given hot coffee and something to eat. With admirable zeal, the charitable ladies of the Blue Cross bathe and clean the

---

[19] *Le petit Parisien*, 31 August 1914.   [20] *The Times*, 2 September 1914.

babies and children, and dispense moral comfort, consolation, and hope ... The Gare du Nord is calm. The number of Belgian and French refugees continues to grow.[21]

This outpouring of charitable activity was common to all three capital cities. In London, *The Times* noted on 23 September 1914: 'yesterday, the Government gave an official welcome to the homeless victims of the barbarian, but the people, as we know, had not waited for an official pronouncement'.[22] At the instigation of the Wartime Refugee Committee, the Catholic Women's League took charge of the welcome of refugees at the stations. There, the latter recognized the League's volunteers thanks to the white sashes they were then wearing with 'Ligue des Femmes Catholiques' written in black letters across them.[23] Similar charitable work was also carried out by the Jewish War Refugees Committee.[24]

Miss Essington-Nelson recorded her experience as a volunteer and described the meeting of trains at Victoria and Charing Cross:

When the trains arrived we helped in the sorting, ourselves trying to find the Belgians from French, Russians, American & even Armenians. Girl guides were there with coffee, soup, etc. & the women's emergency corps was doing excellent work. At one end of the station, a man, appointed for the task, sat on a raised platform with lists of hotels, boarding houses & lodgings with the prices, for those who could pay for themselves.

British railwaymen offered help to Belgian railwaymen.[25] The concomitant presence of refugees and commuters, for instance, encouraged spontaneous and individual acts of solidarity. Parisian commuters reached into their pockets to provide some help for the refugees they had come across on their daily journey.[26]

Such spontaneous sympathy had its limits. As the war went on, refugee mothers and children were assisted, but male refugees occasionally found less support. Madame Vandervelde, wife of the Belgian socialist leader, toured the United Kingdom to denounce misunderstandings and abuses that often occured in the metropolitan railway stations.

---

[21] *Le petit Parisien*, 30 August 1914.   [22] *The Times*, 10 September 1914.
[23] Imperial War Museum, London, Essington-Nelson, Miss A. 86/48/1.
[24] *Report on the work undertaken by the British government in the reception and care of the Belgian refugees*, 1920, BDIC O 10164.
[25] 'Memorandum (n°2) for the use of Local Committees for the Care of Belgian Refugees', in *Report on the work undertaken by the British government in the reception and care of the Belgian refugees*, 1920, BDIC O 10164, 94.
[26] *Le petit Parisien*, 29 August 1914.

On one occasion, when 300 brave Belgian soldiers had arrived at Liverpool Street Station . . . a comment was made in the press as to why these men were making a hiding place of England . . . Several times young Belgians had come to her in her office in the most absolute despair because they had been insulted in the streets by people who said they ought to be fighting.[27]

Adjusting to war: the daily life of wartime stations: London

London's transport overcapacity rapidly became an enormous asset in allowing a smooth adjustment to wartime conditions. A government overwhelmingly concerned with not disrupting the life of the nation adopted the slogan of 'business as usual' and nowhere was business more usual in 1914 than at London's railway stations. Remarkably London passenger services were announced by the Railway Executive Committee to be fully back to normal by 8 August 1914. This was a slight exaggeration. Mobilization was proceeding at full pace, and there was some disruption to services south of London, but basically the normal business travel which was the lifeblood of the metropolis, particularly of the City which had recently resumed trading, was easily accommodated.

British mobilization had, inconveniently, occurred on the worst possible day of the year, 4 August, the summer Bank Holiday Monday, perhaps the railways' busiest day for vacation travel. But it appears that many merely postponed rather than cancelled their holidays. On 22 August, whilst the British Expeditionary Force was fighting for its life at Mons and Le Cateau, the railways were doing 'good holiday business'. An additional 8.15 a.m. excursion train from Victoria to Brighton was provided and the same occurred with the 10.15 a.m. from Charing Cross to Margate.[28]

Beneath the placid surface, the first indications of future pressures on the system were building up. By September 1914 the railway companies had already lost a substantial part of their labour force to the armed forces. By January 1915, 70,000 railwaymen had enlisted in Britain out of a total pre-war work force of 625,723. Across the war as a whole 184,474 railwaymen enlisted or 49 per cent of the military-age workforce in 1914.[29] Other railwaymen were lured into munitions work by higher pay. Was London particularly hard hit? Company records suggest so. London-based and London-centred companies tended to shed significantly more of their workforce than the national average. The major

[27] *The Glasgow Herald*, 7 November 1917.
[28] E. A. Pratt, *British railways in the Great War* (London, 1921), vol. I, p. 127.
[29] Ibid., p. 354.

exception was the London and South-Western Railway, which was a route heavily used by military traffic. The haemorrhage of staff was slowed, if not checked, by the introduction of 'badging' in June 1915, which removed moral pressure on railway staff to enlist. Railway workers were exempted from blanket conscription under the Military Service Act, although they would be subject to occasional 'comb outs' of Grade A and later Grade B men of military age.

One response to mobilization was the substitution of female labour. In 1913 the big companies had employed 13,046 women and girls; by 1916 this figure had risen to 33,000 and would reach 55,000 by 1918. But this replaced less than half of the men enlisted, and there can be little doubt that conditions of work for both male and female railway workers deteriorated in the early years of the war.

The mass recruitment of female staff by the railways was one of the most visible signs of wartime substitution. In many respects the female railway worker was as iconic as the female munitions worker during the war and more visible and ubiquitous. Newspapers commented on this newly visible presence in 1915, 'There are now more than 30 girl ticket collectors at London Bridge station ... By the end of the week ticket collectresses will be on duty at Victoria.' The girls were interviewed and identified by their previous jobs, 'I used to work at dress making ... but I much prefer this.' An ex-waitress stated, 'It was a bit funny the first morning I stood at the barrier ... but it only took an hour or two to get over the novelty of it.' Novelty was also the sensation of the passengers: 'Of course all sorts of men come by train ... Some of them were inclined at first to be facetious and pass remarks, but it does not take them long to get over it.' Women transport workers, the *Daily Mail* noted, 'get on very well with the workmen ... They know we are earning our livings and replacing men who have gone to war and they are quite civil.'[30]

Furthermore many of these female workers were *uniformed* and the combination of uniforms at the London stations – civilian women and military men – was a striking juxtaposition. 'The neat and becoming style of the uniform chosen for them engages the goodwill of the male passengers and pleases the girls themselves. The uniform is a well-cut, tailor made in blue serge ... The hat is a flat topped peaked cap in dark blue, cut like a military staff cap.'[31]

Female employment on the railways was much remarked upon and often praised, but internal records of the companies suggest that there were real doubts about the effectiveness of substitution. High staff

[30] *Daily Mail*, 1 June 1915.   [31] Ibid.

turnover was a serious problem. Of 1,483 women employed at one London Station, 633 had resigned within a month, 126 more within two months, and another 124 within three months. The companies assumed unreliability and indiscipline on the part of female workers, but poor working conditions and competing employment opportunities in munitions and government service are more plausible. There were also accusations of poor time-keeping: out of 152 women working at a London goods station, 116 of them lost a total of 165 working hours through lateness. Again the accusation was unreliability, but the generally increased burdens on women's time in wartime conditions is a more plausible explanation.

The first suggestion of real pressure on civilian travel came in early 1915. On 22 February there was a massive reduction in the numerous categories of cheap-rate fares. This was accompanied by the first London station closures: Walworth Road, Clapham, Wandsworth, Battersea, and Camberwell. It soon became apparent that curtailing Londoner's fondness for the railway was going to be a difficult task; furthermore, increased employment and more disposable income had actually begun to *increase* the demand for certain forms of civilian travel. In June 1916 there was an overall increase of 18 per cent in Whitsun holiday travel over June 1913. Patriotic appeals to reduce this traffic were an utter failure; amongst the rich stock of wartime vocabulary, the phrase 'joyriding' took on the clearly pejorative connotations that have persisted ever since.

A crisis was approaching. In November 1916 the British Expeditionary Force, mindful of the increased strain that it was facing on the Western Front, requested 370 locomotives to support its logistics. The railways were also major consumers of two other resources in increasingly short supply: coal and labour. Something would have to be done.

The gates of leave: men on leave

Paris! The Gare de l'Est
    When you get there, you are always greeted by the fading odour of steam and coal, mixed with the scent of urine.[32]

So French soldiers recalled their arrival at the Gare de l'Est or the Gare du Nord. British soldiers arriving at Victoria were greeted, at least in theory, with free mugs of tea; the other odours were no doubt present as well. In Berlin, the Red Cross was at the termini, supplying the troops with food. There 'attractive' Red Cross volunteers greeted the men. This

---

[32] Paul Vaillant-Couturier, *Une permission de détente* (Paris, 1919), pp. 31–2.

was one of those rare places in wartime Berlin where class barriers broke down, that is to say, the troops were largely working-class or agrarian, and the Red Cross women were generally bourgeois. Still, it seems to have been an agreeable homecoming for men on leave.

Paris was the quintessential destination for Allied soldiers on leave. Its centrality to the French battlefront meant that it played this role from early in the war. Consequently, the French army early represented a large proportion of the city's population.

The Paris railway stations had been a centre for the activities of *permissionnaires* even before the war. The laws of 1873, which permitted occasional leave, and of 1905, which granted Sundays and holidays off to peacetime conscripts, meant that every Sunday there was an invasion of the stations by soldiers and a degree of chaos.[33]

The bloody and fluid fighting of the first months disrupted peacetime leave arrangements in the French army; only in July 1915 was regular leave resumed. The stations that received the troops on leave constituted a military area. On 2 August all stations in Paris came under the authority of the War Ministry. Authority to preserve order was placed in the hands of the 4th Bureau of the Army General Staff. The result was that the interiors of the Gare de l'Est and the Gare du Nord were, at least theoretically, dominated by a mass of uniformed manhood; French soldiers and their allies, mobilized railwaymen, and military police. The space supposedly excluded women and civilians. In other words French soldiers on leave arrived at stations which were essentially extensions of the Front.

Some caution must be applied to this generalization. Civilians do seem to have been present on occasion, despite the rules. References in soldiers' songs and in some personal accounts suggest that the stations were less exclusively military than they were supposed to be. Victor Christophe, returning from leave with his family in Paris in November 1917, records that his wife accompanied him to the train. Two *chansons* of the same year, *La perme de poilu* and *La guerre souterrain*, make reference to being met at the station. The precise topography is unclear and the *chansons* may well be fantasies of wish fulfilment.[34]

The intensity of leave traffic for the French Army grew inexorably from 1915 to 1917. By 1918, there were eight times as many trains bringing

---

[33] F. Pinget, *Les permissions dans l'armée: leur influence sur l'instruction, la discipline, l'esprit militaire* (Paris, 1896), p. 18.
[34] Cited in A. Becker, *Journaux de combattants et de civils de La France de la Nord* (Paris, 1998), p. 86; Préfecture de Police, BA 721, BA 710.

them to the capital than had been available three years earlier.[35] In November 1916, between 5,000 and 6,000 men were returning from leave *each day* through the Gare de l'Est alone.[36] The volume of peak traffic was quite extraordinary: 420,000 *permissionnaires* passed through Paris in *five days* at the end of May 1917 as opposed to a 'mere' 280,000 at the start of the month. The transit station Orry La Ville was sending 9,300 *permissionnaires* daily to Paris Gare du Nord in June 1917.[37] The traffic into Paris remained enormous.

The regularized schedule can be seen in snapshot for 15 October 1917, five leave trains arriving daily at both the Gard du Nord and the Gare de l'Est. Five departing trains each day left the Gare du Nord and six departed from the Gare de l'Est. The arriving trains came into the stations beginning with a 6.15 a.m. arrival at the Gare de l'Est. A further four trains arrived before 9 a.m. The returning trains began to depart from 9.30 a.m., with eight trains leaving the stations before 11 a.m. Five trains arrived and one departed in the mid to late afternoon and finally there were two late departures from the Gare du Nord, the last leaving at 11.18 p.m.[38] There were also two leave trains each day arriving at and departing from the Gare de Lyon, depositing and collecting *permissionnaires* from the provinces, to connect with the Paris traffic to the Front.

If we estimate 1,000–1,500 men per train, we can see a series of 'rush hours' at the stations, a morning and an afternoon influx, a big departure in the late morning, particularly at the Gare de l'Est where three trains left in less than half an hour, and a smaller late one specific to the Gare du Nord. The developed system appears to have arriving and departing troops kept well apart. At the Gare du Nord there was always a gap of at least an hour and a half between any arriving and departing train and usually more than two hours. The minimum gap at the Gare de l'Est was between the 8.40 a.m. arrival and the 9.30 a.m. departure, but this was exceptional; an interval of two hours was more usual.

The system was not without its problems. Some soldiers in transit found themselves forced to travel the capital alone at night between the Gare de l'Est and the Gare de Lyon. In the process they could become vulnerable. For example, Albert Moreau, a machine gunner of the 138th

---

[35] 'Les Chemins de Fer (1871–1914) et la Guerre 1914–18', in ANOST, no. 265, October 1995.

[36] Service Historique de l'Armée de Terre (SHAT) 16N2851: Note de la Direction des Chemins de Fer aux Armées pour la Direction des Chemins de Fer, 22 November 1916.

[37] SHAT 7N1989 Conference 9 June 1917 'mesures concernant discipline dans les trains de permissionnaires'. SHAT 16N2820, Journal N. 19 du Réseau du Nord, 28 May 1917 to 10 April 1918, entry dated 13 June 1917.

[38] *Indicateur du permissionnaire, Service du 15 Octobre 1917.*

regiment, was relieved when a couple of urchins offered to help him with his kit outside Gare de l'Est. But before getting to the Gare de Lyon they had robbed him of 150 francs and his pass.[39]

It appears that prior to 1917 very little official attention was paid to the leave traffic. But during the crisis of French army discipline in the spring of 1917 there was a significant increase in official surveillance. Control became imperative due to fears that a collapse in morale at either the front or the home could be easily transmitted through this interface. The General Staff inquiry into the role of men on leave during the recent trouble recommended 'the most complete possible separation of the public and the *permissionnaires* in the stations'.[40] This will to control faced practical realities. The sheer volume of men involved caused problems for checking documentation. An official report regarding the Gare de l'Est in November 1916 pointed out that 'serious control was impossible' because six trains were leaving in the space of an hour and a half. The report concluded frankly that orderly checking was dependent on 'the good will of the *permissionnaires,* which gives no guarantees of a successful outcome'.[41]

Apparently the Gare du Nord was more successful in controlling the in-flow than the Gare de l'Est where checking remained poor from summer 1917 to the end of the war. During demobilization, discipline came close to collapse. Inspection of passes was often minimal, with all that implied about the possibility of desertion. Men on leave developed strategies to take advantage of this, to take unauthorized leave and to delay the return to units. The Parisian urban frontier turned out to be very permeable. By 1918, more orderly transit arrangements were being imposed in order to prevent troops from deliberately or accidentally getting lost along the way.

The closely adjacent (300 metres) Gare du Nord and the Gare de l'Est created a zone of services in their shadow. As we note below, the *permissionnaires* tended to look outside the stations to the immediate vicinity for their needs. But the stations had some basic facilities; canteens, lavatories and a free canteen existed in each station for 'indigent' soldiers on leave, although it turned out to be difficult to finance them. Between August and November 1915 the free canteen at the Gare de Lyon, in space

---

[39] Répertoires des commisariat parisiens, CB 48.51, affaire 78, 12 January 1918.
[40] SHAT 7N19189, Conference 9 June 1917, 'mesures concernant la discipline dans les trains de permissionnaires'.
[41] SHAT 16N2851, Note de la Direction des Chemins de Fer aux Armées pour la direction des Chemins de Fer, 22 November 1916.

offered by the management and served by civilian volunteers, served 18,000 meals each month to soldiers in transit.

The Gare de l'Est had a wealth of voluntary agencies providing facilities by spring 1917: the Cantine des Deux Drapeaux, sponsored by the American Dupont foundation; the Restaurant du Soldat run by the American Red Cross; and a military canteen run by L'Union des Femmes de France. Generally provision seems to have been better at the Gare de l'Est than at the Gare du Nord. Facilities such as these may have been more important to troops in transit and those awaiting departure; those returning from the front, particularly those with family in Paris, had a more immediate priority than a meal; they wanted to clean up. In October 1916, the trench journal, Le Poilu, noted that no adequate facilities existed at the Paris stations and that everyone before meeting his family wanted at least to have a wash; the author of the article welcomed the initiative of M. Bordes of the hygiene council to provide shower rooms at the stations.[42]

French leave trains had no lavatories; they were non-stop services and men were drinking. The lavatory facilities at the two arrival stations could not possibly have been adequate. The stations must in effect have been transformed into massive toilets, as men relieved themselves on arrival, an inauspicious beginning of the individual entry of the soldier to the city. The two main stations had different topographies. The Gare de l'Est was a huge ante-room; by contrast the platforms at the Gare du Nord were very close to the exit.

Leaving these stations was for Parisians a homecoming, albeit an ambiguous one to a city that had become unfamiliar.[43] They were decanted rapidly into a strange no-man's land: the 10th arrondissement, the administrative *quartier* of St Vincent de Paul. It rapidly became the 'wild North-East'. This was already an area with a criminal reputation and to some extent the disproportionate number of military and civil police reports originating from the area may reflect obviously heightened surveillance. This was 'leave land', an area colonized by men in uniform. The rich tapestry of wartime life at its most vivid could be observed in the district; the playing out of private emotions in public space, the appearance and disappearance of combatant travellers in the capital.

Families were not easily able to meet the soldiers outside the stations, even if the men had wanted this in their unkempt state; reunions were

---

[42] *Le Poilu du 6–9*, no. 3, 1 October 1916.

[43] See E. Cronier, 'Leave and schizophrenia: *Permissionnaires* in Paris during the First World War', in J. Macleod and P. Purseigle (eds.), *Uncovered fields: Perspectives in First World War studies* (Leiden-Boston, 2004), pp. 143–58.

difficult to schedule due to uncertainties about time of arrival. Waiting around for men arriving was an unappetising prospect in this area. Ways could be found; Marie-Joseph Boussac, a resident of the 14th arrondissement, wrote to her husband at the end of July 1915, 'I'll wait for you on August 2nd, which will be almost a year since you left. I believe you got my letter where I suggested we meet at St Laurent, the church near the Gare de l'Est which I assume will be your station . . . if the church is closed I'll wait by the door.' Why the church? Marie-Joseph was a respectable young Catholic woman, and this may explain why she had selected a quiet church to allow some privacy during the first moments of reunion. But also she would be aware of the area's reputation; the station entrance, a cafe or the street would not feel safe for a bourgeois woman on her own and she might attract unwanted attention.[44]

It was only in September 1917 that an official circular concerned itself with the possibility of providing a pass for the wives of *permissionnaires* to allow them to wait in a controlled area outside.[45] Women of the lower social orders generally did not have much time to wait around for arriving trains. Another deterrent to waiting around was that working-class women could well be picked up by the police as suspected street walkers. In these cases their appearance would not clearly distinguish them. The result, ironically, was that the more respectable women stayed away, the more the prostitutes came to dominate the area.

Arrival and departure for Parisians were emotional moments. Men fantasized about leave, and the reunion was central to the fantasy. Contemporary diaries and letters of combatants rarely provide a full account of this. On the contrary they only indicate between the lines the tensions between fantasies and realities, effacing the actual moment of reunion; it is ironically the weight of absence that dominates the evocation of leave. Later memoirs and novels capture this ambience best.[46]

Jean-François Durand, an orientalist painter serving in the 107th Regiment, recounted the sensations of arriving, in his 1922 memoir. He described the arrival of a leave train at the Gare du Nord:

In the hall, amongst us, a big lad marched, just ahead of me. Before going down the stairs to the exit, he checked himself, looking all around. Detaching herself from the scrum, a young woman shouted his name with a poignant voice and with immense élan hurtled herself at his chest. He wrapped her inside his great arms furiously . . . This moment they had waited for desperately for months . . .

[44] *Correspondance de Jacques et Marie Joseph Boussac* (Paris, 1996), p. 378.
[45] AG 7N149, cited in circular no. 2633-Q/O of the Under-secretariat of State for War, dated 1 April 1918.
[46] Cronier, 'Leave', pp. 150–2.

Oblivious to everything they were immensely alone. Their mouths locked, they rediscovered in this intoxication, in this deep communion, the deep marriage of their bodies.

In this moment the author saw time suspended. But he had far greater difficulty waxing lyrical about his own experience on coming home.[47]

The idea of the *silence du permissionnaire* described by Carine Trevisan in her analysis of war novels, can be found to have its roots in the difference between descriptions of arrival and departure in contemporary writings.[48] Numerous post-war novels attempted to describe the arrival of soldiers in the Parisian promised land. Paul Vaillant-Couturier described in 1919 the nervous tension of those disembarking at the Gare de l'Est :

The unsteady crowd of men burdened with flasks, packs, German guns, drums, all evidently exhausted and happy, clog the platform. I stand on my toes to see what awaits me at the exit. But there are too many people. My impatience makes me shake under my pack ... This whole world, immobile, noisy like the sea, dragging muddy boots, necks straining towards the gates, eyes trying to see through the bodies in front of them. Calls ring out. Everything is so slow! Everyone pushes at shoulders, stomachs. I see a group of people waiting, with confused joy and deep agitation: women physically moved, mothers who feel as if they have just given birth, timid children facing fathers who do not recognize them ... Martha is certainly there, in the crowd; my parent must be there too. They got my cable. My heart leaps. I don't know ... I gaze at the crowd, try to penetrate it, search through it, undress it ... The crowd moves on, replete with exclamations and kisses. All that are left are one woman in black, with a little girl, and I. The official closes the gate noisily, looks at me and says: 'Men on leave? You go to the right.' They had not received my cable.[49]

This captures the emotions assaulting the men on their arrival, the culmination of their waiting and their dreams, the brusque confrontation with a reality for which they were unprepared, heightened by the particular atmosphere of the stations, packed and noisy, permeated by the palpable excitement of the men. The strange solitude of arrival in the crowd struck most of the *permissionnaires* and is recaptured in many accounts.

Regarding departure, the unspoken and unsayable is manifest in the writing, and emotional detachment appears often to have preceded the physical separation. Paul Vaillant-Couturier described a family parting at the station; he was present but already 'gone':

---

[47] Ibid., p. 16.

[48] Carine Trevisan, 'Le silence du permissionnaire', in Catherine Milkovitch-Rioux and Robert Pickering (eds.), *Ecrire la guerre* (Paris, 2000), pp. 201–9.

[49] Paul Vaillant-Couturier, *Une permission de détente* (Paris, 1919), pp. 31–2.

The separations of this morning were very painful. As much as I preferred to be expected on my arrival, so it was painful to be accompanied on my departure.

I dread nothing more than this prolonged intimacy outside one's home in the crush of crowds.

This misery, which I dare not mourn, this love which can be constrained no longer, this prolongation of a peaceful life in the midst of this wartime indifference, all these things created an unbearable disorientation.

This evening, my people will return home to their daily tasks, sad, tormented . . . There will be tears, but we will start up again this strange world in which we find ourselves, this agreeable life of ordinary things.

I didn't want them to accompany me to the train. I couldn't stand the traditional shuffling of feet on the pavement before the guard.

Now that I have returned to the war, I have to accept it completely. The quicker the change, the less painful is the emptiness. We have to finish quickly.

– Goodbye Mama. Goodbye dear father. Farewell for a while, a long while, dear Martha. Let us hug each other tightly. Get going, don't look back . . . Keep loving me. I carry you with me. Farewell.

They are gone.

The crowd of men on leave is swallowed up in the vast mantrap of the station . . . .

And in this grey crowd of men returning to the war, in the midst of this rippling field of helmeted men, my family stands there, erect, dignified, holding all the used-up happiness of nine days of leave.

I drank a whole quart of wine.[50]

Is it at all surprising that leave induced *le cafard* (the blues) on the return to the trenches? Here is the source of the nearly universal tropes of alienation and dissatisfaction in writing about leave in war fiction and memoirs, which are often naively extrapolated into generalizations about the relationships between soldiers and civilians. There is an internal world of emotion in this encounter as well.

For non-Parisians on leave the issues were very different. Theirs was not a return to hearth and home, but an adventure in 'the city', and their relationship with the city and its citizens was very different. As ever the quality of the reception of these tourists was usually a matter of hard cash. Those lacking it were discouraged by the military authorities from hanging around, they were to head off home. For those who could pay their way, the objective of the military authorities was to try to alleviate their loneliness in order to maintain morale. A particular concern was the soldiers from the occupied regions. The work of *Parrains de Reuilly* specialized in those, 'deprived of their hearths',[51] and waited for them

---

[50] Ibid., pp. 168–9.
[51] AN F7 13370 B3, pièce 1065, Lettre du Préfet de police au ministre de l'Intérieur, 11.6.1917.

at the station. 'And there was no formality in our reception. Not even the need to tell them we are coming. We were led peacefully by men we knew from the 22nd section by metro to the barracks.'[52] By contrast Allied soldiers were treated pretty much purely as tourists, expected to pay as they went.

The similarities with the rites of passage performed at London's major rail termini is striking. Robert Saunders, visiting London at the height of the Somme offensive, described the spectacle of this same wartime railway station in a letter to his son in Canada: 'In the afternoon, however, London Bridge Station was just plug full and I spent 40 minutes going about the crowd. There were soldiers of all kinds going & coming with Canadians, Australians etc., Red Cross Men & Military Police, people coming to meet, some others seeing friends off. I wish I could photograph some of the sights to send you.'[53] For Charles Sheridan-Jones, writing in 1917, Victoria Station at midnight was the place where these changes in 'life and habits' could be seen 'in a flash'. The imagery of death recurs, 'Before the war the station was ablaze with lights and vibrant with activity. Now you will find a scene of profound gloom, of almost funereal sombreness.' There was also a sense of a 'world turned upside down' of carnivalesque reversals. 'Perhaps the man who pestered you to buy matches has won a commission ... the actor from whom he cadged may be one of the soldiers whom he leads.' There is also a sense of deteriorating continuities; what was bad has become worse; 'the city clerk, who works harder than ever for less money, finds that he must go straight home without that stroll in the brightly lit West End, which was often the one event of colour and interest in his drab and sombre life'. Descriptions of railway stations at night take on the air of a descent into Hades, a grim 'underworld', the very image that Eliot would exploit.[54] But there was more to the railway station in wartime than this.

The most dramatic feature of railway stations in wartime London was the playing out of private emotion in public. As we have seen above, the ritual of leave-ending meant leave-taking from families in public; this environment added awkwardness and embarrassment to what was inevitably a difficult moment. The same was true for those being met by their families on their way home on leave. Here the commonalities among these capital cities are overwhelmingly clear. To be sure, German soldiers mobilized at their barracks, but the complexities of wartime travel made it

---

[52] *La Fusée*, no. 13, 5 November 1916, p. 3, *Avis aux permissionnaires originaires des pays envahis*.
[53] R. Saunders, letter to his son, 16 July 1916, Imperial War Museum.
[54] C. Sheridan-Jones, *London in wartime* (London, 1917), pp. 26–7.

inevitable that family scenes of separation and reunion happened at all major stations.

In London the key theatres were the railway termini linking London to the Channel ports, particularly Victoria Station (to a lesser extent Waterloo). One of the best descriptions of the drama of departure is to be found in the diary of Harold Cousins:

This morning I went to Victoria Station to see Capt. Cobbold, one of our Directors, off to the front by the 1.15 train. The scene was most impressive as the station gradually filled with soldiers and friends come to see them off. The Officers had a train to themselves – mostly Pullmans – and left first . . . There were many sad scenes, but everyone tried to be as cheerful as possible. It seemed a pity that most of the parting could not have taken place in private, but the wish to see the last of husbands and sons is apparently too strong for most people. I went on to the platforms, but there were many spectators who were not allowed beyond barriers which were erected to keep order at the station. It is strange to think that of these men so many will never come back again.[55]

As well as the rather obvious point of a highly visible class distinction in operation and the policed and controlled nature of the space, the language of this passage indicates an awareness of the 'theatricality' of what is happening and a real unease about it.[56] Private versus public leave-taking was something all families had to face. Eva Isaacs never accompanied her husband to the station, choosing to say good-bye at home. She did, however, see her brother, Henry Mond, depart from the station and she wrote that evening to her husband. It had started with an unpleasant surprise: 'Beloved I am back from seeing Boy off to France, as I was going to my work the odd-man appeared with the news that they were leaving at 11.30. As he [Henry] was told that he would not be wanted until the 10th it came as rather a shock.' As a result the family was emotionally unprepared:

Daddy and I went to see him off, Daddy feels it dreadfully, he is devoted to Henry . . . Beloved, you were so right never to let me come to the station. I know I couldn't bear it, it was difficult enough to keep a firm hand seeing Henry go – I wonder how people have the courage: I thought they were marvellous this morning, saying good-bye dry eyed, with almost a smile . . . He went away bravely, he has got stuff in him the lad, for I know he hated going.[57]

Class attitudes may have played a part in Eva's attitude, a public display of emotion might have been less easy to contemplate for the upper strata of London society, either the departing officers or their relatives. It is

[55] H. Cousins, Diary, 13 November 1916, IWM.   [56] See chapter 5.
[57] E. Isaacs to 2nd Lt G. R. Isaacs, 6 March 1917, Marchioness of Reading Letters, IWM.

noteworthy that Eva Isaacs also never met her husband at the station when he returned on leave, whereas, by contrast, Edie Bennett, a lower-middle-class woman, quite literally dreamt of the train pulling in and of meeting her husband. This raises the point that these same stations saw a second, somewhat lighter performance, namely the arrival of the leave trains. Again Harold Cousins gives a good description, this time as he tried to meet his cousin arriving on leave. Not un-typically the train was late:

I went down to Victoria Station today to try to meet Mervyn on his way from France on leave. The train usually comes in at 10 o'clock, but today I was told that it would be in at 2.30. I went down at 2.30 and was informed it wouldn't come until 4.30 . . . Must have missed Mervyn – if he came – for though I took up my position on the gangway & scrutinised everyone in the dim light, I did not see him. I believe there was to be another train, but I couldn't wait for that on the chance.

I was glad to have an opportunity to see the leave train arriving as well as going off again. There were many joyful mothers & relations waiting and I noticed one in particular as she led her son in triumph to satisfy a desire he had expressed for something to eat. The men came mostly by a second train, tired and loaded up with their kit. There were plenty of people waiting to help them, with the Military Police & National Guard, who inquired where each wanted to go and gave them useful advice.[58]

Again class distinctions and the regulation of the space are apparent, but the scene is necessarily a happier one. Yet the point to note is tucked away in the passage. The leave train was a 'turn around'. The striking implication of this is that far from being two distinct scenes at Victoria, arrival and departure overlapped. This must have been difficult for all concerned. Families in the process of being broken up could see others in the midst of reunion, but families in the midst of reunion were being forcibly reminded of the transience of leave and the imminent departure of loved ones. Although probably not a conscious consideration, the regulation of the station to get both groups through as quickly as possible had important implications for public morale.

Even the appearance of *normality* could itself be disorientating. Vera Brittain, returning from Malta in 1917, wrote in her diary of her arrival: 'It seemed very strange to be in Victoria again; same old crowd around the barriers, same old tea rooms, same old everything. One began to believe that one hadn't really been away.'[59]

Same old everything. The most disorientating aspect about the stations was that simultaneously the war changed everything and nothing.

[58] H. Cousins, Diary, 6 December 1915.
[59] Diary entry for 27 May 1917, V. Brittain, *Chronicle of youth* (London, 1982), p. 428.

Symbolically and emotionally they were at the heart of the war, yet functionally and in their physical space they were still recognizably their peacetime selves, evoking unavoidable 'metropolitan nostalgia'.

The service sector: legitimate and illegitimate

There was certainly an edgy and sometimes predatory aspect to the world of railway stations in wartime. The area around the stations fostered an informal 'war economy', part black, part grey. Arriving and departing men sought presents and souvenirs, last-minute purchases and things unattainable elsewhere. They fuelled a service culture orientated towards the hurried pleasures of rest and recreation; gastronomic, alcoholic, and sexual.

Facilities for a last-minute meal or drink had always clustered around stations. But the war created its own favoured venues; for example, according to a report in 1918: 'The cafés surrounding the Gare du Nord and the Gare de l'Est are busy at all hours with *permissionnaires* and refugees. The Café Barbotte, headquarters of the Comité du Nord, is the most invaded.'[60] This café-restaurant at 25 rue de Dunkerque, opposite the Gare du Nord, sold 'articles de Paris' on its terrace and, through the Comité du Nord, helped with the reception of refugees from the occupied areas. The regional clientèle of this business was very marked and reflected a well-established presence of migrants from the north in this district. In this context, the policing of railway stations and especially of the Gare du Nord and its vicinity led to a fierce denunciation of the police. Its indiscriminate round-up of refugees in the Gare du Nord area led to an unfortunate depiction of the exiles, subsequently lumped together in the official press release and in the newspapers with ex-convicts and vagrants. Hence the stern protest addressed in September 1915 to the Interior Ministry by M. Deguise, Député for the Aisne:

Two days ago, there were articles in the press about our compatriots, refugees from the invaded regions; they were maliciously entitled 'A successful round-up', and described refugees as 'invaders' who brought 'disorder' to the Gare du Nord district. Among them, 'hardened criminals' were apprehended and others, 'simple vagabonds', were headed to the base camps behind the lines where they would work on the trenches. I want to protest solely against the collective designation of 'vagabonds' applied to people who deserve nothing less than indulgence and pity.[61]

The new clientèle of *permissionnaires* created a gold rush for all businesses. In August 1915, some of these merchants complained strenuously

---

[60] PF, BA 1587, Physionomie de Paris, 23/10/1918.
[61] *Bulletin des réfugiés du département du Nord*, 11 September 1915.

about legislation restricting sale of alcohol to men in uniform.[62] Those with stores near the Gare de l'Est were most annoyed. The new restrictions on opening hours meant that they had to close before the leave trains arrived; this was less of of a problem for their neighbours at the Gare du Nord. Inevitably other businesses moved in to provide 'under the counter' drink for the thirsty *poilu*. Word of mouth directed men to a drink, street walkers quickly adding this to their services and their appeal.

'Leave Land' was a profitable sex market. From all over France prostitutes mobilized and followed the armies. The station areas of the Gare du Nord and the Gare de l'Est became the new centre of clandestine prostitution in Paris, ascending from fourth place before the war. A doctor at the hospital of Saint-Lazare Le Pileur stated, 'the stations have become the most important pick-up points', and that prostitutes 'found amongst men on leave the most numerous and easy customers, the steadiest market in Paris'.[63] There was concern about the un-regulated and unhealthy nature of much of the trade, which had grown rapidly simply due to the fact, recognized by officials, that 'the *permissionnaires* can't be satisfied by 6,000 girls registered with the *préfecture de police*'.[64]

Around the two stations, the invasion of prostitutes and soldiers led to an explosion of open-air sex. Many girls were arrested for public indecency. Couples were caught in the act in 1915 and 1916, near the church of Saint-Vincent de Paul and by the Lariboisière hospital. Such reports are not found after 1916.[65] But this says little about the extent of the trade. Indeed, for the unimaginative, a '*brochure des 32 positions*', was sold for 2 francs under the counter in 1917.[66]

It is clear that both this market and the official response to it adapted during the war. Increasingly prostitutes portrayed themselves as women who were having sex with a soldier friend who in return had given them a little monetary gift. A case in December 1917 exemplifies this development. The arrested woman claimed that she 'was not a prostitute, but had met someone who had given her a bit of cash for her company. Since she was married, and the mother of two young children, they let her go'.[67] Statements to police included 'now and again, when I need some cash', 'just for two or three days', 'to get me some ready dosh', or a claim, 'her

---

[62] AN F712936, pièces 807, 810, 816, 817, Rapport sur l'état d'esprit des populations pour août 1915, 13/9/1915.

[63] Docteur Le Pileur (infirmerie Saint-Lazare), *Indications sur la prostitution vulgivague à Paris depuis le début de la guerre* (Paris, 1918).

[64] PF Cb 37.44, Cb 37.45, Cb 37.46.   [65] PF Cb 37.44, Cb 37.45, Cb 37.46.

[66] See, for example, PF Cb 37.45, affair 1932, 26/6/1916.

[67] PF, CB 37.48, no. 3209, 8/12/17.

daughter needed some help'.[68] It appears by 1918 that a lot of the arrests were of first-timers.

In this context the police evidently began to show some sympathy, no doubt reflecting their powerlessness in face of this self-renewing and demand-driven market, and simply let the girls off with a warning. Sometimes the cases revealed poignant stories of wartime family life. In June 1917, when one woman arrested for prostitution was released, 'her wounded husband had his left leg amputated'.[69] It is likely that after their brush with the law, many of these amateurs retired from the trade. However, the rising cost of living meant that the sex trade was bound to provide supplements to female wages, coinciding with the mass influx of men on leave in 1917.

For some, casual sex for cash was an answer to the loneliness of leave in the big city. For homosexuals searching for partners, the station area was a good place to cruise. According to one witness in November 1916, there was a daily trade near the Gare du Nord and Gare de l'Est enabling him to bring men to his flat.[70] Heterosexual or homosexual, money was the universal language, the key to all doors.

The sex market changed as one moved away from the the stations. Indoor venues were largely absent from the quartier of Saint-Vincent-de-Paul, but were more easily available elsewhere in the same arrondissement. Around rue de Chabrol and the side streets of boulevard de Strasbourg, a crush of tiny hotels catered for the 'hourly trade'. At number 10, rue de la Fidélité, a doctor provided 'after service'. A near neighbour was the hotel, 'London and Brazil', at number 18, where fifteen prostitutes were arrested in a police raid in August 1918. The proprietor, quizzed about the morality of the clientèle, said that he had tried to discourage the trade, but that he had found it difficult to prevent the place from becoming a resort for whores and their customers from the Gare de l'Est. He did not consider the trade commercially desirable, due to the problems of order and security it brought with it, and promised to suppress it.[71] This was unlikely, since the trade was extremely lucrative. A room was being rented for 4 francs an hour, and beer was being sold at 1.50 francs a bottle.[72]

The economy of instant gratification came to dominate the area. To help fund it, another trade arose. Soldiers sold items of kit and the area

---

[68] PF, CB 37.48, matters reported as 'racolage' or 'clandestine prostitution'. Trans. Gregory.
[69] PF, CB 38.41, 27/6/1917.
[70] PF, CB 37.46, no. 1786, 18/11/16.   [71] PF, CB 37.49, no. 2316, 24/8/1918.
[72] PF, CB 38.39, no. 213, March 1916.

became a centre for the traffic in military items: sold, stolen, and forged. *Permissionnaires* were both vendors and customers. Nearly 18 per cent of all those who overstayed their leave were in possession of false papers. Of those stopped near the two stations, this rose to 21 per cent. But deserters were ill advised to hang around the area. In Paris 28 per cent and 18 per cent of such men arrested as absent without leave were respectively from the districts of Saint-Vincent-de-Paul and Port Saint-Denis, compared to 43 per cent for all the Paris suburbs combined.[73]

In contrast, the smaller absolute scale of leave traffic to London meant that 'leave land' was less marked out as an area of sex traffic. Regulation was somewhat easier. Perhaps the best regulation of all was the organization of the Belgian army on leave, where each individual soldier was met by a gendarme or military policeman and guided on his way either to the stations exiting London or to accommodation in the city.

The troops passing through London were largely strangers to the city. Most of the troops passing to and from these stations were not accompanied by relatives, being from further flung parts of the United Kingdom or even overseas. It should be noted that these overseas troops were overwhelmingly from the white Dominions and some later from the United States. Indian troops, present on the Western Front in large numbers from 1914 to 1916, were not encouraged to take leave in London. Indeed most may not have had regular leave at all until home leave to India was instituted in 1916.[74]

Many British troops spent a good deal of the war in Britain, and this meant that the process of departure by units to the front was prolonged. One observer, Sheridan-Jones, describes an anonymous late-night departure in 1917: 'Then a faint hum fills the air, a hum not unlike the sound of waves breaking on the beach . . . suddenly it dawns on us that it is borne in front of a body of men, men in khaki, loaded with rifles and kit bags, who are marching to Victoria to entrain. On they come with no cheers to encourage them, no voices to hearten them or wish them God Speed.'[75]

The contrast with the scenes of 1914 are clear enough. But by this time most of those departing were doing so as individuals returning from leave. Unaccompanied young men predominated. Particularly early in the war, a fairly high proportion of men returning to the front were inebriated from a 'final drink'. Amongst the reminiscences in the *Pioneer Policewoman*, an

---

[73] The grouping 'Paris and suburbs' which we use here corresponds to the lists of buildings which we have. These lists cover 64 Parisian and 12 suburban police districts.

[74] See David Omissi (ed.), *Indian voices of the Great War* (London, 1999).

[75] Sheridan-Jones, *London in wartime*, p. 27.

account of the work of the Women's Police Service, this point is made with emphasis:

> Occasionally it was imperative to get the soldier, hopelessly drunk, to the boat train in time to join up before leaving for the front. His arrival, in whatever condition, prevented his being treated as a deserter, and saved him and the authorities endless trouble. Superintendent Goldingham laughingly recalls one patriot, a canny Scot, who wanted her to carry his kit bag, his rifles, some mementos and a whole cargo of stuff, in addition to keeping himself upright with his arm across her shoulders. A perfect gentleman he gallantly offered to carry her attaché case in exchange. It was a relief to know he caught his train.[76]

Incoming trains posed more serious problems. As with Paris, the transition from the front to London was remarkably rapid. The strains of combat were not always left behind. One soldier on leave, early in the war, thought that he had lost his ticket home and tried to commit suicide with a razor, only to be tackled by one of the women police who took him to the 'rest room' at the station and calmed him down. Even more serious was a case where a soldier suffered a flashback as he was entering the tube and believed himself to be storming a bunker. He fixed his bayonet and charged the ascending crowd. Again, he was tackled by a woman officer. These very extreme cases are doubtless the tip of an iceberg of difficulty with adjustment among troops passing through wartime London. In his 1917 account of London in wartime, Sheridan-Jones was damning about the failures of reception:

> After all, despite all that has been said and done for, and written about him; the leagues and committees and charities that exist for his betterment, the fact remains that Tommy in London feels an outcast. Go to Victoria Station or Charing Cross as I have done, any evening and see him fresh from the trenches, weighed down with accoutrements, caked with mud, a stranger in a strange place, often with no one to welcome him, to give him the right hand of fellowship and bid him be of good cheer.[77]

Policing the railway station presented its own problems. Technically the major railway stations were private property where the Metropolitan Police were unable to take action, as they had no jurisdiction. This is not to say that the stations were un-policed, on the contrary:

> I find, however, that the Military Police, acting in concert with the Railway Police, do at present exclude from the platforms all persons who have not a permit from the Provost Marshall's Department to be present and that the Railway Police, acting under the Special Powers, exclude all known undesirable characters from the precincts of the stations.

---

[76] *The pioneer police woman* (London, 1925), p. 86.
[77] Sheridan-Jones, *London in wartime*, p. 32.

It is possible to exclude persons from the platforms because they can be checked at the barriers, but it would not be practicable to extend the permit system to the station premises as a whole ... the measures taken by the Military and Railway Police are successful in keeping the station premises clear of women of loose character.

But this merely relocated the problem, 'The exclusion of undesirable women from the railway premises naturally leads to them congregating in the streets outside ... The Police do everything in their power to cope with this evil.'[78]

Not all street walkers in London walked the streets. For example in 1917 it was reported that Annie Young had been sentenced to twelve months' imprisonment with hard labour for running a disorderly house (brothel) within easy distance of Waterloo station, and when it was raided most of the men present were soldiers.[79]

This was the point that Sheridan-Jones had made the year before. He believed that it was unsurprising that the disorientated soldiers fell, 'easy prey to the harpies and humbugs that the war has attracted to London.'[80] In the end, the channelling of the soldiers represented the best hope, according to the Home Secretary: 'Much good work is done by voluntary agencies who get hold of the men upon arrival and arrange for their transport across London or to hostels so as to prevent them falling into bad hands.'[81]

By introducing closing hours in pubs, the authorities failed to acknowledge one of the central desires of soldiers on leave. Sheridan-Jones praised the 'excellently managed' recreation huts of the YMCA but then qualified his approval: 'Man does not live by texts alone, and Tommy gets tired of the severe, not to say bleak interior of these huts with their patriotic and scriptural instructions.' The result was that men would naturally seek out more sociable places, particularly the illegal drinking dens. According to him these were 'as thick as blackberries in August', in the vicinity of Waterloo Bridge Road. The end result was the shameful sight of seeing soldiers, 'some of whom have crossed the oceans to fight our quarrels, asleep on park benches'.[82] Soldiers slept rough on service; it was harsh indeed to turn them into vagrants when they got to the metropolis on leave.

Commemorative art

The abiding image of a railway station in the Great War would be created in another capital city far away. But London, Paris, and Berlin never had a

[78] Simon to Davidson, 8 October 1918, Dav. 355/285, Lambeth Palace, London, Davidson Papers.
[79] *The Times*, 26 February 1917, p. 5.   [80] Sheridan Jones, *London in wartime*, p. 34.
[81] Simon to Davidson, ibid.   [82] Sheridan Jones, *London in wartime*, pp. 36–7, p. 32.

Finland Station. The revolution did enter Berlin through the railway stations when trains delivered mutineers from the Navy at Kiel to the capital in November 1918. But the stations were never the focal point of that revolution. Indeed, Lenin once bitterly quipped that revolutionary prospects would be poor in Germany because the revolutionaries would be held up in forming orderly queues to obtain platform tickets at the stations.

Official memory concentrated on simple commemoration, but it contained an implicit politics of re-integration and ascription of meaning to the war. London saw the major rail companies commemorate their employees at their main stations. A total of 21,522 railwaymen had been killed or died of wounds.[83] The biggest monument was at Waterloo, an arch replete with classical symbolism. All stations had their rolls of honour. But perhaps the most effective memorial was performance art, the regular stopping of the trains at 11 o'clock on 11 November, which began in 1919.[84] The great stations were transformed briefly into cathedrals dedicated to the dead, staff and travellers alike transformed into statues with heads bowed, time frozen in remembrance.

Another major work of commemorative art with the railway station as its focus is a series of paintings at Victoria Station in London. These portray the moments of separation and reunion which we have described above. The official task of representing the railway stations at war in London was conferred on an immigrant, a Russian-born Jew, Bernard Meninsky, who was a naturalized British citizen and until June 1918 a serving soldier. The Ministry of Information had already commissioned photographs of the arrival of leave trains at Victoria in 1917, but in 1918 attention turned to creating a painted record.

Meninsky was born in the Russian Empire in 1891 and had been brought to Liverpool as a baby. He studied art in Liverpool, and was part of a remarkable generation of Anglo-Jewish artists who were present at the Slade School of Art between 1911 and 1913. In 1913 he contributed to the first exhibition of the 'London Group' and in 1914 was employed at the Central School of Art in Bloomsbury. He enlisted in the army after the outbreak of the war, serving in the 42nd Battalion of the Royal Fusiliers as a clerk. In late 1917 he was categorized B2 and hospitalized with what was later diagnosed as 'neurasthenia'.[85]

The prominent society painter Walter Sickert, who had followed Meninsky's pre-war career, recommended Meninsky to the Ministry of

---

[83] Pratt, *Railways*, p. 375.

[84] A. M. Gregory, *The silence of memory* (Oxford and Providence, 1994).

[85] IWM, First World War Artists Archive, File Number 261/6 (Meninsky) B. Meninsky to A. Yockney, 22 January 1918.

Information, which in early 1918 was turning its attention to a permanent memorial collection. According to Sickert, Meninsky would be suitable 'for Govt. pictures. He is a most accomplished painter.'[86] The head of the British War Memorials Committee wrote to Meninsky on 4 May 1918 seeking, 'to secure your services as an artist in connection with "war records"'. He was offered an 'honorary commission, the pay of your rank, a salary and the cost of materials'. Meninsky agreed.[87] He worked on the painting in the later part of 1918 and early 1919. The final picture was delivered on 30 April 1919.[88]

The Meninsky paintings were thus part of the first great post-war exhibition of 'war record' paintings. The scenes he painted are not cluttered with a mass of detail; the emphasis is broadly on form. The sequence of paintings nevertheless has an implied message. Meninsky's preliminary oil-on-paper sketch is the most stylized, the most anonymous. Faces are largely absent. The finished paintings of the platform scenes also give little individuality to the men in uniform. It is only in the scene near the exit where the faces are clearly individualized. The subjects of the painting slowly mutate from *soldiers* to *men*. The war is ending and they are going home. But return would always be problematic. Thinking about railway stations in wartime had been permeated with bittersweet memories of peace. Now, unavoidably, the peacetime railway station would evoke memories of war, shared by millions of Londoners as well as by those who had passed through the city during the conflict.

In Berlin such social consensus was never established. The memory of the war and the stations' part in it was more problematic. Two representations stand out. The army railway workers' memorial, situated in the suburb of Schöneberg, was consciously political. It was an attempt to integrate the railway workers into the front ideology and in particular the 'machine war'. The association made specific reference to the courage required to drive a train into the 'storm of steel', a conscious attempt by the railway workers to assimilate themselves into this potent myth.[89]

The memorial, designed by Otto Siepenkothen and Willy Meller, is topped by two heroic male nudes and has a plinth with a bas relief

[86] IWM, Artists Archive, File number 261/1, Letter from W. Sickert to A. Yockney, January 1918.

[87] Ibid., A. Yockney to B. Meninsky, 4 May 1918, B. Meninsky to A. Yockney, 5 May 1918.

[88] Meninsky to Yockney, 25 September 1918, 2 December 1918, 18 December 1918, 30 April 1918.

[89] 'Oder gehört nicht ganzes Herz dazu, im Stahlgewitter feindlicher Artillerie . . . Die Züge auf das Kampffeld zu fahren', Max Heubes (ed.), *Ehrenbuch der Feldeisenbanner* (Berlin, 1931), Preface.

realistically depicting the activities of the railway troops. The iconography is relatively unexceptional, but the unveiling ceremony in 1929 was much more clearly and intentionally political. Attended by Generals Groener and von Mackensen, it included two plays with explicit right-wing messages. The second play, *Deutsches Hoffen*, written by Professor Dr Burghardt-Oldenburg and performed by the youth wing of the local right-wing veterans' movement, was a retelling of the Siegfried-Hagen story explicitly centred around the 'stab in the back', the *Dolchstoß*. It contains revanchist references to lost territories: Danzig, Tirol, Schleswig-Holstein, and the Saar.[90]

In Paris the great mural at Gare de l'Est commemorated the war, a permanent reminder of the time from 1 August 1918 when this site became the ever-beating heart of France at war. The mural was painted by an American muralist who intended it as a memorial to his son, killed fighting in defence of Paris with the American forces at Belleau Wood in 1918. The scene of mobilization depicted encapsulates the ideology of the citizen soldier. Unlike Meninsky's uniform masses, this highly traditional depiction shows the French soldiers as civilians, not yet in uniform as they part from their families on the platform. The scene is entirely fictional; in the early days of mobilization families were generally excluded from platforms. This was mobilization as it perhaps should have been, poignant and personal. The mural is clearly un-ironic in intention; this was a straightforward commemoration of the loyalty and sacrifices of French citizens in defence of the Republic. But there could increasingly seem to be an ironic sub-text to such representations of 'enthusiasm'.

Such continual reminders may have been unnecessary for any with actual memories of the place; for many of them it would always be the first station of the cross. The addition of the honorific 'Verdun' to the name of the Gare de l'Est firmly located the station as a start point of the 'voie sacrée'. The stations and the trains embedded the memory into everyday life, for example through the signs still present on the Paris metro reserving seats for those 'injured in the war'.

Memory can be ritualized, but it can also arise unbidden in a sound, a sight, or a smell. How often did middle-class men on their way to work or suburban women on a shopping trip find themselves transported back on arrival at Victoria, the Gare de l'Est, or the Potsdamer Bahnhof, to another time in their lives? A generation of Europeans were subject to these capricious but unrecorded memories. In brief moments in these stations and in

---

[90] *Ehrenmahls für die gefallen Kameraden der Deutschen Eisenbahntruppen* (1929), Landesarchiv Berlin, Gesch, 1921.

other settings, they crossed the frontier of time, passing through the 'gate of heartbreak' once more. Rousing songs were inflected with multiple moods, most of which captured the critical role of railway stations in the history of metropolitan life in wartime. These two verses are iconic:

> Goodbye-e, Goodbye-e.
> Wipe the tear, baby dear, from your eye-e
> Though it's hard to part I know,
> I'll be tickled to death to go . . .
> Bonsoir old thing
> Cheerio, Chin-Chin
> Napoo, Toodle-oo
> Goodbye-e . . .[91]

Focus of nostalgia, site of the exchange of identities, information, and cash, railway stations symbolized the sombre turbulence of the war. Beginnings, endings, missed connections – all these happened daily, and gave to the metropolis a sense of possibility and expectation that clearly antedated the war but which took on new and ominous meanings over the fifty months of the conflict.

---

[91] Max Arthur, *When this bloody war is over. Soldiers' songs of the First World War* (London, 2001), p. 45. Music-hall song of the war written in 1917 by R. P. Weston and Bert Lee. Napoo is wartime slang derived from 'il n'y en a plus'.

3 The street

Emmanuelle Cronier

By 1914 the streets of capital cities had long since become a natural topic for debate on metropolitan identity, both because they were the only wholly accessible public location and because it was where experience, symbolism, and imagination met, blended, and evolved in perpetual renewal, locating the street as the basic unit of metropolitan life.[1] For this reason, cultural images of the modern metropolis are fundamentally associated with representations of the street: arteries representing the rhythm and activity of the metropolis, populated by the individual stroller and the crowd and, above all, symbolizing the diversion and freedom characteristic of capital cities.[2] The myths which existed in 1914, of Paris as the City of Light, of London as capital of world trade, or of Berlin as the city of entertainment, are therefore rooted in a tradition of decoding urban space which was to reach its peak in the quest for meaning undertaken by populations at war. The widely perceived need for sobriety during the bloodbath as well as the omnipresence of politics and the stakes of power in metropolitan public space tell us some of the reasons for a reconfiguration of street life in wartime.

Throughout the war capital cities provided a fertile field for representations of war. In particular the cities stood for the home front, the rear, in

Emmanuelle Cronier wrote this chapter, contributions to which were made by Belinda Davis, Jan Rüger, and Armin Triebel. Additional research was provided by Thierry Bonzon, Adrian Gregory, Sarah Howard, Jon Lawrence, Patrick Porter, Pierre Purseigle, Aribert Reimann, Catherine Rollet, and Danielle Tartakowsky.

[1] Karlheinz Stierle, *La capitale des signes. Paris et son discours* (Paris, 2001); Christophe Charle, *Paris fin de siècle. Culture et politique* (Paris, 1998); Rick Allen, *The moving pageant. A literary sourcebook on London street-life, 1700–1914* (London, 1998); Stanford Anderson (ed.), *On streets* (Cambridge, Mass., 1986); Deborah Nord, *Walking the Victorian streets* (Ithaca, 1995); Deborah Parsons, *Streetwalking the Metropolis* (Oxford, 2000); Joachim Schlör, *Nights in the Big City. Paris, Berlin, London 1840–1930* (London, 1998); Thomas Lindenberger, *Straßenpolitik. Zur Sozialgeschichte der öffentlichen Ordnung in Berlin, 1900 bis 1914* (Bonn, 1995), pp. 49–55.

[2] On 'urban arteries' see Richard Sennett, *Flesh and stone. The body and the city in Western civilization* (New York, 1994), ch. 10; see also Parsons, *Streetwalking the Metropolis* (Oxford, 2000).

opposition to the battle front. This was not merely a geographical distinction, but a normative one. In all three cities, the gloomy image of a city relatively safe from the guns, egotistical, prey to speculation and licentious pleasure, is thus contrasted with the mythology of a front line inhabited by true patriots, men of unlimited self-denial and sacrifice. Mobilization feminized these cities. Within this framework, city-dwellers were implicitly and sometimes explicitly reproached for being detached from military realities. This was the image. The reality was otherwise.

Wartime identities were configured and displayed on the streets of each of these cities. The streets were perennially adorned with signs, rituals, and symbolic displays, mostly commercialized before the war, and nationalized after 1914. In wartime a different normative order constrained their exuberance. The appearance and atmosphere of the capitals reflected the fact that so many men were away and at risk in combat. The order of the day was to observe a kind of aesthetic sobriety rather than to indulge in pre-war spectacle. Limits on coal, gas, and therefore illuminations helped keep the streets sombre. But so did the tensions of everyday life.

The metropolitan front

General mobilization transformed the face of Paris, London, and Berlin in wartime. Space was mobilized alongside men and materiel. Almost immediately there was a change in the rhythms of street life. The capitals seemed to return to an earlier period, less mechanized, less well illuminated. Darkness was in part protection against aerial or artillery bombardment, but at night the cities lost their lustre. Shadows proliferated. In daytime, the streets were plastered with posters. Some offered critical information; others were exhortatory, rallying morale. Commercial notices appeared too, but the walls of the streets were occupied. There, on the streets, as Michel de Certeau put it, metropolitan populations 'spoke' the war.[3]

1914: from turbulence to an uneasy calm

The calm that fell on the capital cities from the end of the summer of 1914 was all the more remarkable because it followed the great animation of the period of mobilization, from the end of July to the beginning of August.[4]

---

[3] Michel de Certeau, *The practice of everyday life*, trans. Steven F. Rendall (Berkeley, 1984), pp. 97–8.
[4] Jean-Jacques Becker, *1914: comment les Français sont entrés dans la guerre* (Paris, 1977); Hew Strachan, *The First World War*, volume I: *To arms* (Oxford, 2002); Verhey, *The spirit of 1914*.

During this early period, the capitals played a central role in the circulation of news about the war and in assembling soldiers from various geographical origins at metropolitan stations. In August 1914, the streets of the metropolis remained full of noises and crowds, as usual, but there was now excitement and tension over whether each country would go to war. In Berlin, clusters of people, sometimes gathering into crowds, waited in strategic spots, particularly before the palace at the end of Unter den Linden, but also in the newspaper district in the centre of the city. Once war was declared, Antoine Delécraz noted in Paris, the ordinary noises of the streets disappeared, swallowed up in 'an almost silent agitation' and a 'continuous murmur' of conversations and traffic.[5] Robert Saunders also describes the atmosphere of 'restless excitement' in the streets of London.[6]

At the beginning of September, when the Battle of the Marne was about to begin, metropolitan residents in Paris became aware of reduced levels of street activity, a daily reminder of the absence of men who had left for the front. As we noted in volume I, approximately 350,000 Berliners, 880,000 Parisians, and more than a million Londoners were mobilized in the course of the war.[7] Perhaps half of that number left in the very first months of the war, rendering Parisian streets 'sad', according to one observer.[8] Soldiers were not the only ones to leave. The massive emigration of well-off Parisians fleeing the war, the departure of the government which left for Bordeaux on 3 September, as well as the free rail transport provided for foreigners at the beginning of September, entailed large-scale population shifts across and away from the city. Many commentators spoke of a powerful feeling of emptiness, of a void. This unease about absences continued later in the war. In London, Robert Saunders noted in July 1916 that he had never seen so few people in the streets, and a year later he had the impression of being alone.[9]

The appearance of streets changed in two respects. First, the war brought an end to overcrowding on the sidewalks and markets, so characteristic of metropolitan streets at the end of the nineteenth century.[10]

---

[5] Aged forty-nine in 1914, he escaped mobilization. Antoine Delécraz, *1914. Paris pendant la mobilisation* (Geneva, 1914). See Baronne Jane Michaux, *En marge du drame. Journal d'une Parisienne pendant la guerre 1914–1915* (Paris, 1916), p. 11.

[6] IWM, Robert Saunders, letter to his son in Canada, 17 September 1914.

[7] This represents 35 per cent of the male population of Berlin, 30 per cent in London and 44 per cent in Paris. *Capital cities at war*, volume I, p. 59.

[8] Fernand Laudet, *Paris pendant la guerre: impressions* (Paris, 1915), p. 31.

[9] Robert Saunders, letters to his son in Canada, 16 July 1916 and 9 April 1917.

[10] A few examples of songs: *Derrière l'omnibus*, J. Jouy and L. Raynal, *c.* 1860; *L'Encombrement*, Léon Xanrof and Jean Varney, 1890.

And secondly, it diminished the number of vehicles dominating the thoroughfares.

In Paris, during the years before the war the annual use of bus and tram services was running at more than 500 million journeys in the Paris area, while eight underground railway lines were operating by 1914.[11] There was a steep decline in this traffic thereafter. From the beginning of August inhabitants of the capital cities were surprised at the great calmness in the streets, as a result of reduced traffic. In Paris, buses had been requisitioned by the army, while the number of taxis available was reduced by two-thirds.[12] This fostered a feeling of strangeness, for the noise of traffic was now replaced by the confused mutter of human voices.[13] Parisian taxis, some of which were indeed mobilized to take men and supplies to the Marne, were in shorter supply, once again suggesting to anyone walking on the streets of the city what and who were absent.[14]

From then on the lack of transport forced metropolitan inhabitants to change their daily pattern of getting around. In Paris it was during the end-of-day rush hour that the change was most obvious: no more buses, rare and intermittent metros, and the few horse-drawn cabs were drawn by army reject animals. The natural consequence was to restrict movement, to slow it down, and to require people to remain in the area of business activity.[15]

As we showed in volume I, Paris suffered an economic and social crisis in the first months of the war; there was hardly any cash in circulation. London and Berlin were better off. But by the second half of the war, Berlin's traffic patterns changed as the economic situation worsened. The tram network carried on until the lack of fuel brought a halt to traffic.[16] The fate of Potsdamer Platz, the greatest commercial centre in Berlin, shows what this meant. Before the war, here was the busiest metropolitan intersection in the world, based on the number of streetcar lines that crossed at this site. By 1917, everything had changed. Potsdamer Platz 'thinned out', losing its density of traffic. Fuel scarcities were to blame.[17]

---

[11] D. Van Boque, *L'autobus parisien, 1905–1991* (Paris, 1991).

[12] Michaux, *En marge du drame*, pp. 4–5.

[13] Antoine Delécraz, *Paris pendant la mobilisation*, 2 August 1914.

[14] Mathieu Flonneau, *L'automobile à la conquête de Paris, 1910–1977. Formes urbaines, champs politiques et représentations*, thèse de doctorat de IIIème cycle, Université de Paris I (Paris, 2002).

[15] Laudet, *Paris pendant la guerre*, pp. 32, 98.

[16] *Berliner Tageblatt*, 4 January 1917, cited in D. Glatzer and R. Glatzer, *Berliner Leben 1914–1918* (Berlin, 1983), p. 301.

[17] BLHA PPA no. 15821, p. 77, Police Report Cortemme, 19 June 1917.

The ebbing tide of vehicles was often interpreted as a form of regression.[18] 'In Paris, since the outbreak of the war old delivery vans have replaced the modern streetcar for public transport', observes the trench newspaper *Marmita*.[19] The new rulers of the street, cyclists, 'speed along silently, without sound warning or light, in the dusk', benefiting from police indulgence.[20] Daily movement around the city was largely pedestrian, a phenomenon observed by soldiers on leave in 1916.[21]

And since August 1914 road access to Paris had been rendered more difficult by the defences set up at the gates to the capital, reintroducing the frontier between Paris and its suburbs. Entry to the capital was closed to cars, cyclists, and pedestrians up to 8 August 1914. Thereafter this traffic was restricted during the day except for cyclists or people using trains or trams. Passes were then only available to people 'who justified the purpose of their movements and presented all confirmation'.[22] Up to the middle of August, passport checks by the civil guards were frequent.[23] Subsequently the supervision became less severe, in particular for 'people of good moral standing', to whom authority was immediately granted, and for all those out of work, for whom it seemed urgent to ensure support.[24] Nonetheless, when this period was over, movement was still difficult between Paris and its suburbs. The gates of the capital remained closed at night, and at the approach to some of them tram travellers had to get out 50 metres before the barrier, to cross the fortifications and then take another tram on the other side.[25]

At the beginning of 1916 vehicular traffic stepped up. Old cries resurfaced, such as that of Abel Hermant: 'An excess of vehicles! The quiet peaceful excess of vehicles! The excess of antiquated vehicles! We hadn't seen this since 2 August 1914. Life starts again.'[26] On 1 June 1916 the reopening of the Madeleine–Bastille bus route was a genuine event,

---

[18] Abel Hermant, *La vie à Paris* (Paris, 1917), fictive letter to his recruit, 6 September 1917, p. 193.

[19] *Marmita*, no. 19, 'Nos tuyaux. Tuyau de permissionnaire', p. 4.

[20] Fernand Laudet, *Paris pendant la guerre: impression* (Paris, 1915), p. 98.

[21] 'Le civil' (continuation and conclusion), *Aux 100000 articles*, no. 3, 26 February 1916, p. 2.

[22] Archives of the Paris police préfecture (APP), DB 343, circular notice from the Prefect of Police on 9 August 1914 quoted by Pierre Darmon, *Vivre à Paris pendant la Grande Guerre* (Paris, 2002), p. 29.

[23] Michaux, *En marge du drame*, 5 August 1915, p. 15.

[24] APP, DB 343, circular of the Prefect of Police, 15 August 1914, quoted by Darmon, *Vivre à Paris*, p. 29.

[25] This occurred at the Porte Maillot. Archives privées, *Heures de guerre de la famille H*, Emile's diary, 28 October 1914, pp. 63–4.

[26] Abel Hermant, *La vie à Paris* (Paris, 1917), fictional letter to his recruit, 6 February 1916.

widely noted by the crowd which gathered to see it.[27] Many Parisians interpreted the increase in automobile traffic as a sign of normalization, deeply reassuring as to the outcome of the war.[28] Traffic would never be as heavy again as before the war, however, for in 1918 only 100 buses were on the move in Paris along 25 routes, as against 43 routes in 1910.[29]

Restrictions, though, were not at an end. From the end of 1915 the lack of fuel further reduced automobile traffic. This lack of fuel was felt in Paris and Berlin, and also in London, which since the beginning of the war had been less deserted by cars than the other two cities.[30] In Paris, petrol was rationed from 19 April 1917: the use of cars was reserved to certain categories of users, essentially civil and military authorities, but also Red Cross staff or army suppliers.[31]

Nonetheless, although the war favoured the return to means of transport considered archaic in the streets, it also, paradoxically accelerated the domination of the car in the metropolis. The reason was the change in the balance between different modes of transport. The war caused the disappearance of the boat-omnibus, which in 1913 transported 13 million travellers each year, despite the competition of the metro, buses, and trams. Suspended in 1917 for lack of travellers, the river service was revived in 1921, although never exceeding 5 million travellers. It was suppressed by the city council in 1934.[32] Cars were more evident in another way. They became the vehicle of choice of the Paris police, which in September 1917 inaugurated its four first automobile wagons with cells, abandoning horse-drawn vehicles.[33]

The changed wartime ambience of metropolitan street life had other facets as well. The sombreness of the capital reflected an acute sense of awareness of the carnage of the war. It was simply impossible to justify perpetuating the festive atmosphere of the pre-war capital cities. There were bans on music, dancing, and noisy gatherings. Parisian dance halls,

[27] Hermant, ibid., 1917, letter of 27 July 1916, p. 91. This event was the subject of BDIC photographs Z2157 of 2 June 1916 and press articles in the daily newspapers of that date.

[28] Hermant to his 'recruit' in October 1916, p. 211. Gabriel Perreux, *La vie quotidienne des civils en France pendant la Grande Guerre* (Paris, 1966), p. 191. *L'Echo des marmites*, no. 8, 19 February 1915, 'les plus grandes joies du poilu'; *L'Artilleur déchaîné*, no. 20, 14 July 1916, 'En débigoisant', article by P. Letourneur.

[29] *Le bus dans la ville* (Paris, 2000).

[30] IWM, Fernside Con. Shelf, Elizabeth Fernside (living in Fulham), letters to her son Fred, 14 September 1916.

[31] Perreux, *La vie des civils*, p. 118.

[32] Louis Lagarrigue, *Cent ans de transports en commun dans la région parisienne* (Paris, 1956), 2 vols.

[33] Hermant, *La vie à Paris*, fictional letter to his 'recruit', 6 September 1917, p. 193. Perreux, *La vie des civils*, p. 189.

transformed in some cases into soup kitchens, were all closed and the notices on their doors contradicted their usual signs, stating firmly: 'No dancing here.'[34] All the great Paris festivals were suspended. Throughout the war, the national day of 14 July was silent, as was New Year's Day; although shops and barracks establishments remained open, all circuses and similar entertainments were suspended.[35] Directives published for 14 July 1915, then repeated regularly until 1918, confirm this: 'This year, because of the war, public rejoicings would be in bad taste. This is not the moment to hang out banners and organize district celebrations. We must think of helping those who are suffering from the rigours of the war.' As a result, 'No displays presenting features of public celebration such as banquets, dances, illuminations, fireworks etc. will be permitted.'[36] Colour and sound faded from the Paris streets. One observer, Abel Hermant, saw the sombre tones of these years as the end of a great era of Paris festivities.[37]

In the wartime silence, loud noises were particularly noted by the population or police agents who tracked down sounds that infringed the regulations or which, in their view, challenged moral standards. Although the human voice was more easily heard in the capitals, the climate of political censorship and spy-mania pushed the authorities to pay closer attention to expressions of opinion. In particular they were determined that songs, or in general terms loud conversations, were not an opportunity to utter views that could be pacifist, unpatriotic, or defeatist. This policy was symbolized in Paris by the poster 'Be quiet! Be careful! Enemy ears can hear you!', often mocked at the Front by the fighting troops.[38]

Police reports show how difficult it was to maintain silence among metropolitan populations who were accustomed to singing in bars or in the street, and whose high spirits continued to use song as their preferred form of expression.[39] But these were deviant protests against the greyness of wartime life. A drinking session or family gathering celebrating in a bar still sometimes ended with singing, and the *Internationale* no doubt

---

[34] Hermant saw in this the 'irony' of the times. *La vie à Paris*, Paris, 20 September 1917, p. 200.

[35] Fernand Laudet observed a certain degree of liveliness in the boulevards thanks to the presence of the 'little New Year's stalls'. *Paris pendant la guerre*, 4 January 1915, p. 111.

[36] AD Paris, VK3 187/189/191/194.

[37] Hermant, *La vie à Paris*, pp. 303–4.

[38] Oliver Forcade, 'Censure, opinion et secret en France', *Matériaux pour l'histoire de notre temps* (April–June 2000), no. 58, pp. 45–53.

[39] APP, Répertoire des mains courantes de commissariats parisiens. CB 59.30, CB 59.31, CB 59.32, CB 59.33, CB 79.34, CB 79.35, CB 79.36.

seemed even more subversive when it was heard in streets that were overall quieter than usual.[40]

Restrictions weighing down on traffic and noise, as well as the reduction in human activity in the streets, made them much quieter, creating a strong sense of unfamiliarity among contemporaries who associated all capitals with noisy animation. Henceforward, images of these capital cities insisted on the absence of noise and animation, to the point that all three were compared to provincial towns or villages. London had returned to its bucolic past, as a correspondent of *The Times* noted in August 1916 in his observations on London's new aural identity. 'Calm London Evenings' was the title of the article in which he took pleasure in the disappearance of 'the most hideous uproar and cacophony'. In 1916 the only perceptible sound was that of people talking, which made him realize 'how rare a thing it is to hear human voices in the streets of London'.[41] With the intensifying effect of the fuel shortage, by 1916 the London streets were 'as quiet as those in a country town'.

Metropolitan anarchy

Mobilization was not a period of calm, though as we have noted above, an eerie calm emerged later in the war. In August 1914, though, mobilization turned Paris into a fairground with the streets full of the animals awaiting dispatch to the front. The Bois de Boulogne now provided pasture for livestock. The same scene could be observed at Auteuil, Longchamp, and Bagatelle, interrupting the tradition of horse-racing which before the war was a major interest for Parisian high society.[42] Although humans and livestock alike were quick to leave the city, plant life extended its coverage over urban space, simply through lack of horticultural control.

When, by 1916, problems of food supply began to challenge the capitals, gardens reappeared in town centres. They were there already in the suburbs, but spread in the inner city too. At the beginning of 1917 the Abbé Lemire's Ligue du Coin de terre et du Foyer ('League of the small

---

[40] APP, index on controls on Paris commissions. For example, CB 33.31, no. 606, 2 September 1915; CB 2.31, no. 2694, 26 December 1915; CB 42.37, 21 September 1917; CB 14.958 no. 3, 1 January 1918. Some incidents concerned *The Internationale*: Archives of the Police Prefecture, index of controls on Paris commissions, CB 1.44 no. 432, 31 May 1916; CB 37.46 no. 1978, 16 December 1916, or CB 42.37, no. 340, 28 May 1917. On this topic, see chapter 8.

[41] 'Voices in the street. Calm London evenings', *The Times*, 24 August 1916, p. 9.

[42] 2,000 head of cattle were assembled at Auteuil and Longchamp, 10,000 sheep at Bagatelle. Perreux, *La vie des civils*, p. 99.

patch of ground and of the home') cultivated the fortifications of Paris, an experiment widely commented on by contemporaries.[43] To watch market gardeners work at ground clearance along the rampart walk became a traditional Sunday walk: 'The zone is losing its picturesque appearance, but it will become Paris's vegetable garden', observed Abel Hermant.[44] Indeed, by 1917, 3,000 gardens were under cultivation in Paris, and 2,500 in the 21 communes of the Département of the Seine.[45] Similar sights could be observed in Berlin and London.[46] Even on the florists' stands, the bouquets of fine blooms that were the glory of French floral art were replaced by country flowers.[47]

There is a less salubrious side to this story. Attempts at regulating the capitals were disrupted by rubbish and foul air invading public space. In Paris the outer zone, where order was largely absent before the war, appeared even more anarchic as the gates of the city were readied for war. From the beginning of August, Parisians and suburban residents rushed to visit the fortifications to observe their buttressing and to assess whether they would be adequate to resist the Germans. It is important to recall that Paris had been surrounded and defeated within living memory – 44 years before. Although most of the work was complete by the end of 1914, some entry points – such as Porte Maillot – still had a disorganized air.[48]

It was necessary to provide a makeshift façade to the city in order to protect public monuments from bombardment. The most spectacular measures were the works undertaken in London and Paris at the beginning of 1918 in the context of the Gotha raids. In the French capital, although the Louvre museum had already sent its masterpieces to the south of France, what was to be done with everything that could not be moved – fountains, columns, statues, monuments? The stained glass windows of the Sainte Chapelle were removed, the windows of the Louvre were blocked up, many monuments were protected with sandbags, planking, fabrics, mummifying the national heritage in order to protect it in the long term. The Eiffel Tower, the Place de la Concorde, the Sorbonne, and all the public areas populated with statues all changed their appearance, while gardens were henceforward occupied by air-raid posts.[49]

[43] Perreux, *La vie des civils*, p. 99, and Dir.b. Cabedoce and P. Pierson, *100 ans d'histoire des jardins ouvriers 1896–1996* (Paris, 1996).

[44] Hermant, *La vie à Paris*, 8 March 1917, p. 46.

[45] *Capital cities at war*, pp. 322–3.

[46] IWM, Robert Saunders, letters to his son in Canada, 9 April 1917.

[47] Perreux, *La vie des civils*, p. 205.

[48] Private archive, *Heures de guerre de la famille H*, Emile's diary, 20 December 1914, p. 95.

[49] Thus, photographic album no. 377 produced by the BDIC photothèque on 'Gardens' consists almost entirely of photographs of DCA posts and protection against shelling.

Metropolitan residents soon discovered the disagreeable side of unmanaged streets. In July 1917, Abel Hermant observed that 'the Parisians stay dirty', and commented sarcastically that, 'It is possible to be a victor and be clean.'[50] The urban population no doubt found it all the more convenient to throw its rubbish straight into the streets, as street cleansing and maintenance had been abandoned since the mobilization of the municipal workers charged with their upkeep. In Berlin, even though the streets were spared the hazards of shelling, the sense of increased danger was largely linked to the difficulty of avoiding accidents due to sheets of ice or snow in winter and accentuated by the poor street lighting. The 'obstacles' in the Paris streets were a recurrent theme in the 'frontline press', identifying another way to mock the supposed dangers surrounding Parisians.[51]

The atmosphere and smell of the capital cities was similarly much changed from the first days of the war. Although some witnesses were delighted in August 1914 at the disappearance, with motor vehicles, of 'the smoke, dust and smells of petrol',[52] human odours were in contrast more noticeable, and the impression of their intensification was general. In the street, pedestrians smelled stronger; in Berlin the lack of soap and hot water limited opportunities for thorough washing, and many civilians now depended on a diet based on root crops which caused gastric disturbance. In the street, in public transport and also in spaces where crowds assembled, such as theatres, ventilation was no longer a priority; draughts had to be stopped in order to save on coal and wood. Finally the olfactory and physical presence of men on leave from the front – filthy, their uniforms covered in mud, smelling of stagnant water and, at best, of disinfectant – demonstrated national perceptions of the changes in personal comportment since the outbreak of war.[53] Although this olfactory deterioration may have been bearable in private, in public it created a certain feeling of shame, very strong among the men on leave from the front.[54] After all, they had been forced to live in ditches for months at a time. No more making fun of 'Gilbert the Filbert, Colonel of the Knuts', young men with concern for hair parting and the 'whole grand toilette'.

---

[50] Hermant, *La vie à Paris*, 12 July 1917, p. 139.
[51] *Aux 100 000 articles*, no. 2, February 1916, pp. 3–4, 'le civil' first part.
[52] Michaux, *En marge du drame*, p. 40.
[53] Officers seemed to have been exempt from these images.
[54] Caricature by R. Pallier in *L'Œuvre*, 28 May 1916, p. 2. See also *Le Diable au cor*, no. 13, 10 October 1915, p. 3, 'Les tribulations du permissionnaire'; *Bellica*, no. 1: 1 December 1915, p. 6, 'Le journal d'un permissionnaire'; *L'Echo des marmites*, no. 11, 25 May 1916, pp. 4–5, 'Les Grands étonnements du poilu (…) à Paris'.

Instead French soldiers in London or in Paris on leave were filth-stained, and smelled like it.[55]

Son et lumière: changes in time, light, and sound

The rhythms of daily life were modified strikingly in wartime. As we have noted in volume I, the work week expanded as the war expanded. In Paris, Sunday became a working day. In Berlin, war factory shifts often began earlier and/or finished later, while many workers were frequently forced to work back-to-back shifts. In 1915, the eight or nine-hour shift barely affected many factory workers' senses in that, like proverbial miners, they rarely saw the light of day at all.[56] To meet the demands of the state of siege, from 4 August 1914 opening hours in Paris cafés, bars, and restaurants were reduced. By 1915 the union of restaurateurs and soft drinks establishments achieved a less rigid régime specifically in the Département of the Seine, to satisfy the expectations of men on leave.[57]

As early as September 1914, and partly in reaction to a complaint by Wilhelm II about the 'immorality of his residential city', Berlin authorities had set closing hours at 11 p.m. Daylight-saving time was of some relief to Berliners – though it provided a new source of rancour between urban and rural dwellers.[58] Introduced in 1915, that summer and the next it saved some fuel for the war effort, though by the following year street lights were rarely if ever lit at all. Certainly, then, by late in the war the later sunset meant that some tasks in the street could be carried out in the light rather than in darkness.

In all three capital cities the winter of 1916–17 introduced a period of restricted heating and electricity, reflected in the closing of food shops, theatres, and cinemas on certain days of the week, and by a general reduction in street lighting.[59] For the first time in France and in Great Britain, clocks were put forward by law by an hour in summer from 1916 to save energy.[60] Once peace returned, the Paris norm of 'summer time'

---

[55] Michaux, *En marge du drame*, p. 88.

[56] Belinda Davis, *Home fires burning: food, politics and everyday life in World War I Berlin* (Chapel Hill, 2000).

[57] *Le petit Parisien*, 8 and 11 November 1916, 'l'éclairage des magasins et la fermeture des cafés', p. 2.

[58] Davis, *Home fires*.

[59] In Paris, theatres closed on Mondays, cinemas on Tuesdays, and concerts and music-halls on Wednesdays.

[60] 'Summer time' came into effect in France overnight on 15–16 June 1916 and the return to winter time, in other words the normal peacetime hours, overnight on 30 September–1 October 1916.

was imposed throughout French territory and remained in force until 1940, when German time was substituted for French time.[61]

Meanwhile, late in the war in Paris all shop blinds came down from Monday to Wednesday, when trade began again until the end of the week. The lack of groceries was also responsible for the range and uncertainty of shop opening hours, juggling official regulations with delivery times. In 1917 in Berlin, officials briefly both shifted and limited legal shopping hours, in deference to the women working in war factories who claimed that all goods were gone by the end of their shifts. But these regulations were withdrawn after it became clear that those waiting in line all day for opening time, no matter when it took place, would clearly exhaust supplies before the munitionnettes got home.

The planned or unplanned closing of shops thus reflected the rarity or absence of certain products in the capital cities. In particular, wartime closings affected nightlife, the energy of which was what these cities were all about. The *grands boulevards*, focus of Parisian nightlife before the war, lost their swagger with the 1917 closure of places of entertainment four days a week. Parisians' shorter day provoked a return to home and hearth as the centre of social life, with people generally arriving home earlier than usual. This meant that suburban train services were thronged between 6.00 p.m. and 7.00 p.m. from November 1916 onwards, because of shops' earlier closing time.[62]

Lighting in the capitals, including those of the most symbolic of them, Paris, the city of light, was in fact reduced from the beginning of the war in order to protect the cities from enemy attack, with Paris and London being particularly threatened because of their proximity to enemy forces.[63] When fuel became rationed in 1915, public lighting restrictions also affected Berlin in its turn. In Paris, lamp standards were turned off in an area of 2 kilometres round the Eiffel Tower, and observers were surprised to find Paris 'entirely dark' after 10.00 p.m.[64] The only points of light were now the narrow beams from two large projectors which 'leapt from one point to another, piercing the whole horizon with their vast uncertainty'.[65] The same strange atmosphere reigned in London: 'Can you imagine Tower Bridge, Trafalgar Square, Piccadilly Circus and all the Strand without light?', wondered Baronne Jane Michaux in October 1914.[66] New measures were taken in Paris in 1915 to avoid the

[61] Gerhard Dohrn-van Rossum, *L'Histoire de l'heure. L'horlogerie et l'organisation moderne du temps* (Paris, 1997).

[62] *Le petit Parisien*, 11 November 1916, 'l'éclairage des magasins et la fermeture des cafés', p. 2, and 1 January 1917, 7 January 1917, p. 3.

[63] On the myth of the Ville Lumière, the 'city of light': L. Figuier, *La ville lumière* (Paris, 1914).

[64] Michaux, *En marge du drame*, p. 50.   [65] Ibid., p. 35.   [66] Ibid., p. 103.

lights of Paris being used as guides by German aircraft, of which the first incursions date from the end of August 1914. From sunset to sunrise, facing the rear or on to the streets, curtains and blinds were lowered and lamps wore a small metal hood so that light should not be wasted shining upwards. Coming out of the metro at Porte Maillot 'gives a deep impression of sadness, in addition to what one felt already', commented a resident of a town in the western suburbs of Paris.[67] Indeed, until January 1916 little more than a third of the gas lamps were lit before 10:00 p.m., the number dropping to 20 per cent for the rest of the night.[68]

The growing threat from the air meant that the regulations limiting Paris lighting became tougher again in early 1918 with the new wave of shelling aimed at the capital. By then Berlin was affected too, though not because it was in the line of fire. Coal shortages brought about the reduction in street lighting from the beginning of 1917, creating a particularly noticeable change in the most lively districts, such as Potsdamerplatz and Friedrichßtrasse, as well as in residential quarters in the east of the city where nightlife traditionally took place largely in the streets. Well before regulations on the use of fuel for street lighting, however, the Berlin power company had already begun to 'cannibalize' itself for the war effort, giving up transformers, copper wire, cables, and a whole range of supplies already in use. By the end of 1917, of 44,000 gas street lamps in the city, only 9,000 still burned.[69]

While London suffered similar lighting restrictions, the lighting authorities stated at a Home Office conference in October 1915 that 'the private and shop lighting of the London area has been brought generally within the required limits, which must continue to be observed'.[70] In Paris, police paid particular attention on their night-time rounds to the way in which individuals cooperated with lighting restrictions. The number of fines imposed from February 1918, in particular in the tenth arrondissement where the railway stations to the frontline were located, appears to indicate that this set of rules was still not fully observed.[71]

In France the colour blue – in the sky, in the streets – now lent itself to many slang or metaphorical uses during the war, to mean a telegram, a young soldier, the 'sky blue' of the French uniforms (or 'Joffre blue'), or a

---

[67] *Heures de guerre de la famille; H. Emile's diary*, pp. 122–4.
[68] In normal times, Paris had 55,000 gas lamps. 'Amélioration de l'éclairage de Paris', *La libre parole*, 6 January 1916, p. 2.
[69] Compare Glatzer, *Berliner leben 1914–1918*, pp. 302–3.
[70] 'More light in London streets. An equalizing process', *The Times*, 8 October 1915, p. 3.
[71] Poorly shielded lights attracted fines for the occupants of lodgings and commercial premises. APP, records of Paris police stations.

bad red wine, and became a much-used theme repeated by contemporary descriptions as a substitute for the term 'City of Light' used in nostalgic moments.[72] Marcel Proust saw in these bluish maritime tones a metaphor for mankind during the war, 'men taken up with the immense revolution of the earth ... on which they are mad enough to continue with their own revolutions, and their useless wars, like the one which is drowning France in blood at this moment'.[73] Like many other Parisians, during his nocturnal walks Proust rediscovered the quality of the Paris sky which had supplied a major visual theme for all the avant-garde artists of the late nineteenth century, notably the Impressionists and their successors.[74]

Parisians and Londoners, already accustomed to looking out for the threat of imminent annihilation from the skies, were quick to observe its particular colouring. In August 1916 an article in *The Times* commented on the new way in which Londoners looked at their city, crowding onto their balconies: 'The nocturnal glare of our city has (on account of the Zeppelins) been subdued; and so we can see the moon rising over the chimney-tops of London, picking out the roofs in black and silver and flooding squares and courtyards with a purity of radiance and depth of shadow which were all too unfamiliar.'[75]

We are a long way here from the enchanted evening illumination which was the glory of Paris, Berlin, and London before the war; the vast 'Palace of Electricity' built on the Champ-de-Mars for the 1900 Exhibition seems to belong to a past epoch. Although the poetic appearance of the capitals in this dim blue light was noted by some contemporary observers, most were more inclined to feel thoroughly uneasy at these major changes in the metropolitan landscape, in particular when shelling added to the dislocation and anxiety.

Public representations of war on metropolitan streets

The invasion of public space by representations of the war was a striking feature of this period of metropolitan history. It was apparent first in posters, which since the middle of the nineteenth century had been the

---

[72] *La Fusée*, no. 23, 25 April 1918, p. 4, 'Notes du permissionnaire'. At the same period, the *Bulletin désarmé* describes the new colours of Paris in an article headed 'Echos de Panam. Tout en bleu', no. 2, 1 April 1918, p. 4. ('Panam' was a recognized slang name for Paris.) See also Hermant, *La vie à Paris*, pp. 46ff.

[73] *Le temps retrouvé*, p. 94. In *Le bataillonnaire* (first published in 1920), Pierre Mac Orlan evokes the time when 'Paris presented herself *en veilleuse*' (Paris, 1989 edn), p. 69.

[74] Amélie Chazelle, *Paris vu par les peintres* (Paris, 1987); Frédéric Gaussen, *Paris des peintres* (Paris, 2002); Jacques Wilhelm, *Les peintres du paysage parisien* (Paris, 1933) and his *Paris vu par les peintres* (Paris, 1961).

[75] 'Voices in the street. Calm London evenings', *The Times*, 24 August 1916, p. 9.

preferred basis for images in urban spaces, but which reached their peak between 1914 and 1918. The symbolic significance of certain posters was not limited to the capitals, and it is known that the notices of mobilization marked the outbreak of war for many people at the time.[76] In the open spaces of the capital, however, they sometimes received particular attention because of their historic significance. This is true of the mobilization notice set in a glass showcase in 1917 on a wall in the Rue Royale, where it still exists.[77] Many other military, civilian, or legal notices appeared on walls or Morris display columns, covered in tricolour paper by their licensee and informing the public of accounts of Parliamentary sessions, presidential speeches, or the call-up of reservist classes.[78] Some of the phrases produced here have entered the vernacular: there are Galliéni's words: 'To the very end' (*'jusqu'au bout'*) or Millerand's instruction: 'Keep quiet, take care, enemy ears are listening' (*'Taisez-vous, méfiez-vous, des oreilles ennemies vous écoutent'*).

Exhortations to enlist in London, or to make a financial contribution to the war effort in the three capitals, were unavoidable to those walking through metropolitan streets in wartime. It was impossible to escape the demands of the latest war loan, or 'Kriegsanleihe' in Berlin. Parisian artists did their bit for the war by designing many posters which quickly became iconic.[79]

In a much more diffuse way, the circulation of postcards on a national scale as part of the vastly increased correspondence between front and rear was expressed in the capitals by the permanent and very large-scale display of their propaganda images in kiosks and bookshop windows.[80] The 100,000 designs of cards published in France during the war not only took patriotic images all over the country; in addition their display in Paris, under Parisian eyes – and also those of the Allies and men on leave from the front – ensured the persistence of these images in the minds of their passive observers. Signs and advertisements themselves were also adapted to the war context; placards indicated public establishments offering low prices, charitable undertakings in support of soldiers or auxiliary hospitals. Advertising adapted patriotic symbolism and words

[76] Jean-Jacques Becker, *Comment les Français sont entrés dans la guerre* (Paris, 1977).

[77] It is signed by the mayor of the 8th arrondissement. Perreux, *La vie des civils*, p. 202. Delécraz notes at length the many posters which caught his attention in August 1914.

[78] Perreux, *La vie des civils*, p. 203.

[79] '*On les aura!*' ('We'll get them!) was widely distributed. Véronique Harel (ed.), *Les affiches de la Grande Guerre* (Péronne, 1998).

[80] Marie-Monique Huss, *Cartes postales et culture de guerre. Histoire de famille 1914–1918* (Noisy-le-Grand, 1990); T. and V. Holt, *Till the boys come home. The picture postcards of the First World War* (London, 1977).

for commercial purposes, and commercial symbols were reshaped to support national aims.

City space was colonized by patriotic symbolism of many kinds. For instance in Paris metro stations were renamed. 'Berlin' and 'Allemagne' became 'Liège' and 'Jaurès'. There were spontaneous practices, too; for example, in 1916 a patriotic concierge defaced a metro map from which the name 'Berlin' had not been removed.[81] Early in 1917, Parisians took to the streets to remove the name from the Avenue Richard Wagner in the upper-class district of Passy while, at the same time, new streets were dedicated in 1918 to heroes of the day, such as Gallieni, Guynemer, and President Wilson. At the beginning of April 1918 there were nineteen street names still to be changed, and on 14 July 1918 these baptisms of streets took place.[82] Similarly, certain statues were covered with graffiti denouncing German misdeeds, while someone placed a dummy dressed in a German uniform between the paws of the Belfort Lion on the monument to National Defence in the Place Denfert Rochereau. On the other hand, the statue of Musset in front of the Théâtre Français was capped with a genuine steel helmet, and the statue of the Republic in front of the French Institut bore on its hand a heart pierced with an arrow and a message, drawn in charcoal, 'To the soldiers, forever' ('*Aux poilus pour la vie*').[83]

In all three capitals, lottery drawings, special fund days, flag days, victory celebrations, and numerous appeals followed hot upon each other for the benefit of the combatants and victims of the war, permanently mediatizing the mobilization of the population through the sale of signs, cockades, or banners to be shown or worn by the donors.[84] As early as August 1914 Parisians were showing an excess of enthusiasm for wearing badges, while the invasion of flags in the street was particularly noted, as in London during the spring of 1916. The *Daily Mail* opined that ' "Have you got a flag?" is invariably the first request of a wounded soldier when carried from the field. Today is 'Flag Day' in London and millions of little flags will be on sale in the streets, and every buyer will know that every penny he pays for his flag will buy fourteen cigarettes for a wounded fighter.'[85]

The colouring of the streets on the occasion of patriotic days organized in the three capitals was unusual, and explains the reports made by many

[81] APP, CB32.27, 5 January 1916.   [82] Perreux, *La vie des civils*, p. 251.

[83] Perreux, a pedestrian in Paris, in May 1916, ibid., p. 206.

[84] Days organized in Paris had the following titles: The Day of the 75, of the Serbian Flag, of the Soldier, of French Aid, of Colonial Troops, of Paris, of Belgians, of Orphans, of the Croix de Guerre, of the Americans, etc., Perreux, *La vie des civils*, p. 200.

[85] Michaux, *En marge du drame*, p. 15. On flags: *Daily Mail*, 4 April 1916.

observers. It was part of the scene-setting in the streets, particularly when it was designed to encourage gifts, as shown by the installation in 1917 in the Place de la Concorde of a collection post in front of a genuine Zeppelin and an armed and equipped tank.[86] Similarly, stalls were set up in July 1918 in the large squares of Paris, enabling the most generous donors to win themselves a reputation, such as the American lawyer who arrived at the ticket office at the statue of Lille, Place de la Concorde, to hand over a gift of one and a half million francs in November 1918.[87]

The war further multiplied opportunities for collective sociability. This was true at the time of the mobilization and departure of new recruits, or the arrival and departure of men on leave, experienced by those taking part – usually families – as the model of a common lot, even of a community. In daily life, the dramatic context seemed to bring people together around the search for news or discussion of latest events, encouraging public expression of opinions and feelings formerly more confined to private life, and which were of great interest to authorities who tried to read in the attitude of crowds indications of morale.

The phenomenon of wartime urban sociability in public was all the more remarkable in that gatherings of people were *a priori* suspect, as in Paris where it was forbidden formally to form a group of more than three people in the street. In both Paris and Berlin, popular classes had been attached since the nineteenth century to the idea that the street was theirs, and the war encouraged this symbolism.[88]

Many observers describe the turmoil and tensions which reigned in the streets of the capitals, despite the reduced traffic. There was the separation of families, and the public sign of bereavement in the form of war widows' black clothing and the anxious exchange of news on the well-being of mobilized local men. The expression of these sentiments no doubt reached its peak on Mondays in Berlin, when the lists of the dead and missing were posted in public areas, transformed into scenes of weeping and distress.[89]

And yet the street atmosphere was not always anxious. Perhaps there was some self-censorship here, in that contemporaries may have felt the need not to discuss their distress in public. And yet, there were many times, from August 1914 on, when city-dwellers talked together of things of the greatest importance. Baroness Jane Michaux was surprised that everyone joined in conversation in the trams: 'You would think it was one

---

[86] Perreux, *La vie des civils*, p. 201.   [87] Ibid., p. 201.

[88] *The Berlin of George Grosz: drawings, watercolours and prints, 1912–1930* (New Haven, 1997).

[89] Davis, *Home fires*.

single vast family vibrating with the same emotion in the face of the terrible drama being played out at the front.'[90] In October 1914 one of her American friends, returning from London, confirmed that he no longer recognized the city: people were exchanging newspapers in the Tube and 'the man in a frock-coat deigned to look at his waistcoat-clad neighbour and even speak to him!'[91]

Marie-Josèphe Boussac, who was not given to feelings of social superiority, gained the opposite impression in December 1915 from her contacts with the Paris crowd, which had, in her view, 'become brute-like'.[92] The ambivalence of these experiences and representations owes much to the perpetuation of the conflict's influence on popular morale and perceptions, but also to the vigour of the former representation of metropolitan individualism and anomie, which radically differed from the ideal of fraternity in 1914.[93]

From the outbreak of war, maps of the front were displayed on thoroughfares, such as the *grands boulevards* in Paris, book-store windows, and wine merchants' shops. The crowd which gathered in front of them offered its brisk commentary and saw the little flags defining the front line as a barometer of the overall situation.[94]

The use of maps of the front line as promotional material for the press is a guide to the level of public interest in them.[95] The headquarters of the main Paris newspapers were concentrated in the Grands Boulevards district, between the Opéra and the Place de la République and contributed to the liveliness of a district which remained a metropolitan centre, while a more anaemic air was generally prevalent on the outskirts. The newspapers plunged into an excess of news presentation, with a proliferation of special editions and the use of sandwich-men and advertising. In addition, news items were pinned up in wall-mounted showcases on newspaper buildings, encouraging gatherings on the public streets.[96] *Le Matin*, which in 1914 claimed to be 'the best informed newspaper in the world', reacted to the announcement of the United States' entry into the war by draping American flags across the building's façade.[97]

[90] Michaux, *En marge du drame*, p. 23.   [91] Ibid., p. 96.

[92] *Correspondance de Jacques et Marie-Josèphe Boussac*, letter to Jacques Boussac, 31 December 1915.

[93] Arthur Newton, *Years of change: autobiography of a Hackney shoemaker* (London, 1974), p. 48.

[94] Michaux, *En marge du drame*, p. 27; Perreux, *La vie des civils*, p. 205.

[95] Larousse/Giraudon archives, photograph of 20 October 1918.

[96] Michaux, *En marge du drame*, p. 22.

[97] BDIC, photographic archive, P965, March 1917.

Popular animation in places where military news was made available was also evident in Paris near Les Invalides and the Ministry for War. It was here that families gathered to obtain news of mobilized men, or where certain patriotic demonstrations were shifted.[98] The first captured enemy banner was set up and presented to the nation on these two buildings in succession, a reassuring sight for all those who gathered in front of it.[99]

Public commotion surrounding published news of the war was much more evident on the Parisian boulevards than in London, where Fleet Street, the traditional press district, remained a working area distinct from places of entertainment. Although more widely diffused in public city spaces, military news attracted huge and anxious crowds in several parts of both the British and the German capitals.[100]

It may thus be observed that the search for news lay behind the circulation of human traffic in metropolitan space. Whole districts were kept in a permanent state of animation by rumour and news of the war, exchanged on a daily basis in the street and encouraging contacts between strangers in all public spaces. This applied in particular in markets, the traditional site for the diffusion of public rumours. This aspect was emphasized during the war by the time customers spent queueing and the conditions specific to grocery distribution. Rumours concerning the arrival or exhaustion of grocery supplies for sale were thus amongst the most rapid to be spread, and children were immediately sent to queue in front of the shop with the desired merchandise.[101]

The abundance of representations encouraged the practice of concentrating on printed material as people were motivated by the need to scrutinize their own environment for reassuring signs as to the outcome of the war. And once both Paris and London were under bombardment, the search for news became all the more vital.

Capitals under threat: Paris and London

The possibility of aerial attack meant that the war was no longer simply mediated; it had come to the cities themselves.[102] The first German

---

[98] Laudet, *Paris pendant la guerre*, p. 72.   [99] Ibid., pp. 36 and 44.

[100] IWM, Fernside letters Con. shelf, 6 June 1916.

[101] Michaux, *En marge du drame*, pp. 22–3; Arthur Newton, *Years of Change*, p. 49; and Alice Linton, *Not expecting miracles* (London, 1982), p. 5.

[102] J. Poirier, *Les bombardements de Paris (1914–1918)* (Paris, 1930); Patrick Facon, 'Les villes, objectifs du bombardement stratégique' in CEHD, *La ville et la guerre* (Paris, 1999), pp. 207–17; Joseph W. Konvitz, 'Représentations urbaines et bombardements stratégiques 1914–1945' in *Annales* ESC (July–August 1989), pp. 812–47; Williamson Murray, *Les guerres aériennes, 1914–1945* (Paris, 2000); Danièle Voldman, 'Les

aircraft struck Paris in the night of 30 August 1914: 'a dry sound tore through the air, followed by the duller echo … a flock of pigeons flew past … another outburst, nearer … people running … it was the first *Taube* arriving to terrify Paris', noted a Parisian woman.[103] Parisians felt the irony in the neologism '*Taube*' for these very light aircraft; the word originally meant a pigeon. This threat contributed to demoralization among some Parisians in early September 1914, when the possibility was all too real that the German army would capture the city. 'While there is still time for it, I want to admire the city which will perhaps find its precious beauty suffering', Baronne Jane Michaux noted in her diary.[104]

At '*Taube* time', around 5:00 p.m., a new urban ritual developed, replacing the pre-war Parisian's characteristic stroll with gatherings on balconies, in squares, on bridges or promontories.[105] Those with binoculars scanned the sky: ' "There's one!" shouted a man.' Next the *Taube* is insulted, French aircraft are launched in pursuit, applauded, ammunition gathered up. Certain districts, such as Montmartre, were favoured by the public, who hired chairs, or the very popular Porte Maillot.[106] To some eyes, this Parisian defiance of the *Tauben* constituted the true expression of the Paris crowd: 'The moment when the *Taube* is visible' became the moment when Gavroche laughed at the *Taube* and left. His departure was seen as a collective victory for the crowd.[107] Because these light German bombs claimed few victims, perception of the danger was deferred. It was not until the arrival of the Zeppelins in March 1915 that the people of Paris understood the reality of the threat. The attack was still sometimes described as a 'spectacle' – showing either a lack of awareness of the danger or a wish to deny it.[108] The attack now constituted the horizon of Parisian expectations.

London was targeted in its turn in 1915 by German attacks. Sites that suffered bombing received priestly pilgrimages.[109] A year later a second and final Zeppelin raid, this time on central Paris, came as a surprise so early in the year – a feature widely commented on – and by the number of

populations civiles, enjeux du bombardement des villes (1914–1945)', in Audoin-Rouzeau, Becker, Ingrao, and Rousso (eds.), *La violence de guerre 1914–1945* (Paris, 2002), pp. 151–73.

[103] Michaux, *En marge du drame*, 30 August 1914.

[104] Michaux, ibid., 20 August 1914.

[105] *L'heure du Taube* was thus chosen as the title for a poem by Fernand Hausel which appeared in *La France sauvée*. Quoted in Jacques Bréal, *Les poètes de la Grande Guerre. Anthologie* (Paris, 1992), p. 157.

[106] Michaux, *En marge du drame*, p. 46. Perreux, *La vie des civils*, p. 212.

[107] Hausel, *L'heure du Taube*.

[108] Most of the bombs fell in the suburbs. Michaux, *En marge du drame*, p. 222.

[109] IWM, Robert Saunders, letters to his son in Canada, 20 September 1915.

its victims: 26 dead and 28 wounded, mostly in the popular districts of Paris such as Ménilmontant where a crowd of 300,000 assembled on the following Sunday.[110] The great crowds of Parisians at sites bombed since 1915 rendered press censorship ineffective as to points of impact and the number of victims. Although censorship was designed above all to prevent information reaching enemy forces, it may be surmised that they, like the people of Paris themselves, were aware of the results of the bombing. Abel Hermant emphasized the absurdity of the situation, when he remarked: 'It is entirely senseless that one should not indicate reference points to the enemy, nor reveal to the three hundred thousand Parisians who went on Sunday to judge the effect of explosions, the names of streets where they were strolling, apparently without consulting announcements.'[111] The deliberate decision of French authorities to conceal the number of victims contrasted here with the British decision to publish these figures, a contrast which gave Abel Hermant a subject for mockery: 'In England, the public are told, the same day, about what has happened. Here we can hum the tune next day: If you have nothing to tell me / Why did you make such a fuss yesterday?'[112]

Similarly, images of the damage caused by bombing were widely seen in Britain, particularly in newsreels in the cinema.[113] The number of victims of the *Taube* and Zeppelin bombing, however, remained small, but the symbolic importance of these attacks exceeded the casualties. Here was the moment to denounce yet again German barbarity which took 'the most beautiful city in the world' as its target, focusing on the Eiffel Tower and Notre Dame among other more clearly military targets, the Gare de l'Est and the Gare du Nord.[114]

From 1915 on, news of bombs falling on London created a feeling of fraternity among Parisians, who saw in them an illustration of the alliance between the two nations and, above all, of the common suffering inflicted by Germany on her enemies.[115] London was the first of the two capitals to suffer a raid by Gothas, in May 1917, which caused 95 deaths and wounded 260 in Folkestone.[116] The successful bombing of the British capital a week later, causing 162 dead and 432 wounded, created an

---

[110] Hermant, *La vie à Paris*, pp. 9–10. Perreux, *La vie des civils*, p. 213.

[111] Hermant, *La vie à Paris*, 6 February 1916.

[112] Ibid., 2 August 1917, p. 160.

[113] IWM, film on the raid of 26 September 1917.

[114] By the autumn of 1915, fifty-eight explosive and incendiary bombs had been launched on the capital, killing six people and wounding thirty-four. Danièle Voldman, 'Les populations civiles', p. 156.

[115] Louise Delétang, *Journal d'une ouvrière parisienne pendant la guerre* (Paris, 1935). Entry for 2 June 1915.

[116] Murray, *Les guerres aériennes*, p. 73.

awareness of the danger in their streets. When Paris was targeted in its turn, during the night of 30–31 January 1918, by raids which would continue to focus on the capital on 77 occasions, the bonds of solidarity between the two Allied capitals were strengthened. These raids were on a larger scale. On 31 January the alert was sounded by 27 enormous sirens, and bells rang at full pitch. In all blocks of flats of more than four storeys, inhabitants were required to take shelter in the cellars. Public shelters proliferated, reaching a capacity of 500,000 places in 5,000 shelters. In 37 metro stations electricity was cut off, and Parisians were met by large notices stating 'Shelter'. Many people told of their time in the shelters; their tone varied from telling of an innocent and even festive atmosphere to contrasting scenes of panic, as in the Couronnes metro station on 11 March 1918 where a scuffle in front of doors already closed caused 66 deaths.[117]

From the autumn of 1914 the underground assembly of city inhabitants in shelters seemed to echo the underground existence of the fighting men in the trenches. Elsewhere, private housing blocks were opened to the crowds from February 1918, designated as 'SHELTER' by district commissions, to receive refugees. The concierges of these buildings played a key role at this time. They had been focal figures in the streets and buildings of Paris before the war, and took on new status as agents of surveillance of urban populations during the war.[118]

From 23 March 1918, the fire of new long-range German guns was added to the Gothas. Firing from 120 kilometres away, these artillery pieces were wrongly given the name of 'Big Bertha' by Parisians, a large-calibre cannon with which they were already familiar. Installed in the St-Gobain forest, the cannon had the particular feature of striking during the daytime and of creating incredulity among the population because of its range and the frequency of its firing. The first time that it made itself heard, policemen – armed, as in older times, with drums and whistles – had to range the streets to spread the alert among the residents. Firing until August 1918, the cannon killed 256 Parisians and wounded 628 more, while for their part the Gothas were responsible for 237 dead and more than 500 wounded.[119] The worst day was 29 March 1918, Good Friday, when a single shell falling on the church of St Gervais next to the Paris City Hall, killed 88 and wounded 68.

Until August 1918 the shelling of the capital was the central topic of all conversations, in Paris as among the fighting men at the front who occasionally wrote that they felt heartened that the capital's fate bore some

[117] Perreux, *La vie des civils*, p. 215.   [118] Ibid., p. 217.   [119] Ibid., p. 223.

resemblance to their own.[120] Solidarity in hardship, as it were. In their letters, Parisians commented at length on the shelling; Marie-Josèphe Boussac, for example, reported to her mobilized husband in many letters on where the shells landed, the attitude of the population and in particular the opinions of friends and family. The absence of official figures on the number of victims gave rise to rumours, and everyone did his best to find scraps of information.[121]

Anticipating fate, everyone was constantly occupied in calculations: sounds, the apparently suspect colour of the sky; even silence seemed threatening.[122] In April 1918, a million Parisians fled the city. They returned, and left again in mid-June when shelling that seemed to go on forever swept on to the capital. The bombardment became a major theme in war narratives, driving home the incomprehensibility of ordinary people in the face of the new threat from shells, the fear, the rumours and the exhaustion of nights without sleep.[123] Although many witnesses described the shelling, few admitted to personal fear, preferring to describe the atmosphere of strangeness or excitement.[124]

To be sure there was self-congratulation too in these accounts. The diary of Baronne Jane Michaux was dedicated to 'the people of Paris', who 'showed the *Tauben* their fine mocking face and courageous heart'.[125] Similarly, Abel Hermant saw in the pilgrimage of Parisians to the sites of destruction a sign of moral strength.[126] Those who remained in Paris became, for this reason alone, 'brave defence workers'. Conversely, those who left the threatened capitals were stigmatized, as can be seen in graffiti on the blinds of businesses closed down: 'Closed because of the Gothas', 'Closed because of fear.'[127]

On 28 June 1919, the sound of the last gun heard in Paris inaugurated what many hoped would be an era of peace. This was the last memory

---

[120] Stéphane Audoin Rouzeau, *14–18, les combattants des tranchées à travers leurs journaux* (Paris, 1986).

[121] The Labrousse family were banking friends. *Correspondance de Jacques et Marie-Josèphe Boussac*, p. 293.

[122] The aunts of Marie-Josèphe Boussac, remaining in Paris in June 1918, wrote 'terrified letters': 'as there had not been a Gotha raid nor a cannon bombardment for several days, they wondered what the silence could mean', as Marie-Josèphe wrote to her husband on 17 June 1918. *Correspondance de Jacques et Marie-Josèphe Boussac*, p. 326.

[123] Marie-Josèphe Boussac described the panic of her housekeeper, of a neighbour 'sick with fear' (p. 305), rumours on points of impact and victims (Good Friday 1918, p. 307). See also her letter of 3 June 1918, p. 321.

[124] IWM, Fernside Letters Con., Shelf, Elizabeth Fernside (living in Fulham), letters to her son Fred, July 1917.

[125] Michaux, *En marge du drame*, dedication.

[126] Abel Hermant, *La vie à Paris*, 1917, p. 10; 1920, p. 143.

[127] Perreux, *La vie des civils*, p. 202.

evoked by Elisabeth Boussac, six years old at the time, when she remembered the war seventy years later. She was at the time at a photographer's with her mother, her brother, and her sister:

A woman received us: her husband had been killed in the war and she had taken over his work. While we posed, the gun could be heard firing at regular intervals, every minute, I think, without a break – 'it's the first time I've heard the gun with pleasure' said the photographer. 'They are signing the peace at Versailles', Maman commented. 'It's wonderful', said the photographer, 'to think that it was the last war!' 'The last war!' echoed Mother, 'yes, it's extraordinary to know that our children will never know war again!'[128]

The militarization of the streets

During the war men in uniform passed through the streets of Paris, London, and Berlin the way that working men, blue-collar or white-collar alike, had traversed them before 1914. In Paris this constituted a return to an earlier time. Recalling with nostalgia his life as a Paris child in the 1860s, Fernand Laudet wrote in July 1914 that in his youth 'It was military affairs that most drew the eye.'[129] The same was true after 1914.

In London this high status of men in uniform dominated the recruiting drive of 1914 and 1915. One observer emphasized the effectiveness of popular pressure in Great Britain, as expressed in banners – 'Hurry up, your King is calling' or 'Come in here, there's still room for you': 'Whether you want to or not, you have to read them, then they work quietly on the individual who hesitates or hurries, according to temperament, and always ends up by enlisting.'[130]

In London, 'a lot of comments are made on how the "knut" has turned patriotic and enlisted'.[131] In Paris, the rituals of mobilization followed the precedent of August 1914, maintained throughout the war by the drama of the departure of new classes and volunteers, in particular through parades using conscription rituals from pre-war times.[132] The passage through Paris of young newly mobilized conscripts was the occasion for lyrical descriptions in the press, as in *La vie parisienne*, which wrote in January 1916: 'The young soldiers of the class of '17 departed amidst

---

[128] *Correspondance de Jacques et Marie-Josèphe Boussac*, p. 375.

[129] Laudet, *Paris pendant la guerre: impressions*, p. 2.

[130] Michaux, *En marge du drame*, p. 103.

[131] G. Stedman Jones, 'The "Cockney" and the nation, 1780–1988', in D. Feldman and G. Stedman Jones (eds.), *Metropolis: London, histories and representations since 1800* (London, 1989), pp. 272–324.

[132] Michel Bozon, *Les conscrits* (Paris, 1981); Odile Roynette, *'Bons pour le service'. L'expérience de la caserne en France à la fin du XIXe siècle* (Paris, 2000).

hymns and canticles: in the streets and around the stations, it was a fine spectacle.'[133] There is certainly some exaggeration here, but only some.

In Berlin, the departure of the young men after 1914 does not seem to have been as celebrated as were the departures of the first weeks of the war. Groups of young men, frequently well-off and well educated, on their way to enlist in jaunty groups, were no longer a major cultural feature of the Berlin streets. In complete contrast to Paris and London, it seems that mobilization for the front was a less striking cultural phenomenon. Centred on the barracks, and in a city deeply divided socially, Berlin was quieter about its deep military traditions than were either Paris or London, where the military was less central to the political culture.[134]

Identities are always determined through exclusion. Those who did *not* join up were treated in very different ways. Sexual pressure, applied by women, was not at all hidden. In London, white feathers denoting cowardice were distributed, often by young women, as a well-known ritual of shaming men to enlist in the British Expeditionary Force.[135]

The rituals of denunciation were particularly focused on foreigners in the capitals at the moment of the declaration of war, called on to leave the country if they originated from enemy nations, or to rejoin their own army or the army of their host nation if they were allied or neutral. Military 'neutrality' was in fact inconceivable in the eyes of the nations engaged in this war. The exclusion of foreigners representing enemy nations often took a violent turn, focusing in particular on shops identifiable by their shop sign, public rumour, or local knowledge. The crowd looting the Swiss firm of Maggi, at Neuilly, and then its Paris depots, during which tons of milk were thrown out on the pavement, illustrates well how rumour can pick on the wrong target.[136] The crowd spirit explains why notices were set up in all three capitals, in front of closed shops indicating the proprietor's military status to customers or passers. 'Shop closed, employer and staff mobilized',[137] or, 'Shop closed, open again after the war. *Vive la France* all the same!' could be read in Paris in 1914.[138] In this way, such rituals had a function that was both practical and symbolic, since traders sought to avoid the looting from which their German or

---

[133] *La vie parisienne*, 22 January 1916, p. 69; *La libre parole*, 'Le départ de la classe 1917', 12 January 1917, p. 1. Hermant describes the enthusiasm of the class of 1918 when it reached the barracks in April 1917. 19 April 1917, p. 71.

[134] Brandenburgisches Landeshauptarchiv, Potsdam (BLHA) PPB no. 15810, pp. 112–13, Schwartz report, 16 April 1915.

[135] Nicolette Gullace, 'White feathers and wounded men: female patriotism and the memory of the Great War', *Journal of British Studies* 36 (April 1997), pp. 178–206.

[136] Jean Galtier-Boissière, *Mémoires d'un Parisien* (Paris, 1960), pp. 97–8.

[137] *Heures de guerre*, 30 October 1914, p. 65.

[138] Michaux, *En marge du drame*, p. 15.

Austrian competitors were then suffering.[139] Men who escaped mobilization because of their age, and in particular the veterans of the Franco-Prussian war of 1870 in Paris or Berlin, took pleasure in strolling the streets in search of malingerers.[140]

Ways of excluding foreigners were thus highly visible in the capitals. Anti-Semitic acts towards Russians were particularly salient in London. The socialist journal *Women's Dreadnought* published a long article in May 1917 on 'A Pogrom in London' purporting to expose a wave of deliberate police brutality against 'alien' (mainly Russian) Jews in East London. It describes police raids in Jewish districts of east London leading to mass arrests of men of military age in restaurants, outside cinemas and in streets. This was part of the post-February revolution crack-down on Russian Jews who had managed to avoid being conscripted either to the British or Russian armies. The aim was to hold them and force them to choose between repatriation to fight in the Kerensky armies, or conscription into British units.[141] In Germany too, suspicions prevailed that certain men were shirking military service. In Berlin as in London, officials helped support the illusion through the infamous 1916 'Jew Count' that Jews had found ways to escape their military responsibility (despite good evidence to the contrary). The Social Democratic newspaper *Vorwärts* reported, the 'opinion [was] widely held among the people' that 'in the war industries, there were particularly many "Jewish shirkers"'.[142] This view can be related once again to perceived changes in the profile of the street. The accelerated influx of eastern European refugees from war zones in Galicia touched prejudices very much alive in wartime.

We noted in volume I how deep was popular feeling on questions of fairness in wartime – fairness in paying the *impôt du sang*, the blood tax, and fairness in bearing the economic hardships of the war. More than three hundred letters a day reached the French police or military authorities, to denounce shirkers.[143] It is instructive in this context to examine the lexicon of denunciation found in the weekly session of a special hearing by the Paris judge charged with the examination of complaints from discharged or war-wounded men wrongly accused of being 'shirkers'.[144]

---

[139] Delécraz, *1914*, 4 August 1914.   [140] Ibid., 2 August 1914.

[141] 'A pogrom in London', *Woman's Dreadnought*, 26 May 1917, pp. 758–60.

[142] 'Die Judenzählung von 1916. Ein Protest von Philipp Scheidemann', *Vorwärts*, 21 October 1916.

[143] Perreux, *La vie des civils*, p. 249.   [144] Ibid.

It was true that even though these cities' male populations contributed roughly the same proportion of men to the armies as did rural areas, there were still many men on the streets who never saw the front.[145] There was the bloated military bureaucracy. There were the military drivers who ruled the streets. The esplanades of Les Invalides and the Ecole Militaire, both in the 7th arrondissement of Paris, were the home of many motor convoys to the front from August 1914.[146]

There were other men who had been at the front, but who were either on leave or invalided. In all three capitals, in fact, soldiers on leave were required to wear their uniform while on leave. From then on, the rolling sequence of leave meant a virtually continuous presence of combatant troops from the front in the capitals. It can thus be estimated that between July 1915 and November 1918, between 5,000 and more than 50,000 men on leave simultaneously spent time in Paris. Some 20,000 Londoners were in the British capital at the same time, to which must be added men from the provinces, a certain number of soldiers from the Empire, as well as many Allies – Belgians or Canadians for example, who chose to spend their leave there.[147] In Berlin, the presence of men on leave from the front was no doubt less visible, both because the proportion of Berlin men mobilized was smaller, and also because periods of leave were less frequent in Germany than in France or Great Britain.[148]

In July 1915 the arrival of the first men on leave from the front was described by the press as a major change in the panorama of Parisian life.[149] In the French capital, where apart from Parisians numerous provincial or foreign soldiers spent their time, the mass effect explains how, in the tradition of familiar figures such as the 'rag-and-bone man', the 'sweeper', or the 'local policeman', the soldier on leave became a typical street figure, remarkable for his novelty, visibility, and above all his virtues.[150] From the summer of 1915, the blue of French army uniforms dominated the Sunday-afternoon strolling crowds in Paris, but men on

---

[145] Michel Auvray, *L'âge des casernes. Histoires et mythes du service militaire* (Paris, 1998).

[146] Michaux, *En marge du drame*, p. 54; anonyme, *L'âme de Paris. Tableaux de la guerre de 1914* (Paris, 1915), p. 137. On traffic accidents, see APP, files of Paris police-station day books, notably CB26 (Invalides), CB27 (Ecole Militaire), CB60 (Javel, with the depot in the rue Lacordaire), CB103 (Vincennes).

[147] The number of men on leave who were originally Londoners is calculated on the basis of one ten-day period of leave every fifteen months.

[148] Emmanuelle Cronier, 'Permissions et permissionnaires du front pendant la Première Guerre mondiale' in Jean-Jacques Becker and Stéphane Audoin-Rouzeau (eds.), *Encyclopédie de la Grande Guerre* (Paris, 2004).

[149] 'Choses et autres', *La vie parisienne*, no. 30, 21 July 1915, p. 537. Numerous similar representations can be found, as in 'les premiers poilus arrivent en permission', *La libre parole*, 13 July 1915, p. 2.

[150] *Type de la rue* (Paris, 1920).

leave of all nationalities were also omnipresent in representations of the city.[151] In line with the aspirations of the French military authorities, their presence was part of the long-term mobilization of metropolitan populations. The working woman Louise Delétang used her diary to describe the effect of their presence on civilians: 'If one did not meet so many soldiers, could one believe that there was a war going on?' she questioned.[152]

This revolution in the urban landscape can be seen in popular language in London as well, where the expression 'Khaki fever' arose to designate the genuine and symbolic domination of soldiers in the metropolitan space.[153] In France, the figure of the *poilu* to which was added from 1915 that of the *permissionnaire* – in other words a *poilu* on leave – stood in direct opposition to the 'civilian', for whom the quintessence is incarnated by the 'Parisian'. While in Berlin such vernacular distinctions were less evident, it was still true that some civilians in this industrial city suspected that the well-off had ways of staying out of the army.

Over time, wounded or mutilated men became more prominent on the streets. Standing on street corners, crouching in doorways, or moving, often slowly in contrast with other occupants of the street, the war-wounded offered immediate evidence of the horrors of the battle front. Mentally impaired and traumatized veterans picked fights in the street and otherwise created disturbances and distractions in the flow of movement. In Berlin, the designation of war invalids under the heading 'Krüppel' – 'cripple' in the language of the day – in addition to campaigns urging the population to show respect for war invalids, were evidence of the ambivalence the sight of such men evoked. The very need to ask people to show respect for war invalids testifies to the uncertainty of their position. Anyone walking down the street and not in uniform was potentially under suspicion.[154]

Conversely, anyone wearing the uniform of a common soldier was worthy of popular esteem. The term *poilu*, or hairy one, a Parisian term appearing at the end of 1914, came to signify the entire nation at war.[155]

---

[151] Michaux, *En marge du drame*, p. 350, 30 August 1915. See *La vie parisienne*, 18 March 1916, entitled 'Silhouettes de la guerre sur les boulevards', pp. 206–7.

[152] Louise Delétang, Sunday 24 October 1915.

[153] 'Le visage de Londres en guerre', in *Le petit Parisien*, 2 May 1918, p. 1.

[154] Sabine Kienitz, 'Quelle place pour les héros mutilés? Les invalides de guerre entre intégration et exclusion' in *14–18. Aujourd'hui, Today, Heute*, (2001) no. 4, '*Marginaux, marginalité, marginalisation*', pp. 151–65. Eric J. Leed, *No Man's Land. Combat and identity in World War I* (Cambridge, 1979); H. Whalen, *Bitter wounds. German victims of the Great War, 1914–1939* (London, 1984).

[155] *Le poilu*, of the 108e RIT; the first issue appeared on 15 December 1914, or *Le poilu du 303e*.

As Gabriel Perreux stressed, as time went by, 'the *poilu*, a civilian institution, remained the *poilu*; he even ended up by imposing himself on the whole front, on the whole of France, on the whole world, on posterity'.[156] The term *poilu* added prestige to any other phrase or title. In the spring of 1915 several front-line newspapers changed their title to emphasize the expression *poilu*.[157] The trench press, whose legitimacy was based on the definition of a combatant community independent of the home front, undoubtedly played an important role in the diffusion of the expression among the combatants themselves. They could turn its meaning depending on context and inflection, to be critical, modest, or self-important, depending on the case. Over all, it was a term which separated 'us' from 'them', as in *L'Echo du ravin* of November 1915, 'With us, with the *Poilus* as the civilians say.'[158]

In Parisian representations, men on leave showed civilians what the war was really like. Their physiognomy and attitude were seen by everyone as evidence of morale at the front. The front-line newspaper *Face aux Boches* took pride in this from the autumn of 1915: 'Men on leave are travelling salesmen, agents of courage.'[159] The narrative *La guerre, madame*, by Paul Géraldy, reprinted many times after its first publication in 1916, echoed this in giving a man on leave the words as he arrived in Paris: 'I was a soldier without thinking about it. Now that for a few hours I am no longer one, I remember that I am one.' 'Paris had told them their legend', concluded the author.[160] Combatants were very concerned about their image and both sought and feared the eye of the civilian, in particular that of the women. Many were anxious to show off their stripes and their decorations during their leave periods, and those who had none were tempted to wear them illegally.[161]

The *permissionnaire* was 'a somewhat savage type', whose otherness helped separate civilians from soldiers.[162] Bearded, their complexions

---

[156] Perreux, *La vie des civils*, p. 253.

[157] Founded in 1915, *L'Anticafard* adopted from its third issue the title *Les poilus et Marie-Louise*, explaining that the old title was criticized by combatants who found that it applied to civilians and not to themselves. According to the editors, the new title was better suited to combatant's identity. In April 1915 *A-boche-que-veux-tu* became *Le poilu déchaîné*.

[158] 'Conte pour les futurs permissionnaires', in *L'Echo du ravin*, no. 15, November 1915, p. 2. *Le ver luisant*, April 1917, quoted by Jacques Meyer in *Les soldats de la Grande Guerre* (Paris, 1966), p. 16.

[159] 'Permissionnaires', *Face aux boches*, no. 2, September 1915, p. 1.

[160] Paul Géraldy, *La guerre, Madame* (Paris, 1916).

[161] A song on the officers' parade: *Avez-vous peur?* (APP, BA698, 18 January 1916). Many cases of illegal wearing of decorations appear in the day-book files of Paris police stations (APP).

[162] *Le petit Parisien*, 7 August 1915, pp. 3–4.

burnished by the open-air life, their uniforms shabby, often dirty or even muddy, equipped with a knapsack full of *pinard*, the *poilu* was also marked out by his smell and his obscure turn of phrase, the slang of the front line. In 1915 *La vie parisienne* congratulated itself that the indomitable Parisian workers could now stroll along the boulevard, holding their girl-friends' hand, 'like true and idyllic peasants in a painting by Bastien-Lepage' – the naturalist artist.[163] Some combatants felt cheated by the identity assigned to them, founded on appearance, while their own criteria of value prized front-line experience above all. After all, if it was appearance that mattered, then what about the frauds?

The active trade in military decorations and uniforms in the capital enabled many men to take on a flattering combatant identity.[164] Public opinion was not ignorant of such practices, and from then on suspicion weighed on all men in public areas. Combatants were caught in the trap of the myth constructed around their identity in 1914 and 1915 and broke away from it when in their turn they became the object of a critical eye.

This rapid shift in cultural norms explains why the 'trench press' published numerous manifestos on the concept of the combatant identity, blending the flattering criteria produced by the home front since the beginning of the war with the values that it bestowed on combatants.[165] Those who talk about their exploits in public are henceforward suspect and, like many of the front-line newspapers, the *Echo des marmites* opted for modesty and called for more restraint in the shrill judgments of Parisian opinion.[166]

There is some truth in this accusation. The Paris street was one of the places were identities were performed, be it in or out of uniform. The constant evolution of representations produced in Paris, as at the front, no doubt explains the supposed feeling of unease among men on leave during their stay in the capital, where the proliferation of cultural support, the clash of contradictory norms, and the presence of many soldiers of differing status made it difficult for soldiers disoriented by the violence of the front to find their place, to assert who they were. Jules Romains was to

---

[163] *La vie parisienne*, no. 30, 21 July 1915, p. 537.

[164] There are hundreds of cases of this type in the day-book lists of Paris police stations.

[165] *L'Echo des marmites*, no. 14, 20 October 1916. In 1917, the journal published a manifesto which attacked caricaturists, challenging the name of *poilu*, the search for the picturesque, the rusticity of manners and enthusiasm ascribed to the fighting men (no. 7, 25 January 1917, p. 2, 'Les caricatures à la mode. Les poilus protestent'). See *Le petit echo du 18ème RIT*, which criticized the *permissionnaires'* supposed dirt (no. 41, 22 August 1915, p. 4, 'la toilette du poilu').

[166] *L'Echo des marmites*, no. 6, 10 December 1915, pp. 3–5, 'En permission'.

depict in *Verdun* the pride and the nobility of these men returning from an 'impossible land which defies imagination'.[167]

Under these conditions, the identity of the combatant was set and reset when soldiers and civilians met, in particular in Paris.[168] It is there, in the streets of Paris, that we can see evidence of the uneasy relationship between the community of men on leave and the men of the home front. The front was not far away, after all. There is an element of Jacobin egalitarianism here too. In Paris, soldiers on leave defended their ranking in the moral hierarchy created by the war by parading and defying in the streets everyone whom they identified as a shirker, often supported by a crowd of onlookers. In particular soldiers focused on police agents, whom they had to face daily in checks on their leave passes, and who, in their eyes, were the supreme incarnation of the shirker, sheltered at the rear and at the same time endowed with a power seen by soldiers as unearned and unjust. Whenever there was a case of disturbance to public order which concerned men on leave from the front, insults came quickly and mostly referred to the military status of the police agents sent to sort out the trouble.[169] Agents in uniform were constantly threatened by men on leave, who attacked them verbally and, in certain – rare – cases, physically.[170] In most cases the aggression remained verbal, with agents being accused of being 'cowards', 'idlers', or 'shirkers', along classic lines.[171] These habits of men on leave generally aroused public support, who saw the *poilu* as men who deserved a break or two.[172]

Feminization of the streets

There was only one subject which held the attention of the metropolitan population as strongly as that of the *poilu*. That subject was the feminization of the streets. In all three cities, women were already a central element of the metropolitan landscape and labour force before 1914. They formed the majority of the Paris population in 1914, and 58 per

[167] Jules Romains, *Verdun, les hommes de bonne volonté*, vol. XVI (Paris, 1956), p. 317.

[168] *L'Echo de Tranchéesville*, no. 9, 16 September 1916, p. 3. *Bellica*, no. 1, 1 December 1915, 'le Journal d'un permissionnaire', p. 6. See also *L'Argonnaute*, no. 16, 15 July 1916, p. 2. For the definition of shirkers, see for example *Le Rat-à-Poil*, no. 8, 1 March 1916, 'Aller-Retour', p. 5, *Le diable au cor*, no. 22, 20 February 1916, page 8, 'L'arrière et l'avant'; *Sans tabac*, no. 26, 8 October 1916, p. 1.

[169] APP, listings in Paris police stations' day-books.

[170] APP, listings in Paris police stations' day-books. CB 22.40, case no. 385, July 1917; CB 77.27, case no. 813, 17 September 1916, report on the Belleville district.

[171] APP, CB 22.40, case no. 544, 3 October 1917.

[172] APP, CB 30.43, case 19, 8 November 1916.

cent of Parisian women aged over fifteen were employed outside the home, which they left every day to go to their place of work.[173] By mobilizing the greater part of the male population, the war greatly enhanced the visibility of women in the three capitals. Marlene Dietrich described Berlin in this respect as 'a woman's world',[174] an impression shared by all observers in the capitals and which no doubt contributed to the feeling of a world that was changing radically. As husbands, sons, and fathers left for the front, and as shopping took so much longer than before, women appeared in the streets – and remained there – in larger numbers than ever before, both proportionately but also in absolute terms. The physical presence of women as consumers for the household was visible notably in the queues that stretched, day and night, in searing heat and freezing cold, along streets throughout the poorer areas (including *petite bourgeoisie* districts and, at least initially before alternatives were found, in wealthier quarters too).[175] Photographs of queues in front of supply stores, retail shops, and market stalls clearly indicate women's predominance.[176]

Women were all the more visible in the streets because they overwhelmingly replaced men in the street trades which had hitherto been a male monopoly. In Paris, the female workforce increased by 100 per cent and transport was one of the sectors in which it increased most substantially.[177] From November 1916 the first female employees of the Compagnie du Gaz were seen in the streets, while at the end of May 1917 post-women made their appearance in Paris: this was a new form of employment for women in the capital, although some towns were already employing women in this role before the war. But women were also at work as sweepers, municipal water-cart drivers, lighters of gas street lamps, delivery staff, bill-posters, newspaper saleswomen, car drivers – all these street trades which ensured a continued female presence in the street, beyond the hours when they had widely been seen in the street

---

[173] *Capital cities*, vol. I, pp. 32–6.
[174] Quoted in Barbara Gutt, *Frauen in Berlin. Mit Kopf und Herz und Hand und Fuß* (Berlin, 1991), p. 61.
[175] Margaret H. Darrow, *French women and the First World War: war stories of the home front* (Oxford/New York, 2001); Susan R. Grayzel, *Women's identities at war: gender, motherhood and politics in Britain and France during the First World War* (Chapel Hill, 1999); Nicoletta Gullace, *Men, women and the renegotiation of British citizenship during the Great War*, (New York and Basingstoke, 2002); on Germany, see Ute Daniel, *The war from within, German working-Class women in the First World War* (Oxford, 1997).
[176] BDIC Photothèque in Les Invalides, album no. 339, 'Avenues, rues, artères', many shots of the Edgar Quinet market. For the rue St Denis market: L679 and L685, 10 and 11 May 1916.
[177] R. Wall and J. Winter (ed.), *The upheaval of war. Family, work and welfare in Europe 1914–1918* (Cambridge, 2004), p. 256. Perreux, *La vie des civils*, p. 58.

before the war. In these new forms of work their dress sought to distinguish them from men and was frequently ostentatious. As drivers of underground trains they flourished a red armband and the allied flags pinned on their bodices, before subsequently adding a black smock.[178]

Women had to get around on foot more than before the war because of the lack of public transport, either on their way to food shops along what became regular routes once rationing was established, or travelling between home and place of work. It was above all the popular and the middle classes who were affected by the multiplication of urban routes, but these changes also affected the better-off too.

The *midinettes* were there on the streets in demonstrations. Active in May–June 1917, women demonstrated on their own account on three occasions in 1919 on the occasion of garment-workers' strikes, and on 6 July 1919 in favour of women's right to vote. They also took part more prominently than before the war, according to police reports, in demonstrations of national unity through their associations alongside 'their husbands, their brothers, their parents', according to Marcel Cachin.[179] Women, whose presence in the German paid labour force had been largely unacknowledged (unlike in France), now were not merely encouraged to work outside the home in war factories; they had to do so. This too meant considerably more street visibility for even those women whose work did not take place in the street itself (though there were plenty of those now). In contrast with pre-war home work, such as piece-work, women now had to travel, often across the city, to get to and from work. By late in the war, they were also particularly prominent in strikes and demonstrations that took place near their work sites, now scattered about much of the city.

In contrast to the Paris landscape, largely feminized through women's work, the feminization of Berlin came about largely because of the absence of men, since Berlin did not see the same spectacular increase in the female workforce as did Paris.[180] Even as the figure of the woman became stronger – indeed, masculinized in contemporary understanding, in both a positive and negative sense – men feared becoming feminized, including through an inability to fight at the front, or injury that brought a soldier home permanently. There are many indications that German masculinity was braided together with notions of military service; in

---

[178] Perreux, ibid., pp. 190–1.

[179] *Journal officiel de la République française*, débats parlementaires, Chambre des députés, 6 May 1919, p. 2.

[180] Ute Daniel, 'Women's work in industry and family. Germany, 1914–1918' in Wall and Winter (eds.), *The upheaval of war*, p. 267.

symbolic language, German men, the soul of the nation, were hard and virile, carriers of a 'Kultur' superior to an imagined degenerate French 'civilization' that culturally had invaded Germany, and that had to be rooted out. Thus women who represented vulnerability – whether through their unthinking love of French consumer finery (i.e. lingerie and perfume) or through their sexually predatory nature (i.e. as prostitutes) – could be turned into a threat to the German nation. These fantasies were no less powerful for being illusory.

One worrying element for many men was that in wartime women were defined in terms of what they did outside the home. That is to say, as their public location in urban space changed, so did their place and prominence within the metropolitan population. The mobilization of women in war factories, of which a great number existed in or near the capitals, made them workers in different places and at different times of the day. Women, who before the war formed a large part of the clientèle of shops, now became the main customers. This was a mixed blessing at best, since they were the first to be targeted in the denunciation of mass consumption expressed in wartime campaigns for 'self-restraint'. In London, the 'ladies who shop' came in for serious criticism by 1917, as can be seen in the propaganda film, 'Women and War' which set the female crowd in Oxford Street for whom 'luxury shopping is not helping' in contrast to 'women who are helping', illustrated by a war factory. It ended on this question: 'Can you help?'[181] Social class distinctions matter here, to be sure. The indulgent wives are identified with the profiteering, non-combatant beneficiaries of the war – the picture is simplified to omit wealthy women whose husbands or sons were at the front. These representations were disseminated in France, where popular narratives took up for themselves the ideal of the disappearance of Londoners' idle pastimes.[182]

A dark image of the Parisian woman also emerged during the war.[183] In 1915, during a speech on 'The Parisienne and the War', Maurice Donnay thus contrasted the woman of 1914, frivolous and materialistic, with the new woman whose life was henceforward focused on the household.[184] This was evidently untrue, but comforting to conservatives. When the 'eternal Parisienne' – a woman of public space – was evoked in civilian

[181] Imperial War Museum (IWM), 479, *Women and war*, 1918, Topical Film Company. See C. Sheridan Jones, *London in wartime* (1917), pp. 96–7.
[182] A. Norec, *Tommies et Gourkas* (Paris, 1917), p. 29.
[183] Jean-Louis Robert, 'La Parisienne aux Parisiens', Colloque 'Etre parisien', 26–28 September 2002, University of Paris I.
[184] Maurice Donnay, *La Parisienne et la guerre* (Paris, 1916).

representations, it was in general to condemn her.[185] Soldiers heard these condemnations, and those who needed to, started to worry.[186]

These puritan representations were eclipsed time and again by the location of feminine eroticism in urban space; for the troops, single or married, its incarnation in figures such as the Parisienne continued to represent an absolute fantasy in which conquest remained the ideal. Sexual frustration and the need for female companionship or love among those separated by the war thus formed the foundation of representations of women easily seduced by soldiers. This paradox is evident in the review *La vie parisienne*.[187] While in each issue the review published drawings of semi-naked Parisiennes throwing themselves at French and Allied soldiers on leave, those who read it in the trenches – who were numerous – were bound to be flattered by the 'Don Juanism' attributed to them – but also to nourish the worst suspicions about the faithfulness of their own wives.

In the heightened atmosphere of moral austerity, blaming women was a relatively easy matter. Fashions were seen as provocative or frivolous.[188] In almost every public discussion of women in wartime, images of prostitution emerged rapidly. In the Berlin police reports, *Kriegerfrauen* appear as a main source of sexual transgression and clandestine prostitution. *Kriegerfrauen* was a general term for wives of enlisted soldiers who received state benefits while their husbands were at the front.[189] Receiving a 'separation allowance' (as the British equivalent was called) involved a moral expectation. In official rhetoric the role of the *Kriegerfrau* was associated with 'home', children, and faithfulness. She was not meant to be seen 'in the street' without any obvious purpose, where she occupied a morally suspicious position, at best as a *flâneuse* who abused state benefits, at worst as a 'secret prostitute' ('amateur prostitute' was the derogatory term used in Britain). 'Secret prostitution' encapsulated the ambiguity that official role-modelling associated with the *Kriegerfrau* 'in

[185] Paul Géraldy, *La guerre, Madame*; published anonymously in *La Grande Revue* in March 1916, then under the author's name in 1922 (Paris, 1916).

[186] *L'artilleur déchaîné*, no. 25, 17 February 1917, p. 1, 'Woman in general, and the Parisienne in particular' or 'The jealous *poilu*'. *L'Echo des marmites*, no. 11, 25 May 1916, pp. 6 and 7.

[187] *La Vie Parisienne*, no. 49, 4 December 1915, 30 December 1916.

[188] Darrow, *French women*, pp. 64–71.

[189] Birthe Kundrus, *Kriegerfrauen: Familienpolitik und Geschlechterverhältnisse im Ersten und Zweiten Weltkrieg* (Hamburg, 1995); Ute Daniel, *Arbeiterfrauen in der Kriegsgesellschaft. Beruf, Familie und Politik im Ersten Weltkrieg* (Göttingen, 1989); Ute Daniel, 'Der Krieg der Frauen, 1914–1918. Zur Innenansicht des Ersten Weltkriegs in Deutschland', in *Keiner fühlt sich hier mehr als Mensch: Erlebnis und Wirkung des Ersten Weltkriegs*, ed. Gerhard Hirschfeld and Gerd Krumeich in connection with Irina Renz (Essen, 1993), pp. 131–49.

the street': it referred both to soliciting and to sexual relationships outside marriage.[190]

Military mobilization did indeed give a new lease of life to metropolitan prostitution. We have already noted their work around the railway stations. In Paris, prostitutes remained in the district round Les Halles, the classic setting for nocturnal prostitution.[191] In Montmartre, near the fortifications, or in the woods around Paris – but also in Saint-Germain-des-Prés, by the Madeleine or the Opéra – sex was performed in public, as police reports reveal.[192] Women workers solicited near war factories, for example around the Citroën premises. In more central districts, such as the *grands boulevards*, measures were taken to reduce the visibility of girls, sometimes very young, who contravened standards of modesty.[193] In August 1915 a large café put its terrace out of bounds to unaccompanied women who invaded it, 'doing their best not to stay there long'.[194] The girls and their pimps were often judged by their potential damage to the war effort.[195] This rhetoric, while exaggerated, fed rumours on the number of soldiers suffering from venereal diseases contracted while on leave.[196]

Is all this fantasy? Some of it certainly was a shocked reaction to the appearance of groups of girls on city streets. Thus in June 1917, and following the Bishop of London, *The Times* deplored what it took to be a female invasion of London parks. Since the beginning of the war, 20,000 women had been prosecuted for soliciting, stated Sir Edward Henry, Commissioner of Police, who confessed his inability to eliminate prostitution in the parks, while it seemed relatively limited in the streets. In effect, with only 130 policemen for the whole city, the task was not simple.[197] How many of these women were simply taking a stroll?

In Berlin, police redoubled their pre-war efforts in that city to contain prostitution (though not to illegalize it). As early as September 1914, and partly in reaction to complaints by Wilhelm II about the 'immorality of his residential city', the Berlin authorities forbade those identified (somehow)

[190] LA Berlin, Pr. Br. Rep. 30, Titel 94, 11361, Lit. K, no. 1293, vol. II, Bl. 319; Hoppe to Jagow, 26 July 1916.
[191] Song by Jean Rodor and Vincent Scotto, 1916. Jean-Louis Robert, 'Paris enchanté – le peuple en chansons (1870–1990)', in *Paris le peuple XVIIème–Xxème siècle* (Paris, 1999), pp. 195–206. Alain Corbin, *Les filles de noce* (Paris, 1982), p. 207.
[192] APP, files of Paris police stations' day-books.   [193] APP, CB41.39–41.
[194] *La vie parisienne*, no. 32, 7 August 1915, p. 559. 'On dit … on dit …'.
[195] APP, BA 1689, letter of 2 June 1916.
[196] APP, BA 1689, letter of the Prefect of Police, undated. Jean-Yves le Naour, *Misères et tourments de la chair durant la Grande Guerre. Les mœurs sexuelles des Français 1914–1918* (Paris, 2002).
[197] 'Hyde Park by night. Oversea soldiers and London morals', *The Times*, 28 June 1917, p. 3.

as prostitutes to enter any public café, bar, or restaurant; indeed, they were meant to disappear from the streets altogether, as a traditional source of immorality.[198] Still, there were few efforts to eradicate prostitution altogether, in part because even anti-prostitution campaigners seemed to think it better that German soldiers find German prostitutes (who worked under official aegis at the front lines) rather than seek out 'foreign' prostitutes, who were perceived to be (on what grounds?) likely sources of venereal disease. Prostitutes gathered particularly around Friedrichstraße, where by no coincidence soldiers entered and exited the city. Their rising numbers, which continued meteorically after the war, spoke above all of the economic crisis in which city residents found themselves.

Foreigners and strangers in the capitals

General mobilization created massive movements of people throughout the three mobilized nations, resulting in August 1914 in the flow of soldiers towards the Belgian and German frontiers and, in a corresponding move, by the flight of residents from their homes in threatened areas. These flows were felt in the capitals, emptied until the first leave of men mobilized into fighting units and, in a contrary movement, colonized by new populations which arrived in the urban space. Thus it was that the capital cities became international at the same time as they witnessed conflicts of a xenophobic nature which reactivated ancient tensions and contradicted the myth of the fraternity of allies.[199]

Paris, the inter-allied capital of twenty-five nations at war, was in the front rank of a series of celebrations of her Allies, whose troops internationalized the city. Some Allies like the Americans, were more welcomed than others.[200] The arrival of Americans was all the more celebrated because it had been long awaited, and was marked by the Americanization of a whole district located round the Opéra, from the Madeleine to the Palais Royal, site of the Canadian and American military administrative premises. It was there that most American soldiers en poste or on leave chose to live in Paris.[201] This communal occupation of districts was also noticeable near

---

[198] LA Berlin, Pr. Br. Rep. 30 Berlin C, Titel 94, 11361, Lit. K, no. 1293, vol. ii, fol. 301: Telegram, Wilhelm II to Jagow, 16 July 1916. LA Berlin, Pr.Br.Rep.30, Titel 94, 11361, Lit. K, no. 1293, vol. ii, Bl. 352: Polizeipräsident Charlottenburg to Jagow, 24 July 1916.

[199] E. Benbassa, *Histoire des juifs en France* (Paris, 2000); L. Dornel, *La France hostile. Sociohistoire de la xénophobie 1870–1914* (Paris, 2004); R. Schor, *L'opinion française et les étrangers. 1919–1939* (Paris, 1985).

[200] Marcel Proust, *Le temps retrouvé* (Paris, 1954), pp. 95, 140, 151.

[201] APP, CB3.44 – CB3.46; see also J. Dos Passos, *Trois soldats* (Paris, 1921, 1993 edn).

the Gare du Nord, where Belgian and French refugees were concentrated. In front of the premises of refugee associations, an animated and talkative crowd exchanged news, enabling Parisians to listen to the 'picturesque patois of Flanders'.[202]

The Parisian atmosphere was profoundly affected by this massive presence, which changed the sounds to be heard in the streets. In August 1915 the end of the Ramadan fast in the Centre for Islamic Friendships of Paris gave rise to press accounts, reflecting awareness of the voice of the muezzin audible through the open windows.[203]

A similar, though more muted, cosmopolitan atmosphere reigned in London, city of refuge for Belgians, Serbs, and where the French sometimes attracted popular curiosity when they sang the *Marseillaise* at the news of an Allied victory.[204] In September 1914, *The Times* described the attention brought to bear on these populations: 'One might almost suggest that London's new motto should be *"ici on parle français"* for in certain parts of the City the language of our Allies is heard almost as frequently as our own.'[205]

Though the war was indeed a time for discovery of 'the other', the massive intermixing of populations of different origin and culture was also the source of tensions. They were apparent in Paris in the sexual competitiveness between Frenchmen and their Allies. In effect, the evolution of representations of seduction exercised by the combatants over the Parisiennes favoured officers and Allies. Although one could find two representations of the French *poilu*, the one virile and the other showing him as very sentimental and somewhat frustrated, representations of the Allies were much more unequivocal and flattering. The aesthetics of the uniform, the haughty bearing and exoticism attributed to the Allies, and to a lesser degree to soldiers from the colonies, seemed to place them in the lead in the competition for the Parisienne.

The popularity of coloured men among women also raised lively criticism from Western soldiers present in the capitals. The Mission Française with the American army noted the indignation of Americans in the face of any public intimacy between 'white women and blacks', which they witnessed during their leaves in Paris in 1918.[206] *La vie*

---

[202] *Bulletin des réfugiés du Nord*, 24 March 1915.

[203] 'Le ramadan à Paris', *La libre parole*, 14 August 1915, p. 2.

[204] 'London the city of refuge, official welcome to Belgian victims of war', *The Times*, 10 September 1914.

[205] *The Times*, 10 September 1914. An identical description was made by Robert Saunders. IWM, 17 September 1914.

[206] SHAT, 7N2258, confidential report of the French military mission to the American army on black American troops, 7 August 1918.

parisienne in fact frequently represented the triumph of colonial soldiers with Parisiennes, a notion which clashed with the racial prejudices at work in the American army and beyond.[207]

In Paris, the labour force of colonial origin, concentrated in certain districts and occupying communal premises, suffered criticism or even violence reflecting the weight of racism among the French.[208] The rumour that Annamites (Vietnamese) were widely employed by the Paris police to repress women's demonstrations was widespread at the front, and in general terms foreign workers were the object of far stronger criticism than were colonial soldiers. Even between combatants, jealousies existed and were expressed during leave periods which brought together men who had served in different units at the front. *Le carnet d'un permissionnaire*, written by civilians, gives a résumé of these prejudices with mockery of English 'dandies', concerned only with their appearance, and showed the Senegalese as brutal and more bestial than the Germans.[209]

The ambivalence of the metropolitan population's view of the foreigners they took in from the outbreak of war can be seen in the evolution of the image of Belgian refugees. In this case, two representations competed with and succeeded each other, the one marked by pity for these uprooted victims, the other relating them to parasites as the war was prolonged and their presence was seen as a burden. The arrival of 5,000 Belgian refugees in Paris on 27 August 1914, in a deluge of rain, was described with emotion by Baronne Jane Michaux, who saw in it the 'arrival of terror' in the capital.[210] Similarly, between the end of May and the beginning of June 1918 the journey through the capital of populations fleeing the invaded French regions gave rise to press articles on this 'exodus', as in *Le petit Parisien*.[211] In Paris, the dominant representations remained sympathetic, explained no doubt by the identification of refugees with the occupation of national territory by the enemy, and the unification of Belgians and the French of the north in a single category, 'refugees'.

In London, on the other hand, the refugees were initially seen as foreigners whose welcome came under the heading of philanthropy. This explains that the pity roused by their arrival sometimes included

---

[207] 'Le retour d'un vainqueur', *La vie parisienne*, no. 50, 11 December 1915. On the barbarity of native morals, see: 'abou Amadou en quête d'une nouvelle conquête', *La vie parisienne*, 9 December 1916, drawing by C. Hérouard; R. Lortac, *Le roman d'un Sénégalais* (Paris, 1918).

[208] APP, CB37.47, no. 1348, 13 June 1917.

[209] Roger Boutet de Monvel and Guy Arnoux, *Carnet d'un permissionnaire* (Paris, 1917).

[210] Michaux, *En marge du drame*, p. 39.

[211] *Le petit Parisien*, 27 May, 31 May, and 7 June, 1918.

mixed feelings or even open criticism. The diary of a London woman shows the development of feelings towards them:

Everyone was Belgian-mad for a time . . . But the Belgians are not grateful. They won't do a stroke of work and grumble at everything and their morals . . .! It may be true enough that Belgium saved Europe, but . . . save us from the Belgians! As far as I am concerned, Belgianitis has quite abated.[212]

In Berlin, it was the Jews, and particularly refugees from Eastern Europe, who were the focus for criticism. Before the war Jews were four times more numerous in Berlin than in the rest of Germany, a proportion that grew even larger during the war when another 70,000 East European Jews came to Germany – despite massive protests from right-wing organizations. About half of these came as war workers, which put many of them in Berlin, the major armaments centre that lay furthest east in the country. The other half came as prisoners of war and civil internees. They would have been recognizable through both their clothing and their accents/language difficulties, and, again, were reviled by many as being simultaneously eastern European (therefore uncultured – or 'enemy'-cultured), often not from the city and thus 'bumpkins' and as religiously/'racially' different, figuring as another sign of the negative transformation of the city in wartime.[213]

The cynical or the twisted associated Jews with prostitutes, both dangerous parasites. From 1916 onwards there seemed to be a stronger tendency to interpret the perceived moral decay of Berlin's 'street life' not only along gender but also along racial lines, an interpretation that corresponded to a racialized construction of 'the nation at war'. In such readings 'the street', linked with prostitution, immoral women, Jewishness and crime, symbolized what was opposed to Germanness and the nation's war effort.[214] The anti-Semitism that was expressed in Berlin, London, or Paris was often the racist expression of more general economic tensions evident in the capital cities' markets, which during the war were more than places of commerce. They were theatres of resentment and anxiety.

---

[212] IWM, Coules, Miss M., 97/25/1, June 1914–November 1915.

[213] Michael A. Meyer and M. Brenner (eds.), *German-Jewish history in modern times*, vol. III (New York, 1997), pp. 379–80.

[214] LA Berlin, Pr.Br.Rep. 30, Titel 94, 11361, Lit. K, no. 1293, vol. II, Bl. 352: Polizeipräsident Charlottenburg to Jagow, 24 July 1916. Verhey, *The spirit of 1914* and Aribert Reimann, *Der große Krieg der Sprachen. Untersuchungen zur historischen Semantik in Deutschland und England zur Zeit des Ersten Weltkriegs* (Essen, 2000).

Markets, places of custom and entitlement

Street markets are critical junctures in the trajectory of street life. Here both goods and opinions were exchanged on a regular basis. As we noted in volume I, the rules of consumption in wartime were different from those in peacetime. The civilians who shopped and heckled and talked at markets were regularly judged on their fidelity to the war effort. Noncombatants who were living in the metropolis were evaluated by what and how they spent – and what they went without. Markets were spaces in which people's civic virtue was assessed.[215]

Sheridan Jones's *London in war time*, written in 1917, divided the city into two markets. The market of the poor, the bereaved, and the decent contrasted with the hectic pursuit of luxuries and delicacies by the affluent, mostly linked to women, as we have seen. Market life became shorthand for two clashing forms of civilian behaviour, those who responded to the war through self-sacrifice and those who responded through self-gratification. In the markets of the poor and bereft, costs were rising and certain produce was becoming 'scarce. Shadows also fell over these markets, literally and figuratively. Literally, because the lights that had once illuminated street-stalls and vendors were dimmed or put out by the orders of the government in the interests of the war economy. A cartoon in the London journal, *The passing show*, shows a soldier multiply-wounded, 'injured not on the Somme or in Salonika but in the Strand'.[216] More sombre comments noted the presence of the bereft, mourners and widows, and the anxious, whose husbands, brothers, sons, or friends were 'Somewhere in France'.[217]

Such perceptions were laced through with nostalgia. The more that funerary gloom pervaded street life, the more the pre-war markets were remembered as cheery and vibrant, the metropolitan memory of a lost world.

By 1915 the word 'profiteer' passed into common vocabulary, as we have noted in volume I, at the same time as the British government was appealing for domestic economies, such as reduced meat consumption.[218] This rhetoric appeared in Paris too, where emulation of the display of sacrifice at the front was urged on consumers.[219]

In London, the importance attached to civilians exercising restraint in purchasing food was accentuated by the voluntary nature of the recruiting

[215] Jean-Louis Robert, 'The image of the profiteer', in *Capital cities*, vol. I, pp. 104–32.
[216] *The passing show*, 13 January 1917.   [217] Sheridan-Jones, *London in wartime*, p. 95.
[218] G. J. De Groot, *Blighty: British society in the era of the Great War* (London, 1996), p. 73.
[219] Perreux, *La vie des civils*, p. 204.

drive in the first two years of the war. British war culture celebrated its nation's Protestant voluntary tradition: it had *chosen* to go to war ostensibly on behalf of an invaded neutral nation. Similarly, its citizens were not forced into rationing until the final months of the war. They were encouraged to *elect* to make sacrifices for the greater good; hence the government's appeals for voluntary self-denial and meatless days; hence the reading in places of worship of the Royal Proclamation on saving grain. Because they were free agents, people's choices about what products or produce to enjoy were treated as indicators of their commitment to the war effort.

When rationing of food was finally introduced, in the early months of 1918, it lent a new order and calm to consumer activity. The journalist Michael MacDonagh reported its effects on London:

> The queues have practically disappeared ... Many a butcher who at week-ends recently dared to open only the narrow door of his iron-shuttered front, with a policeman to regulate the slow entrance of the long line of women drawn up outside, had his shop open today as freely as ever.[220]

Londoners discovered that there had been sufficient quantities of food throughout the war, and that food shortages were due to poor distribution rather than overall supply.

Moral hierarchies were defined in the food queues: the place that each person occupied in the queue was a source of tension. In Berlin the wait might last a full night without any guarantee of obtaining anything. The privileges which some individuals exacted were the object of frequent discussion, even if police reports tended rather to underline the extraordinary patience of customers, which they divided into two categories in Berlin: women, generally patient, and young men, sometimes drunk, described as the principal trouble-making *Radaulustige*.

The police reports describe other tensions as well. The police noted that soldiers think that, as soldiers, they can just go to the front of a line for food or tobacco. Soldiers who tried were yelled at and pushed back by those in line, who summoned the police to direct them to the back of the line. Should soldiers' wives have special privileges? Not according to their neighbours. Berlin police reported 'jealous utterances ... in many circles', particularly among the *petite bourgeoisie* and working class, condemning soldiers' wives, when it was rumoured that the latter now regularly spent the afternoons 'consuming quantities of cake and whipped cream with their children'.[221] Now they saw the 'sombre' clothes of a soldier's wife in

---

[220] Michael MacDonagh, *In London during the Great War* (1935), p. 269.
[221] BLHA PPB, no. 15809, p. 292, Report König, 26 March 1915; ibid. no. 15809, p. 293, Report Klonicki, 26 March 1915.

the streets as a sign that she sought preferential treatment, when these other residents perceived the mass unemployment that initially hit the city and other economic dislocations to have made life just as hard for them.[222] When pregnant women, the ill or aged, by virtue of regulations declared, try to pass by, then those in the lines won't allow it to happen. By 1916 many families with small numbers of children actively protested against the perceived advantages of those who were pregnant or who had many children, whose rations they claimed to be disproportionate to their needs.[223] In deference to the protests of those standing in line, as reported to higher authorities by Berlin political police, all such special benefits were withdrawn.

It is possible that these reports indicate a higher level in Berlin of what might be termed brush-fire social conflict evident in these markets as compared to Paris or London. These street-level grumbles turned to anger and bitterness in the German capital in 1917 and 1918. But we should not underestimate how stressful at times was the struggle for a minimum level of consumption in the other two cities as well.

In Paris, there was no legal definition of status enabling some to jump the queue, but police agents tended to tolerate men on leave, whom they would sometimes allow to go first, particularly near the stations where soldiers formed most of the crowd.[224] Indeed, many combatants considered that they should naturally have priority in distribution and denied that the common rule should be be applied to them.[225]

In these confrontations, men on leave frequently spoke out for their rights – an attitude that brought them the approval of the street crowds, who generally conceded soldiers' right to be served first.[226] Combatants moreover defined themselves according to their privileges: 'a man on leave [*permissionnaire*] that's a man who has leave to have all permissions', wrote *La Mitraille*.[227] For civilians, it was all the more difficult to cut into queues because distribution was largely a local matter, settings where people knew each other and where reputations were at stake, and where everyone watched everyone else.[228]

---

[222] BLHA PPB, no. 15810, pp. 112–13, Report Schwarz, 16 April 1915.

[223] BLHA PPB, no. 15817, p. 94. Report Klonicki, 16 March 1916; ibid., no. 15817, pp. 121–3, Mood Report Ludwig, 21 March 1916; 'Die Vorräte an Mehl und Kartoffeln in Groß-Berlin. Die Butterkarte für Groß-Berlin', *Berliner Tageblatt*, 10 March 1916, GStAPK-M 2.2.1. Rep. 197 A Nr. ɪɪ K, p. 106, Letter from Homeowner to Michaelis, 7 March 1917.

[224] APP, BA 1587, Physionomie de Paris, 4 December 1918.

[225] APP, CB 20.35 case no. 341, 2 April 1917.

[226] APP, BA 1587, Physionomie de Paris, 14 December 1917.

[227] 'Le permissionnaire', *La Mitraille*, no. 10, November 1916, p. 5.

[228] Louis Delétang, 28 January 1915.

Everywhere there was a consensus that money did not confer privileges. On moral grounds, the peacetime market could not be allowed to resurface when men were dying at the front. But in Berlin, the old order never really changed. Those in the streets asserted that 'customer lists' and the movement of goods from poorer to wealthier neighbourhoods in branch stores were unfair and immoral. In such circumstances, the maze of barter on the black market became a supplementary source of tensions between consumers, increasingly angry at those who had means and connections to gain access to these parallel networks of distribution.

The black market developed on three different sites: in shops where the best products were sold at prices above the set standard, through home deliveries in prosperous districts, and finally in farms close to the cities where Berliners went in vast numbers at the weekend – a custom little seen before the war. The black market was less developed in Paris and London, since distribution networks fulfilled their role better than in Berlin, where the army, industry, and the state produced a system so complicated that it had to break down. In Paris, police reports appeared to indicate that the main trafficking concerned stolen coal, and was essentially concentrated round the depots near the Seine, where coal stocks were stored.[229] In London, there was a 'grey market', a system of favouritism, of supply through connections among various strata in the population, including the poor. Publicans played a central role in this parallel economy, as indicated in several accounts. The pub belonging to John Gray's father thus experienced no shortage.[230]

The main sites for provisioning Berlin were the thirty-five weekly markets, where the small-scale farmers from Brandenburg came to sell their produce. By late 1914 people in food queues had already formed demonstrations, against both individual retailers and the government. A year later, these demonstrations were daily affairs – and often hours long, growing in one neighbourhood and another in the early evening, then growing in numbers by late evening. These protests, accompanied by shouting, jeering, whistling, and the throwing of objects could move easily to the city's new grand boulevards.[231] Late in the war, things got worse. Random hopeless acts of violent protest and criminality were common in the streets. Women in despair, neglected children, 'delinquent' youth, and physically and mentally damaged former soldiers

---

[229] APP, CB 26.26–7 (Invalides and the port of La Bourdonnais), CB 28.37–9, CB40, 42–4, CB 64.29–31 (Port Debilly), CB 89.48–50, CB 90.21–6 (Suresnes, Nanterre).

[230] John Gray, *Gin and bitters* (London, 1938), pp. 110–11. See also E. Flint, *Hot bread and chips* (London, 1963), pp. 95, 105. A. S. Jasper, *A Hoxton childhood* (London, 1969).

[231] BLHA PPB, no. 15809, p. 18, Report Rhein, 17 February 1915.

roamed the streets in search of food and other needs, with little hope. This situation accounts for the difference in the imagery of street life in Berlin during the war, dominated by a sense of danger due to social conflict, and in Paris and London, dominated by a sense of danger from aerial or artillery bombardment.

By 1918, stallholders at markets had simply stopped coming to Berlin. The risks were too great, and they could make more money selling produce from home. Would-be consumers demonstrated such fierceness that many farmers themselves stopped coming to market, particularly in Lichtenberg and in the north-east of the city.[232] Several scandals bore witness in Berlin to the daily battle between customers and traders, such as the butter war launched by residents of east Berlin against dairymen.[233] The summer unrest also regularly included trips by women to local offices of official agencies, to express their demands directly and to exact a direct reply. As a recurrent practice, this represented a quantum escalation in confrontation.[234] This situation explained why from 1916 the police were frequently present to contain the practices of traders in the markets, near the municipal central wholesale market.

Tensions were less widespread, and expressed less violently, in Paris, where distribution was carried out under better conditions; rationing was not introduced until 1917. Even then, intervention by the police in cases of attempts at looting coal stocks was sufficient to discourage the isolated individuals who tried it, and the rare attempts when groups tried to get at the stocks failed.[235] Practices of protest stayed at the rhetorical level.[236] One critical difference was the better performance of municipal stores, as well as municipal butcheries and groceries.[237] They were known for taking into account consumer's complaints; they were securely enclosed, well organized, and seen as places where fair prices were maintained. Still some criticism persisted, in particular of middle-men working in Les Halles.[238]

Faced with such criticisms, the response of the traders was identical in all three capitals: they accused the newcomers in their trade, the 'dagos'

[232] Ibid., pp. 233–4, Report Kurtz, 13 July 1917. Cf. Annemaria Lange, *Das wilhelminische Berlin: Zwischen Jahrhundertwende und Novemberrevolution* (Berlin, 1967), p. 750.
[233] Davis, *Home fires*; Bundesarchiv Lichterfelde, Provinz Brandenburg Repositur 30, Berlin C. Polizeipräsidium, no. 15821, pp. 229–30, Mood Report Schneider, 28 June 1917.
[234] BLHA PPB, no. 15821, Report Kuhlmann to van Oppen, 4 July 1917. See also 18 June 1917.
[235] APP, CB 79.35, cases 398 and 403, 25 April 1915.
[236] *Le petit Parisien*, 5 November 1916.   [237] *Capital cities at war*, vol. I, ch. 7.
[238] Debates of the Paris city council, November and December 1915, widely reported in the press.

and Jews who were allegedly supplanting the local small traders.[239] In London, significant parts of the pork-butchery trade were believed to be in German hands and the banking trade had significant German and Russian Jewish participation. Resentment at competition may have been a factor in attacks on these shops in 1915, during the period of voluntary recruitment and in 1917.[240] Certainly the imagery of the 'alien' shopkeeper sheltered from military service played a role in pro-internment campaigns for 'allied' aliens. In June 1917 the 'Shop Tenants League' passed a resolution calling public attention to the large number of aliens who allegedly opened new businesses and captured the trade of Englishmen called to the colours.[241] This was almost certainly a myth.

Even city council and other officials in Berlin feared going through the streets; their anxiety was that irate women would follow them or chase them, as one factory worker recalls.[242] The general picture that emerges in the streets and the street markets of Berlin is of a precarious existence and an enormous level of stress.

All the tensions described here contradict the myths of national brotherhood current during the war. There was more than one *culture de guerre*,[243] right from the beginning of the war. Even with the Armistice, these cultural and social differences did not vanish. The spring of 1919 was a turbulent time in both Paris and London. But nothing in the Allied capitals came close to the bitterness of street life in Berlin in the period of revolution from November 1918 to January 1919.

Conclusion

Capital cities suffered physically from the war, in part through the run-down of public and private housing at a time of rent control. But more dramatic was the damage inflicted on parts of London and Paris by aerial bombardment. Less prominent, though more pervasive, was a drabness, a dimness of lighting, reinforcing a sense of wartime melancholy. The cities were greyer, less elevated, less sparkling than at any time in the age of electricity.[244] This muted atmosphere emerged earlier in Paris and

---

[239] Delécraz, *1914*, 4 August 1914.

[240] P. Panayi, *The enemy in our midst* (Oxford 1991). D. C. Woodehouse, *Anti-German sentiment in Kingston upon Hull: The German community and the First World War* (Kingston upon Hull, 1990).

[241] HO 45 10825/320732, cited in Panayi, *Enemy*, p. 142.

[242] Worker Martha Balzer, cited in Glatzer and Glatzer, *Berliner Leben*, pp. 307–8.

[243] Jay Winter and Antoine Prost, *The Great War in history: debates and controversies from 1914 to the present* (Cambridge, 2005), chapter 7.

[244] Adrian Gregory, 'Lost generations', in *Capital cities at war*, vol. i, pp. 57–103.

London, because of the bombardment that Berlin was spared, and was extended in 1915 when the return to a kind of normalcy was limited to the central commercial districts. The contrast with the darker outlying areas was even more acute, in particular at night when social life in these quarters was often non-existent. Although a certain recovery in animation in the streets was apparent in 1915, the winter of 1916–17 was a desolate and dark time. This was a time of restrictions affecting lighting, heating, and fuel, leading to the early closing of many shops and public spaces. Much of social life, by day or night, turned back to home and except occasionally was no longer to be found in the streets. At the beginning of 1918 the camouflage of Paris and London reached a new level following a campaign of German air raids.

The older mythical metropolitan glitter did not fade in the nostalgic recollection of many city-dwellers. 'La belle époque' was never more beautiful than during a war which dimmed its brightness and damped down its gaiety. After the war, with reconstruction and the return of their inhabitants, the capitals gradually regained their welcoming style, but the signs of trauma remained numerous – the omnipresence of war wounded and of invalids is a good example – to the extent that the contrast between the lustrous face and the dark face of the metropolitan streets was deepened in the inter-war years.

There was another level of transformation of the urban landscape, particular to Paris. In 1919, the mounds of earthworks or fortifications surrounding the city were permanently levelled. Thus core and periphery began to merge in a way already well advanced in Berlin, which became Greater Berlin in 1920, and in Greater London, which was already a mammoth before the war.

During the war itself, street life in these three cities helped establish stereotypical definitions of national identities. Many of these were normative myths, pointing to the national virtues of sobriety in a metropolitan environment which had symbolized its very opposite. Metropolitan nostalgia was there too, harking back to a world that was, one the very defence of which had swept away much of its pre-war glitter.

Some of this cloud lifted at the Armistice, when tension abated. In the following months, Paris in particular faced an influx of foreigners who came to participate in or to influence the framing of the peace. The streets of Paris were opened to these people, from every corner of the world. There in the French capital, was assembled 'the world, symbolically'.[245] And there the victors enacted the humiliation and symbolic

---

[245] Stierle, La capitale des signes, p. 3.

punishment of the vanquished, forced to sign the Peace Treaty at Versailles on 28 June 1919.

The streets of Berlin were marked by other events in the six months following the Armistice. The new regime tried to restore a semblance of order, but failed to do so. Armed men were everywhere. Demobilized soldiers swarmed through the streets of Berlin; some joined the *Freikorps* or auxiliary forces, and wiped out the Sparticist uprising of January 1919. Assassinations and other political crimes proliferated. Berlin remained a dangerous place to be for a long time after the war. If the darkness of war lifted in the streets of the Allied capitals, in Berlin the darkness of civil war, war in the streets, had just begun.

4 Entertainments

Jan Rüger

'But all the time London is calling; it calls in the middle of our work, it calls at odd moments like the fever of spring that stirs each year in the blood. It seems to offer romantically, not streets paved with gold but streets filled with leisure.'[1] When Ford Madox Ford wrote this in *The Soul of London* (1905), popular entertainment was already at the heart of the urban experience. London was 'the place', as one of the workers cited in the book put it, because of the vast offerings of diversion: 'it's the Saturday afternoons and Sundays ... It's when ye have your leisure'.[2] Much of this leisure time, Ford found, was spent in the parades and entertainment districts with their music halls and cinemas, 'with the glamorous fall of light and shade, with titillating emotions, with inscrutable excitements, rustling, supremely alive and supremely happy, with here and there a violent heartache, and here and there a great loneliness'.[3]

Cinemas, music halls, and popular theatres, Ford observed, were essential constituents of urban culture at the beginning of the twentieth century. As part of a modern and metropolitan public sphere, they had expanded vigorously since the 1890s, turning into highly visible social, cultural, and economic sites in the urban landscape. By 1914 London, Paris, and Berlin all had distinctive entertainment districts where spectacles, performances, moving images, and a range of other amusements were on offer. Commenting on urban life as much as they constituted it, these sites of entertainment produced a metropolitan modernity that could be bought and consumed daily by a mass public.[4] How this vibrant

This chapter was written by Jan Rüger (convener), in collaboration with Martin Baumeister and Emmanuelle Cronier. Additional research was provided by Sarah Howard, Jon Lawrence, and Peter Martland. Jan Rüger would like to acknowledge the generous support of the Leverhulme Trust, which facilitated the research for and writing of this chapter.

[1] Ford Madox Ford, *The soul of London. A survey of a modern city* (London, 1905), p. 73.
[2] Ibid., p. 72.   [3] Ibid., p. 92.
[4] Kaspar Maase, *Grenzenloses Vergnügen. Der Aufstieg der Massenkultur 1850–1970* (Frankfurt am Main, 1997), pp. 16–114; Schlör, *Nights in the big city*, pp. 235–74; Erika Rappaport, *Shopping for pleasure: women in the making of London's West End* (Princeton,

urban culture responded and changed with the First World War is examined in this chapter.[5]

Focusing on popular theatre, film, and music, we ask how urban audiences made use and sense of the cities' entertainment culture during the war; how that culture changed and adapted between 1914 and 1919; and how the war was put on the stages and screens of London, Paris, and Berlin. To explore the role of urban entertainment during the war thus means to combine three perspectives: the wartime function of entertainments; the political, moral, and artistic discourse surrounding them; and the representations of war they produced. To do so requires us to acknowledge the limits of comparative cultural history. A strictly symmetrical comparison of the sites and forms of entertainment in London, Paris, and Berlin is impossible in the space available. Not only are there substantial gaps in the sources about and our knowledge of urban entertainment during the First World War, what is more, each city had its own range of unique entertainments, each with its peculiar and 'incomparable' cultural context. The London music hall did not have a direct equivalent in Berlin or Paris. Nor can the Paris *café-concert* or the Berlin *Kabarett* be translated into the other cities' experience without losing much of the cultural context.

As a result, this chapter is written in what Jay Winter, in chapter 1, calls the 'relational' mode of comparative history. Acknowledging these limitations, this chapter progresses thematically rather than geographically. We move from an inquiry into the challenge that the war brought to urban entertainments, via an analysis of their role as sites located at the intersection between home and front, to an interpretation of the fundamental shift in representations of war and conflict offered by cinemas, theatres, and music halls. Taken together, these issues lead to an interpretation of the relationship between 'old' and 'new' in wartime urban culture, that is, the resilience of traditional patterns of representation in view of the new, often 'unrepresentable' reality of modern mass warfare. Ultimately, this

---

2001), ch. 6; Vanessa R. Schwartz, *Spectacular realities: early mass culture in fin-de-siècle Paris* (Berkeley, 1998); Concetta Condemi, *Les cafés-concerts. Histoire d'un divertissement 1849–1914* (Paris, 1992).

[5] On sport: Jay Winter, 'Popular culture in wartime Britain', in Aviel Roshwald and Richard Stites (eds.), *European culture in the Great War: the arts, entertainment, and propaganda, 1914–1918* (Cambridge, 1999), pp. 339–40; and D. Birley, 'Sportsmen and the deadly game', *British Journal of Sports History*, December 1986, pp. 288–310. For specific kinds of wartime sports see Tony Collins, 'English Rugby Union and the First World War', *Historical Journal*, 45 (2002), pp. 797–817; Colin Veitch, ' "Play up! Play up! And win the war!" Football, the nation and the First World War', *Journal of Contemporary History*, 20 (1985), pp. 363–78; and Tony Mason, *Association Football and English society, 1863–1915* (Brighton, 1980), ch. 9.

chapter aims to explain how the tensions between 'home' and 'front', between 'city' and 'war', were mediated by urban entertainments with their peculiar combination of modern, nostalgic, and transgressive impulses.

In August 1914, the *Kinematograph*, the leading trade journal of the German film industry, described the threefold experience of cinema, urbanity, and the outbreak of war. Under the headline 'War and Cinema' it wrote:

> The general restlessness that has gripped the public out of uncertainty has been mirrored by strongly increased numbers of cinema visits, at least in Berlin. The public waits eagerly for definitive news. Well into the late hours the streets are densely populated, and for many the cinemas offer a welcome opportunity to spend a few hours calming their anxiety, restlessness, and agitation with the help of flickering pictures. The colourful change of images on the screen, from serious to cheerful, from educational to entertaining, from pictures of landscape to military scenes, corresponds to the mood of the human psyche more than any other medium. In these restless days ... the seemingly randomly and accidentally arranged pictures give a fitting representation of the human state of mind.[6]

The cinema was, in this reading, the mirror of the urban psyche, reflecting the city's frame of mind: restless, chaotic, challenging, anxious, fractured, modern. The metropolitan experience corresponded with the fast-changing, flickering images the cinema produced, and especially so during the days in early August 1914 when urban populations began to engage with the reality of war. The tension between serious and cheerful, educational and entertaining, military and kitsch, which the *Kinematograph* saw as essential to this experience, was to dominate the role of entertainment in London, Paris, and Berlin.

The optimism displayed by the journal, hoping for an increased demand for diversion in times of war, emerged despite an acute sense of crisis in the entertainment industry in early August 1914. Not only was this highly internationalized business suddenly cut off from important supplies and markets, especially where music and film were concerned. What was more, urban entertainment, highly sensitive to changing popular moods and trends, depended on the means available or made available for the consumption of its goods. Going to the music hall or the cinema, buying records or theatre tickets, could seem a luxury, unaffordable in times of war. On 10 August 1914 Alfred Clark, managing director of the London Gramophone Company, wrote about the prospects of

---

[6] 'Krieg und Kino', *Kinematograph*, no. 397, 5 August 1914.

selling music records: 'There is no business and it would be foolish to attempt to do any.'[7]

Beyond the initial sense of crisis illustrated by such voices, however, the *Kinematograph's* optimism was justified. While threatening avant-garde and more exclusive forms of entertainment, the war offered vast opportunities to the entrepreneurs of popular entertainment.[8] In all three capital cities the war accelerated the formation of an urban entertainment industry that had begun in the pre-war decades. In this process intervention from above and initiative from below played equally important parts. A comparably small number of expanding companies were most successful at addressing the new markets and economies that the war had created. The authorities' awakening to the propaganda value especially of film led to further consolidation, most spectacularly in Berlin with the founding of the *Universum Film AG*, or *Ufa*, in December 1917, incorporating some of the most important production and distribution companies in a government-owned holding. The arrival of new audiences underpinned the centralization of entertainment, in London and Paris more strongly than in Berlin. As G. S. Street observed in 1918 in an essay on 'The war and theatre', London entertainments were profiting from new audiences whereas in the provinces most theatres were struggling to survive:

London has had a constant influx of soldiers on leave, of whom a majority want to see a few plays before they return. There are also a great many war-workers living in London who are not normally there, and many of these refresh themselves in the theatre.[9]

The comparably cheap forms of entertainment, such as cinema and music hall, were to profit most from the war. Attendance at them, though fluctuating, expanded between 1914 and 1918 in all three cities. In London, the weekly attendance at cinemas rose from seven million in 1914 to twenty-one million in 1917.[10] 'The cinematograph cinemas are more crowded than ever', *The Times* found in November 1915. Its explanation: 'the coming of war, which means the departure of spare

---

[7] Johnson Museum, Dover, Delaware, USA, Clark Papers: Alfred Clark to E. R. Johnson, 10 August 1914.

[8] Louis Sterling, manager of the Columbia Phonograph Company, embodied this success, see Peter Martland, *Since records began: EMI: the first 100 years* (London, 1997), pp. 108–9.

[9] G. S. Street, 'The war and theatre', *At home in the war* (London, 1918), p. 108. Martland, *Since records began*; Peter Jelavich, 'German culture in the Great War', in Roshwald and Stites (eds.), *European culture in the Great War*, pp. 36–42; and Winter, 'Popular culture in wartime Britain'.

[10] Nicholas Hiley, 'The British cinema auditorium', in Karel Dibbets and Bert Hogenkamp (eds.), *Film and the First World War* (Amsterdam, 1995), p. 162.

cash, has even greatly increased the popularity of this cheap form of amusement'.[11] In Paris, 800,000 cinema tickets were sold in December 1914 and 960,000 in January 1915. A year later, this had doubled to 2 million tickets. The average monthly cinema attendance remained between 1.6 and 2 million until the end of the war.[12] No monthly attendance figures are available for Berlin, where 350 cinemas existed in 1914, with a total capacity of about 120,000 seats.[13] With the exception of a short period in 1916, the number of cinemas remained constant throughout the war in the German capital, while the numbers of visitors expanded.[14]

Legitimacy, morality, and transgression

It was not so much the shrinking disposable income of audiences, the 'departure of spare cash' as *The Times* had it, which redefined the role of urban entertainment during the war.[15] What mattered more, ultimately, were the interlinked issues of moral legitimacy and control. Soon after the outbreak of war, the cities' administrators, the military, the entertainment industry, and a range of often self-acclaimed moral authorities found themselves in a debate about the legitimacy of entertainment. In the course of it three moral arguments were advanced against urban entertainment: that it resulted in physical and moral degeneration, especially amongst the young; that it encouraged sexual immorality; and that it was in itself immoral in times of war.

The first argument drew on late-nineteenth-century ideals of education and physical exercise which moralists of different political persuasions saw endangered by modern urban entertainment. In many schools discipline had been relaxed and school hours shortened,[16] while cinemas

---

[11] *The Times*, 26 November 1915.

[12] Jean-Jacques Meuse, *Paris-Palace ou le temps des cinémas 1894–1918* (Paris, 1995), pp. 430–1.

[13] Brunner, *Kinematograph von heute*, pp. 8–9. These numbers are for Greater Berlin. They are confirmed by Gary D. Stark, 'Cinema, society, and the state: policing the film industry in Imperial Germany', in Gary D. Stark and Bede Karl Lackner (eds.), *Essays on culture and society in modern Germany* (Arlington, Texas, 1982), pp. 122–66, p. 124.

[14] This was despite only very few new cinemas opening, due to the ban on new licences that was in practice for most of the war. Stark, 'Cinema, Society, and the State'; Gertrude Bub, *Der deutsche Film im Weltkrieg und sein publizistischer Einsatz* (Berlin, 1938), p. 63; David A. Welch, 'Cinema and society in Imperial Germany 1905–1918', *German History*, 8 (1990), pp. 28–45.

[15] Jon Lawrence, 'Material pressures on the middle classes' and Jonathan Manning, 'Wages and purchasing power', both in Jay Winter and Jean-Louis Roberts (eds.), *Capital cities at war*, vol. I, pp. 229–54 and 255–85.

[16] See chapter 6 below.

and music halls were frequented by young adults more than before the war. This exposure to entertainment, moralists worried, would seriously undermine recruiting and military training. In Germany, a conscripted Catholic schoolteacher wrote an open letter in April 1916, alerting the home front to the 'pain it causes us, who have been in enemy territory for so long now, when we read in letters and newspapers that the youth at home are deteriorating'.[17] Many pedagogues and moralists blamed popular entertainment for this 'decay', which they saw in opposition to the physical and moral strengthening that the war seemed to demand. A joint committee of justices and members of the London County Council Education Committee reported in January 1917 that 'nearly all the witnesses were agreed that constant attendance at cinematograph theatres had an injurious effect on juvenile mind and character'.[18] Instead of encouraging physical exercise and moral invigoration, the entertainment industry seemed to promote passivity and apathy. It provided spaces where people simply 'sit and are amused', as the *Manchester Guardian* criticized. The palaces of entertainment turned out 'street-urchins and vacuous boys and girls' rather than the soldiers of tomorrow. It was 'grotesque' that large urban audiences should be entertained in front of the screens while physical education was needed to instil the qualities needed for war, such as 'discipline, courage, esprit de corps and a sense of honour'. The *Manchester Guardian*, not traditionally an advocate of privileged private schools, concluded: 'If Waterloo was won on the playing-fields of Eton – what success in future battles will be due to picture palace performances?'[19]

The second moral argument against urban entertainment was about the loose sexual morals that moralists in all three cities saw encouraged by urban entertainment. Lax sexual morality, they argued, was promoted by the halls and palaces of entertainments in two ways: by showing 'indecent' scenes; and by providing spaces that were conducive to 'immoral behaviour'. Again and again, the licensing and censorship authorities dealt with complaints about shows and films that were perceived to be too overtly sexual. The Theatres and Music Halls Committee of the London County Council faced a growing number of objections to the renewal of licenses for variety theatres that were seen as showing 'indecent scenes'. The London Pavilion and the Euston Theatre of Varieties

---

[17] *Freiburger Tagespost*, 17 April 1916, in Bernd Ulrich, *Die Augenzeugen. Deutsche Feldpostbriefe in Kriegs- und Nachkriegszeit 1914–1933* (Essen, 1997), p. 132. See also *The Times*, 6 October 1916.

[18] *The Times*, 16 January 1917.

[19] *Manchester Guardian*, 9 November 1916. See also Dean Rapp, 'Sex in the cinema. War, moral panic and the British film industry 1906–1918', *Albion*, 34 (2002), p. 434.

were the focus of such complaints in November 1916. The chief attraction of these houses, the opponents of license renewals argued, were revues 'of which the outstanding features are scantily dressed females going through a series of evolutions that are vulgar and immodest, and jokes that have indecent double meanings'.[20]

It was not only the scenes shown on stages and screens that critics found objectionable. They judged the entertainment establishments themselves to be the location of 'indecent conduct'. The darkness or semi-darkness of cinemas and music halls made them public sites that were private enough for social and sexual transgressions. Early on in the war, the police in London, Paris, and Berlin had begun systematically to monitor entertainments as sites of sexual transgression and prostitution. We have a variety of reports by undercover officers, employed to observe bars, theatres, and music halls in Paris. They show the range of transgressions deemed as 'immoral' or 'indecent' by the police. In January 1916 one officer found that in some establishments women allowed strangers to embrace them in public.[21] 'Every evening, the exits of concert halls and cinemas, [and] the space on Place de l'Opéra, in front of the Métro exit, are turned into a veritable market of women. One cannot walk through these places any longer', wrote another officer in July 1916.[22] At times, the reports listed instances of drug abuse at sites of entertainment; at others they recorded homosexual couples kissing publicly.[23] What was remarkable about such reports was not only the moral taxonomies they revealed, but also how much the authorities saw urban entertainments as sites where social and sexual transgressions took place in times of war.

In London, the authorities recorded a rising number of what came to be called 'amateur prostitutes'.[24] These women, the critics of urban entertainment argued, were encouraged by the loose morals in music halls, cinemas, and varieties. Moralists appealed to the authorities in particular 'to prevent the use of the promenade by unaccompanied women or to prevent them from soliciting'.[25] Common to most of such criticism was

---

[20] London Metropolitan Archive, LCC/MIN/10, 737, p. 554: Meeting of the Theatres and Music Halls Committee, 2 November 1916.

[21] Archives de la préfecture de police, BA, 1587: report of 23 January 1916.

[22] Archives de la préfecture de police, BA, 1689, prostitution.

[23] Archives de la préfecture de police, BA, 1587: report of 3 March 1918. See also ibid.: report of 1 October 1915 (Cintra Bar, Place Edouard VII).

[24] Lucy Bland, 'In the name of protection: the policing of women in the First World War', in Julia Brophy and Carol Smart (eds.), *Women-in-law. Explorations in law, family and sexuality* (London, 1985), pp. 23–49 and Angela Woollacott, ' "Khaki Fever" and its control: gender, class, age and sexual morality on the British homefront in the First World War', *Journal of Contemporary History*, 29 (1994), pp. 325–47.

[25] *The Times*, 1 November 1916. See chapter 2, p. 48.

that it alleged that many of the urban sites of entertainment not only showed immoral scenes, but also encouraged immoral behaviour amongst the audiences. People should wake up to the fact, wrote the Bishop of London in October 1915,

> that the numerous night clubs of London were for the most part the haunts and hunting grounds of sharks and loose women, whose business consists of exploiting the follies and weaknesses of those who are induced to visit them, and that the existence of these places in war-time is a danger not only to the individuals who resort to them, but also, through them, to the nation ... I do not hesitate to say that the continued existence of some, if not most, of these so-called clubs is a danger to the capital of an Empire at war.[26]

To bring light into cinemas and music halls, both in a metaphorical and literal sense, became a main aim of the numerous committees and societies set up to inquire into the moral implications of urban entertainments. When the National Council of Public Morals published recommendations for the reform of London's cinemas in October 1917, its key suggestions included that each picture house 'should be lighted sufficiently by means of screened lights during the showing of the pictures to ensure that no objectionable practices shall be possible in the auditorium'. Between films 'there should be short intervals in which the theatre should be suffused with light'.[27] Such efforts at improving cinemas and music halls 'morally' point to the presence of powerful anxieties associated with urban sites of entertainment. They illustrate how the war reinforced and expanded the moral discourse on entertainment that had developed in parallel to the rise of popular culture and especially the cinema in the late nineteenth century.[28]

The third moral argument against urban entertainment challenged its very essence: entertainment was about amusement, diversion, and pleasure. The war called these emotional needs, and even more so their public satisfaction, radically into question. In times of death, suffering, and sacrifice, urban entertainment had to justify its moral legitimacy. Entertainment was 'light hearted', 'cheerful', and 'frivolous' while the

---

[26] *The Times*, 4 October 1915.   [27] *The Times*, 10 October 1917.

[28] After the war, Magnus Hirschfeld, the Berlin physician and founder of the Institute for Sexual Science, interpreted wartime entertainments as spaces where the boundaries of 'decent' and 'immoral' had been increasingly blurred and took this as evidence for a general loosening of morals in urban societies during the war. See his *Sittengeschichte des Weltkrieges*, 2 vols (Leipzig and Vienna, 1930) and also Manfred Herzer, *Magnus Hirschfeld* (Frankfurt, 1992); John C. Fout, 'Sexual politics in Wilhelmine Germany: the male gender crisis, moral purity, and homophobia', *Journal of the History of Sexuality*, 2 (1992), pp. 388–421.

times were 'serious' and 'critical' (*ernst* or *schwer* were standard usage in German, *dure* or *grave* in French). In the words of the Bishop of London, frivolous entertainment was not suitable 'in these critical times'.[29] Soon after the outbreak of war, authorities started to demand seriousness in wartime entertainment.[30] Many of the soldiers who took to the cinemas and music halls for diversion while on leave, *permission* or *Heimaturlaub* did feel the moral dilemma posed by urban entertainment: was it 'right' to amuse yourself while your fellow soldiers were fighting and dying in the trenches? The 'trench newspapers' as well as the journals and letters written by soldiers illuminate this ambiguity. On the one hand, many front-line soldiers were offended by the idea of amusement and laughter in the capital city while there were hundreds of thousands dying at the front. A German soldier wrote: 'We come from the battlefield, where we experience nothing but sorrow, pain, and death, and in the big cities they party into the night.'[31] *La Chéchia*, a French soldiers' newspaper, quoted a *poilu* on *permission* in March 1917:

I was disgusted during my last leave. And they talk about a recruiting crisis [*la crise des effectifs*]. Paris is full of people, old boy, strong men like you and me; and young and prim and proper, you should see them! And then they walk the boulevards, they take a seat at the cafés and they lounge on the terraces. They rush to the *pâtisseries* and they laugh at the *cafés-concerts*! As if there was no war! And the theatres are at their height and the cinemas make their fortune. To think that we are fighting for this![32]

However, whilst being offended by such aspects of civilian decadence, many soldiers acknowledged how much they themselves craved and enjoyed urban entertainment. 'I *confess* I have been recaptured more rapidly by exterior life and things from the street. And here I am, all over Paris', wrote one soldier on leave.[33] The trench newspaper *La Chéchia* highlighted the morally ambiguous experience of urban entertainment for soldiers in a characteristic piece of parody in March 1917. The same *poilu* who, in the above quotation, derided civilians for their decadence before he left for his *permission*, is portrayed as complaining

---

[29] *The Times*, 4 October 1915. For a similar conflict see Maureen Healy, 'Exhibiting a war in progress. Entertainment and propaganda in Vienna, 1914–1918', *Austrian History Yearbook*, 31 (2000).

[30] For an example see LA Berlin, A Prf. Br. Rep. 30 Titel 74, no. 16: 'Das Organ', no. 299. See also chapter 5 in this volume.

[31] Quoted in Peter Jelavich, *Berlin cabaret* (Cambridge, Mass., 1993), p. 125.

[32] *La Chéchia*, no. 50, 1 March 1917, p. 2; similarly *Le Diable au Cor*, no. 17, 9 December 1915, p. 3. See also *Echo des marmites*, no. 17, 10 February 1917, pp. 9–11. *Poilu*, literally 'hairy one', was the colloquial term for French infantry soldiers.

[33] *Le Poilu, 108ème*, no. 20, April 1916, pp. 1–2 (our italics).

about the lack of entertainment when returning from leave: Paris is no longer full of amusement, laughter, and debauchery; it is an altogether dull affair. By demonstrating his disgust for civilian decadence *before* embarking on his *permission* and belittling the experience of entertainment *afterwards* this figure offered a rhetorical strategy for coping with the moral dilemma that urban entertainment 'at home' presented for many soldiers.[34]

The soldiers' ambiguous experience was mirrored by the difficulties the authorities faced when trying to develop an approach towards urban entertainment in times of war. While finding many aspects morally objectionable and potentially damaging for the war effort, they appreciated the need for entertainment and the opportunity for propaganda. It took both the authorities and the entertainment industry some time to find a vocabulary and practice that accommodated this ambiguity. In the course of this process, the overriding question became less *if* some aspects of urban entertainment had to be curbed in order to 'purify and elevate the moral tone of London', as the London Council for the Promotion of Public Morality put it in August 1916.[35] Instead, the question became much more *which* aspects of urban entertainment should be curbed. In trying to convince civil, military, and church authorities that cinemas and music halls were in tune with the patriotic demands for morality and 'seriousness', the entertainment industry went beyond co-operating with censorship and control 'from above'. It took an active part in the inquiries and committees set up by voluntary organizations and churches for the moral reform of urban entertainment. Thus the London Cinema Commission, whose aim it was to prepare suggestions for the 'moral improvement' of cinemas, was set up by the National Council of Public Morals at the request of the Cinematograph Trade Council. This allowed the film industry to claim that they were actively engaged in reforming those aspects of cinematography that had been found morally wanting.[36]

The inquiries led by such committees and the debate accompanying them developed a moral taxonomy that allowed a differentiation between acceptable and non-acceptable entertainment, or, as the Bishop of London had it, between 'healthy distraction' and 'immoral diversion'.[37]

---

[34] *La Chéchia*, no. 50, 1 March 1917, p. 2; similarly *Le Diable au Cor*, no. 17, 9 December 1915, p. 3.

[35] *The Times*, 7 August 1916.

[36] Stark, 'Cinema, society, and the state'; Annette Kuhn, *Cinema, censorship and sexuality, 1909–1925* (London, 1988); and Lise Shapiro Sanders, ' "Indecent incentives to vice": regulating films and audience behaviour from the 1890s to the 1910s', in Andrew Higson (ed.), *Young and innocent? The cinema in Britain 1896–1930* (Exeter, 2002), pp. 97–110.

[37] *The Times*, 4 October 1915.

In the course of this process, the moral argument that had threatened the whole industry was deflected on to those avant-garde or bohemian sites of entertainment that did not qualify as 'comparatively reputable'. This moral finger-pointing fitted well with the censorship and control carried out by the authorities.

As a result, the experimental entertainment culture that had blossomed in the years before 1914 came under siege. Avant-garde cabarets and clubs relocated to private, clandestine spaces or closed altogether. This was accelerated when sensationalist journalists and right-wing agitators targeted underground entertainments as sources of conspiracy and treason, with Noel Pemberton Billing perhaps the most notorious example.[38] A dearth of more challenging entertainment followed the upsurge in patriotically redefined middle-class morality. Peter Jelavich, the historian of the Berlin cabaret, concludes that the 'artistic quality [of cabaret] was negligible for the duration of hostilities'.[39] Contemporary critics, too, lamented the increasing dominance of the lowest common denominator. As one of them wrote in 1916, the departure of more challenging forms of entertainment paralleled the unrivalled success especially of the cinema:

There is no dislodging the picture palace; it has become one of the institutions of modern life. Its strong appeal lies in the fact that it is cheap, that it is available not at any fixed hour, but continually, that it is dark and restful, and that it affords entertainment on the easiest terms ever devised by man. You have not even to think – only to look. In addition, it provides or is supposed to provide variety; nothing lasts long; and if you do not like one thing you wait in hope for the next.

Accepting popular taste as the yardstick by which cultural production should be judged could however be immoral in itself, he argued:

These entertainments are all standardized to suit the conventional kind of morality which is the only kind considered by their censors, but there are more kinds of immorality than that which incites people to steal or murder or otherwise misbehave themselves. There may, for example, be such a degree of stupidity as to amount to immorality. The cinema has proved that it can do beautiful and useful things; but unless it does them in rather larger measure it would be as well that the highly explosive substances of which these thousands of miles of celluloid film are made should be employed not against ourselves, but our enemies.[40]

---

[38] Judith R. Walkowitz, 'The "vision of Salome": cosmopolitanism and erotic dancing in central London, 1908–1918', *American Historical Review*, 108 (2003), pp. 337–76; Jodie Medd, ' "The cult of the clitoris": anatomy of a national scandal', *Modernism/Modernity*, 9 (2002), pp. 21–49; Philip Hoare, *Wilde's last stand. Decadence, conspiracy and the First World War* (London, 1997).

[39] Jelavich, *Berlin cabaret*, p. 126.

[40] *The Times*, 25 February 1916. See also *Le Film*, 5 March 1917 and *Le Film*, 27 August 1917.

The popularization that this critic lamented was a symptom of the process in which notions of taste and morality were redefined during the war, not only by censors and governments, but similarly by audiences and the entertainment industry, aiming to align a patriotic image with financial success. After August 1914 the entertainment industry, the authorities, and parts of the press developed a shared rhetoric that brought together entertainment and patriotism, *divertissement* and *patriotisme*, *Unterhaltung* and *Patriotismus*. Crucial to this rhetoric was that it identified 'immoral' forms of non-mainstream entertainment that could be blacklisted and curbed in the name of public morality. It was by reference to such 'immoral' establishments that the flourishing of cinemas, theatres, music halls, and *cafés-concerts* was legitimized. The threefold wartime argument against entertainment was thus overcome by an unwritten contract between the industry and the authorities, which committed the one side to upholding 'patriotic' morality and cooperating with censorship and controls, and the other side to limiting official interference with the entertainment industry. The arrangement underlined the central public role that urban entertainments played during the war.

Negotiating the ties between home and front

This role, in turn, was only partly about the provision of distraction in times of suffering and hardship. Beyond their immediate function as sources of diversion, entertainments were key sites for negotiations between home and front, between civilian and military roles and identities. In November 1914 the film companies distributing the *Eiko-Woche* and *Messter-Woche*, the main weekly newsreels in Berlin's cinemas, advertised their latest pictures of the war. A main feature of this advertising was the claim that the newsreels would bring the front home. One announcement boasted that 'injured soldiers on leave, who are given free entry to all cinemas, have recognised themselves in our images. We are receiving similar statements from families who have had the joy of seeing their sons on the screen.'[41] As much as such claims were informed by advertising purposes, and as much as they hid the fact that these newsreels showed a censored and sanitized version of 'the front', they did point to a central function of urban entertainments in all three cities during the war: they provided sites for the symbolic exchange between front and home, *le front* and *l'arrière*, *Feld* and *Heimat*.

---

[41] *Kinematograph*, no. 413, 25 November 1914; similarly in *Kinematograph*, no. 449, 4 August 1915.

The multi-layered intersection of 'home' and 'front' took place as much on the screens and stages as in the audiences themselves. In all three cities injured and disabled soldiers were given special seats in cinemas and music halls. Marked by the war, they offered a view that most urban audiences had not been exposed to before. Soldiers and civilians alike noted that this could cause conflicts within audiences, often additionally charged with gendered meanings.[42] As we shall see in chapter 7, entertainment and family life were braided together in new ways. This was intensified with the increasing presence of soldiers on leave who mixed with civilian audiences in music halls, cinemas, and theatres. Troops were regularly entertained at Earls' Court and in the Strand in London and in the theatres and varieties of Berlin's Friedrichstraße. However, this rarely reached the level of Paris where soldiers on leave, the permissionnaires, as we saw in chapter 3, became a defining feature of urban entertainment.

The official image of the *permission* was that of a soldier returning to his home, as father or son, and spending time in the family circle. This image was evoked by the Conseil municipal de Paris in April 1917 when it claimed that 'those who come from the front to enjoy some days of leave with their family, those soldiers don't even think about going to places of pleasure'.[43] However, the reality was more complicated than the official image of the permissionnaire as a *bon père de famille*. Not every soldier on leave had a family, nor did the permissionnaires always want to spend their leave in the family home. It was here that urban entertainment came to play a key role. In November 1915, four months after leave had been introduced in the French army, a memorandum by the Prefect of the Paris Police spoke of 'unusual crowds in theatres and cinemas'. A report in December 1917 concluded that 'the entertainment halls have never seen such crowds'.[44] In March 1918 the Conseil municipal de Paris estimated that between 40,000 and 50,000 permissionnaires usually spent their leave simultaneously in Paris and that they now made up 'the main part of the theatre audiences'.[45] Allied soldiers added to these numbers considerably.[46]

---

[42] *Bombardia*, no. 19, 30 September 1917, pp. 2–3. For the London Old Vic offering entertainment to blind soldiers see Cicely Hamilton and Lilian Baylis, *The Old Vic* (London, 1926), pp. 201ff.

[43] Conseil municipal de Paris, April 1917.

[44] PF, BA1587, Physionomie de Paris, 14 December 1917. G. Cerfberr, *Paris pendant la guerre* (Paris, 1919), p. 91.

[45] Conseil municipal de Paris, Comité du budget, 13 March 1918, p. 24. Thierry Bonzon, 'Les assemblées locales parisiennes et leur politique sociale pendant la Grande Guerre (1912–1919)', doctoral thesis in history, Paris I, 1999.

[46] For an evocation of wartime Paris as a place of amusement for British and American troops see George Orwell, *Burmese days* (London, 1967), p. 27.

The popularity of Paris as a centre of entertainment with the troops posed a range of potential problems for the military and civilian authorities. When introducing the *permission*, they had been especially alarmed by the prospect of masses of soldiers on leave in Paris who did not have a home or family in the capital. Two cultural institutions helped with this problem. First, the *marraines de guerre*, the voluntary 'godmothers' who, for the duration of the war, 'adopted' young soldiers who did not have parents to come back to. It became standard practice for the *marraines de guerre* to take their adoptive soldier-sons to the cinemas and theatres of Paris. Already by 1916 the *permission*, with its negotiation of civilian and military roles under the auspices of the *marraines de guerre*, had turned into such an institution that novels took them up as themes. *Papa en permission* by Charles Bazhor, for example, featured an entire chapter dedicated to how the *marraines de guerre* take their 'adoptive son' to the entertainments, including a cinema, where a military revue and the saluting of the colours is followed by a film about a *permissionnaire* killing an *embusqué* (shirker).[47]

Secondly, there were initiatives aimed at those soldiers who had neither their own family nor a *marraine de guerre* to accommodate them during their leave. The most famous of them, *Les Parrains de Reuilly* (literally the 'Godfathers of Reuilly'), were invented for the very purpose of controlling and entertaining crowds of soldiers whom the Paris authorities and police saw as a threat.[48] Scores of *permissionnaires* were brought from the main train stations directly to the barracks of the *Caserne de Reuilly* in the twelfth arrondissement. Here, they were given a bed, food, and an extensive programme of diversion. *Les Parrains de Reuilly* had, inside the military compound, their own cinema and theatre, hosting many of the stars of the Parisian stage. There were excursions to specially organized shows in Paris and to places of interest such as Versailles. These excursions took place under strict supervision and in police buses.[49]

The *permission* with its ritualized visits of cinemas, music halls, and *cafés-concerts*, became an eagerly awaited feature of soldiers' calendars. For many of them, 'leave' turned into shorthand for amusement and raucous fun. Indeed, the French word, *permission*, signalled that this was an exceptional, liminal phase in a soldier's calendar when radically different roles, usually kept carefully apart, collided; and when a range of transgressions seemed possible. The popular French film *Le flirt*

---

[47] Charles Bazhor, *Papa en permission* (Paris, 1916), ch. 12.
[48] Association des parrains de Reuilly, *Statuts* (1916), p. 13.
[49] Emmanuelle Cronier, 'Les permissionnaires du front à Paris, 1915–1918', doctoral thesis, University of Paris I, 2004.

d'Hector, for example, had one Mrs Beauvisage waiting for her *poilu*, Hector, 'who is coming to Paris on leave, and with whom she is ready to be unfaithful to her husband'.[50] The experience of overlapping civilian and military spheres was a recurrent theme in descriptions of the *permission*, especially in soldiers' magazines and journals.[51] Soldiers on leave brought the front 'home' to the audiences in London, Paris, and Berlin – and were confronted with the cities' readings of and reactions to the war. Entertainment thus went far beyond the obvious function of distracting and amusing; it offered a space for the negotiation of wartime experiences and emotions between people whose ideas of the war could be radically different. As a result 'entertainment' could at times be a challenging or uncomfortable experience. Léon Chancerel captured this aspect in his *Chanson des dix jours* published in 1917, where he evokes the emotions of a soldier on leave who watches with his wife a revue in a Parisian music-hall. The revue features naked or half-naked women singing patriotic songs. In the poem this 'spectacle de guerre', the clash between light-hearted, erotic scenes and the serious language of patriotism, with its gendered undertones, produces feelings of awkwardness and discomfort:

> Spectacle of war
> The other night, we were at the Revue
> In the great music hall 'tapageur' – and
> Suddenly, among the crowd, a 'gêne imprévue'
> Took us over, where we were seated.
> The author, juggling bereavement and suffering,
> Spoke out and offered three couplets.
> Bloody heroism became the air of a dance
> And glory figured the path of a ballet.
> And there, at the front of the chorus girls
> We saw Verdun, described in a musical poem.
> Commerce, wearing a flag on her chest,
> Exalts the soldiers and shows us her legs.[52]

However, not only was the front present in the cinemas, theatres, and music halls. The sites of urban entertainment were present at the front, too. A large share of the language by which the troops ascribed sense to the alien world of 'the front' was borrowed from the cinemas, music halls, and popular theatre. Many of the names given to trenches referred to urban locations of entertainment such as 'Haymarket', 'West End', 'The Strand', and 'Piccadilly Circus'.[53] Comedians such as Charlie Chaplin,

[50] PF, BA 772, Casino de Fontenay-sous-Bois, 29 April 1916.
[51] For a poignant example see *Bombardia*, no. 19, 30 September 1917, pp. 2–3.
[52] Léon Chancerel, *La chanson des dix jours* (Paris, 1917), p. 23.
[53] William Redmond, *Trench pictures from France* (London, 1917), pp. 35–8.

Harry Tate, and Harry Lauder came to be associated with a range of front experiences. The British Expeditionary Force was regularly referred to as 'Harry Tate's Army'; the chaotic rush to evade incoming shells could be 'a bit of Charlie Chaplin'; and there were songs in which the 'little tramp' stood for 'the Tommy' in general:

> Oh, the moon shines bright on Charlie Chaplin
> His boots are crackin'
> For want of blackin'
> And his little baggy trousers they need mendin'
> Before we send him
> To the Dardanelles.[54]

It was not only in borrowing the icons of amusement and comedy for soldiers' slang that urban entertainment was present in the trenches. Surprisingly, many soldiers mention the gramophone as a source for at least a glimpse of the 'normality' that was associated with 'home'. Record companies and war charities regularly made gifts of gramophones and records to the army.[55] Gramophones are frequently mentioned in letters sent home by officers and sailors in German submarines.[56] Christopher Stone, the writer and broadcaster, described how the 'Decca arrived with half-a-dozen records while the battalion was in reserve billets at Bouzencourt, near Albert, in January 1917, and from that moment life in the headquarters mess was altered'. The gramophone travelled with his battalion, a portable evocation of 'civilized life', as Stone put it:

Strange homes that old Decca has had, up and down the villages of France in ruined houses, in huts, in tents, in transport lines. Only once, I think, did it get as far forward as the support line and that was in the Dyke Valley, in front of Courcellette . . . It was always waiting for us, with our kit and baths and pyjamas, to welcome us back to a semblance of a civilized life.[57]

In a letter to his wife he wrote: 'We are sitting in the mess with the gramophone playing a selection from *Zig-Zag* [a popular London music-hall hit], quite a domestic pleasure: but every crevice of every entrance is blanketed and has been for two hours as we are being bombarded with

[54] John Brophy and Eric Partridge, *Songs and slang of the British soldier: 1914–1918* (London, 1930), p. 210.

[55] Edison Bell, for example, donated 48,000 records to British troops fighting in France in July 1915. For Christmas 1916, his company sent 100,000 records and several hundred gramophone needles to British service personnel. See *Talking machine world*, July 1915; ibid., December 1916, p. 331.

[56] *Das U-Boot*, issue 8 (1917), p. 503.

[57] Christopher Stone, 'A Decca romance', *The Gramophone*, vol. 1, no. 2, August 1923, p. 56.

gas shells this evening.'[58] By reproducing music-hall hits and songs that would have been shared with family and friends the gramophone became a portable link with 'home' – so much in fact, that the gramophone itself became the theme of songs. In 'Take Me Back to Dear Old Blighty', popular both with the troops and in the music halls of London, the gramophone is instrumental in taking soldiers 'back to dear old Blighty':

> Jack Dunn son of a gun
> Over in France today,
> Keeps fit doing his bit
> Up to his eyes in clay.
> Each night after a fight
> To pass the time along,
> He's got a little gramophone
> that plays this song:
> CHORUS
> Take me back to dear old Blighty
> Put me on the train for London Town.[59]

Although separate cultures developed in urban centres and on the front, these were never entirely divorced from one another.[60] Throughout the war entertainment proved a powerful link between 'home' and 'front', one that could be imagined, enacted, and performed. In a two-way process, cinema, theatre, comedy, and music functioned as arenas for symbolic exchange. The troops brought songs from the music halls they had visited to the trenches and adapted them; urban entertainment in turn took up soldiers' songs and staged them in the cities. A similar process can be seen with the theatre groups and comedy shows touring the trenches. Some of these were organized 'from above' as mass entertainment for the troops. Others, and often the most successful, resulted from the initiative of soldiers themselves. Both forms of 'trench entertainment' staged the experience of 'home' at the front.[61]

Entertainment troupes became a standard feature of most of the British army's divisions. One of the most popular was the *Verey Lights* of the 20th Division. Run by two captains and a bandmaster, and featuring a soldiers'

---

[58] G. D. Sheffield and G. I. S. Inglis (eds.), *From Vimy Ridge to the Rhine: Great War letters of Christopher Stone* (Marlborough, Wilts., 1989), p. 117.

[59] Arthur, *When this bloody war is over*, p. 37.

[60] Regina M. Sweeney, *Singing our way to victory. French cultural politics and music during the Great War* (Middletown, Conn., 2001).

[61] L. J. Collins, *Theatre at war, 1914–1918* (Basingstoke, 1998), ch. 5; J. G. Fuller, *Troop morale and popular culture in the British and Dominion armies, 1914–1918* (Oxford, 1990); Andrew Horrall, *Popular culture in London c. 1890–1918. The transformation of entertainment* (Manchester, 2001).

orchestra, their performances famously opened with the 'Verey Lights Song', performed by the entire company:

> Verey Lights – Verey Lights – V -E - R - E –Y
> Carnoy Camp might be damp,
> But the Colosseum's dry.
> Now you know where to go
> To enjoy yourselves at night.
> As you are near us,
> Just come and hear us
> For we are the VEREY LIGHTS.
> You can leave the war outside the door
> When you come to our show.
> Forget the Huns, their shells and guns
> We'll make your troubles go.
> Fritz may send up his S.O.S.
> Lots of green and white.
> But the lights they send up best
> Are the VEREY LIGHTS.[62]

This 'front theatre' replicated urban entertainment in the trenches, re-created a 'home' experience at the front. Soldiers were given an 'Ersatz' experience of what the cinemas and music halls in the three cities offered. 'You can leave the war outside the door' was the *Verey Lights* slogan. It could have been the slogan of any revue or comedy show in London, Paris, or Berlin. By staging the 'home experience' at the front, entertainments addressed what Siegfried Sassoon called the 'Blighty hunger' of soldiers. In his fictionalized biography he described a concert party, which, improvised and amateurish as it might have been, served this central function of connecting home and front cultures:

It wasn't much; a canvas awning, a few footlights; two blue-chinned actors in soft, felt hats – one of them jangling ragtime tunes on a worn-out upright; three women in short silk skirts singing the old, old soppy popular songs; and all of them doing their best with their little repertoire.

They were unconscious, it seemed to me, of the intense impact on their audience – that dim brown moonlit mass of men. Row beyond row, I watched those soldiers, listening so quietly, chins propped on hands, to the songs which epitomized their 'Blighty hunger', their longing for the gaiety and sentiment of life.[63]

When explaining popular entertainment as a catalyst for cultural exchange between home and front, we need to stress that the transfer between the three cities and the front worked in both directions. Not only

---

[62] Arthur, *When this bloody war is over*, xxi–xxii.
[63] Siegfried Sassoon, *The complete memoirs of George Sherston* (London, 1937), pp. 740–1.

did concert parties emulate the 'home experience' at the front and famous actors tour the trenches with classics of urban entertainment. This process was reversed when soldiers' troupes played in the cities and when music halls and popular theatres integrated elements of 'trench culture' into their urban programmes. The famous *Anzac Coves*, a pierrot troupe of Australian soldiers, illustrates that this was a two-way process of symbolic exchanges in which urban entertainment took up the 'theatre from the front line' and the soldiers' troupes quoted and mimicked their urban role models. Having toured the trenches for much of 1917, the *Anzac Coves* played London theatres with great success in early 1918. 'From France to Sloane-Square' ran the headline announcing their arrival in London:

When the *Anzac Coves* come from France to the Court Theatre next Monday London will be able to enjoy an entertainment which the men of Australian battalions in reserve, close behind the lines, visit nightly. The performances will not be brushed up specially for a London audience, or elaborated in any way.

Stressing that Londoners would be able to see 'real' trench entertainment, London's newspapers and magazines advertised the *Anzac Coves* with the slogan 'Direct from the Firing Line'. On 18 February 1918 the military actors were invited to play before the King and Queen at Buckingham Palace and in March they started playing a second theatre, the Ambassadors on Shaftesbury Avenue.[64]

In Germany, the most spectacular example for such transfers between 'home' and 'front' was the play *Der Hias*, written and performed by soldiers. It was remarkable not only for its huge success, which came despite the play not being an official military production, but also for the way it offered an unusual symbolic exchange between 'home' and 'front'. *Der Hias* had first been performed as a charitable initiative in March 1916 in a Bavarian town by an obscure group of soldiers. Half a year later it premiered in Berlin, watched by the highest ranks of the military, state, and society. Its success was ultimately to become bigger than that of any other war play in this period. Not only was it a massive hit in the theatres of Berlin's Friedrichstraße from August 1916. It started to tour the whole country with four troupes and despite the high costs of travelling, theatre leases, and advertising, the play earned one million marks in war bonds the following year. The play's representation of war will be examined below. What is noteworthy here is how *Der Hias* reversed the direction in which entertainment related 'home' and 'front': it was soldiers who

---

[64] *The Times*, 19 February 1918.

brought a play to the capital city, rather than actors bringing the theatre to the front.[65]

The function of entertainment as a symbolic exchange became the more important the longer the war continued. Recent scholarship has uncovered how soldiers and their families found varied forms and modes of communication between 'home' and 'front' – despite the alienation that many felt and despite the identity politics involved on public and private levels in cultivating 'home' and 'front' as opposite and gendered spheres.[66] Here, popular culture played a key role. Cinemas, revue theatres, and music halls produced easily accessible genres and modern techniques of communication. In the language and imagery that they provided, but also spatially, as sites where private and public intersected, they facilitated the negotiation of wartime roles and identities. Entertainers and theatre directors were acutely aware of this role. They addressed the fundamental changes that the war brought to their audiences often directly, in particular where gender relations were concerned. Comedy, nostalgia, and the eroticization of war were the predominant modes aimed at accommodating changing gender roles.

Otto Reutter, the inventive and highly popular actor-director of Berlin's *Palasttheater*, provides a case in point. His productions paid strong attention to the transformation of gender relations and offered an albeit comically spiced recognition of the new status that women enjoyed as they entered masculine realms. Yet Reutter's plays also emphasized that these changes were appropriate only in the exceptional circumstances of war. His first wartime revue, 'Let Mummy Speak' (*Muttchen hat's Wort*), focused on the metamorphosis of a housewife into a successful entrepreneur. With this figure Reutter introduced a new female self-consciousness in theatre; and he did so without caricaturing or ridiculing the more traditional female characters that had populated the patriotic plays until then. Yet he also set sharp boundaries to the re-evaluation of women's roles. The stage appearance of the lead figure observed the conventions of comic role-reversal, which the war required, but it did not challenge the dominant gender hierarchy. Reutter was not only concerned with the actual situation of women in war here. He regarded the feminization of the home front much more as the symbolic

---

[65] Heinrich Gilardone, *Der Hias: Ein feldgraues Spiel in drei Aufzügen* (Berlin and Munich, 1917); Bayerisches Hauptstaatsarchiv Munich, Abt. IV, Kriegsarchiv: Stv. Gkdo. I. AK, no. 643. For the reception of the play in Berlin see *Vossische Zeitung*, 24 August 1916.

[66] Benjamin Ziemann, *Front und Heimat. Ländliche Kriegserfahrungen im südlichen Bayern 1914–1923* (Essen, 1997); Stéphane Audoin-Rouzeau, *Men at war, 1914–1918. National sentiment and trench journalism in France during the First World War*, transl. Helen McPhail (Oxford, 1992).

displacement of power, in the face of which traditional hierarchies were reaffirmed as if they represented the natural order. The threat to the home front, which was itself conventionally portrayed as the 'female' sphere, justified the war in the first place, but the same threat also demanded the subordination of this sphere to the masculine world of the soldiers, and a female commitment to unconditional gratitude and selfless support.[67]

Comedy could thus give space to issues otherwise too serious or too contentious to be staged in an entertaining fashion. It presented perhaps the most successful cultural mode in the symbolic exchange between home and front. This is underlined when soldiers' reactions to entertainment are considered. When on leave they were frequently opposed to allegedly 'authentic' representations of war in cinemas, music halls, and theatres. They tended to view such representations as 'fiction' that stood in painful contrast to their war experiences. Instead they asked for 'pure entertainment', for comedy, adventure, detective stories, and mystery shows. These genres not only allowed for an exciting if temporary escape from the war. They also offered a shared vocabulary to soldiers and civilians. As one officer put it, most soldiers preferred those genres of popular entertainment that provided them with 'the one link with the gaieties and the comparatively carefree existence they knew before the war'.[68] Urban entertainments offered images and characters that helped to frame an approach to a war that was at once distant and close, concrete and intangible. And if it failed to do so, this entertainment culture provided at least a shared space between war and home, in imagination and communication as well as in fact. Cinemas and theatres, pubs and cafés were, after all, public sites at which combatants and civilians, men and women, could meet. Much of the cultural production in the three capital cities at war became engaged in offering such a space for the negotiation between military and civilian roles, between 'front' and 'home'.

The war on the screens and stages

In August 1914 'the nation' and 'the war' conquered the screens and stages in London, Paris, and Berlin. Most of the sites of urban entertainment engaged in a cultural mobilization for war: the rallying to the colours and the ceremonious departure of soldiers, cheered by families and crowds, were recurrent themes. In Paris, the '*fleur au fusil*' became a

---

[67] Cf. Margaret Higonnet and Patrice L.-R. Higonnet, 'The double helix', in Margaret Higonnet *et al.* (eds.), *Behind the lines: gender and the two world wars* (New Haven and London, 1987), pp. 31–47.

[68] H. C. Owen, *Salonica and after* (London, 1919), p. 122.

standard in the repertoire of music halls and revues.[69] In Berlin, one of the most successful of the 'patriotic plays' or *vaterländische Schauspiele* was *Extrablätter* ('Special editions'). From the premier in October 1914 Berlin witnessed a staggering 300 performances of *Extrablätter* within a single year. In 'eight cheerful scenes from a serious time', as the subtitle went, the play illustrated the adventures of the *Kleinbürger* (petit bourgeois) family Hempel.[70] In following a 'family story' *Extrablätter* exemplified the basic scheme of the popular patriotic dramas of 1914: a Berlin family is usually presented in the beginning right at the outbreak of the war. Mobilization creates much excitement. The male members of the family arrive at the front. After a heroic and short fight all of them return to Berlin. With this basic plot plays such as *Extrablätter* contributed to the creation of the 'myth of August', in which the war was portrayed as a transformative experience of the nation, the *Volksgemeinschaft*. Under a local guise these patriotic plays constructed 'the nation' on the stages of Berlin.

Defining 'the people' and 'the nation' was, of course, a political act. The unity and bonding that the patriotic dramas of 1914 showed was by no means all-embracing. Presenting a national collective, they simultaneously highlighted minority positions, usually associated with class, gender, and ethno-religious affiliation. In these plays, socialist workers converted to nationalism, and subsequently died for the fatherland under the motto *Heute rot, morgen tot* ('red today, dead tomorrow'). Women, who had begun to explore and enjoy new gender roles, were now knitting socks for the soldiers at the front or became selfless motherly nurses. Effeminate bourgeois turned into 'real men' by entering the army. Aristocratic officers, naturally, continued to embody the spirit of the 'true soldier'. Jews represented 'good' foreigners or were pictured rushing to the colours with patriotic enthusiasm. This did not, however, prevent their otherness from being articulated. Their national integration remained an open question in these plays. The community represented in the Berlin 'patriotic plays' of August 1914 was thus highly stratified: difference, hierarchies, and borders remained stronger than ever.

With this highly conservative picture of society, the 'patriotic plays' provided a central medium for the staging of the 'spirit of 1914'. Of the 72 plays performed in Berlin theatres between September and December

---

[69] For an example see the popular song '*Chut! Fermons-la!*' of December 1915 (PF, B A843).

[70] LA Berlin, A Prf. Br. Rep. 30 Titel 74, no. 6058: Rudolf Bernauer, Rudolf Schanzer, and Heinz Gordon, 'Extrablätter: Heitere Bilder aus ernster Zeit'. For a detailed analysis see Martin Baumeister, *Kriegstheater: Großstadt, Front und Massenkultur 1914–1918* (Essen, 2005), pp. 70ff. and Jelavich, 'German culture in the Great War', pp. 33–6.

1914, 45 were plays that re-enacted, in one way or another, the *Augusterlebnis*, the experience of the outbreak of war in August 1914. Plays such as Ludwig Thomas's *The First of August* and Fritz Hillmann's *Mobilization* contributed to the cultivation of the 'August experience', mythologized as the moment when the 'nation in arms' had overcome all internal differences. Only shortly after the outbreak of war, urban entertainment thus enshrined the 'spirit of 1914' and helped to canonize the memory of mobilization, to be invoked by politicians and military leaders throughout the war.[71]

The 'patriotic plays' had their equivalents in the heroic war movies that the film industry was quick to bring to the cinemas. In Berlin, this genre was called *Kriegs- und patriotische Filme*, typical titles were: '*Ein Heldenstück unserer Blaujacken*' ('A heroic deed of our Jack Tars'), '*Für's Vaterland*' ('For the Fatherland'), '*Auf dem Kriegspfade*' ('On the War Path'), and '*In Feindesland*' ('In Enemy Territory'). '*Bismarck*' and '*Michels eiserne Faust*' ('Michel's Iron Fist') were especially popular during the first weeks of the war. These were *Kriegsschlager*, 'war hits', as their distributors called them. The weekly newsreels, *Eiko-Woche* and *Messter-Woche*, similarly aimed to bring the war onto the screens. 'For the first time in film! 30.5 cm mortar in firing position! Field guns under fire!' ran an advertisement for a weekly newsreel in November 1914.[72] Similar scenes were on show in London and Paris. Commentators praised what they saw as authentic pictures. *The Times* claimed in 1915 that 'the realities of this war are being more truly brought home to the British public through the agency of the picture palace than by any other means'.[73]

However, neither the topical newsreels nor the 'patriotic war films' can be seen as realistic representations of the war. In all three cities elaborate censorship mechanisms were in place, ensuring that no sensitive material or damaging images were shown. Military authorities strictly limited cameramen's access to the front. And the censorship departments had to clear every film before it could be shown in cinemas.[74] Film companies soon lamented the 'lack of topicalities': if cameramen did gain access to the front, they were rarely allowed to film anything newsworthy. Pictures

[71] Jeffrey Verhey, *The spirit of 1914. Militarism, myth and mobilization in Germany* (Cambridge, 2000); Carola Jüllig, '"Ja, Frankreichs Geist, du bist verbannt für ewig ..." Die erste Kriegsspielzeit der Berliner Theater', in Rainer Rother (ed.), *Die letzten Tage der Menschheit. Bilder des ersten Weltkrieges* (Berlin, 1994), pp. 137–48.

[72] *Kinematograph*, no. 413, 25 November 1914.

[73] *The Times*, 28 January 1915.

[74] Martin Loiperdinger, 'Filmzensur und Selbstkontrolle', in Wolfgang Jacobsen, Anton Kaes, and Hans Helmut Prinzler (eds.), *Geschichte des deutschen Films* (Stuttgart, 1993), pp. 479–98; Welch, 'Cinema and society'; Stark, 'Cinema'; Olivier Forcade, *La censure politique en France pendant la Grande Guerre*, thesis, University of Paris X, 1999.

of the front showed 'rarely anything that was clearly distinguishable'.[75] As one historian of film has concluded, 'hardly ever could any really topical or representative pictures of the front be shown' in the cinemas.[76] The public in London, Paris, and Berlin was treated to an idealized and sanitized vision of 'the front': soldiers having lunch in the trenches or playing cards, guns firing, but no wounded or dead to be seen. The monstrosity of trench warfare, the devastating experience of a modern mass war, could thus remain hidden from the public eye.

A rare, but important exception to this overriding trend was presented by the *Battle of the Somme*, that was shown in London's cinemas from August 1916, only weeks after the beginning of the Allies' offensive. This was the most successful British war film, watched by unprecedented numbers and now widely regarded as a landmark both in war cinematography and propaganda.[77] It prompted the French and German authorities to produce their own propaganda films about the battle. 'L'offensive française de la Somme, July 1916' was screened in Paris in August 1916, 'Bei unseren Helden an der Somme' in Berlin in January 1917. Neither, however, met with the success of the British film. The first part of the British film featured the stock images of newsreels from the front: smiling soldiers marching past the camera and seemingly content troops in reserve. It was the second part of the *Battle of the Somme* that brought pictures to the cinemas in London and the rest of Britain that had never been seen before. It showed, for the first time, the distinguishable faces and bodies of individual soldiers going into battle and staggering back from combat.

The sequence that had the strongest impact on audiences showed men going 'over the top' into action. Historians have since demonstrated that this sequence and a number of other scenes were staged or re-enacted.[78] However, the question whether the *Battle of the Somme* showed 'real' or 'fake' images misses the point. For most contemporaries there was nothing wrong about re-enacting scenes for the camera: this was an accepted

---

[75] *Kinematograph*, no. 400, 26 August 1914.

[76] Klaus W. Wippermann, 'Die deutschen Wochenschauen im Ersten Weltkrieg', *Publizistik* 16 (1971), pp. 268–78.

[77] Jay Winter and Blaine Baggett, *The Great War and the shaping of the twentieth century* (New York, 1996), ch. 4.

[78] Roger Smither, ' "A wonderful idea of the fighting": the question of fakes in "The Battle of the Somme" ', *Historical Journal of Film, Radio and Television*, 13 (1993), pp. 149–69; Nicholas Reeves, 'Through the eye of the camera: contemporary cinema audiences and their "experience" of war in the film Battle of the Somme', in Hugh Cecil and Peter Liddle (eds.), *Facing Armageddon. The First World War experienced* (London, 1996), pp. 780–98; Nicholas Reeves, 'Cinema, spectatorship and propaganda: "Battle of the Somme" (1916) and its contemporary audience', *Historical Journal of Film, Radio and Television*, 17 (1997), pp. 5–28.

means of producing topical newsreels and rarely seen as impinging on a film's value or its 'authenticity'. The significance of *The Battle of the Somme* lies elsewhere: in its radical departure from the standard representations of the front that are best described as sanitized or 'aseptic'.[79] *The Battle of the Somme* showed a glimpse of what modern warfare could mean for the combatants on both sides; it hinted at the effect that the unprecedented scale of violence could have on human bodies and souls; it showed images of pain, exhaustion, apathy, shock, and death. The worst devastation was depicted among German troops: a dead soldier in a trench; another being led away, staggering, under shock. The overall impression was one of different degrees of devastation. 'It shakes the kaleidoscope of war into human reality', was how one critic described the film's impact.[80]

The Battle of the Somme remained an exception. It did not herald a new genre of war cinematography, not until after 1918. On the contrary, those films, revues, and plays that dealt directly with the war continued to cultivate a harmless and sanitized image of the front. This is exposed by the reactions of soldiers. In letters, journals, and soldiers' magazines they mocked the idealized pictures of the war that urban audiences got to see. In December 1915 a soldier recalled from his visit to the cinema in Paris:

> Between the adventures of *Le Bon Prince de Rigadin* and the unavoidable 'drama' we can watch some "scenes from the frontline" of a guaranteed authenticity ... But the only link to reality is the presence of machine guns.[81]

For many soldiers the harmless and idyllic 'scenes from the frontline' shown in cinemas and theatres amounted to comical entertainment – or bitter irony:

> And so we will get them
> This evening at the cinema
> Let's see military films
> I love that stuff
> The hall is jammed
> I watched, amazed
> How the men, in disguise, took 50 trenches
> Just like that, without taking a breath.[82]

---

[79] Martin Baumeister, '"L'effet de reel". Zum Verhältnis von Krieg und Film 1914–1918', in Bernhard Chiari, Matthias Rogg, and Wolfgang Schmidt (eds.), *Krieg und Militär im Film des 20. Jahrhunderts* (Munich, 2003). On the 'asepticization' of the front in French newsreels see Laurent Véray, *Les Films d'actualité de la Grande Guerre* (Paris, 1995), p. 199.

[80] James Douglas, 'The Somme pictures. Are they too painful for public exhibition?', *Star*, 25 August 1916, cited in Reeves, 'Cinema, spectatorship and propaganda', p. 21.

[81] *Petit Echo du 18° régiment territorial d'infanterie*, no. 57, 12 December 1915.

[82] *Rigolboche*, no. 30, 30 November 1915, p. 3. For similar voices see the trench journals *L'artilleur déchaîné*, no. 10, 25 November 1915, p. 3 and *L'Echo des marmites*, no. 11, 25 May 1916, pp. 4–5.

The longer the war continued, the less did urban audiences want to see it represented on the screens and stages. There is strong evidence that suggests that this had become the dominant attitude by late 1916 and early 1917.[83] Throughout 1917 the attendance for topical war films dropped in the British capital.[84] In Berlin, the wave of patriotic plays and revues showing 'the nation in arms' began to fade as early as 1915.[85] Overtly patriotic and propagandistic films and plays, showing the city mobilize and men volunteer, had all but disappeared by the end of 1916.[86] The year of 1916 must therefore be seen as a watershed in urban entertainment cultures and the popular attitudes they reflected. The war was increasingly either avoided, as by the genres of the detective, adventure, and fantasy story; or it was framed and accommodated in nostalgic, comic, and erotic terms.

Nostalgia and entertainment

In February 1916, as the Battle of Verdun was beginning to unfold, a Viennese operetta with the title *Dreimäderlhaus* ('The house of the three girls') premiered in Berlin. Its success was repeated by *Schwarzwaldmädel* ('The maid from the Black Forest'), a similar musical drama. Both were highly popular – by 1918 seven of the largest theatres in Berlin, with about a quarter of the city's entire seating capacity, played the two operettas – and both stood for a new trend that was emerging in commercial entertainment. With soothing tunes and touching stories they took their audiences to an idealized world, beyond the stark wartime realities.[87] Both operettas showed how ostensibly apolitical musical dramas appealed to the perseverance of an increasingly exhausted public. Nostalgia and sentimentality were mobilized against the harshness of the times. People increasingly preferred plays that 'calmed the nerves' and generated a 'pleasurable atmosphere of love', as critics put it.[88]

The cinemas also turned away from direct representations of war. While military images receded more and more, melodramatic films and

---

[83] Nicholas Reeves, 'Official British film propaganda', in Michael Paris (ed.), *The First World War and popular cinema* (Edinburgh, 1999), p. 31. Similarly Horrall, *Popular culture*, p. 209.

[84] Horrall, *Popular culture*, p. 222.   [85] Baumeister, *Kriegstheater*, ch. 2.

[86] Jerzy Toeplitz, *Geschichte des Films*, vol. I (Berlin, 1979), p. 138.

[87] A. M. Willner and Heinz Reichert, *Das Dreimäderlhaus. Singspiel in drei Akten. Musik nach Franz Schubert. Für die Bühne bearbeitet von Heinrich Berté* (Leipzig and Vienna, n.d.); Berard Grun, *Kulturgeschichte der Operette* (Berlin, 1967), pp. 401–3, p. 399; Otto Schneidereit, *Berlin wie es weint und lacht* (Berlin, 1968), pp. 180–3.

[88] *Berliner Neueste Nachrichten*, 12 February 1916; *Berliner Lokalanzeiger*, 12 February 1916.

kitsch stories expanded. Many of these did not refer to the war at all; others took it as a backdrop for stories of love and romance. A classic example was the film '*Die Glocken von San Martino*' ('The bells of San Martino'), shown in Berlin cinemas from July 1915. The film was set in the Austrian–Italian borderlands, with a young German–Austrian couple at its centre, a reserve officer and the daughter of his employer, who lived happily – until the war. The reserve officer is called to arms and taken prisoner by the Italians during a patrol. He is sentenced to death on the spot, while his rival, an Italian lieutenant, makes a move on his bride, personifying the '*Verrat der Welschen*', the treason of the Italians who had joined the war on the side of France and Britain. The bride, however, comes to the rescue of her beloved by ringing the church bells of the town, triggering a happy ending in which Austrian troops overpower the Italian captors. As in so many other films of this genre, the war was narrated through traditional imagery of love and loyalty. It was idealized as an honourable and ultimately harmless fight between two men over a woman. On the screens of Berlin the First World War, the most brutal mass warfare Europe had ever seen, could be a love battle.

This significant shift away from direct representations of war can be traced in film catalogues and contemporary advertisements. Out of the 57 'film hits' which the *Monopol-Vertriebsgesellschaft* distributed in 1915, for example, only two bore a reference to the war.[89] As early as November 1914 the *Kinematograph* explained in an editorial that the patriotic films that had 'naturally dominated the cinema programmes during the weeks after the outbreak of the war' were no longer *en vogue*: the cinemas now showed more entertainment and fewer pictures of the war. Apart from love stories and melodramas, crime and 'action' were in high demand. The genre of detective stories was especially popular, with Sherlock Holmes and other explorers of the urban underworld appearing in a series of films.[90]

The authorities, too, observed this change. In November 1915 the police department responsible for censoring films lamented the dominance of detective films and '*Schund- und Schauergeschichten*' in the Berlin cinema.[91] Wartime cinema, the police observed, turned away from the war. Sentimentalism instead of realism, traditional idyll and intimacy instead of the modern and anonymous face of mass warfare, were what

[89] *Kinematograph*, no. 447, 21 July 1915.
[90] *Kinematograph*, no. 410, 4 November 1914. Gerhard Lamprecht, *Deutsche Stummfilme 1913–1914* (Berlin, 1969); *Deutsche Stummfilme 1915–1916* (Berlin, 1969); *Deutsche Stummfilme 1917–1918* (Berlin, 1969). See also Jerzy Toeplitz, *Geschichte des Films*, vol. I, 1885–1928 (Berlin, 1972), pp. 134ff.
[91] LA Berlin, A Prf. Br. Rep. 30 Titel 74, no. 16: Memorandum, Head of Abteilung VIII, Berlin Police, 25 November 1915.

it put on the public stage. The more gruesome the reality of war became, the less it was shown on the screens. And the longer the war continued, the more the cinema looked the other way, pretending a backwards-orientated normality and an idyllic innocence which – if it ever existed – had long since been shattered.

Parisian entertainments provide further examples for this shift. There is ample evidence that the soldiers on leave in the French capital preferred love and adventure stories to the pseudo-realistic 'scenes from the front-line' or directly propagandist shows. A journalist reported in May 1917 that *permissionnaires* had protested against patriotic songs during the revue *Ohé, Ohé!*, asking to be entertained by girls instead.[92] Highly popular were the *romans-cinémas* such as *Les Mystères de New-York* distributed by Pathé in December 1915 or the dramas by Maurice Leblanc. Also in high demand were romances such as *Le Flirt d'Hector*, featuring a *poilu's* adulterous adventures.[93] These films employed the narrative scheme of the traditional *théâtre de boulevard*: the trio of wife, husband, and lover was turned into wife, *embusqué*, and *permissionnaire*. As in the Berlin examples quoted above, the love triangle represented a nostalgic normality that accommodated the challenges of war.[94]

Nostalgic vocabulary and imagery came to dominate British popular music in a similar fashion. The initial rush to outrightly patriotic and propagandistic 'war songs' was soon reversed. As Louis Sterling of the Columbia Record Company observed, the 1914 and early 1915 releases of 'patriotic' records proved to be of little relevance to the longer-term musical needs of the British engaged in a total war:

There exists in England today a tremendous demand for straight popular songs and there is also a notable increase in the call for good music. I refer particularly to high-class ballads and the many fine string and orchestral selections. We are shipping many thousands of records per month to the boys at the front, and the orders for these records almost invariably call for fifty per cent of popular music, and the remainder good standard selections and operatic numbers. The demand for the so-called patriotic popular number has practically passed into oblivion.[95]

Again, a trend to represent the war in romantic language and the imagery of love and intimacy can be observed. Thus the popular 'There's a long long trail a'winding' was about the long trail of war that separates lovers

---

[92] *Le Journal*, 26 March 1917.

[93] PF, BA 772, Casino de Fontenay-sous-Bois, 29 April 1916.

[94] On the 'turn to nostalgia' in Parisian musical entertainment see Sweeney, *Singing our way to victory*, ch. 4.

[95] Louis Sterling, 'Conditions in the talking machine industry in England', *Talking machine world* (April 1918), p. 55.

from each other, a distance that could be conquered in their dreams. The extremely successful 'Roses of Picardy', written in 1917 by Haydn Wood and Herbert Weatherly, was similarly about love, parting, and death. The image of the rose and expressions such as 'the shadows veil their skies' came straight from the pre-war lexicon of romantic poetry and ballads, now set against the background of Picardy, the scene of the Battle of the Somme.

A second musical trend can be observed in the preoccupation with imagined worlds far-away. It became a key component of popular songs to evoke lands and fantasy worlds away from war and war-related experiences. This was highlighted in a 1916 list of Columbia's seven best-selling records published in *Talking machine news*. These included three versions of 'Down Home in Tennessee', 'Kentucky Home', 'If You were the Only Girl in the World', 'Pack up Your Troubles', 'There's a Long, Long Trail', 'My Mother's Rosary', 'Every Little While', and 'The Broken Doll'.[96] In February 1917 a second list derived from more general sources appeared in *Talking machine news*.[97] Amongst the most popular of its songs were: 'It's a Long, Long Way to My Home in Kentucky', 'Are You from Dixie?', and 'When You Wore a Tulip'. These songs created a fantasy world, a conjured space, in Kentucky, Tennessee, or Dixie, as far removed as possible from the Western front or the urban experience of war.

Laughter, comedy, and war

Parallel to such nostalgic representations of pre-war 'normality' were the return of laughter and the expansion of comedy. While patriotic moralists thought laughter to be immoral during times of war, the entertainment industry and growing parts of their audiences clearly disagreed. What they sought was a return of humour and fun, of innocence and laughter. But was one allowed to laugh in times of war? *S'amuser pendant la guerre*? As the authorities in London, Paris, and Berlin observed with the course of the war, a certain degree of transgression in public sites of entertainment could not be denied where humour and amusement were concerned. The Paris police observed in December 1915, 'un besoin de se griser, d'oublier' in the boulevards and cafés.[98] In enjoying light-hearted entertainment, urban audiences took 'a turn away from what one would

---

[96] *Talking machine news*, October 1916, p. 247: 'Which are the best sellers?'
[97] *Talking machine news*, February 1917, p. 398.
[98] Archives de la préfecture de police, BA, 1587: report of 15 December 1915. See also the observations by Guillot de Saix in *Le Journal*, 26 March 1917.

have rightly expected', as an undercover Paris police officer reported in December 1917.[99]

'Serious plays about the war are not wanted', a London theatre critic noted in February 1915. Plays and scenes about the war, he wrote, could still draw crowds, but only as long as they were humorous or offered an 'engrossing mixture of laughter and tears'. As an example of the latter he cited M. Fonson's *La Kommandatur*. In contrast to such combinations of humour and melodrama, 'pictures of atrocities and frightfulness meet with no welcome; again and again they have been tried and quickly discarded'. Theatres and music halls acted increasingly 'on the principle that the audience comes to be distracted from all thought of war'. And while some moralists viewed humorous representations of the war with moral objections, the critic wrote that laughter and the 'love of pleasure' should not be mistaken as 'lightness of mind'.[100]

Such an interpretation of the uses of amusement gained increasing currency. Ernest Barker, later the Principal of King's College in London, lent academic credit to it in an open letter against the 'new Puritans' and the 'Catos to all delights'. Amusement was needed, rather than serious representations of war or stern patriotic appeals, he argued:

> There is no tragedy more tragic than war. There has been no war more terrible than this war. Unless we mix some laughter we shall crack. If we falsify Nature's wise economy, and rack ourselves to the pitch of tragic intensity, we are undone. Let us not, like the Puritans of old, close theatres, or suppress race meetings, or even shut down alehouses overmuch.[101]

The longer the war continued and the more totalizing its impact was perceived to be, the stronger, it seems, did the need for laughter become. The unprecedented success of comedians such as Charlie Chaplin or Harry Lauder suggests that Barker had read the cultural need for amusement correctly.

Just as in Paris and London, the theatres, cafés, and cabarets of Berlin opened a space for laughing and joking in times of war. *Späße*, *Humoresken*, and *Schwänke* drew the crowds, rather than war films and patriotic pieces. As one film historian has put it, the war was 'no longer a novelty', and it was too painful to be reminded of it every day in the cinema.[102] Urban entertainments, as central locations for the city's self-image and its coming to terms with the war, could thus show the limits of official propaganda. It was entertainment and distraction more than any

[99] Sweeney, *Singing our way to victory*, p. 137.   [100] *The Times*, 5 February 1915.
[101] Ernest Barker, 'New Puritans', *The Times*, 18 March 1915.
[102] Toeplitz, *Geschichte des Films*, vol. I, p. 138. Similarly Werner, *Skandalchronik*, p. 70.

direct 'education of the public' that became the dominant features of Berlin's cinemas and popular theatres. As the *Kinematograph* explained towards the end of the war, '[t]he propaganda film has been a fiasco'. Official propaganda films had 'not struck a chord with the audience' because they were too serious. What was needed in wartime entertainment was humour not war, amusement not indoctrination.[103]

The Berlin authorities, civilian and military, might not have liked the rush to light entertainment and cheap comedy. Yet despite their clamouring for seriousness, they never effectively curbed the culture of amusement. Rather, official rhetoric in Berlin came to see 'true' laughter as maintaining the war effort and hence permitted as a 'civil duty', as exemplified by the humorous shows in Reutter's *Palasttheater*. Reutter suggested 'comic relief' as a theatrical solution against the burdens and sorrows of urban everyday life in wartime.[104] In Paris laughter was also increasingly seen as boosting morale rather than endangering it. And here, too, a strong difference remained between laughter with one's own soldiers and laughter about the enemy's troops. The organized soldiers' entertainment of the *Parrains de Reuilly* staged a sketch in April 1918 called *Un poilu pour deux marraines*, encouraging the soldiers to identify and laugh with the central character.[105] Whether in the form of reaffirming comedy and slapstick, or whether directed against 'the enemy' or minority groups, what these examples had in common was that they cloaked the war in parody and laughter. This corresponded to the kitsch romances and love stories examined above. Both phenomena reflected a strong tendency to hide the real face of war, to present normality and idyllic order where there were rapid change and transformation.

However, there were limits to the wave of nostalgia and kitsch, parody and comedy that came to dominate representations of war. In two respects, urban entertainment never withdrew entirely from the actuality of the war, although that was the dominant trend. First, a small number of the 'patriotic plays' in the style of August 1914 survived. The most well-known in Berlin was *Immer feste druff* ('Hit 'em harder'), played until the end of the war, contrary to all trends. It performed in Berlin more

[103] *Kinematograph*, no. 592, 8 May 1918: 'Propaganda- und Aufklärungsfilme'.
[104] Otto Reutter and Max Reinhardt, *Muttchen hat's Wort! Volksstück mit Gesang in drei Akten, Musik von Max Schröder und Otto Reutter* (1915); Otto Reutter and R. Liebmann, *Berlin im Krieg: Revue in drei Akten* (1917); Otto Reutter, *Geh'n Sie blos nicht nach Berlin: Revue-Posse in drei Akten, einem Vorspiel und einem Zwischenspiel, Musik von Hugo Hirsch* (1917). The censor's copies of these plays are held at LA Berlin, A Prf. Br. Rep. 30 Tit. 74, nos. 6146, 6635, 6787.
[105] See also *Le Film*, 21 October 1918, on the comical film *Huit millions de dot*, and Sweeney, *Singing our way to victory*, p. 138, on the ridiculing of the enemy in music halls and *cafés-concerts*.

than 800 times. The title contained an aggressive call to violence, picking up on a chauvinistic quote by Crown Prince Wilhelm from 1913. It carried a peculiar mix of cheerfulness, courage, and aggressive patriotism. The play's ideology was designed around the celebration of military heroism and the nationwide departure of men to the front. Its consistent popularity stemmed from its rousing music and two highly popular comedians performing a 'typical' couple of Berliners. Their songs were recorded on to gramophone and played even in the trenches. The play's success lasted almost until the end of the war.[106]

Secondly, in all the three cities the war did provoke artistic responses that tried to capture its new and modern character, despite the dominance of nostalgia and comedy. It was especially modern technology, the symbol of the 'machine age', that was employed in such films and shows. In London, Paris, and Berlin urban entertainments staged new weapons such as the tank and the submarine as symbols of modernity and national prowess. On 15 January 1917 *The advance of the tanks* opened simultaneously at 107 London cinemas, showing moving images of tanks in action at the Western front.[107] This was an official War Office film, intended to be the successor to *The battle of the Somme*; it was hardly surprising that it contained scenes in which soldiers cheered and were, as *The Times* put it, 'in the highest spirits'.[108] In this sense the *Advance of the tanks* kept in line with previous war films. However, the film's main message was novel: the soldiers mattered less than technology. The pictures taken by G. H. Malin showed tanks as the main actors, suggesting that technology rather than human individuals might decide the war. Critics captured the stylization of machines as the new soldiers, describing the tanks on the screens as 'lumbering into action with a majestic roll, and emerging from the ordeal of battle'.[109]

A similar tendency was on display in the show '*Torpedo los!*' performed by the Dresden-based circus *Sarrasani* for Berlin audiences in the summer of 1918. The powerful spectacle, performed by 500 actors and extras employing a wide-ranging technical apparatus, aimed to portray the modernity of the war: it tried to capture processes of mechanization and industrialization as main features of 'total' war. It counted on overwhelming the audience by employing vast numbers of actors and extras (as well as bringing animals into the performance). Elaborate special effects

---

[106] Hermann Haller and Willi Wolff, 'Immer feste druff! Vaterländisches Volksstück mit Gesang in 4 Bildern', *Textbuch der Gesänge* (Munich and Berlin, 1914).
[107] *The Times*, 15 January 1917. See also ch. 6, below.
[108] *The Times*, 16 January 1917.   [109] Ibid.

underlined the anti-individualist emphasis. The audience saw a race between a car and a train, scenes from submarine warfare and a climax in which London was being bombed by Zeppelins. The vision of super-power and destruction drew on the pre-war German techno-nationalism that had expressed itself in the enthusiasm for Zeppelins and the cult of the navy.[110] The show's main impression was one that brought 'the people' into abstraction: this was a uniformed and disciplined mass, enthusiastic for battle and employing a deadly arsenal of modern weaponry.[111]

However optimistic the message of *Torpedo los*, its monumentalism has to be read as the symptom of a deep crisis of representation. While demonstrating how the war could be portrayed as a modern spectacle by the entertainment industry, *Torpedo los* was symptomatic in that it denied any reference to the city, its residents, and their circumstances. This absence indicated the desperate state in which Berliners found themselves in the last months of the war. *Torpedo los* thus presented the last stage in the development of war plays in wartime Berlin. While strength and victory were staged with all available means, the city itself was overwhelmed with social unrest and a longing for peace. At the same time the Western front was beginning to crumble.

Modern representations of war such as *The advance of the tanks* or *Torpedo los* remained exceptions. When assessing the trends, modes, and genres by which urban entertainments dealt with the war, it is hard to avoid the distinct impression of a shift from topical to nostalgic, from direct representations of war and mobilization, as seen during the first months of the war, to a traditional language of harmony and comical amusement. This finding is underlined by contemporary analyses. The London Cinematograph Commission of Inquiry found in January 1917 that 'scenes of love-making, vulgar buffoonery, horseplay, practical joking of a mischievous type, and successful imposture' were dominating in London's cinemas.[112] A survey conducted by the *Kinematograph* towards the end of the war came to similar conclusions. In May 1918, the journal invited a debate about the future of film and popular taste. Anticipating

---

[110] Peter Fritzsche, *A nation of fliers. German aviation and the popular imagination* (Cambridge, MA, 1992); Guillaume de Syon, *Zeppelin! Germany and the airship, 1900–1939* (Baltimore, 2002); Jan Rüger, *The great naval game: Britain and Germany in the age of empire* (Cambridge, 2007).

[111] LA Berlin, A Prf. Br. Rep. 30 Tit. 74, no. 6860: Hans Stosch-Sarrasani, *Torpedo-los! Das hohe Lied vom U-Bootmann. Großes Bühnen- und Manegenschaustück*. See also Hans Stosch-Sarrasani, *Durch die Welt im Zirkuszelt* (Berlin, 1940), p. 149; Ernst Günther, *Sarrasani wie er wirklich war* (Berlin, 1985); Marline Otte, 'Sarrasani's Theater of the World: Monumental Circus Entertainment in Dresden, from Kaiserreich to Third Reich', *German History*, 17 (1999), pp. 527–42.

[112] *The Times*, 16 January 1917.

changing times, the journal put a questionnaire to authors, film directors, and producers as well as cultural functionaries. Would 'in future (in peace time) everything be accepted uncritically that is shown at present with the current hunger for entertainment, or will the public be more choosy', it asked. The answers were illuminating. Almost all critics agreed that wartime cinema had been dominated by images of a dated and false idyll and that this was partly to be explained by the cinema's catering to the lowest common denominator of taste. Otto von Gottberg lamented the 'excesses of amusement', Ferdinand Gregori the 'foolish clownery', and Max Kretzer the 'appalling kitsch' shown in cinemas. Throughout the war a 'craving for entertainment' had been dominating, wrote M. G. Conrad. Another critic, Arthur Zapp, commented that he had seen films in Berlin that were of such 'childish harmlessness and of such antiquated taste that one would have thought that a metropolitan audience would have turned away from them with protest. On the contrary, the audience was much satisfied.' Most critics agreed in calling for a renewal of cinema after the war and for a dramatic improvement in the industry's standards.[113]

Metropolitan nostalgia and the cultural history of the First World War

The *Kinematograph's* survey revealed that the entertainment industry itself was aware of the predominant wartime trend: the 'need for laughing and forgetting' that the authorities observed was addressed predominantly in nostalgic terms. Integrating the war into stories of love and romance or comical and humorous programmes had a paradoxical effect: urban entertainments staged and displayed the *status quo ante bellum*, but accommodated the war in this status. Again and again, film, music, and theatre offered an idealized pre-war version of private and civilian life that was able to embed the war in traditional vocabulary and imagery that was not corrupted or swept away by modern forces. In this sense the past was the future, a nostalgic, idealized, and illusionary past that was able to accommodate needs in a way which the present all too evidently failed to do. The proliferation of nostalgia and kitsch, in turn, meant that the city itself was pushed into the background: urban imagery receded while many programmes turned to distant or imagined places.

These findings complicate traditional interpretations of the war's impact on urban societies and cultures. Historians have engaged in a

---

[113] *Kinematograph*, no. 593, 15 May 1918.

series of assertions about the effects of the war. One of the main themes has been the 'brutalization' and 'trivialization' that the war meant for men and women.[114] A second debate has focused on the question whether the war provoked predominantly 'modern' or 'traditional' responses in the cultural landscape of the belligerent countries.[115] There is little doubt that the war presented fundamental challenges to urban cultures and that the populations of London, Paris, and Berlin felt and acknowledged these changes. The question is rather how, in what modes of representation, these challenges were addressed and negotiated. Here, this chapter's findings stand in contrast to interpretations that see the war as evoking radically new, modernist responses in urban European culture. There was very little 'new visual language' (Modris Eksteins) in the cinemas, theatres, and music halls of London, Paris, and Berlin.[116] Cultural representations that challenged traditional imagery or popular taste were exceptions. A monumentalist techno-spectacle such as *Torpedo los* stood out in a landscape dominated by nostalgic harmony, slapstick comedy, and escapist adventure stories. Moreover, such rare examples of modernist interpretations of war drew on a language of technology, masculinity, and power that was well established before the war.[117]

As noted by critics and directors, the entertainment industry in London, Paris, and Berlin withdrew from the artistic advances and avant-garde styles that it had begun to champion before the war. In fact, the combination of censorship, middle-class morality, and self-acclaimed patriotism forced a range of challenging and experimental forms of entertainment to abandon the public stage. Outside the grotesque stereotyping designed to reaffirm the conservative values of the 'nation in arms' public representations of 'otherness', be they in relation to sexuality, gender, or race, were near impossible.

---

[114] George L. Mosse, *Fallen soldiers. Reshaping the memory of the world wars* (Oxford, 1990), esp. pp. 159–81.

[115] Modris Eksteins, *Rites of spring. The Great War and the birth of the modern age* (London, 1989); Jay Winter, *Sites of memory, sites of mourning. The Great War in European cultural history* (Cambridge, 1995); Jay Winter, Geoffrey Parker, and Mary R. Habeck (eds.), *The Great War and the twentieth century* (New Haven, 2000).

[116] Modris Eksteins, 'The cultural impact of the Great War', in Karel Dibbets and Bert Hogenkamp (eds.), *Film and the First World War* (Amsterdam, 1995), pp. 201–12.

[117] Stephen Kern, *The culture of time and space 1880–1918* (Cambridge, Mass. and London, 1983), ch. 5; Daniel Pick, *The war machine: the rationalisation of slaughter in the modern age* (New Haven, 1993), ch. 12; Bernhard Rieger, *Technology and the culture of modernity in Britain and Germany, 1890–1945* (Cambridge, 2005), ch. 2; Jan Rüger, 'Nation, empire and navy: identity politics in the United Kingdom, 1887–1914', *Past & Present*, no. 185 (2004), pp. 184–7; Robert Wohl, *A passion for wings: aviation and the western imagination, 1908–1918* (New Haven, 1994), ch. 3.

Where the effect of the war on everyday life and social behaviour is concerned, a 'brutalization' might well have taken place in all the three cities. However, the ways in which urban entertainments dealt with these challenges were, as this chapter has suggested, overwhelmingly traditional. Only sporadically were the actual, physical effects of modern warfare on display; very rarely did they become a topic in urban entertainment and the leisure industry. The more the war expanded, revealing totalizing forces on an unprecedented scale, the more did urban entertainment engage in what this chapter has addressed as metropolitan nostalgia: an essentially backward-oriented impulse, idealizing and moulding the pre-war past for wartime usages. In the theatres, the cinemas and music halls of the three cities the war was cloaked in love stories and romances while the forces of change that it unleashed remained largely unaddressed. Going to the cinema, the theatre, or the café-concert offered a way of visiting an idealized time before the war and of reinforcing a feeling of having rescued something of that time for the present and the future. As Ernest Barker explained in 1915, it was an experience that made audiences 'feel something of the old world survive the Deluge'. It was here, at the sites of urban entertainment, that audiences could convince themselves, in Barker's words, that '[m]en still go about the old streets in the old way'.[118] When trying to demonstrate to his readers that 'life was still the same' in 1918, G. S. Street used London's entertainments as evidence in a similar way:

London, no doubt, wears a different aspect from that of peace time; the place is full of soldiers serving at home or on leave from the Front; innumerable civilians are on jobs new to them; we are all thinking and talking about the war. But the structure of our life remains the same; we go to offices in the morning and manage to meet one another at lunch, and take a walk if we have time in the afternoon and dine as usual, if less amply, and take our recreation afterwards. Theatres go on and picture shows are opened and novels are published.[119]

This function of entertainment as a demonstrative affirmation of 'normality' remained powerful throughout the war. The cinemas, music halls, and cafés-concerts in the three capital cities offered a predominantly nostalgic narrative of the urban experience of war, a narrative in which the pre-war past moderated the wartime present. Popular entertainment thereby contributed centrally to the formulation of the language, imagery, and sound through which contemporaries made sense of London, Paris, and Berlin at war.

---

[118] Ernest Barker, 'New Puritans', *The Times*, 18 March 1915.
[119] Street, *At home in the war*, p. 84.

Part II

Civic culture

5   Exhibitions

Stefan Goebel

Exhibitions – or in contemporary usage, expositions – for the general public occupied a prominent place in the cityscape and cultural life of Paris, London, and Berlin before the First World War. The nineteenth century was the classical age of the metropolitan exhibition. World's Fairs showcased or juxtaposed countries' manufacturing and commercial prowess; colonial expositions visualized the fruits of imperial expansion; art galleries prescribed national styles and good taste; and public museums, originating or burgeoning in the nineteenth century, defined and classified the respective nation's cultural heritage. Although they varied significantly in thematic focus and means of display, all types of exhibitions fulfilled the same basic function: the imposition of order and meaning on objects, signifiers of technology, geography, art and history.

As the exhibition reinforced the established order and reduced the complexities of the modern world and its inheritance within a strictly limited space, it also proved an effective medium for fashioning and disseminating images of modern war for consumption by a civilian audience. Order was a key theme. By carving up this world war in manageable categories and spaces, wartime exhibitions showed that the ongoing conflict had pattern and purpose. Exploring a diverse range of exhibition activities – from patriotic expositions and war landmarks to private collections, national museums, and commercial art galleries – this chapter will first chart the proliferation of sites for the display of the war effort and, second, trace the transformation of a quintessential nineteenth-century, metropolitan mode of representation in the era of the Great War.

The history of exhibitions in wartime Paris, London, and Berlin reveals a paradoxical trend towards an expansion in the space available for cultural expression in general on the one hand, and a contraction in the field of cultural innovation on the other. All three capitals, although to different degrees and with notable exceptions, saw the rise of propaganda

Stefan Goebel wrote this chapter, with Kevin Repp and Jay Winter.

spectacles and war kitsch and the demise of traditional exhibitions and the pre-war avant-garde. While patriotic displays of military achievements and metropolitan solidarity boomed, institutional exhibitions and art galleries often struggled hard to survive. The pressures producing this trend were political and economic, mixing a sense of government priorities, in which pictorial propaganda was a must but civilian cultural life a luxury, with a sense of shortages, in which the expenditure on galleries and museums was easily sacrificed for more urgent tasks and projects. This was one of the constraints on exhibitions in all three capital cities, largely a product of government policy at the national level.

There was a second force, located in the market, which moved in a similar direction. The grave circumstances of war demanded more serious and sober forms of diversion for the masses. Wartime exhibitions were sites of entertainments that channelled and satisfied the audiences' desires for cultural consumption.[1] Patriotic expositions, war landmarks and displays of sentimental art became popular – and legitimate – forms of home-front amusement that corresponded with the much discussed 'seriousness' of the age. They satisfied a resurgent demand for the spectacular and the beautiful as the boring and ugly war dragged on. By contrast, the market for more experimental, non-figurative art dried up fast as soon as hostilities began, and pushed artists to sell what they could, which was art in older forms. This trend, though, was stronger in London and Paris than in Berlin. Here is market-driven nostalgia, a strategy for artistic survival.

Patriotic exhibitions

Temporary patriotic exhibitions resembled commercial fairs, but were intended to be more explicitly educational. Celebrating tokens of military might and civilian morale, this type of exhibition evolved into a focus of the rhetoric and rituals of the metropolitan home front in all three capital cities, creating by participation and not coercion a sense of the totality of the war. Provisional in character, patriotic shows were the product of a long-drawn-out struggle which had not yet come to a close, they thrived especially in the mid-war phase between 1915 and 1917. In a sense, patriotic exhibitions counterbalanced the shift away from direct representation of war characteristic of commercial entertainments, notably the wartime cinema, after the first year of war.[2]

---

[1] Maureen Healy, 'Exhibiting a war in progress. Entertainment and propaganda in Vienna, 1914–1918', *Austrian History Yearbook*, 31 (2000), pp. 56–85.
[2] See chapter 4.

War trophies – principally, flags and guns (often heavily damaged) – taken from the battlefields to Berlin were one of the first visible signs of the military conflict in the metropolis. While looted flags created an illusion of face-to-face combat, enemy guns familiarized Berliners with modern weaponry of often impressive size. Such displays gave the civilians an impression of the war they had read about in the newspapers. Above all, war trophies spoke of German superiority. 'Defeated' guns suggested strategic and tactical supremacy, while damaged guns revealed the effectiveness of German military technology. Victory seemed imminent. In order to drive this point home, enemy guns were integrated into the late-nineteenth-century landscape and ritual of victory: the Siegesallee, originally built to commemorate the Bismarckian wars, provided the setting and Sedan Day (2 September), marking the victory over France in 1871, was the date chosen for the parade of war trophies in autumn 1914.[3] Further trophies were on display in front of the Royal Palace, in the Kronprinzenpalais, and in the Zeughaus army museum.[4]

As the war became increasingly 'total', a mere show of war trophies along the lines of nineteenth-century army museums could not adequately represent the experience of the Great War. The representation of modern warfare demanded both a different kind of display and a different agenda. The unimaginative exhibition of trophies in the Zeughaus museum failed, first, to combine education with entertainment and, second, to acknowledge the connections and overlaps between the military and civil society in the war. The *Deutsche Kriegsausstellung*, opened in the exhibition halls at the Zoologischer Garten in January 1916, employed a more innovative – broader and interactive – concept to enframe the war. Divided into twenty-one sections, it comprised war trophies (notably uniforms, guns, vehicles, aeroplanes – the military censors forbade the display of German weaponry) alongside an array of bric-à-brac, artworks, a cinema, a trench, an iron-nail figure, and a souvenir shop.[5]

As the first comprehensive war exposition in Germany, the *Kriegsausstellung* in Berlin played a pioneering role. Other German cities

---

[3] Susanne Brandt, *Vom Kriegsschauplatz zum Gedächtnisraum. Die Westfront 1914–1940* (Baden-Baden, 2000), pp. 74–5; Christine Beil, *Der ausgestellte Krieg. Die Präsentationen des Ersten Weltkriegs 1914–1939* (Tübingen, 2004), pp. 76–103.

[4] Hans Land, 'Kriegstrophäen von 1914/15', *Reclams Universum*, 31 (1915), pp. 1006–7; see also Heinrich Müller, *Das Berliner Zeughaus. Vom Arsenal zum Museum* (Berlin, 1994), pp. 194–204.

[5] *Deutsche Kriegsausstellungen 1916. Amtlicher Führer*, ed. Zentralkomitee der Deutschen Vereine vom Roten Kreuz (Berlin, 1916); see Brandt, *Vom Kriegsschauplatz*, pp. 88–98; Brandt, 'The memory makers. Museums and exhibitions of the First World War', *History and Memory*, 6, 1 (1994), pp. 103–6; Beil, *Der ausgestellte Krieg*, pp. 160–207; Britta Lange, *Einen Krieg ausstellen. Die 'Deutsche Kriegsausstellung' 1916 in Berlin* (Berlin, 2003).

followed suit. All expositions were similarly designed; even the catalogues were standardized. In Berlin alone, as many as 500,000 people visited the exposition in the four months between January and April 1916 (not counting soldiers who had free entry after one o'clock).[6] The proceeds from the sale of tickets and souvenirs went to the Red Cross, which had organized the exposition at the suggestion of the Prussian War Ministry. A hybrid between charity and show, the *Kriegsausstellung* both supported and depicted the war effort. The show focused on military objects, notably heavy guns such as trench mortars, in order to 'give those who stay at home an insight into the modern war technology and equipment'.[7]

The aim of the *Kriegsausstellung* was to represent the totality and novelty of mass-industrialized war, or, in the words of one scholar, 'to synthesize the many facets of war into a unified event, held in a single complex, comprehensible to the individual viewer'.[8] In doing so, it assumed the mantle of the World Fairs of the previous century. International expositions had not only helped to close geographical distances, but also proved an accessible vehicle for translating technological innovations to a parlance discernable to the layman.[9] Like its civilian predecessor, the wartime fair showcased the latest technological 'wonders' (or horrors) and thus helped shape understanding in a society going through unsettling change. Visitors seemed to have come away from the *Kriegsausstellung* with an enhanced awareness of and enthusiasm for military technology.[10]

However, there was now a brutal edge to the optimistic and inquiring spirit of the World's Fairs. In the second half of the nineteenth century, international expositions were believed to exert a 'civilizing influence' on industrial nations or, as one observer put it after the 1878 Paris Universal Exposition, to 'give an impulse to trade, create keen competition and by a mutual interchange of compliments and civilities bring the

---

[6] Susanne Brandt, 'Kriegssammlungen im Ersten Weltkrieg. Denkmäler oder Laboratoires d'histoire?', in Gerhard Hirschfeld, Gerd Krumeich, and Irina Renz (eds.), *'Keiner fühlt sich hier mehr als Mensch . . .', Erlebnis und Wirkung des Ersten Weltkriegs* (Frankfurt am Main, 1996), p. 292.

[7] 'Deutsche Kriegsausstellung in Berlin', *Das Illustrierte Blatt*, 4, 23 January 1916, p. 11.

[8] Healy, 'Exhibiting a war in progress', p. 60, on the Viennese war exhibition of 1916.

[9] See Paul Greenhalgh, *Ephemeral vistas. The Expositions Universelles, Great Exhibitions and World Fairs, 1851–1939* (Manchester, 1988); Jeffrey A. Auerbach, *The Great Exhibition of 1851. A nation on display* (New Haven and London, 1999); Bernhard Rieger, 'Envisioning the future. British and German reactions to the Paris World Fair in 1900', in Martin Daunton and Bernhard Rieger (eds.), *Meanings of modernity. Britain from the late-Victorian era to World War II* (Oxford, 2001), pp. 145–64. Alexander C. T. Geppert offers a historiographical review of older and recent works in 'Welttheater. Die Geschichte des europäischen Ausstellungswesens im 19. und 20. Jahrhundert', *Neue Politische Literatur*, 47 (2002), pp. 10–61.

[10] Beil, *Der ausgestellte Krieg*, pp. 178–85.

whole world into harmonious & peaceful contact with each other'.[11] The erstwhile concept of peaceful competition between nations imploded after 1914, as a statement of national pride and strength. The 'trophies of civilization', as they were referred to at the time of the Great Exhibition of 1851, were replaced by the trophies of war and violence. The Great War saw the perversion of a nineteenth-century utopia and cultural form.

The exhibition concept in 1916 relied on a subtle interplay between the illusion of authenticity and alienation effects. The showpieces seemed tangible and remote at the same time, notably the open-air *Musterschützengraben*, the model trench. Dug by the Garde-Pionier-Ersatz Bataillon III. Rekrutendepot, this full-scale model (complete with shelters for officers and ranks, protective saps, obstacle pits, wire entanglements) represented allegedly 'an exact reconstruction of the best-equipped trenches on the battlefields in the east and west'.[12] According to the *Berliner Lokal-Anzeiger*, the model trenches built in the capital (a second trench was dug in the West End) and in provincial cities were 'events which allow us to see, guess and discover the reality of war'.[13] The visitors blended into the exhibit, like in an open-air museum. They were invited to walk in the trench and imagine themselves soldiers. What was missing though, were noise, dirt, and blood.[14]

The War Ministry had explicitly given orders for 'no exhibits with bloodstains' to be displayed.[15] The *Kriegsausstellung* downplayed or trivialized death and suffering. Instead, visitors learned about new developments in the treatment of war wounded. A whole section was devoted to the wonders of military medicine – after all, the show was organized by the Red Cross. Previously, between December 1914 and January 1915, the Red Cross had sponsored another exposition, the Reichstag exhibition on wartime care of wounded and sick soldiers, which had greatly exceeded expectations. Within just two months, approximately 80,000 people attended this touring exhibition in Germany's parliamentary building. Inspired by fin-de-siècle hygiene exhibitions, it featured original equipment and employed the latest presentational techniques, such as photographs, films, charts, and models. Lectures on the subjects of surgery in

---

[11] Cited in Peter H. Hoffenberg, *An empire on display. English, Indian, and Australian exhibitions from the Crystal Palace to the Great War* (Berkeley, Los Angeles, and London, 2001), p. 4.

[12] Ibid., p. 111.

[13] Alfred Holzbock, 'Schützengraben und Kriegsbeute-Museum', *Berliner Lokal-Anzeiger*, 275, 1 June 1915.

[14] Brandt, *Vom Kriegsschauplatz*, pp. 78–84; Beil, *Der ausgestellte Krieg*, pp. 143–53.

[15] Cited in Brandt, 'Memory makers', p. 104.

the field or the control of pandemics rounded off the show.[16] The visitor was left reassured that if a close relative suffered injuries in battle efficient aid was close at hand; the German army and navy not only possessed 'the best and most efficient instruments', but were also staffed with 'doctors of a high scientific niveau' familiar with 'the marvellous progress' of medical research.[17] The modernity of military medicine could remedy the side-effects of the machine war.

In terms of scale and perfection, Berlin's *Deutsche Kriegsausstellung* was without parallel in either Britain or France. In wartime, Berlin, which had never seen a Universal Exhibition, outstripped London and Paris, hitherto the capitals of great exhibitions and *Expositions universelles*. State authorities, notably the War Ministry, were instrumental in bringing about patriotic spectacles in Berlin. In London, the authorities exhibited captured German guns at The Mall or at special events such as the Lord Mayor's Show,[18] but more characteristic were a series of mostly low-key expositions held by private organizations that were indicative of the continued vibrancy of civil society in the metropolis. Two examples will stand for many more.[19] What they shared was the notion that citizenship had to be performed, and that by attending exhibitions Londoners were performing it. In a nutshell, Berliners flocked to patriotic fairs as consumers, Londoners turned up as citizens.

As in Berlin, attendance was as much a working-class phenomenon as a middle-class one. Consider the Economy Exhibition at the People's Palace in Stepney, at the heart of the East End. There, in September

---

[16] Beil, *Der ausgestellte Krieg*, pp. 130–9; Deborah Cohen, *The war come home. Disabled veterans in Britain and Germany, 1914–1939* (Berkeley, 2001), p. 64; Bernd Ulrich, ' "... als wenn nichts geschehen wäre". Anmerkungen zur Behandlung der Kriegsopfer während des Ersten Weltkriegs', in Hirschfeld, Krumeich, and Renz (eds.), *'Keiner fühlt sich hier mehr als Mensch'*, pp. 145–6; on pre-war hygiene exhibitions, see Stefan Poser, *Museum der Gefahren. Die gesellschaftliche Bedeutung der Sicherheitstechnik. Das Beispiel der Hygiene-Ausstellungen und Museen für Arbeitsschutz in Wien, Berlin und Dresden um die Jahrhundertwende* (Münster, 1998).

[17] *Ausstellung für Verwundeten- und Krankenfürsorge im Kriege. Berlin 1914, Reichstagsgebäude* (Berlin and Leipzig, 1914), p. 6; see also the special exhibition of artificial limbs, Ständige Ausstellung für Arbeiterwohlfahrt (ed.), *Führer durch die Sonderausstellung von Ersatzgliedern und Arbeitshilfen für Kriegsbeschädigte, Unfallverletzte und Krüppel* (Berlin, 1916); Joanna Bourke, *Dismembering the male. Men's bodies, Britain and the Great War* (London, 1996); Sabine Kienitz, ' "Fleischgewordenes Elend". Kriegsinvalidität und Körperbilder als Teil einer Erfahrungsgeschichte des Ersten Weltkrieges', in Nikolaus Buschmann and Horst Carl (eds.), *Die Erfahrung des Krieges. Erfahrungsgeschichtliche Perspektiven von der Französischen Revolution bis zum Zweiten Weltkrieg* (Paderborn, 2001), pp. 230–4.

[18] 'A great naval and military and war-work pageant', *Illustrated London News*, 151 (1917), pp. 594–5.

[19] 'Trenches in London', *The Times*, 41117, 17 March 1916, p. 5.

1916, George Barnes, the mayor of Stepney, and other stalwarts of the London labour movement pressed the case for household economies. Visitors saw displays on various means of making scarce food supplies last, including Jewish cooking, deemed to be very economical and little known to those outside the faith. Even though this was an educational exposition of a purely practical sort, visitors could also admire a spectacular war trophy. The remains of a captured German Fokker aircraft were said to be the only one in the country.[20]

The second example of a London exposition of a patriotic kind had no explicit social agenda, although its proceeds were in aid of the King George's Fund for Sailors. It was a display of paintings and objects illustrating the history of British sea power, held at the Grosvenor Galleries in New Bond Street after the Armistice. Here the guard of honour was not babies but sailors from HMS *Excellent*, escorting into the exhibition the First Lord of the Admiralty and the First Sea Lord. Stirring speeches echoed the rhetoric of pre-war navalism affirming the grandeur of the navy and its essential role in securing victory. The price paid for it was conveyed by objects from lost vessels: lifebuoys from the *Hogue* and the *Cressy*, torpedoed in 1914, remnants from the *Lusitania*, and the log book of one wireless officer, D. M. Harris, killed while writing the entry displayed to the visitors. The combination of charity and show bore a resemblance to the *Deutsche Kriegsausstellung*, yet the relics from sunken ships gave the London exhibition an elegiac undertone, in sharp contrast to the triumphalism and optimism evident at Berlin.[21]

Places like the Berlin war exposition 'do not meet a public need', concluded the London Society, a private body whose aim it was to improve the city's physical environment. 'Apart from the technical interest which will always be maintained by the scientists, they give undue prominence to that side of our life which we hope to forget.'[22] Parisians appeared to harbour a similar aversion against grand shows of war trophies and celebrations of military technology. On the one hand, there was not the same need to mediate distance as in Berlin, that is, to display the war of *matériel* on a grand scale in the capital; the artefacts of war were omnipresent in the French capital which was not only the hub of military communications but also the target of German artillery and air raids. On the other hand, exposition as a cultural form had a particularly Parisian

---

[20] 'Economy illustrated', *The Times*, 41276, 19 September 1916, p. 5; see also Eva Zwach, *Deutsche und englische Militärmuseen im 20. Jahrhundert. Eine kulturgeschichtliche Analyse des gesellschaftlichen Umgangs mit Krieg* (Münster, 1999), p. 50.

[21] 'Relics of the war at sea', *The Times*, 41964, 4 December 1918, p. 3.

[22] 'The war museum', *Journal of the London Society*, 15, December 1917, p. 1.

tradition which made it impossible to renew it during the war. The idea of a Berlin-style *Kriegsausstellung* at the Champ-de-Mars in the shadow of the Eiffel Tower bordered on the obscene. The nineteenth-century utopia of peaceful competition among nations, the guiding principle behind the *Expositions universelles*, was built into the Parisian cityscape. Thus the German concept of *Kriegsausstellung* went against the grain of the physical geography of the French cosmopolis.

Long before the *Deutsche Kriegsausstellung* opened its doors, the front page of *Le Figaro* featured an article on 'L'Exposition qu'il faudra faire' in September 1915. Ought Paris to start planning the next Universal Exposition for 1920, the author asked rhetorically, but only to reject the proposition. Instead, he argued, the city should stage a comprehensive *Exposition de la guerre*. The cinema and illustrated press had merely pictured the battlefields yet failed to capture the 'reality' of war: 'Mais qu'est-ce que tout cela, auprès des réalités que nous imaginons, que les lettres de nos amis, de nos enfants nous racontent ou nous font devenir, et desquelles le photographe n'approche pas? Ce sont ces réalités-là qu'on voudrait qu'une Exposition de la Guerre nous fît voir.'[23] Comprising inter alia a trench, a listening gallery, a store of explosives, the exhibition would employ war veterans, especially decorated and wounded soldiers, as guides, *Le Figaro* suggested. This was a kind of civilian's gateway to the soldier's war experience.

The fact that such a large-scale *Exposition de la guerre* did not take place in the former capital of Universal Expositions is significant. It testifies to a symbolic void in the cultural landscape of wartime Paris, and it confirms that the concept of exhibiting the war and displaying the cultural credentials was nationally and locally inflected. To be sure, smaller patriotic exhibitions were not completely absent from the Parisian scene.[24] Notably, trophies of war like captured German artillery pieces could be seen throughout the city, for instance in Place de la Concorde in 1918, but first and foremost in the quadrangle of the Invalides, the public space that most completely symbolized national resolve in wartime. Both at the Spree and at the Seine, captured guns were exhibited to reassure the civilian population about military superiority over the enemy. However, soldiers on leave sometimes found such patriotic displays unnerving.

---

[23] Emile Berr, 'L'Exposition qu'il faudra faire', *Le Figaro*, 266, 23 September 1915, p. 1.

[24] See Nicholas Saunders, *Trench art. Materialities and memories of war* (Oxford and New York, 2003), pp. 175–6; Nicola Lambourne, ' "Moral cathedrals". War damage and Franco-German cultural propaganda on the Western Front 1870–1938', PhD thesis, University of London, 1997, pp. 171–5, 301; Mark Levitch, 'Young Blood. Parisian schoolgirls' transformation of France's Great War poster aesthetic', in Pearl James (ed.), *Picture this! Reading World War I posters* (Lincoln, Neb., 2007).

An American soldier visiting the Invalides noted that 'Looking into the German cannon muzzles gave one a rather sinking feeling, as the same types of weapons will be firing at us shortly.'[25]

Paris saw also a number of patriotic displays of private enterprise of which two events stood out. In October 1918, the *Panthéon de la guerre* was inaugurated in rue de l'Université – a significant location, for the street linked the exhibition and military landmarks (the Eiffel Tower and the Invalides) with the Latin Quarter (and thus the historic Panthéon). This gigantic panorama of the Great War and its heroes, 120 metres by 15 metres in size, was composed by a group of 128 artists headed by the painters Pierre Carrier-Belleuse and Auguste Gorguet over a period of four years. It depicted the faces of 20,000 people ranging from famous air aces like Georges Guynemer and martyrs like Edith Cavell to an anonymous woman in mourning. Exhibited in its entirety, this monumental 'musée de personnages' was meant to allow the viewer to 'revivre en quelques minutes les émotions que leur apportèrent quatre ans de communiqués'.[26] As a memorial to both the French nation and her allies, the *Panthéon de la guerre* did not fail to impress international visitors when it was later exhibited in almost the centre of the exhibition grounds at the 1933 Chicago World Fair, even though the exhibit strangely contrasted with the exposition's overall theme of a 'Century-of-Progress'.[27]

At certain patriotic *journées* held by organizations such as the Touring Club de France during the war, shop windows along the fashionable boulevards were frequently decorated with patriotic badges (to be worn in the buttonhole of a coat or jacket); these were on sale in support of war charities. At the suggestion of the musician Gustave Charpentier, Paris fashion houses designed colourful cockades, named 'La Cocarde de Mimi Pinson', a kind of talisman for soldiers. Prior to their dispatch to the front, the cockades were shown in an exhibition at the Petit Palais opened by President Raymond Poincaré on 11 November 1915.[28] The newspaper *L'Eclair* commented on the following day: 'Mimi Pinson s'est souvenue qu'elle avait une cocarde à son bonnet. Elle l'en a détachée. Et d'un geste hardi, grave et mutin, elle l'offre à nos combattants. L'idée est

---

[25] William Yorke Stevenson, *At the front in a flivver* (Boston and New York, 1917), p. 19; 'British trophy in Paris', *The Times*, 41878, 26 August 1918, p. 8.

[26] F. H[onoré], 'Le Panthéon de la guerre', *L'Illustration*, 152 (1918), p. 398; see René Bazin, 'Le Panthéon de la guerre', *L'Echo de Paris*, 12551, 17 November 1918, p. 1.

[27] 'Pantheon shown at Chicago fair', *New York Times*, 27519, 29 May 1933, p. 3; on the Chicago exposition generally, see Robert W. Rydell, *World of fairs. The Century-of-Progress expositions* (Chicago and London, 1993).

[28] Archives de Paris, VK 240, 'L'Exposition des "Cocardes de Mimi Pinson destinées aux soldats du front"', November 1915.

jolie et parisienne et comme elle est femme! Elle a naturellement fleuri dans les parterres des quartiers de la Paix et de l'Opéra.'[29]

Nevertheless, the concept of exposition was by and large peripheral to patriotic culture in wartime Paris. Nor did patriotic shows leave their mark on the cityscape of the French capital – in stark contrast to the Universal Exhibitions of the fin-de-siècle which had literally reinvented the French capital. During the war, the *grandes places*, above all the Place de la Concorde with its statues dedicated to the great cities of France (including Strasbourg), became foci for public demonstration of nationalist fervour, but not sites of pictorial propaganda-cum-entertainment.[30] By contrast, patriotic displays and war landmarks reconfigured the urban landscapes of central Berlin and London, as we shall see in the following section.

War landmarks

An added attraction of the *Deutsche Kriegsausstellung* in Berlin was an iron-nail war landmark, sponsored by the Krupp shipyard in Kiel, featuring a German submarine.[31] Like patriotic expositions, war landmarks or *Kriegswahrzeichen zum Benageln* fulfilled a dual purpose: they fashioned representations of war and functioned as war charities. War landmarks sprang up throughout Germany in 1915 and 1916. In the course of month-long celebrations, these wooden statues or plaques were described or outlined by a series of iron nails. All citizens, young and old, male and female, rich and poor, were called upon to drive nails into war landmarks. Initiated and organized by local worthies and societies, the success of this signifying practice ultimately depended on widespread participation. By means of collective action, the wooden objects were – or, sometimes, were manifestly not – turned into steel figures symbolizing the community's iron will to wage war.[32]

The participants had to pay for the privilege by contributing to charities (such as the Red Cross) in aid of war victims, notably the families of wounded and fallen soldiers. The success of this practice reinforces the

---

[29] Ibid.   [30] See chapters 2 and 8.

[31] *Deutsche Kriegsausstellungen 1916*, p. 109; Lange, *Einen Krieg ausstellen*, pp. 71–2; see also Gerhard Schneider, 'Über hannoversche Nagelfiguren im Ersten Weltkrieg', *Hannoversche Geschichtsblätter*, 50 (1996), pp. 242–4.

[32] Stefan Goebel, 'Forging the industrial home front: iron-nail memorials in the Ruhr', in Jenny Macleod and Pierre Purseigle (eds.), *Uncovered fields. Perspectives in First World War studies* (Leiden and Boston, 2004), pp. 159–78; Gerhard Schneider, 'Zur Mobilisierung der "Heimatfront". Das Nageln sogenannter Kriegswahrzeichen im Ersten Weltkrieg', *Zeitschrift für Volkskunde*, 95 (1999), pp. 32–62; Aribert Reimann, *Der große Krieg der Sprachen. Untersuchungen zur historischen Semantik in Deutschland und England zur Zeit des Ersten Weltkrieges* (Essen, 2000), pp. 48–61.

Der „Eiserne Hindenburg" auf dem Königsplatz
in Berlin nach der Enthüllung. — Das Luftschiff
„Hansa" während der Nagelung über dem Standbild.

Fig. 5.1. The 'Iron Hindenburg' depicted on a contemporary postcard: an airship flies over Königsplatz.

view that the meaning of citizenship broadened to include provisions for populations especially hit by the war.[33] War landmarks expressed the gratitude of the *Heimat* to the 'front-line fighters', by means of symbolic gesture and real gifts of money. The civilians' pecuniary sacrifice was meant to emulate the soldiers' blood sacrifice, thus forging an iron bond of solidarity between home and front. Like all war charity, iron-nail war landmarks had above all symbolical value; each nail or donation testified to the civilian's unfailing support of the nation's war effort; each repaid the debt of honour.

Berlin's central war landmark, the 'Iron Hindenburg', was launched on 4 September 1915 to mark the first anniversary of the German victory in the battle of Tannenberg. In order to strengthen this association, war trophies (four Russian guns) were brought from Tannenberg to Berlin to flank the figure of the triumphant field marshal. This was a display of confidence in victory. The unveiling ceremony culminated in an air show with two immense airships, commonly regarded as the miracle weapon and zenith of modernity, overflowing the figure.[34] The 'Iron Hindenburg' stood stiffly erect, his hands clasped in front of him on the pommel of a huge sword which he held tip down.[35] Evocative of the design of the Roland-style statue of Bismarck in Hamburg, the Berlin war landmark suggested continuity between the Bismarckian wars and the Great War, between the Iron Chancellor and the Iron General. Significantly, Germany's largest and foremost (though not its first) war landmark, was erected in the middle of Königsplatz opposite the Siegessäule and the memorials to the heroes of 1871: Bismarck, Moltke, and Roon.[36]

Like the surrounding monuments, the 'Iron Hindenburg' was a symbol of the nation in the heart of its capital city. It denoted the intimate link between the nation and Berlin, the political capital and its inhabitants. There was ample opportunity for both the local populace and visitors to the capital to do their bit. Twelve and a half metres in height, the wooden figure provided space for over two million nails. For a donation of

---

[33] *Capital cities*, vol. I, p. 550.

[34] See Peter Fritzsche, *A nation of fliers. German aviation and the popular imagination* (Cambridge, Mass., 1992) on the cultural significance of airships.

[35] 'Der eiserne Hindenburg von Berlin', *Berliner Börsen-Courier*, 414, 4 September 1915, pp. 1–2; 'Der Hindenburg von Berlin', *Berliner Tageblatt*, 452, 4 September 1915; 'Bei Hindenburg auf dem Königsplatz', *Berliner Tageblatt*, 453, 5 September 1915; 'Die Enthüllung des "Eisernen Hindenburg"', *Berliner Lokal-Anzeiger*, 452, 4 September 1915.

[36] Maximilian Rapsilber, *Der Eiserne Hindenburg von Berlin. Ein Gedenkblatt* (Berlin, 1918), pp. 26, 38–43, 59; on pre-war memorials, see Reinhard Alings, *Monument und Nation. Das Bild vom Nationalstaat im Medium Denkmal – zum Verhältnis von Nation und Staat im Deutschen Kaiserreich 1871–1918* (Berlin and New York, 1996).

one Mark, the donor purchased the right to hammer an iron nail into the 'Iron Hindenburg'. Black and silver nails cost five Marks each; golden nails were sold at a price of a hundred Marks per nail; revenues were shared in equal parts between the National Foundation for Surviving Dependants of Fallen Soldiers, the *Luftfahrerdank*, and the city of Berlin *Kriegssammlung*.

Did the mobilized crowd on the Königsplatz on 4 September 1915 provide a glimpse of things to come? Did the 'Iron Hindenburg' restate the nationalist promise of 1914, mobilize the masses and thus help to turn Germans into Nazis?[37] This interpretation does not stand scrutiny. True, Berlin's war landmark acted initially as a magnet to sightseers; 20,000 nails were sold on the first day. In addition, the spectacle received extensive media coverage in Berlin's liberal and conservative press (the social-democratic *Vorwärts* devoted a mere paragraph to the unveiling ceremony).[38] Soon, however, the novelty lost its attraction and the 'Iron Hindenburg' lagged behind provincial war landmarks. In the event, it was never completely clad with nails. In August 1917, the takings for nails amounted to 650,000 Marks, reported the British press with obvious *Schadenfreude*.[39] *The Times* noted that 'the late-comers, even though they may average thousands a day, are not enough to make noticeable progress' – the 'Iron Hindenburg' was simply too grand a figure.[40]

Intended as a symbol of national unity, the 'Iron Hindenburg' became a bone of contention. Many art critics felt that the 'Iron Hindenburg' did not do justice to the great field marshal. They dismissed the colossus, which smacked of carpentry, as gigantic kitsch. One journal seemed to hit the nail on the head when it referred to the figure as the *eiserne Kitschener* or 'iron *Kitsch*ener'.[41] The same journal considered the practice of nailing images of living persons utterly distasteful (to be sure, only Hindenburg's garments were made iron while his face and hands were omitted). The Royal Academy of Arts and a number of Berlin artists, too, objected to this kind of artistic barbarism, that is the infliction of bodily harm on wooden statues.[42] Critics of the 'Iron Hindenburg' recognized that the

---

[37] Peter Fritzsche, *Germans into Nazis* (Cambridge, Mass. and London, 1998), p. 50.
[38] 'Der Eiserne Hindenburg', *Vorwärts*, 245, 5 September 1915; see Reimann, *Der große Krieg*, pp. 67–8.
[39] 'Imperial and foreign news items', *The Times*, 41571, 31 August 1917, p. 5.
[40] 'Too few nails for Hindenburg', *The Times*, 41054, 4 January 1916, p. 7; see also 'The waning of faith', *Punch*, 152 (1917), p. 273.
[41] Hans Sachs, 'Vom Hurrakitsch, von Nagelungsstandbildern, Nagelungsplakaten und andren – Schönheiten', *Das Plakat*, 8, 1 (1917), p. 11.
[42] Ibid., pp. 9–11; 'Der Eiserne Hindenburg', *Kunst und Künstler*, 17 (1918–19), pp. 464–6; 'Hurrakitsch-Hochflut', *Der Kunstwart*, 29 (1915–16), pp. 31–2; for a positive appraisal, see 'Fetischdienst', *Kladderadatsch*, 37, 12 September 1915.

figure was effectively playing into the hands of Allied propaganda.[43] In fact, French journalists and intellectuals were quick to suggest that the statue of Hindenburg catered to a quintessentially German fetishism. In a public lecture to the French Scientific Association in Paris in February 1917, the speaker emphasized that such practices were no longer encountered except 'among the half-savage tribes of central Africa and the Congo', associated with other 'mental attitudes that are all related to deficient cerebral control, proof of very clear inferiority, psychological as well as moral'.[44]

Due to its sheer size, the 'Iron Hindenburg' attracted a lot of attention in Germany as well as abroad. The historian, however, should be careful not to exaggerate the importance of the monument. In a sense, the 'Iron Hindenburg' was just one amongst many war landmarks in Berlin. Although it is not possible to determine the exact number of iron-nail objects in the capital, it is reasonable to assume that virtually every quarter or suburb (spurred on by local pride and rivalries) established a war landmark of its own. For instance, Lichtenberg nailed a 'German Sword', while Schöneberg cooperated with Wilmersdorf in creating an 'Iron Door' (designed by Peter Behrens).[45] Furthermore, the practice was widespread in neighbourhoods, schools, and clubs. These were mostly small-scale landmarks which vanished without trace after 1918. (For the purpose of comparison, note that thirteen war landmarks have been recorded for the city of Hanover, though the actual figure must have been higher.[46]) War landmarks did not necessarily consist of iron nails. War mosaics, like the one sponsored by the Red Cross in Wittenbergplatz, Charlottenburg, represented an alternative yet less popular commemoration-cum-charity.[47]

Arguably, local initiatives absorbed a great degree of the popular enthusiasm for war landmarks at the expense of the 'Iron Hindenburg' which was both a metropolitan event and national symbol. The relative

---

[43] Times Newspaper Limited Archive, London, Marked copies, 'The German military idol', *The Times*, 40930, 11 August 1915, p. 6.

[44] Edgar Bérillon, 'La Psychologie de la race allemande d'après ses caractères objectifs et spécifiques', in Assocation française pour l'avancement des sciences (ed.), *Conférences faites en 1916–1917* (Paris, 1917), pp. 139–40; for a similar statement, see also Baronne Jane Michaux, *En marge du drame. Journal d'une Parisienne pendant la guerre 1914–1915* (Paris, 1916), p. 356; see also Annette Becker, *War and faith. The religious imagination in France, 1914–1930* (Oxford, 1998), pp. 100–2.

[45] 'Die "Eiserne Tür" in Schöneberg-Wilmersdorf', *Neue Preußische Zeitung (Kreuz-Zeitung)*, 413, 15 August 1915; Sachs, 'Vom Hurrakitsch', pp. 9, 15.

[46] Schneider, 'Hannoversche Nagelfiguren', p. 219.

[47] Sachs, 'Vom Hurrakitsch', pp. 13–14; 'Impressions of Berlin', *The Times*, 41229, 26 July 1916, p. 5; Lange, *Einen Krieg ausstellen*, p. 68.

failure of the 'Iron Hindenburg' compared to success of Berlin's local and suburban war landmarks confirms that the identity of quartiers was never completely subsumed by the capital city as a whole.[48] War landmarks were by definition local ventures: locally organized, they were meant to help local people in need. Donations to the 'Iron Hindenburg', by contrast, assisted anonymous war victims somewhere in Germany rather than the next-door widow or orphan.

Ironically, the war landmarks of Neukölln and Friedrichshagen bore a striking resemblance to the 'Iron Hindenburg'. The 'Roland of Neukölln' at Hertzbergplatz showed Hindenburg in the guise of a crusader knight. What is more, the medievalist iconography went hand in hand with a modernist choreography on the occasion of the ceremonial unveiling on 12 September 1915. Instead of Zeppelins, three aeroplanes circled round the Hertzberg Platz and dropped little flags.[49] A few days earlier, on 5 September, another 'Hindenburg Roland' had been inaugurated in Friedrichshagen on the outskirts of Berlin. Interestingly, this war landmark was made of a tree trunk from Friedrichsruh, Bismarck's final resting-place, donated by Princess Bismarck herself.[50] The failure of the third German High Command to achieve victory did not dampen the Hindenburg cult. Long after the wave of communal war landmarks in 1915 and 1916 had abated, a 'Hindenburg Gate' was nailed at the barracks of the 3rd Garde-Regiment zu Fuß. Between 22 March 1917 (the 120th birthday of Wilhelm I) and 2 September 1917 (Sedan Day), it generated an astonishing net profit of over 32,000 Marks. To be sure, the regiment was most successful at mobilizing corporate organizations; the city of Hanover (which had recently made Hindenburg an honorary citizen) alone purchased golden nails worth a thousand Marks.[51]

Iron-nail landmarks were an innovative form of patriotic display transforming public space. The practice was without parallel in either Britain or France. The nearest equivalent in Britain was the tank bank, launched by the National War Savings Committee in London on 26 November 1917. Tanks, exhibited in central squares from Bristol to Glasgow, solicited money from the populace for war bonds rather than war charity. Similar to the iron-nail landmarks, tank banks were places of both

---

[48] *Capital cities*, vol. 1, p. 6.
[49] 'Die Enthüllung des Neuköllner Roland', *Neue Preußische Zeitung* (*Kreuz-Zeitung*), 442, 31 August 1915; 'Die Nagelung des "Ritters von Neukölln"', *Neue Preußische Zeitung* (*Kreuz-Zeitung*), 466, 13 September 1915; on medievalist imagery, see Stefan Goebel, *The Great War and medieval memory. War, remembrance and medievalism in Britain and Germany, 1914–1940* (Cambridge, 2006).
[50] 'Ein Hindenburg-Denkmal in Berlin', *Hannoverscher Kurier*, 31949, 18 August 1915.
[51] Schneider, 'Hannoversche Nagelfiguren', pp. 255–6.

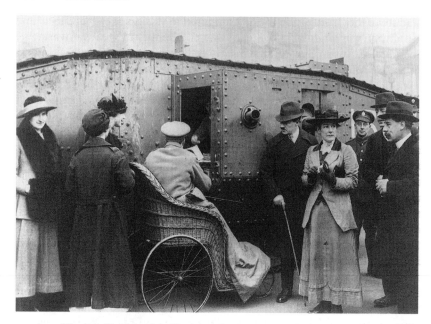

Fig. 5.2. Tank bank in Trafalgar Square: a wounded officer pictured as the purchaser of the first bond. [Imperial War Museum IWM, Photograph Archive, Q. 54248, 'Sale of war bonds from the tank in Trafalgar Square. A wounded officer buying the first bond', November 1917.]

spectacle and performance, sites where not only the organizers but also the audience played an active part. Both practices elevated ordinary people from mere viewers to true participants. Timing, though, was different. While the nailing ritual flourished in the mid-war years, the tank banks only got rolling in the final year of the conflict. By then, German savings had been eaten up by inflation and civilian morale reached a low ebb. Tank banks mobilized financial and symbolic resources in Britain that had long dried up in Germany.

In autumn 1917, the National War Savings Committee, feeling that its campaign to attract small investors needed a fresh stimulus, came up with the idea of the tank bank. The first one was opened in Trafalgar Square, with a brand-new tank attractively positioned between Nelson's Column and the National Gallery and surrounded by war booty.[52] For a sum of only 15s. 6d., Londoners could buy a war savings certificate (to be

[52] 'War bonds from a tank', *The Times*, 41645, 26 November 1917, p. 5; on the symbolism of Trafalgar Square, see chapter 8, and Rodney Mace, *Trafalgar Square. Emblem of empire* (London, 1976).

redeemed for £1 after five years), and inspect the inside of the war machine. (Alternatively, war bonds of the value of £5, £20, and £50 were available, too.) The press celebrated the first purchaser at Trafalgar Square: a wounded officer in a wheel-chair.[53]

The small investor certainly got his money's worth, for the organizers provided a special programme of entertainments in the 'Tankland of Trafalgar-square'.[54] On the last day, a squadron of seven aeroplanes and a naval airship appeared over Trafalgar Square dropping pasteboard discs with patriotic messages.[55] At times, the square resembled a Victorian music hall. Public figures – politicians, aristocrats, and entertainers – led on by Prime Minister Lloyd George and Chancellor Bonar Law, banked on the tank, addressed the queuing crowds or gave musical offerings from the top of the vehicle. The tank became a magnet for the patriotic and the amusement-seeking public alike. Those who avoided the crowds at Trafalgar Square could visit the tank's comrade, the 'wandering tank', which went the rounds through central London.

The campaign proved a tremendous success. Within a fortnight, 3.5 million pounds were raised. Hence it was decided to extend the savings drive, Tank Week, throughout the country. In the provinces, some tank banks produced even more spectacular yields: 4.5 million pounds in Manchester, 6.6 million pounds in Birmingham, and, breaking all records in this inter-urban competition, 14.5 million pounds in Glasgow. Like iron-nail land-marks in Germany, the returns of tank banks in provincial conurbations surpassed the results in the capital city. Compared to the enormous takings in Glasgow, the millions invested in the first tank bank in Trafalgar Square appeared like a trifling sum.

But Londoners were given another chance when the tanks returned for Business Men's Week in March 1918. 'Egbert', a battle-scarred model, was stationed in Trafalgar Square. A second tank was posted outside the Royal Exchange, while four 'wandering tanks' toured the metropolitan boroughs and urban districts of Greater London. Advertisements placed in the London press appealed to the citizen's pride: 'In the records of the Tanks, London with its teeming millions has had to give way to other

---

[53] 'The tank "bank" in Trafalgar Square for the sale of war bonds and war-savings certificates', *Illustrated London News*, 151 (1917), p. 661; Patrick Wright, *Tank. The progress of a monstrous war machine* (London, 2000), pp. 81–100; Trudi Tate, *Modernism, history and the First World War* (Manchester and New York, 1998), pp. 127–34; Reimann, *Der große Krieg*, pp. 60–8; National Archives, Public Record Office, Kew (hereafter PRO), NSC 7/2, 'Report on special activities during October, November, December 1917', 16 January 1918.

[54] 'Towards the third million', *The Times*, 41655, 7 December 1917, p. 4.

[55] 'The tank bank's triumph', *The Times*, 41657, 10 December 1917, p. 5. The air show was later repeated, see 'Bank and tank receipts', *The Times*, 41733, 9 March 1918, p. 7; 'London's tank week', *Daily Telegraph*, 19622, 4 March 1918, p. 7.

cities of less renown and less rich in power and wealth. This week represents London's great effort to take her place at the head of the Roll of Honour of the Tanks.'[56] By using the term 'Roll of Honour', the organizers drew a parallel between the citizens' pecuniary sacrifice and the soldiers' blood sacrifice.

The second campaign was a success. This time, investments totalled 43 million pounds (including a number of big company cheques). For the Londoners, visiting the tank was an activity both patriotic and entertaining; this was a unique wartime spectacle that was not to be missed. In a letter dated 6 March 1918 to her son Fred, Elizabeth Fernside of Fulham described her impression of the campaign:

We also visited the Tank in Trafalgar Sq. On the great canvas stretched across the National Gallery, is a lovely oil painting of the Armada coming, + Drake going out in his old 'Wooden Walls to meet them'. The cheering legend 'Britain is again threatened' is attached on this. The dirty, rusty old tank, 'Egbert' was doing a roaring trade (25,000 up to noon). The 'lions' at the base of old Nelson were *not* roaring, but had a green + a red electric light inside their mouths which looked strange lighted up in the day, there was an Italian aeroplane in which Laureati flew from Turin to Hounslow aerodrome on Sept 14 + a Gondola from a rigid air machine . . . not to forget the Band, which played Egmont overture [*sic*], popular songs + Revue music + some Chu Chow, of course.

Six days later, Mrs Fernside wrote to her son that 'We have the Tank coming to Fulham on Friday, so I am taking £15 from the Bank + intend speculating in 3-£5 bonds in your name (as you practically consented to that, when we were discussing the subject some time ago).' After the event, she reported 'The Tank "Nelson" rolled into Fulham . . . "with an independent air", + the total was just over 130,000 for the day. Several local celebrities spouted from the top of it, but nobody listened.'[57] Mrs Fernside's account shows that tank banks, like other wartime displays, were dynamic and fluid texts. They carried certain messages authored by the organizers, but their meaning was, ultimately, shaped by the fantasy of public participation. Surviving first-hand testimonies are, unfortunately, scarce and difficult to trace in the archives.

Unsurprisingly, the silent majority are the working classes. However, banking on the tank was as much a working-class phenomenon as a middle-class one. Interestingly, the East End gave particularly generously. In absolute terms, Shoreditch and Stepney outdid (the however less

[56] *Pall Mall Gazette*, 16474, 4 March 1918, p. 5.
[57] Imperial War Museum, London (hereafter IWM), Con. Shelf, Letters of Elizabeth Fernside, Elizabeth Fernside to Fred Fernside, 6 March, 12 March and 20 March 1918, original emphasis.

populous boroughs of) Kensington and Chelsea. To be sure, a middle-class man would typically buy a war bond near his workplace in the City, at Trafalgar Square, or in Holborn (the three most successful venues), while a housewife would normally visit the local tank bank in a residential area such as Fulham. Most striking are the figures for Woolwich, the rapidly growing industrial centre on the lower Thames with more than 70,000 workers at the end of 1917. The large sum invested at the Woolwich tank bank – only surpassed by four other boroughs and the City – reflected not only recent population flows but also the confidence of (now relatively well-off) London's (munitions) workers in the national war effort.[58]

'There has been no more popular appeal to investors, large and small, than the Tank', concluded the National War Savings Committee by March 1918. 'This mysterious engine of war has excited the imagination and curiosity of everybody. Coming as it did out of the trenches direct to the homes of British people, it touched the hearts of those whose part it was to remain in Blighty.'[59] Like iron-nail memorials, tank banks allowed the home front to demonstrate its spirit of sacrifice and support of the fighting men. To be sure, corporate investors boosted the results. In both Britain and Germany, philanthropic individuals and prosperous companies bought savings certificates or iron nails, often to distribute them among the local working classes or their own employees.[60]

There are striking similarities between Berlin's 'Iron Hindenburg' and London's tank bank. Both were iron colossuses, exhibited together with war trophies and military hardware, to suggest victory through iron endurance; and both were meant to symbolize the civilian's iron will to see the military campaign through. What is more, both blended into nineteenth-century ensembles of victory and greatness, Trafalgar Square with Nelson's Column and Königsplatz with the Siegessäule respectively. The tank bank and the iron-nail landmark, novel forms of patriotic spectacle, transformed established *lieux de mémoire* into new arenas for symbolic exchanges, at least temporarily.

Like patriotic expositions, war landmarks were not monuments but ephemeral phenomena which temporarily transformed the cityscape. True, a few months later a 'Feed the Guns' campaign was staged along the lines of the tank bank in Trafalgar Square (now turned into a model

---

[58] 'The coming of the tanks', *Woolwich Herald*, 1871, 8 March 1918, p. 2; 'The tank', *Woolwich Herald*, 1871, 15 March 1918, p. 1; see *Capital cities*, vol. I, p. 193.

[59] PRO, NSC 3/1, 'The tank campaigns', *War Savings*, 2, 7 (1918), p. 79.

[60] See note 53 above, and Jay Winter, *Sites of memory, sites of mourning. The Great War in European cultural history* (Cambridge, 1995).

battlefield with guns, trenches, and debris to stir the imagination of those at home), but the tanks never returned to the square after the war.[61] In Berlin, the 'Iron Hindenburg' was publicly disgraced in the aftermath of the revolution. The scaffolding was stolen, the figure dismantled, stored away in a shed, and partly used as firewood. Moreover, Königsplatz was demonstratively renamed into Platz der Republik or Square of the Republic (by contrast, a deputy of the right-wing German National People's Party had suggested 'Siegesplatz' or 'Victory Square'). Only the statue's massive head survived, rediscovered by the police in 1934. A new odyssey began with intermediate stops at the Märkisches Museum and the Air Museum in Adlershof. Stranded in the Air Collection at Lehrter train station, it was destroyed during the Second World War.[62]

War collections

Both patriotic expositions and war landmarks generated an enormous amount of cheap memorabilia, that is, secondary representations. War trinkets allowed individuals to rehearse and replicate domestically what the collective did in public. All contributors to the 'Iron Hindenburg' received a certificate with a *Denkspruch*, a sentiment, in facsimile of Hindenburg's handwriting and a medal. The merchandizing of the 'Iron Hindenburg' included miniature statues available in two sizes (42 or 110 centimetres) and materials ('war metal' or plaster).[63] On Trafalgar Square, street vendors, trying to capitalize on the tank craze, sold tank-shaped brooches, handbags, and teapots. Kitsch and charity went hand in hand with commemoration and mourning. The newspapers reported about purchasers who intended to keep their bonds in memory of loved ones killed in the war, 'and their subscriptions will form a gift to the nation for the purposes of the war'.[64]

War expositions also met the popular demand for souvenirs. At the *Deutsche Kriegsausstellung*, a bookshop catered for the bibliophiles. In fact,

---

[61] 'Our great financial offensive', *Illustrated London News*, 153 (1918), p. 425; 'No guns on Monday', *Daily Telegraph*, 19807, 5 October 1918, p. 6.

[62] Harald von Koenigswald, *Das verwandelte Antlitz* (Berlin, 1938), pp. 64–5; on Königsplatz after 1918, see Maoz Azaryahu, 'What is to be remembered. The struggle over street names in Berlin, 1921–1930', *Tel Aviver Jahrbuch für deutsche Geschichte*, 17 (1988), pp. 241–58.

[63] Jay Winter, *Sites of memory, sites of mourning. The Great War in European cultural history* (Cambridge, 1995), pp. 82–3; Sachs, 'Vom Hurrakitsch', p. 7.

[64] 'War bonds', *The Times*, 41651, 3 December 1917, p. 5; see Wright, *Tank*, pp. 84, 93; Barbara Jones and Bill Howell, *Popular arts of the First World War* (London, 1972), pp. 70–1.

the heavily illustrated guidebook to the exposition itself was designed as a memento. Yet many a visitor wanted to take home with him and possess something more authentic, a genuine relic of the war. A souvenir stand offered a variety of war paraphernalia; prices for shell splinters, for example, ranged between 10 Pfennigs and 20 Marks.[65] The souvenir sale was not only a lucrative business, but also a means of reinforcing law and order. War booty shown in open spaces had been prone to theft and vandalism; fanatic collectors had tried to remove bits and pieces from the guns exhibited in front of the Zeughaus and the Schloß.[66] The official vending of war items both channelled the trade with war souvenirs and solved a public-order problem.

Patriotic expositions and war landmarks were part of the thriving industry of wartime kitsch. For Karl Ernst Osthaus, the great supporter of modern art, this industry elevated bad taste to new heights. In an attempt to stem the tide of popular culture, he helped organize an exhibition of both worthless kitsch and quality design in the rooms of the Secession on the Kurfürstendamm in February 1916. Visitors to the exhibition could see, for instance, Ernst Ludwig Kirchner's models of a war landmark for Hagen in Westphalia. The section on *Kriegsschund* showed mouth-organs shaped like U-boats or rosaries made of bullets.[67] A thorn in Osthaus's eye, wartime kitsch acquired the status of a collector's item, nonetheless. A number of individuals and institutions started systematically collecting objects of everyday life, and Berlin became the capital of private and public war collections. A 1917 survey of war collections listed twenty-five depositories for Greater Berlin (principally libraries, museums, ministries, schools) that could potentially form the nucleus of a future war museum.[68]

Collecting was by and large a civilian operation and understood as a patriotic duty. The most ambitious private initiatives in Europe were the Bibliothèque et musée de la guerre of 1917 (now the Bibliothèque de documentation internationale contemporaine) and the Weltkriegsbücherei of 1915 (now the Bibliothek für Zeitgeschichte), both founded by wealthy

---

[65] *Deutsche Kriegsausstellung 1916*, pp. 20, 108; see also Healy, 'Exhibiting a war in progress', pp. 83–4.

[66] Beil, *Der ausgestellte Krieg*, pp. 84–6.

[67] Kathrin Renken, ' "Die Kunst im Kriege". Eine Wanderausstellung des Deutschen Museums für Kunst in Handel und Gewerbe (Februar 1916–Juli 1917)', in Sabine Röder and Gerhard Storck (eds.), *Deutsches Museum für Kunst in Handel und Gewerbe. Moderne Formgebung 1900–1914* (Krefeld, 1997), pp. 400–8.

[68] A. Buddecke, *Die Kriegssammlungen. Ein Nachweis ihrer Einrichtung und ihres Bestandes* (Oldenburg, 1917), pp. 7–15; Detlef Hoffmann, 'Die Weltkriegssammlung des Historischen Museums Frankfurt', in *Ein Krieg wird ausgestellt. Die Weltkriegssammlung des Historischen Museums (1914–1918)* (Frankfurt am Main, 1976), pp. 62–74.

industrialists, Henry Leblanc and his wife and Richard Franck respectively. The Leblancs had started collecting documents and ephemera as soon as the war broke out. By the time the Bibliothèque et musée was formally founded in 1917, the collection occupied two spacious apartments containing some fifteen rooms in all, in Avenue Malakoff. British journalists were greatly impressed at this venture without parallel at home.[69] Yet once the couple had left their collection in the efficient hands of a group of historians and archivists, the museum character was silently dropped from the agenda.[70]

In Berlin, Richard Franck had originally been a supporter of the Royal Library's special war collection, a monumental effort to impose an all-encompassing *Katalogik*, 'cata-logic', on the war.[71] Later, Franck used his money and international connections to build up his own collection of German and foreign materials. His employees and members of the general public, too, collected ephemera and curiosities on behalf of the Weltkriegsbücherei. Total war requires total documentation was the guiding principle. Franck spared neither effort nor expense to amass a great variety of material such as food-rationing cards, trench journals, and propaganda posters. By 1917, the collection occupied four flats in Franck's private house in Potsdamer Straße 12 and had a staff of over twenty.

Franck pursued above all two aims: to improve war propaganda and to create a storehouse of memory. Having recognized the significance of mass mobilization, he hoped that the documentation, study, and comparison of international war propaganda would help to secure a German victory in the war of words. But Franck's library was more than an exercise in propaganda. Collecting, as Walter Benjamin has pointed out, is a form of practical memory, a manifestation of 'proximity'.[72] Franck himself regarded the upheaval of war as a pivotal moment in German history that had to be recorded for posterity. The collection was meant to furnish a war museum and to provide a basis for future research into the history of the Great War. The original plan was set aside in the aftermath of the German defeat. Franck moved to Stuttgart where

---

[69] 'A national war museum', *The Times*, 41407, 20 February 1917, p. 11.
[70] Daniel J. Sherman, 'Objects of memory. History and narrative in French war museums', *French Historical Studies*, 19 (1995), pp. 54–7.
[71] Peter Berz, 'WELTKRIEG/SYSTEM. Die "Kriegssammlung 1914" der Staatsbibliothek Berlin und ihre Katalogik', *Krieg und Literatur*, 5, 10 (1993), pp. 105–30.
[72] Daniel J. Sherman and Irit Rogoff, 'Introduction. Frameworks for critical analysis', in Daniel J. Sherman and Irit Rogoff (eds.), *Museum culture. Histories, discourses, spectacles* (London, 1994), p. xiv.

he opened his library to the public in 1921. The idea of a war museum did not become a reality until 1933.[73]

The war museum of the Weltkriegsbücherei called for revenge and promised redemption in the Third Reich. Unsurprisingly, the exhibition passed over the appalling character and cost of trench warfare. By contrast, the dead and the deformed featured prominently in Berlin's International Anti-War Museum, opened in Parochialstraße 29 in the very centre of Old Berlin in 1925. Founded by a pacifist activist, Ernst Friedrich, the museum displayed an array of shocking photographs, artworks (notably, by Otto Dix, Käthe Kollwitz, and Heinrich Zille), war souvenirs, and toy soldiers. But enlightening Berliners was not enough for the museum's founder. Friedrich, a committed internationalist, envisaged opening branches in metropolises worldwide. By 1926, he had established a line of contact with like-minded pacifists in Paris and Vienna.[74] Yet Friedrich's plans did not materialize; his Anti-War Museum remained a unique institution.

The gruesome images of mutilated or disfigured soldiers in particular clashed with the previous glorification of war (and military medicine) in war exhibitions. The Anti-War Museum was also an Anti War-Exhibition Museum, for it demystified the sanitized image of modern warfare that war expositions and army museums, notably the Zeughaus, had conveyed. 'Berlin has a very special *"Zeug"-Haus* where all the many things [*Zeug*] are shown, which – from Philipp the Lunatic to Wilhelm the Deserter – was used for mass murder.'[75] In displays of savage images of the mayhem caused by the war, Friedrich graphically pointed out the dangerous selectivity of the patriotic collectors of wartime memorabilia, documents, and books. However, Friedrich realized that ultimately every attempt to represent war, even a pacifist one, trivialized reality: 'However horrible these pictures may be: the reality is even more horrible.'[76] A tourist attraction but a thorn in the (police) authorities' side during the Weimar Republic, the Anti-War Museum was eventually closed down in 1933 to accommodate a museum of the Nazi party's storm troop (SA).[77]

---

[73] Brandt, 'Kriegssammlungen im Ersten Weltkrieg', pp. 287–90, 296; Brandt, 'Memory makers', pp. 113–14; Lange, *Einen Krieg ausstellen*, p. 8.

[74] Ernst Friedrich, *Das Anti-Kriegsmuseum* (Berlin, 1926), p. 13; see also Ernst Friedrich, *Vom Friedens-Museum ... zur Hitler-Kaserne. Ein Tatsachenbericht über das Wirken von Ernst Friedrich und Adolf Hitler* (Geneva, 1935); Zwach, *Deutsche und englische Militärmuseen*, pp. 110–16.

[75] Friedrich, *Anti-Kriegsmuseum*, p. 3.

[76] Cited in Brandt, 'Kriegssammlungen im Ersten Weltkrieg', p. 298; see the catalogue *Nie wieder Krieg! No more War! Plus jamais de Guerre!* (Amsterdam, 1929).

[77] Friedrich, *Vom Friedens-Museum*, pp. 22–5, 74–9.

National museums

Provisional plans for a state-funded national war museum in Berlin had been under discussion during the war. In summer 1916, the director of the National Gallery, Ludwig Justi, submitted a memorandum on the subject of a Reich War Museum in central Berlin to the Minister of the Interior. The world war was, according to Justi, the greatest event in German history, and, therefore, had to be commemorated in a museum of its own. However, neither conventional art and army museums (like his own house, the National Gallery, or the Zeughaus) nor war expositions (such as the *Deutsche Kriegsausstellung*) had adequately captured the over-whelming experience of total war, Justi argued.

The museum director envisaged a new type of didactic exhibition which showed the totality of modern war from many perspectives. Mixing objects, pictures, and texts, Justi's ideal type covered both the home front and the battle front, the privates and the generals. Thematic sections included sites of mobilization, the trenches, factories, railways, and hospitals. Justi suggested, in effect, tracing the cultural history of the war through a series of significant sites. The ideal location for the national war museum had to be found in the historic centre of Berlin in close proximity to the memorials to Wilhelm I and Frederick the Great. Thus it would blend into the historic topography of national grandeur. As a temporary measure, Justi suggested utilizing the Kroll Opera at Köngisplatz, near the General Staff, the Siegessäule, and Siegesallee.[78]

In the end, Justi's vision came to nought. Put on ice during the war, the project was ultimately thwarted by military defeat. To be sure, the viability of a national war museum was not simply a function of the fortunes of war. London's Imperial War Museum is a case in point. The museum's eventual success mirrored its public acceptance and emotional appeal as a site of memory and mourning, serving both the nation and the empire. The making of this institution signifies the search for a symbolic form that could express collective bereavement and celebrate imperial unity at the same time. It tells us much about London's cultural life, for it discloses in unmistakable ways the imperial character of the British capital, a feature which distinguishes it clearly from that of Paris and Berlin. In both these cities, imperial elements were visible; in London they were dominant.

[78] Bundesarchiv, Berlin, R 1501/108997, fos. 7–17, Memorandum by Ludwig Justi, August 1916; see Beil, *Der ausgestellte Krieg*, pp. 59–70; on Justi, see Alexis Joachimides, *Die Museumsreformbewegung in Deutschland und die Entstehung des modernen Museums 1880–1940* (Dresden, 2001), pp. 166–77.

The story of the funding of the Imperial War Museum has been told before.[79] Initiated privately by influential figures (inter alia Charles ffoulkes, curator of the Tower Armouries, and Sir Alfred Mond, MP and First Commissioner of Works), it was originally to be called the National War Museum. Soon it took on an imperial mantle, in order to gather together and preserve relics and other items which would tell later generations about the war and inculcate a sense of belonging to a larger empire. The imperial collecting policy did not go unchallenged, since Canada and Australia launched war museums-cum-memorials of their own.[80] In part the urgency of the task was related to the surge of interest in commemoration during the war itself;[81] in part it arose out of fear that many items would vanish, or be bought by dealers, or be exported abroad, in particular to the United States. To avoid turning sacred material into merchandise, the Imperial War Museum served as a repository for the material memory of the war.[82]

'The War Museum, by the nature and character of its exhibits forms a Memorial of the War', argued Sir Alfred Mond.[83] Here was a permanent exhibition configured as a war memorial. But such a notion was rejected by many politicians since it lacked the simplicity or the sacred elements of a war memorial. This was neither a utilitarian offering nor monumental tribute to the dead.[84] The decision as to the memorial character of the Imperial War Museum was shelved in 1917, and it became what it is today: a site of artefacts, documents, and works of art illustrating all facets of the Great War.[85] To be sure, the museum concept glorified the war effort and took on an air of propaganda. This might have helped political circles to warm to the idea of a memorial museum. Significantly, its foundation coincided with the formation of the new Department (later Ministry) of Information. In wartime, memorialization and mobilization were inextricably intertwined.[86]

In January 1918, the Imperial War Museum organized a temporary exhibition at Burlington House in Piccadilly in aid of the Red Cross, and

---

[79] Gaynor Kavanagh, 'Museum as memorial. The origins of the Imperial War Museum', *Journal of Contemporary History*, 23 (1988), pp. 77–97; Kavanagh, *Museums and the First World War. A social history* (London and New York, 1994), chs. 9–11; Sue Malvern, 'War, memory and museums. Art and artefact in the Imperial War Museum', *Historical Workshop Journal*, 49 (2000), pp. 177–203.

[80] See K. S. Inglis, 'A sacred place. The making of the Australian War Memorial', *War & Society*, 3, 2 (1985), pp. 99–126.

[81] Winter, *Sites of memory*, ch. 4.   [82] Generally, see Saunders, *Trench art*.

[83] PRO, CAB 24/22, GT 1650, fo. 191, Memorandum by Sir Alfred Mond, 8 August 1917.

[84] Alex King, *Memorials of the Great War in Britain. The symbolism and politics of remembrance* (Oxford and New York, 1998).

[85] *A short guide to the Imperial War Museum* (London, 1938).

[86] Winter, *Sites of memory*, pp. 80–1.

though it actually lost money, the idea of bringing the new museum to the public's notice was a good one.[87] Again, relics were powerful objects to promote the idea that a museum was indeed a memorial, whatever the government decided. Although the museum could not allow the physical suffering that the war created to be shown, the presence of death was pervasive. There was a bayonet displayed, with the floppy hat of an Australian soldier on it, plunged into the soil of Pozières to mark its capture in 1916. The soldier was killed, but this gesture was preserved. There was also the silver hunting horn which Colonel J. V. Campbell used to rally the Coldstream Guards during the Battle of the Somme.[88]

The series of patriotic expositions organized or sponsored by the burgeoning Imperial War Museum in 1918 were common to many other parts of Britain. Yet, it signalled the arrival of a new establishment on the London scene. What made London unique was its cultural institutions which provided the focus for cultural activity of many different kinds in wartime. However, as a newcomer, the war museum had yet to find a permanent home. In October 1918, city planners discussed a proposal that placed the war physically at the heart of the imperial city by rebuilding Westminster as an empire war memorial. The scheme (drafted by one Charles Pawley with the backing of Lord Leverhulme) envisaged an ideal city including an Empire Avenue, a war memorial chapel, and war memorial picture galleries in the rough triangle bounded by Vauxhall Bridge Road, Victoria Street, and Millbank–Whitehall. The projected building for the Imperial War Museum in Whitehall incorporated Inigo Jones's Banqueting House.[89] The overall plan would have literally imposed the *culture de guerre* on the cityscape of London, but in a manner unacceptable to most Londoners. It 'would, if carried out', a critic remarked, 'cover Westminster with a fine reminiscence of the "Siegesallee". If Major Pawley had propounded it as the German General Staff's scheme for remodelling a conquered London no one would have been greatly surprised.'[90]

After the Armistice, objects and collections poured steadily into the new museum. It acquired the Ministry of Information's rich collection of artworks, including paintings, sculptures, and posters, and its library also grew exponentially. A mere fraction of these items was on display when the institution was formally inaugurated, in the presence of the King and

---

[87] Kavanagh, 'Museum as memorial', p. 90.

[88] 'Modern war methods', *The Times*, 41681, 8 January 1918, p. 3.

[89] 'Proposed empire war memorial', *Builder*, 115 (1918), p. 278; 'The empire war memorial for London', *Building News*, 115 (1918), pp. 286–7; generally, see David Gilbert, '*London of the Future*. The metropolis reimagined after the Great War', *Journal of British Studies*, 43 (2004), pp. 91–119.

[90] Lawrence Weaver, 'Westminster Abbey and Major Pawley', *Outlook*, 43 (1919), p. 395.

Queen on 9 June 1920 in its temporary home in the rebuilt Crystal Palace at Sydenham.[91] The Crystal Palace was a meaningful setting, which exemplifies how metropolitan nostalgia was triggered by particular sites. The symbol of the Great Exhibition of 1851, and place of the colonial exhibitions of 1905 and 1911, this glasshouse had been used as a naval supply depot during the Great War.[92] There George V referred back to the idea that the empire's war museum was a memorial to the sacrifices made in the struggle for a 'democratic victory'.

The museum boasted looted weapons, but also hinted at the carnage which hit virtually every household in Britain. There were a Cenotaph Court with the top half of Edwin Lutyens's temporary monument for Whitehall and a Women's War Shrine reminiscent of an altar flanked by a sculpture of Edith Cavell by Sir George Frampton.[93] What is more, the museum's stores contain, to this day, thousands of portrait photographs of men killed in the war, mounted on card and filed alphabetically. These were originally sent at the request of the museum by the bereaved. The initial idea had been to obtain a portrait photograph of every single soldier serving. Overwhelmed by the enormity of the project, the curators failed to find an exhibition space for this moving collection.[94] Nevertheless, the hidden portrait photographs are a powerful reminder of the way in which the relatives of servicemen came to see the museum; for them, this was a site of memory that located family stories in bigger, more universal narratives. The curators had, probably, a very similar conception of their task. Consider a photograph kept in the museum's archives. It shows a women holding up a small child so that it has a better view of the portrait painting of a soldier exhibited at the museum. The caption suggests that the child recognizes a relative in uniform.[95]

The masterminds behind Britain's war museum had been inspired by the repository of wartime records collected by the Leblancs in Paris.[96] Both were hybrids between archive, library, museum, and memorial. At the Bibliothèque et musée de la guerre documentation soon took precedence over commemoration. Like its Berlin sister, the *Weltkriegsbücherei*, the Leblanc collection became primarily a research library. To be sure, the

[91] Kavanagh, 'Museum as memorial', p. 94.
[92] Auerbach, *The Great Exhibition*, pp. 210–11.
[93] Malvern, 'War, memory and museums', pp. 185–7.
[94] Catherine Moriarty, ' "Though in a picture only". Portrait photography and the commemoration of the First World War', in Gail Braybon (ed.), *Evidence, history and the Great War. Historians and the impact of 1914–18* (New York and Oxford, 2003), p. 38.
[95] IWM, Photograph Archive, Q. 31176, 'A child recognizes a relative in Photographic Galleries at 10 Coventry Street', n.d.
[96] Kavanagh, *Museums*, pp. 123, 131.

Fig. 5.3. Exhibition of war photographs at the Imperial War Museum: a child identifies a relative.

underlying tension between storehouse of artefacts and site of remembrance was never resolved at the Imperial War Museum either, yet, in the initial phase, it was clearly projected as a memorial. In terms of its memorial character and national scale, it equalled the Reich War Museum. Like its German equivalent, the Imperial War Museum was embedded in a nineteenth-century *lieu de mémoire* and fulfilled a double task: the commemoration of the war dead and the celebration of wartime unity. Unity, however, connoted the empire in London, and the Reich in Berlin.

The Natural History Museum and the Victoria and Albert Museum in South Kensington, as well as the British Museum in Bloomsbury were all celebrations of both national and imperial grandeur. What was the Rosetta Stone doing in Bloomsbury, if not testifying to the history of the imperial presence in Egypt, a presence first occupied by the French, and then forcibly by the British?

The British Museum was a London fixture and an imperial beacon. Its exhibitions were among the glories of the realm, in defence of which six million British men had been mobilized. It is surprising, therefore, to note the indifference, bordering on the callous, marking government dealings with this museum, among others in wartime London.[97]

The need for simple cost-cutting might be sufficient to explain why ministers of various political persuasions thought that the British Museum was an expendable asset in wartime. But there was, too, a sense that cultural life was not necessary for war-related work, and that if a man or woman wanted to renew his or her spirits after a dozen hours in war office or factory, then that was a private matter.

In March 1916, the exhibition galleries of the British Museum closed. Many of the most precious possessions were relocated, rare books in the National Library of Wales in Aberystwyth, and removable antiquities (including the Rosetta Stone and the Parthenon friezes) in an underground tunnel in Holborn. In their place, all kinds of people and objects were stored in the museum. The effects of interned Germans from the Cameroons and other German colonies found a home in the British Museum, making it resemble, in the words of the director, nothing so much as the 'left-luggage office of a London terminus'.[98] With great difficulty, the director and his allies fought off an attempt to house the Air Board in the Bloomsbury buildings, a move which made administrative

---

[97] 'National thrift', *The Times*, 41067, 19 January 1916, p. 5; *Parliamentary debates. House of Commons official report*, 5th ser., vol. 80, 6th session (1916), cols. 422–3, 1291–308.

[98] Frederic G. Kenyon, *The British Museum in war time. Being the fourth lecture on the David Murray Foundation in the University of Glasgow delivered on June 11th, 1934* (Glasgow, 1934), p. 19.

sense, but which would have made the museum a legitimate military target.[99] In the end, the move was blocked, not without difficulty, but that it nearly came off tells us much about the marginal place traditional museums occupied in official thinking in wartime London.

In January 1916, the chairman of a committee set up to reduce the civil service estimates, delivered a public speech on the importance of national thrift. Some of the interests affected by cost-cutting, he complained, seemed to forget Britain was at war. 'All museums were shut in Paris, but for 16 months of the war rows of policemen and officials trooped into London museums, despite a dwindling attendance.'[100] The stenographer noted laughter at this point. But did the audience laugh about the absurdity of the situation in London or about the absurdity of the speaker's statement? Newspaper readers knew very well that since the outbreak of war the number of visitors to London museums had actually shown in some cases a tendency to increase as compared to peace time. What is more, the London press had just reported on a proposed partial reopening of the Louvre.[101]

An international magnet for lovers of art, high-brow tourists, and art historians alike, the wartime fate of Paris's most magnificent museum was in the world's public eye.[102] Although the Louvre's masterworks were removed from the galleries for safe-keeping in September 1914, they continued to arrest contemporaries' imagination. As images they lived on in Europe's cultural memory. During the war, international art journalists rather than the museum's custodians assumed the role of guardians of this cultural repository of images. In Britain, *The Times* had reassured its readers in October 1914 that precautions to protect the Louvre's chief treasures had been most carefully executed.[103] However, the German art journal *Der Cicerone* noted in 1916 – partly out of spite, partly out of sincere concern about the condition of the artworks – that a number of pieces from the Louvre had suffered severely during the transport from Paris to the south of France two years earlier.[104]

Only the most spectacular exhibits had left the capital for safer places; others had simply been removed from the public galleries to the dark

[99] Ibid., pp. 23–8; John Sandys (ed.), *The British Museum. A selection from numerous signed letters, and from leading articles, and resolutions of learned societies [...] protesting against the proposal for taking over the British Museum as offices for the Air-Board and for other purposes of war* (Cambridge, rev. edn 1919); 'Attempted usurpation of the British Museum', *Museums Journal*, 17 (1917–18), pp. 97–8.

[100] 'National thrift', *The Times*, 41067, 19 January 1916, p. 5.

[101] 'General closing of museums', *The Times*, 41071, 24 January 1916, p. 5.

[102] M. H. Spielmann, 'Museums in Paris' (letter to the editor), *The Times*, 41678, 4 January 1918, p. 7.

[103] 'Safeguarding the Louvre', *The Times*, 40674, 23 October 1914, p. 7.

[104] O. G[rauthoff], 'Paris', *Der Cicerone*, 8 (1916), p. 111.

vaults of Paris. By 1918, the undercrofts of both the Louvre and the Panthéon were piled with notable artworks. The Panthéon, in particular, was transformed into a refuge for the material remains of France's past, housing statues from the Luxembourg Museum alongside lustres from the Château de Compiègne and stained glass from Reims Cathedral. This unlikely ensemble was, in the words of L'Illustration, 'un nouvel abri pour les dieux en exil, condamnés à l'humiliation de fuir la foudre des hommes'. Even in a state of 'pittoresque désordre', this collection did not fail to capture the imagination of the (privileged) visitor: 'voici le grand christ de bronze que la férocité des hommes a fait descendre une seconde fois au tombeau, jusqu'au jour de la résurrection de la paix sur la terre'.[105] Closed to the general public, the Parisian press, however, took its readers on virtual tours of this exquisite subterranean museum.

The removal of the chief treasures from Parisian museums for safe-keeping left a noticeable gap in the exhibition halls of the capital, a gap that the French government and museum curators attempted to fill with new, war-related displays. September 1916 saw the opening by President Poincaré of an exhibition of official war photographs at the Louvre. Organized by the government, the photographs documented the war effort of both France and her allies. The British War Office contributed two hundred pictures (shots of torpedo-boats, aeroplanes, the King and his generals among others) which had first been displayed at the head-quarters of the Ministry of Munitions. Together with the photographic collection, the War Office sent over a piece of a propeller of a German Zeppelin shot down at Cuffley in Hertfordshire.[106]

While the Louvre never ceased to be a museum during the war (despite temporary closure, it even continued acquiring new collections),[107] the very existence of the British Museum was called into question in 1916. The desecration of a national shrine was a measure so drastic that any French official would have refused to entertain it, but in London it became a reality. However, the launch of the Imperial War Museum opened up new perspectives. In 1917, the Royal Institute of British Architects suggested including the war museum as a part in the projected extension of the British Museum, effectively killing two birds with one stone. In the additional galleries important war trophies could be housed, thus giving the old institution a new significance. Widely discussed in

---

[105] 'Panthéon de guerre', L'Illustration, 152 (1918), p. 243; 'Les trésors du Louvre mis a l'abri des bombardements', L'Illustration, 151 (1918), pp. 561–2.

[106] 'War picture gallery', The Times, 41276, 19 September 1916, p. 5.

[107] Georges Rémond, 'Au musée du Louvre', L'Illustration, 153 (1919), pp. 184–8; 'Le Louvre rouvert ses portes', ibid., pp. 61–4.

architectural circles, this idea never came to fruition.[108] Meanwhile, the staff of the British Museum bent but did not break under the pressure. They organized a temporary exhibition, attended by a hundred thousand people between August and November 1918. In it were exhibits showing the glories of Britain and its empire and the perfidy of Germany, through images of the coins and medals struck in wartime to celebrate particular brutal acts such as the sinking of the *Lusitania*.[109] Signifying practices of this kind showed clearly the narrowing field of vision of cultural work in wartime London.

Galleries and the art market

'London ... is practically denied the use of its great museums, not through any indication of a failure in the interest of the public, but merely because the Government in its wisdom decided to close them.'[110] Thus concluded the president of the Museums Association in summer 1916. The Tate Gallery, the National Portrait Gallery, and the Wallace Collection were shut; the Victoria and Albert Museum was partly closed; the National Gallery remained open, yet its most important paintings were stored away in strong rooms. All purchase grants were suspended.

The crisis, however, was not confined to the national museums. When we turn from public institutions to the world of commercial art, we enter a field where the market dominated. And given the constraints of that wartime market, the business of art took a beating after 1914. Gallery owners were hard hit, and made – like museum directors – every effort to generate a link between the work they displayed and the war effort. Likewise, auctioneers had to establish their wartime credentials. At Christie's, for example, the Red Cross held a series of benevolent auctions between 1915 and 1919.[111] Yet the primary losers were artists themselves, especially the young, unable to secure patronage or sufficient sales to keep their work going.

What this economic constraint did to the production and consumption of art in London is a complex question. First, it seemed to make experimental or avant-garde art less attractive than it had been before 1914. Figurative art was easier to sell, and therefore safer to produce. What we have called in this

---

[108] 'The British Museum proposal', *Builder*, 113 (1917), pp. 178–9; 'The war museum again', *Builder*, 113 (1917), p. 198.

[109] Kenyon, *British Museum*, pp. 34–5, 40; *A short guide to the temporary war-time exhibition in the British Museum* (London, 1918).

[110] E. Rimbault Dibdin, 'Presidential address', *Museums Journal*, 16 (1916–17), p. 32.

[111] 'Third Red Cross sale', 41370, *The Times*, 8 January 1917, p. 11; 'Red Cross silver', *The Times*, 42053, 20 March 1919, p. 13.

volume 'metropolitan nostalgia' had its equivalent here, in that works of art of a familiar or conventional kind sold in wartime. Market pressure turned the clock back on cultural innovation; it pushed artists away from the abstract and back to the figurative. It is important to note, though, that there was still room for iconoclasm in the London art world. Ironically, it was the cost-conscious authorities which created, as we shall see, a niche for experimental art by seconding talented painters to the propaganda bureau.

The second dimension of nostalgia which had a metropolitan dimension in wartime art was the renewed and deepened quest for works that embodied what Nikolaus Pevsner later called the 'Englishness of English art'. Much comment about art dealt with its capacity to isolate and express facets of Englishness which were taken to be essential to the war effort, especially at the front. Not everyone, it was suggested, could grasp these features of national character; by implication, only those born in Britain could do so. This kind of nativism helped to nationalize art, and make it the product of the native-born population. Such chauvinism, occasionally shading into anti-Semitism, had its critics, to be sure, but it pointed to a narrowing of the space available for independent and iconoclastic painting and sculpture in wartime. The world of exhibitions reflected these very material developments.

Exhibitions represented a taxonomy of 'our' side versus 'theirs', but, at times, the crusade for 'English art' was culturally integrative rather than exclusive. This led to a plethora of displays of the art of the Allies in London.[112] Not only did such exhibitions promote solidarity among the Allies, but they also provided a framework for the argument that English artists were, through their art, defending the Allied cause just as were French, Russian, Belgian, Italian, or Serbian artists.[113] A second concentric circle was drawn around the work of English and Dominion war artists, in particular the Australians, and the Canadians.[114] Sir Max Aitken, the Canadian-born Conservative MP and owner of the *Daily Express*, was named Lord Beaverbrook in 1917 and Minister of Information in 1918. He was the moving force behind the Canadian War Memorials Exhibition, opened at Burlington House on 4 January 1919.[115] Over 400 paintings illustrating the Canadian war effort were on display. Lord Beaverbrook was a powerful patron of war artists, and the

[112] 'Guildhall war pictures', *Daily Telegraph*, 18846, 6 September 1915, p. 7.
[113] 'Art at the front', *The Times*, 41799, 25 May 1918, p. 9.
[114] 'Battle scenes', *The Times*, 41799, 25 May 1918, p. 9; Maria Tippett, *Art at service of war. Canada, art, and the Great War* (Toronto and London, 1984); Meirion and Susie Harries, *The war artists. British official war art of the twentieth century* (London, 1983).
[115] 'War story in pictures', *The Times*, 41989, 4 January 1919, p. 9; Royal Academy of Arts, *Canadian War Memorials Exhibition* (London, 1919).

guiding force behind the Canadian War Records Office, whose work laid the foundations for the creation of the Canadian War Museum in Ottawa. Beaverbrook himself selected twenty-five artists in uniform to express in pictorial art their own individual ideas, notions, and views of war. This was an essential component of propaganda, he said. 'Pictures were an excellent way of appealing to the public. Through the eye they reached the minds of men and brought home to them a realization of the things we were striving for.'[116] Moreover, official war art was essential to overcome the acute shortage of visual material from the front.

Beaverbrook commissioned English-born painters to work for the Canadian War Records Office, again highlighting the imperial character of both the war effort and its artistic representation. In 1918, as Minister of Information, he also set up a British rival scheme, the British War Memorials Committee (later renamed Pictorial Propaganda Committee).[117]

Among the painters involved in both the Canadian and the British schemes was C. R. W. Nevinson, an exhibition of whose works the propaganda minister opened at the Leicester Galleries on 2 March 1918; Nevinson was also represented in an exhibition of war pictures by British artists shown in the Luxembourg Museum in Paris later in the same week.[118] London-born and bred, Nevinson was the son of the radical journalist Henry Nevinson and his wife Margaret, both active in reforming London before the war. He studied first at the Slade School of Fine Art, where he met Mark Gertler and Stanley Spencer, and then in Paris. After the outbreak of war, as a conscientious objector, he volunteered for the Red Cross. He worked as a stretcher-bearer and orderly, and then in 1915 joined the Royal Army Medical Corps. He helped care for seriously wounded men at the Third General Hospital in London, until he contracted rheumatic fever and was invalided out of the army in 1916.

An exhibition of his paintings in London in 1916 brought his work to the attention of the Liberal politician Charles Masterman, who was running the government's war propaganda bureau at Wellington House. Nevinson was commissioned as an official war artist and sent back to France. He produced sixty paintings in this period, and showed

---

[116] 'Battle pictures', *The Times*, 41727, 2 March 1918, p. 3.
[117] Sue Malvern, *Modern art, Britain, and the Great War. Witnessing, testimony and remembrance* (New Haven, 2004), ch. 3.
[118] 'War realism by a former futurist', *Illustrated London News*, 152 (1918), pp. 272–3; 'Imperial and foreign news items', *The Times*, 41732, 8 March 1918, p. 5; see also Michael J. K. Walsh, *C. R. W. Nevinson. This cult of violence* (New Haven and London, 2002), pp. 164–83.

many of them at the Leicester Galleries in March 1918. One of his paintings was so troubling to those who commissioned him, that it was displayed with a diagonal notice on it, saying 'Censored'.[119] What is most striking about this exhibition is that it included Nevinson's painting, even though it was clearly offensive, and labelled so. On this painting, visitors to the gallery were shown the limits of the public expression of artistic sentiment. Nevinson had the authority of direct experience as his shield; he had seen what he had painted, and though the sensitive needed to be protected from such sights, the painting was not suppressed. In fact, it was purchased along with seven others in the exhibition by the trustees of the Imperial War Museum. What helps to account for this partial freedom enjoyed by Nevinson and others is that their paintings were memorials as much as representations of war. The uneasy balance between the two marked all public exhibitions of war art at the time.

After the war, exhibitions of war art, filled with complex images of the battlefield, continued to attract the London public. On 12 December 1919, the Royal Academy of Arts displayed the works of war artists, including those of Stanley Spencer, whose pictures were described in *The Times* 'as a kind of dance', a choreography of the arrival of the wounded at a dressing station in Mesopotamia. The work of men like Spencer, who had seen what war was, constituted, so the newspaper's critic said, a kind of 'revolution' in painting.[120] The same quality was appreciated in another painting in the exhibition, Wyndham Lewis's 'Battery Shelled', a kind of symphonic poem, through which one could 'almost see and hear the shells'. Equally iconoclastic was Paul Nash's 'The Menin Road', with its 'strange, unexpected trails of desolation . . . something made by man and yet surprising to him, as if the earth cried out at his inhumanity'. In short, the exhibition marked a set of bold departures. 'What we would insist upon in the exhibition is the promise of something much richer, more interesting, more spiritual, than has been in English painting since the Middle Ages.'[121]

This notion that the war stripped away convention to expose a more English kind of English art was characteristic of other parts of the London art scene in wartime, too. When Eric Kennington's 'The Kensingtons at Laventie' was displayed at the Goupil Gallery – proceeds to go to the Star and Garter building fund for severely disabled soldiers – art critics hailed

---

[119] The censored image was reproduced in *Daily Mail*, 6836, 2 March 1918, p. 4; see also Malvern, *Modern art*, pp. 45, 52–3.

[120] 'Art's fresh start', *The Times*, 42281, 19 December 1919, p. 15.

[121] Ibid.; on Lewis, see David Peters Corbett (ed.), *Wyndham Lewis and the art of modern war* (Cambridge, 1998).

it as a miracle of English art. No romance here; the artist has painted what he saw – ordinary men, whose dignity and sense of common cause and duty survived the hardships and weariness they had endured. The painting was 'like the best of English pre-Raphaelite pictures, and here, we may say, English art has become itself again. It is a picture of Englishmen, and of the manner and spirit in which they fight.'[122] 'Soldiers Painted by a Soldier' was the title of an account of one of Kennington's later exhibitions.[123] The title captured the respect war artists commanded. They could speak of Englishness through their art in a way that non-combatants could not do. This distinction was essential to an understanding of the reception of the work of other artists who did not serve during the war. Their position was more exposed to criticism.

One such case is that of the American-born sculptor, Jacob Epstein, who settled in London in 1905 and became a naturalized British subject in 1911. He redesigned a sculpture entitled 'Rock Drill' during the war, eliding completely the human and the inorganic. It was hard to miss the reference to what the war was doing to human beings. But Epstein was not a soldier, not a true-born Englishman, and not a Christian.

All three negative attributes made him anathema to one spokesman of English art, the symbolist sculptor and craftsman Sir George Frampton. It is difficult to distinguish between genuine artistic difference between the two and pure irrationality, but Frampton made it his business to stop Epstein from gaining any commissions during the war.[124] He wrote a letter to the editor of *The Times* on 26 July 1916, claiming that the absence of artists on duty at the front – the first official war artists were not appointed until late in 1916 – opened the door to other, lesser men receiving commissions for commemorative work.

There is a grave danger that whilst these brave men are doing their duty in the fighting line aliens – though naturalized – may be given a preference and allowed to suck the juice from the grape (which should be the birthright of our own flesh and blood), leaving but the dry husk to the men of our race, whose development we have watched with such pride and pleasure.[125]

Leaving artist's egos and exaggeration aside, the incident does raise three issues which framed the nature of exhibitions in wartime. The first was their status as sites for the work of men in uniform, or men who saw

---

[122] 'A real war picture', *The Times*, 41172, 20 May 1916, p. 9.
[123] 'Soldiers painted by a soldier', *The Times*, 41818, 17 June 1918, p. 11.
[124] Stephen Gardiner, *Epstein. Artist against the establishment* (London, 1992), pp. 180–2; King, *Memorials of the Great War*, p. 156.
[125] George Frampton, 'War memorials', *The Times*, 41542, 28 July 1917, p. 9; see John Drinkwater, 'War memorials', *Burlington Magazine*, 31 (1917), pp. 126–7.

the war at the front. The taxonomy is here between those who were there, and those who were not. The second point which emerges from the Frampton–Epstein quarrel is how easily such distinctions elided with ones about Englishness and who had the right to express it. Epstein was an iconoclast, and Frampton was not. There was space for both in the London art world, but the tension between the two describes a wider set of tensions in the art world as a whole. The third point relates to the wartime market for art. Much exhibition work looked back to a happier time, or simply affirmed a common past for which the British army was fighting. This was the domain of the Framptons of the art world. But as the numerous reports in the London press indicate, there was space, too, for the more adventurous, the more daring, the more shocking. When the iconoclasts wore uniform, they were immune from most criticism. But those who remained civilians were not so fortunate, either in terms of reception or in terms of livelihood. The war was harsh for everyone, but market pressure made it less harsh for the conventional and harsher for the experimenters.

Berlin's experimenters, by contrast, were often only too eager to fall into line with the wartime mainstream, pronouncing the Germanic qualities of their art. In the heyday of 'German' art in autumn 1914, modernists like Adolf Behne were in the vanguard of the nationalization of art. In Berlin, nostalgic yearning for the national spirit was by no means exclusive to the traditionalist camp. Leaders of various factions – the Royal Academy, Secession, Free Secession, among others – set aside their differences to proclaim the 'irreplaceable value of German art' for the 'verve of the nation'. In an effort to suit the actions to the words, they set up a war aid fund in September 1914 in support of local artists especially hit by the war.[126] Over the coming months, displays of artistic and patriotic solidarity became a common sight in the capital. Retrospective shows for German artists drew crowds to the salons of the city's Impressionist art dealers, who had but recently come under fire from cultural nationalists for their role in creating the fin-de-siècle 'fad' for 'decadent', 'foreign', and above all French paintings.[127]

Calls for a united, monumentalizing 'German style' mirrored the quest for Englishness in London studios and exhibition halls. In search of German art, advocates of both fine and commercial arts vied to denounce

---

[126] 'Allgemeine Sozialpolitik', *Soziale Praxis*, 26 (1914), p. 6.

[127] E. Plietzsch, 'Ausstellung deutscher Meisterwerke des 19. Jahrhunderts im Salon Gurlitt-Berlin', *Die Kunst*, 31 (1914–15), pp. 270–7; 'Von Ausstellungen', *Die Kunst*, 33 (1915–16), pp. 162–3; Ignaz Beth, 'Berliner Ausstellungen', *Die Kunst für alle*, 32 (1916), pp. 390–1; Adolf Behne, 'Dürfen wir uns noch mit Kunst beschäftigen', *Sozialistische Monatshefte*, 20 (1914), pp. 1181–4.

the impotence of *l'art pour l'art* and to assert the seriousness of their engagement in a life-and-death struggle for the present. Inspired by the Kaiser's declaration that he knew no parties but only Germans after the outbreak of war, the Royal Academy invited the Secession – once denounced by Wilhelm II as a refuge for 'gutter art' – to display works in the winter show of war pictures held at its exalted rooms on Pariser Platz.[128] Charity balls, benefit shows, and raffles helped pay for studio space, art supplies, job listings, even soup kitchens and shelters in an outpouring of public sympathy. City hall also chipped in, allocating 25,000 Marks 'war aid for the support of needy artists' and another 12,000 for the Grand Berlin Art Show. By the following winter, the artists' war aid fund had gathered almost 80,000 Marks for the cause on its own.[129]

Yet, despite such shows of solidarity, the outbreak of war in 1914 did not – could not – erase the deep pre-war antagonisms that continued to divide the Berlin art world. Angry tensions between young and old, Expressionist and Impressionist, pure and applied arts, which had emerged in the last decades of peace, remained strong and indeed grew stronger as the war appeared to raise the stakes of contestation.[130] Far from bringing these conflicting parties together in a civic peace grounded in cultural nationalism, the impact of the Great War exacerbated tensions within the Berlin art world for three main reasons. First, the war demanded severing the very ties to European art markets and international commerce that had put Berlin on the map as a centre of artistic and cultural production alongside Paris and London since the turn of the century.[131] While the concentration of national resources in the capital might serve to sustain centralization of the arts within Germany, the forced autarky brought on by the war was anathema to the city's artistic functions, and therefore to the interests of partisans on all sides. This is certainly not to say that outbursts of cultural xenophobia were unknown

---

[128] Wilhelm von Bode, 'Hoffnungen und Aussichten für die deutsche Kunst nach dem Krieg', *Die Kunst*, 31 (1914–15), p. 332; Wolfgang J. Mommsen, 'Die Herausforderung der bürgerlichen Kultur durch die künstlerische Avantgarde. Zum Verhältnis von Kultur und Politik im Wilhelminischen Deutschland', *Geschichte und Gesellschaft*, 20 (1994), pp. 424–44.

[129] Bruno Rauecker, 'Zur wirtschaftlichen Lage der bildenden Künstler', *Soziale Praxis*, 25 (1916), pp. 459–61; 'Zur Kriegsnotlage der Künstler', *Der Kunstwart*, 28 (1914–15), p. 103.

[130] von Bode, 'Hoffnungen und Aussichten für die deutsche Kunst nach dem Krieg', p. 332.

[131] Robert Jensen, *Marketing modernism in fin-de-siècle Europe* (Princeton, 1994), esp. pp. 67–80, 187–219; see also Peter Paret, *The Berlin Secession. Modernism and its enemies in Imperial Germany* (Cambridge, Mass., 1980).

early in the war. Shortly after his election as president of the Secession, Lovis Corinth attacked the 'perverse frivolity' of Paris fashions and rejoiced that 'a wall of warriors' now stood guard along the borders of 'the holy Fatherland'.[132] Yet among insiders in the Berlin art world, such outbursts were remarkably rare.

The second major obstacle to *Burgfrieden* among its various factions lay in the distance between home front and front lines, in the displacement of the Reich capital, especially in its cultural pretensions, from centre to periphery in the German national consciousness. The most palpable and visible indication of this shift in priorities came with the immediate loss of the Moabit Exhibition Palace which had been commandeered for military purposes during the mobilization, forcing the annual Grand Berlin Art Show to squeeze into the smaller rooms of the Royal Academy. After being allowed to return the following year, the Grand Berliner had to move again in 1917, when it was held in Düsseldorf and without its popular exhibits of Berlin sculpture, which could not be shipped due to the transport emergency.[133]

The precarious position of Berlin's cosmopolitan art world was all too obvious to insiders, who feared the war would make art appear superfluous and perhaps even traitorous under conditions such as these. Given this fear, visibly surmounting the distance between the home and battle fronts thus quickly became the most urgent and singularly important legitimizing function of Berlin's exhibition system. Images of battlefields, desolated villages, marching soldiers, and officers in field grey poured into public and private display rooms throughout the city. In addition to the war pictures show held at the Royal Academy in the winter of 1914–15, the Free Secession organized an exhibition on 'Art in War' in its new rooms on the Kurfürstendamm while the 1915 Grand Berliner on Pariser Platz featured two rooms of war pictures. Private dealers such as Cornelius Gurlitt, Paul Cassirer, and Schulte featured artists who died in combat, while Berlin artists scrambled to transform old landscapes into war scenes by painting in 'a few soldiers' or by adding a sabre to polo players.[134]

---

[132] Lovis Corinth, 'An die Herren der neutralen Presse', *Velhagen & Klasings Monatshefte*, 30 (1915–16), pp. 203–4.

[133] E. Plietzsch, 'Die Große Berliner Kunstausstellung 1915', *Die Kunst*, 33 (1915–16); Walter Cohen, 'Die Große Berliner Kunstausstellung in Düsseldorf', *Die Kunst*, 35 (1916–17), pp. 457–8, 472.

[134] Julius Elias, 'Deutsche Kunst 1916', *Neue Rundschau*, 27 (1916), pp. 975–6; 'Kriegsbilderausstellung in Berlin', *Die Kunst*, 33 (1915–16), pp. 314–15; Ignaz Beth, 'Die Grosse Berliner Kunstausstellung', *Die Kunst*, 33 (1915–16), pp. 434, 439–40; E. Plietzsch, 'Ausstellung der Königlichen Akademie der Künste zu Berlin', *Die Kunst*, 31 (1914–15), pp. 336–41.

By far the most widely acclaimed new talent in the race to supply Berliners with an authentic link to the battlefield via artistic representation was Ludwig Dettmann, a previously unknown forty-year-old graphic artist who had rushed to the Eastern front in 1914 and sent back over a hundred drawings in time for them to be displayed in the Academy's war pictures show. Already a sensation during the first winter of combat, Dettmann's 'war impressionism' became a staple of exhibitions in Berlin throughout the war, even after initial enthusiasm for such spectacles quickly waned. In contrast to the pomposity of the Academy, what critics especially liked in Dettmann's pictures was his 'pathos' in confronting the ugly realities of 'study materials ... more fragmentary and coarse than can be conceived'.[135] They particularly lauded the novice's evocative portrayal of the 'dark sides' of war: his gritty naturalism, quick strokes in 'forceful yellow and burning red', and the use of symbol to evoke the uncanny.[136]

In terms of style, Dettmann was neither as radical an artist as Nevinson, nor was he, as an independent painter, granted the immunity of an official war artist. On the contrary, his attempts at representing the nation at war attracted harsh criticism from the traditionalist circle around Wilhelm von Bode, director of the Kaiser-Friedrich-Museum, who accused Dettmann of 'pictorial excesses and rapes'.[137] Far from healing wounds from past battles, the mounting pressure to bridge the gap between home and front lines only intensified the dispute over technical mastery and artistic authenticity on both sides. Here tempers ran high and invectives ranged from complaints of opportunism and dilettantism to 'rape', 'prostitution', and downright treason.[138]

However bitterly Berlin's Academy, Secessions, Impressionists, Expressionists, Cubists, and many others may have fought over the stylistic right to represent the war, as champions of the fine arts all sides had a stake opposing the commercial artists, illustrators, graphic designers, and advertising specialists who stood to gain the most from the wartime mobilization of cultural production and spaces in the city. Dettmann himself was indeed 'merely' an illustrator, though his innovation in breaking through older models of battle depiction stemming from

---

[135] Elias, 'Deutsche Kunst', pp. 977–9.   [136] Ibid.

[137] Ignaz Beth, 'Von Ausstellungen und Sammlungen', *Die Kunst für alle*, supplement, 32 (1917), p. 241; Elias, 'Deutsche Kunst', pp. 983–4, 977–9; for more on the reception of Dettmann's war pictures, see Bode, 'Hoffnungen und Aussichten', p. 332; Plietzsch, 'Ausstellungen', p. 341; 'Kriegsbilderausstellung', pp. 314–15; Cohen, 'Grosse Berliner Kunstausstellung', p. 459; Ferdinand Avenarius, 'Kunstausstellungen', *Der Kunstwart*, 30 (1916–17), p. 51.

[138] Bode, 'Hoffnungen und Aussichten', p. 332.

the Franco-Prussian war won him recognition from most art critics (not, however, the venerable Bode).[139] Others who flooded the market with clichéd heroic representations of the war destined for quick consumption by the masses were not so lucky, but were ostracized by the artistic establishment.[140]

The boom in wartime kitsch – from oil portraits in field grey at up-market art salons to war-loan posters and iron-nail figures – brings us to the third major obstacle to *Burgfrieden* in the Berlin art world: commercial success. Contrary to all expectations, after a brief tightening of the market in the first months of the war, the demand for artworks in Berlin did not dry up as it did in London and Paris. Instead, prices for art objects of all kinds began to skyrocket at an alarming rate that could 'even shock the most cold-blooded auctioneer' by the spring of 1917. Considered by contemporaries one of the greatest surprises of the war, the paradoxical trend continued unabated until the collapse of the regime in 1918, fuelling a proliferation of sites for the display and sale of artworks of all kinds in a fit of *Ausstellungswut*, exhibition mania, that in turn mirrored the public interest and excitement Berlin's booming art market had attracted.[141]

Largely a result of the loss of German access to foreign markets through forced autarky and the subsequent flight of capital into domestic tax shelters, the sudden flow of money into the city's salons and exhibition halls was bound to destabilize the Berlin art world in ways that only aggravated pre-existing conflicts. On the one hand, the record sales achieved by established artists of the older generation – who found dealers eager to promote their works as 'safe investments' in lavish retrospective exhibitions – understandably stirred up resentment on part of the younger artists still struggling for recognition.[142] On the other hand, the unabashed commodification of exhibitions during the war clearly posed a danger to young and old alike, who staked both reputation and livelihood on maintaining the distinction between the

[139] See Frank Becker, *Bilder von Krieg und Nation. Die Einigungskriege in der bürgerlichen Öffentlichkeit Deutschlands 1864–1913* (Munich, 2001), on paintings of the Bismarckian wars.

[140] Beth, 'Ausstellungen und Sammlungen', pp. 241–2; G. I. Kern, 'Der Krieg und die deutsche Malerei', *Die Kunst*, 31 (1914–15), pp. 292–3.

[141] Lothar Brieger, 'Das Kunstsammeln', *Westermanns Monatshefte*, 124 (1918), p. 178; Emil Waldmann, 'Kunstauktionen', *Neue Rundschau*, 27 (1916), pp. 1642–3; Viktor Ottmann, 'Der deutsche Kunstmarkt im Kriege', *Die Woche*, 19 (1917), pp. 1303–4.

[142] 'Von Ausstellungen', *Die Kunst*, 33 (1915–16), p. 162; Ignaz Beth, 'Die "Freie Secession" 1917 in Berlin', *Die Kunst*, 37 (1917–18), p. 41; Ignaz Beth, 'Die Herbstausstellung der Berliner Secession', *Die Kunst*, 37 (1917–18), p. 113.

aesthetic purity and disinterestedness of the fine arts and the crass commercialization of wartime design.[143]

The carnivalesque, race-track-like atmosphere that intruded into Berlin's salon and exhibition hall posed a particularly subversive challenge to the sanctifying functions of these institutions, as insiders were all too keenly aware, threatening to blur the boundary between high and popular culture. If the Berliners' loss of the Moabit Exhibition Palace to military purposes was a concrete reminder of one danger the arts faced – impotence, isolation, insignificance vis-à-vis the German war effort – the opposing threat of absorption into popular commercial culture had its own corresponding symbol in another of the city's physical landmarks: the Free Secession's lavish new home on the Kurfürstendamm, which had been abandoned to auctions shortly after its completion early on in the war. More than one observer found the irony of this particular triumph of commercialism unusually rich, since the Free Secession had been founded only three years earlier as a pure artistic rebellion against the 'dictatorship of the art dealer'.[144]

Despite initial fears that the Great War would see the demise of the arts, exhibitions, dealerships, and private galleries thrived, garnering both fine and commercial arts a strong visual presence in the capital city that continued right through until the end of the *Kaiserreich* – and beyond. 'Whoever went through the streets of Berlin in the year of 1919, the year of tax-dodging "friends of art", could see an "art dealership" peering itself on almost every street corner', remarked the secretary of the National Economic Association of Artists in 1922.[145] Art galleries mushrooming over the city were a phenomenon peculiar to Berlin. The London art world, by contrast, was often on the verge of bankruptcy after 1914, and in Paris, in the small quarter around rue La Boëtie with its opulent galleries, the mood was equally sombre. Some revival was evident by 1917, and with the arrival of the Americans, and the recovery of the Paris art market after the scare of the Second Battle of the Marne, artists in London and Paris as well as elsewhere could finally earn a living again.[146]

Certainly not everyone in Berlin profited from the wartime boom as the commercial artists and well-established painters of reputation did nor was

---

[143] 'Hurrakitsch-Hochflut', p. 31; see also Jensen, *Marketing modernism*, pp. 91–10, 187–99.

[144] Beth, 'Herbstausstellung der Berliner Secession', p. 157.

[145] Fritz Hellwag, 'Die derzeitige wirtschaftliche Lage der bildenden Künstler', in Ernst Francke and Walther Lotz (eds.), *Die geistigen Arbeiter* (Munich and Leipzig, 1922), p. 166.

[146] Malcolm Gee, 'The avant-garde, order and the art market, 1916–23', *Art History*, 2 (1979), pp. 96–100; J. M. Winter, *The experience of World War One* (Basingstoke, 1988), p. 230.

cultural patriotism or the 'irreplaceable value' of 'German art' the basis for Berlin's booming art markets. 'The German art industry is establishing itself, but this nationalism is surely only a superficial and temporary sign', one critic observed, no doubt correctly, in 1916.[147] Neither pressures to bridge the gap between home front and battle front, and still far less common international commitments, could bring the diverse interests of the local art world to consensus. Driven by profits, the spectacular successes that made 'Berlin ... into a centre of artistic interest not unequal to a Paris or a London' proved in fact to be more divisive than unifying, aggravating old antagonisms – especially between young and old, commercial and fine art – that had already riven the art world of the German capital in the 'bad old days' before the 'spirit of 1914'.[148]

Conclusion

Exhibitions had been an integral part of the metropolitan environment before the First World War. They had functioned, in the words of one scholar, as 'venues of socially constructed, mediated, and consumed knowledge. Unlike the private act of reading, participation at the exhibition was a public and mass-oriented textual experience.'[149] After 1914, visual displays continued to be a powerful medium, combining war propaganda and popular entertainment at the same time. Wartime exhibitions were an influential and accessible mode of representing material and cognitive inventories that helped to structure the wartime world. The reduction of the complexities of total war to a strictly limited space was one of the ways city-dwellers tried to understand the dangerous world in which they lived. The history of wartime exhibitions illustrates the central contention of this volume, namely that contemporaries experienced and understood the global conflict and the national war effort through close reading within specific locales and venues.

Wartime exhibitions in London, Paris, and Berlin reconfigured physical space.[150] On the one hand, exhibitions in these cities bridged the distance between home and front. Sending a predominantly civilian audience on imaginary tours through space to the battlefields, wartime exhibitions represented a metropolitan window to a landscape unknown to most viewers. On the other hand, public displays inscribed new meanings on existing cityscapes. Firstly, the war years saw the spread of exhibition

---

[147] Elias, 'Deutsche Kunst', pp. 975–6.   [148] Brieger, 'Das Kunstsammeln', p. 178.
[149] Hoffenberg, *Empire on display*, p. xviii.
[150] Martin Baumeister, *Kriegstheater. Großstadt, Front und Massenkultur 1914–1918* (Essen, 2005).

activity into the open, spilling over into central squares like Königsplatz and Trafalgar Square. Notably, 'wandering tanks' in London, and iron-nail landmarks in Berlin mapped out a new geography of wartime fervour. Secondly, wartime exhibitions transformed nineteenth-century *lieux de mémoire* such as the Crystal Palace, the Panthéon, or the Siegessäule, sites resonant with images of military might and/or national grandeur. Thirdly, there was a noticeable militarization of established exhibition spaces. Not only did civic squares feature military hardware, but also national museums and privately owned exhibition venues (like art galleries and auction houses) turned to military and patriotic themes. Those who did not go with the tide like the British Museum or the Moabit Exhibition Palace faced the threat of closure or insignificance.

Our survey of wartime exhibitions points to a struggle for and reconfiguration of physical space available for cultural work in these cities. Space was a precious resource in all three wartime capitals, and the demands of both civilian and military authorities were enormous. Non-combatant institutions who staked a claim to the capital's spatial resources had to establish their wartime credentials. The political economy of urban space was governed by both official policy and commercial forces. The allocation of exhibition space through the government or the market reveals the unstable equilibrium of wartime cultural life: a paradoxical trend towards expansion in the field of cultural activity in general and a contraction in the field of cultural innovation in particular. Propaganda spectacles and patriotic kitsch flourished whereas the demand for or support of traditional exhibitions and experimental art declined. While the war set limits on what could be pictured and displayed, there remained, nevertheless, pockets of resistance which blossomed, sometimes even with official approval as in the case of the official war artists in London.

The comparative approach has shown that, in London, the wartime reconfiguration of urban space was most enduring. Even though the most visionary plan, the empire war memorial in Westminster was doomed from the start, the Great War changed the cultural topography of inter-war London. While the Reich War Museum at Berlin was never built, the Imperial War Museum (moving from Sydenham to South Kensington and eventually to Lambeth) became a new London fixture and imperial beacon that put the war on the city map. It institutionalized a window both metropolitan and national to a world dominated by loss and pain. Part of the museum's appeal was that it located family stories in bigger, more universal narratives that linked individual suffering to national and imperial survival. Characteristically, the war also featured prominently in the government's pavilion at the 1924 British Empire Exhibition at Wembley – an attempt to rekindle Britain's tradition of international fairs. Here the visitor could, for instance, witness a restaging of the 1918 raid on the German submarine base at Zeebrugge thus reminding 'him of the part that he played as a member of the Empire in the Great War'.[151]

Interestingly, exhibitions occupied a marginal place in the cityscape and cultural life of *the* erstwhile capital of grand exhibitions and the avant-garde: Paris displayed its cultural credentials in *fêtes patriotiques* rather than exhibitions. First, the expo as a cultural form, as an assertion of cosmopo-litanism, had a particularly Parisian history which made it impossible to renew it during the world war; second, due to the capital's proximity to the front, there was neither need nor desire to exhibit the war of *matériel* on a grand scale. By contrast, Berlin's geographical isolation made it necessary to hold large exhibitions that mediated distance between the front lines and the home front. The German capital, hitherto a city on the periphery of the international exhibition circuit, reinvented itself as a, if not the, major cultural centre in wartime. Art shows, patriotic expositions, and war land-marks helped the city to gain in national stature, especially vis-à-vis the Bavarian capital of art and exhibitions, Munich. In wartime, the Prussian capital matured into *the* hub of cultural work in Germany; the war marked a turning point in the cultural history of the city overlooked in most accounts of Berlin's meteoric rise in the legendary 1920s.

However, the ascent of Berlin to a truly German metropolis was a development concurrent with the severance of international ties. The war disrupted the cosmopolitan nature of pre-war exhibitions in Europe (as was most noticeable in the case of the disrupted series of Universal Exhibitions) and forced organizers and participants to conceive of cul-tural life in predominantly national (or nationalist) terms. Berlin exem-plifies this turning inward of exhibition and artistic activity under the impact of war. Cultural work after 1914 became increasingly introspec-tive and nationalized. Arguably, Berlin's wartime exhibitions achieved not only national fame but also international notoriety. London and Paris observed closely cultural events in Berlin; the international press invoked the 'Iron Hindenburg' and the *Deutsche Kriegsausstellung* as negative foils or held them up to ridicule. In doing so, it recognized Berlin as Germany's cultural centre. Thus the metropolitan exhibition functioned, at least for the outsider, as a gateway to the nation's cultural life.

---

[151] *The pavilion of H.M. Government. A brief record of official participation in the British Empire Exhibition, Wembley, 1924* (London, [1924]), n.p.; on the exhibition generally, see Alexander C. T. Geppert, 'True copies. Time and space travels at British imperial exhibitions, 1880–1930', in Hartmut Berghoff, Barbara Korte, Ralf Schneider, and Christopher Harvie (eds.), *The making of modern tourism. The cultural history of the British experience, 1600–2000* (Basingstoke, 2002), pp. 223–47.

6   Schools

Stefan Goebel

The history of schools in Paris, London, and Berlin between 1914 and 1918 illustrates the double burden of maintaining a semblance of 'business as usual', while mobilizing the youngest members of the metropolitan community to fight the war. Schools had to devote most of their energies to educating children and accomplishing that under conditions of material and staffing shortages, not to mention emotional duress. By examining how this was accomplished, our analysis will add another dimension to our understanding of the quotidian life of the capitals during the war. Particularly, in elementary schools – the main focus of this chapter – we see schools educating and protecting children and thus, to a certain extent, insulating them from the war. Yet, at the same time, schools were used to inculcate patriotism and to build a supportive home front. This balancing act had to be performed in all three capital cities, but the school systems faced different challenges and responded differently even to similar circumstances.

Schools represented a social crossroads where the agendas and relationships of the larger society had to be negotiated and where the national and local state had to join forces with the local community and both had to work with and through the powerful mediation of the teacher. This chapter explores both the impact of war on normal school functions and also compares the production, adaptation, and consumption of representations of war in very specific material settings. In particular, it aims to show how the 'child army' (to cite one London teacher) was drawn into the logic of total war.[1] To this end, we concentrate on two sets of representations. First, we discuss the cultural fabric of the wartime community, showing how social inclusion and exclusion operated through rituals of cultural

Stefan Goebel wrote this chapter, with Eberhard Demm, Elise Julien, and Dina Copelman.
[1] 'School attendance', *London Teacher and London Schools Review* (hereafter *LT*), 34 (1917), p. 121. Special thanks are due to Aribert Reimann for providing us with important source material on Berlin schools.

alliances and representations of the enemy other. Second, since the war blurred older demarcations between the civilian and military spheres, we examine how schools helped to bridge the gap between home and front and conveyed the 'home-front experience' to children. Throughout our account one theme in particular is central: the meaning of citizenship and civic responsibility under the impact of total war.

Education: disrupted and continued

The educational systems

On the eve of the war, the populations of the three capital cities were younger than those of the nations to which they belonged. London, in particular, was a city of youngsters. 38 per cent Londoners were under the age of twenty compared with 33 per cent of Berliners and 25 per cent of Parisians.[2] Under the Education Act of 1902, the London County Council (LCC) was to exercise its extensive powers through an Education Committee of 97 members, consisting of 36 elected members, 36 representatives of the metropolitan councils, and 25 co-opted educational 'experts'. Although it was less independent and democratic than its predecessor, the School Board for London set up in 1870, the LCC Education Committee was a more transparent body than other Council committees; its minutes were printed and placed on public sale.

The LCC had oversight not only over all the state elementary and secondary schools (583 schools with 593,024 pupils in December 1914) but also the independent schools (364 schools with 139,883 pupils in December 1914) ranging from confessional schools and endowed grammar schools to a small number of elite 'public schools' (private, fee-paying establishments, in spite of their name) with boarding facilities.[3] In addition, neighbouring county councils such as Essex and Middlesex supervised some metropolitan and suburban schools, while the ancient Corporation of the City of London administered five establishments within the City's square mile. Almost all state elementary schools were de facto three schools housed in one building divided into infants', girls', and boys' departments. Although many schools took younger children in special 'babies' classes, the infants' departments enrolled children over the age of

---

[2] *Capital cities*, vol. I, pp. 30–2, 78.

[3] 'The London County Council', *Times Educational Supplement* (hereafter *TES*), 52, 1 December 1914, p. 192; on the English system of schooling generally, see Gillian Sutherland, 'Education', in F. M. L. Thompson (ed.), *The Cambridge social history of Britain 1750–1950*, vol. III, *Social agencies and institutions* (Cambridge, 1990), pp. 119–69.

five. Promotion to the boys' and girls' schools occurred between ages seven and eight. After the 1902 Education Act elementary education went up to the age of twelve at which point students received some sort of secondary education at least up to the age of fourteen.

Alongside the complex local educational establishment, educational policy was set by the national Board of Education housed in London. The Board, represented by its powerful His Majesty's Inspectorate which could make or break the reputation of a school, had an enormous impact on all schools through the national Education Code mandating curricular and other practices. There were also other bodies shaping educational discourses and everyday practices of schools, the London-based National Union of Teachers being the most important one. It had a strong local affiliate, the London Teachers' Association. By contrast, the law forbade Prussia's teachers to organize themselves into trade unions.

The city of Berlin, too, administered and financed its elementary school system locally.[4] Old Berlin (without the neighbouring cities like Charlottenburg or Wilmersdorf which were incorporated into Greater Berlin after the war) maintained 310 municipal schools (*Gemeindeschulen*), and 23 establishments for handicapped children, altogether catering for about 226,000 pupils.[5] In addition, the Prussian state also provided a small number of peoples' schools (*Volksschulen*). Children were separated according to their sex and denomination (with Jews and atheists normally attending Protestant establishments). Elementary education between the ages of 6 and 14 had been free in Prussia since 1888, but the well-to-do classes preferred to send their children to privately run preparatory schools which, for an annual fee, offered special tuition for the entrance examination to secondary schools.

Like their London counterparts, Berlin's state secondary schools charged an annual fee, but also awarded scholarships to gifted students from poor backgrounds (approximately 10 per cent of the annual student intake). As in the case of elementary education, most secondary schools were maintained by the city of Berlin rather than the Prussian state. The private sector was by and large marginal, with the exception of secondary schools for girls. In 1916, Old Berlin housed fifteen all-male *Gymnasien* with a preponderant instruction in ancient languages, eight

[4] *Statistisches Jahrbuch der höheren Schulen Deutschlands, Luxemburgs und der Schweiz und der höheren deutschen Schulen im Ausland*, vol. XXXV (Leipzig, 1914); H. Schöbel, 'Unterrichtswesen im Jahre 1912/13', in M. Neefe (ed.), *Statistisches Jahrbuch deutscher Städte*, vol. XXI (Breslau, 1916), pp. 686–736; *Berliner Statistisches Jahrbuch*, vol. XXXIV (Berlin, 1920).

[5] The official statistics refer to Old Berlin prior to 1920. However, this chapter concerns schools within the boundaries of the future Greater Berlin, unless otherwise indicated.

Realgymnasien for boys where both Latin (but not Greek) and modern languages were taught, and four *Oberrealschulen* (plus fifteen *Realschulen*) with an emphasis on modern languages (principally English and French). Girls in secondary education attended one of the twenty-four *Lyzeen*, half of which were privately maintained. In addition, there were intermediate schools (*Mittelschulen*) for boys and/or girls, which offered instruction in one foreign language only. Institutions peculiar to the German educational landscape of the time were vocational schools for trainee artisans run under the auspices of the city and the business community.

Schools in Berlin, like all schools in Prussia, fell under the jurisdiction of the Prussian Ministry of Education and Religious Affairs. Yet it was the Provincial School Committee (*Provinzial-Schulkollegium*) of Berlin which supervised the state of education in the schools of the capital. The general inspection and day-to-day administration was delegated to the Municipal School Deputation (*Städtische Schuldeputation*) of Berlin comprising six representatives of the Magistrat, twelve members of the House of Deputies, twelve independent citizens, a Protestant pastor, a Catholic priest, and a rabbi. The deputation consisted of 260 sub-commissions made up of 3,300 citizens engaged on a voluntary basis.[6] Neighbouring 'cities' like Charlottenburg or Wilmersdorf (to be incorporated into Greater Berlin in 1920) had school deputations of their own, but these bodies were smaller and did not always comprise church representatives.

Similar to London and Berlin, Paris had a two-tier school system which reflected and cemented class boundaries; education was a function of cultural and economic capital. The vast majority of Parisian children attended *écoles primaires* (1,722 schools with 408,817 pupils in the Department of the Seine in 1913). Schooling between the age of five or six and twelve or thirteen at *écoles primaires élémentaires* was compulsory and free of charge. A small number of gifted pupils went on to study at *écoles primaires supérieures* and technical training schools. Even more selective were the *écoles normales primaires*. The Parisian upper classes during the Third Republic, however, did not send their children through the same system of primary schools. Instead, bourgeois offsprings went straight to fee-paying *lycées*, essentially secondary schools, which held special elementary classes for younger pupils (12 *lycées* for boys with 13,070 pupils; 11 *lycées* for girls with 5,031 pupils).

---

[6] Wilhelm Münch, Arnold Reimann, and Hans Rettberg (eds.), *Das Unterrichts- und Erziehungswesen Groß-Berlins. Eine Übersicht über seinen gegenwärtigen Stand zur Orientierung für Fremde und Einheimische* (Berlin, 1912); generally, see Christa Berg (ed.), *Handbuch der deutschen Bildungsgeschichte*, vol. IV, *1870–1918. Von der Reichsgründung bis zum Ende des Ersten Weltkriegs* (Munich, 1991).

Here they received the training needed to advance to university or the *Grandes écoles*. As in the case of London and Berlin, few children moved from one system to the other.[7]

In France, the central state played a far more powerful role in the administration of the school system than in Britain or Germany. While almost all state schools in London and Berlin were locally maintained and supervised, Paris schools (with the exception of a small number of private, principally confessional, foundations) belonged exclusively to the Ministry of Public Instruction and Fine Arts. The minister not only formulated educational policies for the whole of France, but also acted as Rector of the Academy of Paris which comprised nine departments, including the Seine. He devolved his duty to maintain educational standards and general discipline in schools to an inspectorate, led by the Directors of Primary and Secondary Education. In close contact with the schoolmasters, the inspectors were key figures in the development of wartime teaching. The structural conditions spelled out above proved both resilient and inadequate when confronted by the realities of war, as the following section will show.

Disruptions

The war literally caught children and educators on vacation. Some teachers were out of their respective countries replenishing their minds and spirits by travelling; others were at home, but quite unprepared even to imagine what lay ahead. For some children summer meant play, but for many it meant work. In rural Hertfordshire, for instance, the Local Education Authority readily accepted the need for child labour on farms and in factories and relaxed existing bye-laws regulating school attendance.[8] After all, the rural areas around London had a long tradition of releasing schoolchildren during harvests. The LCC, however, tried to keep disruptions to a minimum. Its Emergency Committee initially took a very firm stand against the employment of schoolchildren. In August 1914, the committee forbade an experiment at six schools where girls made garments for the War Office, 'garments which would otherwise be worked and paid

---

[7] Antoine Prost, *Histoire de l'enseignement en France 1800–1967* (Paris, 1968); *Statistique générale de la France. Annuaire statistique, année 1913*, vol. XXXIII (Paris, 1914); on the wartime elementary school in general, see Valérie Dehay, 'L'école primaire en France pendant la guerre de 1914–1918', doctoral thesis, Université de Picardie, 2000. We are grateful to Antoine Prost for his comments on this chapter.

[8] David H. Parker, ' "The talent at its command". The First World War and the vocational aspect of education, 1914–39', *History of Education Quarterly*, 35 (1995), pp. 244–7; see also Geoffrey Sherington, *English education, social change and the war 1911–20* (Manchester, 1981), pp. 49–50.

for on commercial lines'.[9] Yet the authorities could not prevent older boys and girls from leaving school much earlier than formerly. The headmaster of Sir John Cass School, managed by the City of London, complained about the unprecedented demand for boy labour and begged parents to encourage their children to complete the school course.[10]

Restricting children's labour was one example of London's educators' determination to carry on business as usual, but disruptions to the school routine were inevitable. Reviewing the experience of war in February 1919, the LCC Education Committee produced a list of five disruptive factors: reduced and inexperienced staff, air raids and warnings of air raids, lack of parental control, scarcity of fuel, and teaching material shortages.[11] The demands of war work (and thus the problem of absenteeism generally), and the occupation of schools by the military are curiously missing in the official summary. *Mutatis mutandis*, the same disruptive factors also prevailed in Paris and Berlin – though to different degrees. Berlin schools, for instance, did not experience bombardments, but suffered most acutely from growing coal shortages, especially in the severe winter of 1916–17.[12] In addition, local practices are to be blamed for disruptions to the normal routines of schools, such as frequent *siegfrei* days after 'victorious' battles in Berlin.[13] In all three cities, war-related disruptions had disastrous consequences for the state of orderly learning. The Société libre pour l'étude psychologique de l'enfant concluded with regard to Paris in 1917 that war had caused a severe decline in teaching standards and pupils' skills.[14] Let us consider each of the major disruptive forces in turn.

Requisitions In volume I, we discussed how welfare practices and social rights conceptualized the metropolis as a polity in which civic

---

[9] London Metropolitan Archives (hereafter LMA), LCC/MIN/4367, Emergency Committee, Signed papers, August 1914–March 1915, p. 15.

[10] Guildhall Library (hereafter GL), MS 31098, Sir John Cass Foundation School, Headmaster's report, 1915, pp. 6–7; see also Richard Wall, 'English and German families and the First World War, 1914–18', in Richard Wall and Jay Winter (eds.), *The upheaval of war. Family, work and welfare in Europe, 1914–1918* (Cambridge, 1988), pp. 96–7.

[11] London County Council Education Committee, *Minutes of proceedings. January to December, 1919* (London, 1919), pp. 61–2. The signed minutes are deposited in LMA, LCC/MIN/2909-15, 1914–20.

[12] Bundesarchiv, Berlin (hereafter BArch), R 8034 II/6940, 'Der Frost und die Schulen', *Vossische Zeitung*, 7 February 1917; ibid., 'Schließung der Spandauer Schulen wegen Kohlenmangels', *Berliner Lokal-Anzeiger*, 30 January 1917; generally, see *Capital cities*, vol. I, ch. 11.

[13] BArch, R 8034 II/6939, 'Wie oft hatten die Schulen siegfrei?', *Vossische Zeitung*, 5 June 1916.

[14] *Nos enfants et la guerre. Enquête de la Société libre pour l'étude psychologique de l'énfant* (Paris, 1917), p. 75.

entitlements in wartime stemmed from social functions. In 1914, a new hierarchy of urban citizenship emerged, highlighting the contribution of soldiers to the survival of the nation.[15] For one historian this translated into the attitude that 'nothing was too good for the troops, and anything was good enough for the children'.[16] Perhaps that is why, in many cases, the armed forces requisitioned school premises for recruiting and drilling purposes or to house military hospitals.[17] In Berlin, over a hundred schools – or roughly one-third of municipal schools – were occupied by the troops between 1914 and 1916, and about thirty schools remained closed during the entirety of the war. The crisis worsened in the aftermath of the Armistice. In the process of demobilization, 158 school buildings were turned into barracks – more than at any point of time during the war; for the pupils of 35 schools, alternative accommodation could not be found in Berlin.[18]

In London, three elementary schools in Woolwich were the first school buildings requisitioned in December 1914.[19] By June 1915, however, the Board of Education concluded that by and large the capital's school system could cope with the temporary occupation of buildings for war purposes.[20] It is noteworthy that not all requisitions were forced on the schools; some headmasters of London independent schools voluntarily offered buildings for temporary use.[21] In all three capitals, arrangements were made for double sessions (mornings and afternoons) held in other school buildings. Unfortunately for displaced children in Berlin, alternative accommodation could not always be found in neighbouring schools.[22] Yet Berlin administrators abreast of the *Zeitgeist* found a very special solution to the dilemma: *Ersatz* school buildings made of wood.[23]

---

[15] *Capital cities*, vol. I, p. 530; see also Susan Pedersen, 'Gender, welfare, and citizenship in Britain during the Great War', *American Historical Review*, 95 (1990), pp. 983–1006.   [16] Parker, 'The talent at its command', p. 242.

[17] *Capital cities*, vol. I, pp. 93–4.

[18] Ernst Kaeber, *Berlin im Weltkriege. Fünf Jahre städtischer Kriegsarbeit* (Berlin, 1921), p. 511.

[19] London County Council Education Committee, *Minutes of proceedings. January to June, 1915* (London, 1915), p. 72.

[20] 'The president's last report – the war and the schools', *LT*, 32 (1915), p. 395.

[21] Corporation of London Records Office (hereafter CLRO), City of London Freemen's Orphan School Committee, Minute book, vol. 43, May 1914–March 1916, pp. 34, 39; and City of London School Committee, Minute book, vol. 73, October 1913–February 1915, p. 114.

[22] Landesarchiv Berlin (hereafter LAB), Sta Rep. 49–05/8, no. 49, fo. 25, Hochbau-Amt to Gemeindevorstand Pankow, 24 February 1917; BArch, R 8034 II/6939, 'Die Volksschule im Kriege', *Berliner Tageblatt*, 11 January 1916; London County Council Education Committee, *Minutes 1915*, vol. I, pp. 268, 420.

[23] BArch, R 8034 II/6938, 'Die Parkschule auf dem Tempelhofer Feld', *Berliner Tageblatt*, 8 April 1915.

In Paris, in particular, the military's demands put a strain on already stretched resources. To understand the full extent of the crisis, consider the case of the 15th arrondissement. In the summer of 1914, the lycée Buffon was turned into a military hospital and forced to relocate most of its pupils to the Miollis girls' school, which itself was partly occupied by the military. The remaining students were dispersed over a number of schools in the neighbourhood. The situation was further aggravated when an automobile depot was established at the school complex in rue Lacordaire in autumn 1914. In summer 1915, the army requisitioned yet another school, this time in rue Saint Charles, and things went from bad to worse. All the pupils from rue Saint Charles plus three hundred from rue Lacordaire had to be accommodated in the school in rue Rouelle, with disastrous results.[24] Alarmed by severe overcrowding and a progressive deterioration of hygienic conditions in rue Rouelle, the Director of Primary Education complained to the Prefect of the Seine:

In the primary school ... the air was so polluted that it was disturbing even to enter some classes ... If ever there were a panic in these overcrowded schools, we should fear very serious incidents ... The reason this place, under the conditions I will outline, had to be used was because the Saint Charles school was requisitioned by the army. It is detrimental to the health of these children and perhaps, in certain cases, a danger to their security. It can only be kept open for reasons of absolute necessity.[25]

The Prefect turned to the military administration to remedy the situation. The outcries of teachers and administrators had hitherto proved no match for the rhetoric of soldiers' rights, but in April 1916 the army requisitioned an alternative location (the national printing house) and vacated the buildings in rue Saint Charles. But now the entire fabric of the school building needed renovation. Eventually, in 1917, almost two years after the school had been requisitioned, lessons resumed in rue Saint Charles.

Staff shortages In addition to the constraints of space, schools struggled hard to replace teaching and support staff serving with the forces. At the outset of hostilities, roughly 1,200 (out of a total of 3,561) Berlin primary-school teachers were called up. Although some returned to their schools during the war, the overall number increased steadily after 1916. In 1917–18, more than 2,000 teachers were in uniform. While approximately half of Berlin's teaching staff

---

[24] Archives de Paris (hereafter AP), D2T-1/47, Rapport groupe scolaire rue Saint Charles, 20 November 1917.
[25] Ibid.

was conscripted, the Prussian average was below 35 per cent.[26] The school authorities endeavoured to recruit female support teachers and also repealed the law which forbade the employment of married women teachers, but the situation could not be remedied.[27] In October 1915, not more than ninety women taught at Berlin *Gymnasien*; the 436 female teachers employed in municipal schools in 1916–17, too, were little more than a drop in the ocean. As a consequence, school lessons had to be reduced considerably with only 10 per cent of the pupils receiving the compulsory thirty-two lessons per week. For the overwhelming majority (77 per cent) tuition varied between twenty-four and sixteen weekly lessons.[28]

In London, 2,353 teachers in total served in the war.[29] 'For the majority, the clear path lies in the performance of duty in the familiar school', impressed the education authorities on London's male teachers.[30] And yet, everywhere, temporary teaching staff, principally teacher trainees, retired and women teachers filled in. Schools were caught between the need to find a large number of auxiliary teachers and the desire to maintain pre-war standards. They faced a Sisyphean task. Take the boys' department of Hanover Street School, Islington. In February 1916, the Council's inspector reported that six out of the seven original assistants had enlisted long before the group system was in vogue. The headmaster, too, tried to join up, but was rejected. In addition, some of the replacement staff had left to join the forces. 'In other words, there has been a succession of teachers during the last eighteen months and there is now a considerable amount of women therein.'[31] Although throughout the history of state elementary education women teachers outnumbered their male colleagues and before the war women comprised 70 per cent of London's teaching force, the education authorities became increasingly concerned about

[26] Kaeber, *Berlin im Weltkriege*, p. 511; BArch, R 8034 II/6938, 'Von den Kindern des Volkes und ihrer Schule', *Berliner Volkszeitung*, 19 March 1915; BArch, R 8034 II/6940, 'Die Berliner Gemeindeschule im Kriegsjahre 1916/17', *Berliner Volkszeitung*, 8 September 1917.

[27] BArch, R 8034 II/6920, 'Frauen in Berliner Gymnasien', *Berliner Tageblatt*, 15 October 1915; ibid., 'Die Aufhebung der Zölibatsbestimmung für Lehrerinnen', *Reichsbote*, 29 October 1915; ibid., 'Die verheiratete Lehrerin', *Vossische Zeitung*, 13 February 1916.

[28] BArch, R 8034 II/6940, 'Die Berliner Gemeindeschule im Kriegsjahre 1916/17', *Berliner Volkszeitung*, 8 September 1917.

[29] *Capital cities*, vol. I, p. 81.

[30] LMA, LCC/EO/WAR/3/1, Education Officer to all teachers, 21 September 1914.

[31] LMA, LCC/MIN/2972, LCC Education Committee, Council inspector's report on Hanover Street School, 20 February 1916.

the progressive feminization of schools and planned to redress the balance after the war.[32]

Yet by summer 1917 administrators were alarmed at a growing desire among women teachers to swap teaching for factory work. 'The Ministry of Labour concur with the Board [of Education] in the view that it is desirable to impress on women teachers generally that their work in the schools is of the greatest national importance at the present time.'[33] Material pressures rather than patriotism might have driven the women to take up manual work; the middle classes suffered disproportionately from inflation and taxation vis-à-vis war workers.[34] What is more, the LCC made economies at the expense of supply teachers and thus undermined the official rhetoric of sacrifice and duty. Temporary women teachers were treated as day labourers and not paid by the month like the permanent staff, but by the number of days they taught. This practice represented a major set-back for the equal-pay movement.[35]

Absenteeism In July 1915, the LCC Education Committee decided on another spending cut. As a result of increased cost of labour and material, the award of medals to pupils for regular and punctual attendance (and cleanliness, tidiness, and good conduct) was suspended for the duration of the war – 'an unnecessary economy and detrimental in effect upon the progress of scholars' as the Bermondsey Borough Council complained.[36] The protest was of no avail, but certificates were issued in lieu of medals. The certificate for 1915–16 gave the metropolitan experience of war a chivalric flavour: it showed two medieval knights silhouetted against the skyline of London.[37]

---

[32] LMA, LCC/EO/GEN/5/21, Some problems of education in London, 1915; on the pre-war situation, see Dina M. Copelman, *London's women teachers. Gender, class and feminism 1870–1930* (London and New York, 1996); on Paris, see Alain Dejean, 'Les lycées parisiens pendant la prèmiere guerre mondiale', master's thesis, University of Paris X-Nanterre, 1993, p. 31; Serge Lesmanne, 'L'école et la guerre (1914–1918)', *Mémoires de la société d'histoire et d'archéologie de Pontoise* (1985–6), p. 7.

[33] London County Council Education Committee, *Minutes of proceedings. January to December, 1917* (London, 1917), p. 431.

[34] *Capital cities*, vol. 1, pp. 229–54.

[35] '"Supply" salaries', *TES*, 71, 4 July 1916, p. 88; generally, see Copelman, *London's women teachers*.

[36] London County Council Education Committee, *Minutes 1917*, p. 535; see London County Council Education Committee, *Minutes of proceedings. July to December, 1915* (London, 1915), p. 99.

[37] LMA, LCC/EO/PS/11/2, Certificate for attendance, 1915–16; on chivalry, see Stefan Goebel, *The Great War and medieval memory. War, remembrance and medievalism in Britain and Germany, 1914–1940* (Cambridge, 2006).

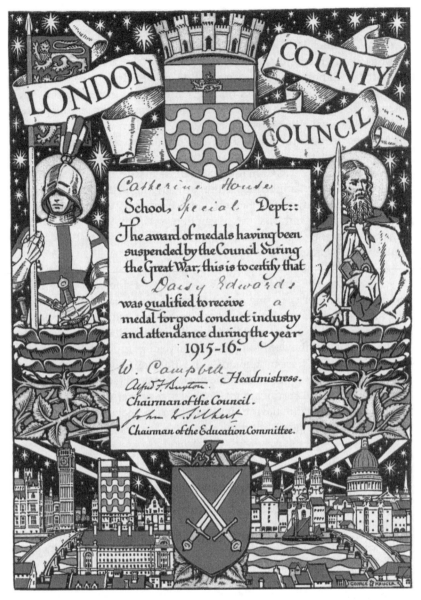

Fig. 6.1. Wartime certificate for attendance and good conduct issued by the Education Committee of the London County Council, 1915.

Attendance, however, dropped significantly during the war, notably at the outbreak (many pupils were still on holiday or kept away to help in the home) and conclusion of hostilities.[38] Due to the influenza pandemic, average attendance in some schools fell below 70 per cent in autumn and winter 1918. The young ran the greatest risk of infection, but the Board of Education intervened little, convinced that their role was purely one of prevention. The LCC school medical officer did not consider either 'that the closure of schools would serve any useful purpose in preventing the spread of the disease'.[39]

Judging from the reports of the inspectors of the Academy, absenteeism in Paris was – as in London – particularly acute in the initial and final phases of the war.[40] However, statistical data tend to obscure the true scale of the crisis in the French capital. Official statistics refer to the number of pupils formally registered rather than those actually in attendance. Moreover, the absence of Parisian pupils was to some degree remedied by the influx of refugee children into the capital. By comparison, absenteeism posed a much graver problem in Berlin. All German cities saw a dramatic increase in pupils cutting classes, from approximately 15 per cent in 1914 to almost 50 per cent in 1917. Although headmasters alerted the authorities, there was a progressive erosion of compulsory education in the capital. The police, theoretically in charge of enforcing attendance, felt overwhelmed by the resistance put up by negligent pupils, their parents, and neighbours. The Pankow police reported 'ugly street scenes' and outbursts of violence against officers taking children to school by force.[41] The inevitable consequence was a breakdown of school discipline unheard of in Imperial Germany before 1914.

The war produced social conditions which loosened the relationship of authority. In both the French and the German capitals, pupils skipped lessons for similar reasons: to mind younger siblings, to earn a supplementary income for the family, and, particularly in Berlin, to secure food stuffs by means of queuing (in front of shops), begging (in the countryside), or

---

[38] LMA, LCC/EO/DIV1/MUN/LB/8, Munster Road School Girls' Department, Log-book, 1913–19, pp. 92–3, 209–10, 213; 'School attendance', *LT*, 34 (1917), p. 121.

[39] 'London education committee', *TES*, 186, 7 November 1918, p. 482; see *Capital cities*, vol. I, p. 483.

[40] Lesmanne, 'L'école et la guerre', p. 7.

[41] LAB, Sta Rep. 49-05/8, Nr. 54, fo. 473, Polizei-Kommissariat Pankow to Amtsvorsteher Pankow, 8 December 1917; see also BArch, R 8034 II/6939, 'Einwirkung des Kriegs auf die Schule', *Deutsches Tageblatt*, 27 March 1916.

stealing.[42] To be sure, pupils also played truant for more trivial reasons. Especially in Paris, the hub of communications in France, students frequently missed school in order to welcome *permissionnaires*, that is conscripted fathers, brothers, and uncles visiting from the front. The Société libre pour l'étude psychologique de l'enfant noted: 'But in Paris ... there are so many cousins and relatives. For these children the additional holidays come more frequently than once in four months!'[43] By contrast, it appears that the problem of absenteeism did not destabilize the London school system to the same degree as it did in Berlin and Paris. However, autobiographical accounts suggest that headteachers simply sanctioned the inevitable, for instance by exempting a pupil from school for the return of a close relative in the forces.[44] Yet it is impossible to ascertain how common this practice of permissive absenteeism was in London.

War lessons Finally, the war caused a disruption to established syllabi. The outbreak of hostilities necessitated the introduction of what the Germans called *Kriegslektionen*, war lessons, that explained the events which were to engulf the children's lives. Particularly subjects like history, geography, or literature, which lent themselves to propagandistic purposes, were remodelled.[45] Yet even religious education and mathematics contributed to the 'moral pollution' of children and teenagers. Especially in Paris and Berlin, and to a lesser extent in London, educational canons were disrupted and militarized at the expense of traditional learning objectives. To be sure, during the nineteenth century educators on the Continent had already seen (primary) education as a key vehicle for promoting the construction of national identity.[46] Nevertheless, after 1914, many a teacher in Paris or Berlin readily sacrificed pre-war educational standards to the exigencies of the war effort. In effect, school curricula broke down. Didactic styles, too, changed as teachers appealed increasingly to their pupils' emotions rather than their intellects.

---

[42] Ingo Materna and Hans-Joachim Schreckenbach (eds.), *Dokumente aus geheimen Archiven*, vol. IV, *Berichte des Berliner Polizeipräsidenten zur Stimmung und Lage der Bevölkerung in Berlin 1914–1918* (Weimar, 1987), p. 90; Eberhard Demm, 'Agents of propaganda. German teachers at war', in Eberhard Demm, *Ostpolitik und Propaganda im Ersten Weltkrieg* (Frankfurt am Main, 2002), p. 62, first published in Cecil and Liddle (eds.), *Facing Armageddon*, pp. 709–18.   [43] *Nos enfants et la guerre*, p. 50.
[44] Gibson Cowan, *Loud report* (London, 1938), p. 42.
[45] Rainer Bendick, *Kriegserwartung und Kriegserfahrung. Der Erste Weltkrieg in deutschen und französischen Schulgeschichtsbüchern (1900–1939/45)* (Pfaffenweiler, 1999.)
[46] The literature in this field is vast. See Antoine Prost, 'The contribution of the republican primary school to French national identity', in Antoine Prost, *Republican identities in war and peace. Representations of France in the nineteenth and twentieth centuries* (Oxford and New York, 2002), pp. 73–89.

War lessons tended to reinforce official propaganda, but in a cruder, more child-like manner. No aspect of the war, even the most gruesome and disturbing, was to be concealed from the children. War lessons were meant to transform classrooms into imagined battlefields.[47] Significantly, a French teachers' professional journal equated school-work with combat: 'Youngsters, to work! Or rather, to arms, because you too are in the fight.'[48] Taking his cue from George Mosse, Stéphane Audoin-Rouzeau has argued that the *culture de guerre* successfully invaded French schools and brutalized children.[49] The war was more than just a fresh item on the curriculum; according to ministerial circulars, *all* teaching was to be built around the events of the day. However, evidence from the three capital cities suggests that war lessons instilled principally a sense of public duty rather than a cult of military brutality. Moreover, official instructions and local practice were rarely congruent. Whether a pupil was indeed bombarded with the propaganda of hatred or informed about the war in a matter-of-fact style depended largely on the individual teacher, notably at the outset of war. In the absence of new, war-related teaching materials in autumn 1914, teachers everywhere had to improvise.

On 10 August 1914, teachers and headmasters in Berlin were officially asked to support the patriotic spirit and to modify, if deemed desirable, the teaching schedule. Yet, teachers did not receive specific guidelines, for the Prussian Ministry of Education did not expect the war to last very long. Three months later, the minister encouraged teachers to deal with the recent events in lessons but still refrained from more explicit instructions.[50] The ministry seemed to put its trust in a teaching force (and its provincial or local supervisors) accustomed

---

[47] Stéphane Audoin-Rouzeau, 'Children and the primary schools of France, 1914–1918', in John Horne (ed.), *State, society and mobilization in Europe during the First World War* (Cambridge, 1997), pp. 39–52; Demm, 'Agents of propaganda', pp. 63–6; see also *Les enfants dans la Grande Guerre*, ed. Historial de la Grande Guerre (Péronne, 2003); Manon Pignot, *La guerre des crayons. Quand les petits Parisiens dessinaient la Grande Guerre* (Paris, 2004).

[48] *Revue de l'enseignement primaire*, 1, 30 September 1917, p. 3.

[49] Stéphane Audoin-Rouzeau, *La guerre des enfants 1914–1918. Essai d'histoire culturelle* (Paris, 1993); Stéphane Audoin-Rouzeau and Annette Becker, *1914–1918. Understanding the Great War* (London, 2002), pp. 110–12; George L. Mosse, *Fallen soldiers. Reshaping the memory of the world wars* (New York and Oxford, 1990).

[50] 'Pflege vaterländischer Begeisterung bei den höheren Lehranstalten', *Zentralblatt für die gesamte Unterrichtsverwaltung in Preußen*, 58 (1914), p. 740; on German war pedagogy generally, see Eberhard Demm, 'Zwischen Propaganda und Sozialfürsorge – Deutschlands Kinder im Krieg', in Eberhard Demm, *Ostpolitik und Propaganda im Ersten Weltkrieg* (Frankfurt am Main, 2002), pp. 73–6, first published in *Militärgeschichtliche Zeitschrift*, 60 (2001), pp. 52–5; Andrew Donson, 'War pedagogy

to implementing militarist curricula since the 1890s, even though some primary schoolteachers had sympathized with the pacifist movement before 1914. Similarly, London teachers were initially left to their own devices. In some schools, war lessons were a stopgap measure, for attendance at the beginning of the school year was so low that normal teaching could not resume for several weeks. One teacher at Munster Road School girls' department, Fulham, noted in a log-book on 17 August 1914 that 'So many girls are still absent that Special Lessons will not be taken ... this w[eek] but talks will be given during time on "War Topics".'[51]

In late autumn 1914, however, the LCC Education Committee assumed a more proactive role. It supplied school libraries with copies of documents and books relating to various aspects of the war (such as Friedrich von Bernhardi's *Germany and the next war*), and, occasionally, sent out teaching suggestions.[52] A circular of October 1914, urged geography teachers to produce in pupils a mindscape of war, a specific way of looking at the conflict in Europe. It stressed that it was of paramount importance to consider the main geographical factors at work in the ongoing conflict. 'Anyone who has read Bernhardi's "Germany and the Next War" will realise that the ambition for material progress, or in other words, geographical expansion, is at the root of the Germany policy of military aggression.'[53] Whether or not geography was really taught along the lines specified in the circular is impossible to say. It is unlikely, however, that this was indeed the case, since many London teachers still harboured a fear of excessive jingoism that dated back to the pre-war period.[54]

Although the demand now was for teaching directed at current affairs, a revolution of the content and methods of learning did not take place. As the war dragged on, the LCC Education Committee became less and less concerned about intellectual mobilization by means of war lessons. The committee members seemed to be content with the way teachers handled the subject. Instead, the future of London education after the war loomed large on their mind. In 1915, a report was commissioned evaluating the state of schooling in the capital. The point was made that, since wartime

and youth culture. Nationalism and authority in Germany in the First World War', PhD thesis, University of Michigan, 2000, esp. chs. 2–5. We are grateful to Andrew Donson for his advice on this point.

[51] LMA, LCC/EO/DIV1/MUN/LB/8, Munster Road School Girls' Department, Log-book, 1913–19, pp. 92–3.

[52] London County Council Education Committee, *Minutes of proceedings. July to December, 1914* (London, 1914), pp. 385, 707, 865.

[53] LCC/MIN/2970, LCC Education Committee, Papers accompanying reports, 1914.

[54] Copelman, *London's women teachers*, pp. 119–20.

conditions prevented the undertaking of any major projects, this was a good time to assess and think ahead.[55]

Post-war education was also a bigger issue than wartime mobilization in some establishments of the private sector. In February 1916, the committee of the City of London School passed a motion that science education be reformed to enable pupils 'to take their part successfully in the economic struggle it is anticipated will follow the termination of the War with Germany and her Allies'.[56] The demands of the war effort notwithstanding, London schools continued to define themselves as centres of learning. In fact, the war became a catalyst for educational reform. While local educationalists discussed the future of schooling in the metropolis, the national Board of Education was busy drafting a major education bill. Fisher's Education Act of 1918 ended part-time employment for schoolchildren and raised the school-leaving age to fourteen. Even though few sections of the act came into effect, it nevertheless stands out as one of the two significant pieces of domestic legislation passed before the Armistice.[57]

War lessons in Berlin followed a very different trajectory. After a spell of inactivity in 1914 due to high expectations and a shortage of paper supply, the Prussian authorities tried to resume the initiative in 1915. Berlin was to become the intellectual hub of war lessons. March 1915 saw the opening of the Central Institute of Education and Teaching (Zentralinstitut für Erziehung und Unterricht) in Potsdamer Straße 120. Nominally an independent foundation (so as to guarantee political 'impartiality'), the institute was entirely dependent on state subsidies. It developed into a kind of coordinative body of wartime education, organizing exhibitions, conferences, and workshops for teachers and publishing teaching materials. The institute targeted teachers nationwide, but cooperated closely with Berlin schools. Its permanent exhibition on 'School and War' displayed above all Berlin examples, such as the fruits of the Berlin War Drawing Week.[58]

Naturally, the institute's staff preferred examples of schoolwork replete with accounts of German heroism, elegies to soldiers, and

---

[55] LMA, LCC/EO/GEN/5/21, Some problems of education in London, 1915.
[56] CLRO, City of London School Committee, Minute book, vol. 77, February 1913–February 1915, p. 114.
[57] Sherington, *English education*, ch. 5.
[58] 'Eröffnung des Zentralinstituts für Erziehung und Unterricht', *Berliner Börsen-Courier*, morning edn, 22 March 1915, p. 3; Hermann Reich (ed.), *Das Buch Michael mit Kriegsaufsätzen, Tagebuchblättern, Gedichten, Zeichnungen aus Deutschlands Schulen*, ed. in co-operation with the Zentralinstitut für Erziehung und Unterricht (Berlin, 1916); *Schule und Krieg. Sonderausstellung im Zentralinstitut für Erziehung und Unterricht Berlin* (Berlin, 1915), p. 76.

Fig. 6.2. The war as imagined by a pupil of a Berlin municipal school. This drawing was on display in the exhibition 'School and War' at the Central Institute of Education and Teaching, Berlin.

disparagements of the enemy, that is, works which reflected the successful militarization of children's minds. But did Berlin schools really regress to a state of being mere *Dressuranstalten für den Krieg*, 'training institutions for the war', as the socialist leader Karl Liebknecht claimed?[59] One scholar has recently argued that teachers throughout Germany abandoned rote memorization and embraced instead innovative teaching methods (which had been developed before the war, to be sure). Far from a one-sided process of indoctrination, war lessons encouraged individual fantasy and personal opinion. War compositions in particular offered schoolchildren a space to reflect on their wartime experiences. While grief and deprivation feature in children's essays, the stresses of war were generally subsumed in narratives of self-sacrifice and endurance for victory.[60] Not all schoolteachers, though, were convinced of their pupils' sincerity. Suspicious about essays that echoed war lessons, some dismissed the pupils' apparent enthusiasm as *bloßes*

[59] Karl Liebknecht, *Gesammelte Schriften und Reden*, ed. Institut für Marxismus-Leninismus, vol. VIII (East Berlin, 1966), p. 535.
[60] Donson, 'War pedagogy', ch. 3.

Nachgeplapper, a calculated attempt to obtain good grades.[61] However, different milieux inculcated different stories. One teacher noted striking differences in German children's receptiveness to war lessons depending on gender and social milieu. Unsurprisingly, upper- and middle-class boys proved most manipulable. Girls, by contrast, were more resistant to war lessons.[62]

French teachers, too, complained about the lack of imagination of pupils repeating war lessons parrot-fashion. Pupils' essays smelled of conformism, not conviction.[63] Ultimately, it is impossible to establish whether educational authorities and nationalistic teachers won or lost the propaganda battle. There was, to be sure, a measurable decline in war lessons in both France and Germany from 1916–17. The editors of the *Bulletin administratif du Ministère de l'Instruction publique* issued fewer and fewer patriotic circulars, none being published in 1918.[64] Also in German elementary schools, the war tended to become a 'side issue' in the second half of the war. Now, the main challenge of war was not to mobilize for the national war effort, but to keep the schools and thus the local state going at all.[65] War lessons might have petered out as the link between education and the war became weaker, but a return to teaching as usual was no longer an option: years of requisitions, staff shortages, and absenteeism among students had sapped the pre-war system of schooling in Paris and Berlin.[66]

[61] Alfred Mann, 'Aufsätze von Kindern und Jugendlichen über Kriegsthemata', in William Stern (ed.), *Jugendliches Seelenleben und Krieg. Materialien und Berichte*, Beihefte zur Zeitschrift für angewandte Psychologie und psychologische Sammelforschung, 12 (Leipzig, 1915), pp. 84, 89. See the war essays by thirteen-year-old Johanna Welz, 'Berlin im Zeichen des Krieges', 23 April 1915, and 'Die Frau im Weltkrieg', 17 November 1916, private collection, Berlin; on Johanna Welz, see chapter 9.

[62] Kurt Walther Dix, 'Beobachtungen über den Einfluß der Kriegsereignisse auf das Seelenleben des Kindes', in William Stern (ed.), *Jugendliches Seelenleben und Krieg. Materialien und Berichte*, Beihefte zur Zeitschrift für angewandte Psychologie und psychologische Sammelforschung, 12 (Leipzig, 1915), pp. 165–71.

[63] Stéphane Audoin-Rouzeau, 'Die mobilisierten Kinder. Die Erziehung zum Krieg an französischen Schulen', in Gerhard Hirschfeld, Gerd Krumeich, and Irina Renz (eds.), *'Keiner fühlt sich hier mehr als Mensch ...' Erlebnis und Wirkung des Ersten Weltkriegs* (Frankfurt am Main, 1996), pp. 187–8, 196; see also Mona L. Siegel, *The moral disarmament of France. Education, pacifism, and patriotism, 1914–1940* (Cambridge, 2004), pp. 35–6.

[64] Audoin-Rouzeau, 'Die mobilisierten Kinder', pp. 193–5.

[65] Demm, 'Zwischen Propaganda und Sozialfürsorge', pp. 118–20; see also Donson, 'War pedagogy'.

[66] Olivier Loubes, *L'école de la patrie. Histoire d'un désenchantement, 1914–1940* (Paris and Berlin, 2001).

The school as wartime community

Enemy aliens

The structural conditions outlined above were in large part assumed and/or invisible before the war and when hostilities first broke out. Instead, among the first issues to demand attention was the question how the enemy – more specifically the enemy alien and the enemy's language – should be treated. Ethnic tensions had raised relatively few fundamental issues of national identity in Victorian and Edwardian Britain compared to Imperial Germany and the French Third Republic. Before the war, British xenophobia was far more subdued than on the Continent.[67] However, after August 1914 'alien enemies' were ostracized, attacked or interned. Outbursts of public anti-alienism played a major part in persuading the British government to take discriminatory measures. The Aliens Restriction Order of October 1914 forbade enemy aliens to assume new names, unless they obtained permission from the Home Office.[68]

Wartime paranoia created an unfriendly climate in London schools for teachers and pupils perceived or stigmatized as 'alien enemies'. British-born teachers with foreign-sounding names were anxious to change their surnames in order to dissociate themselves from enemy aliens. Even distant German ancestry was enough to arouse suspicion. For instance, in July 1915, the boys in Ethelburga Street School, Battersea, learned that Mr Klein, born in London, was now called (or rather spelled) Mr Clyne. The LCC Education Committee dealt with a number of such cases in 1915. The timing confirms that Germanophobia escalated in the aftermath of the sinking of the *Lusitania* in May 1915.[69]

The LCC Education Committee, too, actively engaged in defining who was and who was not a worthy member of the metropolitan community. The redistribution of educational 'functions' and 'capabilities' – which Amartya Sen defines as the freedom or the ability to achieve various living conditions – was an effective means of renegotiating wartime society.[70]

[67] J. M. Winter, 'British national identity and the First World War', in S. J. D. Green and R. C. Whiting (eds.), *The boundaries of the state in modern Britain* (Cambridge, 1996), pp. 261–77.

[68] Panikos Panayi, *The enemy in our midst. Germans in Britain during the First World War* (Providence and Oxford, 1991), p. 54; generally, see Aribert Reimann, *Der große Krieg der Sprachen. Untersuchungen zur historischen Semantik in Deutschland und England zur Zeit des Ersten Weltkrieges* (Essen, 2000), pp. 168–90; Sven Oliver Müller, 'Who is the enemy? The nationalist dilemma of inclusion and exclusion in Britain during the First World War', *European Review of History*, 9 (2002), pp. 63–83.

[69] Panayi, *Enemy in our midst*, pp. 229–39, 283.   [70] *Capital cities*, vol. I, p. 11.

Armed with new powers, the Education Committee restricted, after December 1914, entrance to central (secondary) schools to British subjects. 'Admission to this type of school', they explained, 'is in the nature of a privilege, and the number of places is limited' – too limited to leave room for the children of enemy aliens.[71] Remarkably, the new policy did not affect foreign pupils already in attendance at central schools. Likewise, the children of enemy aliens attending central schools were not considered as eligible for the award of exhibitions (scholarships), but existing exhibitioners were allowed to retain their awards.[72]

Prussian officials, too, went about reorganizing the entitlements of citizenship. In Berlin schools, the children of enemy aliens were subjected to harsher and more far-reaching discriminatory policies than in London. However, news about anti-German riots in British cities influenced administrative thinking in Germany.[73] One headmaster suggested that the mere expulsion of British pupils from Berlin schools was a relatively light retaliation for the outrages committed in Britain.[74] However, as early as 30 August 1914, the Prussian Minister of Education had decreed the wholesale removal of enemy nationals from all educational establishments.[75] Although this measure was resented in Social-Democratic and liberal circles and even criticized in the press and the Prussian lower house, the policy was quickly implemented at universities and secondary schools.[76] The School Deputation, however, complied hesitantly and planned to appeal to the ministry about the expulsion of foreign children from primary schools. The headmasters of Berlin's municipal schools were enlisted in what would become a recurring response: preparing numerous lists and statistics on the issue. In this instance, though it is unclear how many enemy alien children were involved, the final draft of

---

[71] London County Council Education Committee, *Minutes 1914*, vol. II, p. 831.

[72] London County Council Education Committee, *Minutes of proceedings. January to December, 1916* (London, 1916), pp. 182, 521.

[73] Generallandesarchiv Karlsruhe (hereafter GLA), 236/22730, Report by Reichskommissar zur Erörterung von Gewalttätigkeiten gegen deutsche Zivilpersonen in Feindesland [Jan. 1916]; on the nationalization of citizenship generally, see Dieter Gosewinkel, *Einbürgern und Ausschließen. Die Nationalisierung der Staatsangehörigkeit vom Deutschen Bund bis zur Bundesrepublik Deutschland* (Göttingen, 2001), pp. 328–38.

[74] LAB, Sta Rep. 20-01, no. 410, fo. 81, Rektor Rossins (18. Gemeindeschule) to Städtische Schuldeputation, 9 January 1915.

[75] Ibid., fo. 1, Minister der geistlichen und Unterrichtsangelegenheiten to Städtische Schuldeputation, 30 August 1914.

[76] BArch, R 8034 II/6938, 'Ausländische Kinder in preußischen Schulen', *Berliner Tageblatt*, 18 November 1914; see also the speech by the Social Democratic politician Konrad Haenisch on 3 March 1915 in *Stenographische Berichte über die Verhandlungen des Preußischen Hauses der Abgeordneten*, 22. Legislaturperiode, II. Session 1914–15, vol. VII, cols. 8633–4.

the report listed 273 children for whom the School Deputation intended to ask for exemption.[77]

There remained a conspicuous gap between the rhetoric of ministerial directives and the reality of their enforcement locally. Journalists reported with astonishment in February 1916 that there were still 38 English-speaking (probably American) pupils and 57 half-Italian, 21 half-French, and 1,786 Polish children in attendance at Berlin schools.[78] To be sure, the overwhelming majority of alien children, most of them Russian Jews, was banned from attending school. (The ban was lifted after the conclusion of the Brest-Litovsk Treaty.) Even though many of them were born and raised in Berlin, legally they remained foreigners. Only American pupils were granted exemptions for fear of retaliatory measures against Americans of German descent.[79] Even one Swiss pupil appeared in the list of children from enemy countries. The prevailing notion of 'encirclement' seems to have had somewhat erratic consequences for national minorities in wartime Berlin.[80]

The discriminatory measures taken by the administration fostered hostility towards the remaining aliens in Berlin classrooms. In September 1915, the Municipal School Deputation dealt with the harassment of two Italian girls, Lucie and Elsa Mastrogiacomo, by one of their German classmates at the 51st municipal school. Lucie, the elder girl, was involved in a fight, but the headmaster inflicted corporal punishments on both sisters. As their parents' complaint fell on deaf ears with both the headmaster and the school inspector, Mr Mastrogiacomo turned to the Swiss embassy for help.[81] By then, Switzerland had assumed responsibility for Italian nationals resident in Germany. A full-scale investigation was ordered and the parents, teachers, and classmates were summoned to testify. One girl recalled the scene when the headmaster interrogated Elsa: 'The girl said somewhat insecurely: "It is true; besides, the [German] girl always says that we were going to be expelled from school because we are Italians." The

[77] LAB, Sta Rep. 20-01, no. 410, fo. 12, Minister der geistlichen und Unterrichts-angelegenheiten to Provinzial-Schulkollegium, 12 December 1914.

[78] BArch, R 8034 II/6939, 'Berliner Schulkinderstatistik', *Berliner Tageblatt*, 14 February 1916.

[79] GLA, 236/23189, Staatsminister August von Trott zu Solz to Staatssekretär Arthur Zimmermann, 8 April 1917; ibid., Staatssekretär Arthur Zimmermann to Preußisches Ministerium der geistlichen und Unterrichtsangelegenheiten, 15 April 1917.

[80] LAB, Sta Rep. 20-01, no. 415, Städtische Schuldeputation Berlin, Ausschließung von schulpflichtigen Kindern vom Schulunterricht, 1914–18. Special thanks are due to Aribert Reimann who provided this and further material.

[81] LAB, Sta Rep. 20-01, no. 410, fo. 167, Schweizer Gesandschaft to Stadtschulinspektor Dickhoff, 21 September 1915.

headmaster made it clear to her that such a little girl could not possibly know about these things. He slapped her in the face, too.'[82]

In the course of the investigation, the tide turned against the Italian girls. The School Superintendent (*Schulrat*) threatened Mrs Mastrogiacomo, herself a native German, with the expulsion of both her daughters from the school: 'We are not obliged to teach the children of foreigners.'[83] What had begun as a quarrel among children became an investigation into the integrity of a whole family. The case even spread to the family's home in Kopenhagener Straße in the Prenzlauer Berg district, where neighbours were mobilized to give evidence against the family. Anything that could prove an anti-German attitude on part of the Mastrogiacomo family was documented in the files of the Municipal School Deputation. The girls' geography teacher reported an incident in May 1915 which, according to the headmaster, seemed indicative of their parents' anti-German attitude:[84]

Immediately after Italy's declaration of war on Austria, Lucie Mastrogiacomo stood with some of her classmates in front of a map during a break. Suddenly, she said: 'Damned German bastards.' One of the pupils retorted and reported the matter to me. I informed the children that in Germany there would be no war between children and that I would severely punish any abuse from either side.[85]

In the end, the whole issue was laid to rest. The headmaster was cleared of charges of xenophobia, and the Mastrogiacomo siblings were allowed to return to their school. A trivial case? The Mastrogiacomo affair mirrors the multifaceted impact of war on metropolitan ways of life: resources of the city's infrastructure were redistributed and this administrative action caused irritation and hostility among children who even at an early age were sucked into the maelstrom of the conflict. The imagined national community at war split the school and the neighbourhood from top to bottom.

Foreign languages The redistribution of educational 'functions' and 'capabilities' was one way in which schools distanced themselves from contamination by contact with enemy aliens; changes to the curriculum were another. In all three cities, instruction in foreign languages came under the close scrutiny of civil servants, teachers, and parents. As

[82] Ibid., fos. 177–8, Testimony by Charlotte Wachholz, 26 September 1915.
[83] Ibid., fo. 186v, Report by Stadtschulinspektor Dickhoff, 29 September 1915.
[84] Ibid., fo. 172, Rektor Krusemark (51. Gemeindeschule) to Stadtschulinspektor Dickhoff, 27 September 1915.
[85] Ibid., fo. 185, Testimony by Ella Gentsch, 27 September 1915.

the key to an understanding of foreign societies, the teaching of foreign languages was critical to the cultural construction of wartime alliances and enmities. In line with popular Germanophobia in Britain, German as a foreign language came under fire in London schools – though, surprisingly late in the war. The German Roman Catholic St Boniface's School, Stepney, discontinued the instruction of German in 1917.[86] The popularity of languages of friendly nations, by contrast, increased during the war.

It is worth noting that, on the whole, the instruction in German continued during the war in both London and Paris. At least in this field, educationists were often able to discriminate between pedagogical needs and political aims. The Corporation of the City of London discussed substituting another foreign language for German at the City of London School. But the chairman of the school's committee argued that pupils themselves had not expressed any such desire and, moreover, that 'German was an important part of their education.'[87] Parisian pupils, however, were apparently inclined to abandon German in favour of English. It was reported that the mere pronunciation of German vocabulary made some students shudder. One child could not talk German 'without wiping his mouth on his apron, since he had the sensation of soiling it'.[88] At the insistence of the parents, the lycée Victor-Duruy, in the 7th arrondissement, managed to circumvent the problem by teaching passive rather than active language skills: 'the argument in favour of these exercises is that the children will not soon have the occasion to speak German'.[89]

Schools became hotbeds of xenophobia, but, in the case of foreign-language instruction, the sentiment backfired on the institution. French teachers of German, anxious to justify their *raison d'être*, argued that sufficient command of the *boche*'s language was a Frenchman's patriotic duty, not despite but because of the war: 'I tell you: learn it more than ever. Defeated, Germany will not disappear from the map of Europe, and it will be in our interest not to ignore what happens inside her borders', one teacher at the lycée Voltaire, 11th arrondissement, impressed on his pupils: 'Prepared henceforth, you will penetrate Germany better than before.'[90]

---

[86] LMA, LCC/MIN/3287, Elementary Education Sub-Committee, Minutes, vol. 30, 3 April 1917–19 March 1918, p. 157.

[87] 'News in brief', *The Times*, 40992, 22 October 1915, p. 5.

[88] Marthe Serrié-Heim, *Petit Bé et le vilain Boche* (Paris, 1915), p. 8; see Audoin-Rouzeau, *La guerre des enfants*, p. 86.

[89] Mme Hollebecque, *La jeunesse scolaire de France et la guerre* (Paris, 1916), p. 54.

[90] Ibid.

In Berlin, too, educational pragmatism prevailed over linguistic provincialism. Secondary schools continued to offer lessons in English and French. To be sure, some Berlin teachers wanted to eliminate both French and English from the curriculum altogether.[91] Others recognized the necessity of teaching conversational skills but wanted to dispense with the study of English and French literature. They advocated giving priority to the auxiliary language, Esperanto, or Swedish as the language of what was practically the last country left with some sympathies for the German cause.[92]

In practice, English and French survived the onslaught by war propagandists for it proved difficult to substitute Turkish or Bulgarian for mainstream European languages. Nevertheless, the war necessitated the introduction of new teaching methods and new content. Now language teachers were supposed to discuss the imperialistic war aims of the Entente in general and the 'pernicious character' of the English people in particular. In addition, schoolchildren translated German propaganda material such as the White Book into English. Thus language tuition was effectively subsumed into war lessons.[93]

To be sure, the whole issue amounted to much ado about nothing. Only a small elite actually received language training, notably at *Realgymnasien* and *Oberrealschulen*. Furthermore, ancient rather than modern languages dominated the syllabus of traditional *Gymnasien* (as they did in British public schools). However, teachers set out to restore the purity of the German language. The use of many German words borrowed from foreign languages, notably French, were strictly forbidden in German classrooms. Pupils who used, even inadvertently, words of French origin such as *interessant* were reprimanded or fined.[94]

---

[91] BArch, R 8034 ɪɪ/6938, 'Erziehung zum Staatsbürger', *Berliner Tageblatt*, 30 April 1915; ibid., 'Der vergiftete Friede', *Rheinisch-Westfälische Zeitung*, 17 July 1916.

[92] BArch, R 8034 ɪɪ/2536, 'English lernen?', *Deutscher Kurier*, 8 March 1915; ibid., Albert Stechle, 'Soll der höhere Schüler weiter Französisch und Englisch lernen?', *Deutscher Kurier*, 12 March 1915; BArch, R 8034 ɪɪ/2537, Cay von Brockdorff, 'Das Schwedische in deutschen Schulen', *Der Tag*, 5 November 1915.

[93] Staatsarchiv Münster, Schulprogramme-Sammlung, no. 57, Königstädtisches Gymnasium, *Bericht über das Schuljahr Ostern 1914 bis Ostern 1915* (Berlin, 1915), p. 8; BArch, R 8034 ɪɪ/6938, 'Schule und Krieg', *Deutsche Tageszeitung*, 19 May 1915; ibid., 'Der Krieg und die schulpflichtige Jugend', *Deutsche Tageszeitung*, 9 September 1915; generally, see Karl König, *Kriegsstoffe für die Unter- und Mittelstufe*, 3rd edn (Strasburg, 1916).

[94] Franz Führen, *Lehrer im Krieg. Ein Ehrenbuch deutscher Volksschullehrer*, vol. ɪɪ (Leipzig, 1936), p. 27; Jo Milhaly, '… da gibt's ein Wiedersehn!' *Kriegstagebuch eines Mädchens 1914–1918* (Freiburg and Heidelberg, 1982), pp. 16–17; Dix, 'Beobachtungen über den Einfluß der Kriegsereignisse', p. 169; BArch, R 8034 II/2536, 'Englisch lernen?', *Deutscher Kurier*, 8 March 1915; see Demm, 'Agents of propaganda', p. 63; Verhey, *The spirit of 1914*, p. 87.

Refugee children

Social ostracism of (often assimilated) 'alien enemies' went hand in hand with the integration into metropolitan society of new arrivals from abroad. The refugees from Russia settling down in Berlin were mostly of German descent and thus readily accepted and swiftly naturalized. Their children were admitted to municipal schools where they received extra language tuition in German (up to twelve hours per week) to help them settle into the new system – blood proved thicker than linguistic problems in Berlin schools.[95]

Likewise, the integration of refugee children from the occupied French territories and Belgium (notably, French-speaking Wallonia) into Parisian schools went by and large smoothly. Although the newcomers further aggravated the problem of overcrowding in classrooms, the Municipal Council managed to accommodate all 12,000 refugee children and also provided them with clothes and shoes.[96] Support for the most innocent victims of war was considered a civic duty.[97] The compassion shown in public statements, however, tended to blur over the private reservations of teachers. In a 1917 survey, teachers complained about the lowering of standards due to the integration of refugee children.[98]

In contrast to Berlin and Paris, the arrival of refugee children in London – the encounter with the 'friendly alien' – was less significant in quantitative terms, but the rhetoric of solidarity left its imprint on the fabric of the wartime community. Belgian refugees were positively welcomed at local schools. A headline in *The Times* envisaged 'A school Entente. Belgians and British side by side.'[99]

Administrators, too, were eager to support the Belgians. In October 1914, the LCC Education Committee offered free secondary school education to gifted Belgian children.[100] This privilege was not offered

---

[95] LAB, Sta Rep. 20-01, no. 410, fo. 110, Staatsminister August von Trott zu Solz to Provinzial-Schulkollegium, 8 February 1915; ibid., fo. 145, Staatsminister August von Trott zu Solz to Provinzial-Schulkollegium, n.d.; Kaeber, *Berlin im Weltkriege*, p. 513.

[96] A.-E. André, 'L'école primaire française et la guerre', in Ministère de l'Instruction publique (ed.), *Rapports présentés au Congrès pour l'examen des questions concernant le 'cours populaire'* (Paris, 1916), pp. 53–4; see also AP, D2T-1/47, Rapport groupe scolaire rue Lacordaire, 29 June 1917.

[97] *Association amicale des anciens élèves du lycée Charlemagne* (Paris, 1920), p. 18.

[98] *Nos enfants et la guerre*, p. 18.

[99] 'A school Entente', *The Times*, 40805, 18 March 1915, p. 7; see Kevin Myers, 'The hidden history of refugee schooling in Britain. The case of the Belgians, 1914–18', *History of Education*, 30 (2001), pp. 160–1; Tony Kushner, 'Local heroes. Belgian refugees in Britain during the First World War', *Immigrants and Minorities*, 18, 1 (1999), pp. 1–28.

[100] London County Council Education Committee, *Minutes 1914*, vol. II, pp. 439, 622.

to Serbians for another two years.[101] Younger children were sent to state elementary schools. London schools in particular had considerable experience in integrating foreign children often ignorant of English into the system.[102] Yet throughout the war, the LCC Education Committee (like their colleagues in Paris) struggled to find extra accommodation for refugee children. By 1919, special classes for Belgian refugees (offering between 60 and 220 places per school) had been established at the nine institutions (all but one of them Roman Catholic) within the county.[103]

By and large, Belgian relief was a more popular cause than aid to deserving Serbians, and received greater attention. For instance, the Munster Road School girls' department supported Belgian refugee children with gifts of money, vegetables, and garments made by the girls in winter 1914–15, and, in general, school relief efforts tended to favour the 'starving children of gallant little Belgium'.[104] Serbian youngsters, in contrast, sometimes seemed an afterthought, and until autumn 1916, free secondary schooling had been withheld from Serbian children. But around 1916 there does seem to have been a shift. Not only were secondary schools now an option, but Serbian relief seems to have penetrated the consciousness of British schoolchildren; at Munster Road, the girls 'were strongly in favour of making for Serbians as much as has been done by them for Belgians'; in September 1918, for instance, they completed fifty-two pairs of socks for Serbians.[105]

In 1916–17, the LCC Education Committee initiated a Belgian and Serbian Children's Clothing Fund on a grand scale. Boys and girls were asked to bring their pennies to school, and the headmistresses sent in orders for the necessary material and arranged for work to be carried out by their girls as part of their needlework instruction. The garments were then packed up (often accompanied by letters written by the children to their Belgian and Serbian friends) and deposited in a local store, supervised by a special committee under the auspices of the Education Officer. 'It was one of the essential features of the scheme that the whole of it should be a gift from children to children; all the money was to be the children's own money, all the work the children's own work.'[106] The total

---

[101] London County Council Education Committee, *Minutes 1916*, p. 524.
[102] Myers, 'Hidden history', pp. 158–9.
[103] London County Council Education Committee, *Minutes 1919*, pp. 249, 548.
[104] 'Letter from "sunny New Zealand"', *The Times*, 41267, 8 September 1916, p. 11.
[105] LMA, LCC/EO/DIV1/MUN/LB/8, Munster Road School Girls' Department, Log-book, 1913–19, pp. 93, 250–5, 277–8, 300.
[106] LMA, LCC/MIN/2972, LCC Education Committee, 'Belgian and Serbian Children's Clothing Fund', November 1916, p. 4; and see LCC/EO/WEL/5/1, Central Committee for the Provision of Clothing to Belgian and Serbian Children, Minutes, 1916.

sum collected amounted to over £4,270, and the total number of kits supplied was about 10,000 (over 70,000 garments).[107] Both the LCC and the schools aggressively publicized these activities, organizing a central exhibition of 450 kits of clothing in the London Day Training College and a number of smaller exhibitions in different parts of London.[108] A picture of Belgian refugee children dressed in garments made by London schoolgirls appeared in the *London Teacher*, the London Teachers' Association publication.[109]

The school as home front

War charities and war savings

Charitable ventures boomed during the war, and schools in all three capitals made significant contributions to relief efforts, both symbolically (through the aura of childlike goodness) and in reality (as children collected *and* invested monies to produce goods needed at home or in the trenches). In schools, war charities were part and parcel of 'war work'. War work as an assertion of civic worth represented the civilians' claim to membership in the wartime community. Relief efforts conveyed two distinct messages: first, that the meaning of social citizenship had broadened to include provision for populations especially hit by the war, and, second, that the shared hardships of the trenches demanded shared hardships at home. The reordering of entitlements and redistribution of incomes was paralleled by the appearance of a language of moral judgement separating the stingy and idle from the charitable and dutiful citizen.[110]

In September 1914, the lycée Louis-le-Grand, 5th arrondissement, launched the *œuvre du petit sou*. Under this scheme all pupils donated the small, but symbolically significant sum of two sous (ten centimes) per week, a sum which even the poorest of schoolchildren could afford. This set a precedent that other schools followed. In support of the 1914 *Noël du soldat* campaign, the pupils of Parisian state schools contributed about 530,000 francs in total and thus showed their debt of honour to the soldiers. Occasional *Journées nationales* also appealed to the children's spirit of sacrifice.[111] War charity had above all symbolic value, and

[107] London County Council Education Committee, *Minutes 1917*, p. 507.
[108] LMA, LCC/MIN/2972, LCC Education Committee, 'Belgian and Serbian Children's clothing fund', November 1916, p. 4; generally, see chapter 5, 'Exhibitions'.
[109] *LT*, 34 (1917), p. 26.   [110] *Capital cities*, vol. I, pp. 14, 530, 550.
[111] Hollebecque, *La jeunesse scolaire*, pp. 15–17.

Parisian schoolchildren advertising the universality of wartime patriotism performed a vital part in the politics of civic gratitude.

However, the child was both the object and instrument of war charity. Relief efforts such as the *Journée de Paris*, held by the Municipal Council on 14 July 1915, used children to help target adults. The inspector of the Academy of Seine-et-Oise remarked rather cynically that children especially had the power to 'persuader les hésitants, les timides et les faux calculateurs'.[112] It is important to note that, generally, collection drives were not centrally choreographed, but emerged from within the schools. Nevertheless, the administration tried to muscle in on the success of small-scale charities. In 1916, the Prime Minister introduced the *diplôme d'honneur* as a reward for particularly active schools and pupils.[113]

London and Berlin schools saw a similar interplay between auto-mobilization and official intervention. Britain's National War Savings Committee, a governmental agency set up in 1916, aimed to control campaigns in schools and to foster a competitive climate through the formation of a war savings association for London schools. This scheme was part of the authorities' intensification of efforts, or 'remobilization', in the second half of the war.[114] Yet representatives of the headmasters and headmistresses regarded this scheme as an intolerable interference in school affairs; 'the best results in every school will be obtained by leaving the teachers entirely to act on their own initiative', they claimed.[115] In fact, between 1915 and 1917, war savings had essentially been initiatives from below. For example, Hitherfield Road School mixed department, Wandsworth, formed a war savings association in June 1916, which raised £2,037 within two years by means of regular savings and special events such as a 'war savings fête'.[116]

By autumn 1917, however, the National War Savings Committee and the London Teachers' Association joined forces and established the London Schools War Savings Committee. In no more than two months, some 400 war savings associations had been formed under the new

---

[112] Cited in Lesmanne, 'L'école et la guerre', p. 22.
[113] 'Circulaire du 23 octobre relative à l'emprunt national', *Bulletin administratif du Ministère de l'Instruction publique* (hereafter *BAMIP*), 2247, 4 November 1916, p. 871.
[114] Generally, see John Horne, 'Introduction: mobilizing for total war', in John Horne (ed.), *State, society and mobilization in Europe during the First World War* (Cambridge, 1997), pp. 1–17.
[115] LMA, LCC/EO/GEN/3/2, Central Consultative Committees of headmasters and headmistresses, Minutes of miscellaneous resolutions and sub-committees, 1909–21, p. 134.
[116] LMA, LCC/EO/DIV9/HIT/LB/3, Hitherfield Road School Mixed Department, Log-book, 1913–19, pp. 100, 266, 286.

committee, but about 260 schools opted to work under other schemes.[117] The LCC Education Committee, too, chose not to cooperate with the National War Savings Committee on the tank bank campaign. Early in March 1918, tanks toured several London boroughs to advertise and popularize war savings. In Britain's provincial cities, tank banks had particularly enthused children, and their attendance had been of paramount significance to the spectacle. Some local education authorities had released pupils for a day to visit the tanks and cheer on reluctant adults. The LCC Education Committee, however, refused to allow elementary-school pupils to attend the tank banks during school hours.[118]

Later in the same year, the London Teachers' Association decided that the war savings campaign needed a fresh stimulus. Week by week, it now devoted a column in its journal to arithmetical problems based on war savings certificates and national war bonds. Thus the children – and indirectly the parents, too – would 'become authorities on the subject of War Savings Certificates – and by taking home this knowledge to their elders and their parents they will be helping the War Savings movement'.[119] For instance: 'A family saved 3d. a day by giving up the use of sugar in tea, & c., and the father saved 5d. a day by giving up beer. After saving in this way for the months of March, April, May, and June, how much more did they require in order to be able to buy a War Savings Certificate for each of the six members of the family?'[120]

British war mathematics and German *Kriegsrechnen* were virtually interchangeable. Like their British contemporaries, German schoolchildren calculated the economic gains from sensible consumption and war savings.[121] In both countries, schools also took an active role in the collection of monies and, in Germany, gold for national war bonds. The pupils were expected to spread the gospel of economic prudence and patriotic duty outside the classrooms. Zealous students not only pestered their families and friends for subscriptions, but also – following the instructions from their teachers – pressured neighbours and strangers

[117] National Archives, Public Record Office, Kew, NSC 7/2, 'Report on special activities during October, November, December 1917', 16 January 1918. The London Teachers' Association cites slightly different figures, see 'War savings certificates for London school children', *LT*, 34 (1917), p. 433; 'London schools war savings associations', *LT*, 34 (1917), p. 618.

[118] LMA, LCC/MIN/3287, Elementary Education Sub-Committee, Minutes, vol. 30, 3 April 1917–19 March 1918, pp. 472, 487; see Patrick Wright, *Tank. The progress of a monstrous war machine* (London, 2000), pp. 90–3; on the tank bank campaign, see chapter 5, 'Exhibitions', above.

[119] 'War savings associations in schools', *LT*, 35 (1918), p. 242.   [120] Ibid.

[121] M. Hantke, *Die Schule und der Krieg*, Pädagogisches Magazin, 603 (Langensalza, 1915), p. 28; ibid., p. 97.

into subscribing to war loans. The prospect of a day off provided an incentive to students to campaign hard.[122] At one of Berlin's most successful schools, the Körner-Realschule III, Schöneberg, pupils received a crash course on propaganda before they were set after the local residents. The quarter was divided into a number of smaller sectors so that nobody could slip through the net. In his report to the School Deputation, the director boasted about the efficiency of his campaign for the fourth war loan which had generated the tidy sum of 186,600 Marks in 1916.[123]

Teachers, particularly headmasters, driven by a combination of war enthusiasm and careerism, were instrumental in launching war loans locally. They achieved mixed results. It is hardly surprising that secondary schools collected large sums of money, but most municipal schools, too, produced considerable results. Special schools, ranging from establishments for children with special needs to institutes for apprentices, often struggled in vain to mobilize their pupils. Directors of the former type reported that, despite indoctrination, pupils with learning difficulties simply did not grasp the national importance of war loans. Most illuminating is the meagre response to the fourth war loan at vocational schools. Only 30 per cent of pupils at vocational schools made a subscription. At the IV. Pflichtfortbildungsschule für Jünglinge, Dorotheenstadt, the majority of trainees bluntly refused to do their bit: 'Who knows where we will be two years after the war', they argued – 'not without justification', as the director remarked frankly.[124]

Normally, headmasters of vocational schools were anxious to hush up poor results and their political implications by blaming material constraints rather than low morale.[125] The blatant disregard for war loans in vocational schools clearly indicates the waning of faith among Berlin's working classes. Generally, however, subscriptions to war loans in schools do not provide a reliable barometer of the war enthusiasm of pupils and their families. The outstanding results achieved at some schools are particularly misleading. Pupils' zeal for war loans sprang from a combination of youthful passion, social conformism, and cynical manipulation by teachers. For the fourth war loan in 1916, students were mobilized on a hitherto unknown scale. As a result, the fourth war loan

---

[122] BArch, R 8034 II/2536, 'Ein pädagogischer Unfug', *Der Tag*, 6 March 1915; generally, see Donson, 'War pedagogy'.

[123] LAB, Sta Rep. 20-01, no. 421, Report of Direktor Greif (Körner Realschule III), 29 March 1916.

[124] Ibid., Report of Direktor Behm (IV. Pflichtfortbildungsschule), 7 April 1916.

[125] Ibid., no. 422, Städtische Schuldeputation Berlin, Berichte der Rektoren und Hauptlehrer über die Zeichnung der vierten Kriegsanleihe, 1916, for instance, Report of Dirigent Weinberg (Fachschule für Sattler), 7 April 1916.

proved a huge success in contrast to the second war loan of 1915 when merely 60 per cent of schools participated.[126]

War work

To some degree, all three belligerents regarded schoolchildren as a reservoir of cheap labour which could be legitimately mobilized for the survival of the nation. Compulsory education no longer protected children from the economic exploitation. In September 1914, the Parisian Director of Primary Education demanded that winter clothing for soldiers be produced at girls' schools during needlework lessons.[127] Already in August 1914, the Prussian Ministry of Education had ruled a decree to the same effect. As the war dragged on, cloth became an increasingly scarce commodity. Now Berlin teachers took their pupils to forests to collect large stinging nettles needed for the production of *Ersatz* cotton. *Ersatz* became the norm in wartime Germany, and schools started to resemble storehouses of junk: cherry kernels (used for *Ersatz* cooking oil), scrap metal, waste paper, etc., piled up in and outside Berlin school buildings while awaiting further distribution.[128]

The wholesale economic mobilization of London schoolchildren, starting in 1916, followed a similar trajectory. In February, the LCC Education Committee issued a pamphlet entitled *How we can all help* in which suggestions were given for talks to children 'on the subject of the war, and how everyone can help to win it, by saving as much as possible, by avoiding useless or wasteful expenditure ourselves, and by influencing others to do likewise'.[129] Theoretical instruction in civic duty and practical ventures went hand in hand. From 1916 onwards, the Education Committee used the school organization (or gave permission to charities to do so) for the purpose of making collections among pupils, like the collection of waste paper organized by Royal Commission on Paper in November 1917.[130]

By contrast, in August 1914, the LCC Emergency Committee had refused collections in schools in aid of the National Relief Fund and

---

[126] BArch, R 8034 II/2536, 'Die Anleihzeichnung der Schulen', *Vossische Zeitung*, 27 March 1915.

[127] 'Circulaire du 29 septembre relative à l'œuvre du "tricot" dans les écoles de filles', *BAMIP*, 2146, 17 October 1914, p. 516.

[128] Demm, 'Zwischen Propaganda und Sozialfürsorge', pp. 85–6; Kaeber, *Berlin im Weltkriege*, pp. 522–3; BArch, R 8034 II/6939, 'Die Betätigung der Schuljugend an den vaterländischen Bestrebungen', *Deutsche Tageszeitung*, 27 September 1915.

[129] London County Council Education Committee, *Minutes 1916*, p. 42.

[130] London County Council Education Committee, *Minutes 1917*, p. 593.

Fig. 6.3. Pupils of a Berlin intermediate school collecting woollens and metals, 1915. This picture was part of the exhibition 'School and War' at the Central Institute of Education and Teaching, Berlin.

other similar funds – after all, hitherto many pupils themselves had been and, indeed, continued to be the recipients of charitable donations.[131] In 1916, however, the LCC set the legal and propagandistic framework for the self-mobilization of schools. One girls' department in Fulham raised funds for refugees (sporadically in 1914–15, but mainly between 1916 and 1918), maimed soldiers (March 1916), the Red Cross (October 1917), and collected chestnuts (December 1917), and eggs (May 1918).[132]

In 1916, a psychologist conducted an investigation of London children's ideas as to how they could help in time of war, examining 1,300 papers written by boys and girls aged between 11 and 15. He noted that gender was an important factor:

---

[131] LMA, LCC/MIN/4367, Emergency Committee, Signed papers, August 1914–March 1915, p. 23; on the pre-war period, see Anna Davin, *Growing up poor. Home, school and street in London 1870–1914* (London, 1996).

[132] LMA, LCC/EO/DIV1/MUN/LB/8, Munster Road School Girls' Department, Logbook, 1913–19, pp. 276, 295, 299.

The fact of the children being in mixed schools gave the boys an opportunity of watching the girls at needlework for the troops, and while the average boy praised his sister's efforts, one youth was sceptical, adding in his essay, 'I saw some knitted things that Lady Jellicoe had sent to be re-knitted.' The girls, however, kept their strictures for boys who could not knit, one remarking: – 'Although they cannot knit, they can join the Boy Scouts'; another maiden finished up with the comment, 'Boys cannot sew, but they can inform their sisters their clothes are torn.' Children's ideas as to the needs of soldiers were extremely sensible, and range from air pillows to pencil-sharpeners, but whereas many girls suggest sending Christmas puddings, not a single boy mentions them. The War Loan, which one boy says 'broke out in 1915,' evidently did not appeal to some of the youthful essayists. One states that 'if a bomb fell on the Bank of England our savings would be converted to ashes'. Most of the girls state the amount they have already saved at school, but not a boy mentions it.[133]

Parisian and Berlin children proved equally generous and imaginative. One Berlin schoolgirl attending the 270th municipal school knitted a *Schießhandschuh*, a glove for riflemen.[134] Although it was not unheard of for boys to knit socks for soldiers, children's war work tended to deepen gender roles at a time when the sexual division of labour was turned upside down. In London, girls made various garments for soldiers, sometimes at the request of the army or charitable organizations, but also on their own initiative: for example, before Christmas 1917, the girls of Drayton Park School, Islington, knitted a pair of mittens for every scholar's father or brother serving with the forces in France or England.[135]

British boys, by contrast, tended to be employed in agriculture. In summer 1918, the Ministry of National Service took parties of boys from a number of central schools into the country for the purpose of fruit picking;[136] and in September 1918 the Corporation granted an extension of a fortnight of the City of London School holidays so that nearly 700 boys helped in getting in the Lincolnshire potato crop.[137] Both boys and girls from 20 London schools (over 6,000 children altogether) were employed by the Ministry of Food in June 1918 to analyse the agricultural return dealing with the potato acreage. A representative of the ministry told the children that this experience 'had given them their

---

[133] 'Children's ideas in war-time', *The Times*, 41268, 9 September 1916, p. 3.
[134] *Schule und Krieg*, fig. 31. For comparison with Austrian schools, see Christa Hämmerle, '"Wir strickten und nähten Wäsche für Soldaten ..." Von der Militarisierung des Handarbeitens im Ersten Weltkrieg', *L'Homme. Zeitschrift für Feministische Geschichtswissenschaft*, 3,1 (1992), pp. 96–113.
[135] LMA, LCC/EO/DIV3/DRA/LB/5, Drayton Park School Girls' Department, Log-book, 1913–27, p. 240.
[136] LMA, LCC/MIN/3289, Elementary Education Sub-Committee, Minutes, vol. 31, 27 March 1918–4 March 1919, pp. 112, 168.
[137] 'Schoolboys for potato lifting', *The Times*, 41840, 12 July 1918, p. 3.

first insight into the duty of public service'.[138] His statement was characteristic of a social elite which 'placed voluntary social work ... at the centre of a wider vision of social and moral reconstruction'.[139]

One historian argues that war work gave fresh impetus to an expansion of practical and vocational training after the war in Britain.[140] The war transformed, for instance, the character of school gardening classes. Pre-war ideas of experimental work and the cultivation of a wide range of plants gave way to utilitarianism. In 1917, the national Board of Education urged schools to grow 'the most useful vegetables' for they were 'very important at the present time'.[141] Independent schools also dug for national survival. King's College School, Wimbledon, planted vegetables on part of the Royal Wimbledon Golf Club course, and turned some of the school's tennis courts into potato patches. Likewise, the flower beds of Berlin's school gardens in Blankenfelde, comprising 130 Prussian acres (2,553 square metres), became arable land.[142] In addition, schools occupied abandoned land in the heart of the city and planted potatoes there with the help of one pupil's father who donated 300 kilograms of potato seeds.[143]

Berlin's schoolchildren were drafted into farm work on a much grander scale than London or Paris's youngsters.[144] Effectively, the war made the German school an adjunct of the national economy.[145] In 1917 alone, about 68,000 pupils spent several months in the Prussian countryside, ostensibly to improve their health. Private associations selected the children and paid for their medical care, travel, and insurance costs. Still, the parents had to contribute fifty Pfennigs per child per day. The hosts had the right to employ the children in 'light agricultural work', but were not supposed to exploit the undernourished and stressed youngsters. Nevertheless, cases of severe overstress occurred, and approximately 10 per cent of the children preferred to return home prematurely. In secondary schools, work brigades made up of fifteen to twenty students were formed and sent to work on the

---

[138] 'School children's work for the Food Ministry', *TES*, 166, 20 June 1918, p. 260.
[139] Pedersen, 'Gender, welfare, and citizenship', p. 992.
[140] Parker, 'The talent at its command', pp. 237–59.
[141] London County Council Education Committee, *Minutes 1917*, p. 68; see Parker, 'The talent at its command', p. 250.
[142] BArch, R 8034 ii/6941, 'Im Schulgarten Berlins', *Vossische Zeitung*, 29 July 1918.
[143] BArch, R 8034 ii/2536, 'Kriegs-Kartoffelacker des Kaiser-Friedrich-Realgymnasiums in Neukölln', *Deutsche Tageszeitung*, 20 May 1915.
[144] LAB, Sta Rep. 49-05/8, no. 48, fo. 97, Rektor Müller (7. Schule) to Schuldeputation Pankow, 5 August 1914; BArch, R 8034 II/2536, Hanna Gräfin von Pesalozza, 'Erntehilfe', *Berliner Tageblatt*, 30 June 1915.
[145] 'Der Kriegsbericht der preußischen Gewerbeaufsicht', *Soziale Praxis*, 28 (1918–19), pp. 387–8.

large Prussian estates. Again, their experiences varied; some were put up properly and well fed, others slept on rotten straw, ate from dirty common plates, and suffered attacks of diarrhoea.[146]

In 1917, the school authorities of Schöneberg voiced their concern about the physical and spiritual well-being of schoolchildren helping out on farms. They suggested discontinuing the old practice and, instead, setting up a new scheme that would provide for rural colonies of Schöneberg pupils under the supervision of their teachers.[147] The hardships during the final year of war, however, turned the clock back on social experiments. In September 1918, a commission consisting of headmasters and representatives of the Provincial School Committee proposed to establish compulsory service in agriculture for all older students in secondary education.[148] A system of forced labour for offspring of the upper and middle classes was to replace what had once been, at least in theory (and rhetoric), a voluntary institution. Now there was no point in keeping up appearances when everybody knew the survival of the nation was at stake.

Bombardment

In 1917–18, absenteeism among London schoolchildren peaked after air raids. Parents felt that it was safer for their offspring to stay away (at home or in the countryside) from school.[149] What is more, schools sanctioned the inevitable, accepting informally 'permissive late-coming' after night raids. At the suggestion of the London Teachers' Association, the LCC Education Committee arranged that elementary schools opened at ten o'clock instead of nine o'clock on those mornings following an air raid when the all clear signal was given later than ten o'clock at night. The later opening was meant to secure an additional hour's sleep and to guarantee punctual attendance as 'a useful part of the normal discipline and training'.[150]

---

[146] Geheimes Staatsarchiv Preußischer Kulturbesitz, I. HA, Rep. 89, no. 24553, Unterbringung von Stadtkindern auf dem Lande, 1915–18; Kaeber, *Berlin im Weltkriege*, pp. 496–7; Demm, 'Zwischen Propaganda und Sozialfürsorge', pp. 86–8; Demm, 'Agents of propaganda', p. 62.

[147] BArch, R 8034 ii/6940, 'Stadtkinder auf dem Lande', *Deutsche Tageszeitung*, 24 March 1917.

[148] BArch, R 8034 II/2536, 'Hilfsdienstzwang der höheren Schüler', *Berliner Neueste Nachrichten*, 19 September 1918.

[149] GL, MS 31192, Sir John Cass Foundation School (Red Coat School for girls), Log-book, vol. iv, 1913–39, p. 209; LMA, LCC/EO/DIV9/HIT/LB/3, Hitherfield Road School Mixed Department, Log-book, 1913–39, p. 211.

[150] London County Council Education Committee, *Minutes of proceedings. January to December, 1918* (London, 1918), p. 264.

Air war is total war par excellence; airborne raids blurred the boundaries between home and front. The war against civilian targets – a development arising out of mass mobilization for the war – evolved into the cornerstone of the 'home-front experience' in the metropolis. The bombing campaign was, of course, rather limited compared to the Blitz in the Second World War, but air raids had a huge psychological impact on Londoners. Zeppelin attacks were perceived as a 'war on women and children' since 'No soldier or sailor has been killed in any of these raids.'[151] The air raids on London created among teachers a sense of belonging to the community of those at risk of personal loss.[152] Their newspaper claimed that schoolteachers had gained 'first-hand experience of the perils of modern warfare': 'We share now, at any rate in some small degree, the fortunes in the field of our husbands, brothers, sons and comrades.'[153]

Teachers had to deal with stressed children (many of whom were, in addition, undernourished). A number of reports described how pupils suffered from nervous tension and 'a serious diminution in the powers of receptiveness and retentiveness'.[154] The new rules of engagement required amending the form of prayer for use in time of war. Published in October 1914, it contained the line 'Take care of us also, who stay behind in this quiet land.' In March 1918, a churchman drew attention to the need, in view of the frequency of air raids, for the revision of the prayer in so far as it had reference to England being a 'quiet land'; the Council duly dropped the 'quiet land' formula.[155]

The perceived danger of air raids to schoolchildren overshadowed all other issues after summer 1917, and administrators, teachers as well as parents had their say. Both the Education Committees of the LCC and Middlesex County Council were very aware of the possibility of daylight air raids. They issued generic guidelines, but failed to take definite precautionary measures.[156] Initially, the administrators were more concerned about damage to school buildings than the safety of the

[151] 'Zeppelins over London district', *Manchester Guardian*, 21557, 9 September 1915, p. 7; generally, see Andrea Süchting-Hänger, ' "Kindermörder". Die Luftangriffe auf Paris, London und Karlsruhe im Ersten Weltkrieg und ihre vergessenen Opfer', in Dittmar Dahlmann (ed.), *Kinder und Jugendliche in Krieg und Revolution. Vom Dreißigjährigen Krieg bis zu den Kindersoldaten Afrikas* (Paderborn, 2000), pp. 73–92.
[152] *Capital cities*, vol. I, p. 14.   [153] 'Under fire!', *LT*, 34 (1917), p. 369.
[154] GL, MS 31098, Sir John Cass Foundation School, School Managers' minute book, vol. VII, 1914–19, n.p. [20 October 1915, 21 March 1918].
[155] LMA, LCC/MIN/3287, Elementary Education Sub-Committee, Minutes, vol. 30, 3 April 1917–19 March 1918, p. 484.
[156] LMA, MCC/MIN/13/179, Elementary Education Sub-Committee, Minute book, vol. 21, November 1914–March 1915, p. 78.

schoolchildren. Early in 1916, both committees decided to take out a special policy to cover any damage by enemy aircraft.[157]

Proper safety precautions, based on a memorandum by the Board of Education, were not introduced until mid-1917. Both education committees ordered that, on warning of an air raid, the top floor to be vacated and children distributed over the lower floors or basements; the outside gates were to be locked in order to prevent an inrush of anxious parents and the public seeking shelter. Since Zeppelins and, from 1917, aeroplanes attacked mostly during the night, boarding schools were most exposed to air raids. The students at Westminster School were sent to the Norman undercroft beneath the school, the roof of which was five feet thick, and was thought to be safe protection. Air raid drills (in addition to ordinary fire drills) became a routine procedure in all schools from 1915 onwards, particularly in 1917. The boys of Munster Road School practised 'Zeppelin drills' twice in 1915 and 1916, but three times in 1917; at the girls' department, only one drill was held in 1916 compared to twelve in 1917.[158] The example of air-raid drills shows how the war enforced a new set of collective practices and how everyday life was increasingly experienced through larger groups or communities of those at risk.[159]

Schools gave shelter to anxious children, but teachers felt that they were fighting a lonely battle. In January 1915, the Middlesex Elementary Education Sub-Committee stated tersely that the pupils should be kept 'at their ordinary work' during air raids.[160] By July 1917, it had become obvious that 'it may not be possible to carry on work of a normal character during an actual raid'; the LCC's air-raid circular to headmasters, suggested merely to draw the attention of children as far as possible from the raid itself: 'This has been accomplished successfully in many cases by letting the children sing or by telling them stories. Other suitable ways of diverting the children's attention from a raid in process will occur to teachers and these it is considered may be best left to their discretion.'[161] The education authorities had little practical advice to offer; in the words

---

[157] County Council of Middlesex, *Reports of Committees for 1916*, vol. III (London, 1916), n.p. [30 March 1916]; London County Council Education Committee, *Minutes 1916*, p. 10.

[158] LMA, LCC/EO/DIV1/MUN/LB/3, Munster Road School Boys' Department, Logbook, 1913–32, pp. 225–6, 234–7; LCC/EO/DIV1/MUN/LB/8, Munster Road School Girls' Department, Log-book, 1913–9, pp. 225–7; LCC/EO/WAR/3/1, Elementary Education Sub-Committee to headmasters, 20 July 1917.

[159] London County Council Education Committee, *Minutes 1918*, p. 45.

[160] LMA, MCC/MIN/13/179, Elementary Education Sub-Committee, Minute book, vol. 21, November 1914–March 1915, p. 78.

[161] LMA, LCC/EO/WAR/3/1, Elementary Education Sub-Committee to headmasters, 20 July 1917.

of the London Teachers' Association, they showed 'complete incapacity to realise the teachers' difficulties'.

Parents continued to be a force to be reckoned with in school affairs. Before the war, schools had found it necessary to lock the gates during fire alarms to keep out the crowd of excited mothers.[162] Clashes between parents' anxiety for their children's safety and teachers' concern over parental indiscipline intensified during air raids as many parents insisted that their children be handed over to them. In response to their demands, the LCC Education Committee's published a poster (affixed to the outer walls of schools) and handbill (sent to parents) impressing on families the importance of leaving their children in school. First, there was less risk inside school buildings from fragments of bombs and debris, and, second, there was the danger of parents crowding into schools when air raids were expected or in progress and thereby causing panic and disorder. Yet the committee assumed 'that the confidence of the parents in the teachers is so great that any danger of panic due to excitement may by such appeals [i.e. poster] be reduced to the smallest proportions'.[163]

Aerial bombardment during the Great War was life-threatening and traumatic, although less dangerous than the Blitz to come, and seemed to render the conventional distinction between home front and fighting front redundant. London and Paris schools came to regard themselves as part of a new kind of front. By contrast, in Berlin, 'There were no air raids and no bombs. There were the wounded, but you saw them only at a distance, with picturesque bandages', the journalist Sebastian Haffner recalled after the war.[164]

Parisian children, menaced by both aircraft and artillery, shared the experience of bombardments with their London peers. Due to the city's proximity to the main battlefields, the threat of bombardments were a considerable source of anxiety in Paris from the earliest days of the war. But, as in London, actual bombing raids did not cause serious disruptions until late in the war. In spring 1918, the pupils of the lycée Charlemagne, situated in the heart of the capital, in the 4th arrondissement, took shelter in the basement of the school building for the first time. Over the next weeks, emergency evacuations became a routine. In April, the school was hit by a bomb:

Thus we survived the disastrous night of 12–13 April. It was exactly at 10:20 pm; the sirens had not finished sounding the alert when a 50 kg bomb landed on the

[162] Davin, *Growing up poor*, pp. 133–4.
[163] LMA, LCC/EO/WAR/3/1, Elementary Education Sub-Committee to headmasters, 20 July 1917; London County Council Education Committee, *Minutes 1917*, p. 366.
[164] Sebastian Haffner, *Defying Hitler. A memoir* (London, 2002), p. 12.

bursar's office, next to the church of St Paul, creating a crater nearly six meters deep, uprooting trees, destroying the bicycle shed, splitting the pavement and sending pieces in all directions, even into courtyard and that of 111 rue Saint-Antoine, blowing out the windows of the library, the quarters of the headmaster and the bursar and above all the class windows and the window of the hall.[165]

In the aftermath of the air raid, the school closed down for a period of twenty days. Once a week, however, the pupils were supposed to return to school in order to receive their weekly homework. Eventually, when the school reopened, absenteeism had assumed alarming proportions. Even so, the director struggled to accommodate all remaining scholars in a building that was largely destroyed. The crisis dragged on until the summer when the last students joined the schoolmates in the countryside.[166]

Commemorations

The German air raids appeared to be directed against schoolchildren. In a daylight raid on London on 13 June 1917, a bomb hit the Upper North Street School, Poplar, and killed 18 children; over 30 were injured: 'innocent victims of German barbarity'.[167] Accounts of the incident echoed the atrocity propaganda of 1914; the child featured as symbolic victim.[168] The King immediately visited the bombed school, thus manifesting his sympathy with the children. Expressions of sympathy were received from schools all over the world. One school in Australia sent a sum of fifteen pounds towards funds for children who had suffered through air raids.[169] Inaccuracy rather than intention caused the slaughter, but *The Times Educational Supplement* commented that 'Germany of set purpose had set back the clock, had lowered the standard, making an actual pride of brutality and murder, directed against helpless civilians.'[170]

The scale of the disaster called for a permanent tribute to the victims. In November 1917, the LCC Education Committee received the first enquiries as to providing a memorial, and, in June 1918, permission was

---

[165] L. Bernard, 'Le lycée Charlemagne pendant la guerre', in *Association amicale des anciens élèves du lycée Charlemagne* (Paris, 1920), p. 8.

[166] Ibid., pp. 19–21; for another example, see Louis Benaerts, *Un lycée de Paris pendant la guerre. 'Condorcet' 1914–1918* (Montrouge, 1919).

[167] LMA, LCC/EO/GEN/3/1, Central Consultative Committees of headmasters and headmistresses, Minutes, 1908–19, pp. 213–14.

[168] John Horne and Alan Kramer, *German atrocities, 1914. A history of denial* (New Haven and London, 2001).

[169] London County Council Education Committee, *Minutes 1917*, p. 366.

[170] 'The bomb on an East-end school', *TES*, 114, 21 June 1917, p. 236.

granted to affix a tablet to the outside wall of the school.[171] In the event, enough funds were raised to endow several memorials: two cots in the Poplar hospital and one cot in Sir William Treloar's home for crippled children at Alton; a memorial stone in the recreation ground in East India Dock road; and a figurative monument in the cemetery where the children were buried together like fallen soldiers.[172] The cemetery memorial, unveiled by Queen Alexandra, the King's mother, featured a small obelisk surmounted by an angel made of marble.

Traditional imagery was used to accommodate the novel experience of death from the air.[173] The memorial elevated the children to martyrs on a par with the combatants killed in the war. The mayor of Poplar stressed that 'these little ones died as truly for their country as any of our gallant men who have fallen on the battlefield or on the High Seas'.[174] In other words, the London school could legitimately claim to have represented the home *front*, that is the metropolitan community at war. The distinction between civilian and military dead became further blurred in 1934 when the local branch of the British Legion took charge of the annual service of remembrance held at the children's memorial.

War commemorations fashioned the image of the child as both victim and hero; 'innocence was paired with chivalry to mask the ongoing conflict', writes Mosse.[175] Occasionally, the ideal of the boy hero seemed to take on palpable dimensions of reality as stories of frontline bravery began to circulate. The ultimate example of the child hero was Jack Cornwell, celebrated in war memorials and charitable appeals; he became a London cult figure without parallel in Berlin or Paris.[176] Fatally wounded at Jutland, the boy seaman held the position while all around him were killed. His bravery won him the Victoria Cross, but cost him his life at the age of sixteen. His former school, Walton Road School, East Ham – renamed Cornwell School in 1929 – eulogized him as the embodiment of the working-class sense of duty and commitment to the national war effort.

---

[171] LMA, LCC/MIN/3287, Elementary Education Sub-Committee, Minutes, vol. 30, 3 April 1917–19 March 1918, p. 368; and LCC/MIN/3289, Elementary Education Sub-Committee, Minutes, vol. 31, 27 March 1918–4 March 1919, p. 74.
[172] 'Notes', *TES*, 219, 26 June 1919, p. 324.
[173] Mark Connelly, *The Great War, memory and ritual. Commemoration in the City and East London, 1916–1939* (Woodbridge, 2002), p. 89; generally, see Jay Winter, *Sites of memory, sites of mourning. The Great War in European cultural history* (Cambridge, 1995).
[174] As cited in Connelly, *Great War*, p. 89.
[175] Mosse, *Fallen soldiers*, p. 137; see also Audoin-Rouzeau, *La guerre des enfants*, ch. 3.
[176] Connelly, *Great War*, pp. 91–6; Deborah Cohen, *The war come home. Disabled veterans in Britain and Germany, 1914–1939* (Berkeley, Los Angeles, and London, 2001), pp. 30–11; Demm, 'Zwischen Propaganda und Sozialfürsorge', pp. 110–11.

The schoolboys collected funds for a plaque in memory of the famous alumnus which was unveiled by Lady Jellicoe in July 1917. On this occasion, the headmaster eulogized Cornwell as 'a poor boy, a boy of the masses, who rose to heights of bravery and self-sacrifice'.[177] Three months later, the education authority supplied copies of a portrait of Cornwell to all schools in the borough at a cost of 3d. each; the proceeds from the sale went to a children's fund for a monument on Cornwell's grave in Manor Park cemetery. The memorialization drive continued in peacetime and turned every East Ham boy into a Cornwellite. In 1919, the LCC Education Committee awarded certificates commemorating the signing of the peace to well-behaved schoolchildren; it featured Jack Cornwell side by side with George V, Queen Mary, the Prince of Wales, Admiral Beatty, Field Marshal Haig, and Nurse Cavell.[178]

Violent death became a part of everyday life in all three capital cities. Commemorations in schools familiarized children at home with the bloodshed at the front reconfiguring death as a patriotic act of self-sacrifice. The war transformed the school into a nucleus of remembrance, and the school building into a prototypical *lieu de mémoire*. Remembrance as an act of citizenship made pupils connect their shock to public virtue. Generally speaking, schools commemorated the ordinary dead rather than heroes (like Cornwell), and old boys and teachers rather than children (as in Poplar). War remembrance was by and large a grass-roots activity that was locally organized, an activity that originated in the desire to give civic meaning to the slaughter. In Paris, the pupils of école Turgot, a *primaire supérieure*, in the 3rd arrondissement, organized cortèges for wounded soldiers stationed in the school turned hospital who had succumbed to their injuries – long before a ministerial circular ordered schools to pay their respects to the dead.[179] In London, Council schools did not wait for the LCC Education Committee to stipulate a scheme to commemorate fallen teachers and pupils (a goat-leather bound roll of honour and service contained in a shrine made in black wood), but often seized the initiative.[180]

Early in the war, London schools had compiled rolls of service listing former pupils who had joined up or achieved distinctions; as their numbers shifted from life towards death, rolls of honour became widespread. The LCC Education Committee, in turn, arranged for the portraits of

[177] As cited in Connelly, *Great War*, p. 92.
[178] LMA, LCC/EO/PS/11/2/99, Certificate for attendance, 1919.
[179] Pierre Laurant, *Nos potaches pendant la guerre* (Paris, 1932), ch. 3; Hollebecque, *La jeunesse scolaire*, p. 66.
[180] London County Council Education Committee, *Minutes of proceedings. January to December, 1920* (London, 1920), p. 1294.

Fig. 6.4. Children inspecting captured German guns exhibited in the Mall, London.

killed teachers – 11.6 per cent died in the war[181] – to be placed in schools together with a suitable inscription. Wartime commemorations prepared the ground for permanent memorials after 1918.[182] Those range from monumental crosses to simple tablets, and from libraries to sports facilities. In short, school memorials mirror the trends and conflicts – notably, symbolism *versus* utilitarianism – of British war commemoration as a whole.[183] Funding was always critical: it was both a practical necessity – especially for ambitious projects such as the war memorial organ in the Strand School, Brixton[184] – and a means of expression for members of the community (pupils, teachers, and old boys). In a sense, fund-raising for war memorials extended the symbolism of war charity and work in peacetime. In schools, the act of remembrance was cast as a civic responsibility.

[181] See *Capital cities at war*, vol. I, ch. 3.
[182] London County Council Education Committee, *Minutes 1915*, vol. II, p. 99; on casualty figures, see *Capital cities*, vol. I, p. 81.
[183] Alex King, *Memorials of the Great War in Britain. The symbolism and politics of remembrance* (Oxford and New York, 1998).
[184] London County Council Education Committee, *Minutes 1920*, p. 895.

This link was even stronger in Berlin schools where the aspect of commemoration was built into war charity. The remembrance of death in war and the affirmation of wartime community went hand in hand. Iron-nail memorials swept schools all over Germany in 1916. For a donation between two and ten Pfennigs, pupils purchased the right to hammer an iron nail into wooden plaques thus outlining martial symbols such as the German eagle (Gunkelsches Lyceum, Neukölln) a lion (2nd municipal school, Wilmersdorf) or evocative proverbs such as 'All for one and one for all' (Braunersche höhere Knabenschule, Stadt Berlin).[185] Sometimes an inscription would bear the names of teachers fallen in the war. The collected funds, administered by a national charitable society, went to support war orphans.[186] The nailing practice, combining charity with commemoration, expressed the gratitude of pupils to the dead soldiers and their surviving dependants by means of symbolic gesture and real gifts of money. The children's pecuniary sacrifice was meant to emulate the soldiers' blood sacrifice, thus forging an iron bond of solidarity between home and front.

School war museums displaying a plethora of war ephemera fulfilled a similar function. Again, this is a commemorative form peculiar to Berlin and, more generally, Germany (although the London Teachers' Association also toyed with the idea).[187] War trophies, kitsch, and objects of everyday life acquired the status of collector's items during the conflict. Berlin became the capital of such war collections with many schools establishing their own 'war museums'. The students of the Fichte-Gymnasium collected a large range of propaganda material, emergency banknotes, and food-ration coupons.[188] Exhibited in a glass cabinet or stored away in a cupboard, these items were testaments to the local experience of war. Individual schools replicated what the quasi-governmental think-tank, the Central Institute of Education and Teaching, did on a grand scale. Its exhibition, 'School and War', provided

---

[185] We are grateful to Gerhard Schneider for providing us with photocopies from his postcard collection.

[186] Gerhard Schneider, 'Über Hannoversche Nagelfiguren im Ersten Weltkrieg', *Hannoversche Geschichtsblätter*, 50 (1996), pp. 247–53; see also Stefan Goebel, '"Kohle und Schwert". Zur Konstruktion der Heimatfront in Kriegswahrzeichen des Ruhrgebietes im Ersten Weltkrieg', *Westfälische Forschungen*, 51 (2001), pp. 257–81; Benno Fitzke and Paul Matzdorf, *Eiserne Kreuz-Nagelungen zum Besten der Kriegshilfe und zur Schaffung von Kriegswahrzeichen. Gebrauchsfertiges Material für vaterländische Volksunterhaltung durch Feiern in Schulen, Jugendvereinigungen und Vereinen* (Leipzig, 1916); on iron-nail objects, see chapter 5, above.

[187] 'Local war museums', *LT*, 34 (1917), p. 89.

[188] A. Buddecke, *Die Kriegssammlungen. Ein Nachweis ihrer Einrichtung und ihres Bestandes* (Oldenburg, 1917), p. 9; see also Christine Beil, *Der ausgestellte Krieg. Die Präsentationen des Ersten Weltkriegs 1914–1939* (Tübingen, 2004), pp. 123–9.

a comprehensive survey and celebration of the school under the impact of war. It featured primarily artworks and writings by Berlin pupils, inter alia drawings of soldiers' graves by primary schoolchildren and a poem by a student of the Oberrealschule Am Seepark, Wilmersdorf, dedicated to his dead teacher.[189]

Conventional forms of commemoration predominated in Parisian schools. The war years saw an enormous proliferation of *tableaux glorieux*, quite similar to rolls of honour in London schools apart from the almost obligatory inscription taken from Victor Hugo: 'Ceux qui pieusement sont morts pour la patrie. Gloire à notre France éternelle.'[190] The act of naming and cataloguing the dead was an effort to come to terms with the reality of their death. Decorated with flowers by the schoolchildren, these commemorative tokens were prominently displayed in school vestibules throughout Paris. But every classroom was a potential site of memory. All over France, teachers encouraged their pupils to build makeshift classroom memorials using lists of names and photographs.[191]

The naming of the fallen teachers on commemorative tablets was strangely confined to boys' schools or sections. Girls' schools, in contrast, tended to remember the dead as a group without invoking the memory of individuals.[192] After the war, elaborate monuments and plaques, supplemented with books of remembrance, replaced provisional *tableaux glorieux* with their typewritten letters compiled in wartime. There is a notable difference in tone between the war memorials of *lycées* and *écoles primaires supérieures* and those of *écoles primaires*. In the former establishments, war memorials naming alumni were not only foci of shock and bereavement but also vectors for the dissemination of public morals.[193]

The contrast between the commemorations of different types of schools is especially striking in London. Elite public schools could afford to plan on a large scale. The Merchant Taylors' School, for example, established memorial scholarships, purchased a sports ground, and erected a sacred

---

[189] *Schule und Krieg*, figs. 4, 12; Reich, *Das Buch Michael*, figs. 5–6; see also Otto Bobertag, 'Bericht über die Ausstellung "Schule und Krieg" im Zentralinstitut für Erziehung und Unterricht zu Berlin', in William Stern (ed.), *Jugendliches Seelenleben und Krieg. Materialien und Berichte*, Beihefte zur Zeitschrift für angewandte Psychologie und psychologische Sammelforschung, 12 (Leipzig, 1915), pp. 134–64.

[190] Hollebecque, *La jeunesse scolaire*, pp. 66–7.

[191] Mona Siegel, ' "History is the opposite of forgetting": the limits of memory and the lessons of history in interwar France', *Journal of Modern History*, 74 (2002), pp. 781–2; see also Siegel, *Moral disarmament*, ch. 2.

[192] Hollebecque, *La jeunesse scolaire*, p. 66.

[193] Generally, see Antoine Prost, 'Monuments to the dead', in Pierre Nora (ed.), *Realms of memory. The construction of the French past*, vol. II, *Traditions* (New York, 1997), pp. 307–30.

memorial. The inscriptions include 'Faire branche of honor, flower of chevalrie, Joy have thou of thy noble victorie' and 'Nought is more honourable to a knight, Than to defend the feeble in their right.'[194] Public-school memorials evolved into elite foci of reflections on 'the lost generation'; the war, it seemed, had cost elites their most chivalrous apprentices. War memorials conveyed an abiding sense of admiration and guilt for the soldiers' self-sacrifice. Chivalric diction, firmly anchored in pre-war public life, also fulfilled a second purpose: it removed doubts as to the moral character of the bloody actions of the soldiers.[195]

Occasionally, commemorations in Council schools resonated with chivalric overtones, too. At Albert Road School in Romford, Essex, the chaplain – blind to gender – pressed the boys and girls 'to be worthy to stand beside the Albert Road School heroes by the practice of those true manly virtues of courage, courtesy, charity and chivalry'.[196] The young generation was told it had a moral obligation to emulate the chivalrous bearing of the dead, in order to give continuing meaning to their sacrifices. Sport was regarded as the modern equivalent to the chivalrous duel, and the football pitch as a breeding-ground for future knights. When the Duke of York went to Poplar to unveil the Hay Currie School memorial, he told the audience: 'Don't play foul; don't throw in the sponge; go all out to win; and play the game, not for self, but for the honour of the school.'[197]

Conclusion

The logic of total war disrupted the routines, formalities, and procedures that had previously provided the rhythm of educational life. This chapter has charted how schools in Paris, London, and Berlin endeavoured to fulfil two conflicting functions between 1914 and 1918: on the one hand, their traditional educational function to open pupils' eyes and minds – a function vital for the nation's future in a competitive world; and, on the other hand, a symbolic function to affirm community and to exclude those values or people that placed it under threat – a function crucial for the survival of the nation in the present world war. The conflict between these two tasks predated the Great War. In fact, it had been built into the system of public schooling as it had emerged during the nineteenth century. Both the state and parents had expected the school to

---

[194] Charles F. Kernot, *British public schools' war memorials* (London, 1927), p. 236; see also Peter Parker, *The old lie. The Great War and the public-school ethos* (London, 1987); J. A. Mangan, *Athleticism in the Victorian and Edwardian public school. The emergence and consolidation of an educational ideology* (Cambridge, 1981).

[195] Goebel, *Great War*, ch. 4.   [196] As cited in Connelly, *Great War*, p. 87.

[197] Ibid., p. 85.

teach children not only the three Rs but also the essence of citizenship, the meaning of personal duty and collective belonging.

The arrival of total war, however, upset the pre-war equilibrium. After 1914, the symbolic function of schooling, that is, the socialization of children into the martial world of their elders, threatened to override schools' educational mission. Teachers made it their business to encourage children to behave like mature citizens, to make them accept their social obligation to render active service to their country. As against Mosse and Audoin-Rouzeau, we have argued that the wartime school conveyed primarily the importance of civic responsibility rather than the cult of military brutality. In doing so, teachers responded to (and, at the same time, reinforced) the emerging new hierarchy of citizenship in the metropolis during the war, a hierarchy which enhanced the status of those contributing to the war effort. Charitable ventures, 'voluntary' work, and commemorative activities – new enterprises that transformed schools into exemplary 'home fronts' – were underpinned by a rhetoric of civic duty. The appearance of a language of moral judgement separating the responsible from the selfish in the classrooms of the capitals went hand in hand with the administrative reordering of educational entitlements. The exclusion of enemy aliens and the inclusion of refugees configured the school as a nucleus of the wartime community.

The transformation of schools into citizenship academies and schoolchildren into a 'child army' was not a smooth one, but a process accompanied by multiple conflicts. Headteachers assumed increasing responsibility for the physical well-being of their pupils; schools tightened their hold on the children vis-à-vis the parents. At the same time, teachers facilitated and co-ordinated the exploitation of schoolchildren for war work, relief efforts or paramilitary exercise, sometimes seizing the initiative themselves, sometimes reacting to the demands of the army, employers, and charitable organizations. Children became disputed bodies among families, civil society, employers, and the state. To be sure, the war also brought about internal frictions between schoolteachers and administrators, notably over the treatment of enemy aliens and the requisitioning of school buildings in Paris.

Many teachers were caught between two conflicting objectives: their desire to contribute actively to the mobilization of society from top to bottom on the one hand (and thus to advance themselves in the wartime hierarchy of urban citizenship) and their determination to keep disruptions to the normal routines of the school to a minimum. Mobilization for total war transformed work routines and disrupted the rhythms of schooling in all three capital cities; everywhere the internal life of schools was profoundly altered by the war. What distinguished the three cases was their ability to continue to function as institutions of learning on a daily basis. The case of London schools is exceptional, for it underlines the exuberance of the local state as a cultural player throughout the war. While London's school system was on the whole not jeopardized, schools in Berlin and, to a lesser extent, in Paris struggled much harder, and often in vain, to adapt to the dynamics of mobilization. War work, requisitioning, and staff shortages proved more disruptive here and fostered the erosion of the pre-war school as indicated by the rise of absenteeism and breakdown of school discipline. Ironically, from the beginning teachers and administrators helped to unleash the forces of mobilization which eventually undermined many of the foundations of the school system as a place of learning in Paris and Berlin during the Great War.

7   Universities

Elizabeth Fordham

One of the striking characteristics of metropolitan cultural life was the prominent role played by universities and colleges of higher education. Universities were sites, not just of learning and research, but also of professional training, social formation, civic instruction, and political action. This chapter explores how these multifaceted metropolitan sites responded to the war. The approach adopted is deliberately broad. Our purpose is to give a sense of the wide range of functions that the universities performed during the war, and the variety of interests and ideals that guided the academic community. One consequence of this approach is to diminish the emphasis usually given to the university's role in propaganda. Most accounts of the First World War represent university culture exclusively in terms of the public declarations made by professors in support of the national war effort. This chapter demonstrates that such public proclamations formed just one dimension of a response to a crisis that was both practically and intellectually much more complex.

The aim of this chapter is to enlarge our understanding of university culture during the Great War. It is also to investigate, in light of the experiences of academics and students, two notions that have been important in shaping interpretations of the cultural history of warfare. The first is the argument, put forward in the introduction to this volume, that the war years witnessed a resurgence of traditional ideals and practices. By focusing on the discourses of (usually the most conservative) academics, historians have tended to agree that the war did narrow minds and harden conservatism. However, when we look at academic practices – in scientific research, modern language teaching, or university international relations, for example – the war years stand out most remarkably as a period of scholarly innovation. Even in terms of public discourse the picture is more complex. During the war the platform for academic

This chapter was written by Elizabeth Fordham, in collaboration with Nicolas Beaupré and Eberhard Demm.

intervention in public affairs shifted subtly from one of general intellectual authority to one of specific professional expertise. One such special-
ism which grew directly out of the war was the study of political science.

The second notion that this chapter questions is that 1914–1918
witnessed the emergence of a clear 'system' of cultural representations
and practices.[1] What characterizes the experience of universities is both
the extent to which academics refused to adapt higher education to the
dictates of war, and also the degree to which even when they did redirect
their energies towards the conflict, the 'logic' of mobilization was often
defined more by academic concerns than by the needs of war service. This
chapter sets out to investigate how the demands of war were refracted
through strongly entrenched academic interests and practices, creating
within the university community, not a specific form of 'war culture', but
rather a situation of cultural tension between pre-war academic traditions
and the demands of total war.

Capital universities

Universities are understood in this chapter as sites of advanced learning.
We have chosen this broad definition both because it enables us to include
within our study academies, special schools, grandes écoles, institutes, and
colleges, and because by 1914 the classical university – as a single site of
universal instruction – was to some extent in dissolution. By the turn of the
century universities in Western Europe were tending more towards a
'multiversity', a set of loosely related specialist institutions dealing individually with different branches of knowledge and expertise.[2] This tendency
was especially marked in Paris, where throughout the nineteenth century
the French state had intensified its practice, begun with the creation of the
Collège de France in 1530, of fulfilling its growing needs, not by expanding
the existing faculties of the Université de Paris (the Sorbonne), but by
creating independent specialized schools (the grandes écoles). The result
was that by 1914 higher education in the capital was dispersed across a
great variety of independent institutions including, to name only a few of
the most prestigious, the Collège de France, the Sorbonne, the École
Normale Supérieure (ENS), the École Polytechnique and the École
Libre des Sciences Politiques (Sciences Po).[3]

---

[1] S. Audoin-Rouzeau and A. Becker, *14–18, retrouver la guerre* (Paris, 2000). Cf. Winter and
Robert, *Capital cities*, pp. 550–1.
[2] S. Rothblatt, *The modern university and its discontents* (Cambridge, 1997).
[3] G. Weisz, *The emergence of modern universities in France, 1863–1914*, (Princeton, 1983).

The two university colleges (University [UCL] and King's), thirty-one schools and twenty-five other institutions that by 1914 constituted the 'University of London'[4] likewise maintained a more or less autonomous existence. Here however the grounds for their dispersal derived less from the 'divide and rule' policy of a jealous state than from the capital itself. London was a truly metropolitan university, founded and developed to cater for the multifarious needs of a rapidly expanding and modernizing city.[5]

By the outbreak of war the university community of Berlin alone retained a significant degree of unity. In 1914 the Friedrich-Wilhelms-Universität still represented higher education in the capital far more broadly than any single institution in Paris or London had ever done. Nonetheless, several institutions lay outside its reach, including Berlin's schools of art, agriculture, commerce, technology and – most notably – science. No discussion of higher education in pre-war Berlin could afford to ignore the Physikalisch-Technische Reichsanstalt, or the new science institutes of the Kaiser-Wilhelms-Gesellschaft, all of which operated largely independent of the university proper.[6]

Although we cannot focus in detail in this chapter on every capital centre of advanced learning, and have chosen for practical and comparative reasons to concentrate primarily on the more classical universities – the Friedrich-Wilhelms-Universität, the Sorbonne, UCL, and King's College London – we do refer to other sites of higher education when they played a particularly important role in wartime academic culture. We also refer to the great national academies and royal societies that stood above all these institutions, crowning their achievements.

Institutionally diverse, in 1914 the three universities also occupied different positions within the city, the nation, and the world of learning. The Friedrich-Wilhelms-Universität stood in close relation to the imperial regime that in 1810 had founded it. The university was housed in a former royal palace on Unter den Linden at the heart of the capital's government quarter.[7] Through membership of various leagues, societies, and associations based in the city, many Berlin professors enjoyed close

---

[4] N. Harte, *The University of London 1836–1986: an illustrated history*, (London, 1986).
[5] S. Rothblatt, 'London: A Metropolitan University?', in T. Bender, *The University and the City* (Oxford, 1988), pp. 119–49.
[6] D. Cahan, *An Institute for Empire: the Physikalisch-Technische Reichsanstalt* (Cambridge, 1988); B. vom Brocke, 'Die Kaiser-Wilhelm-Gesellschaft im Kaiserreich. Vorgeschichte, Gründung und Entwicklung bis zum Ausbruch des Ersten Weltkriegs', in B. vom Brocke and R. Vierhaus (eds.), *Forschung im Spannungsfeld von Politik und Gesellschaft. Geschichte und Struktur der Kaiser-Wilhelm-/Max-Planck-Gesellschaft*, (Stuttgart, 1990), pp. 17–162.
[7] C. E. McClelland, ' "To Live for Science": Ideals and Realities at the University of Berlin', in Bender (ed.), *The university and the city*, pp. 182–3.

relations with high-ranking civil servants, the Chancellor, and even the Kaiser himself.[8] Berlin professors considered it their role to give advice to statesmen, and also to educate the public at large in the political, moral, and spiritual truths to which they claimed their 'Wissenschaft' gave them special access.[9] Berlin professors did not act in these two spheres as an altogether homogenous body. There was by 1914 considerable disagreement within the professoriate as to the part the feudal Prussian state should play in the modern, industrial world, and also to the direction in which German society should more generally evolve.[10] The university did however possess a powerful sense of its own importance to the survival of the Wilhelmine Empire, and in 1914, when this regime came under threat, the Königliche Friedrich-Wilhelms-Universität zu Berlin rose to its defence as 'the spiritual regiment of the House of Hohenzollern'.[11]

The Friedrich-Wilhelms-Universität was the largest university in Germany and also the most prestigious. In 1910–11 it had around 471 professors and lecturers; the University of Munich had about 248, that of Rostock 69.[12] Thanks to the recruitment policies of the Ministerialdirektor, Friedrich Althoff, the Universität boasted a higher concentration of academic excellence than anywhere else in the Reich.[13] In the immediate pre-war period six new institutes of scientific research had also been created in the capital. Founded by the Kaiser, and largely funded by industrialists, the Kaiser-Wilhelm institutes not only added to Berlin's scholarly pre-eminence; they also represented an innovative experiment in university–industry relations that after 1914 would provide the bedrock for Germany's war effort.[14]

---

[8] R. von Broch, *Wissenschaft, Politik und öffentliche Meinung. Gelehrtenpolitik im Wilhelminischen Deutschland (1890–1914)*, Historische Studien, 435 (Husum, 1980).

[9] E. Demm, 'Autobiographie und Rollenzwang. Autobiographische Zeugnisse deutscher Universitätsprofessoren aus dem ersten Drittel des 20 Jahrhunderts', in *Annali di sociologia/Soziologisches Jahrbuch*, 3, 1987, pp. 299–323.

[10] See F. Ringer, *The decline of the German mandarins* (Cambridge, Mass., 1969).

[11] W. Basler, 'Zur politischen Rolle der Berliner Universität im ersten imperialistischen Weltkrieg 1914 bis 1918', *Wissenschaftliche Zeitschrift der Humboldt-Unversität zu Berlin. Gesellschafts- und sprachwissenschaftliche Reihe*, 10, 1961, pp. 181–203, here p. 201. The university was also called the 'erstes Garderegiment Wissenschaft'. F. Meinecke, *Autobiographische Schriften, Werke*, vol. VIII, ed. E. Kessel, (Stuttgart, 1969), p. 226.

[12] von Broch, *Wissenschaft, Politik und öffentliche Meinung*, p. 107.

[13] B. vom Brocke (ed.), *Wissenschaftsgeschichte und Wissenschaftspolitik im Industriezeitalter. Das 'System Althoff' in historischer Perspektive* (Hildesheim, 1991); F. Stern, *Einstein's German World* (Princeton, 1999), pp. 22, 108.

[14] J. A. Johnson, *The Kaiser's chemists: science and modernization in Imperial Germany* (Chapel Hill, 1990); and J. A. Johnson, 'Akademische Grabenkämpfe und industrielle Ressourcennutzung. Chemie im Spannungsfeld von "reiner" und "angewandter" Forschung', in J. Kocka *et al.* (ed.), *Die Königlich Preussische Akademie der Wissenschaften zu Berlin im Kaiserreich* (Berlin, 1999), pp. 355–80.

At the outbreak of war Berlin was probably the most influential and esteemed university in the world. Although by 1914 academics in Paris and London had begun to assert with increasing confidence the value of their own national academic traditions, and in the process to distance themselves from the Berlin model of university research that for the previous fifty years had been the ideal of academic reformists across Europe, the University of Berlin still remained the benchmark for academic achievement – and the rival for any other university aspirant to international prominence.

'A self-contained city within a city' is how one historian has described the Parisian university community, and this image captures the position of the university within the French capital in at least two respects.[15] First, what the university lacked in organizational coherence, it made up in geographical unity. Most of Paris's main academic foundations stood close together within the Latin quarter, around the Mont Saint-Geneviève, both at the centre of, and slightly above, the larger city around them. In terms of size, too, the Parisian university community can reasonably be described, if not as a city, then at least as a small town. By the outbreak of war the Sorbonne alone had over 19,000 students – the Friedrich-Wilhelms-Universität had just over 8,000, and UCL and King's College London combined, around 5,500. The university community of Paris was not, however, a 'self-contained', or 'autonomous' community.[16] Whilst Parisian professors did not intervene as directly as their Berlin peers in affairs of state, they did identify strongly with the Third Republic, which since its inception had patronized the university as a bastion of Republican values and placed its scholars at the pinnacle of its cultural pantheon.[17] It was as the 'spiritual regiment of the Republic' that academics in Paris had spoken out in 1898 in defence of Captain Dreyfus, for example; and it was in the same capacity that after 1914 they rallied to defend the Republic from German attack.

Although there had been a major expansion of provincial universities before the war, in 1914 Paris still remained unrivalled in terms of the size, number, breadth, and prestige of its institutions.[18] Paris's position in

---

[15] C. Charle, 'Academics or Intellectuals? The Professors of the University of Paris and Political Debate in France from the Dreyfus Affair to the Algerian War', in J. Jennings (ed.), *Intellectuals in twentieth-century France. Mandarins and samurais* (London, 1993), p. 97.

[16] C. Charle, *La naissance des intellectuels, 1880–1900* (Paris, 1990), esp. pp. 231–2.

[17] C. Prochasson and A. Rasmussen, *Au nom de la patrie. Les intellectuels et la première guerre mondiale (1910–1919)* (Paris, 1996), p. 214.

[18] Charle, 'Academics or Intellectuals?', p. 96 and Weisz, *The Emergence of Modern Universities in France*, p. 238.

France far outweighed that of Berlin within Germany; its position within the wider world of scholarship, however, was less certain. On the one hand, Paris could lay claim to international distinction. In the immediate pre-war period the Sorbonne had invested an enormous effort in strengthening its profile abroad, and by 1914 matched Berlin in terms of participation in international conferences and foreign university exchanges, and far surpassed the German capital with regards to foreign-student intake.[19] On the other hand, the capital continued to voice concerns about its inferiority, vis-à-vis Germany, and above all Berlin. 'C'est l'université de Berlin qui a triomphé à Sedan', Ernest Renan had claimed in the aftermath of the Franco-Prussian war,[20] and despite the progress made by French universities since 1870 – and to the degree that this progress had been inspired by Berlin research methods, also because of it – in 1914 Parisian academics still felt that they lived in the shadow of their German rival, and awaited the opportunity to prove their own strength.

The position of the University of London is more ambiguous. The institutions of the university were not centralized like those in Paris, but stretched as 'an acephalous invertebrate' across the entire capital.[21] Although the establishments that most interest us here did lie relatively close together – in Gower Street (UCL) and the Strand (King's) – they in no way formed a university 'centre' as the Latin quarter did in Paris. The university was intellectually, as well as geographically, broadly based in the life of the metropolis. Many of London's academic innovations – the introduction of engineering at King's, the teaching of oriental languages at UCL, the very creation of the LSE – can be understood as responses to metropolitan needs.[22] The emphasis London placed on professional training, likewise, represented a desire to feed into the legal, financial, and government services of the city. But despite this deep engagement in city life, the university of London was not a site symbolic of the capital, as the Friedrich-Wilhelms-Universität was of Berlin, or the Sorbonne and the grandes écoles of Paris.

London was England's largest university: in 1910 its colleges and schools together received around 4,500 students, those of Oxford about 1,000.[23] London was also the nation's foremost postgraduate

[19] C. Charle, *La République des universitaires, 1870–1940* (Paris, 1994), pp. 343–95.
[20] Claude Digeon, *La Crise allemande de la pensée française (1870–1914)* (Paris, 1959) and H. Barbey-Say, *Le Voyage de France en Allemagne (1871–1914)* (Nancy, 1994).
[21] Harte, *The University of London*, p. 24.
[22] S. Rothblatt, 'London: A Metropolitan University?', pp. 127–9.
[23] Harte, *The University of London*, p. 197. L. Stone, 'The Size and Composition of the Oxford Student Body, 1580–1909', in Stone (ed.), *Oxford and Cambridge from the 14th to the early 19th century* (Princeton, 1974).

university.[24] London was the home of England's first 'Godless', co-educational and affordable forms of university instruction. London was a self-consciously imperial university: it set the educational standards for empire, trained men for imperial service, and every year received hundreds of colonial students. By far England's most international university, London was also – to the extent that it was the degree-granting authority for all of the nation's new civic universities – a truly national site of learning. But despite playing such a dominant role in the development of higher education in England and her empire, the University of London still stood in the shadow of Oxford and Cambridge. At the outbreak of war the University of London is best understood as a site of academic potential that had yet to be realized.

The upheaval of war

The lost generation

The most immediate impact of the war on the universities was a drastic diminution in the male student population. The principal colleges of the University of London reopened in the autumn of 1914 with a drop of between 30 per cent (King's) and just under 50 per cent (UCL) in male enrolments, with numbers falling in subsequent years to, respectively, one-half and one-third of pre-war totals.[25] In the first term of war the Friedrich-Wilhelms-Universität suffered a 60 per cent decline in male students, witnessing a fall again in 1915 to just one-quarter of pre-war levels, at which student numbers remained until the end of 1918.[26] During the first year of conflict the number of male French students at the Sorbonne declined by a drastic 80 per cent, to rise only very slightly thereafter.[27] Paris's small elite schools were even worse hit, many barely surviving the mobilization of August 1914. When Sciences Po finally reopened its doors in January 1915 its all-male student population, 800 strong before the outbreak of war, had been reduced to 72, a third of whom were foreigners.[28] There were 211 young men enrolled at the ENS when war broke out. By

[24] R. Dahrendorf, *LSE. A history of the London School of Economics, 1895–1995* (Oxford, 1995), p. 90.

[25] F. J. C. Hearnshaw, *The centenary of King's College London* (London, 1929), p. 462.

[26] *Amtliches Verzeichnis des Personnals und der Studierenden der königlichen Friedrichs-Wilhelms-Universität zu Berlin.*

[27] *Revue universitaire (RU)*, July 1915. R. Thamin, 'L'Université de France et la guerre', *Revue des deux mondes*, 15 July and 1 August 1916, here 1 August 1916, p. 607.

[28] P. Rain, *Naissance de la science politique en France, 1870–1945* (Paris, 1963), p. 65. G. Vincent, *Sciences Po. Histoire d'une réussite* (Paris, 1987), p. 94.

the beginning of 1915 there were around 20: 'une vingtaine d'élèves, exemptés, privés du service militaire, sont présents à l'École', the director Ernest Lavisse lamented, 'ce sont des âmes en peine dans cette maison si vivante et si gaie d'ordinaire, silencieuse aujourd'hui'.[29]

Mobilization rates varied between the three capitals. The shock of war was markedly slower and less complete in London than in Paris or Berlin, although the introduction of conscription seems to have brought an increase in the rate of mobilization at a time when student numbers elsewhere had more or less stabilized.[30] Mobilization rates also differed within the university communities. Somewhat surprisingly, given that the college was socially more elitist, politically more conservative, had a higher public-school intake, and supplied around half the recruits of London's Officer Training Corps (OTC),[31] King's registered a much lower rate of mobilization than its neighbour on Gower Street. The apparent explanation for this lies in the fact that London arts students were slower to enrol than other undergraduates, and that King's had proportionately more such students than UCL. In Paris there were likewise variations between specialist schools and the Sorbonne. Age had an impact here: the average student at the Sciences Po or the ENS was older than at the Sorbonne, where students were still accepted for the baccalaureate. Important too were the 'privileges' bestowed upon students of the ENS, who because of their credentials (not their social background, as was the case in England) were considered more apt for military service and underwent special training during their schooling.[32] In 1914 these men were immediately mobilized as reserve officers.[33] One further factor that contributed to the grandes écoles' high mobilization rate of 1914, and a factor that would be central to the way in which they represented their contribution to the war effort, was the fact that many students who were not yet of age and had had little military training volunteered to fight. It was the enthusiasm of young *normaliens* for war – the 'élan', commentators said, with which they welcomed the conflict[34] – that explains why the ENS was all but emptied of students in the summer of 1914.

---

[29] 'Discours de M. Ernest Lavisse', *RU*, January 1915 and Archives Nationales, AJ/61/85.
[30] The UCL *Annual Reports* (supplement 'Pro Patria') record mobilization figures.
[31] J. M. Winter, *The Great War and the British people* (London, 2nd edn, 2002).
[32] O. Chaline, 'Les normaliens dans la Grande Guerre', *Guerres mondiales et conflits contemporains*, 183 (1996), pp. 99–110, here p. 108.
[33] As in Berlin. B. Thoss, 'Einjährig-Freiwillige' in G. Hirschfeld *et al.* (eds.), *Enzyklopädie Erster Weltkrieg* (Paderborn, 2003), p. 452.
[34] R. Thamin, 'L'Université de France et la guerre', 15 July 1916, p. 299. 'Discours de M. Lavisse', *RU*, January 1915. 'L'example de l'ENS', *RU*, April 1916.

The notion of enthusiasm cannot be rejected so strongly for students as it has been for other sections of society, but it does need to be carefully qualified.[35] Despite the claims made by post-war writers that students left their class rooms 'burning with enthusiasm'[36] to join the army, and despite the image oft propagated in secondary literature that Europe's youth at the turn of the century was animated by a Nietzschean spirit of belligerent heroism, military combat in and for itself seems to have roused the passions of only a minority of students in 1914. In Paris and Berlin the outbreak of war did witness a resurgence of the ideal of the student-soldier, and memories of students who had volunteered to fight in the Franco-Prussian or Napoleonic wars probably did play a role in encouraging students to join up.[37] This was especially true in Berlin where memories of the 'Liberation Wars' against Napoleon had been strengthened by the centenary celebrations of the victory of 1813.[38] But these commemorations encouraged students to join up by pressing on young men a tradition of national service; and it was this, a sense of national duty, rather than an atavistic desire for war, that stands out in the accounts students themselves gave of mobilization.

National service carried a broad range of significations, but one striking theme in student journals and letters is the extent to which the nation was understood as a complex of moral imperatives, much more than as a political or even, with the notable exception of Paris, a territorial unit.[39] Such moral nationalism was broadly prevalent in 1914; it was however particularly powerful within the university communities, which in pre-war Europe closely identified their academic mission with that of the nation. Before the war educational discourse in all three nations strongly associated intellectual achievement with the acceptance of moral absolutes, and the ideal of self-improvement with the dictum of national

---

[35] J.-J. Becker, *1914. Comment les Français sont entrés en guerre* (Paris, 1977); Verhey, *The spirit of 1914*; A. Gregory, 'British "War Enthusiasm" in 1914: a Reassessment', in G. Braybon, *Evidence, History and the Great War. Historians and the Impact of 1914–18* (Oxford, 2003).

[36] E. Jünger, *In Stahlgewittern* (Stuttgart, 1978 [1920]), p. 7. R. Wohl, *The generation of 1914* (Cambridge, Mass., 1979).

[37] G. Mosse, *Fallen soldiers. Reshaping the memory of the world wars* (New York, 1990); T. Weber, 'Studenten', in G. Hirschfeld *et al.* (eds.), *Enzyklopädie Erster Weltkrieg* (Poderborn, 2003), pp. 910–12.

[38] K. Keller and H. D. Schmidt (eds.), *Vom Kult zur Kulisse. Das Völkerschlachtdenkmal als Gegenstand der Geschichtskultur* (Leipzig, 1995). W. G. Natter, *Literature at war 1914–1940. Representing the 'Time of Greatness' in Germany* (New Haven, 1999), pp. 78–121.

[39] A. Becker, 'Les chartistes dans la Grande Guerre', in Y.-M. Bercé (ed.), *Histoire de l'École nationale des chartes depuis 1821* (Thionville, 1997), pp. 200–6; and Chaline, 'Les normaliens dans la Grande Guerre'.

service.[40] It was the extent to which students accepted this broad nexus of moral values that helps to explain why so many were willing to join up in 1914, and continued to fight for the remainder of the war.

However, although enthusiasm was important, the reasons why students consented to fight remain more complicated. The letters that the principal of King's received in 1914 reveal another factor that perhaps played an equally significant role in student engagement: peer pressure.[41] Many young men joined up primarily from the fear that they would be the only ones not to do so. Students did have mixed feelings about the war, but pacifism was rare. In 1914 there was no concerted protest against mobilization in any of the capital's universities, and for the following four years only a couple of isolated students spoke out in opposition to war, and they were promptly silenced.[42]

However, although students did not stand against the war, some did voice reservations about fighting in it. King's theologians were deeply divided as to whether military service was compatible with their spiritual vocation.[43] Others feared losing their place or scholarship if they chose to join up. Most of these men did engage, but only after they had received assurance from the principal Ronald Burrows that this act of national duty would not stand in the way of their future career.

Whilst the attitudes of students to war are difficult to trace, their fate, once they did engage, is tragically stark. Precise figures are lacking, but the picture is clear: student death rates at least equalled the horrific levels of the nation at large, and in many places significantly surpassed them. King's lost around 239 men, over 15 per cent of those who served.[44] At UCL 268 out of the around 2,600 students mobilized did not return.[45] University authorities in Berlin estimated that 997 out of 1,501 in uniform in 1914 and a total of 8,241 student soldiers gave their lives for the Reich.[46] It is more difficult to estimate the death rate of Sorbonne students; however, in 1916 Raymond Thamin reckoned that 20 per cent of Sorbonne students mobilized in the first year of war had lost their lives, and that 12 per cent had fallen the following year. If correct, his calculations would suggest a death rate similar to that suffered by Paris

---

[40] Audoin-Rouzeau and Becker, *14–18*, pp. 112–14. K. Jarausch, *Students, society and politics in Imperial Germany*, (Princeton, 1982).

[41] See King's College London College Archives (KCLCA), KAP/BUR/13.

[42] W. Basler, 'Zur politischen Rolle der Berliner Universität', pp. 195–7.

[43] Hearnshaw, *Centenary*, p. 462.   [44] Ibid., p. 467.

[45] University College London College Archives (UCLCA), 'War memorial fund items'.

[46] *Feier bei der Enthüllung des Denkmals für die im Weltkrieg Gefallenen Studierenden, Dozenten und Beamten der Universität am 10. Juli 1926* (Berlin, n.d. [1926]) and K. Hoffmann-Curtius, 'Das Kriegerdenkmal der Berliner Friedrich-Wilhelms-Universität 1919–1926: Siegexegese der Niederlage' in *Jahrbuch für Universitätsgeschichte*, 5 (2002), pp. 87–116.

as a whole.[47] The picture for the ENS is clearer. Of 833 *normaliens* mobilized, 239 died – around 28 per cent.[48] For some age groups the death rate was higher: 50 per cent of those mobilized from the classes reaching the age of twenty in 1910–13 were killed.[49] If we take into account the numbers of wounded, the losses were even greater still. According to Gustave Lanson, director of the school after 1919, of the 104 students of the 1910–13 classes who survived the war, only six made it through the war untouched.[50] This was a casualty rate higher than that endured at other *grandes écoles*, such as the Ecole des Chartes or the Ecole Polytechnique.[51] It was higher than the death toll suffered by the University of Oxford.[52]

The reasons for this slaughter are many: the massive mobilization of 1914 (around 50 per cent of the 107 deaths from the intake of 1910–13 took place in the first bloody months of war[53]); the large proportion (around two-thirds) of *normaliens* that, because of their privileges, entered the officer corps;[54] the fact that most fought in the infantry, where casualty rates were highest; the 'enthusiasm', perhaps, of these young student soldiers who welcomed the responsibility which their intellectual reputation had bestowed upon them. What is cruelly apparent is that the ENS lost proportionately more men than any other educational institution in the three capitals, and probably in the nations at large.

Student life

For those who did not fight and remained at home, the main casualty of the conflict was the ordinary passage of youth. Not only did the centre of student culture shift during the war from sporting events and *Besäufnisse* to military training and war work, but study itself was severely interrupted. Classes were disturbed by the lack of human and material resources, as well as by loss of buildings, which as we have seen in chapter 6 was also a problem for primary schools. Regular tuition also suffered from the

---

[47] Thamin, 'L'Université de France et la guerre', 15 July 1916, p. 316.

[48] 'Les anciens élèves et élèves mobilisés dans les services armés en 1914–1918', report drafted by Gustave Lanson, director of the École Normale after Lavisse retired in 1919, dated 27 January 1922, AN, AJ/16/2895. The report is reprinted in J.-F. Sirinelli, *Génération intellectuelle, khâgneux et normaliens d'une guerre à l'autre* (Paris, 1988), p. 28.

[49] Chaline, 'Les normaliens dans la Grande Guerre', p. 107.

[50] 'Les anciens élèves et élèves mobilisés dans les services armés en 1914–1918'.

[51] A. Becker, 'Les chartistes', pp. 200–1; B. Villermet, 'Une Grande École dans la tourmente: l'École polytechnique pendant la première guerre mondiale, 1914–1920', *Bulletin de la société des amis de la Bibliothèque de l'École polytechnique*, 10, 1993, pp. 45–6.

[52] J. M. Winter, 'Britain's "Lost Generation" of the First World War', *Population Studies*, 31 (1977), p. 461.

[53] AN, AJ/61/85.   [54] Chaline, 'Les normaliens', p. 100.

redirection of several departments towards war service. 'Many of those who remain at the School are engaged in government work, and are working at very high pressure, which makes it very difficult for them to join in the social life', an editorial of the LSE's student publication, *Clare Market Review*, noted in June 1915. The time that students could afford to spend on study was likewise affected. Increasing numbers of students had to take on jobs alongside study. Those intent on completing their degrees did so through part-time, evening, or vacation courses. Students may have escaped the brutal reality of war that their classmates faced at the front, but the rhythms of their lives had been fundamentally disrupted.

But the brutal horror of war was never really far away. University hospitals shared with the other hospitals of capital cities the burden of caring for the mass casualties of conflict, and the numbers of wounded and dying that passed through their wards gave medical students a direct view of the scale of catastrophe. For instance, UCL hospital, which had been placed at the disposal of wounded soldiers and sailors at the outbreak of war, treated over 6,000 such patients between 1914 and 1918.[55]

The arrival of the war wounded demanded emergency measures, and many university buildings in all three capitals were appropriated and transformed into wards. Berlin's Institute of Dental Surgery in the Invalidenstraße became a military hospital for facially wounded soldiers.[56] One wing of UCL was turned into a recuperation centre for soldiers, and the new, still unfinished Department of Applied Statistics and Eugenics was used by the War Office as a temporary hospital. King's College theological hostel in Vincent Square was requisitioned in 1915 as a nursing hospital and remained so until the end of the war. Regulations of 1888 meant that certain Parisian schools had to turn over their buildings to the Union des Femmes de France. Sections of the École Polytechnique were occupied by the neighbouring hospital, and the School's physics court was temporarily transformed into a mortuary. On 6 August 1914, the flag of the Red Cross was hoisted above the ENS on rue d'Ulm, and the Union des Femmes took over all rooms except for the laboratories and library. Now when the bell rang it was no longer to announce the end of lessons, but the arrival of the wounded – up to 53 a day, and a total of 5,886 by the end of February 1915.[57]

The task of caring for the wounded housed within the universities was one of the new forms of work that occupied students during the war. From 1916 students at UCL organized tea, music, and stage events to

---

[55] W. R. Merrington, *University College Hospital and its medical school: a history* (London, 1976), p. 118.
[56] HUA, Kuratorium/577, Institute of Dental Surgery.   [57] AN AJ/61/85.

make 'the convalescent soldiers as happy as possible'.[58] In Berlin, students worked to help the reintegration of wounded students and staff within the university, and on occasions to assist professors who, because of particularly severe injury, were unable to take up their old functions.[59]

Students everywhere, and in particular female students who after 1914 were increasingly prominent in all university activities, became engaged in many forms of war-related work. The activity of UCL's young ladies was quite remarkable. They were trained as nurses under the Red Cross and the newly formed Voluntary Aid Detachment, and sent to serve both at home and abroad.[60] They undertook canteen work, and under the Board of Trade scheme volunteered for agricultural tasks during the summer vacation. The UCL's Women's Union Society (WUS) was active in raising money to build and equip a rest hut at Le Havre, and also participated in the Student Representative Council's initiative to provide a motor coffee-stall for the Red Cross, one of the rare university-wide aid projects. The WUS organized money and parcels to be sent to the Prisoner of War Relief Fund and to UCL students at the front. The women shared with the men's union the task of forming committees for the night patrol of university buildings to safeguard against air raids. All UCL women were engaged in knitting, a task that according to the editor of the *Union College Magazine* had transformed the face of the College: 'the cloisters resemble workrooms of one of the woollen towns of the North … with bevies of knitters sorting socks of innumerable hues and sizes – not to mention other garments of doubtful purpose – on the window-sills'.[61]

Examples of such initiatives may be given for the colleges and schools of all capital universities. Berlin also had its knitting evenings and its volunteer nurses; Berlin students sent parcels to the front, participated in the raising of war loans, collected books for army libraries, and furnished reading rooms for prisoner-of-war camps in England and Germany.[62] Students in Paris took part in the organization of the 'sou des lycées' charity scheme and helped out in the hospitals and 'ouvriers' that now occupied many

---

[58] 'Social Work', University College London, *Annual Report*, 1916–1917.

[59] BArch, R 8034 ɪɪ/2547, 'Hauptversammlung des Akademischen Hilfsbundes', *Deutsche Tageszeitung*, 25 March 1917.

[60] UCL *Annual Report*, 1914–18.

[61] 'Editorial', *University College Magazine*, December 1914.

[62] See BArch, R 8034 II/2547, 'Die Kriegshilfe der Studenten', *Deutsche Tageszeitung*, 18 December 1914; 'Gründung des Akademischen Hilfsbundes für verwundete Soldatenakademiker', *Deutsche Tageszeitung*, 17 March 1915; 'Hauptversammlung des Akademischen Hilfsbundes', *Deutsche Tageszeitung*, 25 March 1917. T. Maurer, 'Der Krieg als Chance? Frauen im Streben nach Gleichberechtigung an deutschen Universitäten 1914–1918', in *Jahrbuch für Universitätsgeschichte*, 6 (2003), pp. 107–38, here pp. 133ff.

college buildings.[63] Female students were trained as nurses, employed as babysitters for working mothers, and encouraged to volunteer for agricultural work.[64] The main differences between such activities is that in London and Berlin they were largely student-led, and drew on structures of student sociability already in place, whereas in Paris, where student sub-culture was less well developed, war-related initiatives were usually organized by professors.[65] The war did see a growth in student organizations in Paris, with the notable creation at the end of 1916 of the university community's first *Journal des étudiants*. However, most new foundations were orientated towards improving the conditions of students (in particular foreign students) at home, and rarely engaged in the philanthropic tasks for combatant students that occupied so much of the energy of university unions and associations in London and Berlin.

This war work took place outside university hours, replacing regular student activities, many of which proved increasingly difficult to keep going in the context of war. The overall decline in student numbers brought a sharp fall in student-union membership. Many of the small student associations in Berlin almost closed down completely,[66] and in London even the larger unions struggled to keep numbers and funds at an operational level. The annual celebrations of most London colleges were cancelled, and those that did take place did so without the usual pomp, and with the added concern that they were likely to be interrupted by air raids. When the LSE International Students Committee met for its annual dinner in June 1917 those who were still celebrating in the early hours of the next morning had to be marshalled down to the basement when an air raid came near.[67] In December of the same year the Christmas dinner was also threatened by an air raid – though this time London fog saved the party.

Sporting organizations faced a particular struggle to keep going. The absence of men was the main problem, although in London team numbers were for a time made up by female additions. Another problem was space. In August 1914 the UCL Student Union sports field at Perivale was taken over by the Officers' Training Corps OTC as a drilling ground, before being requisitioned by the RAF as a training site for pilots, and throughout the war the college's gymnasium was almost entirely occupied by the Royal Field Artillery. In October 1914 both Ronald Burrows and Gregory Foster, Provost of UCL, had pledged not to abolish games

[63] 'L'Assistance et l'Université. Le "sou des lycées"', *RU*, October–November, 1914.
[64] 'Bulletin de l'enseignement secondaire des jeunes filles', *RU*, January 1915.
[65] G. Weisz, 'Associations et manifestations: les étudiants français de la Belle Époque', *Le mouvement social* (July–September, 1982), pp. 31–44.
[66] HUA Rektor und Senat/809 and 562.   [67] LSE *Director's Report*, 1916–17.

as some authorities had suggested. They argued that it was precisely the importance English education laid on sport that enabled her troops to fight so valiantly at the front.[68] Within a year all student unions reported that most sporting activities had been suspended.

That the war deeply disrupted student life is not in doubt. What remains more problematic to ascertain, is the impact of war on student political views. A number of historians have portrayed the student experience of war in Berlin, and in Germany more generally, as a crucible for radical nationalism.[69] Whilst we do have evidence of student extremism after the war, the extent of far-right radicalism is more difficult to assess. Despite the drop in numbers, the ideas of extremist groups do appear to have hardened after 1914, as is witnessed by the lead that Berlin students took in the formation of a student branch of the German Fatherland Party, and their subsequent engagement in the war aims controversy.[70] More generally, we also find more patriotic demonstrations in Berlin than in the Allied capitals, in particular in terms of marches and 'Fackelzüge' (torch parades).[71]

However, these activities may stem more from the fact that Berlin students had a stronger tradition of parading and a more tightly organized student culture, than that national sentiment ran deeper than elsewhere. Moreover, as before the war, student-society journals do still reveal a variety of political views. *Die Hochschule*, for instance, the journal of the *Deutsche Studentendienst*, reflected a broad spectrum of opinions on war.[72] In its opening edition for 1917 *Die Hochschule* carried the usual patriotic homage to fallen students alongside an essay by Hermann Hesse, but it also published – at a time of rising anti-Semitism – an article celebrating Jewish students at the front. Interestingly, with regard to the politics of female students, it was the more, liberal of the two women's student movements that saw its fortunes grow during the war. Apart from the first heady months of the conflict, the moderate *Freie Vereinigung*

---

[68] KCLCA, KAP/BUR/100. 'Universities and the war. The value of sport in the present time', *Westminster Gazette*, 7 October 1914. King's chose for its war memorial an athletic ground, for 'helping the work and strengthening the character and physique of future students of the college', KCLCA, KAP/BUR/14 and 355.

[69] Mosse, *Fallen soldiers*; M. Steinberg, *Sabers and Brown Shirts. The German's path to National Socialism 1918–1945* (Chicago, 1977); C. Ingrao, 'Etudiants allemands, mémoire de guerre et militantisme nazi: étude de cas', *14–18 Aujourd'hui-Today-Heute*, 5 (2002), pp. 55–71.

[70] BArch, R 8034 II/2547, 'Die Agitation der deutschen Vaterlandspartei in der Berliner Universität', *Berliner Tageblatt*, 29 November 1917; 'Die Berliner Studentische Gruppe der Deutschen Vaterlands-Partei', *Deutsche Tageszeitung*, 19 December 1917; 'Studentische Vaterländische Versammlung', *Deutsche Tageszeitung*, 18 January 1918. Jarausch, *Students, society and politics*, pp. 345–66.

[71] See Basler, 'Zur politischen Rolle der Berliner Universität', pp. 185 and 200.

[72] The journal was founded in 1917.

studierender Frauen Berlin consistently attracted more members than the strongly conservative *Deutscher Akademischer Frauenbund*.[73] The real turning point for the far right came with the indignation of defeat, when the *Deutscher Akademischer Frauenbund* rapidly overtook its more liberal sister organization, which faded away in 1921.

London student reviews also suggest an evolution as well as a considerable ambivalence in attitudes to war. In the *University College Magazine*, there was a sure development from the gung-ho talk about England's 'Great Adventure' that characterized the first months of war, to the publication of decidedly un-glorified accounts of life at the front and the sober chronicling of the College's heavy losses that dominated the review in later years. The *Clare Market Review* was from the start quite balanced in tone, and remarkable for allowing discussion in its review articles of the way war was being waged and even its ultimate purpose.

However, although the deeds of student soldiers at the front were always spoken of with respect, attitudes to soldiers on leave, or to the war more generally, were at times more ironical. The *Clare Market Review* showed little reverence for the 'stalwart khaki-clad beings with bronzed, moustached faces' that periodically invaded the precincts of the School.[74] It showed little toleration either of the few ardent nationalists of the Student Union – the proposals that military law should be imposed, or that censorship should be extended to peacetime, were rejected outright.[75] But it would be a mistake to assume that such irony signified a deep-seated alienation from the war. Irony had always been the main voice of student reviews as they looked on with the arrogance of youth at the folly of their times. Although such irony did become stronger as the war progressed, it rarely hit a note of deep pessimism. It was, for one, interspersed with humour. It was with a degree of tongue in cheek that the *Clare Market Review* launched a 'cursery rhyme' competition, and awarded a prize to this little ditty: 'Twinkle, twinkle, little gun, / Puncture every blooming Hun, / As above the clouds they fly, / Like a sausage in the sky.'[76] Moreover, students also gave much energy to imagining the post-war world, and here they were far more positive. In 1915 Professor Lees Smith found 'a spirit of cheerful optimism still prevailing' at the LSE, and the *Clare Market Review* shows that students were both proud to see their specialized skills of use to the government at war, and also believed firmly that 'in the work of reconstruction after the war the School will have a most vital part to play'.[77]

---

[73] HUA, Rektor und Senat/806.   [74] 'School News', *CMR*, June 1916.

[75] 'Union Report', *CMR*, December 1916.

[76] D. Taylor, *Godless students of Gower Street* (London: UCL Union, 1968), p. 65.

[77] 'The School and the War', *CMR*, March 1915 and December 1915.

Material problems and generosity of spirit In terms of material and human resources, survival for the capital universities was precarious. Balancing the budget, a challenge for authorities at the best of times, proved unmanageable. The decline in student numbers reduced the main source of income, student fees. The other principle source of revenue, state grants, was readjusted to the minimum required to cover necessities. This meant severe cuts in Paris and Berlin. In London, where colleges were more dependent on student fees than in the other cities, and where government contributions were already extremely low, this actually brought an increase in state and county council aid.[78] Without exception, though, the universities entered deep financial crisis, and drastic economies had to be made. All new developments were postponed. Building work was stopped, library orders cancelled, and heavy restrictions laid on the use of paper, ink, and energy resources. As the war continued it became more difficult not just to afford new materials but also to acquire them. Berlin suffered by far the worst in this respect, with wartime shortages rendering the grand lecture halls of the old royal palace increasingly cold and dark, the atmosphere more and more gloomy.[79]

The contradictory policies of state authorities towards the universities increased what Pember Reeves, director of the LSE, described as the 'great element of uncertainty' that reigned over higher education during the war.[80] On the one hand, higher education was an area where cutbacks could be made. Materials were siphoned off to other sites, and buildings were requisitioned. In 1916, the ENS, already seriously strained by the demands of its hospital, was obliged to send all paper (libraries and archives exempt) to the government for use in the Press Office, and all unused cotton to the Department for Artillery and Munitions.[81] King's was a particular object of plunder for the British government. During the war, government ministries took over various departments, and according to the King's historian, F. J. C. Hearnshaw, the entire college barely escaped seizure by the War Office, 'but Dr Burrows was able to save it by demonstrating to the government the importance of the war work that was being done by the surviving members of staff'.[82] Hearnshaw's conclusion may be correct, for on the other hand, there are signs that governments came

---

[78] S. Rothblatt, 'State and Market in British University History', in S. Collini, B. Young, and S. Whatmore, *British intellectual history, 1750–1950. Economy, polity and society* (Cambridge, 2000), pp. 224–42.

[79] HUA, Kuratorium/131.   [80] LSE, *Director's Report*, 1915–16.

[81] AN, AJ/61/86. Letter Liard to Lavisse, 2 May 1916; letter Under-Secretary of State to Lavisse, 16 December 1916.

[82] Hearnshaw, *Centenary*, p. 462.

slowly to recognize the importance of university work to the war effort. Civil and military authorities made increasing demands on university expertise, especially in the natural and medical sciences, but also in modern languages, geography, and social science. In these areas the universities did receive funding, and occasionally staff: the chemistry and physics laboratories of the ENS were the two areas where Lavisse did not see resources cut. However, even here policies were never consistent. Lavisse struggled for months to get trained researchers seconded from the front to the School labs. Burrows frequently complained that the War Office did not pay for the officer language classes that from 1915 the College was required to provide. The Berlin University Institute of Dental Surgery, now a centre for the treatment of the facially wounded, was always understaffed.[83] In 1916 the German High Command even envisaged the temporary closure of Berlin and other German universities.[84]

The task of managing the universities in this context of confusion and cutbacks, fell on an increasingly diminished, and older, body of staff. The expanding capital universities had large numbers of young teachers, or Privatdozenten, and many of these served in the armed forces. Whilst staff mobilization had less of an impact in Paris, where young scholars tended to work their way up to a professorial position by teaching in a provincial and then a Parisian lycée, it has nonetheless been estimated that one in four French academics died in the war.[85] What such a casualty rate suggests is not just that mobilization was far reaching, but also that it was generally indiscriminate of academic abilities. Only rarely were the special skills of mobilized professors recognized, and the latter posted in special geographical, translating, medical, or engineering services. It was only those who could not fight, or had been invalided out of active service, that had the opportunity to put their intelligence to better use, within, for example, the expanding offices of wartime government.

It was thanks to good will and a great deal of hard work that the small professorial body that remained was able to keep the universities open during the war. Professors at home took on (without extra pay) the courses of absent colleagues. Academics engaged in government service occasionally returned to give evening lectures. Retired professors were also asked to help out.[86] Pember Reeves, who did better than most at keeping professors back for war work, complained of the impossibility of planning courses.

[83] HUA, Kuratorium/577.
[84] K. H. Jarausch, *Deutsche Studenten 1800–1970* (Frankfurt am Main, 1984), p. 110.
[85] M. Hanna, *The mobilization of intellect. French scholars and writers during the Great War* (Cambridge, Mass., 1996), p. 57.
[86] HUA, Kuratorium/131, ministerial letter dated 21 October 1916.

Paradoxically, however, such hardship may have had a positive impact on the running of the universities, at least in London. The human and financial shortages of war forced London's chaotic teaching structure into a more streamlined form, and increased positively the degree of cooperation between colleges. As the *Clare Market Review* already reported in December 1914, 'the new solidarity of classes [...] has been one of the indirect blessings of war'.[87]

Academics, like students, took on war work outside classes. London College academics formed relief committees to support the families of mobilized students and staff. In Berlin, Fritz Haber, director of the Kaiser-Wilhelm-Institute for Physical Chemistry and Electrochemistry, organized a war nursery for the children of employees at the front and their working wives; the university theologian Adolf von Harnack, who was also director of the Royal Library, invited his colleagues to send books to the troops and to war hospitals, and helped at home to supply food, clothes, shelter, and even pastoral duties to foreigners in need.[88] To list solely the activities of members of the Institut de France – who funded and managed a hospital in the Hôtel Thiers, formed societies to assist war widows, orphans, and blind veterans, raised money for the Red Cross, and also set up a sewing room in the secretariat of the Académie française to provide work for women impoverished by war – gives a sense of how energetically Parisian academics were engaged in social work.[89] There is no support here for the caricature of professors as 'bloodthirsty old men hobbling along victorious in the absence of youth'.[90] Professors who remained in the universities during 1914–18 were not complacent spectators; they were deeply engaged, both emotionally, and physically, in the national war effort.

Professorial attitudes to refugee students provide one further example of such public-spiritedness, as well as revealing some of its limits. Academics in both Paris and London went to considerable lengths to help refugees continue their studies during the war.[91] A sense of how they did so, and the problems they faced, is given by King's in London, where the refugee experience can be traced in some detail.[92]

---

[87] 'Editorial', *CMR*, December 1914. KCLCA, KAP/BUR/97. 'Report of the Vice-Chancellor on the work of the University during the year 1915–16'.

[88] M. Szöllösi-Janze, *Fritz Haber 1868–1934. Eine Biographie* (Munich: Beck, 1998), p. 267. A. von Zahn-Harnack, *Adolf von Harnack* (Berlin: De Gruyter, 1951), p. 347 and p. 368.

[89] On these and other activities see, M. Hanna, *The mobilization of intellect*, pp. 52–8.

[90] Bertrand Russell cited in S. Wallace, *War and the image of Germany*, British Academics 1914–1918 (Edinburgh, 1988), p. 74.

[91] 'Les étudiants belges et l'Université de Paris', *RU*, October–November 1914.

[92] This section draws on KCLCA, KAP/BUR/43, 44, 45, 46, 70, and 272.

At its peak, early in 1915, King's received around 100 refugees, 70 of whom were Russian, and the rest mainly Belgian. Although refugees only ever made up a small proportion of the overall population of King's, in some classes they were dominant, with refugees accounting for example for half of the college's engineering department in the first year of war.[93]

Burrows was extremely sensitive to refugee needs. Despite serious financial shortages, he allowed students to enrol with a partial or total remission of fees. Burrows tried to have the abilities of refugee students evaluated according to the education they had received at home, and he organized special instruction in English to facilitate their integration. Burrows also ensured the provision of meals, clothes, and housing to refugees in need, which included the majority of the Russians, who usually arrived at King's in dire financial situations. All of this was very time-consuming for King's overworked staff – one critic calculated that the time professors had to take over one refugee was ten times that required by a regular student.[94] Burrows nonetheless felt that refugee students had been a positive feature of College life during the war, and had created at King's a more international atmosphere. He was particularly encouraged by the large Russian contingent, which had helped organize social activities around the newly formed School of Slavonic Studies. Several Russian students themselves seem to have enjoyed their stay at King's, writing to Burrows in 1916, 'we came to England in want and misery and anxiety [. . .] as a beam of light, the welcome given to us at King's College cheered our depressed spirits, reviving in us hope and courage'.[95]

Other college members, however, held less happy recollections of the refugee experience. 'They were a source of embarrassment rather than a strength to the college', Hearnshaw later complained, 'they generally paid no fees, observed no rules, did no work, and showed no gratitude. Many were evading military service, and some were discovered to be spies.'[96] This was in part the hostility of an historian who was conservative and anti-Semitic and after 1917 virulently anti-Russian. But this was also the resentment of a scholar who believed that the College had wasted precious resources on students who rarely showed any thanks. Identical sentiments to Hearnshaw's were expressed by the much more liberal Pember Reeves at the LSE, who in the second year of war resolved to limit college hospitality to those refugees who showed reasonable

[93] KCLCA, KAP/BUR/44.
[94] *Nature, a weekly illustrated journal of science*, 24 December 1914.
[95] KCLCA, KAP/BUR/272. 'Memorandum on Russian Refugee Students'.
[96] Hearnshaw, *Centenary*, p. 460.

attendance, arguing that 'very few of the refugees can be said to have taken very full advantage of the opportunities of study placed at their disposal'.[97]

The academic home front

A defining feature of wartime university life was the way in which even the most patriotically engaged members of staff struggled hard to keep some form of normal education alive. To defend this struggle, academics invoked the ideals by which the war itself was justified: if this was a war for civilization what, they asked, would be the meaning of victory if the very seats of civilization were destroyed in the fight? This was the logic that underlay the speech given by the French Minister of Public Instruction in October 1914, when, with Paris under siege, he called on the university to reopen, 'as if the war did not exist'.[98] The Republic, Albert Sarrault declared, 'is counting on you, and on your collaborators, to maintain straight and clear, above the torment, the flame of French thought'.

However, other reasons, some less noble, were also at play in this stubborn endurance of the academic community. The university is an institution, like other institutions, with its interests, its traditions, and its codes of conduct. The inertia of these traditions, and the professional conceits and social prejudices that underpinned them, were important in the resilience of university culture under the pressures of war.

Academic adaptation After 1914 the Berlin history department witnessed a notable shift towards teaching modern, and especially modern Prussian, history. In 1915 Hans Delbrück and Friedrich Meinecke both updated their lecture programmes: the one taught Clausewitz, the other Franco-German military history.[99] The following year saw the foundation of a new course, inconceivable without the war, on the history of Bulgaria; in 1917 a lecture series was introduced on American History, of more general interest, but directly coinciding with US entry into the conflict. Berlin economists, too, addressed problems of war at the lectern: Heinrich Herkner led his students through a whole set of specific war-related problems, from war-loans and German agriculture, to the economic activities of prisoners-of-war and the social requirements of war widows and orphans.[100]

---

[97] LSE *Director's Report*, 1914–15.   [98] AN, AJ/61/85.
[99] *Verzeichnis der Vorlesungen*, the published catalogue of university courses.
[100] *Chronik der Friedrich-Wilhelms-Universität zu Berlin für das Rechnungsjahr 1914*, 28, and 29 (1915–16); BArch, R 8034 II/2524, 'Aus der Kriegsarbeit der Berliner Universität', *Vossische Zeitung*, 8 September 1916.

Such developments in Berlin were also typical of the schools and faculties of the Allied capitals. At the LSE in 1915–16 Sidney Webb lectured both on 'The War and the Outbreak of Peace: Some Economic Aspects' and 'How to Prevent War', Harold Mackinder taught a course on 'The Geography of the War Area', and in history a series of 'lectures with special bearing on the war' was organized, including R. W. Seton-Watson on the Southern Slavs, and the director Pember Reeves himself on the war and the Balkan States.[101] At the Faculty of Letters in Paris in 1914, Gustave Lanson introduced a course on 'the development of the French ideal of national and human culture amongst the great writers of the three classical centuries'. This set the tone for the renewed emphasis on the classics that became a central part of the university curriculum in France after 1914.[102]

University calendars and reports also reveal a new category of academic achievement: 'war work'. This category applied first and foremost to the near total engagement of university departments of science and engineering in war-related research and manufacture; but it also applied to the humanities and social sciences, where several professors, and their students, used their special expertise directly to serve the national war effort. Such was the case of almost all faculties at the LSE, an institution whose intellectual resources were uniquely attuned to the problems of planning and administration raised by the war. The list of war-work is long: students under Professor Bowley provided statistics for the Ministry of Munitions; a group of geography students worked under Professor Mackinder to provide maps for military headquarters; staff and students of the library gathered information on ocean trade routes, the bread-ticket system in Berlin, and the current conditions of female labour.[103] For the duration of war the LSE acted as a sort of government think tank.

The war excited academic patriotism and realigned the priorities of some faculties and courses. Judging from the tenor of some academic journals, certain professors slipped easily into the language of mindless nationalism, and probably some new courses introduced during the war degenerated likewise into patriotic pedantry.[104] This, though, had also been the case before the war, and whilst academic chauvinism may have

---

[101] LSE, *Calendar*, 1915–16.
[102] Hanna, *The mobilization of intellect*, pp. 142–76. R. Thamin, 'L'Université de France et la guerre', August 1916, p. 608.
[103] 'The school and the war', *CMR*, December 1915; 'The school and the war', *CMR*, March 1916; and 'School news', *CMR*, December 1917.
[104] M. Martin, 'Histoire et actualité. La *Revue historique* pendant la première guerre mondiale', *Revue historique*, 255 (1976), pp. 433–68.

been stronger after 1914, there still remained professors who used their lectures to stimulate debate not indoctrinate, and introduced the war into their courses simply because it posed problems that everyone had to face. Moreover, and as the example of the LSE suggests, war work and academic progress were not always incompatible. The activity of the School during the war lay behind the extraordinary expansion of the LSE under William Beveridge after 1919.[105]

On balance, though, whilst new courses were introduced, the university curricula as a whole remained largely unaltered. This is particularly apparent when one looks at examinations, even in the humanities, for although the war did make some vague incursions, students in general continued to be asked to reflect upon the usual questions of classical, timeless, irrelevance.

Between 1914 and 1918 many measures were passed to adjust university regulations to what was practically possible, and morally justifiable, in a state of war. One of the first steps taken by the Friedrich-Wilhelms-Universität was to rule that mobilized students did not have to be present to defend their theses. In 1917 paper shortages dictated the decree that theses no longer had to be published and in May 1918 the regulation that denied re-inscription after four years' absence was hurriedly lifted.[106] University authorities in Paris and London also introduced various measures to protect the academic status of mobilized students.

In 1915 the University of London introduced an 'Honorary Degree' to be awarded to students who had almost completed their study at home and had served in the war for not less than nine months.[107] Strict safeguards, however, were put in place to avoid abuse of the degree – it was not, the Senate insisted, to be a 'free' degree. Likewise in Paris, in 1915 the authorities awarded an 'honorary' *agrégation* for the class of 1914. The award was granted to candidates who had passed their written exam but had been called up before they could sit their oral. However, it was made perfectly clear that this was an exceptional measure, not a precedent, and the exam was subsequently suspended until the end of the war.

Just how important standards remained during the war can be seen from the example of the École Polytechnique. This is an extreme example to draw, because formal examination procedures were taken more seriously at

[105] Dahrendorf, *LSE*, pp. 130–1 and pp. 137–95; and J. Harris, *William Beveridge. A biography* (Oxford, 1997), pp. 259–60.
[106] Respectively: HUA, Phil. Fak/34; Phil. Fak/35; Kuratorium/219.
[107] KCLCA, KAP/BUR/97. 'Report of the Vice-Chancellor on the work of the University during the year 1915–16.' Similarly in Berlin, from January 1917 medical students were allowed to count six months' service at the front for one term's work in a University Hospital. HUA, Phil. Fak/112.

this military school for engineering than in other capital institutions. It does nonetheless reveal the tensions, even the contradictions, between the demands of war and the demands of education that ran through all schools and faculties throughout 1914–1918, for the management of examinations at the École Polytechnique went completely against the sense of national duty that the school prided itself in embodying. Granted, on some issues school authorities did show some leniency – wounded ex-servicemen received the maximum mark of 20 in all physical tests and the category of 'war services' was included in the examination reports of all veterans.[108] However, on most matters they showed complete intransigence. When examiners noted that in the oral session of the 1917 *concours* a number of students showed signs of nervous depression, the proposal that this be taken into account when awarding grades was rejected outright. The official response to difficulties faced by students at the *concours* of 11 March 1918 was even more obstinate. On the night of 10 March Paris suffered nine hours of intense bombardment. The following day twenty-two exhausted students arrived late at the examination having been delayed by the disruptions to metro and bus services caused by the previous night's raid. The twenty-two students were refused entrance and 'impitoyablement éliminés' from the competition.[109] The student rebellion that such injustice provoked only served to harden attitudes further, and the governing body resolved to take preventative measures against such 'uncivilized behaviour' in the future. War, or not, certain principles were immutable. So, as the question of women shows, were certain prejudices.

The question of women 'The arrival of women students were a godsend', Hearnshaw commented after the war, 'but for their presence the college could barely have maintained a continuity of existence'.[110] The same could be said for all major capital sites of higher education: female enrolments during 1914–1918 kept the student population at a level where teaching could reasonably be justified and the budget at least partially met. These female enrolments were welcomed in London; indeed, the war years even witnessed the conversion of conservative academics, like Hearnshaw, to the cause of women's education. Professors in Paris and Berlin, including those with liberal political leanings, were more ambivalent. They recognized that without the continued

---

[108] 'Concours d'admission à l'École polytechnique', *RU*, February 1916.

[109] B. Villermet, 'Une grande École dans la tourmente: l'École polytechnique pendant la première guerre mondiale, 1914–1920, mémoire de maîtrise, University of Savoy, 1992', pp. 14–15.

[110] Hearnshaw, *The centenary of King's College London*, p. 460.

presence of women many classes would have closed; but they were sceptical as to whether female minds were quite adapted to preserving the spirit of the institutions whose form they kept alive.

Between 1914 and 1918, the Friedrich-Wilhelms-Universität, the Sorbonne, and the main institutions of the university of London – with the exception of King's – witnessed an overall increase in the proportion of women students that far exceeded the rate of growth experienced in pre-war decades.[111] After 1914 the Friedrich-Wilhelms-Universität registered a strong rise in numbers, which in faculties depleted of male students signified a proportional rise from 10 per cent in 1913–14 to over 30 per cent female in 1916–17. In some areas women eventually came to outnumber men. For instance, by the winter of 1915 the Institute of Geography had nearly three times as many women as men.[112] For the Sorbonne, figures are only available for 1914–1915. What even these limited statistics show is not just a steep rise in the proportion of women enrolled, from just over 10 per cent before the war to just over 30 per cent in the summer of 1915, but a marked redistribution of female students. Female enrolment in the amateur arts and sciences dropped, but in professional subjects numbers either remained constant (law and medicine) or grew (doubling in the École de Pharmacie).[113] London figures suggest a similar qualitative gain: during the war UCL women for the first time entered the departments of law, medicine, and engineering. The most far-reaching change in the position of women took place at King's. The war brought the integration of King's College for Women within the main college, enabling women for the first time to participate fully in college activities.[114]

Reponses to the rise in women's educational fortunes varied. The attitude of Berlin's professors to the changing gender of their audience was predictably negative. Having grudgingly accepted the 1908 regulation allowing women entry into Germany's faculties of higher education, the university had succeeded in barring most doors to equal access thereafter.[115] The war did force open some of these doors – shortages in certain service sectors, notably teaching, pushed authorities to allow women to enter courses and exams previously denied[116] – but it seems to have done

---

[111] F. Ringer, *Education and society in modern Europe* (Bloomington and London, 1979).

[112] *Chronik der Königlichen Friedrich-Wilhelms-Universität zu Berlin für das Rechnungsjahr 1914*, Jahrgang XXVIII, Halle, Buchdruckerei des Waisens Lanses, 1915, p. 71.

[113] 'Bulletin de l'enseignement secondaire des jeunes filles', *RU*, July 1915.

[114] KCLCA, KAP/BUR/68.

[115] R. J. Evans, *The feminist movement in Germany, 1894–1933* (Beverly Hills, 1976) and Jarausch, *Students, society and politics*, pp. 109–13.

[116] HUA, Phil. Fak/35. HUA, Kuratorium/155.

little to broaden the minds of those manning them. During the anniversary celebrations of 3 August 1917 the then rector Ernst Bumm gave the first ever formal university speech dedicated to the position of women students in Berlin.[117] Altogether Bumm did not altogether deny their right of entry to higher education, he did express fears that the wartime influx of women tended to render university study a feminine 'fashion'. He went on to note that study had taken women away from their 'natural destiny', marriage and maternity, and he concluded with the observation that what German women needed was 'time and a calm mind' to 'raise numerous progeny'. This, he said, was incompatible with university education.

The rector's views were shared by many other academics, who saw little point in appointing women to academic posts. During the war, absent men were usually replaced by retired professors. If women did on occasion rise to take over the tasks of mobilized men, their positions remained precarious. The example of the classicist Margaret Bieder is revealing. At the request of the distinguished scholars Willamowitz-Moellendorff and Eduard Meyer, Miss Bieder joined the staff of the archaeological faculty. She worked without pay so that the colleague she had replaced could continue to receive his salary. When the director fell ill she was called on to stand in for him, but when another director was appointed, Miss Bieder was forbidden to continue teaching and had to resort to giving private courses. In the eyes of German professors female scholars were considered little more than 'Ersatz'.[118]

The attitudes of male students were similarly reactionary. The rise in female students failed to bring a significant rise in their influence in student bodies. Whilst the number of women in unions did increase, from 77 on the eve of war to a maximum of 116 in the winter of 1916–17,[119] and whilst a few women were allowed to enter the Allgemeiner Studentenausschuss (General Committee of Students), not a single female student was admitted on to the board of directors on the grounds that it would be a mistake to create precedents for peacetime. The sentiment that women should not be allowed to profit from the absence of male students in wartime hardened into outright discrimination in the immediate aftermath of the conflict. The association of student ex-combatants, the Kriegsteilnehmer Verband, included the following

---

[117] E. Bumm, *Über das Frauenstudium* (Berlin, 1917), pp. 19–20.
[118] T. Maurer, 'Der Krieg als Chance? Frauen im Streben nach Gleichberechtigung an deutschen Universitäten 1914–1918', in *Jahrbuch Für Universitätsgeschichte*, no. 6, 2003, pp. 107–38. H. Laitko, *Wissenschaft in Berlin. Von den Anfängen bis zum Neubeginn nach 1945*, (Berlin, 1987), p. 322.
[119] HUA, Rektor und Senat/806.

goal in its statutes: 'to systematically favour the interests of students who took part in the war against those who did not (the women!)'.[120]

Professors at the Sorbonne also met the incursion of women with hostility, though their resentment seems to have stemmed less from fears that this would lead to a fall in the national birth rate than to a decline in intellectual standards. The historian Alphonse Aulard, former Dreyfusard, member of the Ligue des Droits de l'Homme, and champion throughout the war of France's glorious tradition of freedom and equality, was not pleased to note that 'the feminine element' now dominated his courses on the French Revolution at the Sorbonne.[121] Admitting, rather reluctantly, that women had in fact performed better in exams than men, he commented that in general the women in his audience were docile, unoriginal, and lacked initiative. According to Louis Liard, Rector of the Sorbonne, it was important to recognize the courage and resolution of the women in the university, 'but without having any illusion of the force that our Faculties, above all the Faculty of Letters, could draw from the increase in these feminine contingents'.[122] He explained that female students lacked knowledge, method, and depth, and that whilst they tried to supplement these weaknesses with 'the marvellous intuition of women [. . .] the insufficiency of their former baggage soon appears'.[123]

Professorial attitudes to women in London were markedly different. London had long been a pioneer in the educational emancipation of women, and during the war college reports warmly welcomed the rising number of female enrolments, along with the increase in woman on the professorial staff. Such attitudes were not only different from those held by academics in Paris and Berlin, and in other English universities.[124] They were also somewhat ahead of those entertained by male students in London. When student magazines spoke of women during the war it was usually with mockery and condescension. The *Clare Market Review* comment pages give the impression that female students spent the whole war knitting, utterly oblivious to the portent of the events going on around them.[125] Similarly in the *University College Magazine*, UCL women were noted to have organized lectures on 'Some aspects of women's work', and also to have partaken in a large debate on the theme that, 'after the war

---

[120] HUA, Rektor und Senat/874.
[121] *La vie féminine*, 11 June 1916 and 'Les étudiantes à la Sorbonne', *RU*, 7 July 1916. Hanna, *The mobilization of intellect*, pp. 72–3.
[122] L. Liard, 'La Guerre et les universités françaises', *Revue de Paris*, 1 May 1916.   [123] Ibid.
[124] J. M. Winter, 'Oxford and the First World War', in B. Harrison, ed., *The History of the University of Oxford*, vol. VIII: *The Twentieth Century* (Oxford, 1994), p. 14.
[125] 'Union Report', *CMR*, June 1915.

women will be more powerful than men'. The male gloss on the subject was that the women's main concern was the financial position of its Tea Club.[126]

International relations

During the war the international relations of universities were reconfigured in ways that are both more complicated and far-reaching than is usually recognized. As many have argued, European public space was 'fractured' during the war, and ties sharply severed between enemy nations.[127] At the same time, however, other transnational ties were brought into prominence, and new alliances forged. Moreover, in many of these developments the war appears to have acted more as a catalyst than as a cause. By 1914 academics in Paris and London had already begun to voice doubts about the scientific value of German scholarship which had been such a source of inspiration over the previous fifty years, and they had also started to think about new ways of strengthening the international appeal of indigenous academic traditions. Already in the pre-war period European public space appears much less a forum for cooperation than competition; international conferences and exhibitions were opportunities for the glorification of national genius.[128] The nationalist politics of universities between 1914 and 1918 did not mark a break with some sort of idyllic pre-war European community of scholarship, but merely the hardening of national academic rivalries that were already well established before 1914.

Berlin The Kaiser-Wilhelms-Universität broke relations with enemy countries with impressive speed. By the time the Minister of Education von Trott zu Soltz had formally demanded that all alien enemies be removed from the university, staff had already compiled a list of enemy students and professors, and the following day, 31 August, 7 professors and 568 enemy students were expelled.[129] When Italy, Romania, and America entered the war, students of these countries were also promptly struck from matriculation lists. In contrast, and after much debate, the great Berlin

[126] M. F. Lawson, 'College Women in the First World War', cited in D. Taylor, *The Godless Students of Gower Street* (London, 1968), p. 62.

[127] P. Soulez, 'Les philosophes devant la fracture de l'espace public européen', in *Les Philosophes et la Guerre de 14* (Saint-Denis, 1988), pp. 9–23.

[128] B. Schroeder-Gudehus, *Les scientifiques et la paix. La communauté scientifique internationale* (Montreal, 1978), pp. 41–62. R. Jessen and J. Vogel (eds.), *Wissenschaft und Nation in der europäischen Geschichte* (Frankfurt am Main and New York, 2002).

[129] (BArch), R 8034 II/7843, 'Das preußische Kultusministerium und die "Zwangsrussen"', *Berliner Tageblatt*, 19 December 1914. H. Rüdiger Peter (ed.), *Schnorrer, Verschwörer, Bombenwerfer? Studenten aus dem Russischen Reich an deutschen Hochschulen vor dem 1. Weltkrieg* (Frankfurt am Main, 2001).

academies and societies refused to expel enemy professors.[130] However, allied candidatures for certain academy awards were refused – Benedetto Croce, for instance, was ineligible for the gold Leibniz medal in March 1915.[131] Already on 7 September 1914, thirty well-known German academics, the majority of them Berliners, had returned, with considerable display, though not quite unanimous consent, medals received from Allied institutions.[132] Their aim was to make irreversible the rupture with colleagues in the enemy camp.[133]

At the same time, Berlin academics tried to strengthen relations with neutrals. For both political and strategic reasons this offensive was largely unsuccessful. The German manifestos of September and October, and in particular the infamous 'Manifesto of 93', *An die Kulturwelt*, backfired completely. Written to deny the charge that German troops had committed atrocities in occupied territories, these declarations had the result – in part because of their tone, in part because the Allies skilfully misrepresented them – of suggesting that German scholars supported acts of military barbarism. The 'Manifesto of 93' also created the impression that German academics were servile exponents of state policy. The many overtures made by academics to neutrals after October 1914 were, with the partial exception of Sweden,[134] seen as thinly veiled propaganda and viewed with mistrust. Even on an individual level, scientists such as Albert Einstein, who had not signed the manifesto, or Max Planck, who later sought to underplay his role in drafting it, found it difficult to re-establish contact with neutral scholars.[135]

The political hostility provoked by the manifesto was one barrier to academic relations with neutrals; the British naval blockade was another. The blockade not only hindered the transmission of texts abroad – the 'Manifesto of 93' was largely distributed by private letters[136] – it also

---

[130] See Szöllösi-Janze, *Fritz Haber*, p. 260; Basler, 'Zur politischen Rolle der Berliner Universität', p. 190; and T. Wolff, *Tagebücher 1914–1919*, ed. B. Sösemann (Boppard am Rhein, 1984, 2 vols.), 9 July 1915, vol. i, p. 252.

[131] Basler, 'Zur politischen Rolle der Berliner Universität', p. 189.

[132] Schroeder-Gudehus, *Les scientifiques et la paix*, p. 90. Wilhelm Förster, 'Deutsche Gelehrte und englische Auszeichnungen', *Berliner Tageblatt*, 11 September 1914.

[133] Schroeder-Gudehus, *Les Scientifiques et la paix*, p. 90.

[134] E. Demm, 'Les thèmes de la propagande allemande en 1914' (1988), in Demm, *Ostpolitik und Propaganda im Ersten Weltkrieg* (Frankfurt am Main, 2002), pp. 11–26.

[135] Stern, *Einstein's German World*, pp. 45–6 and pp. 114–16. S. Grundmann, *Einsteins Akte. Einsteins Jahre in Deutschland aus der Sicht der deutschen Politik* (Berlin, 1998), pp. 39–75.

[136] B. vom Brocke, 'Wissenschaft und Militarismus: "Der Aufruf der 93 An die Kulturwelt!" und der Zusammenbruch der internationalen Gelehrtenrepublik im ersten Weltkrieg', in W. M. Calder, H. Flashar, and T. Linken (eds.), *Willamowitz nach 50 Jahren* (Darmstadt, 1985), p. 654.

made it difficult for professors themselves to travel. This was a particular handicap with regard to America, where relations, carefully cultivated in the pre-war period, had since the outbreak of war considerably soured.[137]

The isolation caused by the naval blockade and the hostility of neutral opinion had the same result as penury in raw materials: Berlin was obliged to concentrate on allied and occupied countries in Central and Eastern Europe and the Near East for its intellectual, as for its economic, exchange.[138] Under the aegis of the Reichsdeutsche Waffenbrüderliche Vereinigung (the German Association of Comrades in Arms) attempts were made to increase contact with academics in Austro-Hungary.[139] Although a few well-known Austrian professors travelled to Berlin to give guest lectures, and the University of Budapest joined the 'Declaration of German University Professors' against the charge of atrocities, this initiative in general proved disappointing.[140] The same may be said of the moves made to strengthen intellectual relations with Turkey. In the autumn of 1915, seventeen German scholars were sent to Istanbul to teach for five years. Several members of the University of Berlin were included, among them the classicist C. F. Lehmann-Haupt, who at the outbreak of war had lost his job at the University of Liverpool and had since been acting as extraordinary professor in ancient history at Berlin.[141] This mission can be seen as a step towards the realization of the pre-war project of pro-Turkish enthusiasts in Berlin to create a German–Turkish university in Istanbul.[142] It also acted to provide young academics – most of the seventeen envoys were Privatdozenten – with the opportunity to progress in their academic career and, against stiff opposition from the War Office, to defer military service. In both

---

[137] B. vom Brocke, 'Der deutsch-amerikanische Professorenaustasch: preussische Wissenschaftspolitik, internationale Wissenschaftsbeziehungen und die Anfänge einer deutschen Auswärtigen Kulturpolitik vor dem ersten Weltkrieg', *Zeitschrift für Kulturaustausch*, 31 (1981), pp. 128–82 and Schroeder-Gudehus, *Les scientifiques et la paix*, p. 51.

[138] J. Kloosterhuis, *'Friedliche Imperialisten'. Deutsche Auslandsvereine und auswärtige Kulturpolitik, 1906–1918* (Frankfurt am Main, 1994 [1981]), pp. 254 ff.

[139] J. Kloosterhuis, *'Friedliche Imperialisten'*, pp. 505–7.

[140] *Reden in schwerer Zeit* (Berlin, 1915, 3 vols.), here vol. III, pp. 149–76, and pp. 347ff. Politisches Archiv des Auswärtigen Amt (PAAA), Kunst und Wissenschaft, R 64483, Ungarisches Institut.

[141] BArch, R 901/39524, 'Die türkische Universität in Stambul'. Kloosterhuis, *Friedliche Imperialisten*, vol. I, pp. 255–66 and vol. II, pp. 589–93; criticized by E. Demm, 'Die wilhelminische Zeit', in K.-P. Haase (ed.), *Berlin-Istanbul. Katalog der Ausstellung* (Berlin, 2005).

[142] See: BArch, R 901/39531, 'Die deutsche Hochschule in der Türkei Januar 1912 bis November 1913'; and 'Ernst Jäckh, or 'Türkenjäckh', *Der goldene Pflug. Lebensernte eines Weltbürgers* (Stuttgart, 1954), p. 10.

respects, however, the mission failed. War-related inflation undermined the value of teaching salaries, and those who could find jobs back home in Germany left. German professors who still remained in the autumn of 1918 were forced by the Allies to quit the country.

Berlin professors also played a leading role in a broad set of initiatives to expand German intellectual authority in occupied areas, in particular in Eastern Europe. These initiatives certainly complemented larger academic plans for increased German influence in the area, but during the war their organization seems to have been largely improvised, more the result of individual ambition than any concerted programme for academic dominance.

A variety of different schemes were put in place. In Ghent and Warsaw Berlin academics showed marked political pragmatism, playing on local nationalist rivalries to strengthen their support. In occupied Ghent German scholars removed all Walloon professors and re-founded the University of Ghent as a uniquely Flemish institution.[143] Likewise in Warsaw, the university and the polytechnic, Russified since 1869, were reopened in November 1915 as Polish institutions.[144] Dorpat, in Estonia, witnessed even more concerted attempts at influence. The University of Dorpat, once German, had also recently been Russified, and the project to re-found the institution as German was of particular symbolic importance to Berlin scholars. The first move in this direction, after the German conquest of the city in February 1918, was to set up a series of lectures, and in the following months many of Berlin's most prestigious academics came to speak at the university.[145] In the spring of 1918 the Kaiser appointed the Berlin professor of Russian, and his close friend, Theodor Schiemann, to orchestrate the re-opening of the University, which took place with great ceremony on 15 September 1918.[146]

This was Germany's last great intellectual offensive. Little more than two months later the war was lost, and the university closed. There had already been signs of weakness before, however. Schiemann's plans for the complete Germanization of Dorpat, and the exclusion not only of Russian but also of Estonian and Latvian elements, had earned him

---

[143] L. Wils, *Flamenpolitik en aktivisme. Vlaanderen tegenover Belgie in de eerste wereldoorlog* (Louvain, 1974), pp. 161–92.

[144] *Feierliche Eröffnung der Universität und der Technischen Hochschule von Warschau am 15.11.1915* (Warsaw, 1915); M. Handelsman, *Die Warschauer Universität* (München-Gladbach, 1916).

[145] R. von Engelhardt, *Die deutsche Universität Dorpat in ihrer geistesgeschichtlichen Bedeutung* (Munich, 1933), p. 534.

[146] K. Meyer, *Theodor Schiemann als politischer Publizist* (Frankfurt am Main, 1956), p. 66; G. Voigt, *Otto Hoetzsch 1876–1946. Wissenschaft und Politik im Leben eines deutschen Historikers* (Berlin, 1978), p. 70.

the reproach of 'pan-German fanaticism' by moderates at home.[147] Moreover, it remains questionable whether even Schiemann, or any of the scholars who lent their support to his project, really believed that a university in Dorpat could offset the intellectual isolation into which Berlin had been plunged by the rupture of relations with France, Britain, and America.

London The measures taken by UCL and King's with regard to enemy students at the outbreak of war were very different from those introduced by the Kaiser-Wilhelms-Universität and the Sorbonne. Referring with pride to the College's tradition of 'freedom and toleration', the UCL professorial board decided in October 1914 to admit German and Austrian students 'of whose good faith we are satisfied'.[148] At King's, Burrows also accepted German students, considering that it was the duty of the college not only to receive enemy students of sound reputation, but also to protect their rights to just treatment on the question of internment.[149] Burrows struggled against government authorities throughout the war, first to prevent the unfair internment of two of his German students, and later to secure their release. When his appeals failed, he went on to campaign more publicly for the fair treatment of enemy aliens in England, and also encouraged King's students to set up a committee to provide aid to the families of alien interns. Even more strongly than Forster, Burrows believed that London's colleges had a responsibility to uphold liberal traditions in face of the acts of intolerance brought by war.

London was also proud of its internationalism. It recruited more foreign students than any other English university. The curriculum it offered was remarkably open (for its day) to the languages and histories of peoples outside the British Isles. Certain university members also considered that it was London's role to instruct the nation more generally on the importance of foreign affairs, and to challenge what they viewed as the ruinous flaw of the English people – their insularity. The experience of war confirmed Burrows, in particular, in his views that Europe's Great Powers could not survive without the cooperation of other states, and that it was strategically imperative for England's universities, and in particular those of London, to provide the government

---

[147] Hans Delbrück, for instance, in the *Preußische Jahrbücher*, 173, 1918, p. 425. See Meyer, *Theodor Schiemann*, p. 241.

[148] 'Universities and the War. The value of Sports in the Present Time', *Westminster Gazette*, 7 October 1914. Cf. KCLCA, KAP/BUR/100, letter from Foster to Burrows, 9 October 1914.

[149] KCLCA, KAP/BUR/100.

with the requisite linguistic and historical expertise to survive in this new world context. It was towards this end that Burrows helped found in 1915 the School of Slavonic Studies, and in the following years proceeded to establish departments in Spanish, Portuguese, and Modern Greek.[150]

With regard to university foreign policy, the war brought the importance of relations with France more boldly into relief. On 29 September 1914 Forster issued a moving address to the University of Paris, expressing his profound regret to see an ally of his College under enemy attack, and offering the hospitality of UCL to Parisian students and professors.[151] The offer was politely refused by Liard who, echoing the instruction of Sarrault, proudly claimed that 'whatever the circumstances' the university of Paris would continue instruction as usual.[152] UCL did however offer its hospitality to refugees from French occupied territories, and the welcome the College showed to these students, as well as the warm reception given in the spring of 1916 to a visit of French professors to England, helped pave the way for formal exchange programmes to be set up between the two countries at the end of the war.[153] In 1919–20 UCL received over one hundred French students, compared with just fifteen in 1913–14.[154]

One further important dimension of London's foreign relations after 1914 was the stimulus given by the war to the expansion of the Imperial Studies Movement, a loose alliance of academics and political figures dedicated both to improving exchanges between London and imperial (including American) universities, and to coordinating and strengthening of instruction in imperial matters (from tropical medicine to Oriental and African languages).[155] By heightening awareness of the importance of empire, the war opened up sources of funding for the development of such projects. Funds were finally available for the creation in January 1917 of the long-awaited School of Oriental Studies, and at the end of the war the LCC and Rhodes Trust increased donations for the teaching of imperial history, expanding London's single Rhodes lectureship into a University Department of Colonial and Imperial History, with eight new chairs.

---

[150] Hearnshaw, *Centenary*, pp. 465–6. R. Clogg, *Politics and the Academy. Arnold Toynbee and the Koreas Chair* (London, 1986).
[151] AN, AJ/61/85.   [152] AN, AJ/61/85.
[153] *University College Magazine*, March 1915, December 1916. KCLCA, KAP/BUR/132. A. Balz, 'Une mission française dans le Royaume-Uni', *RU*, July 1916, p. 158.
[154] KCLCA, KAP/BUR/251, 'British University Mission to France'.
[155] KCLCA, KAP/BUR/113, 198, 320.

The war also provided London University with the opportunity to demonstrate the expertise it had already acquired in imperial matters. The war years witnessed an increase in public lectures on imperial subjects,[156] and also the tightening of relations between the university and government services, notably the India and the Colonial Offices. Finally, the presence in the capital of dominion forces, including army education officers, provided London academics with an understanding of education abroad that after the war enabled them to formulate effective schemes for attracting foreign students.[157] During the war London University enhanced its reputation as a central site for imperial interchange. It was only fitting, therefore, that one of the schemes of the Empire War Memorial League was to provide new buildings for the University of London right at the heart of Westminster.[158]

Paris The foreign policy of the Sorbonne was even more ambitious. The Sorbonne worked to strengthen ties with Allied nations, as the heavily publicized French university mission to England in 1916 suggests. It was also active in courting the support of neutral countries. Here the Academic Council revealed an interest in university communities as far apart as Bucharest and Dublin, but one particular object of attention nevertheless stands out: America.[159] In this sphere, the Sorbonne sought to win support for the French war effort, and to attract students (and thus income) to its financially strained faculties. Its principal goal, however, was to capitalize on the rapid decline in Germany's reputation abroad after the 'Manifesto of 93', and to increase the international appeal of the Sorbonne.

The campaign to sell French scholarship across the Atlantic drew on a variety of strategies. Exchanges were increased, new chairs in French literature established, special lecture tours organized, and the French contribution to the San Francisco exhibition of 1915 carefully choreographed. The Council believed that the best ambassadors for French culture in America would be American students themselves, and in March 1916 the Council appointed Emile Durkheim to head a commission to look into the most effective ways of attracting young Americans to Paris. Problems of language, social life, lodging, and food were all discussed, and in many areas acted upon. Today's Cité

[156] 'Empire in the Street', *The Times Literary Supplement*, November 1916.
[157] KCLCA, KAP/BUR/198.
[158] 'Empire War Memorial Buildings in London', *The Building News and Engineering Journal*, 30 October 1918. KCLCA, KAP/BUR/33.
[159] AN, AJ/16/2589 and 2560.

Universitaire has its origins in the creation in 1917 of a house for American students.[160] In 1918 a dozen leading French scholars published a volume introducing *La vie universitaire à Paris* to an American audience. The creation at the end of 1918 of the first French chair in American Literature and Civilization lay at least part within this logic of attracting American attention to Paris, as did the grand ceremony held at the Sorbonne at the end of December 1918 to accompany the University's award of the title of doctor *honoris causa* to President Woodrow Wilson.[161]

These initiatives met with great success, not least because they suited American interests. Policies to attract American students were encouraged by American authorities concerned by the lack of support amongst troops for their French ally;[162] professorial exchange programmes were welcomed by a nascent great power eager to show that it was not just a military power, but also an intellectual authority to be reckoned with.[163]

For France, the new special relationship with America far offset the rupture with German universities that had taken place in 1914. Paris had achieved this break with at least as much rapidity as had Berlin. Enemy students had been swiftly crossed off matriculation lists. In October 1914 the Council had ruled that all theses formerly destined for German universities would be sent to universities in Britain, America, Belgium, and Russia instead.[164] Unlike in Berlin, or London, the five Academies of the Institut de France struck the names of all German scholars from their rolls.[165] On 8 August 1914, over one month before the 'manifeste des barbares', Henri Bergson had pronounced his verdict before the Académie des sciences morales et Politiques: 'the struggle against Germany is the struggle of civilization against barbarism'.[166]

[160] 'La maison des étudiants américains', *RU*, October 1917 and AN, AJ/16/7027–44.

[161] J. Prévost, *Dix-huitième année* (Paris, 1929), pp. 100–1.

[162] J. D. Keene, *Doughboys: the Great War and the remaking of America*, (Baltimore, 2001), pp. 105–31. 'Chronique du mois', *RU*, February 1919.

[163] E. Fuchs, 'Wissenschaftsinternationalismus in Kriegs- und Kriesenzeiten. Zur Rolle der USA bei der Reorganisation der internationalen *scientific community, 1914–1945*', in R. Jessen and J. Vogel (eds.), *Wissenschaft und Nation in der Europäischen Geschichte* (Frankfurt am Main, 2002), pp. 263–84.

[164] AN, AJ/16/2589, 1 March 1915.

[165] 'L'Institut de France et la guerre', *Revue internationale de l'enseignement*, 69, 1915; and Hanna, *The mobilization of intellect*, pp. 81–2. Wallace, *War and the image of Germany*, p. 192.

[166] Prochasson and Rasmussen, *Au nom de la patrie*, p. 131.

Innovation

One of the most interesting aspects of university life between 1914 and 1918 was the extent to which the demands of war stimulated the development of modern fields of academic study. We shall focus here on developments made within the domain of science and technology. In the study of modern languages, we should note, striking progress was also made. In London, as well as four new departments at King's, and the creation of the School of Oriental Studies, UCL gained new departments in Dutch studies and (in collaboration with Bedford College) Scandinavian studies, and three new lectureships in Italian.[167] By 1919 the University of Paris boasted new departments in Spanish, Italian, Scandinavian studies, and Russian, the rudiments of an Institute of Slavic studies, and had plans for the foundation of new chairs in Portuguese and Modern Greek.[168] In Berlin too, though to a lesser extent, the war years brought the addition of a new Hungarian Institute, and a special section within the Berlin Oriental Institute for the teaching of Bulgarian.[169] These developments were in part a response to the demands of war. However, they also represent the outcome of long-term academic pressures for curriculum change.[170] For by highlighting the fundamental national importance of scientific and technical training, the knowledge of modern languages, and the mastery of techniques of social and economic management (among other skills) the war gave a crucial impetus to academic reform movements that before the war had struggled to break through conservative opposition to curriculum modernization.

In the fields, then, of science and technology, 1914–1918 were in many respects 'glorious years' for the capital universities.[171] The laboratories of all capital science faculties, colleges, institutes, special schools, and academies were almost totally occupied with war-related work. This work was immensely broad, with innovation taking place in every discernable field. The best-known wartime contribution of German university science was the work of Fritz Haber and his Institute at Dahlem in experimenting with, and then supervising the

---

[167] UCL *Annual Report*, 1917–18.

[168] AN, AJ/16/2560.

[169] PAAA, Kunst und Wissenschaft, R 64483, Ungarisches Institut, 'Berlin – Budapest', *Neue Zürcher Zeitung*, 26 March 1916; BArch, 2523 R 8034 II/2523, 'Bulgarien und die deutsche Wissenschaft', *Deutsche Tageszeitung*, 8 January 1916.

[170] G. E. Sherrington, *English education, social change and the war 1911–1920* (Manchester, 1981). C. Stray, *Classics transformed: Schools, universities and society in England, 1830–1960* (Oxford, 1998).

[171] Michael Sanderson, *The universities and British industry, 1850–1970* (Routledge, 1972), pp. 214–42, here p. 239.

use of, poison gas.[172] However, it is also important to signal, not only the valuable research that went on elsewhere to improve Germany's fighting capacity – such as that carried out by astrophysicists at the Friedrich-Wilhelms-Universität to improve the precision of projectiles[173] – but also the indispensable research led by many Berlin scientists into the production of synthetic materials. It is arguable that Fritz Haber's most important contribution to the war lay not in his work on gas warfare, but in his contribution, alongside Emile Fischer, to the production of artificial nitrogen.[174] With saltpetre stocks near exhaustion, and the British naval blockade preventing further imports from Chile, the production of artificial nitrogen was the only means Germany had of meeting its needs for nitric acid, the source of both explosives and fertilisers.[175]

London University boasted England's first departments in both science and engineering, and led the way in many fields of war-related research, training, and even manufacture.[176] King's, for example, developed the biggest munitions training department in England,[177] and was also one of the nation's main centres for research into the production of optical glass. The most valuable of the many war-related projects in which UCL was engaged was research, on the lines of the Haber process, into the fixation of nitrogen from the atmosphere for use in explosives.[178] The single most important centre for war work in London, however, was Imperial College. Though only formed in 1907, and still partly housed in a hut, Imperial dealt with a wider range of problems than any other English university, and also led research on gas warfare.[179] Indeed, Imperial and other London colleges were so dominantly engaged in this problem that

---

[172] F. L. Haber, *The poisonous cloud: chemical warfare in the First World War* (Oxford, 1986). Szöllösi-Janze, *Fritz Haber*, and Stern, *Einstein's German World*, pp. 59–164.
[173] Basler, 'Zur politischen Rolle der Berliner Universität', p. 191.
[174] F. Haber, 'Die Chemie im Kriege', in *Fünf Vorträge aus den Jahren 1920–1923* (Berlin, 1924), pp. 25–41, here p. 31; L. Burchardt, 'Die Kaiser-Wilhelm-Gesellschaft im Ersten Weltkrieg (1914–1918)', in R. Vierhans and B. vom Brocke (eds.), *Forschung im Spannungsfeld von Politik und Gesellschaft. Geschichte und Struktur der Kaiser-Wilhelm-/Max Planck-Gesellschaft. Aus Anlass ihres 75-jährigen Bestehens* (Stuttgart, 1990). p. 167; G. D. Feldman, 'A German Scientist between Illusion and Reality: Emil Fischer, 1909–1919', in I. Geiss and B. J. Wendt (eds.), *Deutschland in der Weltpolitik des 19. und 20. Jahrhunderts* (Düsseldorf, 1973), pp. 341–62.
[175] Haber, 'Die Chemie im Kriege', p. 31.
[176] M. Sanderson *The universities and British industry 1850–1970*, pp. 214–42, here p. 239.
[177] KCLCA, KAP/BUR/132. Hearnshaw, *The centenary of King's College London*, p. 463.
[178] 'Summary Record of War Work in Scientific Departments', p. cxii. R. MacLeod, 'The Chemists Go to War: the Mobilisation of Civilian Chemists and the British War Effort, 1914–1918', *Annales of Science*, 50 (1993), pp. 455–81.
[179] Sanderson, *The universities and British industry*, p. 240.

William Pope in Cambridge was forced to complain in 1917 that 'no chemist outside London is allowed any effective part in the work'.[180]

The distinguishing feature of war-related research in Paris was the sheer number of centres engaged: the Faculty of Science at the Sorbonne, the Collège de France, École des Hautes Études Pratiques, Musée d'Histoire Naturelle, Institut Pasteur, Institut de Chimie, not to mention the plethora of *grandes écoles* (École Polytechnique, École de Physique et Chimie, École Supérieure de Pharmacie, École Supérieure d'Aéronautique. Even the ENS, all but empty of students, had never been more active before, leading research in wireless telegraphy, long-range of artillery batteries, sonic detection, and 'special projectiles' (gas warfare).[181] The case of the ENS exemplifies the breadth of the work carried out in Paris's science faculties. It also reveals the extent to which the demands of war pressed the capital's multiple centres of expertise into greater collaboration. ENS scientists liaised with their peers throughout the capital, replacing the situation of competition and duplication that had weakened French university science before the war with a far more coordinated structure.[182]

The mobilization of university science in the first years of the conflict was largely voluntary. Scientists appreciated, well ahead of national governments, the role that their expertise could play in the war effort. Haber had placed his Institute on a war footing long before Germany's civil and military commanders had even imagined the potential of his work.[183] Similarly, at the outbreak of war the Paris Académie des Sciences and the Royal Society in London immediately constituted special commissions to look into the application of science to military problems – a year before either Allied government had set itself seriously to the task. 'Par la science, pour la patrie' was the motto of the French association for the advancement of science, alongside most scientists in pre-war Europe.[184]

With the hardening of the Allied blockade, the use of poison gas in April 1915, and the rapid depletion of munitions stocks, national governments came to intervene more directly in the management of university science. For Paris and London the result of this intervention was 'nothing less than a revolution' in state–university relations.[185] University science

---

[180] Haber, *The poisonous cloud*, p. 124.
[181] AN, AJ/61/86. Hanna, *The mobilization of intellect*, pp. 180–1.
[182] O. Lepick, *La Grande Guerre chimique 1914–1918* (Paris, 1998). AN, AJ/61/86 (File 1, 1916).
[183] Szöllösi-Janze, *Fritz Haber* and R. Willstätter, *Aus meinem Leben. Von Arbeit, Muße und Freunden* (Weinheim, 1949), p. 230.
[184] E. Crawford, *The beginning of the Nobel Institution. The Science Prizes 1901–1915* (Cambridge, 1984).
[185] 'Science et guerre', *Revue des deux mondes*, 1 December 1915.

finally gained formal institutional backing. The creation in London of the University Grants Committee and the Department for Scientific and Industrial Research, and in Paris of the Direction des inventions, placed university funding for the first time on a more regular basis.[186] These bodies also helped to promote stronger collaboration between university science and industry.

In Berlin the situation was slightly different. University ties with state and industry were already well developed by the outbreak of war, as the creation of the Kaiser-Wilhelm Institutes shows. What changed after 1914 was the intensity, and the scale, of cooperation. Haber's Institute – 'a kind of Manhattan Project before its time' – worked in alliance with Germany's largest chemical firms, and by the end of the war had a research staff of 150 and employed around 1,500 workers.[187] The war also strengthened the relationship between university science and the military in Berlin. At the end of 1914 Haber had the rank of captain, and his Institute was placed directly under the war ministry and organized along military lines. The war years saw another – the last – Kaiser-Wilhelm foundation, for the science of war technology. Created in July 1917, its aim was 'to bring the army and navy into close contact with representatives of natural sciences and technologies'.[188]

The Great War marked a turning point in the institutional organization of university science, with long-term consequences for academic life in Paris, London, and Berlin. In terms of the representation of science, the impact of war was more ambiguous. The absolute centrality of university science to the war effort was never fully recognized on the level of public academic discourse, not even by scientists themselves. One reason for this was moral. Whilst few scientists went as far as the Berlin pacifist G. F. Nicolai in claiming that science carried out in the service of war was no longer science at all,[189] some did have reservations about extolling their contribution to the war effort in public, and even those who held a less idealistic view of their vocation found it difficult to articulate the value of science within a public sphere that insisted strongly that the factor determining the outcome of war was moral resolve. For scientists in Paris and London such moral restraints were compounded by an obstacle of a

---

[186] R. MacLeod and E. K. Andrews, 'The origins of the DSIR: reflections on ideas and men, 1915–1916', *Public Administration*, 48 (1970), pp. 23–48. Y. Roussel, 'L'Histoire d'une politique des inventions, 1887–1918', *Cahiers pour l'histoire du CNRS*, no. 3 (1989), pp. 19–57. H. W. Paul, *From knowledge to power: The rise of the science empire in France* (Cambridge, 1987), pp. 320ff.

[187] Stern, *Einstein's German World*, pp. 118–19; Szöllösi-Janze, *Fritz Haber*, p. 263.

[188] Feldman, 'A German Scientist between Illusion and Reality', p. 355.

[189] W. Zuelzer, *The Nicolai case: A biography* (Detroit, 1982).

more political nature. By 1914 scientific achievement was strongly associated in the public imagination with Germany's massive industrial expansion after unification. As pro-science reformers had learnt before the war, it was difficult to celebrate the importance of science without suffering the charge of pro-Germanism.

There is a paradox in this association, for while French and British scientists viewed German university research and industrial production as interdependent, German academics retained a strong distinction between pure and practical science, symbolized by the fact that Germany's centres of applied research remained separate from her universities. Berlin's Technical College at Charlottenburg – the embodiment in French eyes of Germany's scientific might, and the inspiration behind the creation of Imperial College – was not considered a scientific institution at all. Industrial and technical research were not *Wissenschaft*.[190] Even though many of Berlin's most prestigious research institutes had by 1914 strong ties with industry, the ideal of scientific progress they represented still lay in theoretical achievements, not big contracts. Indeed, if we judge from Nicolai's 'Appeal to Europeans', for which there was no equivalent in either Allied capital, Berlin scientists were more sensitive than those of other nations to the need for scientific research to remain independent of temporal demands.[191]

The perception abroad that science was German, and that scientific progress required mechanical skills in some way inimical to British and French traditions, was in part strengthened by the war, as national stereotypes more generally hardened.[192] The perception did, however, become more difficult to maintain as the war continued, and as the contribution of science to the Allied war effort became more and more important. Attempts were thus made to separate 'science' and 'German', and to forge French or British ideals of science. These new representations sought to define science as a humanistic discipline, the agent of spiritual progress, not its antithesis: English science was, in the words of UCL students eager to gain recognition for their College's role in the war, 'elastic and spiritual' not 'cast-iron and soulless'.[193] In France the Pascalian distinction between *l'esprit de géometrie* and *l'esprit de finesse*

---

[190] W. König, 'Die Akademie und die Technikwissenschaften. Ein unwillkommenes königliches Geschenk', in J. Kocka *et al.* (eds.), *Die Königlich Preußische Akademie der Wissenschaften zu Berlin im Kaiserreich* (Berlin, 1999), pp. 381–90.

[191] M. Szöllösi-Janze, *Fritz Haber*, p. 259. A. Rasmussen, 'Mobiliser, remobiliser, démobiliser : les formes d'investissement scientifique en France dans la grande guerre', *14–18 Aujourd'hui-Today-Heute*, 6, (2003), pp. 49–59.

[192] Hanna, *The mobilization of intellect*, pp. 184–93.

[193] 'Editorial', *Union Magazine*, March 1916.

played an important role in articulating this difference between a science that uplifted man, and one that reduced him to a soulless automaton. In the process this distinction facilitated the conversion of conservative humanists, like Maurice Barrès for instance, who before 1914 had been arch opponents of 'scientisme'. After 1914 he came to recognize the importance of scientific training to national defence.[194]

What this new Allied discourse did not do was to represent more accurately the real contribution of university science to the war effort. Still couched in moral terms, and still operating on the false assumption that German science was more mechanical and murderous than that of the Allies, it served to obscure the role of science, not explain it. More perniciously, after 1918, the Allied representation of science was used to justify the total ostracism of German scientists from international scientific events, and perhaps, with tragic irony, to pave the way in just twenty years for caricature to become reality.

Conclusion and aftermath

London University's young and forward-looking institutions were strengthened by the experience of war. The university had from its inception taken pride in its capacity to provide 'useful' education, and seen its academic role as one of expanding higher education to meet contemporary needs. In 1914 London's colleges and schools were well positioned to respond to the war's demands for scientific knowledge and skills, and also to recognize the opportunities the conflict created for academic progress. The result of London's wartime activity was to heighten the intellectual profile of the university and to confirm its leadership in several fields of modern education, including modern languages, the social sciences, engineering, and many areas of the natural sciences. The rise in the prestige of London was especially notable abroad, where a pro-active foreign policy, combined with the creation at home of an increasingly international curriculum, had sharply raised the visibility and the attraction of the university.

This wartime academic expansion needs to be set against the background of material hardship and human suffering that marked London's wartime experience, as it did that of the other capital universities. The war had placed great pressure on the physical resources of the university and severely undermined its financial stability. The massive influx of ex-servicemen after 1918, though providing much-welcomed funds,

---

[194] 'Chronique du mois', *RU*, no. 9, 1919. Rasmussen, 'Mobiliser, remobiliser, démobiliser', p. 56.

stretched the teaching and housing facilities of London Colleges, already strained before 1914, to breaking point. The hundreds of students and professors who did not return after the war – as well as those, including Burrows and Reeves, who died shortly after the peace – posed even more painful problems for the university. However, whilst the expansion of departments and the introduction of new subjects could in no way offset these losses, they do seem to have created an underlying spirit of optimism that enabled London's academic community to see in such sacrifices the foundations for a better future. The athletic ground bought by King's after the war, the scholarships the College founded for commonwealth students, and the prizes awarded for achievements in Russian, for example, or the two halls acquired by UCL for public lectures, the new hydraulic laboratories and workshops the College built, as well as the establishment of a new chair in electrical engineering, all of which were funded by memorial benefactions: these were sites of memory, but they were also sites of reconstruction for a university community that had found in war an impetus for innovation.[195]

The impact of war on the University of Paris was more complex. On the one hand, the demands of war galvanized the academic potential of the university, especially within the field of the natural sciences. The war also brought a marked growth in foreign exchange, which continued after 1918, notably with Parisian initiatives to secure French influence in Eastern Europe against former German dominance of higher education in the area. Such foreign activity, whilst serving to increase the international standing of Parisian scholarship, also had important repercussions for learning at home. The extension of wartime improvements in the organization of scientific research, for instance, was strongly influenced by the American experience of Parisian scientists.[196]

On the other hand, such clear examples of academic progress took place within a general context of hardened nationalism and cultural conservatism. One cause for this conservatism was the persistence of fears about German scholarship. Within a year of victory, Charles Andler, prominent Germanist at the Sorbonne, was already warning his colleagues that 'les Universités allemandes [...] songent à leur revanche'.[197] Andler suggested that the best French response to the inevitable rise of Germany would be to encourage

[195] KCLCA, KAP/BUR/14, 278 and 355. UCLCA, 'War Memorial Fund Items'; H. Billett, 'Engineering', in F. M. L. Thompson (ed.), *The University of London and the world of learning, 1836–1986* (London, 1990), p. 173.

[196] Charle, *La république des universitaires*, p. 363.

[197] C. Andler, 'La rénovation présente des universités allemandes et des universités françaises', *Revue internationale de l'enseignement* (November–December 1919), pp. 432–47, here p. 433.

intellectual collaboration between the two countries, but the dominant reaction amongst his peers in Paris was to boycott German scholarship, and prevent German academics from participating in international events. A second basis for conservatism was the high casualties suffered by Parisian students and teachers. From 1914 the University of Paris was marked by a sense of human catastrophe that did not touch London colleges to the same extent. The ranks of Paris's *grandes écoles* had been decimated by war, the nation's 'best men' lost. The *Ecole Normale Supérieure*, the mainstay of classical education in France, had been bled white. The concern, voiced from the arrival of the first casualty lists in 1914, that the death of *normaliens* placed the intellectual future of France in jeopardy, had by the end of war escalated into a bitter lament that the French elite had been massacred and classical civilization brought to the edge of ruin. The war memorial of the *Ecole Normale*, unveiled in 1923 by the President of the Republic, well represents this cultural pessimism, as well as the narrowing of intellectual references of which it was the result. Neo-classical in form, and sculpted in white marble, the memorial presents a young man, naked and frail, lying on the ground, with one arm raised carrying a torch.[198] The *Ecole Normale* may have saved the 'flame of French thought', but those worthy of carrying this light into the future had died in the fight. The elitism of the Parisian academic community deepened its sense of loss, feeding nostalgia for a reified ideal of classical education that prevented academics from recognizing the value of other wartime developments.

The war also hardened conservatism in Berlin, but with the difference that the university refused to believe that the culture it revered had been vanquished.[199] The university did not accept the defeat of its patron, the House of Hohenzollern, or the decline of German power that it had done so much to create. 'Invictis victi victuri!': this was the message of the rector, Reinhold Seeberg in May 1919, at the university's first commemorative ceremony,[200] and these were the words inscribed as well on the war memorial of the Friedrich-Wilhelms-Universität inaugurated seven years later in July 1926, before a patriotic demonstration of over 2,000 people. This memorial, carved in granite – the 'German marble'[201] – represents a soldier

---

[198] P. Wittmer, *Paul Landowski à Paris, une promenade de sculpture* (Paris, 2001), p. 49.
[199] D. Bourel, 'Les mandarins contre la démocratie', in L. Richard (ed.), *Berlin, 1919–1933. Gigantisme, crise sociale et avant-garde: l'incarnation extrême de la modernité* (Paris, 1991), pp. 142–53.
[200] *Trauerfeier der Universität Berlin für die im Weltkrieg gefallenen Angehörigen* (Berlin, 1919), pp. 6 and 17.
[201] K. Hoffmann-Curtius, 'Das Kriegerdenkmal der Berliner Friedrich-Wilhelms-Universität, 1919–1926', p. 102.

crouched with one knee on the ground, holding a shield. The soldier's head is bowed in respect to the dead, but his naked athletic body is poised to rise again in defence of his country. The monument was dedicated to the 'undefeated heroes' of the Great War.[202] It represented, according to the spokesman of the 120 corporations present at the inauguration, 'the terrible and bloody seed from which will emerge the new Reich'.[203]

Although the vision represented by this monument had an undeniably powerful resonance within the Berlin academic community, there is a danger of drawing too simple a conclusion of the impact of war on the university. For one thing, Berlin emerged from war exhausted, and remobilization for a German victory was slow and difficult. In the first years of peace appeals by conservative professors to draw young men into the Freikorps to fight the 'Bolshevik tidal wave' and the 'hydra of the anarchy of civil war' fell largely flat among Berlin students.[204] Secondly, whilst war, and above all defeat, strengthened ultra-nationalist opinion, it did not still other political voices. Berlin students joined the crowds of thousands that congregated in the cemetery of Friedrichsfelde, where Rosa Luxemburg and Karl Liebknecht were buried, for the unveiling of the memorial to the Revolution of 1919 (*Revolutionsdenkmal*) in 1926.

Furthermore, the wartime rise of ultra-conservatism amongst the majority of Berlin professors had had the effect of reinforcing moderate opinion about the need for political reform. For many Berlin professors, though, the most pressing need after 1918 was to break free from intellectual isolation, and re-establish German academic leadership. This drive came in part from concerns about the impact continued isolation would have on nationalism at home; but it stemmed also from the fact that the identity of Berlin's professors had always been closely tied to international prestige. When, at the first post-war Nobel Prize ceremony held in Stockholm in 1920, Max Planck appealed for a renewal of 'the collaborative work of international learning', he expressed the hopes of a number of scientists who during the years of wartime isolation had become acutely aware of the importance of international exchange.[205]

---

[202] Joseph Pompeckj, in *Feier bei der Enthüllung des Denkmals für die im Weltkrieg gefallenen Studierenden, Dozenten und Beamten der Universität am 10. Juli 1926* (Berlin, s. d. [1926]), p. 12.

[203] Ibid., p. 10.

[204] HUA, Kuratorium/131, Appeal from the Minister of Education, Haenisch, 13 March 1919, 'An die akademische Jugend Preußens!' See also the appeal sent by the *Deutscher Volksbund* to the Law Faculty, HUA, Juridisch Fakultät/ 607 (received 21 February 1919).

[205] G. Metzler, '"Welch ein deutscher Sieg". Die Nobelpreise von 1919 im Spannungsfeld von Wissenschaft, Politik und Gesellschaft', *Vierteljahrheft für Zeitgeschichte*, 44 (1996), p. 175.

Planck also expressed the natural expectations of Berlin scientists that their excellence would still matter to men of science in former enemy countries. The award of a Nobel Prize to Haber, among others, in the immediate post-war years, gave substance to his hopes.

Universities were both the cultural repositories of national traditions and sites of international exchange. The experience of war heightened the importance of these two functions and the tension between them. These institutions of higher education located in the three great metropolitan centres were sites of contestation, then as now, between competing and often contradictory trajectories.

8   Public space, political space

Jon Lawrence

Introduction

This chapter takes as its starting point two propositions: first, that politics is pre-eminently a cultural practice, and second, that metropolitan public space provided an important site for the performance of this cultural practice early in the twentieth century. Its focus is thus the politics of public space. It examines the different strategies deployed by state authorities in Paris, London, and Berlin both to maintain control of the symbolically charged public space at the heart of their capitals, and also to impose their own 'official' meanings on that space. At the same time, it examines moments when popular politics spilled over into public space, sometimes as direct attempts to challenge official control of that space, sometimes in more spontaneous outbursts of popular excitement or anger.[1]

Far from being abstract, disembodied entities, nation states tend to invest enormous symbolic meaning in decidedly concrete urban places – in buildings such as Westminster Abbey, the Panthéon, or the Reichstag, and in public spaces such as Trafalgar Square, the Place de la Concorde, or Unter den Linden. In turn, this transforms the urban landscape of capital cities into a politically sensitive stage upon which diverse groups can seek to challenge the state and its status quo by challenging the process of assigning meaning to 'hallowed' urban space. It also allows groups to challenge the hierarchies of urban space – either by resisting their exclusion from that space, or by insisting that other sites have equal

---

This chapter was written by Jon Lawrence. Contributors to this chapter were Elizabeth Fordham, Adrian Gregory, Danielle Tartakowsky, and Jeff Verhey.

[1] See Judith R. Walkowitz, *City of dreadful delight: narratives of sexual danger in late-Victorian London* (London, 1992), ch. 2; Delores Hayden, *The power of place: urban landscapes as public history*, (Cambridge, Mass., 1995); Doreen Massey, 'Places and their Pasts', *History Workshop Journal*, 39 (1995), pp. 182–92; John A. Agnew, *Place and politics: the geographical mediation of state and society* (London, 1987); Henri Lefebvre, *The production of space*, trans. Donald Nicholson-Smith (Oxford, 1991).

(or greater) symbolic meaning – that the national project is not the only project. In this chapter we will study these processes at work in the charged political context of total war.

When it came to the politics of public space, Paris, London, and Berlin had this in common: there was no *right* of public protest as such. In none of the capitals could a political agitator, of whatever hue, summon the public on to the streets by political right and wholly without fear of molestation by state authorities. But here the commonalities end. In Britain, the police could act against a political crowd only if it impeded use of the public highway, caused a breach of the peace, or contravened specific bye-laws relating to the use of certain public parks and squares. They had no absolute right to prevent a meeting, any more than protesters had an absolute right to hold one.[2] Moreover, custom and practice stretching back to the eighteenth century, and beyond, continued to sanction a surprisingly indulgent view of mass participation in public politics. British politicians generally remained deeply attached to the idea that public opinion was an active, demonstrative force, and their ability to hold successful public meetings, both indoors and out, consequently came to represent a vital barometer of political legitimacy. Contests over the right to occupy symbolic public space remained central to British politics down to 1914, and the consequent 'politics of disruption' remained widely tolerated by press, politicians, and public alike.[3]

By contrast, popular politics bestowed no comparable degree of licence on the political crowd under the French Third Republic or the Wilhelmine Empire. In France fear of the 'the crowd', though rooted in the brutal experience of the Commune, found intellectual expression in the writings of harsh critics of demos such as Gustave Le Bon, whose crowd psychology was at heart a plea for the restoration of elite rule. The Third Republic sought to draw a clear distinction between republican traditions of democracy and free expression, and revolutionary traditions of popular street protest. In consequence, when republicans enshrined the new regime's constitutional liberties in the early 1880s, the right to public demonstration was conspicuously absent. In Germany, Nationalist politicians, following Bismarck, became adept at deploying populist appeals to win majorities in the Reichstag, but this did not mean that they licensed an assertive role for the populace in German politics. Old elitist attitudes remained deeply entrenched, not least in Prussia which continued to deploy the three-tier caste system for voting. The

[2] David Williams, *Keeping the peace: the police and public order* (London, 1967).
[3] Jon Lawrence, *Speaking for the people: party, language and popular politics in England, 1867–1914* (Cambridge, 1998), ch. 7.

German constitution of 1871 included formal recognition of the right to public demonstration. In practice, of course, this right was not absolute. The police were very careful to sustain a sacred aura around politically important geographical sites in Berlin – chiefly in the centre of the city. Here, only patriotic rituals, such as the parades on the Kaiser's birthday, were to be permitted, not spontaneous popular demonstrations. Opposition groups such as the Social Democrats held their May Day demonstrations, and their huge anti-war demonstrations in 1911 and 1912, in large parks outside the imperial city centre, and if their supporters sought to 'invade' the centre they were met by brutal displays of state force. In short, there was a very pronounced and sharply contested politics of symbolic public space in Berlin before the war, but one in which the authorities retained a tight rein on all unsanctioned forms of popular expression – tighter even than the Parisian authorities.

July/August 1914

In all three cities the war crisis of late July 1914 brought crowds into the central squares and thoroughfares in vast numbers. Our understanding of the 'spirit of 1914' has been strongly shaped by memories of patriotic crowds supposedly baying for war in each capital, but in practice the crowds took many forms during these days of crisis, and as such they defy easy classification. We shall look at each city in turn in order to assess the similarities and differences between them.

It was a warm July in the German capital, and the people of Berlin mainly waited outdoors to hear news of their fate – expecting, quite rightly, that it would be told to them in 'extra' editions of the city's newspapers. Of the three sorts of crowd in Berlin in the last week of July and the first week of August – the pro-war, the anti-war and the merely curious – the curious always predominated. People waited in the coffee houses, in front of the newspaper buildings, or in the most important public squares. Significantly, according to most accounts they waited quietly. Alongside these curious crowds, occupying in many cases the same public space, were the pro- and anti-war crowds. Already in the last week of July, before the war was actually declared, enthusiastic crowds of patriotic youths, perhaps ten thousand strong, could be seen marching through the 'sacred' national sites of central Berlin, declaring their support for the fatherland.

On 27 July, a Tuesday evening, the SPD staged huge anti-war demonstrations throughout the city. However, because of the regulations on demonstrations these were mainly held in beer-halls in the city suburbs, rather than in the centre. When the meetings ended, the protesters dispersed. But not every Social Democrat went home. Instead a number of socialist youths used the metro to evade the police cordon sealing off the central area. They had clearly agreed on a meeting point, for up to a couple of hundred joined together to sing the worker's 'national anthems' at the same national sites where earlier in the week patriotic youths had congregated and sung. The police, under strict orders not to allow such demonstrations, broke them up – but not as quickly as one might have suspected.[4]

Interestingly, some contemporary observers immediately chose to interpret these rival pro- and anti-war demonstrations as manifestations of broader German 'public opinion'. In the last week of July, before censorship had been imposed, the left-wing, Social Democratic press claimed to see the true spirit of the German public in the anti-war crowds, while, perhaps predictably, the radical, nationalist press took the opposite view: identifying the pro-war crowds as the embodiment of true German feeling. After the outbreak of war, the SPD press fell silent on this issue – in part because of the SPD's willing participation in the war, in part because of censorship – allowing the right-wing press to claim, unopposed, that Berlin's pro-war crowds represented 'Germany'.

In truth, of course, they did not. The claim said more about its authors than about the Berlin public, or even about the crowds who filled its grand public spaces in August. In the heady days of 1914, bourgeois and even aristocratic observers began to break with traditional political discourse by depicting 'public opinion' in terms of the masses and 'mass' enthusiasm. The public response to war was perceived as a transformative experience; moulding a new sense of the people in action. As one pastor wrote, 'the patriotic enthusiasm was and is a powerful one ... There are no longer any Social Democrats: "we were such, today we are no longer such". All differences of class have disappeared behind the awareness of a great commonness.'[5] The inclusive language of 1914 is revealing. It shows that radical nationalists, at least, were aware just how anachronistic elitist understandings of 'the people' had become by 1914.[6] Yet contemporaries disagreed about the consequences of admitting that the monarchical 'world-view' was an anachronism – about the consequences of 'the spirit of 1914'. Democrats, including Social Democrats, argued that the 'spirit of 1914' meant that the German

[4] Verhey, *The spirit of 1914*, p. 112.
[5] ' "Unsere Kirchengemeinden während der Kriegszeit", III. Das hessische Land und Frankfurt a. M. 1. Aus Schlitz, in der Nordostecke von Oberhessen', in *Monatsschrift für Pastoraltheologie* 11, 1. Kriegsheft (October, 1914), p. 16.
[6] 'Ist Gott für uns, wer mag wider uns sein?' *Kreuz-Zeitung*, 6 August 1914, no. 365 (Morgen), pp. 2–3. Also, 'Die eiserne Zeit', *Schlauer Zeitung*, 7 August 1914, for similar archaic language.

constitution must be reformed, that Germany must become a true democracy. Friedrich Naumann, for example, wrote: 'the people have arisen. The broad, good people are saving the state.' He concluded that in consequence, 'the hatred of the people must be thrown into the ditches of the past. The rights of all citizens must be written in the hearts of all Germans.'[7] The Pan-German right, in contrast, supported a populist dictatorship, one which found its legitimation in popular acclamation and the 'spirit of 1914', but stripped these of any dangerous democratizing overtones.

In the excitement of 1914, right-wing German commentators celebrated the 'irrational' aspects of the crowd – the development of a group spirit through an irrational mass psychology. In the words of the Pan-German journalist, Emil Peters:

never before has the present generation experienced something which brought forth such a unity of feeling, thoughts, and wishes. The individual disappeared. The intellectual, nervous, distinguishing man of culture lost control of his feelings and belonged to the masses, in the physical sense, too. This incredible crescendo of the 'mass feeling' has given birth to all the deeply rooted virtues, which unite the people ... And whoever does not have these virtues ... is educated to them, they are forced on him by the masses ... Yes, the masses employ their lively instrument, lynch justice ....[8]

Although Berlin could never stand unproblematically for a nation that was still predominantly rural, the patriotic urban crowd did acquire a new centrality to the iconography of nation. In the mythic understanding of the 'spirit of 1914' the Berlin crowds of late July and early August 1914 came to embody a new sense of unity and national purpose, a German version of the 'Union sacrée'. Significantly, however, it was not a concept embraced with any enthusiasm by the Social Democratic press – here the emphasis was placed on an older, more limited concept: that of the *Burgfrieden* – a medieval concept denoting a temporary truce between warring factions in a city under siege. As the war dragged on, and privations mounted, so the gulf between those who embraced the myths of 1914 and those who merely accepted the need for a *Burgfrieden* widened. For the patriotic right, the myths of 1914 became more rather than less powerful – promoting a vision of a united *Volk* that arguably did much to impair the post-war development of a tolerant political culture capable of accepting diversity and conflict within 'civil society'.[9]

---

[7] 'Die Masse im Krieg', *Die Hilfe*, 21, no. 6 (11 February 1915), p. 85.
[8] Emil Peters, *Deutschlands heiliger Krieg. Der Sieg des deutschen Wesens* (Berlin: Volkskraft, n.d., [1914 or 1915]), p. 27; also Martin Schian, 'Krieg und Persönlichkeit', *Akademische Rundschau* 3, no. 1/4 (October 1914/January 1915), pp. 59–60.
[9] Peter Fritzsche, *Germans into Nazis* (Cambridge, Mass. and London, 1998).

Like Berlin, London witnessed both pro- and anti-war demonstrations in the days before the declaration of war. Like Berlin, it was the patriotic crowds that captured the wartime (and post-war) imagination, perhaps in part because they came to serve the myths of both the anti-war Left, which sought a ready explanation for its failure to prevent war, and the nationalistic Right, which found comfort in the spontaneous mass enthusiasm of 1914, and in the spirit of willing sacrifice it was said to embody.

London's symbolic central squares and thoroughfares thronged with great crowds during the crisis days of early August, especially on 4 August when thousands gathered throughout central London – cheering wildly and singing patriotic songs. Influential accounts of these crowds have stressed their patriotic, even euphoric, character, and have shaped a dominant myth that Britain was gripped by war fever in the summer of 1914. Confronted by cheering crowds as he walked back to Downing Street on the evening of 3 August, Asquith is said to have remarked bitterly that 'war or anything that seems likely to lead to war is always popular with the London mob'.[10] Lloyd George painted a similar picture, recalling 'the warlike crowds that thronged Whitehall and poured into Downing Street, whilst the cabinet was deliberating on the alternative of peace or war', while Bertrand Russell recalled that 'the anticipation of carnage was delightful to something like ninety per cent of the population'.[11]

Historians have begun to question the representativeness of these metropolitan crowds, in London as in Berlin, pointing to the prominence of young and apparently middle-class men, and to the fact that these scenes were all played out in fashionable quarters of the city, and involved only a tiny fraction of the city's population. They have also recognized that Government ministers and anti-war intellectuals had strong, if contrasting, reasons to exaggerate the bellicose nature of the August crowds.[12] Certainly many contemporary accounts paint a very different picture of the London crowd. The Conservative evening *Globe* emphasized the order and discipline around Whitehall, 'Quiet and orderly, this typical English crowd, obviously comprising all classes of people bore itself well. There was no feverish excitement. Downing Street itself was

---

[10] Roy Jenkins, *Asquith* (London, 1964), p. 328.

[11] David Lloyd George, *War memoirs* (6 vols., London, 1938), I, p. 39; Bertrand Russell, *The autobiography of Bertrand Russell* (3 vols., London, 1967–9), II, p. 17.

[12] Niall Ferguson, *The pity of war* (London, 1998), ch. 7; C. Kit Good, 'England Goes to War 1914–15' (PhD thesis, University of Liverpool, 2002. See also Strachan, *The First World War*, volume I: *To arms* (Oxford, 2002), pp. 103–10 for a balanced overview of the issue.

kept clear by police – a duty easily managed by a handful of men, so correct was the behaviour of the crowd.'[13]

The Liberal *Daily Chronicle* concurred – arguing that the crowds in central London were subdued; thirsty for news of the crisis, but in no sense seeking to shape its outcome. In a telling analogy the paper argued that 'it was a scene reminiscent of election times with the difference that the merriment and jest of the electioneering crowd was entirely absent'.[14] Of course these newspapers also had an agenda. As Kit Good has argued, throughout the crisis, the British press proved keen to play down signs of war enthusiasm and to insist that the national mood was very different from the wild scenes of public euphoria witnessed during the South African War at the turn of the century – especially on 'Mafeking night' in May 1900. Hence the *Hampstead Record* stressed that among holiday crowds on the famous Heath 'Nowhere was there the slightest sign of "Mafficking" and it was obvious to the observer that the idea of war was distasteful to all.' By contrast, British newspapers made much of the supposed war fever in Germany, reinforcing the notion that a belligerent aggressor was dragging Britain reluctantly to war.[15]

These 'hidden agendas' make it difficult to draw clear conclusions about the temper of the August crowds in London, but one useful clue is surely the absence of significant disruption at Labour's major anti-war rally in Trafalgar Square on Sunday 2 August. By occupying such a central and symbolic site Labour knew that it was challenging the 'pro-war' camp to mount a counter demonstration. That only 'a negligible contingent of youths' turned up to heckle suggests that Asquith's 'London mob' was not yet bent on war.[16] But if there was no great 'pro-war' movement on the streets of London in August 1914, nor were the trade unionists and socialists who gathered in Trafalgar Square typical of most Londoners. Unlike the labour protesters, most Londoners, like most Berliners, were simply curious spectators – looking on, transfixed, by the momentous historical events unfolding in their capital. In Woolwich the local Labour paper observed that 'war news made a noticeable impact in the street atmosphere', but the reaction they identified was neither enthusiasm nor protest, but rather a deep sense of foreboding that bordered on depression. The Conservative *Woolwich Herald* agreed, noting that throughout the district 'knots of men anxiously discussed

---

[13] *The Globe*, 3 August 1914, p. 5.   [14] *Daily Chronicle*, 3 August 1914, p. 5.
[15] Good, 'England goes to war', pp. 112; *Hampstead Record*, 7 August 1914, p. 2.
[16] *Daily Chronicle*, 3 August 1914, p. 6 – this Liberal paper took a neutral view on the question of intervention, hence its use here.

the situation'.[17] The London crowd did not become the 'emotional centre-piece' of the nation as it marched to war; rather it remained resolutely a spectating crowd, reacting to the stimulus of events, but not shaping those events.

Given its tradition for revolutionary crowd action, Paris in 1914 might be viewed as the dog that did not bark. As Jean-Jacques Becker has demonstrated, the prospect of German aggression engendered a resolute national unity across France in 1914.[18] As the centre of French syndicalist and socialist organization, Paris might have been an exception to this story of national (and nationalist) unity. In some respects it was. Becker identified fifty-two anti-war demonstrations in Paris held between 27 July and 1 August 1914 – all but six organized by socialists. Significantly these socialist meetings were orderly indoor political gatherings – there was no attempt to proclaim the anti-war message in the *grandes places* and boulevards of central Paris. On 27 July, Parisian syndicalists did take to the streets, with tens of thousands protesting against war along Haussmann's grand boulevards amidst scenes of considerable violence. But that was more or less it. The syndicalists' revolutionary rhetoric was not translated into action. In the context of national crisis, talk of organizing mass protests, let alone a general strike against war, simply evaporated.[19]

Spontaneous pro-war demonstrations gathered pace from the proclamation of military mobilization on 1 August 1914. As in Berlin and London, patriotic crowds filled central public sites, rather than private halls – presenting themselves as the authentic voice of the French people, and almost universally being accepted as such. Both left and right rushed to celebrate national unity in action – emphasising not 'war enthusiasm', but rather unity and unshakeable solidarity in the face of German aggression. Maurras and *Action française* celebrated the outpouring of popular nationalism and dropped their bitter opposition to the Republican state. Others, such as Romain Rolland, who would soon re-emerge as bitter critics of war, embraced the mood of August 1914 and praised popular mobilization in the national cause.[20] Indeed even the vast crowds that gathered to mourn the murdered socialist leader Jean Jaurès demonstrated a strong sense of the need to subsume pre-war differences and hatreds in the

[17] *[Woolwich] Pioneer and Labour Journal*, 14 August 1914; *Woolwich Herald*, 7 August 1914, p. 2.
[18] J.-J. Becker, *1914: comment les Français sont entrés dans la guerre* (Paris, 1977).
[19] Ibid., esp. pp. 184–5; on the decline of Syndicalism and its growing reformism after 1908 see John Horne, *Labour at war: France and Britain, 1914–1918* (Oxford, 1991).
[20] E. Weber, *The Action française: Royalism and reaction in twentieth-century France* (Stanford, CA, 1962) p. 92; Romain Rolland, *Journal des années de la guerre 1914–1919: notes et documents pour servir à l'histoire morale de l'Europe de ce temps* (Paris, 1952), p. 23.

common struggle for national survival. In this sense the diverse crowds that flooded the *grandes places* and boulevards of central Paris during the first days of August 1914 represented the embodiment of the Union Sacrée. Socialists and republicans, Catholics and monarchists, bitterly divided throughout the Third Republic, were now to be found side-by-side, both physically on the streets of the capital, and mentally in their determination to avoid a repetition of the national humiliation of 1870.

Public space during wartime

The history of public demonstration in the three cities diverged radically during the long years of war. In both Paris and Berlin, emergency wartime regulations sharply circumscribed the right to public assembly, although perhaps predictably these laws were often used selectively – allowing the authorities to prevent public manifestations of dissent whilst turning a blind eye to the activities of patriotic citizens' groups. In London, by contrast, government control was limited and the politics of public space proved surprisingly volatile throughout the war.

Wartime Berlin, like the rest of Germany, was governed under the 1851 law of the 'State of Siege', which gave the military extraordinary powers over censorship and the control of internal dissent. In 1914 both Bethman Hollweg, as Chancellor, and General von Kessel, the military governor of Berlin, suggested that the State of Siege would only last during the initial phase of mobilization. In fact, it survived throughout the war years. Military governors like von Kessel considered all forms of political activity inimical to the national interest in wartime, and proved very reluctant to sanction meetings and demonstrations of any kind. Perhaps predictably, trades unions and socialist organizations found it particularly difficult to organize meetings, despite their patriotic stance towards the war. Pressure from the civil authorities eventually led to a relaxation of these draconian regulations, and in the case of Berlin the Generals eventually accepted the necessity for concessions in November 1915. Henceforth, meetings could be legally held if they had been approved by the military authorities at least forty-eight hours in advance, but they must be confined to members only, speeches had to be shown to the military censors in advance, and a policeman had to be present throughout the meeting. The policeman had the right to close the meeting at any time. These were therefore very limited rights, intended to allow some resumption of the normal activities of associations within civil society, but not to sanction a full-blown resumption of public politics. Perhaps significantly, the group that complained most bitterly about the loss of civil liberties was not the left (patriotic or anti-war), but the far-right Pan-Germanists. Throughout the war it was these ultra-nationalist groups who most often invoked their 'right' to free expression – not just the right to hold private meetings, but the right to convene public demonstrations expressive of popular feeling.[21]

Much as the authorities undoubtedly feared a resurgence of formal public politics in wartime, by late 1915 it was already clear that a more pressing danger was posed by spontaneous gatherings of hungry, frustrated women unable to buy enough to feed their families. Angry demonstrations were becoming commonplace across Berlin by 1916. Most were confined to the working-class back streets and local markets, but occasionally protest spilled over into more central locations, where the symbolic significance of the revolt from below was hard to overlook. In many respects, social protest was more difficult to police precisely because most of the participants were not 'politicized' workers – the 'masses' that German leaders had long learnt to fear – but 'unpoliticized' women. They did not have the vocabulary to deal with such a situation.[22]

Even the great strike movements in the last years of the war had their origin in the food crisis. In April 1917, it was the lowering of the food ration which led to large strikes in Berlin and Leipzig. Here was protest in a more familiarly 'political' form, and the government's response was rooted firmly in the pre-war mind-set. Strikers and demonstrators were threatened with the full force of military law. By apparently threatening the war effort, strikes allowed the government to represent wartime protest within the old discourse: 'the masses versus public order'. It also made it much easier

---

[21] Johanna Schlellenberg, 'Probleme der Burgfriedenspolitik im ersten Weltkrieg. Zur innenpolitischen Strategie und Taktik der herrschenden Klassen von 1914 bis 1916', doctoral dissertation, Humboldt University (East Berlin), 1967, pp. 34ff. Requests for Berlin meetings rejected by von Kessel are in ZStA Merseburg, Rep. 77, Tit. 162, no. 154, Bl. 128. For pressure on the military authorities to be more lenient see HStA Munich, Abt. IV–Kriegsarchiv, Stellv. GK des I AK, #1917, no. Bl. (2 February 1915). Similarly, 'Schreiben des preußischen Kriegsministers an die stellv. Generalkommandos betr. die Genehmigung von Gewerkschaftsversammlungen', of 25 February 1915 in Wilhelm Deist, *Militär und Innenpolitik*, p. 226; 'Schreiben des preußischen Kriegsministeriums an die stellv. Generalkommandos betr. die Genehmigung von Gewerkschaftsversammlungen', of 9 June 1915, in Wilhelm Deist, *Militär und Innenpolitik*, p. 242; 'Schreiben des preußischen Kriegsministeriums an die Militärbefehlshaber. Richtlinien für die Lockerung der Beschränkungen des Versammlungsrechts', of 17 January 1917 in Wilhelm Deist, *Militär und Innenpolitik*, p. 249, and 'Schreiben des preußischen Kriegsministeriums an die Militärbefehlshaber. Handhabung des Vereins- und Versammlungsrechts gegenüber den Gewerkschaften', in Wilhelm Deist, *Militär und Innenpolitik*, pp. 1052 ff.

[22] According to J. Schellenberger, *Burgfrieden*, p. 21, on 14 to 18 October 1915 there were demonstrations in front of the butter stores of Berlin, as well as a food riot in Chemnitz which lasted four days. (102 people were arrested). See also account of the Justice Minister in the Prussian State Ministry, in ZStA Merseburg, Rep. 90a, Abt. B., Tit. III, 2b, no. 6, Bd 164, Bl. 256.

for them to clamp down on any incursions into public space. In practice, however, the strike movement produced little by way of open, public demonstration. Meetings took place, but as in 1914 they were held in suburban beer-halls near the factories, or in the factories themselves, not outdoors. If there was any sign of protests going public, let alone being taken into the squares and thoroughfares of central Berlin, the authorities clamped down very hard – as they had with Liebknecht and his supporters in 1916. During the strike of February 1918, there were some attempts to organize public demonstrations, notably in Alexanderplatz, a plebeian square just outside the city centre. Police reacted swiftly and in bloody clashes there were many casualties on both sides.

As has been noted, it was the far right, rather than the left, that did most to contest the de-politicization of public space in wartime Berlin. The Fatherland Party in particular tried to organize an extensive programme of public meetings during 1917 to demonstrate popular support for their radical pro-war, ultra-patriotic platform. The authorities clearly viewed such activities as less threatening than those of the socialist left, but even so they were not without controversy. The Fatherland Party's public meetings became the focus for bitter political disputes between far right nationalists and veterans from the Front who argued that war was far from glorious. Such arguments underscored the essentially political nature of the meetings, and consequently usually resulted in police interventions to break them up. In desperation, the Fatherland Party called on the police to prevent disruptive veterans from attending their meetings, but this did little to boost the popularity of their campaign. It did, however, demonstrate two features of the politics of public space in wartime Berlin. First, the strength of the taboos surrounding popular incursions into public space, and second, the far from even-handed way in which the authorities chose to enforce the draconian legal powers conferred under the 'State of Siege'.[23]

In legislative terms the Parisian story was broadly similar. As in Berlin, the outbreak of war led to the declaration of a state of siege specifically outlawing all unauthorized public assembly and introducing draconian penalties for public sedition. The Parisian authorities had always exercised strict control over public assembly, but the war emergency nonetheless greatly strengthened their hand in the suppression of public protest. Moreover, the subsequent militarization of the city during the crisis of late August/September 1914, when the city came under heavy German bombardment and appeared in imminent danger of being overrun, increased further both the physical dangers associated

---

[23] Verhey, *Spirit of 1914*, p. 182.

with public demonstration, and the power of the authorities to control public space. Pre-war traditions of public celebration continued, but only in a much attenuated form, while the politics of public protest all but ceased during the war years. Even those celebrations most intimately connected with the state and national identity (such as 14 July – 'Bastille Day') were much reduced in scale and grandeur. Central squares and monuments were still festooned with flags, and customary charitable appeals still flourished, but the Parisian authorities made it clear that public rejoicing would be in bad taste during wartime.[24] It was not that the authorities sought to prevent all forms of public gathering, rather they sought to control how the people chose to gather in wartime. Public processions associated with suitably patriotic causes, such as war charities, the welcoming of Allied dignitaries, or solemn funerals for the war dead, could all be tolerated, even encouraged, but anything 'unseemly' or divisive was unacceptable.

In June 1916, the elaborate rituals organized to mark the death of General Joseph Gallieni – the popularly acclaimed saviour of Paris in 1914 – represented the epitome of official public ceremony during the middle years of the war. His lying in state at l'église des Invalides, and the solemn grandeur of his subsequent funeral helped to confirm les Invalides, rather than the Panthéon where Victor Hugo had been buried in 1885, as the public space that most completely symbolized national identity and resolve in wartime.[25] However, as the war ground on, the Place de la Concorde resumed its pre-war role as a crucial site for the public demonstration of patriotic fervour. For besides the monument to Strasbourg, lost in the war of 1870, the eight cities memorialized in the square also included Lille, capital of the occupied north. After 1914, the statue to Lille, more even than that to Strasbourg, became the focus for symbolic public displays of patriotism.[26] In 1917, patriotic societies organized a solemn march through the streets adjacent to the Place de la Concorde and past the statues memorializing the two fallen French cities.[27]

Significantly, May/June 1917 also saw the first major unauthorized and, in some senses at least, oppositional demonstrations of the war when striking female dressmakers marched out of the workshop quarters to congregate around the Bourse du Travail, the syndicalist headquarters

[24] Archives de Paris (AP), VK3 187 and VK3 194; Archives de la Préfecture de police (APP, DA 455 Ministre de l'Intérieur aux préfets, directives for 14 July celebrations 1915–1918).

[25] René Weiss, *Hommage de Paris à Gallieni son sauveur* (Paris, 1926).

[26] René Weiss, *La Ville de Paris et les Fêtes de la Victoire* (Paris, 1919).

[27] APP, DA 456.

by the Place de la République.[28] The government made significant concessions to the workers' demands, but they also sought to reassert official, patriotic understandings of the symbolic meaning of central civic space.[29] To mark 14 July 1917, they not only sanctioned a solemn patriotic parade through the Place de la Concorde, but also revived the pre-war custom of the Bastille Day military review. This was the first such commemoration to occur since the outbreak of war, and significantly the authorities broke with tradition by routing the parade through the working-class suburbs of Paris, from Vincennes to Denfert-Rochereau, rather than holding it at remote and affluent Longchamp.[30] Earlier that month enthusiastic crowds had lined the rue de Rivoli on 4 July, American Independence Day, to watch the parade of a detachment of the first American soldiers to arrive in France.[31] It was a sign of things to come. In July 1918, the authorities sanctioned two military revues, one on American Independence Day, proceeding from Place d'Iéna to Place de la Concorde, and a second on 14 July from the Bois de Boulogne in the west to the Place de la Concorde.[32] After the German Spring Offensive, these parades were symbols of Parisian defiance, and symbols too of French faith that American intervention would ultimately ensure victory. Paris already appeared to have been saved a second time from the advancing German armies, and while it was not yet clear that the war had turned decisively in the Allies' favour, hope of victory had been renewed.

The events of July 1918 were unashamedly celebrations of French and American nationalism, displaying little of the restraint characteristic of earlier patriotic demonstrations.[33] It was also no coincidence that the military parades of 1918 coincided with the symbolic renaming of many central Parisian streets in honour of the Allied powers. On 4 July the authorities renamed a major thoroughfare 'l'Avenue du président Wilson', and on 14 July they renamed a series of streets in honour of Britain, France, Portugal, Serbia, and Japan in order to create a symbolic central hexagon of streets celebrating the Allied resistance to Germany.[34]

---

[28] Jean-Louis Robert, *Les ouvriers, la patrie et la Révolution, 1914–1919*, Annales Littéraires de l'Université de Besançon, Besançon, 1995.

[29] John Horne, *Labour at war: France and Britain, 1914–1918* (Oxford, 1991), ch. 5.

[30] AP, VK 193, *L'Illustration*, 21 July 1917.

[31] Maurice Barrès, *De la sympathie à la fraternité d'armes. Les États-Unis dans la guerre* (Paris, 1918) and Daniel Halévy, *Avec les Boys américains* (Paris, 1918).

[32] AP, VK3, 194 and AP, VK3, 94, *Le Journal*, 15 July 1918 on 'La fête nationale de l'Entente'.

[33] AP, VK3, 194, 5 July 1918.

[34] See *Relation officielle de la réception du président Wilson, 16 Décembre 1918* (Paris, 1919); *Réception à l'hôtel de ville de Messieurs les ambassadeurs et ministres des puissances alliés, 14 Juillet 1918* (Paris, 1919).

The national celebrations of July 1918 confirmed both the authorities' physical dominance of public space in wartime Paris, and their ability to impose official meanings on the urban landscape. As we shall see, these celebrations also marked the first manifestations of an intense period of public celebration in Paris that would run through the autumn of 1918, through the Armistice and the opening of the Peace conference, and on to the intense victory celebrations of 14 July 1919. These events still bore the imprint of official choreography, but spontaneous popular forces in ways unimaginable also shaped them during the long years of war.

Despite the implementation of widespread emergency powers in Britain under DORA (the Defence of the Realm Act), there was no legal restraint on the right to public demonstration until 1916, and even in the final years of war, unofficial demonstrations were both common-place, and at times decidedly unruly. In this respect, therefore, the story of the politics of public space in wartime London diverges sharply from the story of our other two capital cities and merits investigation at some length. In the months immediately after the outbreak of war London was unusually quiescent. Most of the principal anti-war groups had chosen either to back intervention, or to keep quiet. Some socialist groups continued to hold impromptu street meetings and paper sells, but these were generally low-key and avoided raising public criticism of the war.[35] Public space was left, by default, as patriotic space – the scene for the more or less joyous sending off of troops, for fund-raising drives by war charities, for the controversial activities of the white-feather brigade, and for loyalist displays such as the famous semi-official women's 'right to serve' march organized by the Pankhursts in July 1915.[36] The definitions imposed on patriotic space were often exclusive and ugly. There were sporadic crowd actions against 'alien' traders throughout the second half of 1914, but it was news of the sinking of the *S. S. Lusitania* off the coast of Ireland in May 1915 that prompted the worst examples of violent crowd action in London during the First World War. These riots left 257 people injured, 107 of them police officers, and led to the arrest of 866.[37]

---

[35] See *Labour Leader*, 20, 27 August and 3 September 1914 (Hackney); and the east-London based *Woman's Dreadnought*, 15, 22, and 29 August 1914.

[36] See Nicoletta F. Gullace, *'The blood of our sons': men, women, and the renegotiation of British citizenship during the Great War* (New York and Basingstoke, 2002), pp. 73–98 and 126–9.

[37] *East London Observer*, 8 August 1914; PRO, HO45/10944/257142/ fos. 4 and 5; Panikos Panayi, *The enemy in our midst: Germans in Britain during the First World War* (Oxford, 1991), 224. See also Panikos Panayi, 'Anti-German riots in London during the First World War', *German History* 7, 2 (1989), pp. 184–203.

From the moment that anti-war forces began to resurface in 1915, they found themselves embroiled in brutal conflicts over the right to occupy public space. Even private, indoor meetings by anti-war groups generated considerable opposition, often culminating in the breaking up of planned gatherings, but it was the proclamation of anti-war politics in London's great civic spaces that created the most explosive situations. The 'anti-alien' violence of 1914–15 had been confined mainly to the periphery since it was about battles over the redefinition of local community, but the violence between pro- and anti-war forces necessarily assumed a broader dimension – it was about who spoke for the metropolitan public. This was a conflict played out in the squares and parks of central London, and in suburban sites such as Finsbury Park, Peckham Rye, and Parliament Hill long associated with public speaking and the politics of disruption that it had generated in pre-war Britain.

Opposition to London's anti-war groups was not simply the result of spontaneous popular anger. On the contrary, from at least the middle of 1915, the city witnessed systematic right-wing efforts to organize patriotic counter-demonstrations that would prevent known anti-war leaders from holding political meetings of any kind. Journalists linked to Beaverbrook's *Daily Express*, the London *Globe*, and the Anti-German Union appear to have played a leading role in this campaign, relying heavily on colonial servicemen garrisoned in the capital for the 'muscle' needed to break up anti-war meetings.[38] After helping to organize the breaking-up of an indoor peace meeting at the Memorial Hall in central London, the *Daily Express* denounced the meeting as 'an act of war against the British nation'. According to the *Express*, those who chose to stop the meeting by over-running the platform were 'as surely fighting for their country as if they were standing in the trenches'.[39]

The Government did little to intervene in this brutal battle over public speech until anti-war groups threatened to bring their conflict with the ultra-patriotic right out of the meeting halls and on to the streets of central London. In early 1916 leaders of a self-styled 'Stop the War' Committee sought permission to hold a demonstration against the war in Trafalgar

---

[38] For details of organized disruption in London see PRO, HO45/10742/263275/ fos. 66, 67, 70, 110, 135, 137, 143; *Daily Express*, 25 November 1915; on the origins and development of the Anti-German Union see Panikos Panayi, 'The British Empire Union in the First World War', in *The politics of marginality: race, the radical right and minorities in twentieth-century Britain*, ed. Tony Kushner and Kenneth Lunn (London, 1990). See also Brock Millman, *Managing domestic dissent in First World War Britain* (London, 2000), pp. 52–7.

[39] *Daily Express*, 25 and 30 November 1915.

Square on Easter Sunday. Ministers and their advisers acknowledged, regretfully, that the application was entirely consistent with the regulations governing meetings in the square, and it seemed inevitable that the metropolitan police would find themselves embroiled in a set-piece battle between anti-war militants and their vociferous opponents. A week before the planned anti-war meeting a crowd of over 1,500, with colonial soldiers again prominently represented, broke up a suffrage meeting in Trafalgar Square organized by Sylvia Pankhurst's radical East London Federation of Suffragettes.[40] The Liberal Home Secretary, Sir Herbert Samuel, came under intense pressure from the Metropolitan Police to find some legal means of banning the forthcoming anti-war meeting. The police commissioner explained that thousands of colonial soldiers on leave in London felt 'intensely strongly' against any talk of a 'premature peace'. He also made it clear that police would find it objectionable to be used against these patriotic servicemen. Until the Pankhurst meeting Samuel had held true to his liberal instincts, arguing that there could be occasions when 'patriotic citizens would be rendering the best service to the country by advocating the ending of a war' and that it was right that the public itself, and not the state, should arbitrate on such questions. As in peacetime, so in war, the mobilization of force and counter-force should determine the fate of claims to 'speak for the people', not the heavy hand of the state. According to Samuel, 'The purpose of allowing the free use of Trafalgar Square for public meetings is to enable the feeling of the public to be demonstrated. If it is adverse to the views of the promoters of a particular meeting and is expressed accordingly no one has a right to complain.'[41]

With the police insisting that they could not guarantee the safety of speakers if the meeting went ahead, Samuel finally agreed to a ban. Though advised that meetings likely to cause a breach of the peace could already be banned under the Common Law, Samuel sought explicit legal powers under DORA (amendment 9A), and insisted that these powers be tightly circumscribed. August Birrell's suggestion, as Chief Secretary for Ireland, to allow the arrest of those organizing proscribed meetings was over-ruled, and there was no support for the idea that police, magistrates, or military authorities should be granted 'standing authority' to prohibit meetings – this power was to reside *only* with ministers of state. Again we can see that there were definite limits to the government's willingness to disregard established understandings of

---

[40] PRO, HO45/10511/130791/ f.22 and 23; *Women's Dreadnought*, 15 April 1916; also Panayi, 'British Empire Union', pp. 120–2.
[41] PRO, HO45/10511/130791/ fo. 22 – Samuel's memo is dated 14 March 1916.

political liberty, even in the context of 'total war'.[42] However, like so many of the state powers created under DORA, amendment 9A marked a definite shift away from nineteenth-century traditions – and hence marked a crucial turning point in the politics of public space in Britain. The new powers to ban meetings were retained under post-war Emergency Powers legislation, and became more routinely available to local police forces under the Public Order Act, 1936.[43]

That said, we should not exaggerate the extent of the British government's crackdown on political demonstration after April 1916. The new powers under DORA were used sparingly. By October 1916 there had already been seven requests to ban meetings using DORA, but all had been refused.[44] Moreover, by 1917 pro-peace groupings were finding it increasingly easy to hold meetings in the capital's outlying working-class suburbs such as Woolwich, Peckham, Islington, Hackney, and Poplar. Socialist groups, notably those linked to Lansbury's 'Herald League' and Pankhurst's renamed 'Workers' Suffrage Federation' played a prominent part in such activity. Government police reports indicate that such meetings were often able to attract large and supportive crowds and generally proceeded without disruption.[45] Significantly, in October 1917, when police were asked to investigate complaints about the regular Herald League meetings in Finsbury Park, they found that problems were mainly caused by the intervention of outside bodies such as the British Empire Union and other anti-socialist groups. Intriguingly, they also discovered that soldiers who had been 'whipped up to attend these meetings, and to expect to find people shouting in favour of Germany' found the reality very different and often insisted on the speakers 'having a fair hearing'. This contrasted sharply with the experiences of 1915–16, although police informers felt the change was due less to an altered temper amongst soldiers, than to the socialists' skilful advocacy of the soldiers' welfare.[46] In many parts of London the anti-war groups had turned to the offensive, leading one speaker working for the government-funded National War Aims Committee to welcome the national crisis caused by the German Spring Offensive of 1918 as a chance to turn the tables on organized *pacifist* disruption at Peckham Rye, Finsbury Park and Parliament Hill.[47]

[42] PRO, HO45/10511/130791/ fos. 23, 26 and 27; PRO, HO45/10810/311932/ fos. 9 and 12a.
[43] See especially, Charles Townshend, *Making the peace: public order and public security in modern Britain* (Oxford, 1993), pp. 80–111.
[44] PRO, HO45/10810/311932 fo. 16.
[45] PRO, HO45/10742/263275/ fos. 194, 208, 209, 214.
[46] PRO, HO45/10742/263275/ fo. 249.
[47] PRO, T102/24 – Jasper Tyrell, 28 April 1918.

As we shall see, his instincts were sound – 1918 did see the tide turn against the Left in the struggle for control of London's symbolic civic spaces.

Besides the escalating conflict between pro and anti-war factions, 1917–18 also witnessed a spate of large, set-piece demonstrations organized by groups from both left and right determined to bolster their rival political programmes. For instance, Labour held a massive rally in Hyde Park in July 1917 as the culmination of its campaign for stricter controls on food supplies. The government did nothing to interfere, just as it did nothing during the summer of 1918 to prevent ultra-patriotic groups such as the British Empire Union, the Discharged Sailors and Soldiers Association and Pemberton Billing's 'Vigilantes' from organizing a series of anti-'alien' demonstrations in key central sites such as Trafalgar Square and Hyde Park. This campaign culminated in a massive rally on 24 August 1918, organized by Henry Page Croft's new National Party and supported by many other ultra-patriotic organizations. After the rally, which was again held in Hyde Park, more than 70,000 protesters marched to Downing Street to present a massive petition demanding tougher measures against German influence in Britain.[48]

Thus, even in wartime, the British Government believed that it was more dangerous to deny the right to demonstrate than to allow public space to be utilized for organized political protest. In part this reflected a deep-seated confidence that public demonstrations would be largely self-policing, and that even violence between opposing factions would be contained within acceptable bounds. Given the considerable violence associated with wartime crowd actions, notably those directed against enemy aliens and their property, this might seem complacent, but it was not wholly unreasonable. Even during the Lusitania riots of May 1915 there had been few serious injuries and no fatalities, and the same was true in the last great waves of anti-'alien' violence to hit London in July and September 1917.[49] During the spring and early summer of 1918, at the height of the German offensive, London witnessed a resurgence of crowd action against pacifist leaders as the organized ultra-right grew in strength and confidence. This was the only time that the Government used its powers under the Defence of the Realm Act (DORA) order 9A to ban political meetings in London, including a proposed May Day rally in Finsbury Park. Once again the catalyst was a sustained campaign in the

---

[48] Panayi, *Enemy*, pp. 212–18.

[49] See Stella Yarrow, 'The impact of hostility on Germans in Britain, 1914–1918', in *The politics of marginality: race, the radical right and minorities in twentieth-century Britain*, ed. Tony Kushner and Kenneth Lunn (London, 1990), p. 101; PRO, HO45/10944/257142/ 186 and 187 and HO45/10810/311932/ fo. 56; Panayi, 'Anti-German riots', pp. 200–1; Colin Holmes, *Anti-Semitism in British society, 1876–1939* (London, 1979), pp. 130–7.

columns of the *Daily Express*.[50] When, later in the month, Labour sought permission for an alternative meeting at Hyde Park, the authorities remained convinced that 'public feeling will be very high so long as the German offensive lasts and rather intolerant of any talk about peace'. However, the government's response was not to ban the proposed meeting, but rather to stall.[51] After waiting almost a month, the north London labour leaders had still not received any reply from the government. In exasperation they called for a major demonstration in Finsbury Park – this time at very short notice. Significantly, the government decided to do nothing unless faced by compelling evidence that there would be significant organized opposition to the meeting. Even a bellicose intervention from the British Workers League (BWL) was ignored. Far from seeking a pretext to ban the meeting, it seems clear that the authorities were searching to find some way of *avoiding* having to court political controversy by proscribing a meeting that had the backing of both the London Trades Council and the London Labour Party – even though it is clear that many radical Left groups including the 'Herald League' were also involved.[52] Despite evidence that the National War Aims Committee was given access to CID intelligence on pacifist activity in London in order to organize 'out-door or indoor meetings as a counterblast', there is no evidence of government connivance with ultra-patriotic disruption. On the contrary, it is clear that within Whitehall the ultra-right groups were generally seen as part of the problem, rather than as part of its solution.[53]

In the weeks following May Day the Government banned two more left-wing meetings in London, both in response to direct threats from ultra-right groups emboldened by the explosion of patriotic feeling since the German Spring Offensive. At a time when anti-'alien' protesters were taking their campaign on to the streets by holding massive public rallies, groups such as the BWL and the British Empire Union also threatened counter-demonstration and disorder whenever the left sought to march. In June 1918, the BWL complained that a planned Sunday peace demonstration at Tower Hill, organized by an alliance of East End socialist groups, risked allowing 'a crowd of aliens gathered from the East End . . . to be held forth to be the voice of the centre of the City of London'. The

---

[50] PRO, HO45/10810/311932/ fo. 59; *Daily Express*, 6 May 1918; Ken Weller, *Don't be a soldier! The radical anti-war movement in North London, 1914–1918* (London, 1985), p. 57.

[51] PRO, HO45/10810/311932 fo. 65.

[52] PRO, HO45/10810/311932/ fos. 64 and 65; Weller, *Don't be a soldier!*, p. 57.

[53] On CID involvement see PRO, HO45/10742/263275/ fo. 265; for government suspicion of right-wing disruption see HO45/10743/263275 fo. 229 [Anti-Naturalized Aliens League], ibid., fo. 241 [Imperial Defence Union], and ibid., fo. 263 [refuting charges that William Brace had welcomed such disruption]; cf. Millman, *Managing dissent.*

concern here with the symbolism of public space, and the belief that public demonstrations somehow embodied public opinion could hardly be clearer. Perhaps the Government concurred; certainly they displayed few qualms about banning the meeting.[54] A few weeks later the Government also banned a Women's International League meeting planned for Hyde Park on Bastille Day after the BWL, which was organizing a rival, pro-French rally, warned that the clash of meetings would 'expose the women engaged in the [peace] demonstration to physical violence'.[55]

Thereafter, a combination of factors appears to have convinced the government that it should retreat from its politically exposed position and that the politics of public space should again be allowed to follow its own course. Three factors were decisive. First, the considerable political fall-out from the May Day ban, which was exacerbated by damaging allegations, in July 1918, that police officers had connived in the disruption of a Woolwich Labour meeting by members of the Discharged Sailors and Soldiers Association.[56] Second, the general lull in public anxiety about the course of the war as the German retreat of the summer began to gather pace. And third, the absence of widespread public disorder during the short-lived, but near total London police strike of late August 1918.[57] Indeed, the absence of disorder during this unparalleled strike highlights London's great paradox – namely that while public politics remained unruly and at times decidedly violent, public order was not an endemic problem in the city. Rather, political customs with deep historical roots licensed behaviour in the context of public protest that would not have been tolerated in other spheres of everyday life, and would certainly not have been tolerated in wartime Paris or Berlin.

Peace and upheaval, 1918–1919

In November 1918 crowds again filled the great squares and thorough-fares of all three capital cities – crowds on a scale not seen either in the crisis days of August 1914, or at any point during the long years of war. Again the cities followed radically different trajectories, but this time divergence was shaped less by deep-rooted differences of custom and culture, than by the brutal realities of war. Paris and London were united by victory – victory won at a terrible price it is true, but victory nonethe-less. The crowds that thronged the symbolic central districts of each capital were celebratory, captured by an unambiguous spirit of joy that

[54] PRO, HO45/10744/263275 fo. 373.   [55] PRO, HO45/10744/263275 fo. 379.
[56] PRO, HO45/10744/263275 fos. 383, 385, 390, 396, 410, 431.
[57] *Daily Mail*, 2 September 1918.

had been conspicuously absent in 1914. London's politics of protest and Paris's elaborately choreographed patriotic wartime displays both gave way to spontaneous scenes of popular rejoicing. For days after the Armistice, Paris and London became 'people's cities', though, as we shall see, exactly what this meant needs considerable deconstructing in each case. Berlin, by contrast, was gripped by the spirit of revolution, rather than celebration – though in terms of crowd action this was very much revolution in the minor key. Indeed, one could argue that Berlin's tired revolution and the wild rejoicing of London and Paris were both expressions of popular frustrations pent up during the long years of war. Both celebration and revolution were tinged by a sense of fatigue and foreboding forged by war. An examination of the politics of public space in the three cities during 1918–19 suggests that more united them than one might imagine at first glance.

We must turn first to Berlin, because its revolution makes it a special case. It was only here that a capital's great civic squares and thoroughfares provided the backdrop for events that reshaped national history, rather than simply a stage upon which to reaffirm a sense of national history. That said, Berlin's was not a revolution based on mass action in the manner of Petrograd in February 1917 or Teheran in 1979. This was a tired revolution. The fear of resurgent revolutionary crowds was much greater than the reality. There were very few such crowds in 1918, although the emergent Communists certainly sought to summon them on to the streets after the fall of the Kaiser, and were by no means wholly unsuccessful in this aim.

The November revolution began with a mutiny, and in a sense spread out from that mutiny day by day. It reached Berlin when the first sailors arrived in the city. Only then did the city's central streets fill with large crowds. As in 1914 these crowds were far from homogeneous either in composition or motivation – they were crowds of the curious, the scared, and also the avowedly revolutionary. But there was no storming of the Berlin armoury or the Kaiser's palace, because no such classic revolutionary acts were necessary. The government simply collapsed and Germany quickly became a republic. The crowds had been there; the sacred sites of imperial Germany had been over-run by the masses, but the crowds had not made the revolution; they had watched it unfold.

The greatest tension in 1918 was between the different factions within German social democracy, and the question was whether or not Germany would follow the Russian path. From the outset, the majority Social Democrats were principally interested in getting things under control; their motto was 'order and progress'. However, with the end of the war, the provisions against public demonstrations and public speaking lapsed.

In the first weeks after the revolution Berlin witnessed an explosion of crowd activity – especially in the Tiergarten and the Lustgarten (probably the only central locations where really large crowds could gather without causing massive disruption). Despite the short, cold winter days, large crowds gathered to hear radical speakers denounce war and militarism, and to demand radical change in the new Germany – the restless spirit of revolution was in the air, even if, as the bloody events of the January 1919 Spartacist rising underscored, it only touched a small minority.

As one would imagine, Berlin saw nothing comparable to the joyous crowds that filled the heart of Paris and London at the Armistice in November 1918, or the peace celebrations of the following summer. Although the prestige of the 'undefeated' Prussian army remained such that Ebert, the new Social Democratic chancellor, sought to organize something close to a victory parade for its returning soldiers, the event itself was bitter-sweet at best and dwarfed by the grand parades through the real victors' capitals. There were even fewer Berliners who saw much to celebrate in the peace treaty that was finally signed at Versailles in June 1919 – but equally there was no great outburst of public protest. With Berlin's nationalist right disorganized and disorientated, the response to Versailles was essentially individual and private. At this stage, Berlin street politics remained dominated by the left, and it was at the Lustgarten (across from the old imperial palace), that radicals created the new focal point for political demonstrations under the Weimar Republic. At first the largest demonstrations by far were anti-war and internationalist in spirit, but over time new forces emerged to impose themselves on the Lustgarten. The internationalist hopes of 1918–20 largely dashed, the site was increasingly dominated by the right (and later by the Nazis). Indeed after 1933, the Lustgarten became the stage for an annual demonstration celebrating the *Machtergreifung* (the Nazi seizure of power). It was a demonstration that in a sense re-enacted the mythic 'spirit of 1914' – though ironically none of the major actors in this Nazi drama had been in Berlin in August 1914.

As we have seen, Paris in 1918 witnessed a relaxation of the authorities' tight control over demonstrations in public space. Official ceremonies, such as those during July, assumed a more relaxed air, and the authorities began to look more favourably on unofficial demonstrations. On 20 October a demonstration in honour of the rising cohort of military conscripts (the *classe vingt*), turned into a massive celebration of imminent victory, and hence of youth spared.[58] It marked the beginning of a fleeting

---

[58] Archives de Paris, VK3 195, 'Manifestation en l'Honneur des Délégations de la Classe 20'.

period when the public would impose its own meanings on Parisian public space. Months earlier, the authorities had granted the Ligue de l'enseignement permission to organize a march to the Place de la Concorde in honour of Alsace-Lorraine on 17 November 1918. The unexpected signing of the Armistice turned this into a massive semi-official celebration of victory and national reunification. Seven hundred societies participated in this grand patriotic spectacle played out before the President of the Republic and the massed ranks of government dignitaries. In the moment of victory the French Right discovered a new form of civic ritual capable of uniting its long divided factions in a shared celebration of victory and national salvation.[59] The public response was enormous, and organizers were barely able to cope with the crowd that swelled the streets around the Place de la Concorde.[60] A week earlier, on the eve of the Armistice, Paris had witnessed a very different occupation of central public space when 4,000 Parisian workers gathered outside the Bourse du Travail at the Elysée to proclaim their radical demands for the coming peace. Here were two faces of the Parisian crowd: the patriotic, spectator crowd that had been mobilized at key moments throughout the war, and the radical, protesting crowd that many feared would now reassert itself.

In the last months of 1918 the patriotic crowd held the upper hand. The Ligue de l'enseignement's march to the Place de la Concorde represented the culmination of days of joyous celebration in Paris. During the Armistice weekend crowds flocked to the Place de la Concorde, many laying floral tributes to the statue of Strasbourg, which was soon barely visible.[61] A month after the Armistice celebrations, central Paris was again the scene of massive popular demonstrations. This time the focus was not peace itself, but the arrival in Paris of the 'apostle of peace': American President Woodrow Wilson.[62] There had already been impressive demonstrations of patriotic fervour to mark the arrival of other Allied leaders, but the reception for Wilson was of a different magnitude. Wilson disembarked at the port of Brest on 13 December 1918. He was brought to Paris by special presidential train, and descended the Champs-Elysées in an open carriage, flanked by lines of Republican guards. Independent of what people thought of Wilson and his plans for peace, the reception for this statesman, who many felt had turned the war, was an event not to

[59] *BMO*, Paris, 26 November 1918, pp. 3190ff (Corbeiller's assessment of celebrations).
[60] *La Ligue de l'enseignement depuis la guerre, 1918–1920* (Paris, 1920). Archives de la préfecture de police (APP) Ba 1645.
[61] *Journal de l'Abbé Mugnier (1879–1939)* (Paris, 1985), p. 345.
[62] The phrase was Maurras's, *L'Action Française*, 8 January 1919.

be missed. But in fact in December 1918 Parisians of all political persuasions hailed Wilson not just as the national saviour, but as a god-like figure possessing the power and vision to bring permanent peace. According to Maurice Martin du Gard, the crowds that lined the Champs-Elysées to catch a glimpse of the great man, cheered for him, not as a man, but as a messiah.[63]

As we shall see, early spring 1919 saw the radical left assert a strong challenge to the state's tight controls over central public space, but by June and July 1919 it was once again elaborately choreographed official ceremonies that held sway. Between 26 and 29 June Paris celebrated the signing of the Versailles treaty – the definitive declaration of peace. But it was the celebrations of early July that again marked the high-point of the patriotic calendar. Another outpouring of pro-American feeling on 4 July, was swiftly followed by massive public celebrations on 14 July 1919, which was proclaimed a national festival for victory. On 13 July the authorities revived a ritual in which troops re-enacted the triumphal return of the Imperial Guard from the Battle of Jena in 1807 (it had been in abeyance since the German army had performed a mockery of the ritual during the occupation of 1871). On 14 July, it was estimated that a million spectators 'animated by a unique spirit' lined the streets of central Paris to cheer the triumphal procession. At the head of the procession were severely disabled ex-servicemen, behind them two ordinary soldiers escorting an officer, then Joffre and Foch on horseback, followed by units representing the allied armies, and finally the massed ranks of the victorious French army. It was the apotheosis of a year of patriotic celebration that had begun the previous July, but which had now found resolution, or so it was hoped, in a strong 'peace with honour'.

Of necessity the various grand public celebrations of 1918–1919 were fleeting affairs, each generally spanning no more than a day or two. However, in many respects the period between the Armistice and 14 July 1919 represented one long patriotic festival throughout which the boulevards and *grandes places* of central Paris were festooned with patriotic regalia. Flags and bunting decorated prominent buildings, street lamps, and public monuments.[64] Trophies of war, especially captured German artillery pieces, were displayed throughout the city complete with prominent national symbols such as the *coq gaulois*. In keeping with the new spirit of unity that animated most of the French Right, the

---

[63] Maurice Martin du Gard, 'La frère quatorze points', in *Les Mémorables*, (Paris, 1957), vol. I, p. 41. J. Prévost, *Dix-huitième année* (Paris, 1994), pp. 84–94, 97–101.

[64] AP, VK3 196, *L'Intransigeant*, 7 December 1918, and especially AP, VK3 202, BMO, 2 January 1919, 'Projet du monument de liberté'.

symbols of Republicanism and of French nationalism were used interchangeably, as they had been in the great Armistice celebration of 17 November 1918. The urban landscape of central Paris became, for months on end, one gigantic monument to resurgent French nationalism.

On the other hand, Paris also experienced a resurgence of radical protest in the months after the Armistice. Never wholly moribund even during the years of war, the radical tradition of popular protest now explicitly sought to challenge government control of public space. Between the Armistice and May Day 1919 inner Paris was the stage for at least eight significant protest demonstrations – far more than had occurred in any comparable pre-war period. Of these eight demonstrations, five were organized by trade groups and had limited resonance with the wider public.[65] But the other three represented bold attempts to challenge government control of public space – both the physical control of that space, and the ability to impose official meanings upon it. All three emanated from the labour movement, which had emerged greatly strengthened from the war, at least in terms of numbers. French Socialist party membership rose from 36,000 in December 1918 to over 130,000 a year later. For the first time membership of the CGT passed the one million mark, a tiny number compared to trade unionists affiliated to the British TUC, but still an impressive achievement for an organization that retained a strongly political, though perhaps no longer genuinely revolutionary, understanding of labour organisation.[66] The rapid growth in socialist organization, and the aggressive re-emergence of the politics of public protest, led many to fear that 'respectable' Paris might again find itself at the mercy of revolutionary crowds. The events of 1918–19 were to demonstrate that these fears were greatly exaggerated, but they were nonetheless real for that. Significantly, this fear of a disorderly, even brutalized, public taking to the streets was another factor common to all three capital cities in the immediate aftermath of war.

The first significant workers' protest represented an explicit attempt to challenge the official meanings attached to the reception organized for President Wilson in mid-December 1918. The Fédération ouvrière des mutilés and the socialist party, supported by the CGT, voted to present the President with an address honouring him, but disassociating their organizations from the pomp of the official ceremony.[67] Despite

---

[65] Habillement à Paris (AN F7 13367), 1 January 1919; *L'Humanité*, 27 March 1919.

[66] A. Kriegel, *La croissance des effectifs de la CGT, 1918–1921: Essai statistique* (Paris and the Hague, 1966); Jean-Louis Robert, 'Ouvriers et mouvement ouvrier Parisien pendant la Grande Guerre et l'immédiat après-guerre: Histoire et anthropologie' (State Doctorate, University of Paris – I, 1989).

[67] *L'Humanité*, 14 and 15 December 1918.

the ban on political emblems, they chose to march through the central thoroughfares behind the red flag of the Association républicaine des anciens combatants and singing the *Internationale*. In the end they were prevented from entering the Place de la République, but they did signal the Left's refusal to accept the government's right to control the politics of public space.[68] The second great demonstration was organized by the regional leadership of the Socialist Party and the CGT to protest at the controversial acquittal of Jaurès's assassin, on grounds of insanity. The socialists were determined that this demonstration should be a dignified and solemn protest – a fitting memorial to Jaurès as well as a stinging indictment of the authorities who had so mismanaged the affair. They called for a march through central Paris to the Jaurès family home in the west to be held on Sunday 6 April. Expecting strong opposition from the authorities, and determined to march whatever the response, the socialists chose a route that would allow crowds to disperse safely if necessary. In fact this was one demonstration the authorities chose not to ban. The government probably recognized that public anger over the Jaurès case needed to be assuaged, and that the decision to organize the protest as a solemn cortège made disorder unlikely. But the principal factor shaping this unusual decision may well have been a calculation that the demonstration would help boost the socialist cause against that of the more avowedly revolutionary syndicalists. It was the first workers' demonstration to be authorized in Paris since 1909, and according to the organizers it brought 300,000 on to the streets in a dramatic demonstration of working-class solidarity.[69]

Some hoped that the success of the demonstration would mark a decisive shift towards the liberalization of public-order policy in postwar France, but this was not to be. Instead, the march unleashed a new phase of militant class consciousness and mass protest, which in turn bred a new phase of conservative reaction in the state. According to one government observer, the Jaurès march had convinced anarchists and other revolutionaries that they were now 'the masters of the street'.[70] The sense of social and political upheaval was intensified by the beginning of a wave of strikes across Paris and its suburbs in early April, many of which involved public demonstrations, albeit mostly on a small scale. The CGT sought to capitalize on the new mood of militancy by reviving its pre-war call for a massive, unauthorized May Day demonstration. As one anarchist trade unionist put it, this was their chance 'to show the government

---

[68] *Le Populaire*, 16 December 1918.
[69] AN F7 14576, CA CGT, 4 April 1919; *L'Humanité*, 7 April 1919.
[70] APP Ba 1614: observation of the Commissaire of the 8th district.

that the streets belonged to the people'.[71] Determined not to concede ground to the CGT, on 23 April the government moved quickly to appease ordinary workers by announcing the introduction of the legal eight-hour day.[72] Earlier the government had introduced important legislation strengthening workers' rights in collective bargaining (25 March 1919), but in this tense climate they were absolutely determined not to rescind the tough public order legislation that so circumscribed the right to public protest. Trade unionists complained that provincial May Day demonstrations were allowed to proceed without hindrance, but the Ministry of the Interior refused all concessions for Paris.[73] The revolutionary crowd would not again capture the grand streets and squares of the French capital. Mimicking a pre-war tactic, the CGT called on supporters to march from the Place de la Concorde to the Place de la République. The government responded by mobilizing forces to occupy strategic sites throughout the capital. Protesters were not to be allowed to congregate at any point. When 3,000 demonstrators gathered at the Madeleine, in preparation for a march on the Place de la Concorde, they were immediately dispersed. When protesters regrouped and tried to reach the Place de la République and the CGT headquarters at the Elysée, they too were dispersed by force. By late afternoon the syndicalists had been driven from central, 'official' Paris, but they did not abandon their defiance of the authorities. In the more plebeian north of the city, in a triangular area demarcated by the Gare du Nord, the Gare de l'Est, and the Boulevard Magenta, the protesters threw up barricades and used paving stones and other street architecture as impromptu missiles with which to assail their tormentors.[74] These were not simply symbolic battles over who controlled public space; they were bloody confrontations in which serious injury was all too likely. Even on 6 April, serious clashes at the end of the day had left 68 police injured, 17 of them seriously. The clashes on 1 May were much worse, with three fatalities, and 43 hospitalized (the vast majority of them protesters).[75]

Almost the whole of the French Left recognized the 1 May demonstrations for what they were: a colossal misjudgement and a flop. Compared to the dignified mass protest organized a month earlier in memory of Jaurès, the sporadic skirmishing of 1 May was unimpressive. It seemed clear that most Parisian workers were not prepared to take to the streets in the name of

[71] APP Ba 1628, réunion rue Cambronne, 30 April 1919.   [72] L'Humanité, 26 April 1919.
[73] AN F7 13273, CA CGT, 16 April 1919.
[74] Danielle Tartakowsky, Les manifestations de rue en France, 1918–1968 (Paris, 1997).
[75] JO, Débats Parlementaires, Chambre des Députés, Réponse du ministre de l'Intérieur, 6 May 1919, p. 2208.

revolution, even though 6 April had demonstrated that they could be mobilized against a perceived injustice. As in Berlin, the war had left the workers profoundly tired. Material grievances remained acute despite the government concessions of March/April 1919, but few had time for the abstract appeal of 'revolution' after years of conflict and suffering. In addition, the French left conspicuously lacked strong leadership in the wake of Jaurès's murder, and after the debacle of the January Spartacist Rising in Berlin, they also lacked faith in revolution. After the horrors of 1914–18 their first goal was to change Germany, not France, and that now seemed an increasingly unlikely prospect. The Parisian revolutionary crowd had proved to be even more of a phantom than its Berlin counterpart.

In May 1919 the authorities sanctioned the revival of the two great pre-war ceremonies of right and left: those associated with the commemoration of Joan of Arc and the martyred Communards. These orderly public rituals signalled continuity with the pre-war politics of public space. But it was the great victory celebrations of July 1919, discussed above, which most clearly demonstrated that it would be official conceptions of 'la France' and 'la patrie' that continued to hold sway over the civic space of central Paris. The fleeting hope, shared by many on the right as well as the left, that post-war France would embrace a more liberal conception of the politics of public protest had come to nothing.

In London the spontaneous crowd, far from dormant during the war years, asserted itself in dramatic style with the formal signing of the Armistice on 11 November 1918. As in Berlin and Paris, the desire to break free of the limitations and conventions of wartime – to abandon oneself to transgressive behaviour – seemed all but universal at first. As we have seen in chapter 3, peace brought an immediate and striking transformation of central London as the blackout was lifted, the fountains switched on and Big Ben allowed to chime. But these authorized transformations did not go far enough for the crowds that thronged the capital's central thoroughfares. In Piccadilly Circus the crowd smashed a glass box indicating an air-raid shelter – a minor incident that was to mark the beginning of days of riotous celebration in the capital. The following night bonfires were lit around the base of Nelson's Column and at Piccadilly Circus, and soldiers scavenged material from far and wide to sustain the flames (including a captured German artillery piece), while airmen buzzed the crowds. When firemen tried to quell the blaze their hoses were either slashed or 'captured' and turned on them by joyous revellers.[76] These wild scenes attracted even larger crowds the

---

[76] *Daily Express*, 13 November 1918; *Manchester Evening News*, 13 November 1918.

following night, with over one hundred thousand estimated to have packed the vicinity of Trafalgar Square alone, while across central London more than a million were said to have participated in an 'orgy of wild rejoicing'. Throughout the capital major thoroughfares and public squares were said to have become 'open air dancing saloons'. By 14 November even the populist *Daily Express* was telling Londoners to 'steady on'. Two days later it was lamenting that 'roughs' had come to dominate the crowds, and that there had been 'many casualties and much wanton damage'. This, the paper warned, was the 'wrong way to rejoice'.[77] They were right. According to London ambulance records 537 revellers were injured between 11 and 17 November, one fatally. By 19 November the authorities were complaining of a widespread shortage of potatoes throughout the capital because celebrations had seriously disrupted metropolitan transport. There is simply no comparison in either scale or intensity between the crowd action in central London during early August 1914 and the wild scenes of November 1918. Moreover, unlike in 1914, at the end of the war Londoners – including soldiers on leave – really did become participants, stamping their own interpretations upon the meaning of 'Armistice'.

Initially the authorities proved indulgent of popular excess. The prominence of servicemen in the crowds probably helped here – but so too did a more general sense, common to many of the crowd phenomena of 1914–18, that it was very difficult to act decisively against such popular demonstrations of patriotic fervour. It was politically inconceivable that the government would turn to DORA, or to the army, to control the disorder, even when, after days of rejoicing, it was clear that the crowd's actions posed a threat to both life and property at the heart of the capital. We should not, however, exaggerate the threat posed by 'misrule' in these celebrations. This was no revolutionary situation – Londoners were not just celebrating victory, they were celebrating the nation and its traditions. The King and Queen toured the plebeian quarters of east, north, and south London on successive days after the Armistice, walking freely among 'their people'. The *Daily Mail* drew strong political conclusions from the 'fraternization' between people and monarchy,

The climax of the revelry ... was the passing of the King and Queen through the streets. Without escort save for two mounted policemen they drove through the delirious people – the King and Queen who, when thrones are falling like autumn leaves, can ride with only the escort of the people's love ....[78]

---

[77] *Daily Express*, 14 and 16 November 1918.   [78] *Daily Mail*, 12 November 1918.

The East End press took a similar line – boasting that the King could drive about his capital 'like an ordinary citizen', and mocking those who had warned that when 'the strain of war was suddenly lifted' the East would go mad for revolution.[79]

The London crowd thus proved Janus-faced in November 1918: tame and loyal by day, wild and unruly by night. The daytime crowds represented passive spectators who could be welcomed into the nation as evidence of its timelessness and stability, but the night-time crowds sought to be assertive participants in the rituals of nation, embodying dangerous, destabilizing social forces apparently unleashed by mass war. Both crowds would resurface at key moments over the next few months. In December 1918, it was the passive, spectator crowd that greeted Woodrow Wilson – the first American president to visit Britain. According to *The Times* 'a few hundred thousand' lined the streets between Charing Cross and Buckingham Palace, displaying 'the gravity and keenness that befit a great state function'.[80] But during the Peace Day celebrations of June 1919, and in a concurrent series of ugly 'race' riots in waterside districts such as Limehouse, Canning Town, and Poplar, the active, restless crowd reasserted itself. True, central London was again the site for grand official celebrations which summoned forth the spectator crowd, but elsewhere the story of Peace Day was very different. In Vauxhall, south London, children celebrated the peace treaty by lighting street bonfires, much as they would do on Guy Fawkes Night, but when the pubs closed adults joined in the fun by breaking into empty properties and stripping them of timber to feed the fires. There were similar scenes in east London, doubtless encouraged in both cases by the fact that most police had been withdrawn from these poorer districts to protect central London from a repeat of the excesses of the Armistice celebrations.[81]

Before 1914 crowd action had been tolerated in Britain, but only within tightly defined customary limits – hence the considerable licence shown to the election crowd. However, during the war crowds had sought influence on a much broader scale, and all too often they had had to be appeased for fear that confrontations between the state and the populace, even a patriotic populace, would weaken the war effort and encourage the enemy. If they could do so, British officials always preferred to ignore the challenge of crowd action, rather than resort to law. Partly this reflected a desire to deny publicity to militant minorities keen on mobilizing the public as a weapon against the government. But it also reflected a residual

---

[79] *East London Observer*, 16 November 1918.   [80] *The Times*, 27 December 1918.
[81] *The Times*, 2 and 3 February 1922; PRO, HO45/11068/372202 fos. 18, 21, 22.

sense that public demonstrations were legitimate – that they were an aspect of British political culture that should not be sacrificed to the 'logic of total war'. However, the experiences of crowd action during the war, and especially in its immediate aftermath, did much to weaken the perceived legitimacy of public demonstration. London played a large part in this story. It was the stomping ground for the demonized patriotic mob that had supposedly stampeded the nation into war in August 1914, persecuted the nation's racial minorities and crushed political dissent.[82] Perhaps in consequence, the post-war story was one of sharp reaction against the disorderly crowd. Not only was the new assertiveness of the crowd firmly quashed when it resurfaced in events such as the riots of 1919, but older traditions of tolerance towards mild disorder and 'misrule' during elections and industrial disputes were also abandoned. In this way the First World War did much to complete the de-legitimation of the political crowd in Britain. Henceforth, only the passive, spectator crowd would be recognized as a legitimate expression of public feeling, and hence a legitimate presence in public space.

Conclusions

Throughout the period 1914–1919 the politics of public space in our three cities were played out against the backdrop of a greatly heightened sensitivity to questions of political legitimacy and control. As we have seen, they were also played out radically differently in the three cities. In each case one finds struggles over the control of public space and, no less importantly, over the ability to define the social and political meanings attached to that space. If politics is an inherently cultural practice, then the squares, parks, and central thoroughfares of our capital cities were an important front line in struggles to impose meaning on a wartime world where so much suddenly appeared to be fluid and uncertain. At a superficial level one might characterize our story as revolving around the contrast between the deep-rooted liberal traditions of England, which allowed a vibrant, even chaotic, politics of public space to continue almost unchecked throughout the war years, and the Statist traditions of France and Germany where the right to public protest, limited even in peacetime, was simply unthinkable in the context of total war. But this simple dichotomy, whilst accurate enough in its essentials, obscures the fact that, in terms of the politics of public space, our three cities were moving on very different trajectories in the years after 1914. Although it

[82] PRO, HO45/10944/257142/ fos. 151, 185.

was not until 1916 that the British Government introduced emergency powers to limit the right to organize public demonstrations (DORA 9a), and these powers were little used except during the crisis period April/ May 1918, Britain had nonetheless made a decisive step away from its pre-war liberal traditions. As in so many fields, temporary wartime controls were retained under the post-war Emergency Powers Act (1920) – justified by widespread concerns about the ugly temper of post-war popular politics. These powers subsequently became more routinely available to local police forces under the Public Order legislation of the 1930s.

By contrast, it can be argued that, after the initial clampdown on all forms of political association in 1914–15, Germany was moving towards, rather than away from, liberalism in its approach to public order. Despite the iron grip of the military on wartime civil society, this was true even before the revolutionary upheaval of 1918. As we have seen, as the war dragged on, the Wilhelmine authorities increasingly felt obliged to allow political groups to resume normal activities. They remained wary whenever politics spilled over into public space, but even here it was often felt necessary to show discretion in the policing of political protest – especially when this was dominated by 'unpolitical' women angry at wartime deprivations. Moreover, whilst the 1918 revolution may have been a tired affair, it still transformed the politics of public order in Germany, establishing a liberal framework broadly similar to that of pre-war Britain. But the street politics of post-war Berlin were not similarly transformed. Rather, the violent confrontations that had characterized pre-war Wilhelmine public politics flourished unchecked within the shell of the new liberal order, one viewed as legitimate by only a minority of the population. The call to 'order' may have been a watchword for Germany's precarious new SPD government, but Berlin, like other German cities, nonetheless saw the growth of a vibrant, and often brutally violent, politics of public space in the years after 1918.[83]

For a brief moment at the end of the war it seemed possible that in Paris as well public order legislation might be liberalized along British lines, but the bloody clashes of spring 1919 ensured that this was not to be. Fearful that the spectre of political violence could once more disfigure the French capital, official control of public space was decisively reasserted in May

---

[83] Eve Rosenhaft, *Fighting the Fascists? The German Communists and political violence, 1929–1933* (Cambridge, 1983), Andreas Wirsching, *Vom Weltkrieg zum Bürgerkrieg? Politischer Extremismus in Deutschland und Frankreich, 1918–1933/39. Berlin und Paris im Vergleich* (Munich, 1999); Dirk Schumann, *Politische Gewalt in der Weimarer Republik, 1918–1933: Kampf um die Straße und Furcht vor dem Bürgerkrieg* (Frankfurt am Main, 2001).

1919. The brutal battles between the state and CGT were played out much as they had been before 1914. There was an intensification of the trend towards workers organizing demonstrations in their own heartlands – the industrial suburbs, but overall surprisingly little had been changed by more than four years of total war. Even more than in London and Berlin, the capital's symbolic public spaces continued to be monopolized by officially sanctioned national and civic rituals where the public was largely confined to a spectating role. However, even in Paris carefully orchestrated rituals intended to reinforce dominant understandings of the social and political order were always vulnerable to subversion. Rituals of remembrance proved especially vulnerable given the perceived legitimacy of the veterans' demand that they should be able to have their say on how war was remembered. Resistance to 'exclusion' had always been central to the politics of public space in our three capitals, and war gave it a new and emotive edge as marginalized ex-servicemen proclaimed that the truth about the war – their truth – was being excluded from the national memory. Veterans' groups in all three cities struggled to contest the official meanings inscribed on the new post-war rituals of remembrance, but in Paris their efforts took on a special significance given the strict constraints on other forms of public political protest. If anything war and its aftermath had intensified political struggles over the 'power of place' in our three capitals. The events of 1914–1919 had spawned new 'sites of memory' in the three capitals – sites of remembrance yes, but also sites of bombardment in London and Paris, and of revolution and counter-revolution in Berlin. The meanings attached to public space had changed, while the struggle to control those meanings had just begun.

Part III

Sites of passage/rites of passage

9   The home and family life

Catherine Rollet

When the British and French soldiers of August 1914 set off for the front they went, in the generally accepted phrase, to 'defend the country', but also, more specifically, to defend their village or district, their family, their home. The corresponding phrase in German was 'Heim' or 'home', but it was more precisely to defend the 'Heimat', or 'nation', an expression carrying much more emotional impact than the French 'patrie'. To fight for one's home was a universally accessible concept which at the same time represented a collective ideal, with the nation being perceived as the total of all the country's family cellular units.

Was it the case that this intrinsic link between the greater and the lesser 'nation' was a myth, one which was in fact often distorted by the war? What about family realities during the war, for those who lived in a metropolis such as London, Berlin or Paris? How did families live through those terrible years? What were the effects of the war on the home? Did the war create a break in the traditional division of labour? Did it instigate other ruptures, other re-orderings, particularly in connection with relationships within marriages, inter-generational relationships, temporalities and social rituals, modes of management of domestic life? Did the theme of family, hearth, and home become increasingly central to the men in the front line as the war dragged on unendingly?[1] What did they expect in return for their sacrifice, was there a 'debt' owed to them?[2]

This chapter was written by Catherine Rollet, in collaboration with Eberhard Demm, Adrian Gregory, and Emmanuelle Cronier.

We are grateful to the *Berliner Zeitung* for publishing a call for family documents on the wartime years, and also to all the Berliners who have helped us to assemble documents and develop this chapter, in particular Frau Ende, Frau Wanckel, Herrn Luke, and Herr Guthjahrn in Berlin. These materials, and similar documents on Paris, are cited in such a way as to protect family names. Only abbreviations of such family names are used in the text and notes.

[1] Olivier Faron, *Les enfants du deuil. Orphelins et pupilles de la nation de la première guerre mondiale (1914–1941)* (Paris, 2001).

[2] Jean-Yves Le Naour, *Misères et tourments de la chair durant la Grande Guerre. Les moeurs sexuelles des Français 1914–1918* (Paris, 2002), p. 317.

In times of war, the emotions of private life tend to become more closely hidden than in ordinary times. Anguish nonetheless finds expression in terms of uncertainty, despair, boredom, waiting, sometimes in revolt. A variety of sources must be used to guess at these reactions, and the feelings underlying them at a time when civilians were diffident, not having to face the hardships of those at the front. Essentially, what we have are private sources, some but not all of which are deposited in public archives: correspondence, private notebooks, account books. For Berlin, an appeal in the newspaper *Berliner Zeitung* in 2003 for written accounts of the war years brought surprising results: readers gave us access to letters and notebooks of great interest. Such materials in private hands are immensely rich, but they have their limitations. They tend to show the 'positive' side of family life during the war: these are model wives or parents writing to their husband or son and who, beyond the pain of separation, sustain the link, at all costs, despite every difficulty. The war as a generator of tensions and conflicts, even of hatreds, can be perceived more clearly in public documents.

Hearth and home under siege

The idea that a war against Germany would be a war of defence of the 'Englishman's Home' was well established even before the war broke out. Most famously, William Le Queux wrote a series for the *Daily Mail* in 1906 which was entitled 'The Invasion of 1910'. This fictional war of the future emphasized the devastation which would be visited on the homes and families of England in the event of a German invasion. Regarding the specifically metropolitan context, it is worth pointing out that the second part of Le Queux's two-part serial was entitled 'The Siege of London'. This offers a graphic description of London under bombardment and occupation: 'Roaring flame shot up everywhere, unfortunate men, women and children were blown to atoms.'[3] The subsequent description of the occupation of London begins with the Germans behaving correctly, ruling London, 'with a rod of iron ... they are harsh but it cannot be said they are inhumane or brutal.'[4] An uprising of Londoners against the occupying forces changes this and the occupying forces retaliate with atrocious reprisals against the civilian population.[5] This widely read serial established in the minds of many Londoners a graphic sense of the threat involved to their families in the event of a German victory. Although Le Queux had written the work as propaganda for compulsory military service, its main effect was

---

[3] *Daily Mail*, 8 May 1906.   [4] *Daily Mail*, 28 May 1906.   [5] *Daily Mail*, 9 June 1906.

probably to stimulate voluntary recruitment by giving Londoners and other Britons a powerful sense of the personal issues involved.

In London appeals for volunteers centred on the defence of hearth and home.[6] It was tacitly assumed that the first men to enlist ought to be those who had the least immediate domestic responsibilities: young single men. But the increasing demand for manpower and the obvious fact that many married men with responsibilities had enlisted voluntarily clouded this distinction. In July 1915 the editor of the Conservative periodical *The Spectator* wrote: 'It is a splendid reflection on the influence of married life that it is the married men who measure and accept their responsibility with conspicuous readiness. They have learned that a home is a thing worth fighting for.'[7] When conscription was implemented in January 1916 there was outrage that married men were not given significantly preferential treatment, despite the fact that there had been hints (but not promises) to this effect during the debates about conscription.

The concept of 'home' was immensely resonant in Britain (and perhaps particularly in the London suburbs) in 1914. It was particularly important to the middle classes, although substantial numbers of the working class also subscribed to a bourgeois ideal of domestic life. One powerful illustration of this is the Ideal Home Show, an annual event in London sponsored by the popular lower-middle-class newspaper the *Daily Mail* before the war. The first exhibition, at Olympia in London, attracted 200,000 visitors in 1908. It would not be much of an exaggeration to say that many British soldiers were fighting for precisely this 'ideal home' and indeed the success of the election slogan in 1918, 'Homes fit for heroes', underlines this point. In this context the British phrase 'Home front' is a term without equivalence in French or German. The French term 'l'arrière' has a very different connotation and 'l'autre front' sounds vague, whereas the German equivalent, 'Heimatfront', has other echoes, located in a sentimentally charged version of 'fatherland'. In Britain the term has a double edge: the home front had to contribute to the fighting front in a logistic sense by producing munitions, etc., but paradoxically one of its duties was to maintain something of peacetime values for the soldier to return to after the war (as in the popular wartime song 'Keep the home fires burning'). As the introduction to this volume suggests, men were being asked to fight for an idealized home, but the act of enlistment

---

[6] Susan Grayzel, *Women's identities at war: gender, motherhood and politics in Great Britain and France during the First World War* (Chapel Hill, 1999), pp. 46–7.

[7] *Spectator*, 24 July 1915, p. 101. Cited in Nicoletta Gullace, *'The blood of our sons': men, women and the renegotiation of British citizenship during the Great War* (New York and Basingstoke, 2002), p. 114.

at the very least disrupted this home and possibly endangered it (in its pre-war form) beyond the hope of recovery. That is to say, the propaganda appeal was to protect the home from the depredations of the eternal enemy, but enlistment could destroy the home life that was theoretically being protected. Men could argue that the financial, emotional, and general damage to well-being (for example, a deterioration in the health of their spouses or in the education of their children) which would result from their conscription utterly negated any theoretical defence of their own 'home' by their joining the colours. If a man was unable to continue his mortgage repayments as a result of the difference between his civilian earnings and his military allowance (a common situation), then the rhetoric of fighting in defence of home would ring very hollow. It is that tension which was frequently enacted in military tribunal hearings.

Middle-class fears of working-class 'incompetence' in housekeeping complicated the question as to how London families would cope with the absence of the man of the house during the war. A survey by the Women's Co-operative Guild of homes in the London borough of Lambeth suggested that in fact most working-class women were highly efficient domestic managers and cooks, but that inadequate domestic facilities severely limited their capability to exercise domestic economy properly.[8] The issue took on a new significance in wartime as food economy became a patriotic duty. Propaganda films targeted 'working-class' women, subtitled with comic Cockney accents, teaching them not to 'waste' food; the response to such campaigns was unlikely to have been entirely positive. Here is yet another instance of the socially stratified nature of discussions of 'the family'. In Britain, where 80 per cent of the population was working-class, these distinctions were inevitable. In London, more heavily middle-class than parts of the industrial north, family life, located more in owner-occupied dwellings,[9] took on a different character. To be sure, there was no one 'family' in these capital cities, though wartime pressure tended to highlight what families of all social groups had in common.

Did the war strain family ties?

The archives of British military tribunals offer a clear example of the disruptive effects of the war. The war fragmented London families that depended on the earnings of a husband, a son, a father, isolated figures struggling to sustain families that were often fragile. This situation emerged time and again in these conscription tribunals. Men frequently

[8] E. Pember Reeves, *Around about a pound a week*.
[9] See *Capital cities at war*, vol. i, chs. 6 and 8.

lodged appeals against conscription on domestic grounds,[10] under clause 'D', a provision in the Military Service Act that permitted an appeal against conscription on grounds of 'severe hardship'. The cases cited here are ones that were heard by the Middlesex Appeal Tribunal, which covered most of 'outer' London; these are 'second level' cases, of men who had appealed against the ruling of the 'local' tribunal or in some cases where the military representative had appealed against their exemption.

In the first session the Appeal Tribunals until June 1916 heard 136 appeals on grounds principally of 'serious hardship'. Of these, 85 cases were dismissed, 47 received temporary exemption (two to six months) and four permanent exemption under 'conditions' (usually undertaking work of national importance). In November 1916, 75 conditional exemptions on grounds of serious hardship were identified.[11] Overall, about 30 per cent of all appeals were on domestic grounds alone, and perhaps another 10 per cent on domestic and other grounds. In Middlesex the overwhelming majority of these appeals were unsuccessful, but many domestic appeals for temporary exemption succeeded at the local level and never reached the Middlesex Tribunal.

Many letters to these authorities bring out the fact that the war would destroy the household of those who were to leave for the front: 'My being called up for military service,' explains Charles Herrin, a nineteen-year-old volunteer, 'would break up the home and also her [mother's] health, under the present state of her nerves, my father having been dead six months. I am quite willing to take up work of national importance whereby I may still look after my mother.' But the Military Representative did not share this view.[12] A commercial clerk, of Highgate, writes:

I have a delicate wife who is not sufficiently strong to depend on her own living. The army Allowance will not be sufficient to keep her. This will mean giving up our present home only recently got together and she will have to go into one room ... owing to being a new man ... [my employers] will not give me an allowance, therefore it means giving up everything.[13]

It is obvious that in many cases the generosity of employers was vital in allowing middle-class households to be held together. Arthur Peake-White explained: 'my wife (is) in a most delicate and unfit state of health having to shoulder the sole responsibility for six young'.[14]

Mother, wife, even the two, are at the core of the letters of these soldiers: 'Should I have to go, my mother and wife would only have the

---

[10] A. M. Gregory, 'Military Service Tribunals. Civil Society in Action, 1916–1918', in J. Harris (ed.), *Civil society in British history* (Oxford, 2003), pp. 177–90.
[11] Middlesex Appeal Tribunal, PRO MH 47/143.   [12] MH47/92 V 3215 February 1917.
[13] MH47/88 V 2649 November 1916.   [14] MH47/107 V 4810 April 1918.

usual army allowance to live on, that would probably mean losing our home which is retained on the hire purchase system?'[15] wrote Cecil Parsons in November 1916. The burden of a large family is also an argument, as Henry James, a piano maker of Hendon, explains that he had not been able to make any satisfactory arrangement for his wife, his home, and his five children. He had hoped to move his home to the country and to make a personal effort to see the kids 'better clothed and fed and taught to be good citizens'. But the Local Tribunal did not share his point of view.[16] In the case of Alfred Grover (railway porter, Kilburn), the investigators pointed out that the mother who would be 'dependent' was in fact in receipt of nearly £5 income a week, which could be perceived as a very good income.[17]

The problem of potential orphans was treated differently in France. A man with six children dependent was exempt from military service after April 1915, following the decision of Minister of War Millerand. But the same was not the case in Germany. Even fathers with all their sons were sent to war.

Family reconfigurations

Although exaggeration is obvious in some of these attempts to convince military authorities, it is nonetheless accurate to state that in all three cities family and household structure was profoundly disturbed by the war. Following departures to the front line, families reconfigured themselves in new ways. The birth rate dropped, the circle of acquaintanceships grew, and domestic arrangements were transformed.

Many Parisian families who remained in Paris or returned there, many after a period of exodus (until November and December 1914), rearranged their living arrangements: an old man on his own would come to live with his daughter whose husband had been called to the front. The opposite was often true: older parents would take in their daughter or daughter-in-law left alone with her children. There was a temporary move to live with parents or parents-in-law – a 'temporary' arrangement which in many cases lasted for five years. As one family diary has it, Emile H. met Monsieur B. in the avenue de l'Opéra in Paris: 'his three sons and his son-in-law have been mobilised. Two of his daughters-in-law have come to live with him, with their children. He has found work, paying out allowances, in 5 or 6 places around Paris' (22 November 1915).[18] How

---

[15] MH47/86 V 2292 November 1916.   [16] MH47/86 October 1916.
[17] MH47/88 V 2668, December 1916.
[18] *Heures de guerre*, diary, private archives, Family A.

did daughters-in-law and married daughters live in these situations? With acceptance, latent conflict, resignation? Such cohabitation was also part of the domestic pattern in Berlin, and above all in London.

The hypothesis that life in an extended family (without the husband) could become unbearable in London can be confirmed through a glance at the exchange of letters between Edith and gunner Fred Bennett.[19] At first Edith lived alone with her little girl Ruby, and sent news of her regularly in her letters to her husband. Yet she did not hide feelings of distress: 'Well, sweetheart mine, I have no news to tell you and life seems just one misery day & night for ever in fear, but I suppose we must keep smiling for your sake' (12 July 1917). She feels depressed: 'I feel perfectly lost & my life seems nothing & I feel I don't want to see anyone or go out' (14 July 1917). Even though her mother-in-law encouraged her to find distraction, she could barely rise above this sadness. She felt even more strongly the separation from her husband: 'So dear I shall be pleased when you come home to me & we can live together alone as I am fed up and most unhappy. My life's a misery. Mum knows too much of our affairs & she is always remarking about what money I have and so on & Winnie [her sister] is a perfect devil at times & I feel like packing into 2 rooms sometimes. I'm fed up & never no more dear, this has been a lesson, she said she expects I will write to you and tell you a lot of lies, after we done and paid half her holiday last year' (24 January 1918). There were daily squabbles over money matters, domestic chores; on the other hand Edith was always on good terms with her husband's family, whom she saw frequently. She desperately wanted to be alone with her husband and their child: 'When you come home . . . my life will be one of happiness, just your dear self & Ruby & no more 3rd or 4th persons shall ever share our happiness' (21 March 1918)

In other cases, family reconfiguration was the only refuge for a young woman in distressing circumstances, and could work well, as two examples show – one in London, the other in Berlin. The very young Eva Isaacs[20] (aged eighteen in 1914) suffered a miscarriage during the winter of 1914–15 while her husband was in a training camp in Britain. She suffered severely from the consequences of this mishap: 'I am still drowsed with the effects of chloroform and opium which is really a comfort' (21 March 1915); 'I am left with only half myself' (29 March 1915). She spent her convalescence with her parents, very successfully. Nonetheless she hoped to return to her own home although she was aware of her parents' concern: 'How sweet it will be to be back in our little home, at one time I thought I should not be able to get away from here as they

---

[19] Bennett Letters: Imperal War Museum 96/3/1.
[20] Isaacs Letters: Imperial War Museum, Con. shelf.

are so anxious to keep me' (9 September 1915). Her ideal was similar to that of Edith, to live alone with her husband in their own home: 'It seems so strange to be at home again, my little sitting room is looking very sweet and comfy ... we shall have it all to ourselves when you come' (19 January 1916).

In 1914 the Berlin primary school teacher Margarethe Lichey had an affair with her married colleague Fritz Neumann.[21] In March 1915 their child was born and she asked the father to recognize the child and to pay a food allowance. Fritz Neumann, who was serving at the front, made no response. The unmarried mother therefore turned to the *Kinderrettungsverein* (children's aid association), where a participant, Pastor Pfeiffer, became the child's official guardian. Before the appropriate tribunal, Pfeiffer attempted to establish a statement of paternity and to obtain payment of the food allowance. However, Neumann declared that he could not attend the hearing, that he was not the father, and that he had never slept with Miss Lichey. Meanwhile, the unmarried mother's situation deteriorated dramatically. Neumann no longer answered letters and the scandal caused the teacher to lose her job. At this point, her parents intervened. They took her into their own home, her mother – a dressmaker – took up work again and, since Prussia was suffering a severe lack of teachers (of whom 34 per cent were serving at the front), the young woman was soon allowed to teach once again. In the end the family operated so well that she could even take on a domestic servant. In 1920 Miss Lichey found another man, who married her and accepted her child.

Was it because of these problems that during the war the number of illegitimate births in Berlin dropped substantially? The figures are striking: although in 1913 10,017 children were born outside marriage, the figure reached only 4,278 in 1917, representing a drop of 57.3 per cent. But married couples also had fewer children. In 1913, the total number of children born in Berlin was 42,511; in 1917, the figure was only 19,463 – a drop in the birth rate of 54.7 per cent.[22] The proportion of births outside wedlock therefore remained stable during the war at around 22–23 per cent,[23] well above the German average which increased slightly from 9 per cent to 11 per cent. The situation was somewhat different in London, and particularly in Paris. In London, the proportion of births outside marriage,

---

[21] Landesarchiv Berlin (LAB) PR. Br.Rep.106, Kinderrettungsverein, no. 972, Karl Friedrich Lichey. Cf. Eberhard Demm, 'Zwischen Propaganda und Sozialfürsorge: Deutschlands Kinder im Krieg' in *Ostpolitik und Propaganda im Ersten Weltkrieg*, Frankfurt/M 2002, pp. 71–131; here p. 101; first in *Militärgeschichtliche Zeitschrift* 60, 2001.

[22] *Statistisches Jahrbuch des Deutschen Reiches*, vol. xxxvi, Berlin 1915, p. 4 and vol. XL (1919), p. 4; on the general situation in Germany, cf. Demm, 'Kinder', p. 108.

[23] 23.6 per cent in 1913, 22.4 per cent in 1915, and 22 per cent in 1917.

which was very low, increased none the less, from 4 per cent in 1913 to 5.4 per cent in 1917; in Paris, with the highest rate by far, the percentage rose from 24.1 per cent in 1913 to 27.8 per cent in 1915, and highest of all to 31 per cent in 1917.[24] One birth in three in the French capital was illegitimate.

However, the total number of births dropped in Paris and also in London, although less dramatically. From 1913 to 1917, the drop was 33 per cent in Paris, and 27 per cent in London. In all three capitals the authorities became aware of the situation quite quickly and discussed measures of birth-control, but without any dramatic effects. In Berlin, on 11 May 1917 an inter-ministerial commission informed the Kaiser that 'the losses in wartime due to the decline in the birth rate will exceed or at least equal the number of casualties in combat'. The commission proposed an increase in the number of crèches and the use of all means (including forced labour) to oblige the fathers of illegitimate children to pay their food allowances. Finally, the use of contraceptives was forbidden and on 29 July 1918 the Prussian ministry of the Interior made 500,000 marks available to social assistance for infants.[25]

While family networks were reconfigured, the war also added to the numbers of unmarried people who came to the city to work in large numbers in the armaments factories. Such people lived in fairly precarious circumstances and fell easy prey to tuberculosis.[26] Furthermore, the war reduced or even eliminated domestic service in prosperous family households. In Berlin, many servants left the families who employed them, attracted by the higher wages in the arms factories, or were dismissed following their employers' impoverishment.[27] In Paris, one feature of the war was the end of wet-nursing.[28] Women who came to the homes of middle-class families to breast-feed their babies, or who took the babies to live with them in the country, could no longer reach the capital: elsewhere, they were mobilized for field work and found more remunerative work in war factories.

At times withdrawing into itself and at other times resorting to greater openness, the metropolitan family was pulled between very different

---

[24] Catherine Rollet, 'The Other War II: "Setbacks in public health"', in *Capital cities at war*, vol. I, p. 459.

[25] GSTA (Preuß. Geheim. Staatsarchiv) Rep 76 VII, no. 24546, Hebung der deutschen Volkskraft, fols. 93–9, quotation fol. 94.

[26] Michelle Perrot, *Histoire de la vie privée*, vol. IV, pp. 265–78, here p. 459.

[27] Ute Daniel, *Arbeiterfrauen in der Kriegsgesellschaft. Beruf, Familie und Politik im Ersten Weltkrieg* (Gottingen, 1989), pp. 37–47 and 'Women's Work in Industry and Family: Germany, 1914–1918' in Richard Wall and Jay Winter (eds.), *The upheaval of war. Family, work and welfare in Europe 1914–1918* (Cambridge, 1988), p. 285.

[28] Catherine Rollet, *La politique à l'égard de la petite enfance sous la Troisième République* (Paris, 1990), pp. 508–12; Georges D. Sussman, 'The end of the wet-nursing business in France, 1874–1914', *Journal of Family History*, vol. 4, no. 3 (1977), p. 246.

poles during and in the immediate aftermath of the conflict. In sum, no one could be certain that a family would survive the war intact.

Substitutes for home

Although the home was indeed a reference point that fascinated soldiers, it was far from being a universal ideal. What about those who had no family, or those Frenchmen whose family lived in an occupied region? They could make or restore links with parts of their family with whom they had little or no connection before the war. Such was the case with Victor Christophe, an infantryman serving with the 150th Infantry Regiment as a musician. A native of northern France, he spent his leave early in February 1916 with an aunt in Paris. He noted how 'On Sunday we went to Suresnes to dine with the de Ferrières cousins. Another delightful day. On Monday I am going to dine with René, 42 rue de Lagny. In the evening we will have supper at a hotel with the cousins.'[29] We can see clearly here how the arrival of men on leave was an excuse for family events arranged around them. On 2 April 1917, Christophe returned to Paris on leave again:

I am here in the midst of all those who are so good at standing in for my missing family, and I am making the acquaintance of my little god-daughter Renée. I don't have time now to tell you in detail about the baptism ceremony at which, with Marguerite, we had the honour to be godmother and godfather to this little angel (8 April, Easter Day). Next day, the 9th, I went to the funeral of M. Lagneau's father, from rue de la Grotte (Porte de Versailles), who was buried in Bagneux cemetery. On 4 April I went to see M. and Mme Godimiaux at Raincy.'[30]

Who looked after those who did not have even distant relatives in Paris? They might find a *marraine de guerre*, a 'war godmother' – a very French, even particularly Parisian, institution, which did not exist in London or Berlin. The 'war godmothers' were an innovation in 1915, introduced to help soldiers from the front line who were cut off from their families in the occupied regions or, in some case, evacuated to the south.[31] The stakes were substantial in the case of Paris, since having a Parisian godmother enabled the soldier to stay in the capital on leave. Voluntary associations were also created, above all by the élite classes of Paris, and focused round the major newspapers (*L'Echo de Paris*, *La Vie parisienne*); more than 70,000 soldiers were 'adopted' in this way (through correspondence and parcels), but this is a small number compared to the total figure of men mobilized during the war (3,580,000 men, simply between August

---

[29] Annette Becker, *Journaux de combattants et de civils de la France du Nord* (Paris, 1998), pp. 36–7.
[30] Ibid., p. 74.   [31] Le Naour, *Misères et tourments*, pp. 66–74.

and December 1914 in France). In fact the 'war godmother' suffered from an ambiguous image – consoler, a haven of peace and comfort, but also a source of emotional and sexual feeling which was enhanced by distance from home and potentially dangerous. As a result of the cost of announcements, some papers specialized in a prosperous 'clientèle', officers and junior officers. This applied to *La Vie parisienne*, which received nothing but requests of this kind: 'Young officer, pleasing physique and character (at least in his opinion), at the front for 18 months, wishes to correspond with Parisian godmother, young, pretty, affectionate, expecting to make fuller acquaintance during leave period. Send photo. Write: Sub-Lieut. Lucrens, chez Iris, 22 rue St Augustin, Paris.'[32]

The other solution for soldiers without a family took the form of 'war charities' (*œuvres de guerre*) created specifically for them. *Les Parrains de Reuilly*, studied by Emmanuelle Cronier[33] is a good example. This welcoming establishment, set up in a barracks in the 12th arrondissement of Paris, could take in 1,000 men at anyone time. It functioned as an extension of front line life in Paris, but on the lines of an adoptive family community: the pattern was recognized as one of godfathers and godsons. Operated by auxiliaries recruited among administrative workmen-clerks, it was approved by General Galliéni and was largely subsidised by the Paris city council. Rueilly provided accommodation for men on leave and fed them well, gave them pocket money, and organized a wide range of activities, walks, and outings. In this way, everything was done to occupy the men on leave as a group, protecting them from the dangers and temptations of the great city – theft, lack of occupation, drunkenness, commercial sex, and fighting. Supervisory checks, however, operating morning and evening, heavily limited the soldier's freedom of movement and kept him tightly controlled.

Family anniversaries

During the nineteenth century the bourgeois family had established a model of ritualization for social activity, organized around the stages of life and the religious ceremonies that went with them (christenings, communions, engagements, marriages, funerals, etc.) and bourgeois patterns of socialization (New Year's Day visits, wearing mourning, celebrating birthdays and anniversaries).[34] In wartime, questions arose

---

[32] *La Vie parisienne*, 18 March 1916.

[33] Emmanelle Cronier, *Les permissionnaires du front à Paris 1915–1918*, doctoral thesis, Université de Paris 1, 2005.

[34] Anne Martin-Fugier, 'Les rites de la vie privée bourgeoise' in Michell Perrot, *Histoire de la vie privée*, pp. 175–241. Catherine Rollet, *Les enfants au XIXe siècle* (Paris, 2001), pp. 102–4.

about such events. Should there be anniversary celebrations during the war in the three capital cities? Should Christmas be celebrated? No doubt the war did not suddenly interrupt this pattern of rituals and festivities that articulate family life and mark the stages of the life cycle. But baptisms were less frequent because of the diminishing birth-rate – and marriages too – except at the outbreak of war, to regularize an existing relationship and to enable the wife to benefit from separation allowances. These were temporary exceptions. Only funerals increased in number.

In Berlin, Christmas was celebrated as always, although the feast lost its sparkle. The family of Johanna We.[35] could not buy a Christmas tree in 1916 because it was too expensive, and there were no candles to be bought. On Christmas Eve the young girl noted in her diary: 'Christmas Eve! It doesn't look like it here because there is no bright Christmas tree, it doesn't look right.' Gifts were modest: 'a toothbrush, some apples, some nuts and 3 Marks' and also 10 Marks and a book sent by her father from the front.[36] Her father could not be present for Christmas. She felt his absence bitterly: 'When Father celebrates Christmas with us, it's different, much better,' and she sympathized with her father, forced to celebrate Christmas with strangers.[37]

At Christmas 1916, the G. family in Berlin-Weissensee was dispersed.[38] The two sons were in barracks at the rear, waiting to be sent to the front, Johannes at Schmiedeberg in Silesia and his elder brother Adalbert at Worms where he was anxious about the medical examination by a commission whose aim was to send as many men as possible back to the trenches.[39] They were still happy that at the beginning of December the military had released their father Paul who had already been serving at the rear since September. The score drawn by the family at Christmas was mixed:

Thank God we have been spared the worst, but we await the spring with trepidation. Little Gerda is not yet aware of the heaviness that prevents us all from being truly joyful. How happy she will be with her small presents. Paula is more thoughtful . . . and from the outside no one will see the sorrow which sits with us around the Christmas tree.[40]

In fact, at Christmas 1916 the terrible '*Kohlrübenwinter*' (turnip winter) seized hold of Germany, and the parents wrote to their son Adalbert that

---

[35] Private collection, Johanna We., Berlin. The names provided are fictional in the text.
[36] We. collection (Diary 24/12/1916, fols. 2r–2v).
[37] We. collection (Diary 24/12/1916, fol. 3r).
[38] Private collection of Family G., Berlin.
[39] G. collection (Adalbert G. to his parents, 22/12/1916 and 1/1/1917).
[40] G. collection (Adalbert G. to his parents, 22/12/1916).

there was neither bread nor apples to be bought. 'What are people living on now?' he responded, incredulous.[41]

Christmas 1917 was still full of delight for the family of Elizabeth Fernside, a lower-middle-class woman living in Fulham, in south London.[42] On Christmas Eve she received a parcel from her son Fred, who was based in Britain, which gave great pleasure on all sides: she read the books, father admired his pipe, his little sister played with her doll ('office boy'), the electric lamp delighted everyone, since the restricted lighting designed to reduce bombing. 'We had hardly a glimmer and could not use our stove, the gas was so scarce. We can see to read and write now' (24th December). Her wealthy compatriot Eva Isaacs evidently refused herself nothing, but suffered from the absence of her husband. She writes on 16 December 1916, 'How strange Christmas must be out there in the midst of war . . . it is strange here without you.'

Edith Bennet[43] saw the same Christmas in a far more negative light:

Christmas is getting very near, but there is not much to remind one, as things are such an awful price and very scarce except little kiddies' toys and they are triple the usual price & rotten stuff at that, no puddings this year, can't buy currants or raisins. We asked the nip what she wants Santa Claus[44] to bring her, so she said a dollie, some sweets, some money & a baby brother. I am afraid she will be disappointed. (13 December 1917)

Nonetheless, she tried to protect Christmas for her daughter. Although she did not find a new baby brother, 'Ruby was very excited over Santa Claus, she had a doll's bed that Beattie bought, a little stove with frying pans, a box of boats and several other things' (1 January 1918) and later a pearl necklace bought in Jerusalem by the fiancé of her paternal aunt (2 May 1918).

A war-time lullaby mocked the restrictions imposed on the middle classes:

> 'Sing a Song of Wartime'
> If I ask for cake, or,
> Jam of any sort,
> Nurse says, 'What, in wartime?
> Archie, cert'nly not'
> Life's not very funny,
> Now, for little boys
> Haven't any money,
> Can't buy any toys.

---

[41] G. collection (Adalbert to his parents, 19/1/1917).
[42] Fernside Letters, Imperial War Museum, London, Con. shelf.
[43] Bennet Letters, Imperial War Museum 96/3/1.
[44] This term is surprising: Father Christmas was the ordinary epithet; perhaps an American cousin imported the phrase.

Mummie does the housework
Can't get any maids
Gone to make munitions
'cause they're better paid.'[45]

No gifts, or very few, no celebrations, or only very discreet ones; life was bleak for all, but even so children were relatively sheltered from the war.

The family as a network of communications[46]

Correspondence is well recognised as a characteristic of pre-war sociability. There was a considerable and growing volume of middle-class writing,[47] but also popular correspondence – briefer, particularly making use of postcards, in this period. The fashion for postcards is well known, with their varied views of landscapes, monuments, caricatures, humorous drawings about families and babies. The war promoted these forms of informal correspondence, as the simplest way to communicate with those at the front. In contrast, the sending of telegrams was reserved for urgent news, and the telephone was only beginning to be in general use. Collections of wartime correspondence show the intensity in effect of these exchanges, in the double form of letters, of private 'field letter forms' folded rather like air-letter forms, and of postcards. The post office operated rapidly between Paris and the front, a factor certainly aided by the location of the capital in relation to the combat zone. However, at the most acute moments of the unending conflict, and because of postal censorship, delays might take a dramatic turn: no news from Jean between 31 August and 25 September, and his father notes 'What anxiety!'[48] Similarly, between 1st and 15th February 1915, Jean's family received no mail and his father was very disturbed. Apart from that, the family never received certain small notebooks kept by Jean in the trenches and sent by him to them. No doubt they were withheld by the censor.

Correspondence had to travel more slowly to and from London and above all to and from Berlin, not only because of the distances but also because of military censorship.[49] Adalbert G. wrote to his mother that

---

[45] N. Macdonald, *Wartime nursery rhymes* (London, 1918), p. 53.

[46] Eberhard Demm, ' "Maikäfer flieg", dein Vater ist im Krieg'. Wie Berliner Familien den Ersten Weltkrieg erlebten, *Berliner Zeitung*, no. 12, 15./16.1.2005, Magazin, pp. 1–2.

[47] Cécile Dauphin, Pierrette Pézerat, and Danièle Poublan, *Ces bonnes lettres. Une correspondance familiale au XIXe siècle* (Paris, 1995).

[48] *Heures de guerre*, private archives, Family A.

[49] Bernd Ulrich, *Die Augenzeugen, Deutsche Feldpostbriefe in Kriegs- und Nachkriegszeit 1914–1933* (Essen, 1997), p. 78.

a comrade had been upbraided by his superior officer because of his over-critical letters, and a second had been punished with a week's confinement to barracks for a letter full of supposed 'exaggerated and false information'. A third was even taken before a military tribunal because of the contents of his letters.[50] In 1918, when Johannes G. was on the Macedonian front throughout the month of October, he could not write to his parents. In all three capitals the authorities insisted that letters from home to the front should be reassuring. This is certainly the case with the light-hearted letters from Elizabeth Fernside to her son.[51] William Proctor[52] writing to his son takes comfort in God's providence. But Edie (Edith) Bennet[53] shatters the convention: she complains about air raids, shortages, the Spanish Influenza in 1918 and, most disturbingly of all, about her own family. Eva Isaacs[54] is much more stoical, perhaps a reflection of what she understood as the conventions of her social class. Of course, her material conditions were much more favourable, despite inconveniences, and she was able to escape the bombing by going to the countryside. Nevertheless her letters show intense anxiety and longing created by separation and also encompass sadness in 1915 when she miscarried.

The post was a way of ensuring the continuity of family presence, particularly if actual encounters were very widely spaced. The situation was particularly painful for French soldiers for, until July 1915, they were granted no leave periods, while the German authorities authorized them from the beginning of the war. For this reason, the French soldier Jean H., who left at the beginning of August 1914, did not see his parents again until 9 March 1915 during a brief stay of five days in the military zone (Auxi-le-Chateau); he was not to go on official leave until 1 August 1915 and would see his parents during a visit to Champagne on 1 November 1915. As a result, in order to stay in touch, people had to write. The family became a veritable letter factory, turning out all sorts of letters, notebooks, personal diaries, and newspaper cuttings. Contemporaries wrote a great deal, no doubt because they knew they were living through a disturbing and unprecedented period. Emile H., father of Jean, began his war diary a few weeks before the declaration of war, on 15 June, when the family settled in Brittany for the summer. Since this particular parent kept no other diary, we may suspect that he began to write retrospectively when the threats of war were proliferating, or perhaps at the moment of his son's mobilization. It was also his

[50] Private foundation, Family G., Berlin, Adalbert G. to Hulda G., 22/4/1917, 24/9/1917.
[51] Fernside Letters: Imperial War Museum. [52] Proctor Letters: Imperial War Museum.
[53] Bennet Letters: Imperial War Museum. [54] Isaacs Letters: Imperial War Museum.

first summer since his retirement. Apart from the diary, which he wrote from 13 August 1914 until 30 November 1916, the day of his death, he wrote 307 letters of which he kept copies. In addition he recopied all the letters from his son as well as his own diary which he sent to Jean so that at the front he could see his family coming and going on their ordinary activities. On the other hand, M. Remon, a teacher at the Lycée Carnot in Paris[55] seems to have been less assiduous in writing letters to his son-in-law Georges, but he noted his daily activities, and all the day's news, in a Hachette diary filled in every day of the war.

The German soldier Adalbert G. wrote daily from the front because he knew that his parents were concerned and waited impatiently for the postman every day.[56] The surviving correspondence shows that sometimes he wrote twice a day. His brother Johannes, on the other hand, wrote irregularly, and his brother Adalbert complained that he left him without news. Adalbert also corresponded with his former colleagues at the teaching college, and thus received news from other parts of the front.[57]

With the letters, photographs were exchanged too. Everywhere, couples and their children went to be photographed before the departure: many such images were found on the bodies of the dead in the trenches.[58] At the front itself, soldiers had themselves photographed, alone or with their friends, and sent the snapshots to their family. Parents were delighted: he's just the same, he hasn't changed, he's well. The H.s thanked their sons for two photographs: 'How happy we were to see you! So happy that we both began to weep while we looked at it. In fact we think you have grown and your face has filled out: as to your bodily physique, we can see that you are well set up' (2 February 1915). In September 1915, Emile H. was able to look at twenty-one little photographs sent from the front. He put the photo of the trenches in a little frame and could see it when he was writing to Jean.[59] After the death of a soldier, their family would have numerous copies made to distribute to those close to them.[60]

---

[55] DE Fonds Remon, Archives de Paris. These are notes written each day in a Hachette almanac by a teacher at the Lycée Carnot. We thank Elise Julien for alerting us to this source.
[56] Private collection, Family G., Berlin (Adalbert G. to Hulda G., 29/3/1917).
[57] Private collection, Family G. (A. to Hulda, 18/9/1916).
[58] Michelle Perrot, *Histoire de la vie privée*, p. 169.
[59] *Heures de guerre*, private archives, Family A.
[60] Private archives, Family M.; DEI Archives Remon, Archives de Paris.

When leave approached, the soldier's bedroom was scrupulously cleaned, but some families went even further and organized a sort of private cult within the household to bring themselves even closer to their children who had gone off to fight. Emile, father of Jean H., set up what he called his 'army museum', a showcase in which he displayed photos and objects sent by his son at the front: 'Your little photos are in my army museum with your little tuft, the epaulette, cartridge, etc. Send us more of them', he wrote to Jean on 21 May 1915.[61] There was box-wood that had been blessed, and every day the family came together in the room and 'we say hello to you, to your big portrait and also in the group' (8 February 1915).[62]

The family as centre of production and consumption

The circulation of products within families between town and country, and also between towns, was already current practice before the war; children, students for example, were sent packets and cases full of food supplies: butter, wine, cakes, sausages, pâtés, fruit.[63] Such dispatches increased greatly during the war, and created vital links between families at home in Paris, Berlin, or London and soldiers in the trenches – but, depending on the city, the purpose of the exchanges could differ considerably.

From the beginning of September 1914, Jean H. set out precise requests in his letters from the front:[64] apart from money, he wanted a fisherman – style sweater, socks, and tobacco. Purchasing began for him, which would last for the whole war, at a remarkable rate – at some periods, a parcel went off every day. It was not always easy to find what Jean wanted; some items could be found in the Grands Magasins du Louvre where his father had worked, but sometimes specialist shops had to be found – and hands were put to work too. For weeks and months, Jean's mother made up cigarettes, sewed, repaired, and even learned to knit.[65] She made up the parcels very carefully, stitching them into canvas, and then queued at various places to send them off. During the years

---

[61] *Heures de guerre*, private archives, Family A.

[62] Annette Becker, *Maurice Halbwachs. Un intellectuel en guerres mondiales, 1914–1945* (Paris, 2003), pp. 57–8.

[63] Caroline Chotard-Lioret, *La solidarité familiale en province: une correspondance privée entre 1870 et 1920*, thèse, Université de Paris V, 1983; Alfred Weber, *Ausgewählter Briefwechsel*, ed. by Eberhard Demm and Hartmut Soell, Alfred Weber-Gesamtausgabe, vol. x, 1 (Marburg, 2003), letters nos. 6, 7, 12, 14, 17, from the years 1888 and 1889, pp. 53, 57s, 71, 75s, 81, 87, 93.

[64] *Heures de guerre*, private archives, Family A.   [65] Ibid. 18 September 1915.

1914–16 hundreds of pairs of socks, dozens of shirts, underpants, jackets, suits, pairs of boots, lighting materials, batteries (one every week), paper, tobacco, were sent, quite apart from food: canned food of all kinds, spirits, pâtés, chocolate, sweets, from this one Parisian family to their son at the front.

Fortunately the father was retired and the mother did not work outside the home. There she laboured in a small workshop devoted to her son and to the making up of cigarettes, socks and mufflers, to preparing cakes and other sweet items, to wrapping up parcels, writing, cutting out. Emile H. noted that 'She [mother] did nothing but knit the whole time, night and day, like a Fury.' In other families, brothers, sisters, the old aunt who lived with them, all had to work together in a matching spirit of sacrifice, in the hope of improving the comfort, so uncertain, of the combatants. Their hope was to improve their capacity to survive, to stand up to the cold, the hunger, the despair, the loneliness.

Furthermore, Emile H. sent a money order each week for 20 francs. Approximate reckoning shows an overall figure of 2,160 francs sent up to November 1916. The father's pension was 60 francs a month, to which was added income from rents and shares. As Jean himself recognized, his family 'sacrificed itself' for its only son.[66] The specificity of Jean's requests is striking. On 30 October 1914, in the midst of a battle, he wrote, 'In a recent letter you told me to ask for anything I needed. I would like, if you can manage it, in return for taking the money out of what you send me, some *boots*'. There followed a very precise description of the desired boots, with a sketch and a method of despatch. His parents had great trouble in finding the boots, which was not easy. 'There is nothing left, anywhere. The Government requisitions leather and leather-workers.' But this was Paris, a city which was still highly industrialized, with its factories and thousands of small workshops, and someone was found who could make the boots in about two weeks. But even in Paris some articles were unobtainable, with all industrial production directed to war needs. Emile could not find anywhere a camera for taking small format snaphots such as Jean wanted, for all had been sold at the outbreak of war (8 March 1915). On 6 June 1915, still no camera 'in this small calibre format', so Emile's alternative present for Jean's birthday was 'a small Lip chronometer with wrist strap'. On 17 June 1915 Emile sent his son his own compass. Jean asked for a torch and spare batteries. Emile explained: 'This item has become very rare, I was able to get one at the Louvre, which was hidden away' (23 December 1914). Jean also thought of his

---

[66] We should remember that in October 1915 an ordinary soldier was paid 30 sous and a corporal 12 francs per month.

comrades: 'send the L's [friends] the balaclava helmet, I won't wear it but I can give it to someone who doesn't get anything' (26 December 1914). For there were those too: in January 1915, Jean explained, 'all those who like me have money are very happy' – with the underlying message that not everyone was so fortunate, and many were totally without these family relationships.

The contrast between Paris and Berlin was striking. While French families sent parcels to the front, in Germany this support worked in both directions. Of course, small packages were sent to the soldiers with cigarettes, newspapers, woollen socks, books, etc., but, with the terrible crises of food supplies resulting from the British blockade and the chaotic distribution system for food products in Germany, it was the soldiers in the occupied territories who sent home not only small packets but in some cases even great trunks and boxes full of all that was lacking in Berlin.

When Johanna We.'s father[67] came home on leave in December 1916, he brought first a box containing 20 kg of butter – and, next day, a trunk of which the weight was not noted but since its freight cost was the considerable sum of 14 marks (around 100 euros), we may imagine the scale of provisions: meat, sausage, cheese, potatoes. Johanna wrote: 'In heaven's name, no one must know that we have so much food.'[68] Fortunately her father was serving in the rear rather than in the trenches, and he continued to send his family enormous parcels (in particular, pork and smoked meat by the kilo, as well as sugar and matches, even if he had to restrict himself to dry bread and what he called 'cattle fodder').[69] An alternative was also to send such provisions with a comrade going on leave. What could be bought with ration cards amounted to only around 1,000 calories per day, a third of the daily requirement for health.

When the bread ration was reduced yet again in June 1918, Johanna wrote in her diary: 'One can only admire those who are content with 7 pounds of potatoes and 40 g of butter, and from time to time a little jam and gruel. That is not enough for us and if father and Aunt Martha did not send us food fairly often, we would die of hunger.'[70] The father, who was comfortably settled in occupied France, near Aulnoye, and who seemed to have been on reasonably good terms with his lodging housewife (at least once in one of the father's letters, she added some friendly words for his family[71]), even managed to rent a small field where he planted

---

[67] Private collection, Johanna We., Berlin.
[68] Private collection, Johanna We. (Johanna We.'s diary, 7/12/1916, fol.1r).
[69] Private collection, Johanna We. G.We. to J.We. 15/5/1917.
[70] Private collection, Johanna We. (diary 1916/1918, fol. 36r).
[71] Private collection Johanna We., G.We. to J. We., 6/2/1915.

potatoes, onions, salads, beans, and beetroot and raised rabbits, a genuine idyll. He was thus able to send plentiful provisions to his family. The family thanked him by sending cakes.[72]

The artist Käthe Kollwitz, reasonably prosperous since her husband was a doctor, sent her son Hans, who was a medical attendant, initially on the Belgian front and then in Poland, a quantity of small packets because the weight of such items was limited to 500 g,[73] with woollen goods, shoes, confectionery, books, and a pen.[74] When Hans began to spend time with officers, he asked for various articles to be sent for his social encounters, including cigars, Schnapps and cognac, and also language methods.[75] During the 'turnip winter', when food supplies were particularly difficult in Germany, Hans was asked to send items in his turn, including bacon and flour, and his mother even sent him a clean pillowcase for him to fill with flour.[76] A lively exchange of parcels now began, Käthe always sending money, cigars, long trousers, socks, linen underwear and also woollen goods since they were now rationed.[77] For his part, Hans sent some food parcels,[78] but since he was stationed in Rumania, he was able to send vast cases with flour, beans, peas, oil, and even bread, sugar, coffee, and more than 100 eggs.[79] On 7 June 1917, his mother asked him not to send anything more because she had enough provisions for the winter. In December 1917 Hans took up sending parcels once more,[80] and continued to send whole cases with provisions until the war ended.

In less prosperous circles, naturally, the parcels were more modest. Soldier Adalbert G.,[81] son of a minor employee, received packets with soles, a pair of scissors, galoshes, apples, a bar of chocolate, cakes, gooseberries, sweets, sometimes medicaments and, depending on the front, French or Polish dictionaries.[82] Adalbert G. himself rarely had the opportunity or the money to send them anything, although in August and September 1918 his brother Johannes at least managed to send thirty

---

[72] Private collection, Johanna We. (G.We. to J.We. 15/5/1917).

[73] K. Kollwitz, *Briefe an den Sohn 1904–1945*, ed. Jutta Bohnke-Kollwitz (Berlin, 1992) (K.B.).

[74] K.B., 4/1/1915, p. 96; 29/1/1915, p. 100; 8/11/16, p. 131; 18/9/1916, p. 126.

[75] K.B., 8/11/1916, p. 13. 2/2/17, p. 134, 3/2/17, p. 135, 18/2/17, p. 135.

[76] K.B., 11/3/17, p. 139.

[77] K.B., 17/3/17, p. 142; 21/3/17, p. 143; 9/4/17, p. 146, 16/4/17, p. 148.

[78] K.B., 17/3/17, p. 142.

[79] K.B., 26/3/17, p. 145; 22/4/17, p. 150; 1/5/17, p. 152; 31/5/17, p. 154.

[80] K.B., 6/12/17 and 15/12/17, p. 159; 1/2/18, p. 164.

[81] Private collection, Family G., Berlin.

[82] G. collection (A. G. to Paul G., 19/3/1916, 26/7/1916, 26/2/1917, to Johannes G., 26/3/1916, to his parents 21/7/1917).

parcels with meat, peas, and corn flour, and he even had 100 Marks sent to him by his parents to supply them in this way. These examples show the range of styles of exchange between Parisian and Berlin families. Paris sustained the front. Berlin was provisioned not from the front, but above all from the rear, in other words from the occupied territories.

Family relationships

Further detailed analysis of family relationships, as displayed in letters and notebooks, takes us into the heart of a family intimacy under pressure during the war. We can explore diffidently only certain aspects of these son–parent relations, in particular the sorrow of fathers facing up to the departure or death of a son. There is the heartbreak of Emile Durkheim learning of the death of his son and the distress of the mother of Apollinaire throughout his period at the front, and after his death.[83] Such wounds never healed, and historians tread in such delicate terrain with caution. There is an evident limit to what we can know about the history of emotion in wartime.

Fathers and sons

Newspaper clippings kept by a father living at the gates of Paris give a view of the shared sense of war experience some families nurtured and pre-served. The document is called '*Heures de guerre*', like a medieval book of hours, it is the sacred story of the son, on the battlefield, whose life at the front is the centrepiece of the family.[84] Then there is a section termed 'Pendant la guerre', documenting the story of the father (and of his wife from time to time when the father is ill) who day in, day out endures this terrible test and notes all that he does (visits, shopping, walks, adminis-trative activities). The father follows the son and to a degree lives through him and his ordeal. All or nearly all his life turns round him, recalling perhaps the relationship between a mother and her newborn son.[85] After a period of references to the war of 1870, he focuses on defence of the interests of family and home: 'I won't speak to you about the war: you see enough of it as it is, and then anything that is not personal to you is of no concern to me', he wrote on 1 July 1915.

---

[83] Catherine Rollet, ' "The other war" II: Setbacks in public health', in *Capital Cities at War*, vol. I, pp. 484–5.
[84] *Heures de guerre*, private archives, Family A.
[85] T. Berry Brazelton and B. Cramer in their book, *Les premiers liens: l'attachement parents–bébé vu par un pédiatre et par un psychiatre* (Paris, 1991).

The H. family lived in Neuilly, the wealthiest suburb of Paris. Born in 1857, Emile H. was nearly fifty-six years old, suffered from a heart condition and had retired early after a career working for the Grands Magasins du Louvre. Having joined the company very young, he attracted his employers' attention, who gave him increasingly important functions until he ended as the shop's chief accountant. His trajectory was one of social advancement. Of his wife (the couple married in 1889), little is known; she was born in 1868, she looked after the household and accompanied her husband in most of his activities. When he was ill she took her turn in writing to their son. 'And I too, I send you all my love, I am not writing to you since Father and his diary leave me nothing to say; but I sew, and make up parcels, I am working a little bit for you.' (23 February 1915). The closeness of the pair to their son is unmistakable and indeed Jean responds with equal feeling, ending his letters with the salutation 'With all my love'.

He was an only son, twenty-one years old (born on 22 April 1893), and did his military service in the cavalry; on 16 June 1914 he still had 828 days of service to accomplish! Knowing of his father's heart condition, Jean spared him the worst in his letters and even attempted to raise his morale. At his father's suggestion to report sick, Jean even gave him a lesson in ethics: to be discharged for 'neuralgia', and then to find himself 'between a man with a leg missing and another with a bullet in his stomach?' or to hide away at Headquarters? That was not his duty. But sometimes, his despair and sadness were such that he forgot his caution, although he reproached himself for it later. In his letter of 14 December 1914, Jean spoke without dissembling:

I have nothing new to tell you, I am writing virtually out of despair today; I could almost weep with this odd sense of oppression, 130 days spent in which we see nothing but uniforms. I don't even know what to write on this sheet of paper. Far off we can see the light of shell-bursts. When will it be finished? I have a friend who has five brothers who all set out with him, that means six of them. Four are killed, one is wounded, he is unhurt. I am pretty well. You never write about yourselves.

The father spoke of his loneliness: on 28 January 1915 he went for a walk alone in the Bois de Boulogne. It was fine and cold, the sky was blue. At the junction of two avenues, he realized that as far as the eye could see, not a single pedestrian or vehicle was visible. 'I am alone' – the loneliness of a father during the war, at the gates of a capital city.

Finally, in March 1915, a family visit was organized to Montigny-les-Jongleurs in the Somme. Jean advised his parents not to make themselves conspicuous because such visits were not authorized. On 9 March they managed to meet: 'Joy, hugs. How handsome he is, and strong, and well!'

They passed a day together and met some of Jean's friends. These parents, as exemplary as any, had managed to break the taboo of military regulations to meet their son and they declared themselves determined not to hesitate, and even hoped to repeat the exercise: as soon as Jean would let them know, they would 'slip away' to meet him in his rest camp.

Morale was so high that on their return, to his wife's astonishment the father began to sing as he used to do as he dressed in the morning. As in the old days, as before. The correspondence shows clearly the effect of the inter-relationship between Jean's circumstances and those of his father, at the level of well-being and health. Alternating moments of expectation, despair, satisfaction, or joy led the father in particular to the limit of his strength and triggered several cardiac crises before the final one which caused his death in November 1916. The son was to live, and survive even a serious head wound. The father was the casualty of war.

Mothers and sons

Käthe Kollwitz[86] had two sons, Hans and Peter, but felt closer to Peter, the younger of the two. In August 1914 this young man of eighteen enlisted in the German army, with his parents' hesitant blessing. On 22 October 1914 he was killed in Belgium. The story of his parents' mourning and his mother's long journey towards sculpting a war memorial in his honour are well known. Less attention has been paid to the Kollwitz's relationship with her surviving son, Hans.

Hans had enlisted in the cavalry, and was discharged after a fall from his horse. In October he trained as a medical attendant, undoubtedly less dangerous, but who knows? His parents were afraid. His father Karl offered to write to the Ministry so that Hans would not be sent to the front, to his wife's embarrassment.[87] She took comfort in imagining that Peter, dead, took care of his brother as his guardian angel, for it was at the moment of Peter's death in action that Hans had decided to join the hospital service.[88] When Hans was at the front and she received no letters, she was uneasy, but her comments on this point are much briefer than her remarks about Peter.[89] Sometimes she was seized with panic over

---

[86] K.B., p. 168. (K.T.) K. Kollwitz, *Briefe an den Sohn 1904–1945*, ed. Jutta Bohnke Kollwitz (Berlin, 1992) (K.B.) for a psychohistorical interpretation of her diary, cf. R. Schulte, 'Käthe Kollwitz's sacrifice', *History Workshop Journal* 41 (1996), pp. 193–221.
[87] K.T., 27.11.14.   [88] K.B., 25.11.17, p. 157.
[89] K.T., 23.1.16, p. 216; 31.3.16, p. 232.

Hans too: 'One sacrifice is enough, Hans, one is enough', she wrote in 29 January 1915 to her son, and on 29 April 1915, 'Who can promise me that you will return?'[90] When Hans was home on leave, she constantly compared him to Peter and the comparison was not in his favour. 'He is back but Peter will never come back again [. . .] Hans is calm, he has always been calm, Peter was lively. [. . .] Hans is intellectually inactive, he does not think a great deal and he does not like thinking.'[91]

This incessant confrontation with the war through her sons informed Käthe Kollwitz's emerging pacifist and socialist perspective, and her hatred of nationalistic phrases: 'Died for his country – what a horrible tragedy, what a triumph of the hell which hides behind the smooth mask of these words.'[92] In 1917 she took part twice in a peace demonstration in Berlin, although she did not support the cause with particular strength.[93]

Paul G.'s family was much more modest.[94] Paul G., born in 1874, was a minor employee in the Alcohol Control office (*Staatliche Spiritus-Zentrale*), his wife Hulda was a housewife, and the pair had four children: the eldest son, Adalbert, born in 1896, had just completed his training as a junior school teacher and had been teaching for a few months at the Berlin-Treptow primary school,[95] but continued to live with his parents in their small flat in Lehrter Straße in the Berlin suburb of Weißensee – which had neither gas nor electricity and where lighting still meant a petrol lamp.[96] He had socialist leanings, fulminated against the officers' privileges and had works by Karl Marx sent to him at the front.[97] He frequently criticized the authorities: 'But as anyone can see, the authorities do whatever they want with the people', he wrote on 19 January 1917, when no bread and potatoes were available. His younger brother Johannes, born in 1897, began as a minor clerk in the Berlin-Weissensee local authority and also lived at home with their two sisters: Paula, born in 1904, went to a private girls' school and the youngest of the family, Gerda – nicknamed Gerdalein, or 'little Gerda' – was born in 1911.[98] In February 1916 Adalbert G. was conscripted and sent to Rosheim

---

[90] K.B., p.100, p. 109.   [91] K.T., 5/16–5/5/16, p. 241 s.
[92] K.T., 22/4/1916, p. 239.   [93] K.T., 26/11/17, p. 158, 16/12/17.
[94] Private collection, Family G., Berlin.
[95] G. collection (his pupils sent him cards, cf. A. G. to Johannes G., 26/3/1916).
[96] G. collection (A. G. to his parents, 18/8/1917).
[97] G. collection (A. G. to his parents, 18/8/1917).
[98] Unfortunately, this private collection contains very few letters from the parents, but almost daily letters from Adalbert to his parents between March 1916 and September 1917, from which the many references to family life enable us to perceive some aspects of home life in Berlin.

(in Lower Alsace) for military training.[99] Johannes, the younger brother, also risked being called up, but his family hoped that he would be spared for the time being.[100] This was only a respite; one day it would be his turn, and Adalbert wrote to his sister Paula, 'Be happy that you are a girl.'[101] In September their ageing father was called to the army, and in mid-October it was Johannes's turn. He was sent to Silesia for military training,[102] where Adalbert visited him during his second period of leave in Berlin.[103] In January Johannes was sent to the Rumanian front,[104] and his parents feared that he would not return alive. Adalbert tried to dispel their fears, 'Why should he not come back? I have come back after all, and will come back again. And it's not so bad against the Russians as it is against the French and English artillery.' And he explained that he would even volunteer for the Eastern Front in order to avoid being sent back to the Somme.[105]

And indeed he was able to keep this promise: at the end of February he departed on a train to Galicia,[106] where he remained until June in reasonable conditions. Then he was sent to the Western Front again, where the dangers of the situation and the wrangling among the officers exasperated him to the point where he no longer hid the truth from his parents. He was forced to undertake useless and dangerous patrols at night in the rain, to capture a British soldier while the company leader rested in his dugout, well protected from the shells. His unvarnished comments and descriptions from the front exacerbated his parents' fears considerably and in one of the few letters from his mother that have survived, she wrote to him on 3 December 1917: 'I imagined you were already back in the line, and as it is now so cold and stormy, with ice and snow, I was so worried about you yet again . . . Now at least we know that at this moment, you are protected against the cold and danger, at least a little bit . . . Still the war rages. Will the madness never end?'[107] This letter did not reach its destination, but was sent back to the parents marked: 'Returned! Fallen on the field of Honour!' Early in December 1917, Adalbert was killed near Ypres.

[99] G. collection (A.G. to Paul G., 4/3/1916).
[100] G. collection (A.G. to Johannes G., 26/3/1916).
[101] G. collection (A.G. to Paula G., 28/7/1916).
[102] G. collection (A.G. to Hulda G., 12/10/1916).
[103] G. collection (A.G. to Paul G., 20/11/1916 and 11/1/1917).
[104] G. collection (A.G. to his parents, 19/1 and 21/1/1917).
[105] G. collection (A.G. to his parents, 21/1/1917).
[106] G. collection (A.G. to his parents, 21/2/ and 25/2/1917).
[107] G. collection (Hulda G. to A.G., 3/12/1917).

Married couples

Whether a couple was young or old, the separation imposed by the war was in most cases a difficult experience. Opportunities to meet were rare during the conflict. In France, an order of 28 August 1914 ruled out the possibility that men at base camps could bring their wives and families to be near them. Despite the recommendation of the Medical Academy to raise the prohibition, pressures of all kinds and the impressive number of those breaking the order, notably officers, the army maintained this position throughout the war.[108]

The departing husbands were not always young men, and the call-up of older men frequently created difficult situations for wives and families. In the summer of 1916 the family of the low-ranking employee Paul G. already had a son at the front, and it was feared that his younger brother would soon be called up in his turn. But in September, to their great surprise, it was not the son but the ageing father, his hair already white, who was summoned to the colours to serve in the territorial army reserve, and who was apparently to be sent immediately to the front. To the family it seemed barely credible: 'Now this is a cruel blow, and especially hard for you. Papa is in the army ... How can this be possible? I still hope that he will be discharged.'[109] Adalbert tried to comfort his despairing mother, explaining that his father would perhaps serve only in a barracks, and that even at the front, the soldiers were not always in the front line but from time to time put in the reserve or at rest.[110] But he knew his mother, and knew that she would be unbearably anxious: 'I see you now [at 3 a.m.] lying sleepless and restless. You are troubled by images and thoughts of Papa and these cannot help him.' Despite his marxist beliefs, he turned towards God. 'And then, I know you trust in God and plead with him for our sake. I too have gone down on my knees to pray that God give you strength and keep Papa from harm.'[111]

The father's absence also had material consequences for their families, and soldiers knew it. Rationing problems had already affected the family, and the mother was forced to join the 'Nahrungsmittel-Polonaise' a humorous expression referring to queuing for hours, sometimes the whole day.[112] Adalbert was afraid of not getting enough to eat when he was in Berlin on leave.[113] But now, with the father away, the situation was much

[108] Le Naour, *Misères et tourments*, pp. 360–72, on wives who visited.
[109] G. collection (A. to Hulda G., 10/9/1916).
[110] G. collection (A. to Hulda G., 18/9/1916).
[111] G. collection (A. to Hulda G., 18/9/1916).
[112] G. collection (A. to Johannes G., 26/3/1916, to Paul G., 11/6/1916).
[113] G. collection (A.G. to his parents, 26/7/1916).

more dramatic. Could the family live on the allowances available to soldiers' families? Did the traders' mutual support association give them something? The mother chose not to answer these pressing questions from Adalbert.[114]

When the younger brother Johannes was called into the army in October, it was the last straw: alone with her two daughters, the mother could no longer cope. She fell ill and sent an urgent request for Adalbert to return on leave.[115] But Adalbert was unwell after a short period in the trenches of the Somme and was currently in a sanatorium in Belgium. He could not get leave, he wrote: 'Convalescents cannot get a furlough from here.'[116] At the end of October Adalbert, once more at the front, was indeed able to return to Berlin unexpectedly on leave. In mid-November, to his great surprise he had a second period leave of two weeks for convalescence.[117] The family increased its demands to have the father discharged, but the matter trailed on.[118] The mayor of Weißensee advised Frau G. to obtain a declaration from her husband's employer, 'that Paul is an indispensable employee and that the company has war contracts'. But that suggestion was the limit of the company's intervention.[119] Despite this disappointment, Paul G. was lucky, for on 2 December he returned to Berlin.[120] However, he was formally only discharged for a limited period – a very common practice – and his call-up could have happened at any moment. For the rest of the war, the family did not escape the gnawing fear that their father would be called up again.[121] Adalbert wrote home about soldiers who had to return to the front: 'If only Papa could be spared that.'[122] Fortunately, after a sudden recall to the front in April 1917 which was miraculously cancelled two days later,[123] the father was able to remain in Berlin and even seemed better able to earn his living since, several months later, in September 1917, the family moved from the drab suburb of Weißensee to one of Berlin's smartest and most expensive areas, the 'Hansa' district at the heart of the Tiergarten.

The correspondence of the Bennets and the Isaacs in London are also very enlightening on this topic. This time, the main protagonists are

---

[114] G. collection (A. to Hulda G., 18/9/1916).
[115] G. collection (A. to Hulda G., 9/10/1916).
[116] G. collection (A. to Hulda G., 9/10/1916).
[117] G. collection (A. to Paul G., 28/10/1916).
[118] G. collection (Hulda to Paul G., 3/11/1916; A. to Paul G., 4/11/1916 and 16/11/1916).
[119] G. collection (A. to Paul G., 17/11 and 22/11/1916).
[120] G. collection (A.G. to his parents, 2/12/1916).
[121] G. collection (A.G. to his parents, 19/1 and 21/1/1917).
[122] G. collection (A. to Hulda G., 11/1/1917).
[123] G. collection (A.G. to his parents, 15/4/1917).

young women and their husbands. At times Eva Isaacs[124] wrote every day to her husband who was posted first to a home garrison and then to France. This young woman, eighteen years old in 1914, continued to sustain her married life through her letters. 'I am immensely proud of you', she wrote on 12 August 1914, 'and I am glad to think you are soldiering while we are at war, though you know how much I would give to have you with me ... that you are doing the only thing that is right and worthy of a man, makes it easier to bear being apart from you.' And again on 10 December 1916: 'I feel so proud dearest when they ask me where my husband is and I can reply simply "on the Somme".' She tells her husband about her health (after a miscarriage she became pregnant again, following his time on leave); she tells him of her discoveries (such as the role of breast-feeding in the spacing of births); she asks him about his wishes and shares with him her thoughts on the idea of having another baby.[125] She tells her husband about her dreams: 'I dreamed of you again last night: that I was at the front as a big push was in process ... I lifted a curtain and stepped into the trenches, it was all dark and I threw a bomb. The funny thing was that you were in dancing pumps.'[126] Here is a rare glimpse of the emotional life of very young married couples who, despite the difficulties of the separation, constructed their life as a couple, as if their private history was independent of the history of the war, and as if letters helped her create a kind of protective bubble around her husband and herself.

Like Eva Isaacs, Edith Bennet[127] dreamed of her husband. On 16 May 1918, she wrote: 'I had you home in my dreams last night, but you said you were on 12 months leave & was going to take Ruby and I back to India with you. You did look well in civvies, that old grey suit that I am keeping for you', She also kept him informed of all the details of her life, and did not hesitate to share her problems with him.

Eva Isaacs's and Edith Bennet's husbands survived the war: others not so fortunate reacted with violence to their husband's death. The *Daily Express* reported: 'Oh mummie, I have done for myself, I am going to Cecil.' These were the dying words of Mrs Sybil Griffin, the eighteen-year-old widow of an officer who shot herself with a sporting gun at Chester Terrace. 'It was stated at the inquest at Marylebone yesterday that she had been married only seven months when her husband was killed.'[128]

---

[124] Isaacs Letters, Imperial War Museum.
[125] Isaacs Letters, 14 and 23 December 1916.   [126] Isaacs Letters, 23 January 1917.
[127] Bennet Letters, Imperial War museum.
[128] Taken from the *Daily Express*, cited in James McMillan, *The way it was 1914–1934* (London, 1979), p. 73.

Moments of truth?

It should not be thought that all soldiers' wives were model spouses, as shown in personal correspondence. Police and court files often give a very different image. Here we frequently see the woman in another light, the unfaithful wife who amuses herself with other men while her husband sacrifices himself in the trenches. The omnipresent censor suppressed more explicit references to adultery in the media, in novels,[129] and even in songs. The song of a man on leave, 'Oh, how I love you', with the lines: 'I even think that to console yourself/you let yourself be pecked at by the sergeant' was suppressed by the censor,[130] but he could not remove all suspicions over wives' conduct.

Police and court files in London and Paris present much more bloodstained cases: a London soldier explained why he killed his wife: 'I consider that I only did my duty as I did in France' said Henry Stephen Graham, a private in the Machine Gun Corps. 'I shot her with my service revolver. I went to France sixteen months ago and soon after I heard that she had sold up my home with the exception of a few things. She had left the baby to be looked after by anyone and was living an immoral life. I have letters to prove it.'[131]

In Paris, a man on leave went home 'with his suspicions' about his wife. She confessed to him that she had a lover, and he strangled her.[132] Another chose to attack the lover:

Having begged his wife in his letters, in very touching terms, to give up her adulterous relationship, Artilleryman Le Fort returned on leave to Montreuil sous Bois on 20 June last. He went immediately to the home of the man named Bry, where he knew he would find his wife. Unfortunately for him, the lover opened the door himself and was brought down with six revolver shots.

The permanent Court Martial showed great mercy. The defence declared that 'to take the wife of a *poilu* exposed the guilty man to a sort of professional risk' and demanded a light penalty 'on principle'. The man on leave was 'acquitted, to public acclaim'.[133]

Cases of such violence were relatively rare. Sometimes there were bloody reprisals; sometimes couples found reconciliation. In many cases

---

[129] Eberhard Demm, 'Barbusse et son feu: la dernière cartouche de la propagande de guerre française', in *Guerres mondiales et conflits contemporains* 197 (2000), pp. 43–63, here p. 49.

[130] Police préfecture archives, Paris, series B.A. (censor), carton 697; Eberhard Demm, 'La chanson française pendant la Grande Guerre' in: François Genton (ed.), 'La guerre en chanson', *Chroniques allemandes*, 11 (2004).

[131] McMillan, *The way it was*, p. 73.

[132] Police préfecture, daily register, quarter 76 Register 51, case no. 389, 21–4.1916.

[133] PFBA1587, *Physionomie de Paris*, 11–12.1917, Le Palais (de Justice).

the wife invoked the fact of her husband's brutal behaviour before the war, saying that she took the opportunity of his absence to run away or to live with someone else. In these cases the war simply accelerated the break-up of a pair who were already mismatched. For many couples, the war created a coolness: with each of the spouses having lived separately for several years – up to five years – their experiences and ways of life had distanced them from each other.

It is not surprising, therefore, that in Paris the number of divorces, which diminished sharply up to 1915 (only 315 divorces that year[134] against 3,055 in 1913), increased again up to 4,404 divorces in 1920. Related to 10,000 marriages, the number of divorces was nonetheless slightly lower in relation to the pre-war period (956 divorces for 10,000 marriages in 1913, 180 in 1915, and 818 in 1920), for the people of Paris had rushed to remarry at the end of the war (53,820 marriages in 1920 instead of around 30,000 before the war). English (as opposed to London) divorce actions rose from 1,387 in 1915 to 3,033 in 1917, and of these 1,900 were initiated by soldiers.[135] In Berlin, the divorce rate evolved less spectacularly in terms of absolute figures: 2,323 divorces in 1913, 1,295 in 1917, and 2,222 in 1919 – but for 10,000 marriages the increase is much more apparent since the recovery in the rate of marriages was less robust: 1,104 divorces for 10,000 marriages in 1913, 834 in 1915, 980 in 1917, and 1,485 in 1920.[136] Some of these divorces probably concerned hasty wartime marriages, often undertaken to obtain separation allowances or to legitimize children. It is possible that the wartime idealization of marital relationships led to post-war disillusionment within marriages when the business of day-to-day living with the idealized loved-one resumed.

Even if relationships with sons and husbands remain central to our understanding of family life in wartime, there is evidence of other important familial relationships. The experience of the Yorkshire-born nurse Vera Brittain, is particularly arresting on this matter. At the age of twenty she was engaged to a friend of her brother Edward, Roland Leighton. Like, no doubt, many of her contemporaries, 'she would have liked to be a man so as to be able to enlist'.[137] This, indirectly, is what she tried to do by giving up her place at Oxford University and joining the nursing

---

[134] H. Fougerol, *Condition civile des mobilisés*, 1916.

[135] *Daily Mail*, 'War weddings', 18 August 1915; *Daily Mail*, 'Faithless wives', 11 December 1918.

[136] *Statistik des Deutschen Reiches*, vol. 276, Bewegung der Bevölkerung in den Jahren 1914–1919 (Berlin, 1922), p. xxxii, vol. 39, Bewegung der Bevölkerung im Jahre 1913 (Berlin, 1918), p. 49.

[137] Stéphane Audoin-Rouzeau, *Cinq deuils de guerre* (Paris, 2001), p. 20.

service in London, thereby moving closer to Roland and to the war. The long list of men killed in action that she read in *The Times* and which she noted in her diary only increased her anguished feelings about her fiancé. And indeed Roland died on 21 December 1915, at the age of twenty. 'Everything was given to me, and then taken away, in a single year', she wrote.[138] After Roland's death, one of their closest mutual friends was killed, and then it was her brother Edward's turn. He died in Italy in June 1918. Her despair was overwhelming.[139] It took her years to work through her grief and to restart her life with a young man of her own generation.

More restrained, more delicate, but also very evocative is the narrative of Clare, Roland's young sister, aged sixteen at her brother's death. Was it she who decided, with her father, to keep the uniform with its blood-stains of her dead brother? How did she live through this brutal loss? Indeed, in August 1980, in her preface to a new edition of Vera Brittain's war journal, she wrote, 'I feel as shattered as I did after the death of my brother.'[140]

Young children with fathers at the front

In the case of children, historians need to be even more diffident. There is very little direct material, some drawings and school essays, letters, personal diaries written by the older children and then autobiographies – but these recreate the experience of the war after the event. Yet some insights can be gained. At Christmas, parents tried not to let the war weigh too heavily on their young children's lives: protecting them was a concern. Edith wrote to her husband,[141] 'It's the kids that worry you. They must live on something. Can't get milk to make a pudding for them ...' (24 January 1918). In the case of Berlin, the only way not to let them suffer too severely from malnourishment was to send them to rural farms, a disturbing course of action in some cases. The girl Paula G. was sent to Wimpfen, near Heilbronn, as part of the measures for sending under-nourished Berlin children to country households. But she was extremely unhappy there, perhaps because she was exploited, as happened to many Berlin children, by farmers.[142]

---

[138] Audoin-Rouzeau, *Cing deuils*, p. 17.   [139] Rollet, *Les enfants*, p. 45.
[140] Audoin-Rouzeau, *Cinq deuils*, p. 51.
[141] Bennet Letters, Imperial War Museum 96/3/1.
[142] G. Collection, Johannes G. to Hulda G. 20 and 30 August, 1918; Demm, *Kinder im Krieg*, pp. 86–8.

To keep children in capitals such as Paris and London left them at risk from other dangers – aerial attack. Edith Bennet was very frightened of air-raids, and wrote to her husband in uniform

I am sure dear little Ruby and I shall be taken from you in one of these terrible raids which are getting worse every time ... When I shut my eyes I can see these huge things like great blackbirds right over us in immense quantities ... baby and I stood in the passage clenched tightly together expecting the last of our lives, so should anything happen to us your address is stuck on the wall, someone is sure to write to you ... One thing I assure you, I am quite prepared to meet our Supreme father when he calls dear Ruby and I [sic]. (9 July 1917).[143]

Emile H. described in minute detail the passage of two Zeppelins over north-west Paris during the night of 10 March 1915, forewarned by a bugle warning.[144] The couple and their neighbours remained awake from 1.30 a.m. to 3.30 a.m.: 'the clashing noise of the shells, illumination from the Mont Valérien search-lights. Father learned next day that 7 or 8 people had been hit, including one seriously. Fresh alerts on 21 and 23 March. During the air attacks on Paris, Emile and his wife took in a family with two little girls who were very frightened. One night they put the girls into the bed of their son away at the front.'

Parents sought to protect their children from excessive privation and shock, but in a different way the children were involved in the full social environment in a form of psychological combat against the enemy. In France, Britain and Germany children were mobilized at school, at church, in their reading and at leisure.[145] A whole 'war culture' aimed at children was created, so that they too could share in the national effort: school syllabus material, book contents, manual and sporting activities, all were altered to bring children into the great national cause. Overall, children experienced this 'war culture' and even internalized it, as can be seen in the case of Françoise Marette (Dolto), six years old in 1914, in a letter to her father who manufactured weapons: 'You should work harder to make shells to kill the dirty boches who are harming the poor French who are suffering from the wicked boches who are cruel and who kill children of one year and two who are suffering and are crying.'[146] But some children were unaffected by adult propaganda and let their anguish, their despair, their weariness be seen, as for example in the case of a young German girl who in 1916, at the age of fourteen, explained to her mother that 'I am simply no longer excited by the war like most

---

[143] Bennet Letters, Imperial War Museum, 96/2/1.
[144] *Heures de guerre*, private archives, Family A.
[145] Cf. Stefan Goebel, Eberhard Demm *et al.* 'Schools', above, pp. 188–234.
[146] Cited by Audoin-Rouzeau, *Cinq deuils*, p. 173.

people' and who two years later noted in her diary: 'we should no longer let ourselves be duped by the lies with which the older people have brain-washed us'.[147]

There were children who were truly traumatized. A boy of ten became depressed, not playing or eating after his father's departure to the front, and this depression reached the point that his mother was forced to seek medical help.[148] Then there were all those whose fathers had been killed in the war. France recorded a total of around 600,000 widows and 1,100,000 orphans, while Britain had 240,000 widows and 350,000 orphans.[149] This does not include all the children whose fathers were wounded or sick. Some children had only a brief personal memory of their father, departed and so often dead at the front.[150] The majority of French orphans suffered the loss of their father before their tenth year. On the other hand, during and after the war their lives were full of the cult of remembrance, organized both by their mothers as part of family memory and by society as a whole. The war memorial and photograph of the dead father[151] formed the central features of this memory. Death in wartime formed a conclusive reference point for their developing identity: a singular experience, as in the case of the Algerian childhood of Albert Camus. All that remained of his father were shell fragments taken from his body.[152] These were turned into relics, as similar objects were in metropolitan homes. Everything was done to put off the time of forgetting.[153]

With time, direct memory of the father came to be merged with or submerged beneath the memory constructed by the family and by the nation. A significant obligation imposed itself on everyone: the living had a debt they owed to the dead and the children had to play an active part in this duty of remembrance. This was a heavy inheritance to bear: some of these children had in consequence the feeling of not having had a child-hood. Some steps were taken to help them. In France, a law on the nation's 'wards' was adopted late, on 24 July 1917. A child whose father had died on active service, or whose father, mother or family support had been rendered incapable of earning a living because of wounds or illness contracted or aggravated as a result of the war, was a ward of the

---

[147] Jo Mihaly, 'Da gibt's ein Wiedersehen! Kriegstagebuch eines Mädchens' (Freiburg and Heidelberg, 1982), p. 252, p. 314; on other cases of children's autonomy, cf. Demm, *Kinder*, ch. 4, 'Die Reaktion der Kinder auf die Propaganda', pp. 115–22.

[148] K.T., p. 164.

[149] Olivier Faron, *Les enfants du deuil. Orphelins et pupilles de la nation de la première guerre mondiale (1914–1941)* (Paris, 2001).

[150] Faron, ibid., p. 36.   [151] Faron, ibid., p. 36.

[152] Albert Camus, *The first man*, trans. David Hapgood (New York, 1995), p. 82.

[153] Olivier Faron, *Les enfants*, p. 35.

state. The French National Bureau of Wards of the Nation was linked to the Ministry for State Education. The Nation's wards had acquired personal rights through their fathers' sacrifice. But the nature of these rights was not defined uniformly, each individual case being the object of an enquiry. Despite the material and educational support that they received, these children lived a very particular kind of family life: either their mother remained single and had to work, or she returned to her family or her husband's family to remain there permanently, or she remarried, in which case the child gained a step-father. Some children later remembered a sad life without male figures, others knew the complex world of reconstituted families. Here the metropolitan world differed little from that of the nation as a whole.

An uncertain death

One of the most terrible aspects of the war for families was undoubtedly for parents (and wives) not to know the fate of loved ones. Anguish trapped families during long months, and parents exhausted themselves in attempts to find out what had happened: was their son alive, wounded, a prisoner, dead? And in that case, how did he die? Living in one of the three capitals had some advantages. There was a greater range than elsewhere of sources and ways of gaining information, sometimes contradictory: the metropolis hummed with continual rumours.

One Parisian family can stand for many others.[154] A son-in-law and the three sons (out of five children) were immediately mobilized, including the youngest, Jacques, a lawyer and graduate in Oriental Languages and Political Sciences. Before leaving for the front Jacques divided his various possessions between his father (his mother had died in 1890 when he was four), his brothers and sisters and his nephews.[155] Evidently the family had received no news since a letter dated 13 August. On 10 September, the father wrote to his son-in-law: 'I don't know what to think about it. If he'd had an accident I would of course have been informed. I still hope that it's a matter of a badly organized postal service.' One of the brothers was wounded. The son-in-law enquired of the Commandant of the depôt of the 267th infantry reserve regiment to which the young lieutenant had apparently been posted. In his letter he did not hesitate to write that the request came from the two sisters of whom one 'is the wife of

---

[154] Letters. Private archives, Family M.
[155] See also the example of the Lyon soldier Georges Gélibert who made a legacy to his children on 23 September 1914 (Jean-Pierre Guéno and Yves Laplume, *Paroles de poilus. Lettres et carnets de front, 1914–1918* (Paris, 1998), pp. 176–7.

Commandant Le H., Commissioner for Railways at ...' The family mobilized its networks of social relationships at the highest level. Paris headquarters were not far away. No definite news, except rumours indicating that the lieutenant had been very seriously wounded.

The son-in-law continued the quest: he had received eye-witness information at Dreux from a man who had seen his brother-in-law fall near Guise, on the River Oise on 28 August (letter of 26 September 1914). The young man 'was apparently hit in the throat, one of the earliest in this battle in which nine-tenths of the 17th and 18th companies were rendered unfit to continue'. It was still not known whether the wound had been fatal. The father was in a state of collapse; all the family wept together. The son-in-law immediately wrote to the Red Cross and to Geneva at the end of September 1914. Other enquiries were made in the hospitals of Bordeaux. No results. Rumours flew: 'people will say anything'. An announcement in the *Echo de Paris* was tried. Finally, confirmation of Jacques's death on 9 August was given by an assistant head of President Millerand's cabinet in a letter of 29 October. The father was in despair. 'The poor boy died far from us, abandoned. Where is he now? Oh that he may not have suffered too much. I cannot go into his room or even go past it, thinking about him, without pain in my heart, and I cannot believe that he will never return.'

The son-in-law continued his efforts; he wanted to obtain a decoration for his brother-in-law. He contacted the wife of his captain who advised him to visit wounded soldiers and to write to General Franchet d'Esperey. In particular, soldiers who had been imprisoned in Germany might have information. He sought copies of soldiers' testimonies focusing on the circumstances of the battle of Monceau, in the Oise – a battle which lasted forty minutes and which killed 223 men out of 250, including the lieutenant. The twenty-seven survivors were all taken prisoner on the spot. Their stories provided the grounds for the decoration, duly noted by Army Order published on 30 July 1915.

At the time, these letters and documents were of little use to the family. The grief of the father, the brothers and sisters was such that no one went into Jacques's room until 1929. This was when they found the letters and the small legacies he had written before his departure.[156]

The efforts of M. Rémon,[157] a teacher at the Lycée Carnot, to find traces of his son-in-law Georges, traced the same trajectory. As soon as silence from the front created doubts, steps were taken, letters written, visits undertaken, support requested. This quest can be followed step by

---

[156] This older sister played an important role in the family, because of her mother's death in 1890, leaving her husband and five children between four and fifteen years old.
[157] DE1 Fonds Remon, Paris Archives.

step through the short notes written each day in a Hachette Almanach. On holiday in Royan, the family learned of the departure of Georges on 4 August 1914. Every day his father went to the Mairie to read the day's news and write out the mayor's telegrams. On 15 August a telegramme came from Troyes, on 12 September a letter came from Dreux. The family returned to Paris where Georges visited them on 29 September. After this he returned to the front, but from this time on, no news came of him. In late September, the father-in-law and his wife began to make enquiries: they went to La Courneuve, to the 'tramps' dépôt' where they saw 'a man of the 26th who could not tell us anything about Georges'. At the Red Cross, they received the names of wounded soldiers in his regiment. One soldier responded that he had not seen Georges since Troyes, another that he did not know him. The father-in-law went to see the parliamentary deputy for his constituency, as well as a corporal of the 26th. A card signed by a soldier in the train charged to distribute parcels of woollen clothes arrived, saying that Georges was dead. But the information was contradictory, because a sergeant told them that Georges had been seriously wounded on 1 October at Fricourt, on the Somme. In case George was now a prisoner, the father-in-law went to the Red Cross to send a request to Geneva. A witness of the battle at Fricourt, undergoing medical treatment in Paris, recounted the facts but 'thought that Georges could have been picked up by the Germans'. A new approach in the rue François 1 enquired if it was possible to have news of the dressing station at Bray. On 2 November a friend offered to write to the chairman of the Red Cross in Geneva. Fresh letters were sent to the Major of the 26th, to the chief medical officer and to the Colonel of the 26th. Finally, a letter came on 19 November, from the furrier Kohler who confirmed Georges' death and 'took away all hope'. The family prepared a religious service which took place on 2 December. Notices appeared in *L'Echo de Paris*, *Figaro*, *Le Temps*. Two months passed between the date of death and the religious ceremony: two long months of anguish, hopes, efforts, visits, letters written, meetings.

Berlin was the setting for many similar searches. Paul Wo., a university student, was a member of the '*Wandervogel*', the German youth movement, and founded one of its branches at Potsdam. He liked to explore the countryside by foot and even to take to the sea. He also had social interests. He belonged to a workers' social group, in north-east Berlin which organized circles for reading, theatre visits, for young girls and a writing group for workers and their wives.[158] Paul enlisted at the outbreak of war. By the end

---

[158] *Nachrichten aus der Sozial- und Arbeitsgemeinschaft*, no. 4, November, 1914.

of September he was near Potsdam undergoing a brief military training. Life was good, they were served roast duck and his parents could visit him.[159] In mid-October the young volunteers set off for the front.[160]

At the end of October the young volunteer received his baptism of fire and was confronted by the terrible reality of war. Knowing that his father was extremely anxious about him, he did not dare to give him realistic news. In vague terms he mentioned the trenches, but preferred to talk about food.[161] On 9 November his morale had lifted: 'I hope to return to our nation with high spirits.' It was to be his final letter: next day, standing guard, the student Paul Wo. was killed.

His body was not found, and consequently his parents were therefore not informed of his death. They began to be seriously concerned after a friend had returned to Potsdam, seriously wounded. On the day of Paul's death, they wrote to him again: 'We are very worried about you. You were at the heart of the battle', and they begged him, 'Take good care of yourself.'[162] As letters from the front arrived very irregularly, the parents did not at first realise that their son was no longer writing to them, but they became increasingly anxious. On 21 November, eleven days after the death of their son, they wavered between anxiety and hope. On one hand they had received cards that were three weeks old and, of course, explained why more recent ones had not arrived. On the other hand, the general situation near the Ypres canal made them anxious: 'You cannot imagine how worried we are when we read articles in the newspapers, with all sorts of rumours in addition from people who have heard something. There is more and more news of men killed in action.'[163] At the end of November, however, the military authorities returned all the letters sent since 10 November, stamped 'zürück' (returned) or 'Lazarett' (military hospital). The agitation in the family house may be imagined. At the beginning of December, the father wrote to the company sergeant, Robert Fischer, and asked for news. Fischer responded that Paul had been listed missing since 10 November in the attack near the town of Bixschoote and at the front it was thought that he had been taken prisoner.[164]

The despairing father then sent a large number of letters to various organizations to find a trace of his missing son: to the Red Cross, the Prisoners of War Information Bureau, London, to the International

[159] Wo. collection (Paul to Richard Wo., 25/9/ and 30/9/1914).
[160] Wo. collection (Paul to Richard Wo., 11/10/14).
[161] Wo. collection (Paul to Richard Wo., undated, late October, and Paul to Richard Wo., 1/11/1914).
[162] Wo. collection (Richard to Paul Wo., 10/11/1914).
[163] Wo. collection (Richard to Paul Wo., 20/11/1914).
[164] Wo. collection (Fischer to Richard Wo., 19/12/1914).

Committee of the Red Cross, the Swiss and French authorities, and to the Prussian war ministry. All in vain. No one was able to give him any information. The Army 'told him that Paul was reported missing [...]'.[165] London explained that he was not on the list of prisoners-of-war.[166] The Swiss sent only standard replies, and the French did not respond at all.

At the same time, the father tried to get in touch with Paul's friends. He wrote to the Neitzke family, knowing that their son was in a Brittany hospital. The reply was disappointing: their son had been seriously wounded and as he had not written to them for six months they thought that he was dead.[167] Richard Wo. also mobilized an uncle who wrote to say that he knew another of Paul's comrades, a prisoner of the French at Châtellerault.[168] The latter did indeed offer some news: the comrade wrote that the attack had been very hard and costly and after 'quite a number of our dear comrades were missing', but he did not know what had happened to Paul Wo.[169] Another comrade, Herr Gesell, told him that his son was dead. But Sergeant Fischer insisted that this information was false, and that the prisoner had confused him with another man.[170] Further, in April, the company found itself once more near Bixschoote, and they found the dead of the terrible battle of 10 November. None the less, Paul Wo. was not among them.[171]

Rumours circulated, some terrible and others encouraging. On 29 October 1915 the uncertainty came to an end: the regiment officially informed Richard Wo. that his son had been killed in action on 10 November 1914 outside Bixschoote. Three weeks later, Lieutenant Kellermann, Paul's company commander, confirmed this information 'of the heroic death of your son' and sent the student's modest personal effects, around 20 Marks and 35 Pfennigs, his notebook and a pipe, to his family.[172] Paul Wo.'s 'heroic death' was described in detail in the report apparently written at the Saint Nazaire prisoner-of-war camp on 21 September 1916: 'Wo. fell on the morning of 10 November 1914 near Bixschoote when he was standing guard. I myself saw him, dead on the ground.'[173] Paul's father, a bookbinder, put all these documents together

[165] Wo. collection (Richard Wo. to Zentralnachweisbureau, 31/3/1915, to Internationales Komitee, 2/1/1915, 27/2/1915 and undated); (Zentralnachweisbureau to Richard Wo., 5/4/1915).

[166] Wo. collection (Prisoner-of-war information Bureau to Richard Wo., undated).

[167] Wo. collection (Neitzke to Richard Wo., 3/5/1915).

[168] Wo. collection (Richard Wo. to Herrn Bruckmann, 29/4/15).

[169] Wo. collection (Bruckmann to Richard Wo., 30/5/1915).

[170] Wo. collection (Robert Fischer to Richard Wo., 8/5/1915).

[171] Wo. collection (Robert Fischer to Richard Wo., 30/4/1915).

[172] Wo. collection (Kellermann to Richard Wo., 23/11/1915).

[173] Wo. collection (Report by Johann Woveries, 21/9/1916).

in an album. He never managed to console himself for the death of his only son. In January 1923 he committed suicide.

The convergence of these different stories is striking. In order to have news of their family members, all these people, some of them reasonably prosperous, were forced to turn to means closely linked to their residence in the capital cities: telephone, telegrams, newspaper announcements, visits to national or international bodies located in the city, approaches to members of headquarters staff, numerous items of news – often contradictory – which plunged them into the greatest confusion. The wait was appallingly long-drawn-out, and the toll on families, even when the news turned positive, and their sons or fathers were found wounded, or prisoners, was immense.

Conclusion

In a number of ways, these tensions and crises led to the idealization of hearth and home in the inter-war years. A return to conventional gender roles made sense to those who wished to forget everything the war represented: a sombre turbulence, severe material hardships, and a sense of unlimited uncertainty about the future. For those in public life, rebuilding the *foyer* was at the core of rebuilding the nation. But at a much more intimate level, the recasting of the rhythms of family life, within a *quartier*, a neighbourhood, came first. There were wounds to attend to, scars to hide, memories to bury. Perhaps cities were places in which there was less support from neighbours and kin; but anonymity had its virtues too, for those who wanted to turn their backs on the heaviness, the cruelties of the war.

10   Hospitals

Jay Winter

Many institutional histories of nursing, medical care, and hospitals emphasize the heroism of the caring professions during the Great War. Other projects document the powerful legacy of the contributions of this relatively small population trained to deal with the casualties of soldiers and civilians alike.[1] Alongside this body of work stand efforts that, to varying degrees, follow a different agenda, one based on the work of Foucault. He urged us to try to see how, in the clinical environment, the medical profession forges alliances between words and things, 'enabling one', in the context of infirmity and contagion, '*to see* and *to say*'.[2] How these conceptual and therapeutic alliances, professionally constructed and culturally encoded before the war, were reconfigured in wartime has been the subject of scholarly enquiry in recent years,[3] though rarely in a comparative framework. This chapter adopts such a perspective by considering the many clinical and teaching hospitals of London, Paris, and Berlin not only as familiar landmarks on the wartime metropolitan landscape but also as centres of medical treatment and therapy where Foucault's process of 'spatialization and verbalization of the pathological'[4] played out. In these sites, too, the medicalization of identity in wartime took significant form. Here we give the role of the hospital in wartime cultural life, and in the lives of soldiers and civilians who lived

---

Jay Winter wrote this chapter, in collaboration with Sophie Delaporte, Peter Leese, Paul Lerner, and Jeffrey Reznick.

[1] Brian Abel-Smith, *A history of the nursing profession* (London, 1960); Abel-Smith, *The hospitals, 1800–1948; a study in social administration in England and Wales* (London, 1964); Margaret Higonnet (ed.), *Nurses at the front: writing the wounds of the Great War* (Boston, 2001).

[2] Michel Foucault, *The birth of the clinic. An archaeology of medical perception*, trans. by A. M. Sheridan Smith (New York, 1973), p. xii.

[3] Roger Cooter, Mark Harrison, and Steve Sturdy (eds.), *Medicine and modern warfare* (Amsterdam, 1999); Cooter, Harrison, and Sturdy (eds.), *War, medicine and modernity* (Stroud, *c.*1998); Mark Harrison, 'Medicine and the management of modern warfare', *History of Science* 34, no. 4 (1996), pp. 379–410, and Harrison, 'The medicalization of war – the militarization of medicine', *Social History of Medicine* (September 1996), pp. 267–76.

[4] Foucault, *The birth of the clinic*, pp. xi–xii.

in and/or moved through London, Paris, and Berlin, the attention this subject deserves.[5]

Hospitals and the medicalization of identity

Examining aspects of wartime metropolitan medical history in a comparative framework requires contrasting different strategies of medicalizing identity in wartime and locating these strategies in pre-war circumstances. Taken together, spatialization, classification, and social stratification constitute a taxonomy forged during peacetime and wartime. The dominant and governing process in this taxonomy was the rationalization of treatment, a uniformity in the way military-medical authorities identified and distinguished convalescent soldiers from the larger population of hospital patients and noncombatants on the home front. In London, indeed throughout Britain, that uniformity manifested itself through a distinctive blue uniform. Here was an outward sign not only of institutionalized identity but also of a comprehensive medical system involving discipline, efficiency, and economy that aimed to ensure manpower needs by returning soldiers as rapidly as possible to active duty.

Once identified, the patient went through processing of many different kinds. 'Spatialization' of the pathological, or a form of triage, operated in hospitals. This kind of hospital triage performed many distinctions. First were those relating to health, distinguishing between those able to fight and those unable to fight. Secondly, they identified degrees of disability – among those men who could be nursed back to fitness relatively easily and those who needed longer-term treatment. Here the implications are both military and financial, given the implications of such distinctions for treatment and entitlement to a pension. Thirdly, there was the divide between those men who were in hospital as a result of combat – whose conditions bore no stigma at all – and those who were there as a result of non-combat related or illicit reasons – whose flawed physicality or mental state bore substantial stigma. Foremost among the men in this latter category were malingerers who found themselves in the realm of psychiatry. The performative element of wartime medical care, evident in many facets of hospital life, had a particularly striking character in this context.

Triage was a performance. What was performed varied according to the institution and the physician, but the language of the performance was drawn out of the cultural archive of that society. Performance here means the re-presentation of power and powerlessness in different and

---

[5] Jeffrey S. Reznick, *Healing the nation: soldiers and the culture of caregiving in Britain during the Great War* (Manchester, 2004).

overlapping contexts. Thus the element of social class deference and defiance described the interaction of doctors and patients in London and Berlin in overlapping, though distinctive, ways. Doctors occupied multiple social positions as did patients; their interactions were always dialogic, though many doctors refused to see it that way. To such men, mental illness was a sign of social insubordination or congenital weakness as much as psychological or physical disturbance. In Berlin, this issue took on the baggage of the pre-war debate over 'pension neurosis', and brought shell-shocked men up against the accusation that they were unpatriotic and subversive. These differences between the origins, attitudes, and social class position of the doctors on the one hand and the mass of the patients on the other created conflicts in both London and Berlin, but the German case had a toxic element in it which brought the mentally ill in line with others supposedly 'betraying' the national cause. The discourse on insanity contributed to the brew of maliciousness surrounding the claim that Germany was stabbed in the back.

Shell shock therefore was a vexed and problematic category: it lacked the status of more 'legitimate' and clear-cut wounds and illnesses, but was nonetheless accepted by medical and military authorities as requiring evacuation and treatment and in some cases pensioning. On the other hand, the difference between 'real' shell shock and simulation or outright malingering was nearly impossible to verify by any accepted medical standards. These patients, therefore, occupied a liminal status between civilian and combatant, between war casualties and malingerers; as such, they provide an ideal test case for seeing the operation of the medical gaze, the military-medical construction of identity, and the different strategies and negotiations which physicians adopted once the patient's medical 'identity' was established.

In terms of treatment, the clearest classification operated between officers and men. At the extremes, repose for the officers and incarceration for the men presented in these cities as elsewhere a socially stratified world of care, by and large replicating pre-war patterns of medical practice. There was much in the middle, and the notion that all men in the ranks were treated as if they were prisoners is blatantly false. And yet we must bear in mind the fact that a substantial part of the working-class populations who entered hospitals as a result of wounds or illness contracted on active service had never entered a hospital before. And what they saw in these institutions probably did not encourage them to repeat the experience thereafter. Hospital care disciplined an already disciplined population of working-class or peasants in uniform.

One issue which arose time and again was where to put the sick. Could they be seen by the public? Or was it too dangerous for them to appear on metropolitan streets? In every city large and small public visibility of the disabled soldier was both unavoidable and potentially dangerous to the maintenance of civilian morale. There was a consensus as to the need to keep out of the public sight the most severely injured, lest their wounds who would make anyone wonder what could possibly justify such mutilation and pain. Visibility and invisibility not only figured in hospital triage but was central to life within and around metropolitan hospitals.

What was new in wartime therefore was the crossing of multiple binary choices concerning disability, stigma, rank, and visibility. Each society configured the mix in its own way, though the medical professional was sufficiently international to establish norms of which virtually all practitioners in these cosmopolitan environments were well aware. There were clearly distinctive national styles of the practice of medicine in wartime, and indeed of science as a whole. These styles combined with different sets of economic and military priorities to produce different profiles of medical treatment in these three countries. Given the prominence of the great hospitals of these capital cities, it was inevitable that these distinctions would operate strikingly in London, Paris, and Berlin.

Uniforms and uniformity

One of the key vectors of wartime traffic, alongside that from provincial towns where armies were formed and trained and subsequently made their way to the front, was the return of sick and wounded soldiers to centres of medical treatment, along the 'lines of communication' as British military authorities called this route, 'from battlefield to Blighty' as many British soldiers described it, and then back again to the front. This system was designed chiefly to ensure manpower through the return of soldiers as rapidly as possible to active duty or if they were unfit for further service, through discharge to civilian life.[6] Informed both by precedent and by the exigencies of war, these lines constituted a network of distinct sites through which caregivers evacuated men who received a 'Blighty wound' from the front lines to hospitals at home. They included regimental aid posts, advanced dressing stations, casualty clearing stations and general and stationary hospitals. They also included distinct modes of transportation such as motor ambulances, ambulance trains and hospital ships and barges, several of which could provide specialized treatments for illness and injury.

---

[6] 'The Royal Army Medical Corps and its work', *British Medical Journal*, 18 August 1917, 217–24 and 25 August 1917, 254–60.

Passage along these lines, frequently long and painful, ended often but certainly not always in capital cities where medical authorities regularly processed the human wreckage of war. Casualties therefore became a prominent feature of life at Victoria and Waterloo, among other stations. The great teaching hospitals of London, St Thomas's or St Bartholomew's were not far away, and were serviced by cars and taxis dispatched by voluntary-aid organizations integral to the system of receiving and processing men. Traffic and therefore public views of the wounded grew as casualties mounted, especially during the great battles of 1916 and 1917. In Paris, too, where at the Gare de l'Est, cars and taxis met hospital litters en route to the Salpêtrière, Les Invalides or other major centres of treatment. The greater distance from Berlin to the front lines diminished the significance of this vector of the return of the wounded as a facet of metropolitan life, though in the German capital, too, many wounded soldiers regularly arrived at the great metropolitan train stations on their way to receiving the treatment they required.

One way in which we can see how the war required men to perform their 'identities' was in terms of the dress disabled men were instructed to wear in London. In the military hospitals and associated convalescent homes of London and other British cities, a soldier's processing began in part with the requirement that he always wear a distinctive blue uniform, no matter where his location inside or beyond the institution when he received permission from authorities to convalesce in public. This measure was at once of a piece with the broader story of hospitals, workhouses, prisons, and schools, where standard clothing was the norm to ensure personal and communal hygiene as well as institutional discipline and order.[7]

Made of a flannel and flannelette combination the convalescent soldier's 'Rickett's Blue' outfit and its lounge-jacket counterpart resembled ill-fitting pyjamas.[8] The entire ensemble included a red four-in-hand necktie and was the only item of hospital clothing issued exclusively by the government during the war. While military authorities required that the garment be worn at all times by soldiers of non-officer 'other ranks' who were receiving treatment in military hospitals and their associated convalescent facilities, authorities exempted officers from wearing the 'blues', providing them instead with a white armband decorated with a

---

[7] On the use of standard garments in asylums and workhouses see 'The clothing of lunatics: the therapeutic value of a becoming costume', *Hospital*, 3 May 1919, 106.

[8] *Hansard Parliamentary Debates*, Commons, vol. 86 (1916), cols. 970–1 (case 16, item 29), Imperial War Museum, and from 'Convalescent jacket', *Tailor and Cutter*, 20 August 1914 (supplement), pp. 688–90, which also contains the Army Council's special 'sealed pattern' (also called a 'specimen garment') for the 'Convalescent jacket'.

red King's Crown, with a personal clothing allowance, or with fancy silk pyjamas donated by the public and voluntary-aid agencies.[9]

The convalescent blue outfit served hygienic purposes but also symbolized efficiency and economy during a time of scarce goods and high prices. Regulated by the government, its production was carried out either through military contracts with private provincial factories or directly by the army at the Royal Army Clothing Factory at Pimlico, where 'labour-saving devices' and a 'smooth, efficient and economical' factory system dominated every facet of clothing manufacture.[10] The uniform was also designed so that a handful of sizes would fit all recovering soldiers of 'other ranks'. This standardization made the uniform fit poorly, requiring soldiers to 'flap' or 'cuff' their trouser legs and shirt sleeves.

There are indications that soldiers were ambivalent at best about their ill-fitting, brightly-coloured and pocket-less 'blues',[11] after which they popularly became known as 'convalescent blues' and thus familiar features of wartime urban life. Some men appreciated their uniforms for helping to draw the attention of attractive young women. The blues also served as a mark that very likely permitted the public to distinguish Tommy from shirkers who would receive a humiliating white feather.[12] In this respect, praise of the blues had much in common with 'khaki fever', serving as another way to salute a hero.[13]

At the same time some men held a more negative view of the 'blues', suggesting that this standard clothing – a mark of discipline, indeed of the war machine itself, upon his body – failed in large measure to confer a deserved dignity of appearance. In its issues of March and June 1916 the *Gazette of the Third London General Hospital* included two caricatures of blue-clad Tommies, both of which beg comparison of his wear to proper, upper-class masculine 'fashion' of the day.

[9] Abel-Smith, *The hospitals*, p. 275. Lyn McDonald, *The roses of no man's land* (New York, 1993), p. 39. Discharged soldiers who were no longer receiving care in military hospitals did not wear hospital blue but 'their own clothes'. See Charity Organisation Society, 'The Star and Garter Home for Disabled Discharged Soldiers, Commanding Officer's Report (interview with the Matron of the hospital) 27 August 1919', (A/FWA/C/D), London Metropolitan Archives.

[10] 'A visit to the Royal Army clothing Factory', *Tailor and Cutter* (6 August 1914), pp. 636–9. 'The Royal Army clothing department, 1897', Public Record Office, WO 33/78.

[11] Reznick, *Healing the nation*, chapter 5 and *passim*.

[12] Nicoletta F. Gullace, 'White feathers and wounded men: female patriotism and the memory of the Great War', *Journal of British Studies* 36, no. 2 (April 1997), pp. 178–206.

[13] Reznick, *Healing the nation*, chapter 5, and Angela Woollacott, ' "Khaki Fever" and its control: Gender, class, age and sexual morality on the British home front in the First World War', *Journal of Contemporary History* 29, no. 2 (April 1994), pp. 325–47.

Here the heroes depicted in figures 10.1 and 10.2 become comic in the spirit of London music hall. Unlike a proper suit, these images suggest, the blue uniform prompted laughter and ridicule, responses that added nothing to the masculinity of men who have served King and Country. Such ambivalence about the 'blues' helps to reveal how this sartorial requirement forced an unstable public identity for men who convalesced in London and elsewhere in Britain.

Hospital magazines reveal such instability in another way, by suggesting that men saw within the hospital, a site of assumed comfort and healing, the very rhythms of the slaughterhouse and the factory – indeed the 'war machine'.[14] Lieutenant P. Bishop plainly identifies men as lambs, surgery as slaughter and hospital as slaughterhouse in his caricature 'As a lamb to the SLAUGHTER'.

As devils swirl around the head of the helpless soldier, preparing instruments for the kill, angels assist in the process and inform by 'diet sheet' that starvation awaits. Captain C. Rhodes Harrison, one of these cartoonists, plainly evoked hospital as factory in many of his caricatures of hospital life, including the series entitled '3rd L.G. Labour-saving Devices'. Consider 'The Automatic Bed-making and Patient-washing Apparatus,' which, without care for his condition, processes the blue-clad Tommy in a mechanistic, assembly-line fashion, preparing him eventually for another stint in the line.

Here we find not only the notion of hospitalization as dehumanized insertion into a mechanical monster but also a direct allusion to hospitalization as a continuation of what the French army termed the '*noria*', or circular chain bringing men into the line and out of the line, recycling casualties as 'wastage' or as in need of repair, before they are put back on the conveyor belt again. To refer to an assembly line made sense in the German context too, where soldiers who were unfit to return to the front were instead returned to war factories. Designed well before the war to produce efficient workers, such a rationalized approach to medical care informed imperatives during the conflict with greater authority as the face of industrialized warfare grew more distinct.[15] Once again humour enabled soldiers themselves to represent their own sense of what hospitalization meant to them.

The industrial character of hospitalization had another facet evident in the treatment of men who had lost a limb in battle. In the summer of 1916, at the Military Orthopaedic Hospital, Shepherd's Bush, construction

[14] Pick, *The war machine.*
[15] Paul Lerner, *Hysterical men. War, psychiatry and the politics of trauma in Germany, 1890–1930* (Ithaca, 2003).

Fig. 10.1. Picture postcard by Fred Spurgin, "'Tho' still in the 'Blue' –
I'm glad you're in the pink!'"

began on the quadrangle of what authorities called 'curative workshops',
the design scheme for which not only evokes the very mechanical character
of the caricatures by Bishop, Harrison, and others but in linking pre-war
rehabilitation schemes for industrial-accident victims frames the war as the
largest set of industrial accidents in history.[16]

---

[16] Paul Weindling (ed.), *The social history of occupational health* (London, 1985).

Fig. 10.2. Lieutenant-Corporal J. H. Dowd, 'Our Afternoon Excursion', *Gazette of the Third London General Hospital* (October 1916), p. 19.

Hospital Fashions.

By Pte. Vernon Lorimer.

"The Bond Street Cut"—from the
3rd L.G.H. Style Book for 1916.

Fig. 10.3. 'Hospital Fashions: "The Bond Street Cut"' – from the 3rd L.G.H. Style Book for 1916, *Gazette of the Third London General Hospital* (March 1916), p. 152.

Hospital Fashions.

**"The Guardsman Cut"—from the
3rd L.G.H. Style Book for 1916.**

Fig. 10.4. 'Hospital Fashions: "The Guardsman Cut"' – from the 3rd
L.G.H. Style Book for 1916, *Gazette of the Third London General Hospital*
(June 1916), p. 228.

The first three of these shops opened in October 1916, becoming the
nucleus of the hospital's rehabilitation strategy. They included a direct
curative shop, in which disabled soldiers received various forms of
mechanical therapy; a central shop, which contained a smithy fitted

with an electric forge and anvils; and a site for commercial photographic work. The rapid growth of these sites attests to their great success. Within less than a year, hospital authorities used soldier-patient labour to help construct and maintain fifteen additional shops. In engineering shops disabled soldiers repaired motor-car engines, enamelled frames, re-lacquered fittings, and re-upholstered seat cushions. In artistic shops, they made decorations for the hospital chapel and wards. In the carpentry shops, soldiers made hospital furniture, shelves and cupboards for the institution. And in other shops there were materials for them to learn tailoring, cigarette making, French polishing, sign writing, and fretwork.

Here was classification and treatment of the sick, repair and rehabilitation hand in hand to the end of 'reclaiming the maimed,' as R. Tait Mackenzie described it.[17] Authorities at Shepherd's Bush carefully marshalled images of such hospital labour in picture postcards, as means to bolster morale among civilians, to secure public funds for the institution itself, and to give hope that those who lost a limb in service to King and Country could earn a living, a new identity, and renewed dignity upon their return to civilian life.

Shell shock and metropolitan care: spatialization

The function of metropolitan hospitals as triage centres is particularly evident in the case of shell shock. The origins of both the diagnosis and treatment of this set of infirmities lay in the field of industrial medicine and workmen's compensation.[18] The war reconfigured the character of such accidents and their sequelae and turned them into an inescapable element in the medical history of the war. Here lie some of the sources of medical thinking about mental illness in wartime, and some origins of the kinds of care and handling such men received in these cities during the Great War. The war as industrialized slaughter created categories of classification derived directly from pre-war industrial history.

None of this pre-war history diminished the vagueness of the category of war-related mental illness nor the difficulties in diagnosing it. The tasks of classifying and processing the disabled were dealt with differently in the three cities. On this point, geography mattered. The proximity of Paris to the front, and its critical importance as the hub of a national rail network help account for the special position of the city, but so does the presence

---

[17] R. Tait Mackenzie, *Reclaiming the maimed* (New York, 1918).
[18] Weindling (ed.), *Occupational health*; Mark S. Micale and Paul Lerner (eds.), *Traumatic pasts: history, psychiatry, and trauma in the modern age, 1870–1930* (Cambridge, 2001).

of the great military hospital complex of Val-de-Grâce. As against the cases of London and Berlin, Paris was both a fortified city and the centre of the army medical services as a whole, from which point individual cases could be scrutinized and sent on their way.

What happened in Paris was not repeated in either London or Berlin, though similarities did exist. Paris resembled a solar system of care for men of all kinds, and we shall pay particular attention to one group which illustrates this point – those suffering psychiatric ailments. There was a series of satellites located in the suburbs and the adjacent towns of the Île de France. These were connected by road and rail, and provided a complex system of medical classification and treatment which was both specified in Paris and distributed in the surrounding region. The initial triage took place in the capital, after which men were shuttled to different institutions depending on their profile.

By concentrating on only one category of disability, it is possible to see in microcosm how the triage of identities operated in wartime. Here – as elsewhere – rank was the critical variable in determining where and how men were to be treated. There was a hospital at Issy-les-Moulineaux for officers suffering 'benign mental troubles'; this was not considered a site of confinement at all. For the men in the ranks, there was an array of institutions to which they were sent, and all of them had some coercive character. At the 'light end' of incarceration was the asylum of Ville-Evrard near Neuilly-sur-Marne. It was divided into a number of units, of which two, the 'Quartier Pinel' and the 'Quartier Esquirol', were designated for mentally ill people who were not a danger to themselves or others. This institution was termed the 'Maison blanche'. In contrast the asylum of Saint-Maurice at Charenton, where the Marquis de Sade had been incarcerated 150 years before, and the Paul Brousse hospice at Villejuif in the Paris 'red belt' were the places for treating those 'insane men requiring committal to a psychiatric institution' (aliénés vrais ... justiciables de l'internement)'. This was the scene Céline described in a nightmarish section of his fictionalized war memoir *Voyage au bout de la nuit*.

Both the Maison Blanche in Neuilly-sur-Marne and the Paul Brousse hospice on the outskirts of Paris were institutions for treating men who were suffering from what were taken to be real disabilities. Their rehabilitation happened in many different places, but the Salpêtrière hospital offered much in the way of physical and psychological retraining, along the lines of the London teaching hospitals, St Thomas's, Guy's Hospital, and St Bartholomew's, among others.

There was one other category for men who were considered dangerous in several respects. Criminal or 'detained' men – men awaiting trial or prisoners of war – were treated in the hospice of the Fort-de-Bicêtre, also on the outskirts of the city. This massive set of buildings, with its prison façade, held a population of men suspected of malingering or of having committed other crimes.

In sum, there was a sophisticated taxonomy of sites for the treatment of mental illness; this map of care was worked out both spatially and functionally. Critically important were the rank and social class of the patient. First came those officers whose recuperation was organized in the fashion of a pre-war sanatorium, with all the privileges associated with it. Then came the men who were psychologically ill but not dangerous. Then came those who had to be restrained, though not due to criminal intent or activity. Those in custody came last.

The strength of the hospital system in the Paris region helped ensure that metropolitan medicine was well equipped to deal with psychological illness on the outbreak of war. Thereafter, though, the scale of casualties made congestion a constant headache in mobilizing and maintaining psychiatric services, alongside all other medical services. In sum there were 1,500 beds for such men in Parisian institutions, of which up to 200 were located at Val-de-Grâce itself. The Maison Blanche had the greatest capacity. Its two sections had 385 and 300 beds respectively. There were 350 beds at the Ville-Evrard, and about 150 at the Maison Saint-Meurice and at Villejuif. We should bear in mind, to be sure, how small these numbers are when compared to the avalanche of physically wounded men who needed treatment. That some physically injured men also needed psychiatric care was obvious, and yet the classification system rigidly separated the two.

The physical location of different institutions offers us a rough map of treatment. In the city, prison-like conditions prevailed. In the countryside, more pastoral conditions gave psychiatric care a very different face. What both kinds of institutions shared, though, was the power of occlusion, the possibility of helping the disabled without adding to the distress of city-dwellers in whose midst they were hospitalized. No 'Blue Boy' uniforms for these patients. Their condition still retained a stigma, however innocent they were of even the remotest taint of malingering.

Shell shock and the taxonomies of mental illness: the case of Paris

One of the most important tasks for neurologists and psychiatrists was to establish a nosography – a systematic classification of diseases of the mind. It is with this kind of taxonomy that different strategies of treatment could be organized and differentiated. What emerged was anything but a systematic structure. In response to the demands of the Army Statistical Office, individual doctors developed their own taxonomies which overlapped to be sure, but which also differed in fundamental ways.

The director of medical services at Val-de-Grâce, Marcel Briand, subscribed to his own set of categories. He distinguished between and among the following classes of patients. We give the French terminology after the English, since the usages were not the same in the two languages. Herewith Briand's classification system:

1. The 'truly insane'
2. Those 'confused' due to
    1. Mental shock: *commotion cérébrale traumatique*
    2. Simple shock: *psychoses émotives*
    3. Degenerates: *émotifs, impulsifs, obsédés douteux, abouliques*
    4. Epileptics
    5. Hysterics: *paralysie, surdité-mutité, crises convulsives*
    6. Mental deficients
    7. Demented due to cerebral lesions or other causes
    8. Delirium due to addiction to alcohol or drugs
    9. Typhoid fever victims
    10. Those under observation or condemned: amnesiacs and self-mutilators
    11. Recovering soldiers in need of further examination
    12. Prisoners – German soldiers with mental affliction or French Dissimulators

At Maison-Blance, Laignel-Lavastine developed an entirely different system of classification. He divided his patients into four categories. The first was physical, indicating conditions arising from:

1. Nerve lesions – traumatic
2. Nerve lesions – non-traumatic
3. Bone marrow lesions
4. Lesions of the brain lining

The second was psychological, defined not by source but by symptom. Here Laignel-Lavastine identified five sub-categories:

1. Hysterical symptoms: paraplegia
2. Emotional syndromes: mutism, shaking
3. '*Habitude*' or comportment dysfunction
4. Localized reaction syndromes: *syndromes réactionnels locaux*
5. Inhibitions: partial paralysis and mutism

His third category comprised malingering and simulation, which he termed: '*manifestations nerveuses fonctionnelles illégitimes*'. The fourth was neurotic behaviour: *neurasthénie, l'hystéro-neurasthénie, l'asthénie par surmenage de guerre, la tristesse, la psychasthénie.* A fifth was the catch-all residual '*syndromes nerveux divers*'.

The upshot of these different systems of classification was evident both in the treatment of patients and in their physical location. Outside of Paris, the regime developed by Philippe Pinel in the nineteenth century presented patients and doctors with parks and avenues of trees, appropriate for convalescent strolls and the calming effects of the countryside. But inside Paris, and in some of the surrounding institutions, a different regime operated, much more coercive and fortress-like. Classification and spatial distribution of patients clearly went hand in hand.

The varieties of treatment: the case of London

The parallels with the treatment of shell-shocked men in London are striking. The distinction of rank was just as pre-eminent as it was in Paris. The decision to open specialized wards and institutions for officers came when numbers began to increase rapidly in October and November 1914.[19] Lord Knutsford was among the first to help answer this need when he placed an appeal in *The Times* on 4 November for funds to establish a private hospital to treat soldiers suffering from 'severe mental and nervous shock due to exposure, excessive strain and tension'.[20] The sum of £7,700 was raised within three months and the first, most famous of the Knutsford centres, Palace Green, near Kensington Gardens, was open by January 1915.[21]

What became known as 'Hospital II' was opened in a large private house in the fashionable district of Campden Hill in south-west London in April 1915. This institution was closer to a specialist convalescent home of the kind where affluent patients were treated by affluent doctors before the war. After about a month at Palace Green, patients could go to Campden Hill where they would remain for a further six weeks, bringing their total recovery period to around two and a half months.

For the rest of the army, London provided a number of centres for diagnosis and treatment.[22] The 4th London General at Denmark Hill was the largest of the London hospitals, comprising a 400-bed Neurological Section, and a more specialized hospital wing – the Maudsley wing. Denmark Hill was also one of the most important reception centres for

[19] W. A. Turner, 'Nerves and mental shock', *British Medical Journal*, 10 June 1916, p. 830.
[20] 'Lord Knutsford's appeal', *The Times*, 4 November 1914, p. 5b.
[21] 'Lord Knutsford's special hospitals for Officers', *The Lancet*, ii (1915), p. 1155.
[22] T. W. Salmon, 'The care and treatment of mental diseases and war neuroses in the British Army', *Mental Hygiene*, 1 (1917), pp. 509–47.

By ·Lieut. P. Bishop.

Fig. 10.5. 'As a lamb to the SLAUGHTER', *Gazette of the Third London General Hospital* (January 1917), p. 98.

disabled men. Thousands of cases came there directly from France. The Maudsley wing took acute cases of traumatic neurasthenia, hysteria, and the milder psychoses. Of all patients, 20 per cent were discharged from the army, 40 per cent went back to serve on light duty, 38 per cent were deemed to have been totally cured.[23] This recovery rate was extremely high, and it is unclear whether some of the men deemed 'cured' wound up back in the Maudsley or elsewhere in the medical system.

Denmark Hill was also among the most conservative of shell-shock treatment hospitals. Its regime was run along strictly military lines. Its staff included the neurologist F. W. Mott, a pathologist for the London County Council before the war who specialized in neurology, and whose 'biological' view of wartime mental disorders was favoured by military leaders especially in the first two years of the war.[24] Thus in a 1917 survey of 'predisposing factors of war psycho-neurosis', Mott reported that

[23] Turner, 'Nerves and mental shock', p. 831.
[24] F. W. Mott, *War neuroses and shell shock* (London, 1919). Also, 'Chadwick Lecture: Mental hygiene in shell shock, during and after the War', *Journal of Mental Science*, 63 (1917), pp. 467–88; 'Neurasthenia: the disorders and disabilities of fear', *Lancet* (26 January 1918), pp. 127–9.

three-quarters of all cases had a 'positive family history', which might include insanity, alcoholism, or nervousness, and almost as many had a 'previous neuropathic constitution'.[25]

Patients were well aware of the predisposition of many physicians to see them as malingerers. *The Springfield War Hospital Gazette* in 1917 published this imaginary instruction to hospitalized men:

Owing to the pressure of work in the department, it has been suggested to us (unofficially) that much valuable time and labour might be saved if answers to the following important questions were prepared in advance. We added a few useful hints for the guidance of prospective candidates:

(1) State briefly why you should be discharged as 'permanently unfit'. (The shortage of paper only allows six sheets of foolscap for this answer.)
(2) Give fully the reason why you should return to duty. (The back of a visiting card will usually be found sufficient in this case.)
(3) What are the chief causes of your headaches? (The sight of an M.O. and visions of the depot are so obvious that they need not be mentioned.)[26]

The notion that psychiatric treatment was a scarcely veiled form of discipline arose out of the division, evident in the pre-war period, in the kinds of people psychiatrists treated. On the one hand were the fee-paying, upper-class 'neurasthenic'; on the other hand, the non-fee paying, working-class 'hysteric'. This distinction was a cultural construction, and we shall return in the conclusion to its reinforcement by wartime conditions. During the conflict, the officers occupied the first category, and their hospitalization was conducted in an atmosphere of rest and slow rehabilitation, in the manner of a tuberculosis clinic for the well-to-do. The second category of patient – the hysteric – was socially remote from most psychiatrists and specialist physicians, since their professional standing was not enhanced by work undertaken among working-class people, by and large paid for by Poor Law boards of guardians. Psychiatric care for these working-class men both before and during the war took on the austere, and at times harsh, character and social stigma of the Victorian poor law.[27] This interpretation should not lead us to succumb to the temptation to see all such treatment as punitive. Psychiatrists like all other physicians in wartime faced an unprecedented medical

---

[25] F. W. Mott, 'The predisposing factors of war psycho-neuroses', *Nature*, 100 (1917), pp. 1–3.
[26] 'Medical Boards', *Springfield War Hospital Gazette*, 10 (June 1917), 24. See also Peter Leese, *Shell shock: traumatic neurosis and the British soldiers of the First World War* (Houndsmill, 2002), pp. 99–102.
[27] Ben Shephard, *A war of nerves* (London, 2000), pp. 8–9.

emergency, and they had to draw upon the accepted cultural configurations of mental illness.

The National Hospital for Paralysed and Epileptic, in Queen Square, in London's West End, was both a highly effective specialist treatment centre and the site of some of the most controversial cases of what even then appeared to be the harsh treatment of soldiers. While Palace Green and the other Knutsford centres drew most attention from the public in the first year of the war, and while Denmark Hill and Springfield became known as the major reception centres for treatment of the other ranks, Queen Square briefly came to prominence in the aftermath of the Somme with the claim of two distinguished physicians, Edgar Adrian and Lewis Yealland, to having found a quick cure for some of the common neuroses of war by the use of electricity.[28] Adrian won the Nobel Prize in Physiology and Medicine in 1932.

Yealland's use of aversion therapy and electric shock treatment for mute and paralysed men is well known.[29] Yet because he treated only a handful of cases, Yealland's (and Queen Square's) contribution to the shaping of psychiatric therapy was both marginal and largely symbolic of but one approach to the problem of mental illness in wartime. The first men were accepted there in February 1915 when Lord Beauchamp, President of the Board of Directors of the hospital, announced the opening of a specialist ward. War-related cases continued to receive treatment there until 1924, according to the case notes that have survived.[30]

From these notes, it is apparent that after 'shell shock', 'neurasthenia' and 'traumatic neurasthenia' were the most common diagnostic categories used at Queen Square. Yealland's use of what was known in Germany as the 'surprise attack' method – robust persuasion, sometimes tantamount to abusive violence, and a certain degree of mystification to assist it – while probably unethical and certainly draconian, could apparently yield remarkable results. His purpose was to get the patient to feel the weight of medical and military discipline, and then to internalize it so that eliminating the symptom was preferable to continuing the treatment. This was the pathway back to military service Yealland followed in his clinic. Power – and rank – were performed in Yealland's wards; no one had the slightest doubt as to what characterized the identity of the doctor and of the patient. One imposed his will on the other.

[28] E. D. Adrian and L. R. Yealland, 'Treatment of some common war neuroses', *Lancet* (June 1917), pp. 867–72.

[29] Leed, *No Man's Land*; Elaine Showalter, *The female malady: women, madness, and English culture, 1830–1980* (New York, 1985), and Pat Barker, *Regeneration* (London, 1991).

[30] National Hospital Queen Square, Medical Notes and Records 1915–24.

There are surviving case notes supporting the view that Queen Square was an institution in which a range of therapies were practised, well beyond Yealland's idiosyncratic form of medical theatre. One such patient treated at Queen Square was a private soldier, serving in the Northumberland Fusiliers, aged thirty-four. He was admitted on 5 October 1916 and discharged, after two and a half months, as 'cured' on 13 January 1917.[31] This is the core of his medical history:

Hist. On Sept 26th, patient and four comrades became scattered after an attack. After wandering all night they joined an Officer and 50 men in another trench. The whole time they were being heavily shelled. On joining the bigger party, he felt so dizzy and ill that he asked to see the Doctor. In the morning he was sent to Albert and then to No 2 Canadian Hospital. He had a good deal of headache, both frontal and occipital. This came on suddenly and was shooting in character, and lasted for a few minutes. He has continual sensations of dizziness.

Previous Hist. Joined 8th Northumberland Fusiliers in April 1915; went to Dardanelles October 1915; Egypt Jan 1916; France May 1916 ...

Physical. Well built man of 34. Lies quietly in bed with a rather vacant expression. Coarse tremor of both hands. His extremities are very clammy. He speaks in a halting fashion and gives a fairly connected account of his illness Massage etc

Another soldier's file describes the circuitous route the soldier took to Queen Square:[32]

... Was taken to the Dressing Station and from there to Ypres, then to No 10 Dressing station at Poperinghe after that to No 14 General Hospital, Boulogne, where he remained four days. Was sent to No 5 Convalescent Camp where he was sixteen days under observation. For a few was in the Australian Hospital and then was sent to the 1st London General Hospital, Camberwell, at which he arrived on the 31st March. States that his voice has been leaving him for six months ...

Personal ... joined the Gordon Highlanders, has been with them for two years. Went to France 14th August 1914. He has been in the following engagements: Mons, Aisne, La Basse, 1st Battle of Ypres, Kemmel, Hill 60, Hooge and the International trenches ... Cured by faradism.

In contrast to this 'cure' by electricity, there is the case of a sergeant in the 1/8 Royal Warwicks, aged twenty-three. He was treated at Queen Square between early January and mid-March 1916 with 'no change' in his condition:[33]

Complaint: Headache, weakness, Backache, difficulty passing water

Anamnesis – Has been coming for a long time but not until Nov 7 1915 did it become so bad that he had to consult the doctor. He was treated for rheumatism

[31] Dr Tooth, 1916. National Hospital Queen Square, Medical Notes and Records 1915–24.
[32] Dr Taylor, 1916. National Hospital Queen Square, Medical Notes and Records.
[33] Dr Yealland, 1916. National Hospital Queen Square, Medical Notes and Records.

and lumbago and given light duty. At night there were large explosions in which many of his company were killed. Bomb burst just ten feet from where he stood. He believes it was the sight of the Sergt Major who was lying with his legs cut off that caused him to be more nervous than ever. On Christmas (day) he was sent back to the trenches and there shivered all day. When he same off duty he couldn't walk. When the doctor saw him his temperature was 102° f.

Personal He was born in Burmah [sic] and the son of an English Officer. He has been employed as a chartered accountant, was a Territorial and went to France when war first broke out

Nervous System – Patient is conscientious; answers questions very intelligently. Has no delusion or hallucination and is well oriented. There are no speech defects. hyperanaesthesia of ankles & feet + analgesia below knees both legs. High frequency ... three times a week + bromide & massage + disch furlough & ld [Light Duty]

These cases are of men who did recover; it is important to note that the Queen Square regime was not the only way things were done in London. A final case of treatment shows what could be done for some of the men brought to Queen Square.

Case No. 395. – April, 1915, paresis left arm. In hospital and under treatment till 16th December 1915. On admission monoplegia left upper extremity. Did not walk: dreams; wandering attacks; confusion. Lost all manifestations.

Case No. 448. – March, 1917, invalided from Salonica with malaria and inability to walk. In military hospital till January, 1918. Admitted here as ambulance case May 17, 1918. Discharged August 27, 1918. On admission unable to stand or walk – chronic invalid. Frequent hysterical attacks. Did well in engineering shop. Discharged to training in engineering.

These records reinforce the overall sense that there was a varied response on the part of attending physicians trying to unravel the complex cases they had to treat. Their ability to do so was at times robust and at times limited, and it is in part Yealland's claim to 'cure' the mute and the paralyzed in a very short period that reinforced his position. But these medical histories lead us to conclude that Yealland's approach to psychiatric care was highly exceptional. His dramatic assertion of the authority of the officer and the physician through brow-beating, humiliation, and a form of what may appear to be blatant cruelty requiring the patient to thank the doctor for maltreating him must not be taken to characterize the work of hundreds of other physicians who tried a number of different procedures to try to relieve the suffering of their patients.

There was never consensus during the war on how shell-shocked soldiers should be understood or cared for. Their simultaneously heroic, tragic and – to some medical practitioners – 'cowardly' status was reflected in the very different localities and facilities which they were allocated. Added to this were the various and complicated 'tribal' alliances of class, military tradition and medical thinking, all of which affected men as they entered and were processed through the system.

We have information on many cases treated in the Ministry of Pensions First Home of Recovery, on the border between Highgate and Golders Green in north London. This home was set up soon after the Ministry came into operation in 1917, and was intended to serve as a model for other homes throughout the country for the treatment and rehabilitation of discharged neurasthenics.[34] Once again, as at Palace Green in early 1915, a large house was chosen as the premises, adapted from its former role as a girls' school, and with the addition of several other buildings in the vicinity, housed 100 patients and their staff. Like Palace Green, Golders Green was also to be a showcase, but this time to show that men could successfully be cured and retrained for entry back into the civilian world of work rather than back into the Army. To this end it was important that the new home was 'in a beautiful position on the outskirts of London, and when the final arrangements were complete was surrounded by twelve and a half acres of excellent garden'.[35] Opened in May 1917, Golders Green was placed under the management of the Hospital for Epilepsy and other Diseases of the Nervous System, in Maida Vale. A resident Medical Officer, matron, and trained staff together with carefully selected VADs were to staff the Home, and an extensive array of equipment was purchased for the electrical department, including 'high frequency, radiant heat and total immersion electric baths'. More importantly there were well-equipped workshops for therapeutic and re-training purposes where patients could learn carpentry, woodwork, basket-making, boot-making, small iron drilling and filing work, and electrical engineering as well as 'intensive culture in a French garden'.[36] Captain B. Williams described the regime at Golders Green as a modified version of pre-war treatments for neurasthenia, with the additional injunction of 'forgetting' war experiences and cultivating a positive frame of mind:

Work and interest in extraneous life are the best cure for such cases. One of the worst services that can be rendered to them is to lavish injudicious sympathy upon them. From the nature of the disorder the man is apt to pity himself unduly and to welcome greedily well-meaning but ill-advised attempts to make him think himself incapable of exertion. Chiefly in order to save such men from their friends and to give them the bracing treatment they require, a home for neurasthenics discharged from the Army has recently been opened by the Ministry of Pensions at Golders Green.[37]

---

[34] *Joint War Reports of British Red Cross/St. John 1914–18*, p. 240.
[35] *Joint War Reports of British Red Cross/St. John 1914–18*, p. 241.
[36] *Joint War Reports of British Red Cross/St. John 1914–18*, p. 241.
[37] Captain B. Williams, 'Pensions', *Recalled to Life*, 1 (June 1917), p. 127.

3rd L.G. Labour-saving Devices.

(Invented by Capt. C. Rhodes Harrison.)

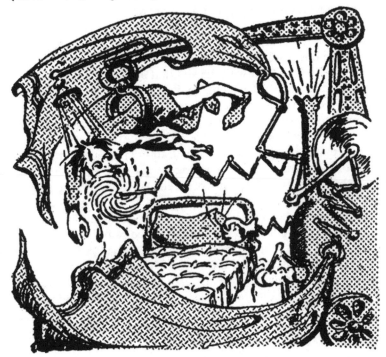

The Automatic Bed-making and Patient-washing Apparatus.

Fig. 10.6. 'The Automatic Bed-making and Patient-washing Apparatus',
Gazette of the Third London General Hospital (December 1916), p. 72.

To this end both the medical regime and the attitude of staff was to
combine a positive outlook and a busy regime of outdoor work or physical
labour.[38]

---

[38] Lieut.-Col. W. Turner, 'Remarks', *Recalled to Life*, ii (September 1917), pp. 251–3;
W. Draper, 'Village centres for cure and training', *Recalled to life*, 3 (April 1918), pp. 342–57;
Major A. F. Hurst, 'Nerves and the men', *Reveille*, 2 (November 1918), pp. 260–8.

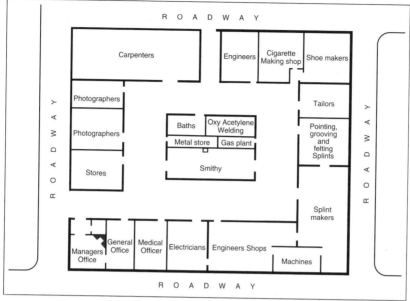

Ground plan of new curative workshops

Fig. 10.7. Plan of the 'curative workshops' at Shepherd's Bush in D. H. Eade (ed.), *Organisation and methods of the Military Orthopaedic Hospital, Shepherd's Bush, London W.* (London: *c.* 1918), p. 48.

John Collie, an experienced civil servant with a commitment to keeping down the costs to the state of medical care, was the Head of the Ministry of Pensions office responsible for ex-servicemen suffering from neuroses. In describing the Golders Green home, he stressed that it was no different from an ordinary convalescent home or neurological unit in a large hospital, but that large numbers of cases necessitated the setting up of small, specialist centres for relatively curable men so more specialist places could go to the chronic and acutely ill. Success depended, however, on a set of basic principles which he outlined: enthusiasm and optimism of doctors, sisters and nurses; ejection of any patient not showing signs of progress; hopeful atmosphere; cheerfulness and industry in administrative arrangements; no overwork or outside interference with a successful resident Medical Officer. Collie also noted that while any kind of gradable work would do for therapeutic purposes, the idea of gardening as a therapeutic tool for the cure of mild cases of paralysis, tremors and stammering had been imported from Paris, where gardens around the city had been turned over to the same purpose. Yet while 'intensive culture is not laborious, and provides full scope for the bodily and mental activities, and a suitable outlet for the activities of many of the men we hope to cure at Golders Green', the longer-term problem of the unemployment of former patients, already apparent towards the end of the war, was more difficult to solve.[39] In an uncharacteristic display of positive thinking Collie concluded by stating:

> Such is the scheme for the salvation by work of the neurasthenic. To those who consider it Utopian, and who from politeness suppress their smiles of incredulity, I say that the scheme has enlisted the active cooperation of many of the best brains and the hardest workers of the country, and it is backed by the sympathy and co-operation of a great Department of State.[40]

Collie's optimism was well placed. According to the *Joint War Reports of British Red Cross/St. John*, out of the 357 patients treated over the period of around twelve months when Golders Green was in operation, 270 (78 per cent) were sent to work or training. This rate of rehabilitation is entirely remarkable.

Varieties of treatment: Paris

The same array of treatments was evident in Parisian hospitals. Dr Briand's reports from his vantage point at Val-de-Grâce presented much information about the flexibility of medical initiatives in this field. French physicians emphasized the singular importance of treatment in forward areas close to the front. The milieux of treatment was critical: the more the soldier retained his military identity, despite his infirmity, the more quickly could he return to his duties.[41]

If the patient had to be invalided out of front areas, then the hospitals of the Parisian region took over, and usually faced a harder task of completing the patient's rehabilitation. Treatments varied from simple rest and water therapy, to a mixed bag of physical therapies, summarized by Dr Laignel-Lavastine: 'rééducation individuelle, massage, électrothérapie, aérothermothérapie, hydrothérapie, gymnastique d'ensemble, promenade thérapeutique'.[42] In this repertoire, gymnastics formed a kind of re-education, a restoration of the rapport between the shell-shocked man

---

[39] J. Collie, 'The management of neurasthenia and allied disorders contracted in the Army', *Journal of State Medicine*, 26 (1918), p. 15.

[40] Ibid., p. 17.

[41] Monthly report, July–August 1915, Médecin-major Briand, Hôpital du Val-de-Grâce, Carton 73, ASSA.

[42] Monthly report, November 1916, Médecin-chef Laignel-Lavastine, Maison-Blanche, Carton 73, ASSA.

and his own body. Here the parallel with the treatment of orthopedic and other injuries is apparent. They all helped to restore the coherence, the integration, of the injured man's body and his own sense of it.

Electricity was used both in stimulating damaged muscles and in various forms of paralysis. There was nothing new in this practice, which was deemed helpful in breaking a blockage in treatment. It could start the recuperative process, but rarely end it just in and of itself. Just as in Queen Square, London, the overall purpose of these medical interventions was to restore a sense of autonomy to damaged men. Their control over their bodies and their minds was either damaged or severed. Whenever possible, a return to *status quo ante bellum*, the sense that a man had of his own physical and emotional integrity, was their objective. That they were incapable of reaching many disabled men is not surprising; perhaps more remarkable is the limited but real assistance they were able in some cases to offer.

Varieties of treatment: Berlin

The German case shows many similarities to the diagnosis and treatment of shell shock in France and Britain, but Berlin did not play nearly as significant a role as either Paris or London as a clearing house for the war's psychiatric casualties. Indeed, Berlin had no Salpêtrière or Queen Square; its closest equivalent, the Dalldorf Asylum (now the Karl-Bonhoeffer-Nervenklinik) to the north of the city, was not a centre for treating such men. There is no evidence that war casualties were housed there, although a great number of war veterans entered the facility in the post-war years for alcoholism, psychosis, and other maladies. While temporary and make-shift facilities for treating the war wounded, including possible shell-shock cases, were created throughout the city – most notably, in Berlin's Museum for Applied Arts, where neurologist Hermann Oppenheim presided over two-hundred beds – Berlin was the last place German military-medical officials wanted shell-shocked men to be sent.[43] Far from the 'solar system of care' that we see in the case of Paris, Berlin lay at a great distance from the front; more importantly, Germany lacked the centralization – politically, militarily, and medically – that so marked France and Britain. Berlin, furthermore, was a relative

---

[43] R. Hirschfeld, 'Zur Behandlung im Kriege erworbener hysterischer Zustände, insbesondere von Sprachstörungen', *Zeitschrift für die gesamte Neurologie und Psychiatrie* 34 (1916), pp. 195–205; F. Mohr, 'Grundsätzliches zur Kriegsneurosenfrage', *Medizinische Klinik* 12 (1916), pp. 90–3; E. Rittershaus, 'Zur Frage der Kriegshysterie', *Zeitschrift für die gesamte Neurologie und Psychiatrie* 50 (1919), pp. 87–97.

newcomer to the status of 'world city'; – until around German unification in 1871 and Germany's belated, but intense industrial take-off, Berlin was not at all comparable to Paris or London in terms of either population or significance. Consequently, the most important developments in the German response to war neurosis occurred not in the capital, but in places like Baden-Württemberg and Bavaria, corps districts much closer to the fighting, which constructed elaborate and highly rationalized systems for processing these cases.

Sending psychiatric casualties to the capital was, in the eyes of German authorities, dangerous for both political and medical reasons. The nineteenth-century notion that the city was a site of degeneration, articulated by such medical and social critics as Max Nordau, resonated in German intellectual circles. Sociologist Georg Simmel's 1903 essay on 'Metropolis and mental life' was perhaps the most articulate and nuanced of a series of fin-de-siècle writings on the city and its psychological and moral dangers.[44] The city's relentless expansion and the fast-paced intensity of Berlin street life threatened to overtax the nerves and strain the mind, argued Simmel. Simultaneously, a number of reactionary and anti-modernist critics took up the call and condemned the city, with its rapidly growing working-class population, its foul, disease-ridden apartment blocks and its political instability as a threat to the (imagined) traditional German way of life and as contrary to the German spirit. Psychiatrists also saw the city as a space that threatened mental and nervous health, and many leading doctors published studies of the increased incidence of nervous illness, alcoholism and suicide in Germany's urban centres.[45] Military and medical officials, thus, sought to keep this category of patients away from Berlin, where, they feared, these highly suggestible men could easily be seduced by a life of malingering, begging, or subversive political behaviour. The alleged role of war neurotics in the November Revolution served as a belated justification for these policies. War neurotics, thus, were to be kept in a strict military environment where these threats could be kept at bay and where they remained fixed by the military-medical gaze.

Shell-shock treatment in Germany, then, was not an urban story. Officers, generally diagnosed with neurasthenia or nervous exhaustion,

---

[44] Max Nordau, *Degeneration* (Lincoln, Neb., 1992); Georg Simmel, 'Die Großstädte und das Geistesleben', *Jahrbuch der Gehe-Stiftung zu Dresden* 9 (1903), pp. 188–95.

[45] Karl Bonhoeffer, 'Ein Beitrag zur Kenntnis des großstädtischen Bettel- und Vagabundentums. Eine Psychiatrische Untersuchung', *Zeitschrift für die gesamte Strafrechtswissenschaft* 21 (1901), pp. 1–65. See also Dirk Blasius, *Umgang mit Unheilbarem: Studien zur Sozialgeschichte der Psychiatrie* (Bonn, 1986); Richard Wetzel, *Inventing the criminal: a history of German criminology, 1880–1945* (Chapel Hill, 2000).

were most likely to be cared for in sanitariums in soothing, bucolic settings far from both the front and major cities. Men were originally treated in regular military hospitals, but after 1916–17, as increasing numbers of specialized war neurosis facilities appeared, they were isolated from other types of war wounded and mentally disturbed civilians and placed in small hospitals specifically devoted to war neurosis treatment.[46] This was because war neuroses were believed to be contagious, and these patients were seen as a bad influence on other types of wounded and as a general detriment to the hospital atmosphere. New psychiatric observation centres were created as sites where psychiatric patients were processed, and war neurotics, once separated from psychotics and other, more chronic cases, were sent on to the new, specialized facilities.

Candidates for these facilities included, above all, sufferers from monosymptomic hysterias, that is, men with a single functional disability such as muteness, deafness, paralysis, or twitching. Such cases were the easiest to treat and were the most likely to be 'pure hysteria' without any accompanying somatic disturbances. For men whose symptoms did not meet the criteria for the new neurosis stations, the director of the observation centre had to determine the appropriate course of action: whether they should be discharged; returned to their troops; sent to state asylums in cases of severe mental illness, disorientation or extreme agitation; treated in other facilities for organic injuries or diseases or dealt with as simulators.

Treatment in the nerve stations consisted of what became known as active treatment – hypnosis, faradization, bath cures, or any number of highly theatrical psychological interventions intended to suggest or force them out of disability and back into health.[47] Work was seen as the key to recovery: agricultural and industrial labour was used as a means to guide the patient back to health and therefore into a useful role for the national community, and the ability to perform this kind of work was likewise taken as a sign of recovery. Thus, a plan pioneered in Baden placed these new psychiatric facilities close to factories enabling the integration of work and treatment and the swift transformation of idle soldier-patients into convalescent worker-patients.[48]

---

[46] Lerner, *Hysterical men*, ch. 5.

[47] Max Nonne, 'Therapeutische Erfahrungen an den Kriegsneurosen in den Jahren 1914–1918', in *Geistes- und Nervenkrankheiten*, vol. IV of *Handbuch der ärztlichen Erfahrungen im Weltkriege, 1914–1918*, ed. Karl Bonhoeffer (Leipzig, 1922), pp. 102–21.

[48] Karl Wilmanns, 'Die Behandlung der Kranken mit funktionellen Neurosen im Bereiche des XIV A. K.', *Deutsche medizinische Wochenschrift* 43 (1917): 427–8 and 'Die Wiedertüchtigung der an funktionellen Neurosen leidenden Kriegsbeschädigten', *Die Kriegsbeschädigtenfürsorge* 2 (1917), pp. 129–50; Ferdinand Kehrer, 'Behandlung und ärztliche Fürsorge bei Kriegsneurosen', *Die Kriegsbeschädigtenfürsorge* 2 (1917), pp. 158–64.

Conclusion

Hospitals were sites for the construction and re-construction of soldiers' bodies, minds, and identities. The objective was to send as many as possible back to the front, or to find ways of enabling them to contribute to the war effort in other capacities. To do so, complex taxonomies were forged and adjusted, enabling the injured to be identified, hospitalized, treated, and returned either to their units or to their homes.

Inevitably, social taxonomies informed medical ones. Officers were diagnosed as having 'neurasthenia', what today we term a nervous break-down, while men in the ranks had 'hysteria', or the conversion of an emotional state to a physical one. There is no evidence that this distinction was accurate or arose through observation. It was ascriptive and deductive. Officers were not diagnosed as hysterics because they were officers; the men in the ranks were from the working population, and thus were unlikely to fit the template of neurasthenia, developed by doctors in their pre-war practices and clinical work.

That such distinctions were made time and again in Paris, London, and Berlin is not proof of the class-bound nature of mental illness, but of the social distinction between those who treated and those being treated. The 'spatialization' and 'verbalization' of the pathological went on day after day in metropolitan hospitals during the war. As indeed it had to do, for what choice did physicians have? They used the equipment – cultural as well as medical – that was at their disposal.

Their work and the presence of thousands of injured men in these three capital cities were unmistakable facets of the metropolitan landscape during and after the war. Some were hidden, to be sure, but many were not. George Grosz's and Otto Dix's sketches of amputees on the streets of post-war Berlin are well known. So is the powerful image of the *grands mutilés de la guerre* at the head of the 'victory parade' up the Champs Elysées in Paris on Bastille Day 1919. London too was filled with men in uniform being treated at dozens of sites and convalescent homes. We have attended to only a few such forms of medical assistance and to the men being treated for war-related conditions. When the war ended they were still there, attesting to the role of these three cities as centres of medical knowledge and treatment, as well as to the enormous difficulties of achieving full rehabilitation from injury.

As a result of their prominence in the field of medical care, Paris, London, and Berlin became centres for embodied memory – the record of war written on the bodies and minds of the survivors. Their inevitably slow pace of recovery meant that the ravages of war were visible, palpable on metropolitan streets long after the war was over.

11 Religious sites and practices

Adrian Gregory and Annette Becker

Cities of man, City of God

The established history of religious practices suggests that cities are engines of secularization, remote from the pieties and practices of the rural world.[1] Many would therefore assume that metropolitan society in 1914 was irreligious. If we compare Paris, London, and Berlin in the war decade, this argument cannot be sustained. London was a city with a vibrant religious culture. The British capital did not suffer from the adversarial metropolitan atmosphere of either Paris or Berlin, where the churches and working-class traditions and history stood against each other. Furthermore, religious practices of many kinds flourished in all three cities after the outbreak of war.

Churches and churchmen

Measured in many ways, formal religiosity in Paris and Berlin was lower than in London. Between 1903 and 1908 Easter Communion in Paris attracted only 17.7 per cent of the population.[2] On 22 February 1914, a typical Sunday in Berlin, only 3.5 per cent of the Evangelical population attended church,[3] and Easter Communion attendance in Berlin in 1913 drew only 14.4 per cent of Protestants.[4] Whilst the wealthier districts

---

This chapter was written by Adrian Gregory and Annette Becker, in collaboration with John Moses, Patrick Porter, and Jeff Verhey.

[1] Bernard Meland, *The secularization of modern cultures* (New York, 1966); Alasdair MacIntyre, *Secularization and moral change*, The Riddell Memorial Lectures, 36th series, delivered at the University of Newcastle upon Tyne on 11, 12, and 13 November 1964 (Oxford, 1964); C. V. G. Van der Burgh *et al.* (eds.), *Secularization in global perspective* (Amsterdam, *c.* 1981); Bryan R. Wilson, *Religion in secular society: a sociological comment* (London, 1966); Owen Chadwick, *The secularization of the European mind in the nineteenth century* (Cambridge, 1975).

[2] Ralph Gibson, *A social history of French Catholicism 1789–1914* (London, 1989), p. 175.

[3] *Kirchliches Jahrbuch für die Evangelischen Landeskirchen Deutschlands* 41 (1914), p. 109.

[4] Martin Schian, *Die Evangelischen Kirchengemeinden* (Leipzig, 1918), vol. II, pp. 200–2; see also Nicholas Hope, *German and Scandinavian Protestantism* (Oxford, 1995), p. 597.

tended towards higher formal religiosity, lower down the spectrum there was much greater variation.[5] In Paris in 1908, the proportion of the population not baptized was 37.9 per cent, whilst civil marriage covered 39 per cent; and those who had no religious burial (in any denomination) was 29.6 per cent in 1913.[6] This figure is comparable with Berlin burial rates, where 34.5 per cent had no religious burial in 1913 (although this figure fell to 19.5 per cent by the end of the war).[7]

The difficulties of ministering to rapidly growing urban populations are evident in the measure of the ratio of clergy to population. Concerned Parisian and Berliner observers in the late nineteenth century feared that their capitals were not cities of God. In 1881, a speaker at the City Synod despaired that Berlin is 'the most irreligious city in the world'.[8] Mgr Guibert, Archbishop of Paris, stated, 'One could say that this is a people without altars ... they do not hear the word of God.'[9]

Berlin's phenomenal population growth from less than a million in 1870 to approximately 4 million in 1914 had triggered an unprecedented church-building campaign, yet (on a very rough estimate) there were only around 200 churches in Berlin by 1914. The larger congregations of Berlin in 1920 had a ratio of approximately 1 pastor to 10,000 parishioners. The ratio of priests to parishioners in Paris, which had 107 Christian sites of worship, was approximately 4,790 parishioners per priest, while the number of inhabitants for each site of worship in Paris was 26,991. In this respect, the low level of clerical presence on the ground was a common concern to church authorities in these cities. Indeed, the level of pastoral supervision directly affected the intensity of worship as well as the definition of the flock. As E. Germain pointed out in Paris in 1914, 'the faithful are defined as those Christians who are under the authority of their legitimate pastors'.[10] If so, the faithful were dwindling. The number of Parisians who could be considered in any practical sense to be under the authority of their pastors must have been low – indeed the largest Parisian parish had a population over 100,000.

Low levels of formal churchgoing were also part of a bitter political conflict between the secular and sacred spheres in Paris and Berlin that had few parallels in London. In Paris, the 1905 Separation of Church and State sparked debate over property of the church of Sacré Cœur. The

[5] Hugh MacLeod, *Piety and poverty* (London, 1996), p. 11.
[6] Gibson, *Social history*, p. 164.
[7] See Schian, *Die Evangelischen Kirchengemeinden*, vol. II, pp. 200–2.
[8] Macleod, *Piety*, p. 6.
[9] Quoted in Yvan Daniel, *L'équipement paroissial d'un diocèse urbain. Paris (1802–1956)* (Paris, 1957) pp. 35–6.
[10] Quoted in Gibson, *Social history*, 56.

building belonged to the City of Paris, but the church itself was granted a 'perpetual affiliation' to the Catholic religion. The city's right of property had first been asserted in 1908 and then confirmed in 1913.[11] In Berlin, a number of prominent Social Democrats had, since 1906, been engaged in a campaign to achieve massive resignations from the churches. The level of formal resignation from the churches in Berlin was rising on the eve of war. The number of church leavers in 1912 and 1913 rose to 10,000 each year as a result of this campaign, the *Kirchenaustrittsbewegung*.[12] Some of these people probably left to avoid paying church tax. This was a significant contrast with London, where organized secularism by the turn of the century was in decline, and politically organized renunciation of religion on a large scale was absent. There were upholders of the cause of popular unbelief – witness Robert Blatchford's 1904 publication *God and my neighbour*, a widely read critique of Christianity.[13] The plays of George Bernard Shaw were intended to annoy believers of any faith. But these were causes without mass support. In 1902 an Education Act incorporated denominational schools within the state-funded system of primary education. The Anglican Church in London as elsewhere benefited clearly from this measure. Ironically, opposition may equally have served briefly to reinvigorate urban Nonconformity.

London's religious resources were richer than those in Paris and Berlin, and even by formal measures levels of religiosity were much greater. Problems of definition make it difficult to be precise about the numbers of clergy and places of worship in London in 1914, but there were comfortably in excess of 1,500 churches and chapels, by any reasonable definition of the city. For example, there were 103 Roman Catholic places of worship in 1914, and this was the poorest and least well served of London's religious communities. Some 25 per cent of these had been built in the previous ten years. These places of worship were serving approximately 700,000 Catholics.[14] During the war, a further five Catholic churches were consecrated, as well as a chapel to serve Belgian refugees.[15] London also possessed fourteen German Protestant churches (as well as one Catholic). To put this in perspective, it is almost certainly the case that in 1914 a German Lutheran or a French Catholic would be

---

[11] Jacques Benoist, *Le Sacré-Cœur de Montmartre. Spiritualité, art et politique (1870–1923)* (Paris, 1992).

[12] Macleod, *Piety*, pp. 25ff.   [13] Ibid., p. 48.

[14] In 1903 the number of Roman Catholics was estimated at 500,000.

[15] Chapel of Our Lady of Hal (1914) – for Belgian refugees; St Patrick, Waterloo (1915); St Augustine, Hammersmith (1916); Blessed Sacrament, Camden (1916); St Wilfred, Kennington Park (1916); and Holy Apostles, Pimlico (1917).

better provided with religious services in London than in his own capital.[16] The overall numbers of clergy in London are difficult to establish, but to give some idea of the scale, at Advent 1914 (one of four annual acts of ordination) the bishops of London and Southwark ordained 59 priests and 22 deacons.[17] The numbers of non-Anglican ministers of religion probably matched those of the Anglicans. The survey of churchgoing conducted in 1903 showed that on a randomly surveyed Sunday, approximately 22 per cent of the adult population of London attended a service of Christian worship. Of these, just over half attended Anglican services.

The feminization of religion in London in 1903 was striking: 372,264 worshippers were male, whereas 607,257 were female. But the degree of feminization varied significantly between denominations. At the elite Roman Catholic Brompton Oratory, women outnumbered men by 4:1, whereas amongst the Nonconformists of West Ham, the proportion by which women exceeded men was about 1.3:1.[18] In London, as in Paris and Berlin, attendance in the wealthy areas significantly exceeded that in the poorer districts. We have no detailed figures for 1914 for London, but if national trends were followed, it can be assumed that Roman Catholic worship and possibly Anglican worship (including in the poorest areas) had somewhat increased since the census, whilst Nonconformist worship had diminished slightly.

Yet while the levels of formal church attendance were perceived as low in 1914, paradoxically all three cities were also the centres of authoritative religious responses to the war. The physical and psychological presence of the sacred was a feature of each of the capital cities prior to the outbreak of the war. Paris and London had very deep links to the religious past and were cities of great significance in the religious histories of their nations. Their status as capitals was not simply a reflection of secular political organization, but incorporated religious symbolism within the very urban fabric. Berlin, by contrast, had less depth of religious sentiment attached, but was a city where the physical presence of the Evangelical church was rapidly taking on specific political and ideological significance. Notre Dame de Paris was the geographical centre of Paris and the pre-eminent symbol of the city until the 1880s; Westminster Abbey was the site of English coronations since the eleventh century, whilst St Paul's Cathedral was not only the heart of the City of London, but the embodiment of the Anglican religious settlement in stone. Hallowed by both tradition and

---

[16] G. Sims (ed.), *Living London* (1902), reprinted as *Edwardian London* vol. II, (London, 1990), p. 241.

[17] *The Times*, 21 December 1914.

[18] R. Mudie-Smith, *The religious life of London* (London, 1904).

the state, the great London cathedrals were still easily the most imposing structures in the metropolis. Lambeth Palace was the London residence of the Archbishop of Canterbury, who sat in the House of Lords.

By contrast Berlin's cathedral was a very recent construction (completed in 1905), a self-conscious attempt to embody the sacral ideology of the Wilhelmine Reich in its new capital. The Berlin cathedral identified Church and State very strongly by providing the site for devotion to the nation's cause and in accepting the Kaiser as the guardian of the faith. Whilst Westminster Abbey spoke of the long association of Crown and Church in England, Berlin's Cathedral symbolized the personal role of Wilhelm II as protector of the Evangelical church, a more operational religious role than George V's position as 'supreme governor' of the Church of England. In its assertive political message, the Berlin cathedral had more in common with the still unconsecrated Sacré Cœur de Montmartre than with Notre Dame. It also reflected the way in which Berlin professors and theologians had played a major role in developing the theological and intellectual underpinnings of the *Kaiserreich* and its imperial ambitions.[19]

Sacré Cœur brings out a second comparative dimension – the traumatic recent history of Parisian Catholicism – which lacked parallels in London and Berlin. No archbishop had been martyred in London since the seventeenth century, no archbishop had ever been martyred in Berlin; by contrast the martyrdom of an Archbishop of Paris at the hands of the Commune, together with significant numbers of priests and nuns, had occurred within living memory. Sacré Cœur reflected both this trauma and the militant reaction to it: bluntly it was a symbol of re-conquest, dedicated to the banner of the militantly anti-Republican Vendée rebels of 1792, planted in the district at the heart of anti-clerical violence as a physical and spiritual reproach to a city which had spawned the Commune and had rejected Christ. This symbolism was well understood and not lost on any Parisian; nor was the counter symbolism of the Pantheon, place of burial for the leading figures of French scepticism beginning with Voltaire. A deconsecrated church, it was unquestionably the 'sacred' site of 'anti-religion', one that had no parallel in London or Berlin.

Paris had a particular place in the demonology of traditionalist European Christians, as the irreligious and anti-religious city par excellence, site of Enlightenment mockery, massacres of priests, the festival of the Supreme Being and the generalized immoral debauchery of the Belle

[19] Karl-Heinz Krill, *Die Ranke Renaissance: Max Lenz und Erich Marcks* (Berlin, 1962).

Époque. Rural French Catholics, German Protestant theologians, and British puritans could all find something to dislike in this image.[20] The famously intense Catholic piety of pre-Enlightenment Paris was largely forgotten. This cultural archive of Christian suffering also acted as inspiration for the embattled pious Catholic minority within the city. In this respect, Paris was the embodiment of modern urban dissolution, but it is important to note that all three cities suffered from the same perception *within* their national frameworks. The irreligious metropolitan masses were the central problem for the religious and social thinkers of the nineteenth century, sometimes coupled with the perception of ever growing scepticism amongst the intellectual elites. Viewed from the provinces, Berlin and London also represented reproaches, 'mission fields', a challenge at least as great as the 'dark continent'.

The over-arching perception of similarities among the metropolitan centres, reinforced by the classical sociology of religion, has tended until recently to obscure vitally important differences between them. London in particular has been misunderstood by trying to force it into a framework of modernization leading to secularization. In particular the low levels of regular church attendance on the part of working-class Londoners in the early twentieth century were taken as conclusive statistical proof of the decline of religion. Counter-statistics such as the steady rise in per capita rates of church marriage, Sunday school attendance, and baptism amongst working-class Londoners from the 1880s to 1914 were dismissed by clerical observers and historical sociologists alike as superficial compared with their chosen measure.[21] The obviously increasing penetration of ideas of Christian doctrine and the framing of community ethical norms as 'Christian' were not considered at all. Nor was the increased identification of localities with 'their' churches and chapels, and the corresponding decline in popular anti-clericalism, popular innovations in liturgy, new forms of religious organization and public ritual – in short, the genuinely dynamic picture of religious development in the late Victorian and Edwardian metropolis.[22] Working-class London in 1914 was not the site of a declining traditional religion, but in fact a series of locales increasingly saturated with a sense of genuinely modern, in the sense of recent, religious values. During the war London soldiers

---

[20] C. Schwarz, *Predigten aus der Gegenwart* (Leipzig, 1869–73), vol. VI, pp. 44–5, cited in Arlie J. Hoover, *God, Germany and Britain in the Great War. A study in clerical nationalism* (New York, 1989), pp. 129–30.
[21] J. Cox, *The English Churches in a Secular Society: Lambeth 1870–1930* (Oxford, 1982).
[22] S. C. Williams, *Religious belief and popular culture in Southwark, c. 1880–1939* (Oxford, 1999).

sang hymns and parodied them. They carried Bibles for both reading and for luck, and were capable of making elaborate jokes about scripture.[23]

At the same time, the *real* story of religious decline in the Metropolis was the gradual decoupling of religious attendance from middle-class respectability. Increased residential segregation and the growth of the suburbs reduced the importance of church attendance as a mark of respectable social status; the middle classes were also more exposed to the challenges that modern biblical criticism and scientific theory posed to conventional faith.[24]

Two other features of the London religious scene should be noted. The first is the more politically neutral nature of religion. The Church of England was no longer the 'Tory party at prayer' and after a final convulsion over the consequences of the 1902 Education Act, Nonconformists were no longer self-evidently Liberal. In addition we must bear in mind that the slow permeation of ideas of 'Christian Socialism' in London meant that the rising generation of London Labour leaders included many with deeply held personal faith. The second point of significance is the atmosphere of religious pluralism in London. The Roman Catholics had their own Cardinal-Archbishop and Cathedral, and London was the headquarters of all the major groups of dissenting Protestants. There was really no overall religious majority, simply a plurality in favour of the Church of England. The establishment of the Church of England had generally ceased to be oppressive. As a result religion was never a stark either-or choice in London, and most religious tastes, including very heterodox ones, could be catered for by a saturated and competitive market place of religions; by contrast Berlin and Paris look to be more simply bifurcated cities. In Paris, the Republican anti-clerical tradition faced a hostile Catholicism with reactionary tendencies, a binary opposition which had been exacerbated by the increased politicization of religion during the Dreyfus affair. Berlin could appear to be a city where the churches faced a counter culture of highly organized Socialist anti-clericalism. But as the London case suggests, these stereotypes may well not tell the whole story.

Outbreak of war: mobilizing the sacred

In Berlin, appeals for patriotic sacrifice were framed from the start in religious terms. On 1 August 1914, the crowd congregated on the

---

[23] *Evening Standard, The 500 best Cockney War Stories* (London, 1921) (introduction by Gen. Sir Ian Hamilton).

[24] J. Morris, *Religion and urban change: Croydon 1840–1914* (London, 1992).

Alexanderplatz started to sing spontaneously – not the German anthem *Deutschland über alles*, but the Lutheran chorale *Gott, tief im Herzen*. On 2 August, Bruno Doehring, a Court Chaplain, had conducted a service in the Königplatz, in which he extolled the virtues of national and military heroes like Bismarck, Moltke, and Roon before their statues, conjuring up the memories of the war of liberation of 1813.[25]

The Kaiser's speech of 4 August, in which he declared that he recognized no political parties but only Germans, was written by Adolf von Harnack, the renowned theological scholar at Humboldt University. On 4 August 1914 Court Chaplain Ernst von Dryander preached in the cathedral to mark the opening of the Reichstag session in the presence of the Kaiser and some parliamentarians. His sermon promoted the notion of a war to defend German *Kultur*:

we are going into battle for our culture against the uncultured, for German civilisation against barbarism, for the free German personality bound to God against the instincts of the undisciplined masses. And God will be with our just weapons! For German faith and German piety are ultimately bound up with German faith and civilization.[26]

There *was* a marked rise in Berlin church attendance in August 1914 and the following months. This may be explained by the popularity of family communion as a farewell ritual for the departing men, which may have been seen as a means of providing protection, as well as a public demonstration of the family's patriotic service.[27] There was also a marked *fall* in contracting out of contributions to the Lutheran church, suggesting the suspension of formal hostility towards the church on the part of the SPD.[28]

Even that greatest advocate of rational modernity demystifying the world, Max Weber, speculated upon the possibility of warfare as a stimulus to religious feeling.[29] Whilst this might be seen as little more than a sophisticated rendering of the English adage that there are 'no atheists in the fox holes', it is certainly reasonable to point to the ways in which an elevated sense of the national 'cause' formulated itself in religious and quasi-religious terms. Messianism, apocalypse, redemption, sacrifice, sin, crusade – such was the rhetoric which inevitably framed what may

---

[25] Bruno Doehring, *Ein feste Berg: Predigten und Reden aus eherner Zeit* (Berlin, 1914), cited in Hope, *German and Scandinavian Protestantism*, p. 590.

[26] Quoted in Klaus Scholder, *The Churches and the Third Reich*, vol. I (Philadelphia, 1988), p. 84.

[27] Hope, *German and Scandinavian Protestantism*, p. 596.   [28] McLeod, *Piety*.

[29] M. Weber, *Essays in Sociology*, H. Gerth and C. Wright-Mills (eds.) (London, 1998), p. 335.

be termed wartime metropolitan religious culture, which respected the frontiers between the dominant or subsidiary Catholicism and Protestantism, according to country, and also acquired a universal meaning which included Jews and those without religious practice. As Robert Hertz, one of Emile Durkheim's students who died in the war, put it, 'How could we not recognise in the war the mysterious forces which sometimes crushed us and sometimes saved us ... this modern and wholly industrial and scientific war, is full of religion'.[30] Hertz wrote in wartime of what he termed a 'war religion' based on the sense of sacrifice and the internalization of an always-possible death. 'Our task', he wrote, 'is the equivalent of a true sacrament.'

The concept of a war of civilization against enemy 'barbarism' was at the heart of Parisian wartime representations. This reading of the war brought together Republican and Catholic millenarianisms, which, given the previously poisoned relationship between the Republic and the Catholic Church, was the most remarkable cultural achievement of the Union Sacrée. Both forms of messianism attributed to France a universalist mission. Whether preachers were Catholic, Protestant, or Jewish, there was no doubt that it was a Godly war. Secular figures similarly celebrated the 'universal mission' of the Republic. The war was thus presented as both a war of religion and a war of civilization, and for the religious, a war of civilization *because* it was a war of religion.[31] Civilization itself would progress through a French victory and regress through a French defeat. The rhetorical requirements of the construction of a united France meant that gestures of reconciliation were prominent; in September 1914 Poincaré sent official representatives to the memorial Mass in Notre-Dame for the recently deceased Pius X, and within a month Poincaré and the Pope had formally exchanged letters.[32]

Paradoxically, the ends being achieved by violent means of warfare could be presented as anti-war; as the playwright Jacques Copeau wrote in 1914: 'This is what is admirable: a peaceful and pacifist nation victorious over a powerful militarism ... destroying war through war!'[33] This did not exclude the celebration of virtuous and 'purifying' violence as an end in itself – such a concept was voiced in the French National Anthem,

---

[30] Robert Hertz, *Un Ethnologue dans les tranchées, août 1914-avril 1915* (Paris, 2002), 3 October 1914, pp. 69–70.

[31] Gerd Krumeich, ' "Gott mit uns", la Grande Guerre fut-elle une guerre de religion?', in *1914–1945, L'ère de la Guerre, violence, mobilisation, deuil*, 2 vols., edited by Anne Dumenil, Nicolas Beaupré, Christian Ingrao (Paris, 2004), vol. I, pp. 117–30.

[32] S. Marchese, *La Francia ed il problema dei rapporti con la Santa Sede* (Naples, 1971), p. 86.

[33] Jacques Copeau, *Journal*, vol. 1 (Paris, 2000), 13 November 1914, p. 624.

and it is significant that Bastille Day 1915 was chosen for the transfer of the remains of Rouget de Lisle, the author of the 'Marseillaise', to the Panthéon. Poincaré gave a speech in which, once more, the murderous struggle was relocated in a fight for the life of the just and universal Nation:

> The whole future of our race, and not only its honour but its very existence, are held suspended in the heavy moments of this inexorable war ... It is not in vain that in every part of France these admirable popular virtues will arise *en masse*. Let them, let them achieve their holy task. They clear the way for victory and for justice.

French Republicans saw the war in terms of the 1789 Revolution and the Declaration of the Rights of Man, which conferred on France the role of universal beacon, the torch of humanity. Radicals of a Jacobin bent, among them Georges Clemenceau, could see the war as a return to Year II (1793–4). French Catholics could recall the position of France in Catholic Christendom as the 'eldest daughter of the Church', thanks to the baptism of Clovis at the turn of the sixth century. When examined logically these visions were highly incompatible. The Year II had seen a concerted effort at dechristianization on the part of the Republic; but these were precisely the things not dwelt upon. In the spirit of Ernest Renan,[34] the Union Sacrée was a concerted effort to create unity by forgetting.

The British likewise defined the war effort as a defence of civilization. The 'Great War for Civilization' was pronounced early as the definition of the British war effort by one of London's most notorious anti-religious figures, H. G. Wells. Significantly Wells softened his hostility to religion in wartime and it was even rumoured (falsely) that he had converted to Christianity. The concept was common to public intellectuals and much of the clergy as well as politicians, some of whom – most notably Lloyd George (a Welsh chapel-goer) – naturally employed explicit religious rhetoric in a manner which was much less instinctive to their equivalents on the French left. In a speech to the Welsh community in London, delivered in 1914, he referred to 'clad in glittering white, the great pinnacle of Sacrifice pointing like a rugged finger to Heaven'.[35] The major dissenters from this view were the self-conscious religious sceptics of Bloomsbury. Their view of civilization saw it as fundamentally incompatible with warfare.

---

[34] Ernest Renan, *Qu'est-ce qu'une nation?* (Paris, 1992, first edition 1882).
[35] *The Times*, 20 September 1914.

The war did not in itself create an upsurge in the public use of religious rhetoric in London because religious imagery already saturated such public rhetoric. Uses of the word 'Crusade' in *The Times* actually *fell* significantly in the first three years of the war compared with pre-war levels, and only began to increase with the Palestine campaign in 1917. The crucial exception is the use of the word 'Sacrifice' which *increased* 25 per cent. In London at least, the rhetoric of Crusade in the classic sense is most marked by its absence, very few clergymen formulated this view of the war, at least in straightforward terms.

The most notable exception was the Bishop of London, Arthur Winnington-Ingram, who infamously went so far as apparently to call for the extermination of all Germans in order to save civilization. This appeal for murder must be read in the specific context of 1914–15 and in light of the outrage which had swept through London at the idea of 'Hunnish barbarism' leading to rioting against Germans and perceived Germans throughout his Diocese: 'Everyone who loves freedom and honour ... are banded together in a great crusade – we cannot deny it – to kill Germans: to kill them not for the sake of killing, but to save the world ... and to kill them lest the civilization of the world should itself be killed.'[36]

Much has been made of this widely reproduced quote, but within the Church of England Winnington-Ingram was considered an over-promoted man of limited intellectual gifts. In 1918 the Dean of Westminster, W. R. Inge, commented that Winnington-Ingram had preached 'a most unchristian sermon, which might with a few words changed have been preached by a court chaplain in Berlin'.[37] Although the Anglican hierarchy was unwilling to reprimand publicly this senior figure for his violation of Christian morality and the Anglican 'just war' theology, they made their opinion known, and Winnington-Ingram later largely retracted these sentiments. Still, as a populist sermon it was probably effective in catching the mood of many of his flock. When a more sophisticated Anglican thinker, Dr Edward Lyttleton, shortly before Winnington-Ingram's diatribe, preached a sermon entitled 'Love your Enemies' at St Margaret's, Westminster, in March, 1915, in favour of reconciliation; a sermon widely admired *within* the Church, Lyttleton was lambasted in the press as 'pro-Hun'.[38] It is even possible that

---

[36] A. Wilkinson, *The Church of England and the First World War* (London, 1978), p. 217.
[37] W. R. Inge, *Diary of a Dean* (London, 1949) p. 43, 6 January 1918.
[38] Wilkinson, *Church*, p. 221. The journalist Michael MacDonagh wrote in his diary of the sermon 'Magnanimous and courageous words, worthily spoken from a Christian pulpit.'

Winnington-Ingram's sermon was an attempt to re-establish the patriotic credentials of Anglicanism which had been cast into doubt.

In June 1917, the Bishop of London appeared in a different light. A German air-raid killed eighteen infants in Poplar. Sixteen of them were buried at the Anglican Parish church, and Winnington-Ingram presided over the funeral service. Amidst the local anger,[39] he spoke out *against* reprisals, 'Never did we expect to have war waged on women and children ... but we must be careful that indignation drives us to right action.' He further stated that, 'he did not believe that the mourners would wish that 16 German babies should lie dead to avenge their dead'. Instead the correct response was 'the increased output of all the instruments of legitimate punishment and military and naval action was the reply to these raids'.[40] This scrupulous application of 'just war concepts' perhaps demonstrates that Winnington-Ingram had been brought into line. Significantly, along with the rest of the Anglican Episcopate, Winnington-Ingram voted in the House of Lords against the bombing of German civilians.

A different mix of theology and politics may be seen in Berlin, where pastors retained the conviction that God had chosen the German nation to be His agents on earth. History was God's tribunal, *Gottes Gericht*. In this way German Protestant theology contributed significantly to the 'militarization' of public discourse during the conflict. Ministers trumpeted the widely held view that Germany was being 'encircled' by those Powers envious of Germany's rise as not only a great military and naval, but also a major commercial and imperial Power. Germany at war was merely defending her homeland, her heritage, her superior *Kultur*. Service to the Fatherland was thus essentially a religious duty.

Lutheran ministers claimed that the German people had realized after all that the source of their strength was their Reformed Christian faith. This is what made them ready to offer themselves to the national community (*Volk*) and the fatherland. The victory over Catholic France on Sedan day had been celebrated as a Protestant victory. This Protestant theology of the just war reached its peak in Berlin in 1917, the 400th anniversary of Luther's (mythical) posting of his '95 Theses' on the door of the church at Wittenburg. This *Lutherfeier*, confirming the survival of German Protestantism, seemed to some to prove the spiritual validity of Germany's cause in the war. The intense publishing output of the Berlin

---

[39] The Wesleyan minister of Poplar, William Lax, wrote of one of the fatally injured victims of this raid, a devout Methodist laywoman, forgiving the German pilots on her death bed with the words 'Father forgive them, they know not what they do.'
[40] *The Times*, 21 June 1917.

Protestant churches was reminiscent of the flood of literature in the Reformation: Berlin-Kölln synod distributed in 1915/16 for home and front consumption 350,000 calendars, 150,000 Christmas stories, 6,342,000 sermons, 10,134,000 'Glad Tidings' (*Frohe Botschaften*) and even more church magazines.[41] Most theologians and pastors had no difficulty in identifying the will of God with Germany's fate. The biblical scholar, Adolf Deissmann, who taught at Humboldt University, and edited the wartime publication, *Der Evangelische Wochenbrief*, claimed that Germany was 'A nation united down to the last man, assembled because its holiest possessions are threatened.'[42] It should however be noted that such public pronouncements do not fully accord with Deissmann's private opinion. During the war, he made a point of reading the King James Bible in English on a daily basis in order to remind himself of his common Christianity with his pre-war English friends.[43] Some even went so far as to equate war with an expression of Christ's love. One nation must have superior knowledge to be in a position to 'educate' its neighbours to live according to God's law. German *Kultur* was infinitely superior to the mere materialism of France or Britain. Protestant virtues were understood to oppose the cosmopolitan values of the Enlightenment, liberalism, popular sovereignty, and western democracy. These were decadent, in contrast to the manly Christian values of the German people engaged in a genuinely holy war. Germany's task was to mete out God's punishment to the arrogant and un-Godly, and to show them the true path to righteousness. The Berlin pastor (and future Nazi theologian) Paul Althaus proclaimed that Germany was 'fighting for the more noble England against the moribund, degenerate England, for the victory of what is true and good among our enemies against the mean, ugly and deceitful'.[44]

The most significant dissenter within the Berlin Protestant community was pastor Friedrich Siegmund-Schulze, who prior to and during the war championed reconciliation and ecumenism. His 'pacifism' was generally regarded by Protestant pastors in Germany as *Gefühlsduselei*, emotional sentimentalism.[45] In wartime Berlin, he implemented several charitable

[41] Schian, *Die Evangelischen Kirchengemeinden*, vol. II, p. 227.

[42] Deissmann quoted in Arlie Hoover, *The Gospel of Nationalism: German patriotic preaching from Napoleon to Versailles* (Stuttgart, 1986), p. 51.

[43] Alan Wilkinson, *The Church of England and the First World War* (London, 1978), p. 229.

[44] B. W. Pressel, *Die Kriegspredigt 1914–1918 in der evangelischen Kirche Deutschlands* (Göttingen, 1967), p. 115.

[45] Julian Jenkins, *Christian Pacifism confronts German nationalism – the Ecumenical Movement and the Cause of Peace in Germany, 1914–1933* (Lampeter, 2002), pp. 82–90.

endeavours that attracted continual harassment from the military authorities. He established the Zentralstelle für Deutsche im Ausland und Ausländer in Deutschland (Central office for Germans abroad and foreigners in Germany). With the help of Ernst von Dryander, he made visits to the Ruhleben camp in Berlin, where 500 foreign citizens were interned. His slogan for this ministry was *caritas inter arma* (charity in the midst of weapons), which he also called the 'workshop of love for one's enemy'. He created the *Hilfausschuss für Gefangenenseelsorge* (Aid committee for pastoral care of prisoners) as well.

The military authorities regarded his efforts with suspicion and harassed him even though he had the support of the Foreign Office from 1915 onwards. He had to face a tribunal after he sent an appeal of the English Quakers to all Protestant clergy. With the possibility of a death sentence hanging over him, he presented the tribunal with a letter from the Kaiser thanking him for sending the appeal. The Kaiser stated that the appeal expressed the right attitude of Christians towards war but that necessity forced him and the German nation to act otherwise. In all, Siegmund-Schultz was arrested over two dozen times because of his charitable activities.

'Pacifist' is misleading as shorthand for Siegmund Schultze's attitude to the war. During the war he was a patriotic ecumenicist who advocated moderation and ultimate reconciliation with the enemy. In November 1914 he extolled the spirit of unity which arose in 1914 and called upon Germans to support the 'holy struggle' of the fatherland.[46] Siegmund-Schultze was a divisive figure in Berlin precisely because he rejected the absolute polarities of oppositional pacifism versus militant nationalism. He disavowed the stance of radical pacifists such as Friedrich Wilhelm Foerster, who were 'rejectionists' in their conscientious objection to military service and their refusal to grant funds to the war. Siegmund-Schultze averred that the good citizen and Christian must remain attached to the national community and must not commit 'ingratitude and betrayal of the Fatherland'.[47] Equally, he demanded that the churches acknowledge that Germany and indeed her churches should share the blame for the origins of the war. The Church of Christ must 'work against hate'. This led him to support Germany's peace offer of December 1916 as a gesture of reconciliation which he denounced the British for refusing.[48]

---

[46] *Kriegsnachtrichten aus der SAG* no. 4, (1914) 77–9 cited in Jenkins, *Christian pacifism*, p. 148.
[47] 'Caritas inter arma' p. 92.   [48] Inge, *Diary*, 29 December, p. 43.

Generally the Protestant churches in Berlin functioned as a pillar of the *Kaiserreich*, and stood squarely behind the war effort. In line with the programme of the 3rd OHL, they advocated the ideal of the united and patriotic community, the *Augustgemeinschaft* that had supposedly been forged in the first days of war. In February 1917 the Evangelische Kirchenrat ordered for 11 March a day of prayer for the war (*Kriegsbettag*) stating that there was only one watchword: with God's help to struggle further and hold out until the final victory.[49] The churches were also involved in Ludendorff's campaign of 'patriotic instruction', the military petitioned the churches in 1917 for pastors to help enlighten the political consciousness of the people.[50] Berlin Protestants also vocally opposed the Reichstag peace resolution as a 'renunciation peace' that would waste the sacrifices of the dead and bring no peace against an enemy 'whose will to destruction is insatiable'.[51] Many clergy joined the Deutsche Vaterlandspartei, launched in Berlin on 24 September 1917. One hundred and sixty Berlin pastors signed a protest statement that Germany must choose between complete victory and ignominious defeat.[52] They were offended by the Reichstag peace initiative 'without annexations or indemnities', and hostile to its proponents, amongst whom were socialists believed to be anticlerical. Bruno Doehring, in a sermon delivered in January 1918 disparaged the leaders of a munitions strike as:

cheap, cowardly creatures who have desecrated the altar of the fatherland with their brothers' blood, . . . who have misled and herded the unfortunate masses into the streets from their peaceful workplaces, pressed deadly weapons into their hands, and bid them attack their brothers from behind, who are still confronted by the enemy.[53]

For clerical nationalists, dissent was treated as a symptom of deliberate political subversion by the ungodly.

---

[49] 28 February 1917, Evangelischer Kirchenrat an Dt. Ev. Kirchenausschuß, cited in Boris Barth, *Dolchstoßlegenden und politischen Desintegration. Das Trauma der deutschen Niederlage im Ersten Weltkrieg 1914–1933* (Düsseldorf, 2003), p. 162, n. 466.

[50] Gottfried Mehnert, *Evangelische Kirche und Politik 1917–1919. Die politischen Ströhmungen im deutschen Protestantismus von der Julikrise 1917 bis zum Herbst 1919* (Berlin, 1959).

[51] Günter Brakelmann, *Der Deutsche Protestantismus im Epochenjahr 1917* (Witten, 1974), pp. 159–71.

[52] Mehnert, *Evangelische Kirche und Politik*, pp. 53f. See also Daniel Borg, *The Old Prussian Church and the Weimar Republic* (London and Hanover, New Hampshire, 1984).

[53] From Presse, *Die Kriegspredigt 1914–1918*, pp. 305–6, trans. in Wolfgang Schivelbusch, *The Culture of Defeat* (London, 2003), p. 361, n. 44.

Adaptation

There was much discussion early in the conflict about a moral revival of each nation at war; such rhetoric faded away as the war turned into a giant industrial siege. Instead, piety took on the more modest forms of service. Among Parisian Catholics, the war provided new opportunities for public service, bypassing though not entirely forgetting earlier conflicts between church and state. Monseigneur Baudrillart was Chairman of the Catholic committee for propaganda in other countries. He knew that Catholics could defend the country in many ways.

> I attended the ceremony in the Madeleine organised by the Cardinal for the [war] loan ... Père Sertillanges spoke with a sort of enthusiasm of our *Président du Conseil*, Clemenceau! ... Clemenceau, who hates our Lord whom he calls Moloch ... Père Sertillanges did not speak of prayer: he said that there are four battlefields, the front, the factory, the Treasury, our hearts. He forgot one of them, the Church. The official world must have been thrilled.[54]

In the course of the war an intense Catholic patriotism emerged in the Paris region as elsewhere. One parishioner of Saint-Jean Baptiste, at Neuilly-sur-Seine, wrote to the curé, Abbé Maurice Salomon, 'In the grace of the all-present God, I will do my duty as a soldier and a Christian ...' (19 August 1914); 'I have sacrificed my life, I don't bargain with it, and I will be happy that my wife can look after herself and bring up our children if some day it is God's wish that I should kick the bucket' (1 December 1914).[55]

Serving the religious needs of soldiers on leave was one function of the metropolitan church which clearly grew in wartime. In London, the church of St Martin in the Fields was transformed by its vicar, Dick Sheppard, into a welcome centre for soldiers.[56] Sheppard had served briefly as a military chaplain, and as a result was convinced that the war was a spiritual opportunity to be grasped. On his return to St Martin's, he approached the challenge of his new role with prophetic zeal. He told his parishioners that at the front he had had a vision of 'a great church standing in the centre of the greatest square of the greatest city in the world'. He then asked, 'will you give a hand in trying, even if we fail, to build up this church?'[57] The doors had to be opened to those remote from Christianity. 'However beautiful Evensong is to those who love the

---

[54] *Les carnets du Cardinal Alfred Baudrillart, 1er août 1914–31 décembre 1918* (Paris, 1990), 10 December 1917, p. 702.
[55] Historic archives of the Diocese of Paris, 4 Z Salomon.
[56] C. Stott, *Dick Sheppard: A Biography* (London, 1977).
[57] Inaugural sermon, 14 November 1914, quoted by Stott, *Dick Sheppard*, p. 68.

church, we must be obliged reluctantly to confess that there are thousands among us who need catering for with something a little more simple and more warm and loving in its appeal to men and women who are beginning their search for Christianity'.[58]

This was the beginning of a year-long clash with some St Martin's parishioners. Sheppard's introduction of colourful ritualism offended some. One well-travelled parishioner wrote 'that he had never seen such absurd ceremonial since visiting a Shinto temple in Japan'.[59] The real contest for power in the church came on Easter Sunday, 1915, when the churchwarden, a local publican, refused communion from Sheppard and, turning his back on the altar, walked out to return to his pub. Sheppard pursued him and barred him from the church. The churchwarden threatened legal action and Sheppard successfully called his bluff.

Having established control over St Martin's, Sheppard announced his radical intention in the *St Martin's Messenger* in December 1915: 'I am quite certain that big central churches like St Martin in the Fields ought to be entirely free and open and no seats reserved. Everyone, poor and rich alike, should sit wherever they choose.' A cowed vestry agreed to this on 16 December 1915. Services were further simplified, the litany was cut, and the psalms removed. Above all the church was opened at night. A member of the congregation recalled:

The troops arrived in London at half past two in the morning when even the YMCA and the cafes were closed. Troop trains didn't leave London until the early morning. So Dick said they must come to St Martin's. There was an uproar. People thought they would bring bugs into church. There was an enormous row, but nothing happened. The troops kept on coming, and people gradually accepted they should come.[60]

By 1917, 1,200 people were cramming into St Martin's for Sunday morning service. A regular churchgoer commented, 'it is easier for a camel to go through an eye of a needle than for a parishioner of St Martin's to get into his own church'.[61] Sheppard, undeterred, instituted a short Sunday afternoon service for servicemen at which he suggested that parishioners should sit in the galleries until they knew how many men from the forces would attend. Seats were reserved for the wounded and provision made for wheel chairs. 1,300 people regularly packed this service, 'the church was full of troops with their wives and girlfriends ... By the autumn parishioners were considering bringing their own camp-stools to church with them and men with poles were stationed at the door

[58] Ibid., p. 73.   [59] Ibid., p. 74.   [60] Ibid., p. 80.   [61] Ibid., p. 85.

to control the crowds.'[62] By the end of the war 4,000 people were visiting the church daily, 'taking communion together and breakfasting together at the room downstairs'.[63]

The war established Sheppard as a rising star of the church. Through his post-war involvements, in radio broadcasting and leading the Peace Pledge Union, by the time of his early death in 1937, he was probably the nation's best-known priest. But the paradox was inescapable: to undertake root and branch reform on the Sheppard model required someone with the charisma of a Sheppard; yet an established church cannot rely on charismatic figures. The Sheppard approach in less able hands was a recipe for disaster, alienating an existing congregation without guarantees of a new one.

Parisian churches also provided shelter for soldiers and city-dwellers alike. The church of Sacré Cœur in Paris never closed. Max Jacob described 'L'Adoration nocturne au Sacré-Cœur de Montmartre' in these terms: 'The eternal light comes through its core, this is the Sacred Heart of Jesus. The light of the Father strikes through the Son to strike through me and this passage is the Holy Spirit. My God! You have wounded me with love ...'[64] Nocturnal prayer was a commonplace in Parisian churches and the homes of believers. Pierre Tisserant wrote:

Poor little mother, I can still see you on pilgrimage to Notre-Dame des Victoires and to the Sacré-Cœur, and above all I see you awake at night, praying incessantly for me. Surely I am well protected by this network of prayer, but you should not be disturbed either on this point above all when I am in a relatively quiet sector ...[65]

While the notion of a rise in religious fervour describes some features of wartime life, in other respects the continuities and adaptation of pre-war religious practices are more evident. It is striking that the four most extensive letter collections of wartime Londoners in the Imperial War Museum all involve families where regular church or chapel going and a serious commitment to faith had been part of the pre-war fabric of family life. To them the war entailed the deepening of existing ties rather than the development of new ones. Each family shows a distinctively modern piety, albeit in very different forms.

Eva Isaacs was a member of London's social and political elite; both her father and father-in-law served in wartime government in senior roles. Yet her piety was not simply a reflection of her social status: it was a deeply personal affair. In essence it was Eucharistic and highly

---

[62] Ibid., p. 85.   [63] Ibid., p. 86.
[64] Max Jacob, *La défense de Tartufe* (Paris, 1964), p. 177 (original edition, 1919).
[65] Pierre Tisserant, *Lettres, 1914–1918*, p. 234, 25 April 1917.

intellectual; she wrote to her non-practising Jewish husband at the front trying to explain her religious experience, and read theological discussions of the meaning of communion. The sense of connectedness it gave her (and in which she wishes to incorporate her absent husband with whom she was deeply in love) was central to her sense of self and also played a role in helping her to cope with her tragic miscarriage in 1915. There is nothing either conventional or traditional about this; indeed she is clearly out of step with most of her family, amongst whom there was no obvious tradition of Anglican piety. Furthermore Eva Isaacs was not particularly conservative (she clearly practised birth control and discusses it with her husband) and her individual faith took her in unconventional directions, as when she attended – and rather admired – a Roman Catholic church service.[66] At the same time, she was critical of Roman Catholicism for being too priest-centred. 'It gives one no form of expression oneself, there is no prayer to join in, no singing one can join, one merely watches the priest conduct the service.'[67] Nevertheless she returned to Westminster Cathedral, drawn by the old English Mass where she told her husband that she would be 'Glad of a quiet hour to sit & think & pray & dream of you.'[68] Despite this flirtation with Rome, she was the very model of a modern Anglican in wartime.

Edie Bennett, another young mother, but poles apart socially – the wife of a clerk in the anomic suburb of Walthamstow – had a very different Anglican piety.[69] She was a simple church goer, who found the church a shelter from a difficult home situation. Unlike Eva she was clearly inclined to private prayer for instrumental purposes, for example during air raids. She was the beneficiary of the mission to the cities and attempted to use the church as a warm heart in a cold world. But it is notable that this was not always a success; she admitted that after one church service she still felt 'rotten'.[70]

Elizabeth Fernside, a shopkeeper's wife from Fulham, was a significantly older mother, parted from an adult son who had been conscripted. Her letters to him are light-hearted and gossipy, and frequently mention their circle of acquaintance from Chapel and the PSA as a way of remaining connected. Fernside's allegiance to the PSA is also distinctly modern,

---

[66] Marchioness of Reading, Letters Collected in the Imperial War Museum. E. Isaacs to G. R. Isaacs, 16 December 1916, 28 January 1917, 4 February 1917, 11 February 1917, 5 March 1917, 6 April 1917, 29 April 1917, 27 June 1917.
[67] Letter to G. R. Isaacs, 5 March 1917.
[68] Letter to G. R. Isaacs, 4 April 1917.
[69] Edie Bennett, Letters to Gunner Bennett, Collected in the Imperial War Museum. Particularly: 17 April 1918, 29 July 1918.
[70] Letter of 17 April 1918.

the 'Pleasant Sunday Afternoons' was a para-religious organization designed to take the Puritan and Sabbatarian edge off Victorian dissenting culture. It fitted well with the warm and fun-loving Fernside family: religion as leisure activity, mixed with cultural self improvement and socio-political discussion.[71]

In the letters of the chapel-going Proctor family of South London – a more traditionally minded Nonconformist clan – the paterfamilias William Proctor, writing to his conscripted son in 1917–18, demonstrated Cromwellian rectitude, including a severe view of the righteous punishments that should be meted out upon the Germans. In 1918, he referred to the outbreak of Spanish influenza in the German army as 'this wonderful disease creeping up amongst the Bosches. It looks as if the Almighty has said "Thus far, and no further." '[72] He had little tolerance for those he saw as weak-minded towards Germany.[73] He also showed a fascinatingly universalist strand of theological-philosophical speculation, recalling the heterodox elements long rooted in London artisanal culture, 'but a knowledge of the goodness of God through our Lord and Saviour Jesus Christ, that's the sum of all religion – all religion (except devil or evil-worship) is good. I have found many good things amongst the writings of Confucius, the Vedas, Zoroaster and others – even the Mahommetans.'[74] The mother was more conventionally pious, signing off her letters with the fatalistic abbreviation DV (Deus Veult, meaning God willing).[75]

None of these strands of piety originated in the war, although all of them were utilized as tools for dealing with the stresses of family separation. All of them reflected the evolving religious scene of pre-1914 London. This may suggest a hypothesis that in coping with separation (and none of these families lost a close family member), familiar religious practices and institutions, already adapted to the rhythms of modern urban life, could be of tremendous use, whereas the impact of sudden loss might call forth a need for something more.

These detailed accounts are biased towards middle-class experience, but some of the same points could be made about working-class religion in London, a picture of intensification, adaptation, and continuity rather than transformation. Sarah Williams has detailed at length some of the wartime religious adaptations in the notoriously unchurched London

---

[71] Fernside Letters, Collected in the Imperial War Museum.
[72] William Proctor to Arthur Proctor, 7 July 1918. Proctor Letters, Imperial War Museum.
[73] William Proctor to Arthur Proctor, 11 August 1918, see also 2 August 1917.
[74] William Proctor to Arthur Proctor, 24 July 1917.
[75] 'Mother' to Arthur Proctor, 5 August 1918, 8 September 1918.

district of Southwark.[76] In particular she studies the continuities in the relevance to the idea of 'magical thinking' and its relationship to formal religion in wartime. Wartime did not create and perhaps did not even accelerate the growth of popular superstition in London, nor did it change its relationship with formal religion. What it did do was to reveal it, particularly when it was noticed by the Army and Religion Survey in 1917. The reason is simple: the world of Weberian rationality simply did not exist in the worst London slums. Life was unpredictable, chaotic, and often short in peacetime; disease struck adults and infants in apparently arbitrary fashion; men were crippled and killed at work, and most working people felt they had little control over 'fate'. The war brought some new risks, for example air raids, but the possibility of sudden violent accidental death had always been there. Gambling was endemic and the hope of influencing fortune led most people to experimentation with supernatural methods. Some of these were old customs of previous generations of rural immigrants, some were new inventions of the slums themselves, a process that continued into wartime. For example, Belgian refugees brought with them new folk remedies such as the use of cat skins as a magical specific against rheumatism, which were eagerly adopted by the inhabitants of Southwark.[77] Many of the formal religious practices involved in the 'occasional conformity' of slum dwellers were associated with folk religion concepts of luck, for example baptizing a baby was seen as protection against disease, whilst marriage in church was a protection against abandonment. Where, if anywhere, did churches as such fit into this milieu, and how did the war affect parish life? Certainly the pre-war function of the church as a feminine space of sociability had value in wartime. Williams describes, for example, the importance of the church 'Mothers' Meetings' as a meeting point for the wives of soldiers where they could provide one another with mutual support.

Can examination of a single church provide a sense of its role in the community? A snapshot view of one slum parish reveals a good deal about the challenge of war and the response of believers and clergymen to it. The mission church of St Silas the Martyr in north London, one of the newest parish churches in London, serving a parish of 10,000 described in surveys as 'poor and very poor', St Silas was emblematic of the attempt to bring the Church to the working class. The vicar, G. Napier Whittingham, had few illusions about the scale of the task. In his annual letter to the mission's supporters in 1913 he described the

---

[76] See Williams, *Southwark*, pp. 54–86.   [77] Ibid., p. 57.

area as 'a hard nut to crack' with 'little opposition, but such mountains of indifference.'[78]

Wartime was a real test for a parish such as this one, heavily burdened with building debts and still finding its feet in the community. The annual report for 1916 reveals something of both the opportunities and problems presented by war. In terms of the core mission of worship, modest success could be reported. In 1908, St Silas had made 634 communions, in 1915 this figure had risen to 3,505 and in 1916, 4,461. This comparison is misleading regarding 1908 – when the church building was uncompleted – but the rise between 1915 and 1916 is apparent. Whether the rise means more communicants or more frequent communion-taking is of course a matter to ponder (does this change represent deeper or wider influence?), but the bald figures cannot tell us.

Either way it is not a record of failure, but modest success. Communion was not the sole measure, and in all likelihood not the most appropriate measure. Engagement with the local community is also in evidence in the accounts, which provide an insight into the wide range of activities of a wartime parish church in London. The biggest items are standard religious expenses, but intermingled are many 'social expenditures', including £60 on 'summer and Christmas treats', £6 for the Scout Camp, £49 for the 'sick and poor' fund, £76 for the 'Mission club', and £2 16 shillings for 'Christmas gifts for our boys at the front'. Finally there was the sum of £6 and 18 shillings for 'war shrines'. Such modest expenditure was made despite the headaches arising out of inflation, pressure on 'middle-class' discretional expenditure, and competing charitable claims. As the vicar frankly admitted, 'These are very difficult times for a poor parish ... with the constant worry of how to keep the work going from a financial point of view.'[79]

Money was not the only problem. The war put pressure on personnel as well. The vicar of St Silas noted in December 1916 that, 'We have lost many of our workers, including our organists ... our Sacristan ... and very many others; Fr Scholefield left at the end of the year to take up Chaplain's duties at Salonika ... the church wardens have given every assistance to the work ... especially since the Verger left on National Service.'[80]

In all St Silas went through eight 'assistant priests' during the war years, of whom three left to become Chaplains, one had a nervous breakdown and two left for other parishes. The 'junior officers' of London

---

[78] *St Silas the Martyr, Annual Letters and Accounts*, December 31 1913. Deposited in the Bodleian Library.
[79] Ibid., 31 December 1916 (published in 1917), p. 5.   [80] Ibid., p. 7.

Anglicanism had little time to develop a familiarity with their flocks. In this context it is perhaps unsurprising that the National Mission was doomed. Still, the vicar tried to make the best of it, 'In November we had a 12 days mission in connection with the National Mission, which, if it did not fulfil all we hoped as regards the parish, was certainly a real revival of our congregation.'[81]

One effect of the war in a poor urban parish was to enable new urban churches to 'put down roots'. A barn-like mission church such as St Silas could in a sense 'invent tradition' through its campaign to erect a war memorial. Indeed, a little noticed facet of the whole street shrine movement is how much of the impetus came in the first instance from the poorest parishes where the church desperately needed to reinforce its focal role, to provide some sense of continuity with the past of the parish. The claims to represent the whole of the parish may explain why such practices could generate hostility from Nonconformists in London. J. H. Kensit, leader of the Protestant Truth Society, considered war shrines 'Papist superstition', and a violation of the Second Commandment. He campaigned against them through 1916 until in 1917 he was comprehensively defeated in public debate with the Bishop of Willesden, and driven out of the meeting where he was denounced as a pacifist, in riotous circumstances.[82]

But at the same time as some parishes deepened their local roots in wartime, their financial weaknesses were exposed. The devolved financing of parish churches by the Church of England meant that the churches with responsibility of ministering to the urban poor were the ones with the least resources. Relatively new foundations, lacking endowment, or even, like St Silas, actually burdened by debt repayment, were heavily reliant on middle-class philanthropy.

The material situation in Berlin was far worse, but it is also clear that war-weariness played a role in a gradual decline in both the effectiveness of the Church's pastoral activities and in the status of the clergy. This is the way one Berlin pastor put it:

The church suffers under the war, if [the war] itself is also often a false excuse. Mothers pretend to have no time for the registration of their children for confirmation. The children sleep in confirmation class, because they must do errands for their mothers. The number of corpses is taken advantage of by coffin dealers ... to receive money for an expensive coffin in their stock. The clergyman is shoved aside when getting on the electric train and treated impolitely by the people in the car. The unheated mortuary doesn't offer the Berliner any convenience either. The Reformation [anniversary] services [in 1917] were as a

---

[81] Ibid., p. 6.   [82] Connelly, *Great War*, p. 43.

consequence badly attended. The war prayer hours were transferred to the confirmation hall. Part of the resident visitors remained distant because they took annoyance at such a narrow room. Given our dire material conditions, the church poor-register suffers from a chronic deficit.[83]

It is possible in addition that the militant pro-war stance of the Berlin clergy made them a lightning-rod for the discontents of the population. In all three cities as the war continued, it became clear that the spiritual opportunity which had been anticipated in 1914 had been a casualty of material realities. This was not, in practical terms, a propitious time for the established churches to attempt to evangelize the 'godless' urban masses. But for other groups, the opportunities presented by the war unfolded differently.

The faith of the 'Other'

Israël Zangwill, a London Jewish writer wrote of Europe, 'The Jews are often more patriotic than the patriots themselves.'[84] There is a good deal of evidence for such statements, but it should be remembered that in a war of nation states it became imperative for the often trans-national Jewish communities to avoid being tainted with accusations of lack of patriotism.

In all three cities, Judaism was the principle religious 'other'. Christianity has tended to define itself in contrast to the major religious traditions with which it is in contact. In Western and Central Europe, this has meant above all Judaism. The three capital cities were major Jewish cities. Each was the centre of national Jewish life and the place of residence of a substantial part of the Jewish population.

Berlin's Jewish community

Approximately 270,000 Jews lived in Berlin in 1914, the largest population of any of the three cities. It is impossible to discuss Judaism in Berlin without reference to the prominence of Reform Judaism in the city. In 1900 only 15 per cent of the Jewish population were categorized as Orthodox. Although the numbers of Orthodox Jews rose with East European migration before 1914, prior to the war the influential position

---

[83] Georg Uehlein (ed.), *Kreuz und Pickelhaube. Großstädische Gesellschaft und Kirche zwischen 1850 und 1945 am Beispiel der Heilig-Kreuz-Gemeinde in Berlin*, p. 100.

[84] André Spire, *Les Juifs et la guerre* (Paris, 1917), p. 16. Zangwill was highly critical of such Jewish patriotism, his own inclinations were both Zionist and Pacifist and spoke in defence of Jewish objectors to military service.

of the Reform strand was unquestionable. Berlin was the world centre for this movement. The second ever Reformed Congregation had been formed in Berlin in 1815 and in 1847 the Berlin Rabbi Samuel Holderhein had pushed the logic of Reform to its ultimate extreme, in the foundation of the Berlin *Reformgemeinde*, which had taken the idea of assimilation to the extent of moving the Sabbath to Sunday, and holding services where men were expected *not* to wear headgear. The *Reformgemeinde* was an extreme manifestation; more typically, Reform occurred within the context of Orthodox synagogues, which adopted Reformed practices. Reform Judaism rejected the concept of the exilic nation in favour of a historicist adaptation to the nation state, in which Jews would think of themselves as Germans of Jewish faith. The great symbolic manifestation of this approach was the New Synagogue in Berlin, dedicated in 1866 in the presence of Chancellor Bismarck. It was in many respects the first great physical embodiment of the new *Kaiserreich*. Capable of seating 3,200, it not only preceded but exceeded the size of the cathedral of Berlin.

In Berlin, it was increasingly apparent that elements of Jewish life had become attenuated even as some others retained their significance. The mikve, or site of ritual purification, was largely given up, and most Berlin Jews ceased to observe the laws of 'kashrut' pertaining to food. These changes were consistent with Reform thinking about the historical flexibility of Jewish law. On the other hand, many life-cycle rituals were maintained, and associational Jewish life increased in significance. 'Above all Jewishness was located in the family home: for urban, increasingly secular Jews the family provided a crucial location for Jewish observance, a central form of religious activity, and indeed a replacement for it.'[85] This association between faith and family life was typical of middle-class German religious practice. Many Jewish families would have Christmas trees, frequently rationalizing them as being for the servants or as 'Hanukkah trees'. In this environment it is perhaps unsurprising that Berlin Jews had a high rate of conversion to Christianity, and that intermarriage was quite frequent. Roughly 18 per cent of Berlin Jews married non-Jews in 1910, and significantly by 1915 this figure had risen to 33 per cent.[86]

These tendencies were reflected in the response of one of the most important Jewish religious leaders in wartime Berlin. Rabbi Leo Baeck took the view that the prevalent idea of Judaism as 'ethical monotheism' was compatible with national citizenship, but that a more mystical and

---

[85] Marion A. Kaplan, 'Redefining Judaism in Imperial Germany: practices, mentalities, and community', *Jewish Social Studies* 9, 1 (Fall 2002) (New Series), pp. 1–33.
[86] Ibid.

ritualistic relationship with God was also essential. Baeck rapidly volunteered as a Feldrabbi on the outbreak of war. One of his congregants recalled the Lützowstrasse Synagogue in Berlin: 'This liberal synagogue, where I had been accustomed to hearing the prayer for the state in the German language since my Bar-Mitzvah, could claim many famous German Jewish members. This was the synagogue I had come to from the front on the final Yom Kippur of the war, and it was there that I had been called to the Torah together with my comrades in arms.'[87] This conjunction of Jewishness with German-ness, whilst probably not absolutely universal (for example, amongst more recently arrived *Ostjuden* who faced considerable prejudice even from within the Jewish community) can probably be taken as typical. Some Berliners saw in the defeat of Britain a step towards their Zionist vision of a Jewish homeland in Palestine. One such person was the philosopher Martin Buber, an immigrant to Berlin from Vienna. During the war he actively promoted the vision of the war as a war of Jewish Liberation and continued to propagandize for Zionism. Unlike most Berlin Jews, he was also sympathetic to the exuberant piety of the Hassidic movement. At the same time he had begun the work which would be published as *I and Thou*, a profoundly influential meditation on Jewish theology. Although Buber left Berlin in 1916, it is perhaps not fanciful to see some aspect of the 'war experience' in the development of his ideas. The sense of mystical connection can be seen also in the writing of his friend and collaborator Franz Rosenzweig, who served in the Balkans. Buber and Rosenzweig together re-translated the Bible.

The war did allow patriotic German Jews new opportunities for demonstrating their patriotism. Yet ironically at the very time this community identified itself with the nation in peril, there was increasing resistance to their assimilation. Jews took it as an insult that rumours as to their shirking their duty had led to an Army Census of 1916. When preliminary figures demonstrated, unsurprisingly, that Jewish military participation was fully in line with that of non-Jews, the census disappeared. The idea of Jewish shirking was allowed to flourish by default.[88] A second example of wartime anti-Semitism involved women's associations. The highly patriotic Organization for Jewish Women, founded in Berlin before the war, was pointedly snubbed in 1915 when it was the only major German women's organization not invited to participate in a general Women's Patriotic Conference.

---

[87] V. Grünefeld, *Heimgesucht* (Berlin, 1979), p. 36.
[88] C. Hoffman, 'The Jewish community in Germany 1914–1918', in John Horne (ed.), *State, society and mobilization* (Cambridge, 1999), p. 98.

Yet to conclude that the war led to the increasing isolation of Berlin's Jews would be inappropriate. As the statistics on intermarriage suggest, in some respects wartime conditions speeded the assimilation of Berlin Jews, and it is notable that the majority of Berlin Jews perceived their relationship with non-Jewish neighbours as friendly and only 3 per cent described it as exclusively unfriendly.[89] This view might not have been shared by the *Ostjuden* whose numbers increased rapidly after 1918.

London's Jewish community

The principal features of the London Jewish community, of around 190,000 individuals, were the numerical dominance of relatively recent immigrants, and at the same time the hegemonic position within the community of an established Anglo-Jewish elite. This elite was capable of exercising influence beyond the bounds of the Jewish community – indeed it is noteworthy that the British Cabinet in 1914 had as one of its members a practising Orthodox Jew, Herbert Samuel. It is too easy to perceive Anglo-Jewry as a monolithic assimilated group. To get a sense of the complexity of the established Anglo-Jewish community the example of the New West End Synagogue in London is illuminating. This well-established synagogue was undoubtedly the most prestigious of the Orthodox synagogues in London and was the preferred place of worship of the Anglo-Jewish elite. On the surface this was the picture of a very comfortably assimilated and socially conservative Jewish community, but in fact the New West End could not avoid the turmoil of the time. Herbert Samuel's presence as a worshipper had led to a suffragette demonstration on Yom Kippur 1914 when young female militants (and congregants) had chained themselves to the railings of the women's section and shouted 'votes for women'.

The outbreak of war further disturbed the congregation: the Chazan, John Lionel Geffen, quickly enlisted to serve as a Jewish chaplain, despite being well over military age. His son had done the same and was killed in action just outside Jerusalem in December 1917. The rabbi, Dr Joseph Hochman, resigned after conflict with members of the congregation over his appointment. He joined the army and after the war gave up the Rabbinate to enter the bar.[90] In the congregation were Zionists,

---

[89] E. A. Johnson and K-H. Reuband, *What we knew: terror, mass murder and everyday life in Nazi Germany: an oral history* (London, 2005), pp. 270–1.

[90] 125 Anniversary lecture on the History of the West End Synagogue by Elkan Levy, ex-president of the synagogue, published on line: www.newestend.org.uk/125Anniv/edl.lecture

suffragists, and trade unionists, men and women who served in many theatres and in many capacities.

Through the organization of the United Synagogues and many charitable organizations, Anglo-Jewry tried to exercise leadership over the much numerically larger, predominantly immigrant (or first-generation) community in the East End of London. Most of these immigrants originated in the Jewish Pale of settlement in the Russian Empire, and a very large number had never become naturalized British citizens. The level of religiosity was high; in a small area of the East End there were twenty-five synagogues, and a large population attending Yeshiva (Jewish religious schools).[91]

Britain's wartime alliance with Russia sat uncomfortably in these districts, and knowledge of pogroms committed by the Russian army in 1915 was widespread. The situation was further exacerbated by the long-standing politics of anti-Semitism in the East End, substantial numbers of East End Jews were attacked during the *Lusitania* riots in 1915. Accusations of Jewish shirking were widespread in the local press, both during the period of voluntary recruitment and after the introduction of conscription in 1916, when initially 'Russian' Jews were exempt from the Military Service Act.[92] For example, a Stepney councillor claimed in the *East London Observer* in February 1916 that only 2 out of 900 children at a local Jewish school had fathers in the army, compared with 52 out 500 at an Anglican Church School.[93] The local Jewish community bitterly disputed such allegations. The highly politicized nature of this argument makes it very difficult to establish the record one way or another. This tension climaxed in brutal form in September 1917 with widespread street battles involving 3,000 Jews and non-Jews in East London supposedly caused by a civilian Jewish tailor insulting Gentile servicemen in a pub.

It is likely that East End Jewish military participation up until 1917 was somewhat below average. For Jews of Russian descent, avoiding harsh military service had frequently been the initial reason for emigration. Occupational concentration in tailoring meant that many men had physical disabilities (such as poor eyesight) which would exempt them from military service, whilst devout Orthodox Jews had genuine religious inhibitions about military service, in particular, the difficulties in Sabbath observation, keeping Kosher and in the case of Cohanim (hereditary priests), biblical injunctions against touching or even seeing

---

[91] Overall London had fifteen large well-established synagogues and some fifty smaller ones.
[92] Julia Bush, *Behind the lines: East London Labour 1914–1919* (London, 1984), pp. 165–77.
[93] Ibid., p. 171.

dead bodies. The extension of conscription to Allied subjects in 1917 turned such issues into a real sense of grievance. The provisions for conscientious objection were framed in an implicitly Christian manner, making little allowance for concepts of ritual purity. It was perfectly consistent for Orthodox Jews to work on army contracts whilst objecting to their personal military service on such grounds, but this was something that military service tribunals found almost impossible to understand. One response was that of the ultra Orthodox Rabbi Avram Kook who ordained many of his Yeshiva students as Rabbis so that they would be exempted as 'Ministers of Religion'.[94]

The low level of East End Jewish military participation was not matched elsewhere. There seem to have been extraordinarily high levels of military service amongst established Anglo-Jewry, desperate to demonstrate a fundamental compatibility between Jewishness and British patriotism. A very high proportion of this group served as officers. The Chief Rabbi was himself keen to encourage military service, and went out of his way to help the Orthodox deal with the difficulties of army life, publishing homilies for Jewish soldiers which were collected together in 1917 as *The Book of Jewish Thoughts* which quickly became a classic of modern Orthodoxy. Nevertheless, Hertz was worried about the possible impact of military service on Jewish observance, and occasionally made speeches to this effect.

Above all else, what transformed the war for many British Jews, including the Chief Rabbi, was its relationship to Zionism. The higher level of Orthodoxy in the London Jewish community meant that the concept of Jewish nationhood mattered far more than it did in Berlin. Coincidentally, the presence of many Jews serving in London regiments in the Palestine theatre made concrete the concept of a Jewish national home, precisely at the moment of the Balfour declaration. Nathan Mindel (born Menachim Mindel) had immigrated from Vilna to London in 1902, and had enthusiastically assimilated, giving up speaking Yiddish and taking out British citizenship in 1912. He enlisted as an officer in 1915 and served in the Middle East. Prior to the war he had shown some interest in Zionism, but it was Palestine which turned this into a true passion. He wrote back to a friend in London that 'The Orient has captured me', and this was what he had been 'dreaming of for a lifetime'. After the war he chose to settle in Palestine, marrying a local Jewish woman. Throughout his life he considered himself both a loyal British citizen and a Zionist pioneer.[95] Such experiences may have become more

[94] S. Kadish, *Bolsheviks and British Jews* (London, 1992), pp. 207–8.
[95] Jonathan Freedland, 'A loyalty divided', *The Guardian G2*, 15 February 2005, pp. 6–7.

commonplace with the formation of the Jewish Brigade (Royal Fusiliers), recruited primarily in the East End by the Zionist leader Ze'ev Jabotinsky, which served in Palestine throughout 1918. Of course, not all British Jews subscribed to the Zionist project, and some were uncomfortable with the potentially anti-Semitic possibilities of a Jewish national home, fearing that the existence of such an entity could call into question their rights as British citizens. But because the policy of a Jewish national home was the stated policy of His Majesty's Government, many – like Nat Mindel – could see their Zionism not as contrary to their Britishness but as an extension of it.

Paris's Jewish community

Because of the historical legacy of the Dreyfus Affair, there has been a particular sensitivity towards descriptions of Jews as anything other than patriotic French citizens. Indeed the historiography reflects this, in its tendency to discuss French Jews as 'Israelites', a term which French Jews used to distance themselves from the idea of Jewish national identity, stressing instead the idea of being a Frenchman of Jewish faith. This is a reflection of the position of the Jewish elite, and especially the Central Consistory, who were socially and culturally the most assimilated group. There is, therefore, a danger of circularity in that the records are dealing with those who already defined themselves primarily as patriotic French citizens; it is an open question as to whether generalizations made about this group would have equal applicability to more recent immigrant groups (who represented 16 per cent of the community). For example, there are clear indications that the 'Israelite' section of the Jewish community were less critical of France's Russian ally than the Yiddish press, which sometimes fell foul of French government censors.

The Jewish population of Paris in 1914 numbered 60,000. Unlike London and Berlin, Paris had a significant Sephardi (Mediterranean) Jewish community as well as Ashkenazi immigrants from Eastern Europe. The fire in Salonika in 1917 led to a significant further immigration of Sephardi Jews to Paris.[96] But their presence was already established prior to the war. The Montmartre Synagogue (built in 1877) had been converted from Ashkenazi to Sephardi use in 1906.

The largest synagogue in Paris, the Temple de la Victoire, seat of the Chief Rabbi, was built in 1874, slightly later than its analogues in London and Berlin, perhaps reflecting the newly favourable conditions for French

---

[96] A. Benveniste, *Le Bosphore à la Roquette. La communauté judéo-espagnole à Paris 1914–1940* (Paris, 1989).

Jews in the early years of the Third Republic. There were fourteen synagogues in Paris in 1914, of which two had opened only the previous year; there was now a reasonable density of synagogue coverage for the population. Berlin with a much larger Jewish population apparently had sixteen.

One consequence of the presence of a foreign Jewish community is that its members were not eligible for conscription into the French army. In contrast to the case of London, these aliens never became eligible for conscription. Paradoxically, this distinction allowed Jewish non-citizens to demonstrate a particularly high level of commitment to the cause of the French Republic by volunteering – which automatically gave them French citizenship. A total of 8,500 Jewish immigrants enlisted in the Foreign Legion (somewhat more than those who 'volunteered' to join Jabotinsky's 'Jewish brigade' in London). In the 11th arrondissement, after the war, Jewish volunteers were commemorated in a plaque placed at a specifically Jewish Veterans' Society, a clear signal of their patriotism.[97]

For foreigner and French citizen alike, fighting for the Republic could take on a particular meaning because of the role of the French Revolution in emancipating European Jews. Recent history provided another powerful motivation: joining up undermined the calumnies of treason hurled without foundation at Jews. There were even some elements of wartime philo-Semitism to celebrate, such as the words of Maurice Barrès about Jewish sacrifice in wartime.

Jewish tradition could merge in a profound way with patriotism. The Parisian Georges Wormser wrote a letter-testament to his parents, designed to be sent to them if he was killed at the front: 'I regret nothing. I have achieved not only my *duty* as a Frenchman but as a Jew who *cannot forget* what *France has done* for his race. *Shema Israel Adonai* . . . I embrace you a last time.'[98] The use of the declaration of Jewish faith, the *Shema* (the assertion of the unity of God), familiar from religious services from childhood and deeply connected to the concept of Jewish martyrdom, as a trope for describing Wormser's feelings towards France carried a complex message. The implication of unity simultaneously affirmed the concept of Union Sacrée, but also asserts a Jewish particularity within it. There can be little doubt that for many French Jews, the experience of fighting for the Republic helped to create a sense of closure after the wrenching period of the Dreyfus affair.

[97] Benveniste, *Le Bosphore*, p. 77.   [98] Private collection.

As in London and Berlin, the wartime history of Parisian Jewry was marked by a robust mobilization of resources, both physical and ideological, in support of the war effort. Yet this proved insufficient to prevent at least some manifestations of wartime anti-Semitism. In all three cities, the aftermath of the Russian Revolution created new problems and challenges for the Jewish community. The influx of Eastern European Jewish refugees and the fear of 'Bolshevik Judaism' provided new ammunition for convinced anti-Semites. The breaking-down of barriers, the fading of stigmatizing the Jew as 'the other', a hope dear to Martin Buber, would prove short-lived.

Other faiths and denominations

Each of the capital cities in 1914 hosted foreign Christian communities of allied, neutral, and enemy nationality. The situation of Russian Orthodox and Anglicans in Berlin, and of German Lutherans in Paris and London, was manifestly precarious, but in the end these churches were to some extent assimilated into the broader story of treatment of enemy aliens.

Paris and London, as imperial capitals, also had a Muslim presence, despite the fact that neither city had a mosque in 1914. Due to the proximity of the front, this need was more significant in Paris than in London. The city accommodated Muslim soldiers on leave. The first leaves occurred in the middle of Ramadan in July 1915. On 13 August 1915 the breaking of the fast was celebrated with the inauguration of the Foyer des amitiés musulmanes, in the presence of Gaston Doumergue, Minister for the Colonies.[99] There are photographs of Muslim soldiers celebrating Eid at the *Foyer* on 10 July 1918.[100] It is widely believed that some of the impetus for the establishment of the Paris Mosque in 1926 was a statement of gratitude for Muslim contribution to the French war effort.

The London Muslim community improvised its own arrangements in wartime; Friday prayers were held under the auspices of the London Mosque fund, initially at Lindsay Hall, Notting Hill Gate, then at 39 Upper Bedford Place, and finally at 111 Camden Hill Rd. In 1916 the British Muslim Lord Headley (Al-Haj El Farooq) approached Austin Chamberlain for the allocation of state funds for the construction of a mosque in London, 'in memory of Muslim soldiers who died fighting for the Empire'. But it would not be until 1941 that the state finally gave aid to the construction of the Regent's Park Mosque.

---

[99] *La Libre parole*, 14/08/1915. Thanks are due to Emmanuel Cronier for this reference.
[100] *La Prière* SPA R4692.

Perhaps the most distinctive spiritual community in wartime London was that of the Society of Friends. The war challenged and split the Quaker community; the Quaker cabinet minister Joseph Pease agonized about remaining in the wartime cabinet, but stayed on – although he did (unsuccessfully) attempt to prevent his son from enlisting for armed service.[101] Likewise George Hall, the treasurer of the Independent Labour party (ILP) in London, enlisted for military service at the outbreak of the war despite his Quaker background – rising to the rank of captain and being wounded in action. After the war he became the president of the radical National Union of Ex-Servicemen.[102] But many London Quakers remained true to their pacifism, particularly amongst the older generation and amongst women. For example, Edward Grubb, sixty years old at the outbreak of war, became the treasurer of the No Conscription Fellowship, and was particularly effective at raising funds from his fellow wealthy Quakers. In May 1916 he was prosecuted alongside agnostic Bertrand Russell for distributing an allegedly seditious pamphlet.[103] Quaker women were at the heart of most wartime humanitarian internationalist and pacifist activity. For example Kate Courtney, born in 1847, veteran peace campaigner and suffragist, insisted on championing 'innocent enemies' and was a regular visitor to German prisoner-of-war camps. In January 1919 the 'Fight the Famine' Committee was formed at her Chelsea home, and in July 1919 she was condemned by the *Daily Sketch* as 'pro-Hun'.[104] Even before Courtney formed the Committee, Dorothy Buxton – a social activist and resident of Kennington, born 1881, who had joined both the Society of Friends and the ILP in 1916 – had campaigned from 1917 against the blockade. Buxton also published, from her own home, *Notes from the foreign press* – a definitive study of antiwar activism in both allied and enemy countries. Quakers also opposed wartime abuses; the veteran feminist healthworker and Quaker Elizabeth Knight organized active opposition to regulation 40D, which allowed the authorities to conduct compulsory

[101] Cameron Hazlehurst, 'Pease, Joseph Albert, first Baron Gainford (1860–1943)', *Oxford Dictionary of National Biography* (Oxford, 2004), [http://www.oxforddnb.com/view/article/35446, accessed 11 December 2005].

[102] David Howell, 'Hall, William George Glenvil (1887–1962)', *Oxford Dictionary of National Biography* [http://www.oxforddnb.com/view/article/33656, accessed 11 December 2005].

[103] Thomas C. Kennedy, 'Grubb, Edward (1854–1939)', *Oxford Dictionary of National Biography* [http://www.oxforddnb.com/view/article/71530, accessed 11 December 2005].

[104] Sybil Oldfield, 'Courtney, Catherine, Lady Courtney of Penwith (1847–1929)', *Oxford Dictionary of National Biography* [http://www.oxforddnb.com/view/article/51372, accessed 11 December 2005].

medical examinations of women suspected of transmitting venereal disease to members of the armed forces.[105]

The politics of the Protestant conscience had powerful consequences in wartime London. This was the only one of the three capitals where conscientious objection was enshrined in law as a legitimate reason not to serve in uniform. The provision of conscientious objection was an absolute necessity in allowing the introduction of military conscription in 1916; only in this manner could many Nonconformist politicians be brought to support the measure. Religious grounds were by far the most common reason for application for exemption from military service, though much historical writing has concentrated on the undoubted sufferings of socialist objectors, whose claims were rarely accepted by tribunals. The chances of success in such an application were far greater for members of acknowledged pacifist Christian sects, principally the Society of Friends but also the Christadelphians – a group that had been formed specifically for non-Quaker Christians with deep objections to military service. This presented a problem for some conscientious objectors, because it had been the outbreak of war which had brought them to join such pacifist sects in the first place. Such men were likely to be suspected of coming in bad faith to Christian objection. Even more difficult was the case of the small 'house churches' of devout believers, which could not be identified as a denomination at all. An example of this is the testimony before the Middlesex tribunal of Charles Atwell, 'Deacon' of the 'London Tabernacle Congregation',

I am a Christian teacher and I have lectured against war and its concomitants. I am a member of the Associated Bible students and in harmony with the religious doctrines taught by them which are that all members avow a full consecration of will, heart and life to God's service – as footstep followers of the Lord Jesus Christ, and the doctrines and teaching of the Kingdom of Peace and good will ... the provisions of the Military Service Act are in conflict with the teachings of the Lord Jesus Christ, as I understand and believe them ... the present kingdoms of the world are not Christ's kingdoms ... I can only render obedience to the 'powers that be' in so far as their laws and requirements do not conflict with the teachings of Jesus Christ.[106]

Atwell's appeal for total exemption was not granted. Such 'testimony' (deeply resonant for fundamentalist Protestants) was probably self-consciously modelled on that of Early Christian and Marian Protestant

---

[105] Elizabeth Crawford, 'Knight, Elizabeth (1869–1933)', *Oxford Dictionary of National Biography* [http://www.oxforddnb.com/view/article/38524, accessed 11 December 2005].

[106] Appeal of Charles Atwell, Springfield Road Tottenham, to the Middlesex Appeals Tribunal 16 April 1916 in PRO: MH 47/8 File M97.

martyrs. Martyrdom simply means bearing witness. One suspects that many religious objectors in London relished their chance to appear before the 'magistrate' and testify for Christ. Men steeped in personal readings of the Bible, unmediated by the advice of the Church Fathers to obey the powers of the world in matters of warfare, tapped straight into the pacifism of the early church. It is noticeable that few Anglicans or Catholics became religious objectors. Indeed, one of the articles of the Church of England explicitly stated that 'it is lawful for Christian men to bear arms at the command of the magistrate'. It is also worth noting that Atwell's millenarianism is quite literal, the powers of the world were coming to an end, the Kingdom of God was at hand and to flinch would be to invite damnation.

This culture of Protestant pacifist dissent was a peculiarly British phenomenon. The small traces of it in Berlin were obliterated under the weight of the *Augusterlebnis*. Apparently not a single German Mennonite was recorded as challenging the duty of military service. The leaders of Seventh Day Adventism in Germany announced at the start of the war that fighting on Saturday did not constitute a breach of the Fourth Commandment and that killing in war did not represent a breach of the Sixth. Some Adventists refused to obey their leaders in this, but it is unknown if any of them were Berliners. The main manifestation of Protestant dissent was an appeal from a group of pacifists who called themselves the Zentrallstelle evangelischer Friedensfreunde (Central Office of Protestant Friends of Peace), who supported a negotiated peace in opposition to the uncompromising war aims of Pan-German nationalists. It included the theologians Martin Rade and Siegmund-Schultze. Its appeal was signed by five Berlin pastors in October 1917 during the four-hundredth anniversary of the Reformation. Siegmund-Schultze decided eventually to remove his signature from the appeal before it was released, as Jenkins suggests, to prevent losing government support for his welfare programmes.[107] Even though it was eventually signed by between 250 and 300 churchmen throughout Germany, it was hotly condemned by nationalist pastors.[108]

As a result, dissent in Berlin was left almost entirely in the hands of anti-religious Socialists, most famously Karl Liebknecht. In his post-war internationalist pacifist museum (ironically located on Parochialstraße), inaugurated in Berlin in 1924, the communist Ernst Friedrich was scathing about religion, presenting a poem 'We have no father in Heaven' which claimed that the horrors of war proved the non-existence of a

---

[107] See Jenkins, *Christian Pacifism*, p. 224, n. 38.
[108] See Brakelmann, *Der deutsche Protestantismus im Epochenjahr 1917*, pp. 175–216.

Deity. A large section of the exhibition was dedicated to war-ruined churches with captions such as 'Why has almighty God not even protected his own places of worship?' Friedrich was particularly fond of long ironic quotations from Pastor Schetller. But there is an irony to this, his images and particularly captions were frequently steeped in Luther's Bible. The picture of a ruined crucifix in a French Church is captioned 'I am Jesus of Nazareth whom thou followest', whilst a picture of an executed corpse is entitled 'God said to Cain, where is thy brother Abel?' Friedrich demonstrates the anger of an Old Testament prophet, but he turns it against organized religion.[109]

Similarly Parisian pacifists, such as Michel Alexandre, Alain or Jeanne Halbwachs, aimed to crusade against war itself. In a mirror image reflection of Ernest Psichari, the young nationalist officer who died in 1914, of whom it was said that he appeared at all moments 'ready to take Communion or to die', pacifist militants like Michele Alexandre mobilized images of martyrdom:

the river of blood floods the earth, batters at our houses, the splashes always higher as the massacre adds victim upon victim . . . Have we accepted the Devil's bargain, death for death? That my son, my husband, my brother, should die to ensure, to buy, the death of the execrated enemy . . . 'Cain, Cain, what have you done to your brother?'[110]

In sum, conscience was a characteristic of men and women in all three cities, but London provided greater opportunities for its exercise in institutional terms. Both the public display of volunteering (and there is some scattered evidence that nonconformist chapels may have yielded a higher proportion of volunteers than Anglican churches) and the ritual drama of conscientious objection, the mobilizing of lay women both in religious charity and religious protest (and in the Quaker case these could be the same thing), the sheer diversity of religious options beyond obedience to the state, helped characterize London at war. R. H. Tawney, economic historian, socialist philosopher, and Anglican, could nevertheless write that when 'conscience and authority collide, it is to God, not to man, that obedience is due'.[111]

The widespread familiarity with biblical precepts and the respect for the ideal of 'the Christian' meant that such impulses could emerge even amongst the apparently secular. For every conscientious objector there may have been ten conscientious volunteers – they could even be the same

---

[109] Ernst Friedrich, *War against war!* (Seattle, 1987).
[110] Archives of the Municipal Library, Nîmes, Michel Alexandre, *Notes de Guerre*, 1917.
[111] 'Christianity and the Social Order', in R. H. Tawney, *The Attack and other papers* (London, 1953), p. 171.

person. Max Plowman came from a fundamentalist and pacifist Plymouth Brethren background in Tottenham. He rejected the faith of his fathers, but not his devout father with whom he stayed in close touch. Plowman became a socialist and agonized over whether to enlist, but in 1915 he did so and became an officer. Yet by 1917 he had rejected the war as immoral, from first-hand experience at the front. In 1918 he resigned his commission and registered his 'conscientious objection'. Under military law this was desertion, for which the penalty was death. It was an act of extreme courage. The authorities, embarrassed and not wanting to create a high-profile martyr, quietly discharged him. For the rest of his life Plowman would campaign for Pacifism, a key member of the Peace Pledge Union, where he worked closely with Dick Sheppard. Plowman never resumed his religious faith, but everyone who knew him believed that the root of his pacifism was his childhood religion.[112]

Ending the war

By 1917, one indication of the impact of the war on metropolitan communities could be found in the fate of church bells. In Paris, they were rung to give the all-clear after air raids.[113] In Berlin, they had been melted down in large numbers for metal amidst tearful farewell ceremonies. The days when Berlin's bells had rung out in celebration of German victory had long passed. Only in London were church bells used for celebration. In December 1917, the bells were rung to celebrate victory at Cambrai, a celebration that quickly turned to disillusionment.

The strains and burdens, particularly those of loss, made it very difficult for the established churches to preach any message of compromise peace. For example, the improvement in relationships between France and the Vatican suffered a setback with the delivery of the Papal Peace Note in August 1917.[114] The response was a sermon preached in the Madeleine by Monsignor Sertillanges with the prior approval of Cardinal Amette, and in the presence of the wife of the President of the Republic. 'Most Holy Father, we cannot for an instant abide your words of peace.' Reaction to this sermon was very positive in Paris, but extremely hostile in

---

[112] Richard A. Storey, 'Plowman, Mark (1883–1941)', *Oxford Dictionary of National Biography* [http://www.oxforddnb.com/view/article/39714, accessed 11 December 2005].

[113] Henri Sellier, A. Bruggeman, and Marcel Poëte, *Paris pendant la guerre* (Paris, 1926), p. 82.

[114] *L'Echo de Paris*, 17 August 1917, described the Peace Note as 'strongly influenced by the enemy.'

Rome. The Vatican was appalled that a clergyman could disagree with the Pope in a sermon, worse still with the active approval of the Archbishop of Paris. Indeed, Sertillanges was subsequently exiled from Paris on Vatican orders, and forbidden to continue propagating his views.[115]

The reaffirmation of the war effort could take on new forms, and the great religious buildings could still serve to mark the evolving course of the war. The entry of the United States into the war provided a new role for St Paul's Cathedral as a symbol of transatlantic Protestant unity. On 20 April 1917, 'a great and solemn service' was held in the cathedral, 'to mark the entry of the United States into the war for humanity'. The prayer for 'the King's majesty' from the Book of Common Prayer was supplemented with a 'prayer for the President of the United States' (a Presbyterian) and after the Grace the congregation sang 'the Battle Hymn of the Republic'.[116]

A deep sense of crisis accompanied the German offensive of spring 1918. For Mgr Baudrillart, the drama of the German offensive escalated to a new level when the bombardment of Paris began again: 'Everywhere felt threatened. I repeated my acts of contrition, of faith, of hope, of charity; I said a prayer for the victims ... we don't know yet how many victims there are ... After all, if I should die, I prefer it to be like this than of illness.' 29 March 1918 was Good Friday, and at 3.30 that afternoon the faithful were assembled for the Service of *Ténèbres* in the various churches of Paris. A shell fell on the church of Saint Gervais, just behind the City Hall; in the rubble, eighty-eight dead and a similar number of wounded were found, mostly women, children, and the elderly. Despite the flight of many of the Parisian bourgeois, Saint Gervais was crowded to hear the church's famous choir sing the Lamentations of Jeremiah. A few moments after the shell struck, the government Deputies in session were alerted. M. Grousseau, who was speaking in favour of refugees, added this strongly applauded protest to his speech: 'At the moment when we are defending other victims, we must mourn new ones. We will not forget a single one of them ... We demand justice from Heaven and in the face of men. Our soldiers will know how to add what is necessary for this justice to be complete.'

This tone of opprobrium was developed in the following days. The Germans were doubly guilty, for this bombardment destroyed a church at the hour when the death of Christ was being commemorated, the most sacred moment of the whole Catholic liturgy. The shell was both atrocity and sacrilege. Those who felt that from the beginning of the war the *poilus*

---

[115] Marchese, *Francia e la Santa Sede*, p. 138.   [116] *The Times*, 21 April 1917.

were sacrificing themselves in imitation of Christ saw here once again the hope of the resurrection for all the French people.[117]

Cardinal Amette, Archbishop of Paris, immediately visited the site and received by telegram the condolences of the Pope. The innocent victims of Saint-Gervais, were transformed into martyrs. The killing of children was particularly abhorrent, 'When children weep for their father who has fallen in action, that is war; but when fathers return from the front to bury their assassinated children, that is the Boche war.'[118] Protestant and Jewish authorities added their protests to those of the Catholics. The Grand Rabbi Israël Levi made the Old Testament speak for him: 'As once upon a time the Grand Priest Zachariah, was assassinated in the temple of the Lord, so the innocent victims of the enemy's bloodthirsty cowardice laid low in a house of prayer, cry to Heaven.'

With the Armistices the churches in London and Paris sought to extend their spiritual war effort. The solemn procession of King and politicians to give thanks in the great London Cathedrals on 12/13 November was seen as an entirely fitting and traditional way for London's war to end, certainly more appropriate in the eyes of staid contemporary observers than the rowdy night-time celebrations in the streets which also took place. The *Te Deum* organized in the cathedral of Notre Dame on 17 November 1918, merged with a more profane celebration:

It was the cry of gratitude and of liberation of a people, all together on their feet after four and a half years in their defence and who, trampled and bloodstained, martyred, had at least twice during this long anguish, nearly died . . . Notre Dame, all rejuvenated in its light coloured drapings of the colours of France appeared truly in its role of Temple in which the soul of a nation took shelter . . . the city's festival penetrated there, purified, and ennobled. But the church is in ardent communion with the crowd . . . It is as if the torrents of blood poured out by France were symbolised there in this solemn glorification of heroes, of martyrs and of our triumphant land . . . there are believers and non-believers. But all, without distinction, are seized with religious emotion . . . Under these vaults which never heard such music before, ceremoniously chanted with unanimous agreement, hear the great organ playing the *Marseillaise*, the national anthem, the hymn of those who fought for freedom, justice, human fraternity and our generous French ideal.[119]

There was no *Te Deum* in Berlin: on 9 November the Primate of the city and of the Evangelical Church, Wilhelm II, had fled into exile. The crisis of the German state was also the crisis of the Evangelical Church and the rituals on the streets of the city were the rituals of anti-religion

---

[117] *La Croix*, 2 April 1918.   [118] *L'Illustration*, April 1918.
[119] Georges Lecomte, *L'Illustration*, 30 November 1918, p. 515.

triumphant – a dimension of the German Revolution of 1918 which has not received sufficient attention.

Defeat and the abdication of the Kaiser presented the German churches with an existential crisis. The Protestant clergy, accustomed to the historical patronage of princes, feared the newly triumphant social democracy and its aspirations to create a parliamentary secular state. Apprehensions were especially high under the rule of People's Commissars during the turbulent period before the elections for the Constituent National Assembly. For six weeks after the revolution, the Ministry for Spiritual and Educational affairs in Prussia fell under the dual leadership of the Majority Social Democrat Konrad Haenisch, a moderate who regarded religion as a private matter, and Adolf Hoffmann, the Independent Social Democrat, whose anticlerical hostility was overt. Hoffmann was appointed Prussian Minister of Education and Public Worship in November 1918.[120]

Hoffmann antagonized former chaplain Reinhard Mumm, a former Nationalist Reichstag deputy, now delegate to the Weimar National Assembly and defender of religious education. In a Philippic against Hoffmann in March, 1919, Mumm cried, 'He must know what he did therewith to the Christian people. Adolf Hoffmann was capable of besmirching the honour of his mother before the gathered assembly building if it was serviceable to hatred against the Christian church.' Hoffmann's appointment was one of the 'indelible cultural humiliations of our fatherland'.[121] Their clash reinforced the mutual alienation of SPD and clergy. The assault on the churches' privileges and social status, especially state financial subsidies, confiscation of property, intervention in ecclesiastical affairs, the dismantling of religious education, were all imminent dangers to the traditionalists.

Perhaps the only way out of this clash was to invite adversaries to join in forming a cult of the war dead. On *Totensonntag*, the traditional day of remembrance on the last Sunday before Advent in November 1918, clergy had been urged to bring mourners 'the faith that these holy sacrifices will contribute to the resurrection of our nation'.[122] After the armistice and with increasing urgency, returning army chaplains and other

---

[120] See J. Wright, *'Above Parties'. The political attitudes of the German Protestant Church leadership 1918–1933* (London, 1974), pp. 12–14.

[121] R. Mumm, *Der Religionsunterricht und die Nationalversammlung. Rede des Abgeordneten D. Reinhard Mumm in der Nationalversammlung am 11 März 1919* (Berlin, 1919), p. 4.

[122] E. K. Bramsted, 'The position of the Protestant Church in Germany 1871–1933', *Journal of Religious History*, 3, 1 (June 1964), pp. 65–6.

pastors would exhort survivors that national resurrection through the dead was an ideal to be pursued.[123]

Religious reconstruction

Consecration ceremonies for the church of Sacré Cœur in Montmartre were held on 16–19 October 1919, to display the strength of Catholicism in this post-war period.[124] Large crowds of the faithful gathered round the building to hear official addresses, by the Papal Legate, His Eminence Cardinal Vico, and the French bishops, presenting the same message. France, punished in 1870–1 with defeat, the Commune, and the abandonment of the papacy, should be grateful for unity in victory and the consecration of the basilica. The consecration was seen as the essential point of the return of France to her own self, from defeat to victory, from religious and political destruction to the hope of reconciliation, not without irony from *La Croix*:

In 1870, on this same hill of Montmartre, Clemenceau saw the blood-stained flower of the Commune surge and pullulate. It would have been very astonishing to hear it said then that, fifty years later, ... the power of Christ would be manifest there, and that a whole nation would watch its triumph with avidity, and he himself would see all this with a disarmed and, who knows! ... perhaps benevolent eye.

The Papal legate announced festivals for the canonization of the Blessed Marguerite-Marie Alacoque (founder of the cult of the Sacred Heart) and Jeanne d'Arc, which would take place in 1920. The canonization of these two French women was accelerated by the war – by devotions at the front and the rear – as was also the case for Thérèse de Lisieux.[125]

Everywhere, war memorials appeared in these cities, in places where men had worked, studied, prayed, lived. The crypt of the basilica of Sacré Cœur would soon be transformed into a war memorial to Parisian Catholics killed in the war. In London's St Silas church, the congregation created two war memorials, one particularly striking. There was a parish war memorial, which listed the names of the 182 dead parishioners, under the inscription 'Who thereafter will surpass the glory of what they have achieved? May God have mercy on their souls.' There was also a second

---

[123] See P. Porter, 'Beyond comfort: German and English Military Chaplains and the memory of the Great War, 1919–1929', *Journal of Religious History*, 29, 3 (October 2005), pp. 258–89.

[124] Benoist, *Le Sacré-Cœur de Montmartre*.

[125] Yves de la Brière, 'Chronique du mouvement religieux, au Sacré-Cœur de Montmartre', *Etudes* (November 1919), pp. 336–62, at p. 360.

memorial brass plaque placed within the confessional boxes, requesting prayers for the souls of sixty-seven specified soldiers who had died in the war. 'Of your charity, pray for those who gave their lives in the war 1914–1918 and praise God for their valour.'[126] In 1920, the Archbishop of Paris was invited to bless the coffin of the Unknown Warrior on the afternoon of 11 November. Although nominally Catholics made up the majority of the nation, who could say whether the unknown soldier was not Protestant, atheist, or Jew?

Conclusion

In broad terms, the wealth of religious resources in wartime London acted as a source of continuity and stability, both during and after the war. Some went so far as to claim that religion in London acted as a check to the growth of Communism as a mass movement.[127] Impulses towards peace, social reform, and internationalism were as apparent amongst the religious as the non-religious, indeed religion was a prime carrier of these ideas. The wartime chaplain to the 56th London Division, Thomas Tiplady, who had been an East End clergyman prior to the war, wrote in 1917 that 'the pale thin faces of the children haunt me as the terrible sights on the Somme will never haunt me, for a ragged starving child is more terrible than a youth blown to fragments.' He concluded: 'Slums are now a reproach to Christianity.'[128] The war experience reinforced the pre-existing tendency in the Anglican Church towards Christian Socialism.

As sources of social welfare and comfort to the bereaved, London churches generally functioned well. Yet this overview needs to be broken down to reflect the reality of a multi-faith city. Zionism complicated the situation of London's Jews, and events in Ireland split the loyalties of London's Irish Catholics. The biggest challenge faced the Nonconformists. Prior to the war, chapel going had been proportially much more male than had been Anglican and Catholic worship. The 'middling' social base of Nonconformity was more heavily drawn into military service.[129] The war deepened the pre-war crisis of Nonconformity in four ways: the death of chapel stalwarts in action; the challenge of arbitrary death to the concept of the 'elect'; the corrosive impact of wartime on Nonconformist moralizing; and the insidious effect

---

[126] www.saintsilas.org.uk.   [127] Lax, *Lax of Poplar* (London, 1927), p. 92.
[128] T. Tiplady, *The Cross at the Front* (London, 1917).
[129] S. C. Williams refers to one part of Southwark as being known as 'too poor for dissent'.

of wartime oecumenicism which eroded the sense of separation from the Established Church. In England as a whole there was a striking fall in ordinations of Nonconformist ministers in the cohort which corresponds to the 'war generation'.[130]

It is reasonable to speak of a lost generation of male Nonconformist activists, which in turn may help to explain the stagnation and decline of the Liberal Party. One constructive response is demonstrated in the case of Constance Mary Todd. Drawn to the preaching of Presbyterian pacifist Edwin Orchard, she became a member of his church at King's Weigh House in London in 1917. In the summer of that year, she and her fiancé received a call to take charge of the Weigh House mission in East London, and on 17 September 1917 they were both solemnly ordained to the Holy Ministry by the laying on of hands, and the invocation of the Holy Ghost. On the following day they were married. Constance Mary Coltman – as she now was – became the first female Christian minister in English history.[131]

To some extent, Parisian Catholicism was a beneficiary of providential theodicy. If defeat and disaster in 1870–1 had been a punishment for apostasy, then surely 1918 was a reward for virtue. Nevertheless, the truce between Catholicism and anti-clericalism was a fragile one, bound together in wartime by parallel ideas of France's universal mission, and sustained to some extent in the post-war period by bourgeois fear of Communism. Yet it is difficult to portray the Paris of the 1920s as a city in the grip of a deep religious revival and even had it been, the clerical nature of French Catholicism limited its appeal and its resources. Marc Sangnier's initiatives towards a 'social gospel' were not insignificant, and in 1920 he received the blessing of the hierarchy for increased lay initiatives of 'patronage' – a marked contrast with the suspicion with which such activities had been viewed prior to the war.[132]

Perhaps the most remarkable legacy of the war for Parisian Catholicism was 'the city of remembrance', a project initiated in 1925 by Abbé Keller with the support of the Archbishop of Paris. This was a low-cost housing

---

[130] K. D. Brown, *A Social History of the Nonconformist Ministry in England and Wales* (Oxford, 1988), p. 230. Frank Richards cited in Michael F. Snape and Stephen G. Parker, 'Keeping faith and coping : belief, popular religiosity and the British people', in J. Bourne, P. Liddle, and I. Whitehead (eds.), *The Great World War 1914–1945* (London 2001) vol. II, p. 409.

[131] Elaine Kaye, 'Coltman, Constance Mary (1889–1969)', *Oxford Dictionary of National Biography* [http://www.oxforddnb.com/view/article/50351, accessed 11 December 2005].

[132] Gearoid Barry, 'Marc Sangnier's war, 1914–1919: Portrait of a soldier, Catholic, and social activist', in Pierre Purseigle (ed.), *Warfare and Belligerence. Perspectives in First World War Studies* (Leiden–Boston, 2005), pp. 163–88.

corporation on the rue Saint Yves in the 14th arrondissement. Each apartment was named after a dead Parisian soldier and the tenants were urged to pray for their souls as well as to help replenish the nation in honour of the dead by being fruitful and multiplying. The benefactors of the project were urged to support it in order to 'facilitate the impact of parish clergy on a population very heavily influenced by communism'.[133] Nevertheless there were limits to how far the clerical, hierarchical, and sacramental vision of French Catholicism could spread within the urban masses and many of the spiritually minded 'Agathon' generation had not survived the war.[134]

For Berlin churches, the war yielded a material and political crisis. The churches as a site of solace and comfort had been overrun by wartime politics. The clergy were instructed by the military to preach patriotism, to gather funds for war loans and other charitable donations, to denounce strikers and moderates who wanted a negotiated peace. Efforts for the care of soldiers meant that the churches could not deliver enough heating and lighting, while the church bells were melted down for metal to the point that none at all rang in the winter of 1918.

In a way not paralleled in the other cities, the fate of the Berlin churches was tied to the tight nexus of throne and altar. Wartime Berlin had been the heartland of the churches' prophecies of national salvation. It was also the place where these visions visibly failed. The fate of the Berlin churches was intimately tied to its royal protector, the Hohenzollern dynasty. The fall of one created crisis for the other. The *Manifesto of the Protestant Supreme Consistory* (*Evangelischer Oberkirchenrat*) lamented the injustices visited on Germany: 'We have lost the world war. We have been compelled to accept unheard of, most cruel armistice conditions from arrogant enemies . . . We have been spared no bitterness and no humiliation.' The declaration diagnosed 'inner discord', the culpable disunity of people, as the cause of defeat.[135] The Weimar churches' understanding of the war was set. War was a trial of the nation's cohesion and capacity for self-renewal, and the wayward civilians had invited defeat. Not only had the war not achieved the ambitious domestic reforms that were articulated in the pulpits, for many church-going people, it had subverted the sacred order of the nation.

[133] A. Becker, *War and faith. The religous imagination in France 1914–1930* (Oxford and New York, 1998), pp. 143–4.

[134] Schivelbusch, *Culture of defeat*, pp. 159–63.

[135] E. K. Bramsted, 'The position of the Protestant Church in Germany 1871–1933', *Journal of Religious History*, 3, 1 (June 1964), pp. 65–6.

Formally constituted in 1919, the Weimar Republic could not elicit real allegiance from the bulk of Germany's Protestant clergy. Dahm estimates that 80 per cent of the German clergy sympathized with anti-republican opinion.[136] This polarization of opinion accelerated official resignations of parishioners from the churches: 41,341 contracted out of the Berlin churches in 1919.[137]

The crisis of the churches entered the home, especially middle-class homes, because of the family-centred nature of piety of Lutheranism. Its main political consequence, with the collapse of the royal dynasty and consecrated political order, was to replace the churches' quietism with active opposition. For the first time since the Reformation, the Berlin churches would become institutions of resistance to the ungodly state, effectively replacing the ethos of Luther with the ethos of Calvin. By opening the door of the doctrine of resistance initially against the secular Weimar Republic, paradoxically the groundwork was being laid for later resistance to Nazism (and later state communism) by a small, saving, pious, God-fearing, minority.

If London shows the greatest continuities over the war decade, Berlin life is marked here as elsewhere with divisions that became chasms. In all three cities churchmen hoped for a new beginning for the churches. This never happened. Religious sentiments had their own rhythms and resources, many of which were located outside of the churches. In these three cities, the wartime struggle brought to the surface elements of spirituality which were there all along. These gestures and acts of faith, prayer, and solidarity were essential elements in the cultural codes and practices through which contemporaries tried to make sense of their world at war.

---

[136] K. W. Dahm, *Pfarrer und Politik* (Cologne, 1965), p. 9.
[137] Daniel Borg, *The Old Prussian Church and the Weimar Republic* (London, 1984), pp. 4 and 298.

12   Cemeteries

Carine Trevisan and Elise Julien

The Great War was the moment when family history and universal history came together. It is not surprising therefore that traces of the war can be seen in these three cities in local cemeteries, which are striking sites of family history, as well as in both small-scale and grandiose monuments in all three cities.[1] It is not clear, however, how contemporaries used these sites of mourning at a time of mass bereavement.

The key difference from the past was that older mourning practices centred on the body, but from 1914 on new rituals had to be found in the absence of the bodies of thousands of soldiers, men who left these cities to serve their country and who never returned. Those killed in action were most often buried *in situ*, on the site where they fell, in makeshift graves and then, after the war, if the remains could be found, gathered into national burial sites or more rarely repatriated at home. This left civilian cemeteries mainly deprived of their dead, deprived of their function as a site to which people could come, remember, and become accustomed to living without their dead. In effect, *rites de passage* concerning the dead became largely disconnected with graves and cemeteries in villages and cities alike.

Metropolitan cemeteries, like those in smaller towns, at best set aside military burial plots for men who died on the home front, sometimes while recuperating from their wounds, or those non-combat deaths, such as the thousands of still-serving men who succumbed to the influenza epidemics of 1918 and 1919. In the capital cities' cemeteries, those plots reserved for soldiers 'Morts pour la France', 'For King and Country' in England, and 'für das Vaterland' in Germany, served metonymically the same role as did front-line cemeteries.

It is important to note the special features of London cemeteries, which raise difficulties of comparison. In Paris, the capital of a predominantly Catholic population, people visited cemeteries on the first two days of

---

This chapter was written by Carine Trevisan and Elise Julien, with Jay Winter.
[1] Annette Becker, Stefan Goebel, Adrian Gregory, Jan Rüger, Danielle Tartakowsky, and Armin Triebel provided documentation and information for this chapter.

November, for All Saints' Day; in Berlin, the capital of a predominantly Protestant population, the visit was traditionally on *Totensonntag,* the Sunday of the Dead.[2] In London, no such dedicated day on the calendar existed, and in Anglican tradition, the physical remains of the dead were less significant theologically, and so were visits to cemeteries to honour the dead. There is as well a geographical fact to consider. The size of the city, dwarfing both Paris and Berlin, meant that it was difficult for families to get to cemeteries, even on an irregular basis.

The placement of military graves in civilian cemeteries tended to modify the character of these sites and how they were used. Cemeteries were not only individual sites for mourning a particular loved one, there was room set aside in these plots for collective mourning. In addition, other sites served funerary purposes, above all the tombs of the Unknown Soldier in Paris and London. Westminster Abbey, London's Cenotaph, and the Arc de Triomphe in Paris became symbolic cemeteries. Here is where the grand funerary spectacles unfolded, requiring us to extend the temporal boundaries of this chapter until 1920.

Finally, new rites to commemorate the war dead emerged in the capital cities' cemeteries, especially on Armistice Day. It was only in 1922 in France that 11 November was deemed to be a national holiday. In Britain, Armistice Day was thus named in 1919, though it remained and still remains a day of ordinary business. In Germany, the issue as to whether it was proper to designate a day of national mourning arose in autumn 1919, but which date was the question. The Volksbund Deutsche Kriegsgräberfürsorge[3] took the lead, and a consensus emerged surrounding the sixth Sunday before Easter.[4] On that date, starting in 1922, the popular day of mourning (*Volkstrauertag*) took place throughout the 1920s, even though it had no legislative standing before 1934.[5]

---

[2] German Protestants celebrated their day of the dead for a century prior to the First World War, beginning in 1816, at the initiative of the Prussian King, Frederick Wilhelm III, in order to commemorate the dead of the war of liberation of 1813–15. The *Totensonntag* is the last Sunday of the religious calendar, before the first Sunday of Advent at the end of November.

[3] German Union for the Care of War Graves. This private organization was founded on 16 December 1919.

[4] From 1926, this day was pushed away to the 5th Sunday before Easter, at the request of the Evangelical Church.

[5] By a law of 27 February 1934, Hitler gave official sanction to the *Volkstrauertag* as a national day of remembrance, and changed its title to *Heldengedenktag*: a day to commemorate fallen heroes, both in the war and those of the Nazi party.

The heavy burden of the dead

The Great War saturated metropolitan cemeteries. In Berlin, this was the result, primarily, of excess mortality among civilians. As we noted in volume I of this project, Berlin registered higher mortality due to tuberculosis and respiratory infections. There were those – particularly the elderly and illegitimate infants – who succumbed to the harsh conditions of war. In parts of the city there was malnutrition; survival rates went down due to a host of infectious diseases. And then there was the multitude who succumbed to 'Spanish influenza', a mutant virus which hit young adults with particular severity. In Paris and London, there were the victims of enemy bombardment to bury. Then there was the use of cemeteries in these cities to bury soldiers re-interred and those who died in the great metropolitan military hospitals. There were enemy soldiers who died in captivity. In Berlin, for example, 1,172 British soldiers lie in the Stahnsdorf cemetery. They died in captivity in eastern Germany, and their bodies, initially dispersed in individual graves, were later grouped together. In Berlin too, the Friedrichsfelde cemetery was completely full for the first time. According to inscriptions in the cemetery registers, there were 7,500 burials and cremations between April 1915 and December 1917. This was twice as high as the figure registered in the immediate pre-war years.

Inevitably, there was an effort to enlarge cemeteries, to the point where there was a fear, in Paris, of seeing them 'extending to infinity, with Paris and the Seine becoming vast cities of the dead'.[6] By September 1914 the military sections in Pantin and Bagneux cemeteries were both full. In July 1916 a section of this type was to be opened in the cemetery of Saint-Ouen. Another few months, and the places still available near the reserved sections were being used; and then in November 1917 the *Invalides* section at Vaugirard was instituted. A vast military cemetery was proposed for Mont-Valérien, but the plan was not realized.[7] In Berlin in 1915, architects and artists working for the war ministry foresaw the enlargement of the Berlin *Garnisonsfriedhof* in order to create 4,000 war graves, a figure which rapidly had to be revised upwards.

The contrast with London on this point is clear. The casualties suffered by France and Germany in the first year of the war dwarfed British losses, and the material pressure first on Paris and then on Berlin was much greater than that which the war brought to London. Consequently, the

---

[6] Danielle Tartakowsky, *Nous irons chanter sur vos tombes. Le Père-Lachaise, XIXe–XXe siècle* (Paris, 1999), p. 83.
[7] Ibid.

authorities running London's cemeteries never faced the challenges their counterparts in Berlin and Paris encountered during the war.

Cemeteries by default

The material concerns of funerary provision in Paris, London and Berlin paled in comparison with the fundamental problem that the majority of those who died in the war had vanished without trace. Thousands were first listed as missing in action, before their deaths could be confirmed. But even when death was confirmed, the problem that most soldiers had no known grave proved to be devastating. *Le Figaro* of 1 November 1915 printed a poem by André Rivoire, dedicated to the dead and entitled 'The Absent':

> They lie at the heart of a distant landscape
> They will not return ... [...]
> These dead do not belong to us.

The same issue of the paper carried an item under the heading of 'Echoes':

Tomorrow is All Souls Day. [...] This year, alas, there will be plenty of graves on which it will be impossible to lay the pious tribute. Most of those who died on the field of battle have been buried near the very site where they were killed, and which is out of reach.

A quotation from Alexandre Dumas followed, aimed at reducing the pain of absence: 'Those whom we have loved and whom we have lost no longer exist where they were but they are always and in every place where we are.'

The fact of absence was particularly difficult for Berliners. In most cases their dead lay in foreign territory. For most of the cemeteries, therefore, above all for the small parish burial grounds on the city's outskirts – cemeteries to which the people of Berlin were very attached – the dead were deemed to be in exile:

There, where one used to be able to go for consolation, to lay some flowers on the grave of a dead person, stopping to think there for a moment or to weep, how things have changed! The number of families who have been able to bury their dead close to home is very limited. The great majority of the dead lie in foreign soil and their parents may never see their grave.[8]

There were many images city-dwellers had of these battlefield cemeteries. Some came in the form of letters from the front or postcards. In France, the journal *Le Miroir* published a number of photographs which

---

[8] Samuel Keller, *Unsere Kriegsgräber. Ein Wort der Gewissheit und Hoffnung* (Berlin, 1915), p. 4.

were unlike those produced in previous wars. They showed precarious graves and rickety crosses in the middle of devastated fields, cemeteries themselves devastated by renewed fighting and bombardment. Then were bodies left without burial. It is thus striking that Jean Ajalbert, whose son died in November 1914, ended his astonishing enquiry 'How to glorify those who died for the nation?' with this bitter reflection:

At the end of this leaflet I learn that a grave, towards which all my feelings had returned for 18 months, in the hope of going there one day to place a flower on it, is threatened with disappearance: the shelling is pounding the cemetery caught between the trenches. The shells will tear the dead apart . . . The heart is swamped with horror; those who know what this is, will understand that I may be indifferent to a few letters carved on a wall [in some civilian war memorial].[9]

More troubling still were the writings of soldiers well aware of the precarious state of war graves. The Parisian newspaper *Le Figaro* printed a soldier's letter to a father, telling him about the death of his son:

He fell beside the frontier marker, and I have noted the spot where the Germans buried him. After the war, if it pleases God to enable me, I will go with my platoon to rediscover this place, I will exhume his mortal remains and I will bring you the body of your son.[10]

This was 5 September 1914. Four years later, the chances of success were infinitely small. Some says that in short order they would be dead, and that their body would literally disappear. J.-E. Blanche cites a letter in his *Cahiers*:

And in so much grey, sky, land, water, I am a little blue dot lost in the plain [. . .] The Yser is flowing again above our heads: we can see it through a rampart of corpses, for here there is no earth, no stone, no wood, nothing but mud. [. . .] To fire, we have to lean our heads against the dead bodies. We are inside death, so close to her that it would be awkward if death did not want us; the path would perhaps, once more, be difficult to follow, less smooth and less straight. I am coming to the point. Soon in the great eternal light, I will find him who preceded me [. . .] Do not look for my body, it already exists only as a little blue dot which will get lost in the mud. I will not have a grave like Gustave, marked near a tree where he was carried by faithful hands. Tell my family not to look for any trace of me. Let them wait! We will all meet again . . . elsewhere.[11]

The tomb is no longer where the dead lie. Even more so, cemeteries at home were not the place to find the dead; instead civilians had to go on pilgrimage to those sites where the dead fought and died, as soon as such a journey had become possible.

[9] Jean Ajalbert, *Comment glorifier les morts pour la patrie?* (Paris, 1916), p. 107.
[10] *Le Figaro*, 5 September 1915.
[11] Jacques-Emile Blanche, *Cahiers d'un artiste*, 2 (Paris, 1916), pp. 37–8.

These pilgrimages expanded very considerably in 1920. 'As in past years ... a vast crowd of Parisians paraded yesterday in the capital's cemeteries ... In the stations, from the first hours of the morning, large numbers of men and women took the train to the front-line cemeteries to bring to the war dead the same homage of gratitude and admiration.'[12] These pilgrims acted out of the 'nostalgic hope to be where the dead soldier they mourned passed his last days'.[13] In England, such visits focused more on how fallen soldiers lived; in France, on where they died. As David Lloyd has shown, one father, aged seventy, walked three miles to the cemetery where his son was buried near Ypres, because 'he would never pass that way again and he wanted to feel that he had traversed the same road that his son had traversed on his last journey on earth'.[14] The key point is that in such places the living could somehow come into contact with the spirit of the dead. In these places, pilgrims found all kinds of objects – flowers, bits of barbed wire, clumps of earth – which enabled them to hold on to a tangible link to the dead. Here we are well beyond a conventional visit to a cemetery.

In some respects front-line cemeteries were identified as the war cemeteries of these three cities. This was the point made by the Volksbund Deutscher Kriegergräberfürsorge (VDK), when it asked for financial help from the city and from churches to help maintain war cemeteries at the front. The same voluntary organization justified its appeal for aid by pointing to the service it provided Berliners in search of information on the graves of loved ones,[15] and by noting its work in maintaining and decorating these cemeteries on certain dates, thus uniting such funerary sites with the families of those buried there.[16] From 1927, the VDK suggested that Berlin adopt a front-line cemetery, as other cities had done. Their function was to maintain the cemeteries, in the form stipulated by the Versailles treaty, to correspond with a local authority who carried out the work, and to publish twice yearly a report on the state of these cemeteries. The organization hoped that locals would choose a particular cemetery to sponsor, on the basis of the number of their war dead.[17] In the case of Berlin, the cemetery chosen by the VDK was at

[12] *L'Echo de Paris*, 1 November 1920.

[13] Suzanne Brandt, 'Le voyage aux champs de bataille', *Guerre et cultures, 1914–1918*, ed. Jean-Jacques Becker, Gerd Krumeich, Jay Winter, Annette Becker, Stéphane Audoin-Rouzeau (Paris, 1994), pp. 411–16.

[14] David William Lloyd, *Battlefield tourism. Pilgrimage and the Commemoration of the Great War in Britain, Australia and Canada, 1919–1939* (Oxford, 1998), pp. 135–6.

[15] Landesarchiv Berlin (LAB), A Rep. 001–02, Box 1024; letter of *VDK* to the *Magistrat* of Berlin, 29 October 1921.

[16] Ibid., letter of 10 November 1922.

[17] Ibid., letter of 24 June 1927 and 3 May 1930.

Sissonne, near Laon, a site which held the remains of 15,963 German soldiers. Berlin declined to act in this way.[18] Even so the VDK made annual collections on *Volkstrauertag*, thereby contributing to the maintenance of cemeteries designated by clergymen as places where family members of a particular parish were buried.[19] The VDK assured local clergymen that in this manner they reinforced the ties between pastor and congregation.[20]

The notion that cemeteries were not the fixed abode of all the men who had died in the war led to a blurring of the boundaries between municipal sites and battlefield sites. They both served the same purpose, though it would never be fully realized, since so many of the dead had simply vanished from the earth. Here is one reflection by Lucien Descaves on this matter from early in the conflict. The date is the second All Saints Day of the war in 1915:

> The crowd who will visit Bagneux cemetery, today and tomorrow, will no doubt come with thoughts that are the same as my own at the moment when I found myself in front of the graves of a handful of our soldiers. Such as they are, these graves are representative, and each cemetery has similar graves. They do not invite meditation and weeping over the men who are buried there, more than over others. It is an anonymous delegation of all the scattered dead, in the woods and fields.[21]

This is confirmed in *Le Figaro* of 2 November 1915: 'Once one only went there [to the cemetery] to visit the graves of those who slept their last sleep there. Now people go there to weep for those, too many – alas! – whose graves are scattered far and wide.' The first All Saints Day of the war thus deeply modified the conventional meaning of the cemetery visit. Jean Ajalbert wrote that: 'All Saints is no longer the calm sad gathering in the city's burial grounds, but the forceful procession of an anxious people towards its thousands of heroes, lost in battlefield graves.'[22]

The new funerary architecture

The design of military sections in civilian cemeteries promoted a new affiliation, founded on a new community: that of 'brotherhood' in arms. Above all, the military burial plot appeared at the very moment (after 1880 and up to the eve of war) when, according to Michel Vovelle, the

---

[18] Ibid., letter of the *Magistrat* to the VDK, 2 August 1928.
[19] Evangelisches Zentralarchiv, 1/A2/525, letter of *VDK*, 17 June 1921.
[20] Ibid., Internal report to the German Evangelical Church, 3 February 1923.
[21] *Le Figaro*, 1 November 1915.
[22] Jean Ajalbert, *Dans Paris, la Grand'ville. Sensations de la guerre* (Paris, 1916), p. 111.

funerary chapel became popular as the chosen place for family burial. The cemetery, exiled outside city walls at the end of the eighteenth century, became reintegrated into the urban fabric from the middle of the nineteenth century as cities expanded. The post-war debate over repatriation of the bodies raised the question as to whether civic virtues or family virtues should predominate. Those who favoured restitution of the body to the family confronted those who defended the principle of retaining them in national burial grounds in terms which are now well known.[23]

Leaving soldiers' remains near the place where they fell was decided for reasons that were both practical (to avoid the scattering of graves, over thousands of kilometres, in fields often under cultivation, also to avoid the transfer of thousands of bodies) and ideological. In effect, family links gave way to those of the combatant community: 'They lived together, they fought together, together they saved the Nation; they should remain united in death as they were in glory', declared Paul Doumer on 31 May 1919.[24] Many soldiers themselves demanded to be buried alongside those with whom they had suffered. Furthermore, the standardization of graves in the national burial grounds was clear evidence of complete equality in the face of sacrifice. State maintenance also ensured for the dead an 'eternal survival' in collective remembrance, for when bodies were returned to their families, their graves lost not only the benefit of a perpetual concession, but might also be gradually neglected. Finally, the front-line burial grounds created, at least in France, a symbolic frontier: in the inter-war years it was considered that the army of dead watched against new threats from the east. As Paul Doumer always declared:

I consider that my son, officer or private soldier, should remain in the midst of those with whom he fought; he led his men into the cauldron and I wish him to remain amongst his comrades, that the fight continues for him, that he should be at the frontier and inspire in future generations, in the case of a new attack, the wish to defend the Nation.[25]

'Having served France to their last breath, the soldiers buried at the front will defend the nation into the mystery of death', declared General de Castelnau. Further, in his view,

to celebrate [the] cult [of the dead], there is no altar more dignified than the battlefields [. . .]; there is no greater sanctuary than this immense cathedral open

---

[23] Yves Pourcher, 'La fouille des champs d'honneur', *Terrains*, 20 (March 1993), pp. 37–56; Annette Becker, 'Les Croix de bois, Sépultures de la Grande Guerre', *Communio*, 20, 2 (March–April 1995); Jay Winter, *Sites of memory, sites of mourning. The Great War in European cultural history* (Cambridge, 1995).
[24] Pourcher, 'La fouille', p. 47.   [25] Ibid.

to heaven whose starry vault envelops the land with light and azure blue. And it is why our soldiers who fell on the field of honour should sleep there, on the altar of their holocaust.'[26]

The same idea was voiced in Germany in the context of defeat. The dead who remained at the front, almost always abroad, served a symbolic purpose: they had prevented the invasion of the country, its violation by the enemy. For that reason, they were the guardians of German history. In his speech on the commemoration of the dead of the University of Berlin, in the *Berliner Dom*, the Rector Reinhold Seeberg, who held the chair of Protestant Theology, said: 'A great mass of pale silhouettes is rising and stands guard before the proud and ancient fortress . . . Our dead stand guard silently before our great History.'[27]

The year in which the Unknown Soldiers were buried (1920), saw the introduction in France of the 'National office for military graves', and promulgation of the law to regulate the great national burial grounds, located near or at the front and designated as a permanent resting place for the ashes of soldiers who had 'Died for France'. Only the Americans and the French were to demand the repatriation of bodies; in France, around 240,000 bodies would be sent home; the exact figure for Paris is not known. But given the proportion of the army coming from Paris, a rough estimate of 30,000 bodies is probably not far from the mark.

In Germany, on 29 December 1922 a law was passed regulating the maintenance of war graves and the return of the remains of war dead to their families. However, there were substantial obstacles to overcome in returning the remains of war dead to Germany. The VDK insisted that German soldiers' remains rest where they had fallen. In the British case, repatriation of bodies was rejected, on grounds of cost and of equity, since the majority of men who died had no known grave.[28] Fabian War, the chairman of the Imperial War Graves Commission, was against repatriation, and insisted that the British war dead remain in small cemeteries near the site of their deaths, making these war cemeteries 'an eternal and supreme memorial'.[29]

In France, the State took charge of these exhumations, despite protests from many prominent families. In *L'Echo de Paris* of 14 October 1920, General Castelnau wrote a letter asking families not to reclaim the bodies of their loved ones. Still, many families demanded the repatriation of

[26] *L'Echo de Paris*, 14 October 1920.
[27] Reinhold Seeberg, 'Invictis victi victuri', *Wir heißen Euch hoffen, vier akademische Reden* (Berlin, 1919), p. 33.
[28] Winter, *Sites of memory*, p. 27.
[29] Winston Churchill's address to the House of Commons, 4 May 1920, as cited by Becker and Audoin-Rouzeau, *14–18. Retrouver la guerre*, p. 221.

bodies, seeing the military burial grounds as post-mortem barracks. The daily newspaper *Le Temps* was particularly outspoken on this topic, featuring in its columns comments of the bereaved questioning the forms envisaged for military cemeteries and the occasional errors of identification. On 21 October 1920 the front page of *Le Temps* carried a letter from a father complaining that his son's body had been exhumed from an isolated grave to be transferred to a national necropolis: 'Just think what these exhumations can be like, without the families [. . .] and what may be their guarantee that it is indeed their child who has been put into a concentration cemetery [. . .] How do such violations of graves take place [. . .]?'

On 3 November 1920 the same daily paper quoted a letter from a woman complaining about the 'disappearance' of her husband's grave: 'the exhumations were undertaken in May 1919 by the Australians [. . .] The sad remains, tied up in sacking, were taken into the cemetery in no particular order. Finally, a father seeking the return of his son protested: 'Will there never be an end to the atrocious despoliation of which we are victims? It is nearly a year now since the war ended: what right does the State have to keep my son who died for France?' The same newspaper concluded: 'Violations of graves do not stop, despite the assurances given by the Chamber in the name of the government. Under the pretext of regrouping, graves of our heroes are opened again and the remains inside them are taken far away, without the knowledge of [their families].' Finally, invoking the law of 31 July 1920 which allowed families to obtain restitution of the bodies, *Le Temps* observed: 'The demobilisation of the dead has been achieved'.[30]

The combatants themselves sometimes expressed their wish to be buried among their own people:

If this letter reaches you, you must understand that it is because France will have wanted the whole of me. [. . .] Perhaps one day you will come and seek my remains here in Belgium, the real one, not the land whose soil has been disturbed by impious barbarians. My only happiness is to think that you will come to find me and that one day I will lie close to you, in Marcey, which I should so much have loved to see again [. . .] Your little Henri, fallen for France.[31]

Or again, these comments by Maurice Briot, dated 4 May 1915 (he died on 9 June):

I wish that my body or what remains of my body should be transported to the little cemetery at Jardres, near to those who were dear to me, and that my favourite flowers

---

[30] *Le Temps*, 4 October 1920.
[31] *La dernière lettre écrite par des soldats français tombés au champ d'honneur* (Paris, 1922), p. 162.

should be placed on my grave. But I may fall perhaps between the lines, where the rats and crows will fight over my body, and then I will be buried in the mass grave.[32]

Overall, transfers in France were complete by 1923.[33] However, specific exhumations were undertaken on family demand throughout the century. In Vaugirard military burial ground, for example, the body of Paul Favier, who died on 12 March 1918, was exhumed on 17 September 1971 at the request of his son, to be re-interred in a family vault.[34]

Military graves

Following the articles of the Treaty of Frankfurt in 1871 establishing the first European military cemeteries, article 225 of the Treaty of Versailles provided for the maintenance of military cemeteries for German or Allied soldiers and sailors who had died in the war. The lay-out and decoration of graves in the military burial grounds were strictly regulated in France: each individual grave had its individual standard monument, with inscriptions indicating the family name and first name, the rank and military posting of the dead man, the place and date of his death, and the statement: 'Morts pour la France.' In addition the monument could bear a religious emblem, according to family wishes.

In the British case, the IWGC offered both uniformity and some personal variation in inscription. The horticulture was particularly English; a country garden cemetery was the model, and to this day, the decoration of flowers and the green of the lawns separate British war cemeteries from French or German. When men died at home, their remains were placed in civilian cemeteries, but the same style of stone design, with name, rank, regiment, and some modest phrase or poem of the family's choice, were used here just as they were in war graves cemeteries abroad.

In Berlin, families had a wider margin of decision. On 5 July 1917 a new set of regulations was published for the *Garnisonsfriedhof*, which could be reduced to two essential points: the upkeep of the graves was assured by the cemetery's management (here joined to the military administration), but parents could arrange the grave of their son as they wished, provided they had obtained permission from the cemetery's administration (sketch to be submitted, material to be used, colour and inscription proposed). Similarly, in the north-east part of the Stahnsdorf cemetery, a military

---

[32] Ibid., p. 51.
[33] Béatrix Pau-Heyries, *Le transfert des corps des militaires de la Grande Guerre, 1914–1939. Etude comparée France-Italie (Belgique, Royaume-Uni, Etats-Unis)*, doctoral thesis, University of Montpellier 3, 2004.
[34] Service des Sépultures militaires, Box 851.

cemetery was established for 173 German soldiers killed during the First World War. A large and simple cross gave this part of the cemetery, laid out in terraces, its sober identity. However, the parents of war-dead also had the right to be buried there.

We should note another feature specific to Berlin, concerning the Invalids' cemetery. In 1925 Treuwerth examined the graves in this cemetery. Of 6,000 existing graves, he drew up a list of 199 people who fell during the First World War or who had died of their wounds in Berlin's military hospitals.[35] More than a strictly military cemetery, this was a kind of burial place of honour (*Ehrenhain*) for Prussia. According to Laurenz Demps, it was during the First World War and the following years that the 'Invalides' cemetery acquired its definitive status as a cemetery for heroes (*Heldenfriedhof*).[36] On the tombs, 'there are in most cases the little crosses brought back from enemy territory, as the finest and most significant ornament, lovingly made by friends and comrades in the turbulence of endless battles, perhaps carved out of timber from trees split apart by grenades'.[37]

Some famous men are buried there. The 'Invalids' cemetery does not, however, contain only generals; there are also military men of lower ranks (although they are all officers). The majority of First World War dead are buried in field B: all kinds of funerary monuments are visible here – from the wooden cross to the martial eagle – set up after the war. On the grave of Lieutenant Werner John, created by Emil Cauer, the inscription reads '*Mutter Erde nimmt ihren Sohn auf*' ('Mother Earth takes back her son').

Airmen were particularly cherished in war propaganda, a fact which explains the burial here in 1925 of Manfred von Richthofen who entered war history as 'the Red Baron'. He was killed in France in 1918 and buried in a military cemetery in the Somme. His family expressed their wish to take his body back to Silesia, but Gerhard Gessler, Minister of Defence, asked that he should instead be buried in the Invalids' cemetery. For the political authorities of the Weimar Republic it was a matter of creating a consensus around a victorious representative of the German army during the war. Those who benefited were the members of an elite which was, to say the least, not particularly democratic. It was for this elite that the meaning of this cemetery developed as 'the monument of history' (*Denkmal der Geschichte*) and the symbol of former times.[38]

[35] Karl Treuwerth, *Der Invalidenfriedhof in Berlin. Eine Stätte preußisch-deutschen Ruhmes* (Berlin, 1925).
[36] Laurenz Demps, *Zwischen Mars und Minerva. Wegweiser Invalidenfriedhof* (Berlin, 1998), pp. 33ff.
[37] Hermann Frankfurth, *Berlin und Potsdam in der Sprache ihrer Kirchen und Friedhöfe* (Berlin, 1924), p. 146.
[38] Demps, *Zwischen Mars und Minerva*, p. 38.

In London, too, there are some arresting monuments to those who died in the air war. In the Brompton cemetery, thanks to donations by readers of the *Daily Express*, there is a monument to the first British aviator who shot down a Zeppelin – Rex Warneford, who died in 1915.

Family vaults

New ways of dying brought about changes in funerary architecture. When the dead had not been repatriated, family tombs in Paris were modified with the addition of plaques bearing the statement: 'In memory of . . .'. In principle these were merely plaques of homage, in memory, the body of the dead man being buried in a national necropolis or never having been traced. Thus there appears on the vault of the Martineau and Daverdin families (Passy cemetery), the mention:

> To
> The memory
> Of my son
> Who died on the field of honour

Or again, on the Maillochon and Genette tomb (Grenelle cemetery):

> To the memory
> Of my dear son
> René Genette
> Killed and buried at Gorcy (Meurthe & Moselle)
> 22 August 1914
> Aged 21 years

The plaque appears to take the place of the absent body. Sculpture refashioned the bodies of the fall in a monumental form. In the *Sankt-Annen-Kirchhof*, Berlin-Dahlem, there is a funerary monument consisting of a sculpture representing a 'dying soldier': a soldier with helmet and weapons, mortally wounded, leaning against a rock; his naked body is wrapped in a flag, his left hand presses a weapon to his breast, while the body leans to the right. Professor Max Sering had this monument erected in memory of his son (of the same name), a university student who was killed in France in 1918 and was buried in the Forest of Mormal. For the installation of this particularly tall monument he had to obtain special permission from the parish in 1922. The *Neuer Friedhof* at Wannsee has another monument of the same type. This time it is a 'soldier's head'. The sculpture in fact represents the upper half of a soldier's body, with helmet and sword-belt, holding binoculars in his left hand. This memorial was set up by Professor Paul Strassemann in memory of his son Hellmuth, a lieutenant in the Reserves who was killed at Tilloy on the Somme and buried in Arras.

Some notation is more complex, relating to the interment of the body elsewhere.

> To the memory of Maurice Maugin
> Machine-gun sergeant
> With the 40th Infantry regiment
> Born in Paris, 11 February 1892,
> Died on the field of honour
> And piously buried
> By his comrades
> 24 August 1915
> At Neuville Saint Vaast

Even when families did not want their dead to rest in a national cemetery or military plot in a civilian cemetery, there were monuments which mixed together family forms and civic virtue. The evangelical Nikolassee parish cemetery contains the grave of Reinhold Klimsch, an aviator who died in 1918 at the age of twenty-one. The funerary monument, created by his father, the sculptor Fritz Klimsch, is surmounted by a triangular relief with a helmet at its centre flanked by a laurel branch and an oak branch.

Some families placed the name or some emblem signifying the man who fell in the war at a prominent place in their sepulchre. Family time and historical time were braided together in the optic provided by the war. An example is visible in the Père-Lachaise cemetery in Paris, the grave of Albert Rapilly: a bronze bas-relief on the top of the family tomb features the portrait of the young dead man, against a neutral background in which can be seen an aircraft crashing into a church. The Fleisch family grave is also surmounted with a bronze bas-relief showing the dead soldier.

Thus the grave site combines features of the family vault and the patriotic altar. In Passy cemetery, the Bluzet family grave bears a sort of monument to the family's dead soldiers on which is carved a woman in mourning holding a laurel wreath, and surmounted with the inscription *Manibus date lavros plenis* ('Hands full of laurels'). On each side of this figure appear the names of family members killed in the war, with their decorations.[39] This tomb manifests the spectacular intrusion of the nation in the familial space of a sepulchre.

At the same time, epitaphs proliferated. In Montparnasse cemetery, for example, on the white stone cross embellishing the grave of René Pinard, killed at Château-Thierry on 2 July 1918, was an extract from one of his letters, carved at his family's instructions:

---

[39] Cécile Prévost, *La mort, le deuil, le souvenir à Paris pendant la Première Guerre mondiale*, MA thesis, University of Paris X, 2002.

'Under arms, 3 December 1916.
Do not tremble for me, my adored Parents. The more this war goes on, the happier I am to be a soldier. If you knew what support and comfort it is at the same time to have to be an example to others, you would not pity me, quite the contrary. Your René'

The epitaph might take on the pattern of a brief historic fable. Thus in Père-Lachaise there is a family crypt on which we can read on a flag enveloping a cross:

> Same prayers
> Same grave
> Same glory
> To the victim of 1870 (father)
> To the victor of 1915 (son)
>   (Buche tomb)

All too frequently, the monument had to accommodate not one but two sons who had died in the war. Here is what is written on the Marot tomb in the Auteuil cemetery in Paris:

> To the memory of my sons who died for their country
> André Nicolas, Sergent of the 143rd Infantry Regiment
> Decorated with the Croix de Guerre
> Fell on the field of honour at Vaux Chapître near
> Verdun on 18 August 1916 at the age of 23 years.
> Louis Nicolas, soldier in the 26th Infantry Regiment
> Fell on the field of honour at Esnes near Verdun
> On 9 April 1916, at the age of 21 years. Eternal regrets.

The age of the dead man is often specified, as if to insist (even obliquely) on the overwhelming burden of grief provoked by a premature death. The cross on the grave of Maurice Charlet-Reyjal in Père-Lachaise states:

> Corporal in the 22nd Infantry Regiment
> Died for France at the age of 20 years
> At the Four de Paris 307
> 1914
> Pupil at the École Centrale

The site where the combatant met his death was also frequently mentioned. Thus the grave of Divisional General Pierre Guignabaudet in Père-Lachaise states:

> Killed by the enemy
> Kemmel region
> 30 May 1918

This desire to localize the site of death was part of the need the bereaved felt to represent this death, to make it palpable. Here is one example of the effort made by parents to find out what had happened to their son. Jean Ajalbert tried every avenue he knew to confirm the fate of his son, who had volunteered at the age of eighteen and from whom he had not heard since 20 November. Over the next six weeks he pulled every string he could, but to no avail. It took until 28 December for him to receive official confirmation of his son's death:

> I went through all the fever of waiting before the ministerial note containing this simple piece of information: Died on 28 November at Clermont-en-Argonne as a result of his war wounds. No detail about the passing of our heroic sons. That would not change anything of what is irreparable. All the same there could, perhaps, be some softening of the terrible pain, to be able to locate the site of the disaster, to know, as far as possible, some of the circumstances. The corpse still exists, under the earth of a grave. It is terrifying to weep in the shadows and the void, in the useless search for the absent one . . . [40]

'C'est la guerre', was not good enough for this father. 'That's war? That I don't know where my son is buried, even though he died in the dressing-station, where he was identified? Come on! And I'm going to have to track down his body through the ruins of the Argonne.'[41]

As if to retain the memory of the circumstances of his death, the Le Blan family (Passy cemetery), burial place of Philippe Le Blan who was killed on 17 April 1916, had the family tomb embellished with two crosses: one is the cross which marked the site of the first grave of Philippe at the front, and which was taken back by the family during the repatriation of bodies.[42]

And some epitaphs, bearing the note 'Killed by the enemy'[43] or 'Killed in the war' are brutal, the second being capable of being read as a form of protest:

> To the memory of our son
> Gustave Drodelot
> Killed in the war on 16 January 1915
> At the age of 29 years
> Much missed by his family
>   (Grenelle cemetery)

One of the most striking examples of these new funerary designs is that of the grave of the son of Jane Catulle-Mendès, Primice, killed in April 1917. Stéphane Audoin-Rouzeau has retraced the long and

[40] Ajalbert, *Paris*, pp. 192–3.   [41] Ibid., p. 214.

[42] Prévost, *La mort, le deuil, le souvenir.*

[43] Marc Boasson, *Au soir d'un monde, Lettres de guerre (16 April 1915–27 April 1918)* (Paris, 1926), pp. 14–15.

painful stages of the mourning of this mother. Informed relatively soon after the death of Primice, the mother set out to find her son's temporary burial place, wanting to have him exhumed in order to bury him somewhere further from the front, in a 'quiet little grave'. She obtained special permission to travel into the military zone and made two separate semi-clandestine trips to the temporary grave. Primice was finally buried in Mourmelon cemetery: 'It does not hurt any less. But it is something, a grave [. . .] I have it. There have been people kind enough to give it to me [. . .] all have shared in the Night which effaces my life.'[44] She wrote a long account retracing the stages of her mourning, *La Prière sur l'enfant mort*, which can be seen as a written tomb. Jane offered her a new grave, 'the little white tomb of a book'. A final tomb would be dedicated to Primice: that in which his mother would herself be buried, in Montparnasse cemetery. This grave features a bas-relief representing the profile of the dead man in the folds of the flag; the profile reproduces the design which is seen on opening *La Prière sur l'enfant mort*.

We should note that in their final letter,[45] often testamentary, soldiers at times stated instructions for their own funeral, and designed their own tombs. In the words of a soldier who fell on 7 March 1916:

He who falls victim to the enemy does not die.

If I should gain this signal honour, I do not want people to weep for me.

In passing on the information of my glorious death, they will announce, with my name, my rank and then my civil ranks as graduate and diploma holder . . ., the whole followed with the words 'killed by the enemy'. No flimflam, field of honour, etc., the truth, that's all.

The make-shift grave that battle will have given me should be respected. On our family graves, my name and the place where I lie.

Opposite my name . . ., the letter 'T' [tué] should be inserted in italics, and this should replace the usual 'M' [mort] for all comrades killed in the war.[46]

Above all, these letters indicate how much the combatants were aware of the future distress of those who would mourn them without a grave to visit. A soldier wrote about his own brother:

When I arrived there, he had already been buried in a grave, all alone, and not like many others who are buried in the same hole. I had a cross made on which I had his name written, his company, his regiment and the date of his death, on one side, in paint and, on the other side, his name carved with a point heated in the fire. He is buried in a small ravine, about two kilometres north of Perthes, on the right of the road from Perthes to Tahure. Take careful note of this information: you will be

[44] Audoin-Rouzeau, *Cinq deuils*, pp. 230ff.   [45] *La dernière lettre.*
[46] Ibid., pp. 194–5.

able to find the place if I do not return myself, and have his body moved so that he can rest in the bosom of the family. Have a great service for him without waiting for the death certificate to reach you, for that may take some time, particularly now when there are so many to be prepared [. . .] I would like you to have a fine grave made now, or at least a beautiful cross in his memory among the family where perhaps he can be laid one day [. . .] One day, when this terrible war will be over, he may sleep his last sleep in the land of his birth.[47]

Finally, cemeteries were modified by the creation of war memorials. In Camberwell, there are numerous monuments, one of which is dedicated to the inhabitants of the Borough of Southwark killed by aerial bombardment. In the Greenwich cemetery, a section was named 'The Great War Heroes' Corner'. There is a Cross of Sacrifice, on which rest plaques listing the names of hundreds of fallen British soldiers. The same gesture was made towards others. A cenotaph designed by Lutyens in memory of South African soldiers who died in the war was erected in Richmond Cemetery in 1915. In the Roman Catholic cemetery of St Mary's, the east wall was dedicated as a memorial to Belgian soldiers who died of their wounds in England.

New funerary customs

The adoption of the dead

A new liturgy emerged in this period in all three capital cities, enabling those unrelated to the individual who had died in the war to 'adopt' his body as a collective symbol. In Paris, ordinary men and women followed the burial cortège of soldiers they could not have known. This form of 'fictive kinship' both established the bond between families who had lost sons in the war and gave some parents the opportunity at last to attend a funeral ceremony denied to them when they received the news that their sons had died.[48] An association (Le salut aux morts pour la patrie) was formed for the welfare of those who died for their country, with the aim of sending its members to soldiers' funerals to form a guard of honour following the coffin:

You have undoubtedly experienced strong emotion on passing in the street the modest bier of a soldier who died for the Nation and who, having no family in Paris, was transported to the cemetery without any following cortège. We felt that in respect of those without families, there was a duty to be fulfilled and we would like to make up for the absence of family and friends.[49]

[47] Ibid.   [48] Winter, *Sites of memory*, ch. 2.
[49] Prévost, *La mort, le deuil, le souvenir*, pp. 47–9.

Sometimes schools were transformed into reception points for wounded men. When some died, the pupils themselves sometimes took the initiative to accompany the funeral convoys and to maintain, in the Pantin cemetery, the graves of these soldiers who died far from their family.[50] These practices mirrored those at the front, where it was companions in arms who took the place of the family at funerals.

For soldiers buried in Paris in military burial grounds, the army and the State organized the funerals and provided the honour guards. The family could not intervene in the organization of military funeral ceremonies – indeed, sometimes family members felt lost amongst the anonymous men who followed the cortège. We should note, particularly during the first months of the war, the sumptuous nature of these obsequies, in contrast to the haste in which soldiers who fell at the front had to be buried:

Yesterday there took place in the church of Saint-Ferdinand des Ternes the funeral of the first soldier to die in the hospital in the rue du Sergent-Hoff. The peaceful population of Ternes was determined to honour this unknown man in person, after he was brought in dying the evening before and died without having recovered consciousness, and in so doing to honour the whole French army and its own children currently under arms. The coffin vanished beneath the wreaths and bouquets of fresh flowers and flags sent by local residents and traders.[51]

The militarization of the cemetery

Funerary customs in wartime changed because in these war years, mourning was both private and public, both familial and national, both intimate and collective. In *Le Figaro* of 2 November 1914, we thus read the following description of the ceremony of All Saints at Bagneux cemetery, which had a military burial plot:

In the avenue, the paved pyramid surrounding the cypress is transformed every fifteen minutes under the bouquets of flowers brought by the crowd. This temporary monument no longer resembles an open-air stage: it is a vast and painful block, it is a church column covered with ex-voto offerings ... Near the flowers brought by each family to honour on the sheltered grave in the cemetery all those graves which on the fields of battle are marked by a wreath made of a belt and a bouquet of *képis*, Paris yesterday brought official palms, the palms of patriotic societies and their prayers.

What choice did these parents have? The front was unreachable, and they sought solace among others who shared their anxieties and their

---

[50] Pierre Laurant, *Nos potaches pendant la guerre* (Paris, 1932), ch. 3, 'Derrière les morts'.
[51] Prévost, *La mort, le deuil, le souvenir*, pp. 56–8.

sorrow. It is hardly surprising therefore that there was a major increase in cemetery visits on this, the first All Saints Day of the war. In 1913, about 400,000 people came to the cemeteries of Paris. In 1914, just about one million came, or nearly half the population. The increase was noted in local cemeteries with military sections, in Ivry, Bagneux, and Pantin. In those cemeteries, rituals emerged throughout the war. A representatives of the nation or the city laid flowers on the temporary memorials to the war dead. The rich and the poor came together just as the armies had done. This is how *Le Figaro* described the scene on 1 November 1914:

At the gates of all the cemeteries, at Bagneux and at Pantin, cemeteries of poor folk but now the richest because our soldiers lie there, of Clichy or Montparnasse [. . .] the brotherly, egalitarian friendship, which has awoken between all French people at the moment of national danger was accentuated on this day devoted to death. Each one felt that he had no right to stand isolated in his sacrifice, since all families sacrificed themselves equally. No one could make distinctions between the dead because the living were visible there, on the field of battle, together and for the same family goal.

All Saints Day came to have a collective character, with new sites of mourning paralleling the ones family had visited prior to the war.[52] This new itinerary continued after the Armistice. As *Le Figaro* of 2 November 1920 put it: 'this year [. . .] pious instinct has extended to three days the journeys to the cemeteries and the ceremonies associating the cult of the family dead with that of the heroes who have sacrificed their life for the nation'. The correspondent of *Le Temps* made the same point:

The cemeteries received an unusual number of visits: the war memorials from the 1870–1871 war, the memorial to the dead of the Great War, monuments to the victims of duty, the graves of soldiers, saw an unending parade [. . .] In front of these monuments and on the graves there was soon a great pile of wreaths and bouquets [. . .] For everyone, the temporary monument set up to the glory of the war dead in the Père-Lachaise cemetery, through the efforts of the city of Paris on the initiative of M. Paul Virot, was the object of pious visits.

This monument took the form of a cenotaph of wood and fabric, with its four faces bearing bas-reliefs portraying 'the departure', 'the trench', 'gas', 'death'. On top was a statue representing 'France weeping for her children'. On the same day in Berlin the French ambassador, Charles Laurent, went to Hasenheide cemetery to salute the graves of soldiers who had died in captivity. On each grave he placed a green palm with tricolor ribbons.[53]

---

[52] Ajalbert, *Paris*, p. 111.   [53] *Le Temps*, 3 November 1920.

From 1914, in Paris, veterans' associations were active in organizing funerary ceremonies. In Berlin these associations were particularly active in the post-war years. Many had a strong local character, reflecting the fact that recruitment was a matter of residence.[54] The war further strengthened the friendly associations of the regiments: the latter supplied a stable framework to maintain their collective memory. For this reason many war memorials were erected in garrison cemeteries of the town and its region: they were financed by veterans' associations of a particular regiment. These 'memory activists', in Carol Gluck's phrase,[55] were almost always officers, and frequently Prussian aristocrats.[56]

These Kriegervereine (veterans' associations) were very anxious to make Germans understand that those close to them had not died in vain, despite the unexpected defeat; recalling the dead, their loyalty, and their sacrifice also served to sustain a certain spirit of resistance to western values, or the *Diktat* of peace treaties. The contrast was particularly sharp with French veterans, who developed a special form of Republican pacifism. The German associations attempted to win the lost battles of the past and the battles to come. For them, the maintenance of tradition was directed towards the restoration of lost glory. Pacifism was not part of their outlook.

To be sure, there were other veterans who wanted none of this idealization of the *Fronterlebnis*. But the people who dominated commemorative ceremonies in Germany were not pacifists. Every inauguration of a war memorial offered these groups an opportunity for expression. As soon as the war ended, enough money was quickly collected to set up memorials: veterans' associations thus succeeded in financing monuments through private subscription, even without State support. The political pressure from these soldier associations on public life made itself felt particularly in the regulation issued by the Prussian Ministry for the Interior on 29 September 1922: meetings of associations of former soldiers' units were permitted in the open air, their members could be buried according to tradition, the inauguration of war memorials by the said associations was permitted (without provocative banners or weapons).

During the 1920s memorials to the dead of many regiments were constructed in the part of the *Garnisonsfriedhof* reserved for First World War burials: there were monuments erected on behalf of several reserve

---

[54] Martin Zippel, *Untersuchung zur Militärgeschichte der Reichshauptstadt Berlin von 1871 bis 1945* (Berlin, 1982).

[55] Carol Gluck, *Past obsessions: war and memory in the twentieth century* (New York, 2006).

[56] Among the 156 authors of regimental histories counted above, 68 bore names with the honorific 'von', and several titles of 'Count'.

infantry regiments. As elsewhere in Germany, these memorials concealed the truth about the defeat. Nowhere was there place to recognize that the German army had been defeated on the field of battle. Instead heroism was the dominant motif. This past of heroism and of unjust defeat prepared the ground for the politics of revenge. Unlike in Britain and France, in Germany, to not forget the dead was an exhortation to carry on the struggle. The funerary monument thus became a political statement visible to all.

Consider just one monument, that dedicated to the Queen Augusta Regiment. The base of the sculpture bears this inscription: 'We died so that Germany might live. We will live through you.' The figure on the monument is a reclining soldier in his shroud. On his chest is his helmet, a laurel, and a sword. He seems about to awaken, raising his fist under the shroud. The ominous implications were there, and gave to commemorative art in Berlin a political edge separating it from that in London and Paris.

Discrediting civilian death

Valorizing the war dead meant devalorizing civilian deaths. 'The sick, the dying, if they are not military, no longer seem worthy of concern', wrote J.-E. Blanche. 'A little boy was watching a civilian funeral, I saw him begin to salute. His friend said to him, "No need to lift your cap, he's on his own!" It is the carts for the dead which count today, or processions with flags and honour guards. The civilian does not count.'[57]

Death had no gravity unless it could be attributed to the deleterious effects of the state of war. Thus it was possible to die of the war. On 1 October 1915, in the church of Saint Thomas d'Aquin, there occurred the funeral of Rémy de Gourmont, founder of the *Mercure de France*, who died on 27 September 1915 and was buried in Père-Lachaise cemetery. Pierre Louys stated:

Remy de Gourmont died yesterday. The war causes deaths beyond the battlefields. The day when the patient philosopher of *Epilogues* took up his collaboration once more with *Le Mercure* after eight months of silence, he confessed that he felt stricken, that he did not really know whether he would ever again be in a state to write and think.

Similarly, Rachilde stated:

Death does not kill only with its iron scythe. With rigid mechanical movement, with its bony arms, it lays low those at the rear who are not directly on its path. It is

---

[57] *Cahiers d'un artiste*, p. 67.

the other side of the war for all those who, condemned to inactivity, none the less stretch their nerves towards news from the front [...] He [Remy de Gourmont] might still be alive, but the abnormal was to kill him [...] It is abnormal, for a France which is literary to its marrow, to see only the brutal side of life.[58]

No metaphor was necessary in adding to the toll of war losses those civilians killed by aerial or artillery bombardment. Civilians did indeed 'die for France', and were recognized as war victims. The victims of the Belleville bombardment of 29 January 1916 received state funerals and were honoured as having died for their country, with burial in Père-Lachaise in a concession reserved for the City of Paris.[59] Here is material evidence of public acknowledgement that the field of battle extended to the streets of these cities as well.

Capital cities in mourning

These three capital cities faced a duel challenge. The first was to find a way to mourn their own. The second was to serve as sites of national funerary rites. This gave to Paris, London, and Berlin, a particularity not known elsewhere in the three countries.[60] Let us consider Paris first. A law of 25 October 1919 provided that a 'national monument in com-memoration of the heroes of the Great War who fell on the field of Honour would be set up in Paris or in the immediate surroundings of the Capital'. The critical point here is that there would be no memorial to the dead of the city of Paris as such. The same was true of London and Berlin. In commemorative history, the cities did not exist as cities. They were either capitals, symbolic spaces of national or imperial life, or a cluster of localities, each of which marked the loss of its own sons. The quartier, the school, the local association commemorated their war dead; but outside of a *Livre d'Or*, a nominal list of all those residents of each arrondissement who had died, a book kept in each *mairie*,[61] there was (and is) no Paris war memorial.

In 1932, at the inauguration of the war memorial of the 9th arrondisse-ment, Fontenay, the chairman of the municipal council declared that:

Paris, we know, has the great honour of possessing the most sacred memorial that anyone could imagine: the tomb of the Unknown Soldier ... but the Capital,

---

[58] *Le Mercure de France*, December 1915.
[59] Prévost, *La mort, le deuil, le souvenir*, p. 15.
[60] Elise Julien, *Paris, Berlin: la mémoire de la Première Guerre mondiale, 1914–1933*, PhD thesis in progress at the University Paris I and the Free University of Berlin.
[61] Archives Nationales, Paris, F/7/223-332.

crushed under the weight of the sacrifices made, still has not set up an altar worthy of the vast holocaust of its sons . . .'[62]

People had to be satisfied with little memorials scattered among the *mairies* in the arrondissements, set up late (sometimes extremely late, after the 1960s), 'of mediocre symbolism, of mediocre visibility'.[63] Similarly, propositions and petitions seeking to set up a monument to the victims of the war inside cemeteries proliferated once peace had returned; no such effort was realized. A 1916 proposition to set up a monument to the memory of all the victims of the war who came from Paris in Père-Lachaise – seen as the true Parisian necropolis – came to nothing.[64]

Berlin too has no national memorial to the dead of the Great War. Voices emerged to demand that the *Garnisonsfriedhof* should have a national war memorial. It was only on 3 August 1924, the anniversary of the Emperor's mobilization order in 1914, that the government expressed the wish to set up a *Reichsehrenmal*, a State monument dedicated to the dead of the war.[65]

Proposals for the site of construction and the form of this monument were varied, and dozens of projects were considered without any of them winning a consensus of support. On the eastern front, for example, the memorial set up on the field of the Battle of Tannenberg is more a site to the glory of the victors in the battle, Hindenburg and Ludendorff, than a site of homage to German soldiers. Two projects for a *Reichsehrenmal* stayed for a long time in competition: the one corresponds to a monument at the edge of the Rhine, the other one consists of a *Heiliger Hain*, a sacred wood, which would be located at Bad Berka in Thuringia, near Weimar. It is this last one which, under the pressure of veterans' associations, was finally approved by the authorities of Reich. The veterans' associations favoured the Bad Berka monument as an open and accessible site in the heart of the countryside, where silence would stimulate a feeling of grandeur and where visitors could reflect on those who sacrificed their lives in the war.

---

[62] Jean-Louis Robert, 'Les monuments aux morts de la Grande Guerre à Paris', in Christophe Charle and Daniel Roche (eds.), *Capitales culturelles, capitales symboliques: Paris et les expériences européennes, XVIIIe–XXe siècles* (Paris, 2002), p. 153.

[63] Ibid., p. 153.   [64] Tartakowsky, *Nous irons chanter*, pp. 85–91.

[65] Bundesarchiv: series R32, boxes 353, 358, 374; series R1501, boxes 125,799 to 125,809. See also Peter Bucher, 'Die Errichtung des Reichsehrenmals nach dem ersten Weltkrieg', in *Jahrbuch für westdeutsche Landesgeschichte* 7 (1981), pp. 359–86 and Benjamin Ziemann, 'Die deutsche Nation und ihr zentraler Erinnerungsort. Das "Nationaldenkmal für die Gefallenen im Weltkriege" und die Idee des "Unbekannten Soldaten" 1914–1935', in Helmut Berding, Klaus Heller, and Winfried Speitkamp, *Krieg und Erinnerung, Fallstudien zum 19. Und 20. Jahrhundert*, pp. 67–92.

Nevertheless, on the initiative of the government of Prussia, Berlin placed a war memorial in the *Neue Wache*, the new imperial guard house built by Schinkel on Unter den Linden, unused since 1918. A competition was launched for the interior adaptation of the building, and the memorial was inaugurated on 2 June 1931. This did not end the argument over commemorative activities in Berlin, a theme to which we shall return.

In London, monuments were built to honour those who died by parish, by Metropolitan Borough, or in regiments. The Royal Artillery Memorial and the Machine Gun Regiment Memorial, both at Hyde Park Corner. If there was a monument to all the city's dead, it was Lutyens's Cenotaph, though Londoners shared it with the entire British empire. Here are some of the reasons why the three capital cities have no war memorial of their own. The weight of Nation, State or Empire was greater than the weight of metropolitan life.

Decentred commemoration: local activity and associational life

The most spectacular effect of the Great War was the mass creation of symbolic graves[66] – temporary or permanent monuments, plaques or altars commemorating the dead and designed for a funerary cult – scattered through the heart of the city, in effect installing the dead among the living. Henri de Montherlant described the symbolic tomb set up in the chapel of Les Invalides for the ceremony of 11 November 1919:

> At the centre of the nave was a mound made of closely piled turf, scattered with dead leaves. And on the mound a plain cross [...] like something that had sprung out of the earth [...] And at the four corners of the mound were four children, and their fathers had died in the war.[67]

This dispersal found a striking form of expression in a text by Maeterlinck which appeared in *Le Figaro* on 2 November 1916, entitled, 'the power of the dead': 'We are the living home of our dead'; 'in each of our houses, of our towns [...] in the palace as in the darkest cottage, there lives and reigns a dead young man'. In response to Jean Ajalbert's question, *Comment glorifier les morts pour la patrie?*, which was the object of a very large survey in 1916, Edmond Rostand proposed that the Arc de Triomphe should be divided up to make plaques bearing the name of

---

[66] Antoine Prost, *Les anciens combattants et la société française, 1914–1939* (Paris, 1977), vol. III, p. 54. Cf. Annette Becker, *La guerre et la foi*, p. 112.

[67] Montherland, *Mors et Vita* (Paris, 1919; ed. 1988), pp. 545–6: 'Le 11 novembre à la chapelle des Invalides'.

each dead soldier. These plaques would then be affixed to his home. 'There will no longer be any streets without their stubborn ghosts mingling with those who pass through'; 'our houses, which are signed by those who built them, will thus be countersigned by those who have prevented their destruction.' Some protested: 'Is there the right to poison the future by perpetuating the mourning of the present: to turn the joyous land of France into a necropolis in which one cannot move without reading a funerary inscription?' This view was clearly shared by only a minority.

This decentred commemorative movement took many forms. On All Saints' Day 1920, in the *mairie* of the 6th arrondissement, the mayor and his deputies had set up in a black-draped hall a cenotaph at which the families of the dead paraded to the sound of the Funeral March. On the same day the Manufacture Nationale de Sèvres inaugurated a commemorative plaque bearing the names of pupils of the factory's school of ceramics who had died; and the national school of horticulture in Versailles unveiled a plaque in honour of its former pupils who died 'on the field of honour'.[68] On 11 November 1920 many commemorative plaques were fixed to sites shelled by the Germans: on the rue des Marais, rue Pelleport, quai de Sèvres and boulevard Ney, the church of Saint-Gervais,[69] the Port-Royal maternity hospital, and the Père-Lachaise cemetery, where the 'most murderous' shells fell.[70]

On 9 December 1923 Paul Landowski inaugurated the memorial which he had designed to honour the pupils of the Ecole Normale Supérieure who were killed during the war. He recalled later the disturbance created by the emotion of parents 'whose children's names are carved in the stone.'[71] Finally, in *Bleu horizon*, meditating on the Panthéon stele bearing the names of dead writers, Roland Dorgelès regarded it as a funerary location: 'the young dead [are] gathered here'; their 'grave' is 'under these resounding stones'.

Commemorative statements proliferated in the same manner in Berlin, to mark the passing of members of organizations, of professional groups, of administrative or public institutions,[72] and even more, in schools and

[68] *L'Echo de Paris*, 1 November 1920.   [69] *L'Echo de Paris*, 18 October 1920.
[70] *Le Temps*, 12–13 November 1920.
[71] Pierre Wittmer, *Paul Landowski à Paris, une promenade de sculpture* (Paris, 2001), p. 51.
[72] Meinhold Lurz, *Kriegerdenkmäler in Deutschland*, Band 4, *Weimarer Republik* (Heidelberg, 1985); Reinhard Koselleck and Michael Jeismann (eds.), *Der politische Totenkult, Kriegerdenkmäler in der Moderne* (Munich, 1994); Ursel Berger, 'Immer war die Plastik die Kunst nach dem Kriege", in Rainer Rother (ed.), *Die letzten Tage der Menschheit. Bilder des Ersten Weltkrieges* (Berlin, 1994), pp. 423–34.

churches. From the earliest days of the war, priests and pastors placed in parish graveyards, where other family members were buried, commemorative plaques to parishioners who died in the war and who were buried in remote places.[73] The inauguration of these monuments took place at two particular times: between October and December, in the period surrounding November mourning rituals, or during the summer, when the early, heady days of August 1914 could be evoked. November inaugurations were commonly the practice of churches and local authorities. The parish of Stralau inaugurated its war memorial on 17 October 1926 in the cemetery along the walls of the church.[74] On 27 November 1921, the Berlin borough of Steglitz inaugurated a plaque in memory of its employees who died in the war; in Tempelhof, a similar plaque was unveiled on 25 November 1928.[75] Summer inaugurations were the province of nationalist groups. For example, the war memorial for students of the University of Berlin, was begun in 1919 but inaugurated on 10 July 1926, in a revanchiste spirit supported by a military parade. The sculpture on the monument was that of an ancient and athletic warrior, weakened but about to rise. The inscription read: "Invictis victi victuri".[76]

London witnessed the same proliferation of decentred 'sites of memory'. The battles of Jutland and the Somme, in particular, in 1916, inspired the construction of war shrines in east London. The first of these makeshift public altars of remembrance appeared in South Hackney in August 1916. A letter in the *Evening News* followed by an appeal from the Lord Mayor of London stimulated the establishment of over 200 such shrines on London streets. Queen Mary brought them to public notice by visiting one in Hackney in August 1916.[77] They were not all designed in the same way, but most were small triptychs, with wings for the names of the serving and the dead, and with a central space for flowers and at times, a cross. Soon enough a commercial design was available to order, patented by Mr T.A. Hand of Longton, Staffordshire. The cost was 6s 6d.[78]

---

[73] Evangelisches Zentralarchiv, 7/2927, letter of the Evangelische Oberkirchenrat, 5 November 1914 and 4 February 1915.

[74] Landeskirchliches Archiv Berlin-Brandenburg, Kirchengemeinde Stralau, File 242.

[75] Landesarchiv Berlin, A Rep. 43, Box 29.

[76] Kathrin Hoffmann-Curtius, 'Das Kriegerdenkmal der Berliner Friedrich-Wilhelms-Universität, 1919–1926: Siegesexegese der Niederlage', *Jahrbuch für Universitätsgeschichte* 5 (2002), pp. 87–116. See also ch. 7 above.

[77] Alex King, *Memorials of the Great War in Britain. The symbolism and politics of remembrance* (Oxford and New York, 1998), p. 50.

[78] *Evening News*, 4, 6, 8, 10 November 1920.

These shrines appealed to Catholics and Protestants alike, and especially to the Anglo-Catholics among them. They reminded soldiers on leave of the moving sight of Calvaries in villages and roads in France and Flanders. There were shrines in working-class streets and in middle-class streets. Mark Connelly notes that the middle-class shrines were more likely to be a product of a local initiative; working-class ones were organized by clergymen.[79] The parish of St Michael and All Angels in Bethnal Green erected eighteen shrines listing 1,506 names. Individual benefactors paid for some; public subscription financed most others. Services of dedication drew local residents to the shrine, where flowers were placed by passers-by in the months which followed.

At the end of the war, many were taken into parish churches, but others remained in place. New ones were built too. One shrine, a site for floral wreaths, was erected in Hyde Park in August 1918. It was in the form of a 24-foot high wooden spire, draped in purple and white cloth, surrounded by the Union Jack and flags of the Allies. In the centre was a Maltese cross. This shrine was deluged with flowers, to the extent that Sir Edwin Lutyens was approached to create a permanent shrine for those who needed a focus for their acts of remembrance. But such a shrine was never built, since the Cenotaph served this purpose. Such local sites became points on the route of a local pilgrimage on Armistice Day. This practice continued in Bow and Bromley throughout the inter-war years.

The appearance of street shrines and pilgrimages to them were prefigurations of the outpouring of public feeling on Armistice day 1919 and 1920. Local settings highlighted the anxiety of families whose men were at the front. Most were built with the idea that they would be dismantled after the men came home. What Lutyens offered in Whitehall, in contrast, was a permanent site for pilgrimage.

Unknown soldiers

The different forms of 'war memorials', commemorative plaques or altars, were thus perceived as symbolic places of burial, a substitute for the absent grave. The most powerful symbol for these practices of mourning the absent body, invented in the Great War, appeared in France and in Britain in the form of the burial of the Unknown Soldier, 'the warrior laid to earth among the living'.[80] In Paris the Arc de Triomphe, raised to

---

[79] Mark Connelly, *The Great War, memory and ritual. Commemoration in the City and East London* (London, 2002), pp. 56ff.

[80] Anonymous, *La flamme sous l'Arc de Triomphe au tombeau du Soldat Inconnu*, p. 9. Carine Trevisan, *Les Fables du deuil, la grande guerre: mort et écriture* (Paris, 2001).

the glory of revolutionary and Napoleonic armies, became a funeral site and created around it the space for collective mourning. Similarly in London, a public area – Whitehall, where in November 1920 the cenotaph designed by Sir Edwin Lutyens was set up, or Westminster Abbey where the British Unknown Soldier was buried – became, for a brief moment, symbolic cemeteries.

We should first note the specificity of Berlin. Not only was it difficult for the city to impose its federal role as the capital, where national mourning could be undertaken, but the Germans had no wish to imitate the victors' action.[81] Above all, for the cult of the Unknown Soldier, an obscure and anonymous being, seemed to be substituted here for that of the exceptional personality. The Unknown Soldier was not dead but living, miraculously reincarnated. Thus Hitler saw himself as 'martyr of the war betrayed by his country'[82] but transformed into the living saviour of his nation. 'I, an unknown soldier of the world war ...' was how Hitler presented himself in many of his speeches. From the 1920s, Hitler planned to build a triumphal granite arch in Berlin, at the end of an official State avenue, similar in style to that in Paris but substantially exceeding it in size (it was to be 120 metres high and thus more than twice the size of the original) and bearing the carved names of 800,000 German soldiers killed on the field of battle.[83] A maquette of this strange monument denying defeat and mourning (for which he had himself offered a sketch in the 1920s) was presented to the Führer in 1939, on the occasion of his fiftieth birthday.

Retracing the history of the French Unknown Soldier in a study on the ceremony of 11 November, General Weygand wrote: 'There were some whose fate was particularly cruel to those who cherished him: they had not been recognised among the dead [...] It was necessary to give these families a grave at which they could pray.'[84] The anonymity of the Unknown Soldier enabled 'families who had the pain of having one of their members lost in the war without being identified' to 'always remain able to suppose that the being who was dear to them, was the object of this supreme homage'.[85] This prototype body thus represented all the missing bodies. He was 'the Son of all the Mothers who had not found their son'.[86] 'He would be the child of a whole nation in mourning', wrote

---

[81] Volker Ackerman, 'La vision allemande du soldat inconnu: débats politiques, réflexion philosophique et artistique', in *Guerre et cultures*, pp. 385–96. See also Ziemann, 'Die deutsche Nation und ihr zentraler Erinnerungsort'.

[82] Ibid., p. 391.

[83] Albert Speer, *Au cœur du Troisième Reich* (Paris, 1972), p. 103.

[84] Général Weygand, *Le 11 novembre* (Paris, 1932), p. 132.

[85] Quoted by C. Vilain, *Le Soldat Inconnu, histoire et culte*, p. 57.

[86] Weygand, *Le 11 novembre*, p. 131.

Dorgelès, 'and each mother will be able to say, as she bends over the stone: "Perhaps he is mine ....." '.[87] But he also represented the gathered army of the dead.

Paris

In Paris it was first envisaged that the Unknown Soldier would be transferred to the Panthéon[88] which had been a place of burial since Mirabeau's interment in 1791. But, symbolizing 'a whole heroic nation', he represents infinitely more than a great man.[89] Les Invalides was also considered, as a site which since the nineteenth century had been used for the burial of military heroes, but 'here sleeps, already, a great man whose individual glory is enough to fill the ancient and illustrious house',[90] Napoleon. The Unknown Soldier, for his part, had to have a 'grave unique in the world',[91] and 'rest on the finest of the hills of Paris, sheltered by the august vault which already, on 14 July 1919, saw the apotheosis of the survivors of the epic'.[92] Above all a militarist memorial, the Arc de Triomphe, which until then was no more than a stage for funeral processions (it received the bier transporting Napoleon's ashes, Victor Hugo's catafalque and finally, in July 1915, the remains of Rouget de Lisle[93]) became a funeral site where the soldier was finally and permanently buried on 28 January 1921. From 1922 (when 11 November became a national holiday in France), the Arc became the site for the expression of mourning both public and national, while 1 November remained the date of family and private mourning, in the cemetery. For several years after the war, All Saints' Day was thus seen as only the first part of a mourning period which extended to include 11 November.

From the cenotaph to the tomb

As if in anticipation of the funeral ceremony of November 1920, a vast crowd kept watch in Paris during the night of 13–14 July 1919, at the foot of a cenotaph set up under the Arc de Triomphe, lit by violet-coloured flares (the colour of mourning in the Catholic liturgy), which bore the

---

[87] Roland Dorgelès, *Bleu horizon. Pages de la Grand Guerre*, (Paris, 1949) pp. 120–1.

[88] Jean-François Jagielski, *Le Soldat Inconnu. Invention et postérité d'un symbole* (Paris, 2005).

[89] *L'Echo de Paris*, 7 November 1920.   [90] *L'Echo de Paris*, 7 November 1919.

[91] *La Flamme*, p. 10.   [92] *L'Echo de Paris*, 7 November 1920.

[93] Avner Ben Amos, 'The Marseillaise as myth and metaphor: the transfer of Rouget de Lisle to the Invalides during the Great War', in Valerie Holman and Debra Kelly (eds.), *France at war in the twentieth century: propaganda, myth and metaphor* (New York, 2000), pp. 27–48.

inscription, 'To the nation's dead.' 'One million five hundred thousand dead men are there in spirit: they have come to the rendezvous [...] which Paris had prepared for them', noted *L'Echo de Paris* on 14 July 1919. During this 'tragic night', the dead responded to the appeal of the living and 'with their mystic presence sanctified the multitude communicating like the waves of the sea around the cenotaph'.[94]

Next day the victory parade was opened by 1,000 severely mutilated veterans, men who seemed to stand on the threshold between the living and the dead: 'After the dead, but ahead of the triumphant, however glorious they may be, we must honour those whose sacrifice will endure as long as they have life.'[95] Insisting, in the description of these mutilated men, on the work of death operating within life – 'men lying on low carts, as if wrapped in a shroud of flowers'; 'blind men holding high the flags of which they will never see the colours again' – General Weygand added: 'At this poignant spectacle, a few rare involuntary cries were uttered: but hearts were too heavy, voices were strangled in throats. Each one watched this extraordinary parade, silent in pity and horror.'[96]

During the victory parade of 14 July, the dead thus remained palpably present: 'They are, although invisible, at the heart' of the procession, 'where the mysterious instinct of widows and mothers will be able to find their beloved image'.[97] The day afterwards, thousands made the 'pilgrim-ages' to the cenotaph, laying flowers with 'touching' gestures of devo-tion.[98] Mourning was the order of the day. *Le Figaro* of 14 July 1919 printed this poem:

> Alone
> My husband and my brother died out there, gloriously.
> I weep for them and my grief is vast.
> Yet one day the others will come and this day is near.
> On that day I wish to be in the front rank to acclaim the sublime
>   phantoms
> On that day my mourning veil will not conceal my face,
> So that my black shadow will not sadden those who will be passing ...
> On that day I will have for them kisses and flowers, this is how I will
>   celebrate my dead, for they died so that those men could come back thus.
> They will pass, handsome, immense, in the midst of hurrahs and clamour.
> They will pass.
> When the last has passed, I will return to my empty house, I will put on
> my black veil and I will weep.[99]

---

[94] *L'Echo de Paris*, 15 July 1919.   [95] Weygand, *Le 11 novembre*, p. 107.
[96] Ibid.   [97] *L'Echo de Paris*, 15 July 1919, p. 2.
[98] *L'Echo de Paris*, 16 July 1919, a text significantly entitled 'After the apotheosis'.
[99] Quoted by Annette Becker, 'Du 14 juillet 1919 au 11 novembre 1920. Mort où est ta victoire?'

These events led directly to the burial of the unknown soldier a year later.[100] At the centre of the capital an unknown hero was to be buried, selected in the citadel of Verdun, a mythic site since 1916.[101] The procession to Paris passed innumerable graves.[102]

Paris, 11 November 1920

The funeral ceremony coincided with the fiftieth anniversary of the Republic. Two 'relics' were therefore on display: the heart of Gambetta, which was to be laid in the Panthéon, and the body of the Unknown Soldier, destined for the Arc de Triomphe. The two corpses were first displayed in the Place Denfert-Rochereau, named for the 'hero' of the war of 1870; the Unknown Soldier's coffin arrived there from Verdun shortly after midnight. 'In front of the bodies of the Unknown Soldier and of the great patriot, women knelt and men stood silently for long periods', in the columns of Le Temps, which described how,

Around Gambetta's heart and the soldier's coffin, infantry men, their weapons at the ready, mounted guard all night long. Women in black came, laid modest bunches of flowers at the foot of the catafalque, knelt and prayed fervently. Some touched their lips with the edge of the tricolor flag which covered the coffin. These silent isolated displays left the watchers, during this freezing night, with a poignant impression.'[103]

Next day the relics were taken to the Arc de Triomphe, past the Panthéon. The coffin of the Unknown Soldier, placed on a gun-carriage and wrapped in a flag, was accompanied by a fictional family. Near the coffin, 'the father of a dead soldier, unidentified; the mother of a dead soldier, unidentified; the widow of a dead soldier, unidentified; and the orphan child of a dead soldier, unidentified, together constitute the symbolic and moving representation of the family of the unknown soldier' according to Le Figaro of 8 November 1920.[104] On 11 November in the evening, seventy-six electric search-lights illuminated the Place de l'Etoile before suddenly switching off, leaving the arch in the vivid glow of a violet lamp. Roland Dorgelès brooded over the scene:

I would like the wind [...] to howl over the cortège, twisting the flag, shaking up black crêpe clothing, putting out the flaming torch-lights, and that the night watch

[100] Becker, 'Du 14 juillet 1919 au 11 novembre 1920'.
[101] Antoine Prost, 'Verdun', in Pierre Nora (ed.), 'Les lieux de mémoire', La Nation, vol. III, pp. 111–42. The destroyer HMS Verdun transported the British Unknown Soldier en route to Westminster in 1920.
[102] Dorgelès, Bleu Horizon, p. 120.   [103] Le Temps, 12–13 November 1920.
[104] L'Humanité, 12 November 1920.

would end like a night in war-time, under the weeping of flares. And then, silent with fear, the crowd would understand perhaps the lesson of the Unknown as they see that beneath the Triumph is dug a grave.[105]

And, like a reminder to a forgetful crowd, he imagined the parade of the army of the dead:

It would take eleven full days, eleven days and eleven nights, without a break, without a moment's halt, to review these five hundred regiments. An army of dead longer than the whole of France's infantry if, on the day after the war, it had paraded ... (...) Victory itself is a festival of the Dead.

Did mourners respond to the appearance of this new grave? We do not know; and perhaps cannot know. Jane Catulle-Mendès said nothing of it in her diary of mourning (*La Prière sur l'enfant mort*) for 11 November 1920, or on succeeding 11 Novembers. She did not take part in the procession of 14 July 1919; on 10 July, her son's birthday, she laid two silver palm leaves on his grave. Her mourning followed an intimate pattern of time, articulated by private rhythms and not by the world's or the capital city's calendar.[106]

London

On 11 November 1920 the body of the British Unknown Soldier was placed on a warship in Boulogne, in the presence of Marshal Foch and General Weygand. On the cover of the coffin was riveted a sixteenth-century sword, a gift from the King of England. A square steel plaque covered part of the blade, with this inscription: 'A British Warrior who fell in the Great War 1914–1918 for his King and his Country.' The body was transported on the destroyer *Verdun*. It was saluted on its arrival at Dover by nineteen gun shots, the salute generally reserved for marshals.

The London ceremonies The day was the occasion for a double ceremony in London. The first, that of the burial of the Unknown Soldier in Westminster Abbey, was both militarist and aristocratic in style, even though the Unknown Soldier remained a democratic symbol. The second, the procession in Whitehall past Sir Edwin Lutyens's Cenotaph was less organized, more democratic, more popular – more than a million people were to file past it during the week – was also more civilian, and with more women. A correspondent of *The Times* noted: 'A phenomenon so moving, so unexpected, and, withal, so thoroughly spontaneous, has to

---

[105] Dorgelès, *Bleu Horizon*, p. 127.
[106] Audoin-Rouzeau and Annette Becker, *14–18*, p. 252.

be seen in order to be understood'.[107] The space between Trafalgar Square and the Abbey became the symbolic cemetery of the nation, even of the Empire. Some compared the event to a pilgrimage to Lourdes, a pilgrimage on a vast scale.

Thousands of poor, homely folk bereaved by the war – folk who have never been in London before – have undertaken long journeys for the purpose of joining in the Great Pilgrimage. One met them everywhere, in tramway-cars, omnibuses, and tubes.[108]

The week following 11 November represents an unparalleled moment in the history of London. Nothing like it had ever happened in the capital. Although despite their reminder of mourning, in Paris the ceremonies of 14 July 1919 and of 11 November 1920 retained an element of dark triumphalism, in London – in a country without obligatory military service – the accent remained on the funerary nature of ritual. The nation's military and political directors had 'their' ceremony in 1919 and at the burial of the Unknown Soldier. On the following days, it was the people who filed past, above all in honour of their dead.

From peace parade to pilgrimage

The history of London's Cenotaph is well established.[109] We will concentrate on the contrast between the first appearance of the Cenotaph in the Victory Parade of 19 July 1919 and its unveiling to the public on 11 November 1920. In 1919, five days after the commemoration in France of the fall of the Bastille, a military parade passed through the centre of London. Lutyens's hastily designed wooden Cenotaph was constructed in one week expressly for this event. It was not initially intended to serve as a permanent memorial.

The day was one for celebration. *The Times* called the event 'a glorious show'. The crowds in attendance were 'light-hearted' and were 'enjoying the prospect of an historic spectacle and the charms of a summer day that was neither broiling hot nor cold and wet, but perfect for the occasion'. The great were on display too. 'Mr Winston Churchill with two ladies drove towards Charing Cross in an open motor car and bowed gaily and frequently to the greetings of a crowd with was not slow to recognize him.' 'It was a merry scene, but the merriment did not jar.' The American

[107] 'The Cenotaph', *The Times*, 15 November 1920.
[108] 'Call of the Cenotaph. A national pilgrimage', *The Times*, 15 November 1920.
[109] Adrian Gregory, *The silence of memory. Armistice Day 1919–1946* (Oxford, 1994) and Eric Homberger, 'The Story of the Cenotaph', *The Times Literary Supplement*, 12 November 1976, pp. 1429–30.

Commander, General Pershing, came by 'now so smiling and cordial'; then came Marshall Foch, 'a soldier of genius'. Then followed the soldiers from many lands; there were 'little contingents from Japan, China, Greece, Siam: for all these the indefatigable crowd kept up a steady enthusiasm', showing 'its feelings joyously'.

This state and imperial pageant contrasted strikingly with the local shrine movement and the pilgrimages organized around them. Woolwich, the County Borough serving as site for both arsenal and military college, is a case in point. In September 1919, just two months after the victory parade, a 'Temporary Cenotaph' was erected by local members of the Discharged Soldiers' and Sailors' Federation. Its location was at the intersection of two main roads on Woolwich Common, 'between the Royal Military Academy and the barracks, and opposite the monument to the Prince Imperial of France, killed in the Zulu wars'. The Cenotaph was intended as a permanent monument, to serve as a destination for pilgrimages. The first one took place on 7 September 1919, attended by 5,000 people representing 'practically every organization in Woolwich'.

On Armistice Day 1919, the King deposited a wreath of 'laurel leaves and immortelles' at Lutyens's Cenotaph in Whitehall, soon to be replaced by a permanent structure through popular demand. This decision was not unopposed. The London Traffic Advisory Committee of the Westminster City Council wanted to move the structure to Parliament Square. Sited permanently in Whitehall, they argued, the Cenotaph would be 'a menace to the safety of the public, and a danger to life and limb'. Viewed 'from the point of expediency only as distinct from that of sentiment, the placing of so substantial a structure as the Cenotaph in the middle of a roadway, having so large a volume of traffic as Whitehall was undesirable'. The Metropolitan Police concurred, but the Cabinet, following overwhelming public feeling, decided otherwise. 'It was felt' by the Cabinet 'that in its present position the Cenotaph had memories which could not be uprooted.'

The following Armistice Day, 11 November 1920, was the time when the local pilgrimage movement was nationalized. This was a two-stage process. The first was the ceremony surrounding the burial of the Unknown Warrior in Westminster Abbey. The second was the unveiling of the permanent, stone version of Lutyens's Cenotaph. Both attracted enormous crowds, but the structure and symbolism of the two events varied.

This sketch [Fig. 12.1] was produced in *The Times* on 11 November 1920. It described a formal, hierarchical ceremony, led by the King, on one side of the Cenotaph, and a 'firing party' on the other. The casket

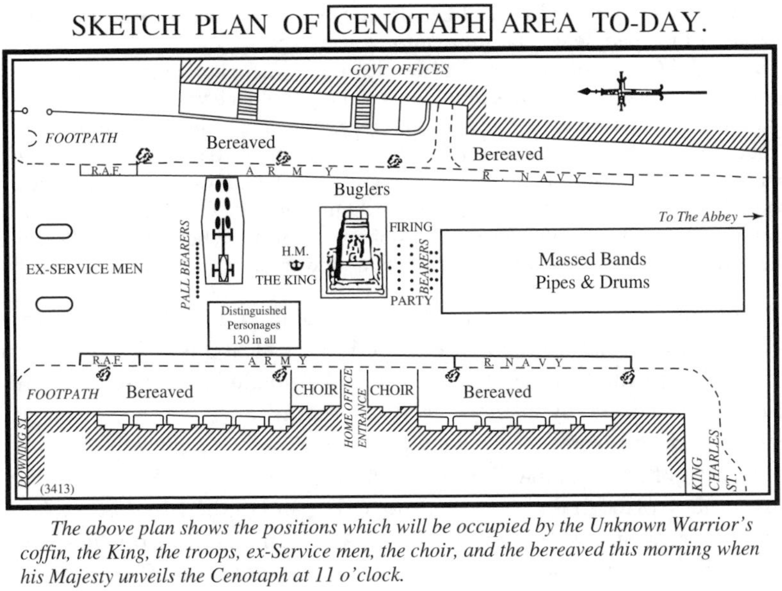

SKETCH PLAN OF CENOTAPH AREA TO-DAY.

The above plan shows the positions which will be occupied by the Unknown Warrior's coffin, the King, the troops, ex-Service men, the choir, and the bereaved this morning when his Majesty unveils the Cenotaph at 11 o'clock.

Fig. 12.1. 'Sketch plan of Cenotaph area today', *The Times*, 11 November 1920.

itself was carried by pallbearers in uniform, flanked by ex-servicemen on one side and 'massed bands, pipes and drums' on the other. The choir of Westminster Abbey, and several hundred bereaved men and women lined Whitehall and were given places in the windows of adjacent official buildings. After the King and dignitaries had laid their wreaths at the Cenotaph, they proceeded to Westminster Abbey, a quarter mile away, where the Unknown Soldier's casket was laid in an open grave dug into the central nave of the Cathedral. For the next week, the procession of pilgrims who came to London described a trajectory from Bridge Street, near Big Ben, northward up Whitehall past the Cenotaph, then circling back around it, four abreast until they came back to their starting point, leading this time to the Abbey.

What a contrast with the 'pageant' of 19 July 1919, when Lutyens's Cenotaph was first on display. This time the pilgrimage was entirely sombre. The crowd of silent mourners, so said *The Times*, 'was always the same and yet always changing'. And it went on and on for days and nights, a never-ending river of pilgrims.

Yesterday the captains and the Kings had honoured the Unknown Warrior. They departed, and then the people – the unknown living – came to pay their respect to the unknown dead. The official celebration was a wonderful pageant, but the homage of the people was far more impressive.

The official ceremonies resembled a series of very deft photographs. They always gave the impression of a series of tableaux. The pilgrimage yesterday was far more like a moving picture. The crowds were never still . . . During their long wait the mourners saw the Cenotaph in many different lights. At dawn it was tinged with faint orange. A gleam of sun just tipped the monument, and the waiting crowds could hardly be seen at all. With daylight came fog. The Cenotaph could not be seen except by those quite close to it. Looking down Whitehall one could see only the end of the waiting queue. It was soon swallowed up in the mist . . .

Women formed the nucleus of every queue and of the women most were in black. They seemed to feel that it was at last possible to give some expression to the feelings that they were compelled to subdue while the war continued. Many of them carried wreaths, and there were few who had not brought some simple token to place by the Cenotaph.

There is little doubt that the Cenotaph came to occupy from that moment on a unique place in the history of the nation and of the Metropolis. At the time, Westminster Abbey and the Cenotaph formed one symbolic space, a surrogate cemetery for the nearly one million men from Britain and the Empire and Dominions who died in the war. It may be true that the interment in the Abbey was an effort by the Anglican Church to reassert its symbolic primacy in the shaping of the commemorative moment. But nothing could take away from the simple power of Lutyens's ecumenical monument. It focused the energy and emotion already directed towards pilgrimage on the local level, both in London and elsewhere in the nation, and thereby reconfigured the symbolic space of the capital. A virtual cemetery emerged in the heart of Whitehall, one which served as the focus for a people's pilgrimage, lacking the panoply of power and rank, but infused by a national consensus that public commemoration was not just a duty; it was a necessity. That is what the Cenotaph came to mean in London. That is what it means today, nearly a century later.

Next to the grave of the unknown soldier and of the Cenotaph we can locate the memorial in honour of Lord Kitchener, a figure at once heroic and popular, whose body was never found (he was lost at sea in 1916, near the Orkney Isles). A chapel dedicated to him in St Paul's Cathedral is also dedicated to 'all those who fell' during the Great War. Through honouring an outstanding figure all those anonymous figures are commemorated here, as if private and national mourning identified with each other.

Finally, in November 1928 and in subsequent years, the bereaved were invited to plant little crosses or poppies, provided by the British Legion Poppy Factory, in remembrance of lost relatives and friends. Like the common act of touching a war memorial, and especially touching names inscribed upon it (as can be seen on photographs of the period), putting tokens in the ground of St Margaret's constituted a ritual of mourning and separation.[110] A British Legion pamphlet noted: 'It is moving and inspiring to see men, women and children planting their Crosses or Poppies in this hallowed lawn nestling in the shadow of the historic Abbey.'[111]

Another and final contrast must be noted. The two-minute silence in London (and throughout Britain thereafter) produced a spectacular auditory effect. Silence formed a heavy blanket on the capital, covered by a November fog. Here is a form of meditation, indeed of silent prayer associated with Anglo-Catholicism, in a capital city otherwise full of the myriad sounds of metropolitan life.[112]

Ghosts

Although it was possible to locate names, to inscribe them on a specific site, the bodies of the dead of the war often remained just out of reach. Hence the importance of an imaginary world of ghosts, of the ghostly presence of the missing men. In *Bleu Horizon* Dorgelès imagines the ghosts of unburied dead above the Arc de Triomphe's flame of remembrance:

To which survivor of the Marne and of Verdun has it not happened, crossing the Place de l'Etoile one evening, to stop, alone, at the anonymous stone to dream of his comrades who were killed? I have done it many times. Dazzled by the flame, I would soon see ghosts surging forward [...] Muddy, shivering, tightly wrapped in their capes with stiff folds as if in a coffin. Around us, the damp night stifled the rumbles, and the few headlights of cars blinking their signals on the Champs-Elysées recalled our flares dimmed in the fog. [...] We could not bring back your bodies, and since then you must prowl in the shadows, seeking the trench of final rest. Yes, there are perhaps dead men without graves who come to warm themselves at night at this camp fire.

Blaise Cendrars' account of the funeral of Apollinaire is particularly striking in this context. The cortège accompanying the poet's coffin, wrapped in a flag, encountered a crowd noisily celebrating the armistice. Cendrars left the funeral procession together with the artist Fernand Léger. When they reached Père-Lachaise, the burial was finished and

---

[110] Winter, *Sites of Memory*, p. 113.

[111] Imperial War Museum, London, Eph. Mem., K 94/113, British Legion Poppy Factory, 'The Empire Field of Remembrance', n.d.; on the symbolism of poppies, see Gregory, *Silence of memory*, pp. 99–104.

[112] Gregory, *Silence of memory*, p. 18.

they had difficulty finding the grave ('There are so many ...' was the grave-digger's reply to their questioning). It was through a strange sign, a drawing in the earth reproducing the shape of Apollinaire's face, with grass marking the scar left by his trepanning operation, that he recognized the poet's grave. He was not dead, they decided. He would soon reappear. Jay Winter links this episode to the famous sequence in Abel Gance's film, '*J'accuse*', in which the dead return among the living as if they were still wandering between the two worlds.[113] At the time of ceremonies commemorating the death of Jaurès, in July 1919, which for socialists represented a counter-balance to the celebrations of 14 July 1919, *L'Humanité* declared:

We can confirm, we who without believing in our eternal life do not stop behaving as if we were eternal: the dead were present among us in all simplicity ... Brothers who were killed, we have not forgotten the pact which unites us, nor the sound of your last words. It was not a cenotaph: for our soul is not an empty tomb.[114]

This wandering of the dead, the potential return of the dead, who would not be entirely dead, was embodied notably in the development of a funeral statuary borrowing from mediaeval imagery. In this setting, the dead were simply sleeping, waiting to reawaken.[115] These figures of modern sleeping effigies proliferated, particularly in Germany, placed like the relics of a saint in crypts, chapels, or sanctuaries designed specifically for this purpose. Clearly they were in part linked, in Germany, to the concept of a military revenge,[116] sometimes of a denial of death. There was hope that the dead, like the Reich, would be reborn.

Stefan Goebel suggests a parallel between the legend of Barbarossa and that of King Arthur – betrayed and wounded by his only son, he is not dead but 'rests' on the Isle of Avalon, waiting to rise again if the nation has need of him. The Arthurian mythology was also mobilized for commemorative purposes at King's School, Chester. An image of King Arthur fills the centre of the memorial window in the school chapel, with the legend 'Such a/sleep they sleep/the men/I love'. This line, slightly misquoted from Alfred Tennyson's 'The Passing of Arthur' (*Idylls of the King*), had been given the Victoria and Albert Museum's seal of approval. In 1919, the museum had issued a booklet of edifying memorial inscriptions

---

[113] Winter, *Sites of memory*, pp. 20–1.

[114] *L'Humanité*, 2 August 1919, p. 1, quoted by Annette Becker, 'Mort, où est ta victoire?'

[115] Stefan Goebel, 'Re-Membered and re-mobilized: 'The "Sleeping Dead" in interwar Germany and Britain', pp. 487–501.

[116] Goebel notes that the source of this imagery lay in the legend of Friedrich I, Barbarossa, sleeping on Mount Kyffhäuser in Thuringia until the restoration of the Holy Roman Empire. This legend inspired belief in the rebirth of a thousand-year Reich.

borrowed from the corpus of English literature. In practice, Tennyson's Arthurian verses did not prove a popular choice for grass-roots commemorations. Far more widespread was John S. Arkwright's hymn 'O Valiant Hearts', particularly the line 'Tranquil you lie, your knightly virtue proved', which conjured up notions of chivalry and enchanted sleep but lacked the Arthurian subtext of political awakening. The hymn was sung at the burial service for the Unknown Warrior – the 'Unknown Arthur' as one newspaper strangely dubbed him – in Westminster Abbey in 1920, and evolved subsequently into a leitmotif of war remembrance in inter-war Britain.

In conclusion, metropolitan cemeteries may be seen as sites of experimentation, where men and women invented new forms of collective remembrance which formed a new liturgy, part spiritual, part familial, and part patriotic. Above all, the Great War was the moment when a new set of funerary practices emerged surrounding the central fact that the bodies of those who died were absent. Here the three cities developed their own different approaches out of earlier historical experience. Paris was the place where the secularization of cemeteries was most marked, and where the old tradition of using public buildings as funerary sites was well established. To be sure, mourning took on many different forms in each of these three capital cities. The war dead were remembered, not only in cemeteries and in the grand ceremonial sites, but also in homes, in places of work and prayer, in schools, in cafes, in fact, throughout civil society. It is the multiplication of sites of remembrance and of signifying practices concerning those who died in the war which left a lasting mark on cemeteries and on the contours of metropolitan life.

13   Conclusion

Jay Winter and Jean-Louis Robert

The Metropolitan comparison

If we are ever to realize a truly European history of the Great War, we need to go beyond the national boundaries which have dominated historical writing on the subject.[1] The comparative history of the war, though, is still in its infancy. This project has aimed to broaden our understanding of nations at war by investigating cities at war. To do so, we adopt a firmly comparative perspective. This is not serial history, in the sense of dealing with Paris, London, and Berlin in sequence. Instead we integrate material on each city in an overall interpretation of the practice of metropolitan life in the period of the Great War.

Our claim is that Parisians and Londoners had at least as much in common with each other as did Parisians and farmers from Provence, or Londoners and Durham coal miners. City-dwellers traversed metropolitan space to get to work by bus, tram, commuter or underground train; they enjoyed metropolitan space and its amenities when the working day or working week ended. They also lived in three of the largest and most spectacular cities in the world, capitals of three imperial powers. They lived in places where their rulers resided and met, and where great hospitals, great centres of learning, and great museums were there for their benefit. The entertainment industry, fully international in 1914, was thriving in all three cities.

In each metropolis there were staggering inequalities of wealth and privilege. In 1914 in all three universal suffrage was yet to come. Social class distinctions were visible on the street, and to a degree social segregation in housing was palpable: working people lived with their like, just as did the wealthier classes.

Before the war, the distance – geographical, social, cultural – between capital city and the provinces was undeniable. In 1914, a visit to Paris by a

---

[1] Jay Winter and Antoine Prost, *The Great War in history: debates and controversies 1914 to the present* (Cambridge, 2005).

Breton fisherman and his family probably seemed to them as likely as a trip to the moon. The war brought people to these three cities who never would have dreamed of striding down Piccadilly or the rue de Rivoli. There is, therefore, an important story to be told about the place of these cities in their national histories in the period of the Great War, and we have tried to tell it.

Metropolitan history does not displace national history; it helps deepen and broaden it. Without comparison, it would not have been possible to establish the significance of the economic crisis in Paris in 1914; nothing similar happened in Berlin or London. Sticking solely to the national framework, the story of the relatively successful defence of the well-being of the civilian population on the Allied side remained a mere assertion. Using a comparative framework on the metropolitan level, we have done better, and thereby deepened our understanding of why one side won and the other side lost.

In both volumes, we do not ignore the national dimension, but assume that the history of cities sometimes follows national trends, and sometimes diverges from them. The distance between the metropolitan and the national is never fixed, and comparison enables us to see whether and when the war brought cities and nation closer together.

One of our findings is that the war tended to 'nationalize' these cities. That is to say, because of the war, Paris, London, and Berlin became not the same as, but more similar to, their respective countries than they had ever been before. Part of the reason resides in the horrific casualties and suffering the war brought to every part of these nations. We have shown that, contrary to popular claims, the war losses in these cities were similar to those of the nation as a whole. Another centripetal force bringing metropolis and nation together arose out of the vast movement of populations, thrown into contact both in these cities and elsewhere with other people they would never have met had the war not taken place. Part was due to the media, and to the effort made by newspapermen, educators, and clergymen to persuade civilians and soldiers that they were all fighting for one cause, for one nation.

At the same time, we cannot ignore the wartime and post-war persistence of regional and linguistic differences. London was not England in 1918, just as Berlin emphatically was not Germany. Indeed, this distinction helps account for the failure of revolutionary efforts in Berlin after the war. These militants were a minority there, and a tiny minority within Germany as a whole. In France too, Paris was not the nation. Regional contrasts were still striking, despite the much more powerful tentacles of the schools and the prefectorial structure of authority, linking the centre with each French department in ways remote from British or German affairs. Linguistic differences persisted as well.

In another way, the shape of these three cities changed in the period of the war. The physical boundaries of Paris and Berlin were transformed. In the case of Paris, the old mounds surrounding the city, earthworks that had served as fortifications after the defeat of 1870, were levelled. The space between the twenty arrondissements and the suburbs was now open. And though the *banlieu rouge* surrounding Paris had a separate cultural and political existence throughout the inter-war years, the city itself was no longer blocked off from its penumbra. The same was true in Berlin, though in this case the cause was administrative rather than physical. Greater Berlin, formally constituted in 1920, incorporated twenty formerly independent townships in the municipality, producing the metropolitan giant that exists today. Greater London, defined as an area inhabited by some 7,000,000 people served by the Metropolitan Police, did not change administratively in this period. It still dwarfed the other two cities, physically and demographically, though its rate of population growth slowed down in the war decade.

Symbolic capital

The cultural authority of these three capital cities as unique centres of sociability and style survived the war. But in another sense these capitals lost some of their symbolic power during the conflict. We have noted in chapter 12 that there are no metropolitan war memorials per se, though there are many local war memorials within these cities. The same is true for Paris and Berlin. Their inhabitants utilized national, local, or imperial symbols instead.

There is thus a significant absence in the system of representations of the war in these capital cities. The attachments described in commemorative forms were to the locality, to the nation, or to the Empire, but not to the metropolis itself. We argued in volume I that a capital city is both an experienced and an imagined community, but apparently not with respect to the community of those who gave their lives or of those they left behind. Here again is a point emerging from comparative metropolitan history which has remained obscure in the national historiography.

Post-war representations of the conflict differed in the three cities. Both Paris and London still had the force to organize a *mise-en-scène* of the war in the form of museums. The Imperial War Museum, on the site of the former insane asylum 'Bedlam' in Lambeth became a permanent landmark, archive, and tourist attraction. Les Invalides in Paris incorporated a section on the Great War, and a Musée de guerre turned into the Bibliothèque de documentation internationale contemporaine (BDIC), now one of the great archives of the war. Given the painfulness of defeat, it is not at all surprising that there was (and is) nothing similar in Berlin.

By focusing on collective representations, we can catch a glimpse of another major theme needing further attention: the extent to which lassitude pervades the history of the immediate post-war years. In some respects, many men and women in these cities were exhausted, and some broken, by the war, and by the family losses they, along with everyone else, had suffered. They went to familiar parts of the landscape – Whitehall and the Arc de Triomphe, nineteenth-century sites – when they joined the great commemorations on 14 July 1919 or on 11 November 1919 and 1920.

Is it surprising that these exhausted populations turned towards the past during and because of the war? There were exceptions: innovators and experimenters were there too. The war was as much a counter-revolution in the art world as it was a moment for the appearance of new experimental groups. The art market mattered, and it wanted the familiar and the accessible, not the bizarre or the shocking. Sales of Monet's water lilies and Degas's dancers brought in millions.[2] Whatever the war was, it was not in these beautiful canvases, evoking a world that seemed very familiar, but unreachable because of the war.

Lassitude is the right word for the mood of many returning soldiers too. They had been through one crusade and most had no interest in another. A return to normalcy was the order of the day; there were families to reconstruct, marriages to restore, jobs and friendships to reclaim. Everyone knew that a full return to the pre-war years was out of the question; too much damage had been done for that. But it is hardly surprising that *la Belle Époque* loomed large in their minds, a time before the deluge, when people had the good fortune of dying one at a time.

Fatigue fuelled nostalgia for a time before the war in other ways too. The subdued character of these cities, the dimming of their lights, made recollections of pre-war illuminations ever brighter. Pre-war night life was one of the great attractions of the metropolis. Wartime restrictions hampered or curtailed the movements of people, many of them soldiers, who simply wanted to wander in search of adventure. There were too many shortages and too many military policemen around to enable them to do so freely.

At the Armistice, in a grey November, there was an outburst of mass exuberance in Paris and London, though celebrations were short-lived. Gratitude and relief that soldiers no longer had to fear for their lives characterized the day. In Berlin there was as well a pall of gloom over the defeat and a sense of fear for the immediate future; the Kaiser had fled, and a revolution had broken out, with what consequences no one

[2] Jay Winter, *The experience of World War I* (London, 1989), p. 121.

could tell. Six months later, thousands had died in street fighting in Berlin, and the political outlook remained uncertain. In all three cities, *La Belle Epoque* may have been an illusion, a cultural chimera, but it is a nostalgic expression of a widely shared sense of what the war had taken away.

'War culture'

Lassitude was certainly not restricted to capital cities in the aftermath of the war. When we see photographs of exhausted men returning home to city and country alike, we cannot avoid concluding that the real distinction was between those who had fought and those who had not seen action at the front. The hardships and endurance of the combatants was written on their faces. Here metropolitan history and national history share the same family stories of separation, anxiety, and with luck, reunion.

The debate is still ongoing about how unified was the civilian population of these countries in wartime. One way of describing this unity is in terms of what Stéphane Audoin-Rouzeau and Annette Becker term 'war culture'. They take the term to mean 'a collection of representations of the conflict that crystallised into a system of thought which gave the war its deep significance'. Intrinsic to 'war culture' was the notion that the fight was between the civilized world and the barbarians, hatred for whom grew from the very first months of the conflict. 'Deep down', they write, 'the 1914–1918 "war culture" harboured a true drive to "exterminate" the enemy.'[3]

In the context of these three cities, this interpretation needs to be qualified. Some individuals and groups found an easy path to hatred of the enemy. Others were more circumspect. Seven professors and 568 alien students were struck from the matriculation lists of the Kaiser-Wilhelms-Universität in Berlin as early as 31 August 1914. In similar manner, the five academies of the Institut de France purged their rolls of German colleagues. But shortly thereafter, the great scientific academies and societies of Berlin refused to expel their British and French corresponding members and fellows. London scientists also refused to expel Germans from their learned societies. Where is 'war culture' here?

The wisest course is to conclude that the mobilization of hatred was part of one 'war culture' among many, but that other elements of a less violent kind infused cultural and social life as well. Among them was laughter, always a corrosive of hatred. In the Great War, the enemy was

---

[3] Stéphane Audoin-Rouzeau and Annette Becker, *Understanding the Great War* (New York, 2000), pp. 102–3.

mocked as much as he was hated. That mockery was visible in virtually every London music hall. The Kaiser has blood on his hands in many press cartoons, but 'putting the kybosh on the Kaiser', a phrase from a well-known London music hall song, sounds little worse than a good spanking. It is hard to hate the Germans captured by Charlie Chaplin in his reverie at the end of 'Shoulder Arms', a very popular film of 1918. The problem with the theory of 'war culture' is that it is too monolithic, too unified for the variegated and chameleon-like cultural practices it is meant to describe.

Once we admit the need to speak of 'war cultures' in the plural, then we can see how at certain times fear replaced swagger and the heaping of calumny on the head of the enemy. In March 1918, when the German army threatened Paris, and no one could be certain as to the outcome of the war, there is anxiety more than hatred in the public and – to the extent that we can tell – in the private language people exchanged about the war. At other moments, for instance, after aerial attacks on Paris or London, or after the execution of Nurse Edith Cavell, loathing predominates. Hatred towards Germany among French soldiers may have gone up after the Armistice.[4] War cultures were polyvalent and polyvocal; no one voice out-shouted them all.

Audoin-Rouzeau and Becker go further and suggest that the hatred imbedded in 'war culture' 'intensifies the violence of war – between soldiers and between soldiers and invaded civilians'.[5] Here we encounter a second facet of their argument from which we dissent. It is that 'war culture' brutalized soldiers and civilians alike, and deepened the violence of combat. With respect to the men in uniform, there were many instances when they expressed hatred for the enemy and behaved brutally, in particular when friends and comrades had been killed. But there is also evidence of solidarities displayed across the front lines, and of irrational kindnesses proffered at the front when and where we would least expect them. It is unpersuasive to argue that the men who showed up in these cities on leave or at the end of the war were 'brutalized' men. True enough, they tended to taunt passers-by and even the police when they felt like it, but these men kept their arms, and never used them on leave, even when provoked. The vast majority of these men were civilians in uniform, men who had lived through a time which marked them for life, but which did not turn them into engines of hatred. Some learned to kill and liked it. Others turned their backs on violence; some were revolted by

---

[4] Bruno Cabanes, *La victoire endeuillée: la sortie de guerre des soldats français, 1918–1920* (Paris, 2004).
[5] Audoin-Rouzeau and Becker, *Understanding*, p. 103.

what they had done. No one interpretation can encompass the impact of trench warfare on the men who fought.

'War culture' may have helped strengthen the determination of soldiers to go on with the war despite almost unimaginable hardships. Here we encounter one of the most hotly contested fields of First World War scholarship, which sets at odds historians who believe that soldiers fought out of consent and those who believe they fought because they had no choice. The Military Police were there if they decided that enough was enough.[6] Again, this argument is phrased in too much of a binary form. Coercion and consent were mixed in countless ways in wartime. Berliners and Parisians were obliged to join their regiments in 1914; British men went voluntarily. Were they coerced into going? Probably not. Did they consent to the war they went on to fight? Almost certainly not, since whatever was their image of war in 1914, the reality they confronted was infinitely worse than they had imagined. Almost all went on in the hope of victory anyway.

A theory of proportionality helps us see how this amalgam worked in practice.[7] Soldiers fought on when they were persuaded that the objective in question was worth the sacrifice they knew in advance would have to be made in taking it. But they did not go on if the level of sacrifice grew beyond what was proportional to the gain they hoped to achieve.

Proportionality was a concept that extended to metropolitan populations as well. One reason why Germany lost the war was that civilians in Berlin as elsewhere came to the conclusion that their sacrifices were both without end and without purpose. The war could not be won. The soldiers on leave among them, as well as those still in the line, came to the same conclusion around the same time, during the early summer of 1918. In contrast, Parisians and Londoners believed firmly that the war could and would be won, and was worth the costs they and their loved ones were forced to bear. It was not hatred which made them go on; it was faith in victory, an absolutely essential element in wartime cultures.

'The culture of war did not die at the Armistice', Audoin-Rouzeau and Becker affirm.[8] Once again, our research suggests that some qualifications should be made to this view. On the one hand, hatreds and bitterness did not vanish over night. The German delegation to the Versailles peace conference was humiliated publicly on the day they were forced to sign the peace settlement. Allied troops occupied the Rhine, and on

---

[6] Winter and Prost, *The Great War in history*, chs. 4 and 7.

[7] Leonard V. Smith, *Between mutiny and obedience: the case of the French Fifth Infantry Division during World War I* (Princeton, 1994).

[8] Audoin-Rouzeau and Becker, *Understanding*, p. 166.

occasion roughed up German civilians who had the temerity not to take off their hats in the presence of French soldiers. German scientists had great difficulty returning to the international learned communities they had dominated before the war; some men of science in London and Paris refused to restore old ties. On the other hand, the Nobel committee awarded its annual prize in chemistry to Fritz Haber, the mastermind behind Germany's poison gas effort during the war. In the same year Albert Einstein's theory of relativity was proven by experiments conducted by Arthur Eddington, a pacifist who was professor of astronomy at Cambridge. Some scientists continued to hate their German colleagues; others believed that science has no nation.

Hatred is not the whole story elsewhere too. Berlin communists joined their Parisian comrades in solidarity with the Bolshevik revolution and rejoiced at its survival in the bitter civil war waged by their own governments to overthrow it. Commerce between Paris and London on the one hand and Berlin on the other quickly resumed after the war. A new French university was established in Strasbourg, in place of the Kaiser Wilhelm Universität, and it became the home of great French scholars, including Marc Bloch and Maurice Halbwachs, who were drenched in German culture and who infused the human sciences with an ecumenical spirit remote from wartime hatreds and animosities. Veterans in Paris vented their hatred on war itself, and created a movement dedicated to its eradication. Their work certainly speaks of a process of cultural demobilization,[9] a defusing of the hatreds of war in the interests of a lasting peace.

In sum, the field of wartime and post-war cultural practices is simply too protean to be contained in any one approach to 'war culture'. An eclectic approach may be less elegant, but it is probably both a more modest and more accurate guide to the cultural history of the front. There was a culture of life at the front, and a separate though overlapping culture of life behind the lines, among soldiers' families, the defence of which was their central allegiance. Metropolitan life had elements of both front-line culture and home-front culture, since millions of soldiers on leave came to these cities for a breather and a good time.

Sombre turbulence

In both volumes of this study, we find evidence of massive population movements. These cities were entrepots for migrants before the war, but the turnover during wartime was greater still. There were those who fled

---

[9] *14–18. Aujourd'hui. Heute. Today*, edited by John Horne in 2002.

Paris in 1914 and 1918 when the German army threatened the city; there were new munitions workers to house, and refugees to be cared for, reluctantly or enthusiastically. There were armies in barracks and men and military material to be transported to the front. There were trainloads of the wounded to be sent to hospitals in the great cities or elsewhere. Men of every colour and nationality strode through these cities, and some stayed to make them more multi-cultural than before the war.

And yet despite the turbulence, the key points in the landscape of these cities in 1914 were still there a decade later. The Kaiser had gone, to be sure, but much of the Kaiserreich endured. The railway stations went back to their older function, bringing commuters to the cities each morning by the tens of thousands. Notre Dame was still there. The Basilica of Sacré Cœur in Montmartre was finally finished, and consecrated in 1919. St Gervais, adjacent to the Paris City Hall, was soon rebuilt, covering over the scars of its bombardment on Good Friday in 1918. Traffic still clogged Whitehall, though after 1920 vehicles had to take a wide berth around the Cenotaph. In terms of urban history, the scars of the Great War pale into insignificance alongside the scars of the Second World War, especially in the case of Berlin.

In volume I, we showed the unplanned ways in which the war changed privileges into rights, and thereby helped narrow the material distance between classes and between strata within classes. The cultural and political implications of this change were very mixed. On the one hand socialist parties benefited from a reduced level of popular deference. Some of the violence of wartime language easily moved on to the plane of domestic conflict. In all three cities in the bitter post-war years, hatred of the class enemy was undiminished by a shared nationality. On the other hand, what Bourdieu termed forms of domination largely remained in place. The notables, the mandarins, the ruling elites in business and in politics were still there after the war. And they were almost all men. Wartime demands deepened gender divisions, despite the granting of votes for women in Britain and Germany. Social inequalities persisted even when economic inequalities diminished.

Clearly there were powerful resources of flexibility and adaptation which enabled these cities to emerge from the Great War by and large intact. Among the many institutions which ensured stability was the home, the *foyer*, which both served as a point of support and a sign of continuity. Much of what we have termed metropolitan nostalgia returns here, to hearth and home, just as the soldiers returned there when they were on leave or discharged from active duty. They fought to preserve these homes, the nuclei of the home front, and much of their understanding of what the war had been about had the domestic sphere at its core.

To be sure, there were millions of hearths and homes which had been destroyed by the war. Too many people were in mourning for anyone to celebrate the defence of the family during the Great War. As we noted in chapter 12, the bodies were absent, most buried far away or simply blown to pieces. Pre-war rituals of mourning were hard to apply. Who knows how effective the great national ceremonies surrounding the Cenotaph or the Arc de Triomphe were in supplementing them? And we must not forget those other victims of the war, the disabled and disfigured. They were there too on metropolitan streets. Others resumed their lives more easily, though the rise in the divorce rate in the post-war period suggests strains on family life related to the difficulties of coming home again.

Here again we confront part of the cultural history of the war which at its deepest level knows no national boundaries. Yes, war pensions varied internationally, and so did forms of assistance and treatment available to ex-servicemen.[10] But the problems of rehabilitation or of adjustment to the loss of a loved one were no different in defeated Berlin than in victorious London or Paris. Triumphalism among the winners was very short-lived. There was too much suffering, too many gaps in families and in the community to sustain it. Moving to the metropolitan level of historical comparison helps us to see and to feel both the mundane and the tragic sides of the war and to retain a sense of astonishment when thinking about the men and women who endured it, and still managed to retain their humanity.

Metropolitan histories: politics, culture, remembrance

In 1913, the Deutsche Bücherei, the national deposit library for all books published in Germany, opened after years of discussion.[11] The enterprise was the fruit of efforts made not by public authorities and not by the state, but rather by the *Börsenverein*, an association of German publishers. The *Deutsche Bücherei* was inaugurated on 2 September 1916, the anniversary of the German victory at Sedan; the date alone suggests the profoundly national reverberations of the event. This library, though, was not located in Berlin. It was in Leipzig, for generations the city of books and publishing in Germany. Berliners had tried to claim the library for the capital. Pressure was exerted by Adolph von Harnack, the director

---

[10] Deborah Cohen, *War come home. Disabled veterans in Britain and Germany, 1914–1939* (Berkeley, Los Angeles, and London, 2001).
[11] Matthias Middell, *Kulturtransfer und Vergleich* (Leipzig, 2000).

of the Prussian Royal Library, but to no avail. Saxony won the contest during the war.

On 6 February 1919 another Saxon city welcomed the new National Constituent Assembly of post-war Germany. There in Weimar's theatre the Assembly voted on 11 August to approve the Constitution of what was to be the Weimar Republic. How ironic it is to compare the two moments: the birth out of defeat of the Third Republic in Paris/Versailles in 1871, and the birth out of defeat of the Weimar Republic in 1919. In 1871 no one dreamt of calling the Third Republic the 'Versailles Republic'.

What a clear demonstration of the way in which Berlin emerged from the war both the political heart of a fragile and incomplete state and the one city whose imperial past was to be left behind in the new democratic order. All at once the German revolution of 1918–19 made the city, like Paris, into a republican bastion. The first democratic municipal elections (without the three-tiered weighted voting system and with votes for women) in February 1919 produced unsurprisingly a landslide for the Social Democratic party, already powerful before the war. Its two wings accounted for 65 per cent of the vote.

On 1 October 1920 the majority pushed through the Prussian Diet a law creating Greater Berlin. Berlin, which in the pre-war period had registered the most rapid population growth of the three capital cities, administratively absorbed its suburbs as London had done well before the war, and as Paris had never done. Berlin – the city of the modern, the city of heavy industry, the city of science – constructed a more rational system of administering its space and social services. The city became even more emphatically than ever before a centre of the avant-garde, and it did so despite economic hardship and chronic police surveillance. The modest and conservative face of the *Deutsches Theater*, presenting in November 1917, 'Young Germany' on stage, was replaced two years later by a much larger theatre seating 3,000 spectators presenting popular theatre directed by Max Reinhardt.

Mass entertainment and the arts flourished in and around Berlin, for instance in the Babelsberg film studios near Potsdam. The multiple cultural forms which had emerged during the war seemed to have created the conditions for a new appropriation of the landscape of their city by Berliners themselves, but this was not to be. The poets of the nineteenth century evoked the Berlin of sadness and of barracks. Goethe and Schiller preferred to live not in Berlin but in Weimar. In this metropolis without tradition, the citizens who promenaded on its boulevards were neither *flâneurs* nor ornaments. This is what Franz Hessel wrote of Berlin: 'We wanted to gaze at it, to feel affection for it, to find its beauty, so that it would be beautiful.'[12] Few succeeded in doing so. Here is the stuff out of which Baudelaire's (and Benjamin's) 'memory city' emerged, that sense of nostalgia for and consolation in being in a city which 'changes more quickly that the human heart'.

The same cannot be said of the other two capital cities. The two volumes of this long study have reinforced the sense that London's cultural and commercial pre-eminence within Britain survived the war intact. Its political life, though, changed fundamentally in these years. The municipal elections of 1 November 1919 produced the first indications that the Labour party was a major political force with national aspirations for power. There were Labour majorities in the working-class districts of Shoreditch, Bethnal Green, Stepney, Poplar, West Ham, and East Ham, the heart and soul of East London. From a total of 26 councillors elected in 1912, the Labour party took 168 out of 222 seats in local elections seven years later.[13] And in Parliamentary elections, the same transformation, albeit moving at a slower pace, may be seen: in these East London constituencies, Labour took 2 seats out of 14 in 1918, 8 in 1922, and 13 of 14 in 1923. The power of Labour in the London County Council grew in the inter-war years, producing a sturdy base for the careers of many politicians, Herbert Morrison in particular.

How do these results fit into our history of capital cities at war? To be sure, we can see traces here of the national wave, common to all three countries, of recognition and support for Labour and Socialist parties in the immediate aftermath of the war. But in London it is the local character of these movements which is most striking. Of all three cities, it was London, that immense imperial capital, which best preserved its local political culture, now expressed in a decidedly working-class accent.

In London, as elsewhere, the war brought politics into every facet of life: in public spaces, in the streets, in the music halls, in the household, in hospitals, even in cemeteries. The state was there to stay, in the economy, in universities, in cultural life. Even London's cabbies, proud citizens of Stepney, made a special mark on the city by striking in 1919, thereby binding together material grievances and the vote. So did the Metropolitan police.

The popular districts and suburbs of Paris had been conquered by socialists well before the war. And the conflict did not change this fact. The war helped complete the creation of the 'red belt' of suburbs. These

---

[12] Franz Hessel, *Promenades dans Berlin* (Grenoble, 1989).
[13] Julia Bush, *Behind the lines. East London Labour, 1914–1919* (London, 1984).

districts were formally outside the jurisdiction of the Municipal Council, which retained the old geographical definition of the city after the war. Thus a post-war spatial divide highlighted the deep political divide in the city's political culture.

As we have noted, in one respect, there is a lacuna in Paris's commemorative history. Part of this story is well known. A site of pilgrimage and of grand ceremonial occasions, the tomb of the Unknown Soldier and the Eternal Flame placed in central Paris a palpable national site for remembering the war. This was not at all the same as a site for remembering all Parisians who died in the war; indeed no such site exists. Paris, the 'memory city' par excellence, apparently had no room for its own collective remembrance of the war. London, the city of Lutyens's Cenotaph and of countless small war memorials, also has no metropolitan memorial of its own.

Let us return finally to the question of what constitutes metropolitan experience, a point we raised in the first chapter of volume I. A novelist like Italo Calvino might conjure up an imaginary city bringing Paris, London, and Berlin together, a place where one strolled from Piccadilly Circus to the Place de la Bastille and then on to Alexanderplatz. Is there such a thing as metropolitan culture which spans these urban spaces as one? In these two volumes there is evidence of a common experience joining together these city-dwellers in their streets, their theatres, their homes. But what divided them for five long years of war was the nation and its relentless mobilization. Was what bound them together as metropolitan citizens more significant than their national identities? In the winter of 2005, a French–German–British film, directed by Christian Carion and entitled 'Merry Christmas', was launched about the Christmas truce of 1914, a time when soldiers on the Western front came out of their trenches, shook hands, and took a break from the war. There they were – Berliners, Londoners, and Parisians alike – in the trenches a few metres from each other, their commonality impossible to miss. To be sure, the film was a fairy tale, but one with a bite to it. As these two volumes show, both at the front and in their homes behind the lines, these men and their families did indeed have much in common, whatever their nationality. And yet it was for the nation, configured in so many different ways, that they fought and sacrificed and died. Identities are like shoes; we do not walk with only one. But there the metaphor ends, for this clash of identities was murderous. To see this collision of affinities and loyalties helps us appreciate better the ways in which the residents of these capital cities of war shared a common experience. For in these places, these millions of men and women entered the tragic history of the twentieth century together.

War and moral thinking

The only way to understand the Great War is in terms of the language of those who lived through it. As our two-volume study has shown, that language was filled with moral metaphors, categories, and judgements. When mass death is an everyday matter, moral thinking is a necessity. Is the cause just? Are burdens being shared equitably? Is the blockade or aerial bombardment a war crime? Are strikes a form of treason? What price victory? To be sure, many politicians emptied these questions of meaning and turned them into mere slogans, akin to advertising. But even when moral issues were debased through propaganda and outright lies, they still refused to go away. Too many people were disabled, too many killed, too many in mourning to allow questions of fairness, of equity, of shared sacrifice to remain unaddressed.

And these moral matters did not vanish with the Armistice. Who stabbed whom in the back was a question which tore Weimar Germany apart. Each 11 November, men and women in the victorious countries meditated on the human toll of the war, and had to consider the question as to whether winning was worth the costs, human and otherwise. Many thought so; many others were unsure. But by the time the first post-war decade had ended, the promise of a new start, a new international order, a new deal for veterans had faded. Moral thinking, so many instances of which are highlighted in this study, informed the post-war veterans' movement in their effort to make war unthinkable. 'Never again' is a phrase tied to the First World War long before it became braided to the Second, and in particular to the Holocaust. And 'never' lasted a mere twenty years.

By then a new regime was in power in Berlin, whose radical thinking both transformed Europe and made a comparison of the kind we have undertaken but covering the period of the Second World War almost impossible. There were affinities in the state of wartime populations after 1939, but the kind of war the Nazis inflicted on the world, and the devastation and mass murder which it occasioned, separate like a chasm the history of the First and the Second World Wars. These metropolitan populations fought a world war in 1914–18, but they also fought a very European war, one in which both sides, if they looked in the mirror at their adversaries, would see people just like themselves. It took the disaster of the Second World War to pull Europeans back to an urgent consideration of their common destiny. When they did so, metropolitan life in Paris, London, and Berlin began to converge again, and to give to the new Europe a dynamism and elegance which, over more than a century, has made living in these capital cities both a privilege and a challenge.

Bibliography

I.   Archives

1.   Berlin

Brandenburgisches Landeshauptarchiv, Potsdam (BLHA)
PPB no. 15810

Bundesarchiv, Berlin (BArch)
R 1501/108997
R 8034 II/6938
R 8034 II/6940
R 1501/125 799 – 125 809

Evangelisches Zentralarchiv
1/A2/525

Geheimes Staatsarchiv Preussischer Kulturbesitz, Berlin (GStAPK)
I. HA, Rep. 89, No. 24553.
I. HA, Rep. 77, Tit. 162, No. 154 (M).
Rep 76 VII, No. 24546

Humboldt Universität
Humboldt Universität Archiv (HUA), Kuratorium
HUA, Kuratorium/577, Institute of Dental Surgery
HUA Rektor und Senat/809 and 562

Landesarchiv Berlin (LAB)
Gesch 921
A Prf. Br. Rep. 30, Tit. 94, 11361, Lit.K, No. 1293, Bd. 2
A Prf. Br. Rep. 30 Tit. 74, No. 16

A Prf. Br. Rep. 30 Tit. 74, No. 6058
A Prf. Br. Rep. 30 Tit. 74, No. 16
A Prf. Br. Rep. 30 Tit. 74, No. 63
A Prf. Br. Rep. 30 Tit. 74, No. 6146, 6635, 6787
A Prf. Br. Rep. 30 Tit. 90 No. 7496
A Prf. Sta Rep. 49-05/8, No. 49
A Prf. Sta Rep. 20-01, No. 410
A Prf. Br. Rep.106, No. 972
A Rep. 001-02, No. 1024

Politisches Archiv des Auswärtigen Amtes (PAAA)
Kunst und Wissenschaft, R 64483

Private collections of letters on family life in Berlin
Familie G. collection
Johanna We. collection

2.　　*Dover, Delaware*

Johnson Museum, Clark Papers

3.　　*Karlsruhe*

Generallandesarchiv Karlsruhe (GLA)
236/22730
236/23189

4.　　*London*

Corporation of London Records Office (CLRO)
Freemen's Orphan School committee
City of London School committee, Minute book

Guildhall Library
MS 31098
MS 31192

Imperial War Museum (IWM)
Bennett papers
Coules papers
Cousins diary

Essington-Nelson papers
Fernside papers
Film on the raid of 26 September 1917
First World War Artists archive
Isaacs papers
Marchioness of Reading papers
Photograph archive
Proctor papers
Saunders papers
Women and War, 1918, Topical Film Company

King's College London archives
KCLCA, KAP/BUR/13.

Lambeth Palace London
Davidson papers, 355/285/360

London Metropolitan Archive
LCC/MIN/10, 737
LCC/MIN/4367
LCC/MIN/2909–15, 1914–20
LCC/EO/GEN/3/2
LCC/EO/DIV1/MUN/LB/11
TD (A/FWA/C/D)

London School of Economics archives
Wallas papers

National Archives, Public Record Office, Kew
CAB 24/22, GT 1650, fo. 191
HO 45/10511/130791/ff. 20 and f. 21
HO45/10944/257142/ff. 4 and 5
HO45/10511/130791/ff. 22 and 23
HO45/10742/263275/ f. 265
HO45/10743/263275 f. 229
HO45/10744/263275 f. 373
HO45/10744/263275 f. 379
HO45/10744/263275 ff. 383, 385, 390, 396, 410, 431
HO45/10742/263275/ f. 194, 208, 209, 214
HO45/10742/263275/ f. 249
HO45/10810/311932 f. 16
HO45/10810/311932/ f. 56

HO45/10810/311932 f. 65
HO45/10810/311932/ f. 64 and 65
HO45/10944/257142/ 186 and 187
HO45/10944/257142/ff. 151, 185
HO45/11068/372202 ff. 18, 21, 22
MH 47/143
MH 47/8 File M97
NSC 7/2
T102/24
WO 33/78

National Hospital Queen Square archive
Medical Notes and Records 1915–24

Times Newspaper Limited Archive
Marked copies of *The Times*

University College London, college archives
'War Memorial Find Items'
'Franco-British exhibition'

5.   *Maidenhead*

      Archives of the Commonwealth War Graves Commission

6.   *Münster*

      Staatsarchiv Münster (StAMS)
Schulprogramme-Sammlung

7.   *Munich*

Bayerisches Hauptstaatsarchiv Munich, Abt. iv, Kriegsarchiv:
Stellv. Gkdo. I. AK, No. 643
Stellv. GK des I AK, #1917

8.   *Nîmes*

Bibliothèque Municipale

9.   *Oxford*

      Bodleian Library
St. Silas the Martyr, Annual Letters and Accounts

10.   Paris

Archives du Ministère de la Défense, Château de Vincennes
Service historique de l'Armée de Terre, 16N2851
Archives de Jean-François Durand, 7N2258

Archives de la Préfecture de Police de Paris
BA 1587
BA 1645
BA 697
BA 721, BA 710
BA 772
BA 843
BA698
CB 22.40
CB 39.68
CB 59.30
CB 59.32
CB 59.33
CB 77.27
CB 79.34
CB 79.35
CB 79.36
CB 103
CB 26
CB 27
CB 32.27
CB 59.31
CB 60
DA 455
DA 456
DB 343
PF Cb 37.44
R40 no. 999

Archives de Paris
D2T-1/47
DE Fonds Remon
VK 240
VK3 187
VK3 194
VK3 195

Archives Nationales
AJ/16/2895
AJ/16/85-6
AJ16/2699
AJ/16/2589
AJ/16/2640
AJ/16/2877
AJ/16/7027-44
F/7/223-332
F7 12936
F7 13367
F7 13370 B3

BDIC, University of Paris – X, Nanterre
O 10164
Photographs, Z2157
Photographs, P965

Conseil municipal de la ville de Paris
Comité du budget, 13 March 1918
Procès verbaux

Diocese of Paris
Historical archives of the Diocese of Paris, 4 Z Salomon

Larousse/Giraudon archives
Photograph of 20 October 1918

Private archives
Heures de guerre de la famille A.
War Essays by Johanna Welz, 23 April 1915 and 17 November 1916. Private
collection, Berlin.

II.   Contemporary newspapers, journals, and periodicals

ANOST (Association nationale des officiers du service militaire des transports)
Bellica
Berliner Börsen-Courier
Berliner Lokal-Anzeiger
Berliner Morgenpost

Berliner Neueste Nachrichten
Berliner Tageblatt
Berliner Volkszeitung
Bombardia
Builder
Building News
Building News and Engineering Journal
Bulletin des réfugiés du Nord
Burlington Magazine
Clare Market Review
Conservative Agents' Journal
Daily Chronicle
Daily Express
Daily Mail
Das Illustrierte Blatt
Das Plakat
Der Cicerone
Der Kunstwart
Deutsche Zeitung
Die Eiche
Die Kunst
Die Kunst für alle
East London Observer
Excelsior
Face aux boches
Freiburger Tagespost
Glasgow Herald
Hampstead Record
Hannoverscher Kurier
Hansard's Parliamentary debates. House of Commons official report
Heimsdorff-Weidmansluster Zeitung
Hospital
Illustrated London News
Illustrierter Kriegs-Kurier
John Bull
Journal Officiel, débats parlementaires, Chambre des deputés
Kieler Zeitung
Kinematograph
Kirchliches Jahrbuch für die Evangelischen Landeskirchen Deutschlands
Kladderadatsch
Kreuz-Zeitung

Kunst und Künstler
L'Argonnaute
L'Artilleur déchainé
L'Echo de Paris
L'Echo de Tranchéesville
L'Echo des Gourbis
L'Echo des marmites
L'Echo du ravin
L'Esprit du co
L'Humanité
L'Intransigeant
L'Œuvre
La Bourguignotte
La Chéchia
La Croix
La Fusée
La Libre parole
La Lune
La Mitraille
La Vie feminine
La Vie parisienne
Labour Leader
Le Canard du Boyau
Le Diable au Cor
Le Figaro
Le Film
Le Journal
Le Petit Echo du 18ème RIT
Le Petit Parisien
Le Poilu
Le Poilu du 303e
Le Poilu du 6–9
Le Populaire
Le Rat-à-Poil
Le Ver luisant
Leipziger Neueste Nachrichten
Liller Kriegszeitung
L'Illustration
London Teacher and London Schools Review
Manchester Guardian
Marmita

Monatsschrift für Pastoraltheologie
Museums Journal
Neue Preußische Zeitung [*Kreuz-Zeitung*]
Neue Rundschau
New York Times
Norddeutsche Allgemeine Zeitung
Outlook
Pall Mall Gazette
Petit Echo du 18° régiment territorial d'infanterie
Punch
Revue de l'enseignement primaire
Revue universitaire
Rigolboche
Soziale Praxis
Sozialistische Monatshefte
Statisches Jahrbuch des deutschen Reiches
Tägliche Rundschau
Talking Machine News
Talking Machine World
The Globe
The Gramophone
The Passing Show
The Times
The Times Educational Supplement
University College Magazine
Velhagen & Klasings Monatshefte
Verhandlungen des Reichstags
Vorwärts
Vossische Zeitung
Westermanns Monatshefte
Woman's Dreadnought
Woolwich Herald
Woolwich Pioneer and Labour Journal
Zeiten und Völker

III.   Books and articles

1.   *Contemporary publications, sources, diaries, and memoirs*

'A visit to the Royal Army clothing factory', *Tailor and cutter* (6 August 1914).
Abel-Smith, Brian, *A history of the nursing profession* (London, 1960).

Adrian, E. D. and Yealland, L. R., 'Treatment of some common war neuroses', *Lancet* (June 1917), pp. 867–72.

Ajalbert, Jean, *Comment glorifier les morts pour la patrie?* (Paris, 1916).

Dans Paris, la Grand'ville. Sensations de la guerre (Paris, 1916).

Alexandre, Michel, *Notes de guerre* (Nîmes, 1917).

Andler, C., 'La rénovation présente des universités allemandes et des universités françaises', *Revue internationale de l'enseignement* (November–December, 1919), pp. 432–47.

André, A.-E., 'L'école primaire française et la guerre', in Ministère de l'Instruction publique (ed.), *Rapports présentés au Congrès pour l'examen des questions concernant le 'cours populaire'* (Paris, 1916).

Anonymous, *La flamme sous l'Arc de Triomphe du Soldat Inconnu* (   ).

Anquetil, Georges, *La maitresse légitime. Essai sur le mariage polygamique de demain* (Paris, 1923).

Association amicale des anciens élèves du lycée Charlemagne (Paris, 1920).

Association des Parrains de Reuilly, *Statuts* (Paris, 1916).

Ausstellung für Verwundeten- und Krankenfürsorge im Kriege. Berlin 1914, Reichstagsgebäude (Berlin and Leipzig, 1914).

Barrès, Maurice, *Les diverses familles spirituelles de la France* (Paris, 1917).

De la Sympathie à la fraternité d'armes. Les États-Unis dans la guerre (Paris, 1918).

Barthas, Louis, *Les cahiers de guerre de Louis Barthas, tonnelier: 1914–1919*, introduction by Rémy Cazals (Paris, 1978).

Bazhor, Charles, *Papa en permission* (Paris, 1916).

Benaerts, Louis, *Un lycée de Paris pendant la guerre. 'Condorcet' 1914–1918* (Montrouge, 1919).

Bergson, Henri, *Les deux sources de la morale et de la religion* (Paris, 1932).

Bérillon, Edgar, 'La psychologie de la race allemande d'après ses caractères objectifs et spécifiques', in Association française pour l'avancement des sciences (ed.), *Conférences faites en 1916–1917* (Paris, 1917), pp. 77–140.

Blanche, Jacques-Emile, *Cahiers d'un artiste*, 2 (Paris, 1916).

Boasson, Marc, *Au soir d'un monde, Lettres de guerre (16 April 1915–27 April 1918)* (Paris, 1926).

Bobertag, Otto, 'Bericht über die Ausstellung "Schule und Krieg" im Zentralinstitut für Erziehung und Unterricht zu Berlin', in William Stern (ed.), *Jugendliches Seelenleben und Krieg. Materialien und Berichte*, Beihefte zur Zeitschrift für angewandte Psychologie und psychologische Sammelforschung, 12 (Leipzig, 1915), pp. 134–64.

Bonhoeffer, Karl, 'Ein Beitrag zur Kenntnis des großstädtischen Bettel- und Vagabundentums. Eine Psychiatrische Untersuchung', *Zeitschrift für die gesamte Strafrechtswissenschaft*, 21 (1901), pp. 1–65.

Boutet de Monvel, Roger and Arnoux, Guy, *Carnet d'un permissionaire* (Paris, 1917).

Brackmann, A. (ed.), *Ostpreußische Kriegshefte auf Grund amtlicher und privater Berichte;* vol. II: Fluchtbewegung und Flüchtlingsfürsorge (Berlin, 1915).

Bréal, Jacques, *Les poètes de la Grande Guerre. Anthologie* (Paris, 1992).

Brecht, Bertolt, *Complete poetry* (London, 2000).

Bridgwater, Patrick (ed.), *The German poets of the First World War* (London, 1985).

Brittain, Vera, *Chronicle of youth*, ed. A. Bishop (London, 1982).

Brophy, John and Partridge, Eric, *Songs and slang of the British soldier: 1914–1918* (London, 1930).

Buchner, Eberhard (ed.), *Kriegsdokumente; der Weltkrieg 1914 . . . in der Darstellung der zeitgenössischen Presse* (Munich, 1914–18).

Buddecke, A., *Die Kriegssammlungen. Ein Nachweis ihrer Einrichtung und ihres Bestandes* (Oldenburg, 1917).

Bumm, E., *Über das Frauenstudium* (Berlin, 1917).

Camus, Albert, *The first man*, trans. David Hapgood (New York, 1995).

Cerfberr, G., *Paris pendant la guerre* (Paris, 1919).

Chancerel, Léon, *La chanson des dix jours* (Paris, 1917).

Collie, John, 'The management of neurasthenia and allied disorders contracted in the army', *Journal of State Medicine*, 26 (1918), p. 15.

Condemi, Concetta, *Les cafés-concerts. Histoire d'un divertissement 1849–1914* (Paris 1992).

Copeau, Jacques, *Journal, 1901–1948* (Paris, 1991).

Correspondance de Jacques et Marie-Josèphe Boussac (Cléry, 1996).

Cowan, Gibson, *Loud report* (London, 1938).

Daniel, Ute, *Arbeiterfrauen in der Kriegsgesellschaft. Beruf, Familie und Politik im Ersten Weltkrieg* (Göttingen, 1989).

Dehay, Valerie, 'L'école primaire en France pendant la guerre de 1914–1918', doctoral thesis, University of Picardie, 2000.

de la Brière, Yves, 'Chronique du mouvement religieux, au Sacré-Cœur de Montmartre', *Etudes* (November 1919), pp. 336–62.

Delécraz, Antoine, *1914. Paris pendant la mobilisation* (Geneva, 1914).

Delétang, Louise, *Journal d'une ouvrière parisienne pendant la guerre* (Paris, 1935).

Delvert, Capitaine Charles, *Histoire d'une compagnie: Main de Massiges – Verdun, November 1915–Juin 1916. Journal de marche* (Paris, 1918).

Demm, Eberhard, 'Zwischen Propaganda und Sozialfürsorge – Deutschlands Kinder im Krieg', in Eberhard Demm, *Ostpolitik und Propaganda im Ersten Weltkrieg* (Frankfurt am Main, 2002).

Deutsche Kriegsausstellungen 1916. Amtlicher Führer, ed. Zentralkomitee der Deutschen Vereine vom Roten Kreuz (Berlin, 1916).

Dix, Kurt Walther, 'Beobachtungen über den Einfluß der Kriegsereignisse auf das Seelenleben des Kindes', in William Stern (ed.), *Jugendliches Seelenleben und Krieg. Materialien und Berichte*, Beihefte zur Zeitschrift für angewandte Psychologie und psychologische Sammelforschung, 12 (Leipzig, 1915), pp. 165–71.

Donnay, Maurice, *La Parisienne et la guerre* (Paris, 1916).

Dorgeles, Roland, *Bleu Horizon. Pages de la Grand Guerre* (Paris, 1949).

Dos Passos, John, *Trois soldats* (Paris, 1993; 1921 edn).

Draper, W., 'Village centres for cure and training', *Recalled to Life*, 3 (April 1918), pp. 342–57.

Dudon, Paul, 'La voix des morts de la Grande Guerre', *Etudes* (5 August 1919), pp. 256–70.

Durkheim, Émile and Lavisse, Ernest, *Lettres à tous les Français* (Paris, 1992 [1916]).

Ehrenmahl für die gefallen Kameraden der Deutschen Eisenbahntruppen (Berlin, 1929).

Engelhardt, R. von, *Die deutsche Universität Dorpat in ihrer geistesgeschichtlichen Bedeutung* (Munich, 1933).

Evening Standard, The 500 best Cockney war stories (London, 1921).

Figuier, L. *La ville lumière* (Paris, 1914).

Fitzgerald, F. Scott, *Tender is the night: a romance* (New York, 1934).

Fitzke, Benno and Matzdorf, Paul, *Eiserne Kreuz-Nagelungen zum Besten der Kriegshilfe und zur Schaffung von Kriegswahrzeichen. Gebrauchsfertiges Material für vaterländische Volksunterhaltung durch Feiern in Schulen, Jugendvereinigungen und Vereine* (Leipzig, 1916).

Flint, E., *Hot bread and chips* (London, 1963).

Ford, Ford Madox, *The soul of London. A survey of a modern city* (London, 1905).

Fougerol, H., *Condition civile des mobilisés* (Paris, 1916).

Francke, Ernst and Lotz, Walther (eds.), *Die geistigen Arbeiter* (Munich and Leipzig, 1922).

Frankfurth, Hermann, *Berlin und Potsdam in der Sprache ihrer Kirchen und Friedhöfe* (Berlin, 1924).

Friedrich, Ernst, *Das Anti-Kriegsmuseum* (Berlin, 1926).

  Vom Friedens-Museum ... zur Hitler-Kaserne. Ein Tatsachenbericht über das Wirken von Ernst Friedrich und Adolf Hitler (Geneva, 1935).

  War against war! (Seattle, 1987).

Führen, Franz, *Lehrer im Krieg. Ein Ehrenbuch deutscher Volksschullehrer*, vol. II (Leipzig, 1936).

Galtier-Boissière, Jean, *Mémoires d'un Parisien* (Paris, 1960).

Géraldy, Paul, *La guerre, Madame* (Paris, 1916).

Gibson, Ralph, *A social history of French Catholicism* (Cambridge, 1975).

Gilardone, Heinrich, *Der Hias: Ein feldgraues Spiel in drei Aufzügen* (Berlin and Munich, 1917).

Glatzer, Dieter and Ruth, *Berliner Leben 1914–1918* (Berlin, 1983).

Gleason, Arthur, *Inside the British Isles* (London, 1917).

Glück, Carol, *Past obsessions: war and memory in the twentieth century* (New York, 2006).

Gray, John, *Gin and bitters* (London, 1938).

Guéno, Jean-Pierre and Laplume, Yves, *Paroles de poilus. Lettres et carnets de front, 1914–1918* (Paris, 1998).

Haber, Fritz, 'Die Chemie im Kriege', in *Fünf Vorträge aus den Jahren 1920–1923* (Berlin, 1924).

Haffner, Sebastian, *Defying Hitler. A memoir* (London, 2002).

Halévy, Daniel, *Avec les Boys américains* (Paris, 1918).

Haller, Hermann and Wolff, Willi, 'Immer feste druff! Vaterländisches Volksstück mit Gesang in 4 Bildern', *Textbuch der Gesänge* (Munich and Berlin, 1914).

Handelsman, M., *Die Warschauer Universität* (München-Gladbach: Volksverlag, 1916).

Hanna, M., *The mobilization of intellect. French scholars and writers during the Great War* (Cambridge, Mass., 1996).

Hannsen, Hans Peter, *Diary of a dying empire*, trans. by Oscar Osburn Winther. Ed. by Ralph H. Lutz, Mary Schofield, and O. O. Winther. Introd. by Ralph H. Lutz (Bloomington, Ind., 1955).

Hellwag, Fritz, 'Die derzeitige wirtschaftliche Lage der bildenden Künstler', in Ernst Francke and Walther Lotz (eds.), *Die geistigen Arbeiter* (Munich and Leipzig, 1922).

Hermant, Abel, *La vie à Paris* (Paris, 1917).

Hertz, Robert, *Un Ethnologue dans les tranchées, août 1914–avril 1915* (Paris, 2002).

Hessel, Franz, *Promenades dans Berlin* (Grenoble, 1989; 1st edn Berlin, 1929).

Heubes, Max (ed.), *Ehrenbuch der Feldeisenbanner* (Berlin, 1931).

Hirschfeld, R., 'Zur Behandlung im Kriege erworbener hysterischer Zustände, insbesondere von Sprachstörungen,' *Zeitschrift für die gesamte Neurologie und Psychiatrie*, 34 (1916), pp. 195–205.

Hobhouse, L. T., *Democracy and reaction* (2nd edn, London, 1909 [1st edn 1905]).

Hobson, J. A., *The psychology of jingoism* (London, 1901).

   The crisis of liberalism: New issues of democracy (London, 1909).

Hollebecque, Mme, *La jeunesse scolaire de France et la guerre* (Paris, 1916).

Holmes, Colin, *Anti-Semitism in British society, 1876–1939* (London, 1979).

Holt, T. and V., *Till the boys come home. The picture postcards of the First World War* (London, 1977).

Huelsenbeck, Richard, 'Dada lives!', in Robert Motherwell and Jack D. Flam (eds.), *The Dada painters and poets* (Boston, 1981).

Hurst, Major A. F., 'Nerves and the men', *Reveille*, 2 (November 1918), pp. 260–8.

Inge, W. R., *Diary of a dean* (London, 1949).

Jacob, Max, *La défense de Tartuffe* (Paris, 1964).

Jarausch, K. H. *Deutsche Studenten 1800–1970* (Frankfurt am Main, 1984).

Jasper, A. S., *A Hoxton childhood* (London, 1969).

Jones, Paul, *War letters of a public-school boy* (London, 1918).

Jünger, Ernst, *In Stahlgewittern* (Stuttgart, 1978 [1920]).

Kaeber, Ernst, *Berlin im Weltkriege. Fünf Jahre städtischer Kriegsarbeit* (Berlin, 1921).

Kehrer, Ferdinand, 'Behandlung und ärztliche Fürsorge bei Kriegsneurosen', *Die Kriegsbeschädigtenfürsorge* 2 (1917), pp. 158–64.

Keller, Samuel, *Unsere Kriegsgräber. Ein Wort der Gewissheit und Hoffnung* (Berlin, 1915).

Kellermann, H. (ed.), *Der Krieg der Geister. eine Auslese deutscher und ausländischer Stimmen zum Weltkriege 1914* (Weimar, 1915).

Kern, Stephen, *The culture of time and space 1880–1918* (Cambridge, Mass. and London, 1983).

Koenigswald, Harald von, *Das verwandelte Antlitz* (Berlin, 1938).

Kollwitz, Käthe, *Briefe an den Sohn 1904–1945*, ed. Jutta Bohnke-Kollwitz (Berlin, 1992).

   Die Tagebücher, ed. Jutta Bohnke-Kollwitz (Berlin, 1989).

König, Karl, *Kriegsstoffe für die Unter- und Mittelstufe*, 3rd edn (Strasbourg, 1916).

Kushner, Tony, 'Local heroes. Belgian refugees in Britain during the First World War', *Immigrants and Minorities*, 18, 1 (1999), pp. 1–28.

L'Ame de Paris. Tableaux de la guerre de 1914. (Paris, 1915).

La dernière lettre écrite par des soldats français tombés au champ d'honneur (Paris, 1922).

Land, Hans, 'Kriegstrophäen von 1914/15', *Reclams Universum*, 31 (1915), pp. 1006–7.

Lansbury, George, *Faith and Hope* (London, National Mission Pamphlet B, 1916).

Laudet, Fernand, *Paris pendant la guerre: impressions* (Paris, 1915).

Laurant, Pierre, *Nos potaches pendant la guerre* (Paris, 1932).

Lax, W., *Lax of Poplar* (London, 1927).

Le Pileur, Docteur (infirmerie Saint-Lazare), *Indications sur la prostitution vulgivague à Paris depuis le début de la guerre* (Paris, 1918).

Liard, L., 'La Guerre et les universités françaises', *Revue de Paris*, 1 May 1916.

Liebknecht, Karl, *Gesammelte Schriften und Reden*, ed. Institut für Marxismus-Leninismus, vol. VIII (East Berlin, 1966).

Linton, Alice, *Not expecting miracles* (London, 1982).

Lloyd, David William, *Battlefield tourism. Pilgrimage and the commemoration of the Great War in Britain, Australia and Canada, 1919–1939* (Oxford, 1998).

Lloyd George, David, *War memoirs* (6 vols., London, 1938).

Lortac, R., *Le Roman d'un Sénégalais* (Paris, 1918).

Loubes, Olivier, *L'école de la patrie. Histoire d'un désenchantement, 1914–1940* (Paris and Berlin, 2001).

Lowell, A. L., *The government of England*, 2 vols. (London, 1908).

Maase, Kaspar, *Grenzenloses Vergnügen. Der Aufstieg der Massenkultur 1850–1970* (Frankfurt am Main, 1997).

MacDonagh, Michael, *In London during the Great War* (London, 1935).

MacDonald, J. Ramsay, *Socialism and society* (London, 1905).

Macdonald, N., *Wartime nursery rhymes* (London, 1918).

Mace, Rodney, *Trafalgar Square. Emblem of empire* (London, 1976).

Mackenzie, R. Tait, *Reclaiming the maimed* (New York, 1918).

McMillan, James, *The way it was 1914–1934* (London, 1979).

Mann, Alfred, 'Aufsätze von Kindern und Jugendlichen über Kriegsthemata', in William Stern (ed.), *Jugendliches Seelenleben und Krieg. Materialien und Berichte*, Beihefte zur Zeitschrift für angewandte Psychologie und psychologische Sammelforschung, 12 (Leipzig, 1915), pp. 78–90.

Masterman, C. F. G. (ed.), *The heart of the empire: discussions of problems of modern city life in England* (London, 1901).

Masterman, C. F. G., *England after the war* (London, 1922).

Materna, Ingo and Schreckenbach, Hans-Joachim (eds.), *Dokumente aus geheimen Archiven*, vol. IV, *Berichte des Berliner Polizeipräsidenten zur Stimmung und Lage der Bevölkerung in Berlin 1914–1918* (Weimar, 1987).

Meinecke, Friedrich, *Autobiographische Schriften*, *Werke*, vol. VIII, ed. E. Kessel (Stuttgart, 1969).

Meiss, Honel, 'Au soldat inconnu du 11 novembre', *L'Univers Israélite*, 26 November 1920, p. 271.

Michaux, Baronne Jane, *En marge du drame. Journal d'une parisienne pendant la guerre 1914–1915* (Paris, 1916).

Mohr, F., 'Grundsätzliches zur Kriegsneurosenfrage', *Medizinische Klinik* 12 (1916), pp. 90–3.

Moniot, A., *Le crime rituel chez les Juifs* (Paris, 1914).

Montherland, *Mors et Vita* (Paris, 1919; ed. 1988).

Mott, F. W., 'The predisposing factors of war psycho-neuroses', *Nature*, 100 (1917), pp. 1–3.

'Chadwick Lecture: Mental hygiene in Shell shock, during and after the War', *Journal of Mental Science*, lxiii (1917), pp. 467–88.

'Neurasthenia: the disorders and disabilities of fear', *Lancet* (26 January 1918), pp. 127–9.

War neuroses and shell shock (London, 1919).

Mudie-Smith, R., *The religious life of London* (London, 1904).

Mugnier, Abbé, *Journal de l'abbé Mugnier: 1879–1939*, edited by Marcel Billot; preface by Ghislain de Diesbach; notes by Jean d'Hendecourt (Paris, 1985).

Mumm, R., *Der Religionsunterricht und die Nationalversammlung. Rede des Abgeordneten D. Reinhard Mumm in der Nationalversammlung am 11 März 1919* (Berlin, 1919).

Münch, Wilhelm, Reimann, Arnold, and Rettberg, Hans (eds.), *Das Unterrichts- und Erziehungswesen Groß-Berlins. Eine Übersicht über seinen gegenwärtigen Stand zur Orientierung für Fremde und Einheimische* (Berlin, 1912).

Newton, Arthur, *Years of change: autobiography of a Hackney shoemaker* (London, 1974).

Nonne, Max, 'Therapeutische Erfahrungen an den Kriegsneurosen in den Jahren, 1914 –1918', in *Geistes- und Nervenkrankheiten*, vol. IV *of Handbuch der ärztlichen Erfahrungen im Weltkriege*, 1914–1918, edited by Karl Bonhoeffer (Leipzig, 1922), pp. 102–21.

Nordau, Max, *Degeneration* (Lincoln, Neb., 1992).

Norec, A., *Tommies et Gourkas* (Paris, 1917).

Nos enfants et la guerre. Enquête de la Société libre pour l'étude psychologique de l'enfant (Paris, 1917).

Omissi, David (ed.), *Indian voices of the Great War* (London, 1999).

Orlan, Pierre Mac, *Le bataillonnaire* (Paris, 1989 [first published 1920]).

Orwell, George, *Burmese days* (London, 1967).

Owen, H. C., *Salonica and after* (London, 1919).

Pember Reeves, Mrs, *Round about a pound a week* (London, 1913).

Peters, Emil, *Deutschlands heiliger Krieg. Der Sieg des deutschen Wesens* (Berlin, n.d. [1914 or 1915]).

Petit, G. and Leudet, M., *Les Allemands et la science* (Paris, 1916).

Pinget, F., *Les permissions dans l'armée: leur influence sur l'instruction, la discipline, l'esprit militaire* (Paris, 1896).

Prévost, J., *Dix-huitième année* (Paris, 1994).

Rapsilber, Maximilian, *Der Eiserne Hindenburg von Berlin. Ein Gedenkblatt* (Berlin, 1918).

Réception à l'hôtel de ville de Messieurs les ambassadeurs et ministres des puissances alliés, 14 Juillet 1918 (Paris, 1919).

Redmond, William, *Trench pictures from France* (London, 1917).

Reich, Hermann (ed.), *Das Buch Michael mit Kriegsaufsätzen, Tagebuchblättern, Gedichten, Zeichnungen aus Deutschlands Schulen*, ed. in co-operation with the Zentralinstitut für Erziehung und Unterricht (Berlin, 1916).

Relation officielle de la réception du président Wilson, 16 Décembre 1918 (Paris, 1919).

Renan, Ernest, *Qu'est-ce qu'une nation?* (Paris, 1992).

Rittershaus, E., 'Zur Frage der Kriegshysterie', *Zeitschrift für die gesamte Neurologie und Psychiatrie*, 50 (1919), pp. 87–97.

Romains, Jules, *Verdun* (Paris, 1956).

Rosenzweig, Franz, *L'étoile de la rédemption* (Paris, 1982).

Royal Academy of Arts, *Canadian War Memorials Exhibition* (London, 1919).

Rühlmann, P., 'Delbrücks "Mittwochabend" ', in E. Daniels and P. Rühlmann (eds.), *Am Webstuhl der Zeit. Eine Erinnerungsgabe an Hans Delbrück* (Berlin, 1928), pp. 75–81.

Russell, Bertrand, *The autobiography of Bertrand Russell* (3 vols., London, 1967–9).

Salmon, T. W., 'The care and treatment of mental diseases and war neuroses in the British army', *Mental Hygiene*, 1 (1917), pp. 509–47.

Sandys, John (ed.), *The British Museum. A selection from numerous signed letters, and from leading articles, and resolutions of learned societies . . . protesting against the proposal for taking over the British Museum as offices for the Air-Board and for other purposes of war* (Cambridge, rev. edn 1919).

Sarraut, Albert, *L'instruction publique et la guerre* (Paris, 1916).

Sassoon, Siegfried, *The complete memoirs of George Sherston* (London, 1937).

Schian, Martin, 'Krieg und Persönlichkeit', *Akademische Rundschau* 3, no. 1/4 (October 1914/January 1915), pp. 59–60.

Die Evangelischen Kirchengemeinden (Leipzig, 1918).

Schobel, H., 'Unterrichtswesen im Jahre 1912/13', in M. Neefe (ed.), *Statistisches Jahrbuch*, vol. XXI, (Breslau, 1916).

Schwarz, C., *Predigten aus der Gegenwart* (Leipzig, 1869–73).

Serrié-Heim, Marthe, *Petit Bé et le vilain Boche* (Paris, 1915).

Sheffield, G. D. and Inglis, G. I. S. (eds.), *From Vimy Ridge to the Rhine: Great War letters of Christopher Stone* (Marlborough, Wilts., 1989).

Sheridan-Jones, C., *London in wartime* (London, 1917).

Simmel, Georg, 'Die Großstädte und das Geistesleben', *Jahrbuch der Gehe-Stiftung zu Dresden* 9 (1903), pp. 188–95.

Sims, G. (ed.) *Edwardian London* (London, 1990, 2 vols.).

Speer, Albert, *Au cœur du Troisième Reich* (Paris, 1969).

Spire, André, *Les Juifs et la guerre* (Paris, 1917).

Statistique générale de la France. Annuaire statistique, année 1913, vol. XXXIII (Paris, 1914).

Stern, William (ed.), *Jugendliches Seelenleben und Krieg. Materialien und Berichte*, Beihefte zur Zeitschrift für angewandte Psychologie und psychologische Sammelforschung, 12 (Leipzig, 1915).

Stevenson, William Yorke, *At the front in a flivver* (Boston and New York, 1917).

Stone, Christopher, 'A Decca romance', *The Gramophone*, vol. I, no. 2, (August 1923), p. 56.

Stosch-Sarrasani, Hans, *Durch die Welt im Zirkuszelt* (Berlin, 1940).

Street, George Slythe, 'The war and theatre', *At home in the war* (London, 1918).

Tawney, R. H., *The attack and other papers* (London, 1953).

Temple, William, *The call of the kingdom* (London, National Mission Pamphlet A, 1916).

The Church's mission to the nation (London, National Mission Pamphlet T, 1916).

Temple, William, *The fellowship of the Holy Spirit* (London, National Mission Pamphlet G, 1916).

Thamin, R., 'L'Université de France et la guerre', *Revue des deux mondes*, (15 July and 1 August 1916), pp. 580–620.

The pavilion of H.M. Government. A brief record of official participation in the British Empire Exhibition, Wembley, 1924 (London, [1924]).

Tiplady, T., *The Cross at the front* (London, 1917).

Tisserant, Pierre, *Lettres, 1914–1918* (Paris, 1922).

Treuwerth, K., *Der Invalidenfriedhof in Berlin, Eine Stätte preußisch-deutschen Ruhmes* (Berlin, 1925).

Turner, Lieut.-Col. W., 'Remarks', *Recalled to Life*, 2 (September 1917), pp. 251–3.

Turner, W. A., 'Nerves and mental shock', *British Medical Journal*, 10 June 1916, p. 830.

Type de la rue (Paris, 1920).

Vaillant-Couturier, Paul, *Une permission de detente* (Paris, 1919).

Wallas, Graham, *Human nature in politics* (London, 1908).

The Great Society: a psychological analysis (New York, 1914).

Weber, Alfred, *Ausgewählter Briefwechsel, Alfred Weber-Gesamtausgabe*, vol. 10, ed. E. Demm and H. Soell (Marburg, 2003).

Weber, Max, *Essays in sociology*, ed. by H. Gerth and C. Wright-Mills (London, 1998).

Weiss, René, *La Ville de Paris et les Fêtes de la Victoire* (Paris, 1919).

Hommage de Paris à Gallieni son sauveur (Paris, 1926).

Weygand, Général Maxime, *Le 11 novembre* (Paris, 1932).

Williams, Captain B., 'Pensions', *Recalled to Life*, 1 (June 1917), p. 127.

Willstätter, R., *Aus meinem Leben. Von Arbeit, Muße und Freunden* (Weinheim, 1949).

Wilmanns, Karl, 'Die Behandlung der Kranken mit funktionellen Neurosen im Bereiche des XIV A. K.', *Deutsche medizinische Wochenschrift* 43 (1917), pp. 427–8.

Die Wiedertüchtigung der an funktionellen Neurosen leidenden Kriegsbeschädigten, *Die Kriegsbeschädigtenfürsorge* 2 (1917), pp. 129–50.

Witkop, Philip (ed.), *Kriegsbriefe deutscher Studenten* (Gotha, 1916).

Kriegsbriefe gefallener Studenten (Munich, 1928).

2.   *Scholarly articles and books*

Abel-Smith, Brian, *The hospitals, 1800–1948; a study in social administration in England and Wales* (London, 1964).

Ackerman, Volker, 'La vision allemande du soldat inconnu: débats politiques, réflexion philosophique et artistique', in Jean-Jacques Becker *et al.* (eds.), *Guerre et cultures, 1914–1918* (Paris, 1994), pp. 385–96.

Alings, Reinhard, *Monument und Nation. Das Bild vom Nationalstaat im Medium Denkmal – zum Verhältnis von Nation und Staat im Deutschen Kaiserreich 1871–1918* (Berlin and New York, 1996).

Allen, Rick, *The moving pageant. A literary sourcebook on London street-life, 1700–1914* (London, 1998).

Anderson, Stanford (ed.), *On streets* (Cambridge, Mass., 1986).

Andrieu, Claire, Le Béguec, Gilles, and Tartakowsky, Danielle, *Associations et Champ Politique* (Paris, 2001).

Appiah, Kwame Anthony and Gates, Henry Louis Jr. (ed.), *Identities* (Chicago, 1995).

Arthur, Max, *When this bloody war is over. Soldiers' songs of the First World War* (London, 2001).

Atkin, J., *A war of individuals. Bloomsbury attitudes to the Great War* (Manchester, 2002).

Audoin-Rouzeau, Stéphane, *14–18, les combattants des tranchées à travers leurs journaux* (Paris, 1986).

Men at war, 1914–1918. National sentiment and trench journalism in France during the First World War, trans. by Helen McPhail (Oxford, 1992).

La guerre des enfants 1914–1918. Essai d'histoire culturelle (Paris, 1993).

'Die mobilisierten Kinder. Die Erziehung zum Krieg an französischen Schulen', in Gerhard Hirschfeld, Gerd Krumeich, and Irina Renz (eds.), *'Keiner fühlt sich hier mehr als Mensch ...' Erlebnis und Wirkung des Ersten Weltkriegs* (Frankfurt am Main, 1996), pp. 180–96.

'Children and the primary schools of France, 1914–1918', in John Horne (ed.), *State, society and mobilization in Europe during the First World War* (Cambridge, 1997), pp. 39–52.

Cinq deuils de guerre (Paris, 2001).

Audoin-Rouzeau, Stéphane and Becker, Annette, *Understanding the Great War* (London, 2002).

Audoin-Rouzeau, Stéphane, Becker, Annette, Ingrao, Christian and Rousso, Henry (eds.), *La violence de guerre 1914–1945* (Paris, 2002).

Auerbach, Jeffrey A., *The Great Exhibition of 1851. A nation on display* (New Haven and London, 1999).

Auvray, Michel, *L'âge des casernes. Histoires et mythes du service militaire* (La Tour d'Aigues, 1998).

Axsom, R. H., *Parade. Cubism as theatre* (New York, 1979).

Azaryahu, Maoz, 'What is to be remembered: the struggle over street names in Berlin, 1921–1930', *Tel Aviver Jahrbuch für deutsche Geschichte*, 17 (1988), pp. 241–58.

Barbey-Say, H., *Le Voyage de France en Allemagne (1871–1914)* (Nancy, 1994).

Barker, Elizabeth, 'The primitive within: the question of race in Epstein's career 1917–1929', in Terry Friedman and Evelyn Silber (eds.), *Jacob Epstein. Sculpture and drawings* (London, 1987).

Barker, Pat, *Regeneration* (London, 1991).

Barry, Gearoid, 'Marc Sangnier's war, 1914–1919: Portrait of a soldier, Catholic, and social activist', in Pierre Purseigle (ed.), *Warfare and belligerence. Perspectives in First World War studies* (Leiden–Boston, 2005), pp. 163–88.

Barth, Boris, *Dolchstoßlegenden und politische Desintegration. Das Trauma der deutschen Niederlage im Ersten Weltkrieg 1914–1933* (Düsseldorf, 2003).

Barthes, Roland, *Mythologies* (Paris, 1957).

Basler, W., 'Zur politischen Rolle der Berliner Universität im ersten imperialistischen Weltkrieg, 1914 bis 1918', *Wissenschaftliche Zeitschrift der Humboldt-Unversität zu Berlin. Gesellschafts- und sprachwissenschaftliche Reihe*, 10 (1961), pp. 181–203.

Baudrillart, Alfred, *Les carnets du Cardinal Baudrillart: 1914–1918*, edited and annotated by Paul Christophe (Paris, 1994).

Baumeister, Martin, ' "L'effet de reel." Zum Verhältnis von Krieg und Film 1914–1918', in Bernhard Chiari, Matthias Rogg, and Wolfgang Schmidt (eds.), *Krieg und Militär im Film des 20. Jahrhunderts* (Munich, 2003).

Kriegstheater: Großstadt, Front und Massenkultur 1914–1918 (Essen, 2005).

Becker, Annette, 'Les monuments aux morts, un legs de la guerre nationale? Monuments de la guerre de Sécession et de la guerre de 1870–71', *Guerres mondiales et conflits contemporains*, 167 (July 1992), pp. 22–40.

'Du 14 juillet 1919 au 11 novembre 1920; mort, où est ta victoire?', *Vingtième siècle, Revue d'Histoire*, no. 49 (January–March 1996), pp. 31–44.

'Les chartistes dans la Grande Guerre', in Y.-M. Bercé (ed.), *Histoire de l'Ecole nationale des chartes depuis 1821* (Thionville, 1997), pp. 200–6.

(ed.), *Journaux de combattants et de civils de la France du Nord* (Paris, 1998).

'Les Croix de bois, sépultures de la Grande Guerre', *Communio*, 20, 2 (March–April 1995).

War and faith. The religious imagination in France, 1914–1930 (Oxford and New York, 1998).

Maurice Halbwachs. Un intellectuel en guerres mondiales, 1914–1945 (Paris, 2003).

Becker, Annette and Audoin-Rouzeau, Stéphane, *14–18, retrouver la guerre* (Paris, 2000).

Becker, Frank, *Bilder von Krieg und Nation. Die Einigungskriege in der bürgerlichen Öffentlichkeit Deutschlands 1864–1913* (Munich, 2001).

Becker, Jean-Jacques, *1914: comment les Français sont entrés dans la guerre*, (Paris, 1977).

Becker, Jean-Jacques, and Audoin-Rouzeau, Stéphane (eds.), *Encyclopédie de la Grande Guerre* (Paris, 2004).

Beil, Christine, *Der ausgestellte Krieg. Die Präsentationen des Ersten Weltkrieges, 1914–1939* (Tübingen, 2004).

Bemmann, Helga, *Otto Reutter* (Frankfurt, 1996).

Ben Amos, Avner, 'The Marseillaise as myth and metaphor: the transfer of Rouget de Lisle to the Invalides during the Great War', in Valerie Holman and Debra Kelly (eds.), *France at war in the twentieth century: propaganda, myth and metaphor* (New York, 2000), pp. 27–48.

Benbassa, E., *Histoire des juifs en France* (Paris, 2000).

Bender, Tom (ed.), *The university and the city* (Oxford, 1988).

Bendick, Rainer, *Kriegserwartung und Kriegserfahrung. Der Erste Weltkrieg in deutschen und französischen Schulgeschichtsbüchern (1900–1939/45)* (Pfaffenweiler, 1999).

Benoist, Jacques, *Le Sacré-Cœur de Montmartre. Spiritualité, art et politique (1870–1923)* (Paris, 1992).

Benveniste, A., *Le Bosphore à la Roquette. La communauté judéo-espagnole à Paris 1914–1940* (Paris, 1989).

Bercé, Y.-M. (ed.), *Histoire de l'Ecole nationale des chartes depuis 1821* (Thionville, 1997).

Berg, Christa (ed.), *Handbuch der deutschen Bildungsgeschichte*, vol. IV, *1870–1918. Von der Reichsgründung bis zum Ende des Ersten Weltkriegs* (Munich, 1991).

Berger, Ursel, 'Immer war die Plastik die Kunst nach dem Kriege', in Rainer Rother (ed.), *Die letzten Tage der Menschheit. Bilder des Ersten Weltkrieges*, Deutsches Historisches Museum (Berlin, 1994), pp. 423–34.

Berghoff, Hartmut, Korte, Barbara, Schneider, Ralf and Harvie, Christopher (eds.), *The making of modern tourism. The cultural history of the British experience, 1600–2000* (Basingstoke and New York, 2002).

Berstein, Serge (ed.), *Les cultures politiques en France* (La Seuil, Paris, 1999).

Berz, Peter, 'WELTKRIEG/SYSTEM. Die "Kriegssammlung 1914" der Staatsbibliothek zu Berlin und ihre Katalogik', *Krieg und Literatur*, 5, 10 (1993), pp. 105–30.

Besier, G., *Die protestantische Kirche im Ersten Weltkrieg* (Göttingen, 1984).

Biagini, Eugenio F., *Liberty, retrenchment and reform: popular liberalism in the age of Gladstone, 1860–1880* (Cambridge, 1992).

Bialas, Wolfgang and Iggers, Georg (eds.), *Weimarer Intellektuelle: Neue Interpretationen* (Frankfurt, 1996).

Billett, H., 'Engineering', in F. M. L. Thompson (ed.), *The University of London and the world of learning, 1836–1986* (London, 1990).

Birley, D., 'Sportsmen and the deadly game', *British Journal of Sports History*, December 1986, pp. 288–310.

Bland, Lucy, 'In the name of protection: the policing of women in the First World War', in Julia Brophy and Carol Smart (eds.), *Women-in-law. Explorations in law, family and sexuality* (London, 1985), pp. 23–49.

Blasius, Dirk, *Umgang mit Unheilbarem: Studien zur Sozialgeschichte der Psychiatrie* (Bonn, 1986).

Bonzon, Thierry, 'Les assemblées locales parisiennes et leur politique sociale pendant la Grande Guerre (1912–1919)', doctoral thesis in History, Paris I, 1999.

Boque, D. Van, *L'autobus parisien, 1905–1991* (Paris, 1991).

Borg, Daniel, *The Old Prussian Church and the Weimar Republic* (Hanover, New Hampshire, 1984).

Bourdieu, Pierre, *Distinction. A social critique of the judgment of taste* (Cambridge, Mass. and London, 1984).

Bourdieu, Pierre, *The field of cultural production. Essays on art and literature* (New York, 1994).

Bourel, D., 'Les mandarins contre la démocratie', in L. Richard (ed.), *Berlin, 1919–1933. Gigantisme, crise sociale et avant-garde: l'incarnation extrême de la modernité* (Paris, 1991), pp. 142–53.

Bourgin, H., *De Jaurès à Léon Blum. L'Ecole normale et la politique* (Paris, 1938).

Bourke, Joanna, *Dismembering the male. Men's bodies, Britain and the Great War* (London, 1996).

Bourne, John, Liddle, Peter, and Whitehead, Ian (eds.), *The Great World War 1914–1945* (London, 2001).

Boyer, M. Christine, *The city of collective memory: its historical imagery and architectural entertainments* (Cambridge, Mass., 1994).

Boym, Svetlana, *The future of nostalgia* (New York, 2001).

Bozon, Michel, *Les conscrits* (Paris, 1981).

Brakelmann, Günter, *Der Deutsche Protestantismus im Epochenjahr 1917* (Witten, 1974).

Bramsted, E. K., 'The position of the Protestant Church in Germany 1871–1933', *Journal of Religious History*, 3, 1 (June, 1964), pp. 50–66.

Brandt, Susanne, 'Voyage aux champs de bataille', in Becker, Jean-Jacques *et al.* (eds.), *Guerre et cultures* (Paris, 1994), pp. 221–34.

Brandt, Susanne, 'The memory makers. Museums and exhibitions of the First World War', *History and Memory*, 6, 1 (1994), pp. 103–16.

'Kriegssammlungen im Ersten Weltkrieg. Denkmäler oder Laboratoires d'histoire?', in Gerhard Hirschfeld, Gerd Krumeich, and Irina Renz (eds.), *'Keiner fühlt sich hier mehr als Mensch ...' Erlebnis und Wirkung des Ersten Weltkriegs* (Frankfurt am Main, 1996), pp. 280–92.

Brandt, Susanne, *Vom Kriegsschauplatz zum Gedächtnisraum. Die Westfront 1914–1940* (Baden-Baden, 2000).

Braybon, Gail (ed.), *Evidence, history and the Great War. Historians and the impact of 1914–18* (New York and Oxford, 2003).

Brazelton, T. Berry and Cramer, Bertrand, *Les premiers liens: l'attachement parents-bébé vu par un pédiatre et par un psychiatre*; translated from American by Isabella Morel (Paris, 1991).

Brocke, B. vom, 'Der deutsch-amerikanische Professorenaustauch: preußische Wissenschaftspolitik, internationale Wissenschaftsbeziehungen und die Anfänge einer deutschen Auswärtigen Kulturpolitik vor dem ersten Weltkrieg', *Zeitschrift für Kulturaustausch*, 31 (1981), pp. 128–82.

'Wissenschaft und Militarismus: "Der Aufruf der 93 an die Kulturwelt!" und der Zusammenbruch der internationalen Gelehrtenrepublik im ersten Weltkrieg', in W. M. Calder, H. Flashar, and T. Linken (eds.), *Willamowitz nach 50 Jahren* (Darmstadt, 1985), pp. 649–719.

'Die Kaiser-Wilhelm- Gesellschaft im Kaiserreich. Vorgeschichte, Gründung und Entwicklung bis zum Ausbruch des Ersten Weltkriegs', in B. vom Brocke and R. Vierhaus (eds.), *Forschung im Spannungsfeld von Politik und Gesellschaft. Geschichte und Struktur der Kaiser-Wilhelm-/Max-Planck-Gesellschaft* (Stuttgart, 1990), pp. 17–162.

(ed.), *Wissenschaftsgeschichte und Wissenschaftspolitik im Industriezeitalter. Das 'System Althoff' in historischer Perspektive* (Hildesheim, 1991).

Brocke, B. vom and Vierhaus, R. (eds.), *Forschung im Spannungsfeld von Politik und Gesellschaft. Geschichte und Struktur der Kaiser-Wilhelm-/Max-Planck-Gesellschaft* (Stuttgart, 1990).

Brophy, Julia and Smart, Carol (eds.), *Women-in-Law. Explorations in law, family and sexuality* (London, 1985).

Brown, K. D., *A social history of the nonconformist ministry in England and Wales* (Oxford, 1988).

Bruch, Rüdiger von, *Wissenschaft, Politik und öffentliche Meinung. Gelehrtenpolitik im Wilhelminischen Deutschland (1890–1914)*, Historische Studien, 435 (Husum, 1980).

Weltpolitik als Kulturmission. Auswärtige Kulturpolitik und Bildungsbürgertum in Deutschland am Vorabend des Ersten Weltkrieges (Paderborn, 1982).

Brunner, Otto, Conze, Werner, and Koselleck, Reinhard (eds.), *Geschichtliche Grundbegriffe*, vol. IV (Stuttgart, 1978).

Bucher, Peter, 'Die Errichtung des Reichsehrenmals nach dem ersten Weltkrieg', in *Jahrbuch fur westdeutsche Landesgeschichte* 7, 1981, pp. 359–86.

Burchardt, Lothar, 'Die Kaiser-Wilhelm-Gesellschaft im Ersten Weltkrieg (1914–1918)', in R. Vierhaus and B. vom Brocke (eds.), *Forschung im Spannungsfeld von Politik und Gesellschaft* (Berlin, 1990), pp. 163–96.

Buschmann, Nikolaus and Carl, Horst (eds.), *Die Erfahrung des Krieges. Erfahrungsgeschichtliche Perspektiven von der Französischen Revolution bis zum Zweiten Weltkrieg* (Paderborn, 2001).

Bush, Julia, *Behind the lines: East London Labour, 1914–1919* (London 1984).

Butler, C. V., *Domestic service: an inquiry by the Women's Industrial Council* (London, 1916).

Butler, Judith, *Excitable speech: a politics of the performative* (London, 1997).

'Giving an account of oneself', *Diacritics*, vol. 31, no. 4. (Winter, 2001), pp. 22–40.

Butler, Judith, Stanley Aronowitz, Ernesto Laclau, Joan Scott, Chantal Mouffe, and Cornel West, 'The identity in question', *October*, vol. 61 (Summer, 1992), pp. 108–20.

Cabanes, Bruno, *La victoire endeuillée: la sortie de guerre des soldats français, 1918–1920* (Paris, 2004).

Cahan, D., *An institute for empire: the Physikalisch-Technische Reichsanstalt* (Cambridge, 1988).

Calder, W. M., Flashar, H., and Linken, T. (eds.), *Willamowitz nach 50 Jahren* (Darmstadt, 1985).

Campos, Edmund Valentine, 'Jews, Spaniards, and Portingales: ambiguous identities of Portuguese Marranos in Elizabethan England', *ELH*, vol. 69, no. 3 (Autumn, 2002), pp. 599–616.

Carleton, John D., *Westminster School. A history* (London, 1965).

Cash, John Daniel, *Identity, ideology and conflict: the structuration of politics in Northern Ireland* (New York, 1996).

Cecil, Hugh and Liddle, Peter (eds.), *Facing Armageddon. The First World War experienced* (London, 1996).

CEHD, *La ville et la guerre* (Paris, 1999).

Certeau, Michel de, *The practice of everyday life*, trans. by Steven F. Rendall (Berkeley, 1984).

Chadwick, Owen, *The secularization of the European mind in the nineteenth century* (Cambridge, 1975).

Chaline, Olivier, 'Les normaliens dans la Grande Guerre', *Guerres mondiales et conflits contemporains*, 183 (1996), pp. 99–110.

Chapman, Michael, 'The problem of identity: South Africa, storytelling, and literary history', *New Literary History*, vol. 29, no. 1 (Winter, 1998), pp. 85–99.

Charle, Christophe and Roche, Daniel (eds.), *Capitales culturelles, capitales symboliques: Paris et les expériences européennes, XVIIIe–XXe siècles* (Paris, 2002).

Charle, Christophe, *La naissance des intellectuels, 1880–1900* (Paris, 1990).

'Academics or intellectuals? The Professors of the University of Paris and political debate in France from the Dreyfus Affair to the Algerian War', in

J. Jennings (ed.), *Intellectuals in twentieth-century France. Mandarins and Samurais* (London, 1993), pp. 80–99.

La République des universitaires, 1870–1940 (Paris, 1994).

Paris fin de siècle. Culture et politique (Paris, 1998).

Chartier, Roger, *Cultural history: between practices and representations*, trans. by Lydia G. Cochrane (Ithaca, New York, 1988).

At the edge of the cliff, trans. Lydia G. Cochane (Baltimore, 1997).

Chassaigne, Philippe and Largeaud, Jean-Marc (eds.), *Villes en guerre* (Paris, 2004).

Chazelle, Amélie, *Paris vu par les peintres* (Paris, 1987).

Chiari, Bernhard, Rogg, Matthias, and Schmidt, Wolfgang (eds.), *Krieg und Militär im Film des 20. Jahrhunderts* (Munich, 2003).

Chotard-Lioret, Caroline, *La solidarité familiale en province: une correspondance privée entre 1870 et 1920*, thèse du 3ème cycle, Université de Paris V, 1983.

Clarke, D., *The Angel of Mons* (London, 2004).

Clogg, R., *Politics and the Academy. Arnold Toynbee and the Koreas Chair* (London, 1986).

Cohen, Deborah, *The war come home. Disabled veterans in Britain and Germany, 1914–1939* (Berkeley, Los Angeles, and London, 2001).

Collini, S., Young, B., and Whatmore, S., *British Intellectual History, 1750–1950. Economy, Polity, and Society* (Cambridge, 2000).

Collini, Stefan, *Liberalism and sociology: L. T. Hobhouse and political argument in England, 1880–1914* (Cambridge, 1978).

Collins, L. J., *Theatre at war, 1914–1918* (Basingstoke, 1998).

Collins, Tony, 'English Rugby Union and the First World War', *Historical Journal*, 45 (2002), pp. 797–817.

Condemi, Concetta, *Les cafés-concerts. Histoire d'un divertissement 1849–1914* (Paris 1992).

Condette, J.-F., 'L'Université de Lille dans la première guerre mondiale, 1914–1918', *Guerres mondiales et conflits contemporains*, 197 (2000), pp. 83–102.

Confino, Alon, *The nation as a local metaphor. Württemberg, Imperial Germany, and national memory, 1871–1918* (Chapel Hill and London, 1997).

Connelly, Mark, *The Great War, memory and ritual. Commemoration in the City and East London, 1916–1939* (Woodbridge and London, 2002).

Cooter, Roger, 'Medicine and the Goodness of War', *Canadian Bulletin of Medical History* 7 (1990): 147–59.

Surgery and society in peace and war: orthopaedics and the origin of modern medicine, 1880–1940 (London, 1993).

'War and Modern Medicine', in *Companion Encyclopedia of the History of Medicine*, ed. W. F. Bynum and Roy Porter (New York: Routledge, 1993), pp. 1,536–73.

Cooter, Roger, Harrison, Mark and Sturdy, Steve (eds.), *Medicine and modern warfare* (Amsterdam, 1999).

War, medicine and modernity (Stroud, c1998).

Copelman, Dina M., *London's women teachers. Gender, class and feminism 1870–1930* (London and New York, 1996).

Corbett, David Peters (ed.), *Wyndham Lewis and the art of modern war* (Cambridge, 1998).

Corbin, Alain, *Les filles de noce* (Paris, 1982).

Cork, Richard, *Jacob Epstein* (London, 1999).

Cox, J., *The English churches in a secular society: Lambeth 1870–1930* (Oxford, 1982).

Crawford, E., *The beginning of the Nobel Institution. The science prizes 1901–1915* (Cambridge, 1984).

Cronier, Emmanuelle, 'Permissions et permissionnaires du front pendant la Première Guerre mondiale', in Jean-Jacques Becker and Stéphane Audoin-Rouzeau (eds.), *Encyclopédie critique de la Grande Guerre* (Paris, 2004).

'Leave and schizophrenia: *Permissionnaires* in Paris during the First World War', in J. Macleod and P. Purseigle (eds.), *Uncovered fields: perspectives in First World War studies* (Leiden and Boston, 2004), pp. 143–58.

Les permissionnaires du front à Paris, 1915–1918, doctoral thesis, University of Paris I, 2005.

Culler, Jonathan D., 'Philosophy and literature: the fortunes of the performative', *Poetics Today*, vol. 21, no. 3 (Autumn, 2000), pp. 503–19.

Cyrulnik, Boris, *Le murmure des fantômes* (Paris, 2003).

Dahlmann, Dittmar (ed.), *Kinder und Jugendliche in Krieg und Revolution. Vom Dreißigjährigen Krieg bis zu den Kindersoldaten Afrikas* (Paderborn, 2000).

Dahm, K. W., *Pfarrer und Politik* (Cologne, 1965).

Dahrendorf, Ralf, *LSE. A history of the London School of Economics, 1895–1995* (Oxford, 1995).

Daniel, Ute, 'Women's work in industry and family. Germany, 1914–1918', in Richard Wall and Jay Winter (eds.), *The upheaval of war. Family, work and welfare in Europe 1914–1918* (Cambridge, 1988), pp. 250–67.

Arbeiterfrauen in der Kriegsgesellschaft. Beruf, Familie und Politik im Ersten Weltkrieg (Göttingen, 1989).

'Der Krieg der Frauen, 1914–1918. Zur Innenansicht des Ersten Weltkriegs in Deutschland', in *Keiner fühlt sich hier mehr als Mensch: Erlebnis und Wirkung des Ersten Weltkriegs*, ed. Gerhard Hirschfeld and Gerd Krumeich in connection with Irina Renz (Essen, 1993), pp. 131–49.

Daniel, Ute, *The war from within, German working-Class women in the First World War* (Oxford, 1997).

Daniel, Yvan, *L'équipement paroissial d'une diocèse urbain. Paris (1802–1956)* (Paris, 1957).

Darmon, Pierre, *Vivre à Paris pendant la Grande Guerre* (Paris, 2002).

Darrow, Margaret H., *French women and the First World War: war stories of the home front* (Oxford/New York, 2001).

Daunton, Martin and Rieger, Bernhard (eds.), *Meanings of modernity. Britain from the late-Victorian era to World War II* (Oxford and New York, 2001).

Dauphin, Cécile, Pézerat, Pierrette, and Poublan, Danièle, *Ces bonnes lettres. Une correspondance familiale au XIXe siècle* (Paris, 1995).

Daviet, M.-B., 'De l'honneur de la corporation à l'honneur de la patrie. Les étudiants de Göttingen dans l'Allemagne de la Première Guerre mondiale', *Le mouvement social*, 194 (2001), pp. 39–65.

Davin, Anna, *Growing up poor. Home, school and street in London 1870–1914* (London, 1996).

Davis, Belinda, *Home fires burning: food, politics and everyday life in World War I Berlin* (Chapel Hill, 2000).

Davis, Natalie Zemon, *The return of Martin Guerre* (Cambridge, Mass., 1983).

De Groot, G. J., *Blighty: British society in the era of the Great War* (London, 1996).

Dehay, Valerie, 'L'école primaire en France pendant la guerre de 1914–1918', doctoral thesis, University of Picardie, 2000.

Deist, Wilhelm (ed.), *Militär und Innenpolitik im Weltrieg 1914–1918*. (Düsseldorf, 1970).

Militär, Staat und Gessellschaft: Studien zur preussisch-deutschen Militärgeschichte (Munich, 1991).

Dejean, Alain, 'Les lyceés parisiens pendant la Prèmiere Guerre mondiale', master's thesis, University of Paris X–Nanterre, 1993.

Delacy, Margaret, *Prison reform in Lancashire, 1700–1850: a study in local administration* (Stanford, 1986).

Demm, Eberhard, 'Autobiographie und Rollenzwang. Autobiographische Zeugnisse deutscher Universitätsprofessoren aus dem ersten Drittel des 20. Jahrhunderts', in *Annali di sociologia/Soziologisches Jahrbuch*, 3, 1987, pp. 299–323.

Demm, Eberhard, *Der Erste Weltkrieg in der internationalen Karikatur* (Hanover, 1988).

Demm, Eberhard, *Ein Liberaler in Kaiserreich und Republik. Der politische Weg Alfred Webers bis 1920, Schriften des Bundesarchivs*, 38 (Boppard on the Rhine, 1990).

Demm, Eberhard, 'Anschluss, Autonomie oder Unabhängigkeit? Die deutsche Litauenpolitik im Ersten Weltkrieg und das Selbstbestimmungsrecht der Völker', *Journal of Baltic Studies*, 25 (1994), pp. 185–200.

Demm, Eberhard, 'Barbusse et son feu: la dernière cartouche de la propagande de guerre française', in *Guerres mondiales et conflits contemporains* 197, (2000), pp. 43–63.

Demm, Eberhard, *Ostpolitik und Propaganda im Ersten Weltkrieg* (Frankfurt am Main, 2002).

Demm, Eberhard, 'Zwischen Propaganda und Sozialsfürsorge – Deutschlands Kinder im Krieg', in Eberhard Demm, *Ostpolitik und Propaganda im Ersten Weltkrieg* (Frankfurt am Main, 2002).

Demm, Eberhard, 'La chanson française pendant la Grande Guerre', in François Genton (ed.), 'La guerre en chanson', *Chroniques allemandes*, 11 (2004).

Demm, Eberhard, 'Die wilhelminische Zeit', in K.-P. Haase (ed.), *Berlin-Istanbul. Katalog der Ausstellung* (Berlin, 2005).

Demm, Eberhard, ' "Maikäfer flieg', dein Vater ist im Krieg". Wie Berliner Familien den Ersten Weltkrieg erlebten', *Berliner Zeitung*, no. 12, 15./16 January 2005, Magazine, pp. 1–2.

Demps, Laurenz, *Zwischen Mars und Minerva, Wegweiser Invalidenfriedhof* (Berlin, 1998).

Dibbets, Karel and Hogenkamp, Bert (eds.), *Film and the First World War* (Amsterdam, 1995).

Digeon, Claude, *La crise allemande de la pensée française (1870–1914)* (Paris, 1959).

Dohrn-van Rossum, Gerhard, *L'Histoire de l'heure. L'horologie et l'organisation moderne du temps* (Paris, 1997).

Donson, Andrew, 'War pedagogy and youth culture. Nationalism and authority in Germany in the First World War', doctoral thesis, University of Michigan, 2000.

Dorgeles, Roland, *Bleu Horizon. Pages de la Grand Guerre* (Paris, 1949).

Dornel, L., *La France hostile. Sociohistoire de la xénophobie 1870–1914* (Paris, 2004).

Dumenil, Anne, Beaupré, Nicolas, and Ingrao, Christian (eds.), *1914–1945, L'ère de la guerre, violence, mobilisation, deuil* (Paris, 2004, 2 vols.).

Eksteins, Modris, *Rites of spring. The Great War and the birth of the modern age* (New York, 1989).

'The cultural impact of the Great War', in Karel Dibbets and Bert Hogenkamp (eds.), *Film and the First World War* (Amsterdam, 1995), pp. 201–12.

Erikson, Erik H., *Young man Luther; a study in psychoanalysis and history.* (New York, 1962).

Identity and the life cycle (New York, 1980).

Esoavelomandroso, Manassé, 'Identity and history', *Ethnohistory*, vol. 48, nos. 1–2, Emerging Histories in Madagascar (Winter–Spring, 2001), pp. 319–22.

Evans, Richard J., *The feminist movement in Germany, 1894–1933* (Beverly Hills, 1976).

Facon, Patrick, 'Les villes, objectifs du bombardement stratégique', in CEHD, *La ville et la guerre* (Paris, 1999), pp. 207–17.

Faron, Olivier, *Les enfants du deuil. Orphelins et pupilles de la nation de la première guerre mondiale (1914–1941)* (Paris, 2001).

Farred, Grant, 'Endgame identity? Mapping the New Left roots of identity politics', *New Literary History*, vol. 31, no. 4, Is there life after identity politics? (Autumn, 2000), pp. 627–48.

Feeley, Francis, 'French school teachers against militarism, 1903–18', *Historian*, 57 (1995), pp. 315–28.

Feldman, David, *Englishmen and Jews. Social relations and political culture 1840–1914* (New Haven and London, 1994).

Feldman, David and Stedman Jones, Gareth, *Metropolis: London, histories and representations since 1800* (London, 1989).

Feldman, Gerald D., 'A German scientist between illusion and reality: Emil Fischer, 1909–1919', in I. Geiss and B. J. Wendt (eds.), *Deutschland in der Weltpolitik des 19. und 20. Jahrhunderts* (Düsseldorf, 1973), pp. 341–62.

Ferguson, Niall, *The pity of war* (London, 1998).

Flonneau, Mathieu, *L'automobile à la conquête de Paris, 1910–1977. Formes urbaines, champs politiques et représentations*, doctoral thesis de IIIème cycle, University of Paris I, 2002.

Forcade, Olivier, *La censure politique en France pendant la Grande Guerre*, thesis, University of Paris X, 1999.

'Censure, opinion et secret en France', *Matériaux pour l'histoire de notre temps*, no. 58 (April–June 2000), pp. 45–53.

Foucault, Michel, *The birth of the clinic. An archaeology of medical perception*, trans. by A. M. Sheridan Smith (New York, 1973).

Fout, John C., 'Sexual politics in Wilhelmine Germany: the male gender crisis, moral purity, and homophobia', *Journal of the History of Sexuality*, 2 (1992), pp. 388–421.

Fraenkel, Ernst, 'Öffentliche Meinung in Deutschland', in *Deutschland und die westlichen Demokratien* (Frankfurt am Main, 1991), pp. 232–50.

Freedland, Jonathan, 'A loyalty divided', *The Guardian G2*, 15 February 2005, pp. 6–7.

Friedman, Terry and Silber, Evelyn (eds.), *Jacob Epstein. Sculpture and drawings* (London, 1987).

Fritzsche, Peter, *A nation of fliers. German aviation and the popular imagination* (Cambridge, Mass., 1992).

Germans into Nazis (Cambridge, Mass. and London, 1998).

Fuchs, E., 'Wissenschaftsinternationalismus in Kriegs- und Krisenzeiten. Zur Rolle der USA bei der Reorganisation der internationalen *scientific community, 1914–1945*', in Ralph Jessen and Jakob Vogel (eds.), *Wissenschaft und Nation in der europäischen Geschichte* (Frankfurt am Main, 2002), pp. 263–84.

Fuller, J. G., *Troop morale and popular culture in the British and Dominion armies, 1914–1918* (Oxford, 1990).

Gardiner, Stephen, *Epstein. Artist against the establishment* (London, 1992).

Gaussen, Frédéric, *Paris des peintres* (Paris, 2002).

Gee, Malcolm, 'The avant-garde, order and the art market, 1916–23', *Art History*, 2 (1979), pp. 96–100.

Geppert, Alexander C. T., 'True copies. Time and space travels at British imperial exhibitions, 1880–1930', in Hartmut Berghoff, Barbara Korte, Ralf Schneider, and Christopher Harvie (eds.), *The making of modern tourism. The cultural history of the British experience, 1600–2000* (Basingstoke and New York, 2002).

'Welttheater. Die Geschichte des europäischen Ausstellungswesens im 19. und 20. Jahrhundert', *Neue Politische Literatur*, 47 (2002), pp. 10–61.

Gibson, Ralph, *A social history of French Catholicism* (Cambridge, 1975).

Gilbert, A. D., *Church, Chapel and social change 1740–1914* (London, 1976).

Gilbert, David, '*London of the Future*. The metropolis reimagined after the Great War', *Journal of British Studies*, 43 (2004), pp. 91–119.

Glasgow, G., *Ronald Burrows. A memoir* (London, 1924).

Glück, Carol, *Past obsessions: war and memory in the twentieth century* (New York, 2006).

Goebel, Stefan, ' "Kohle und Schwert". Zur Konstruktion der Heimatfront in Kriegswahrzeichen des Ruhrgebietes im Ersten Weltkrieg', *Westfälische Forschungen*, 51 (2001), pp. 257–81.

'Medievalism in the commemoration of the Great War in Britain and Germany, 1914–1939', doctoral thesis, University of Cambridge, 2002.

'Forging the industrial home front: iron-nail memorials in the Ruhr', in Jenny Macleod and Pierre Purseigle (eds.), *Uncovered fields. Perspectives in First World War studies* (Leiden and Boston, 2004), pp. 159–78.

'Re-membered and re-mobilized: the "Sleeping Dead" in interwar Germany and Britain', *Journal of Contemporary History*, vol. 39 (2004), pp. 487–501.

The Great War and medieval memory. War, remembrance and medievalism in Britain and Germany, 1914–1940 (Cambridge, 2006).

Goldstein, Eric, 'The Round Table and the new Europe', *The Round Table*, 346 (1998), pp. 177–90.

Good, C. Kit, 'England goes to war 1914–15', PhD thesis, University of Liverpool, 2002.

Gosewinkel, Dieter, *Einbürgern und Ausschließen. Die Nationalisierung der Staatsangehörigkeit vom Deutschen Bund bis zur Bundesrepublik Deutschland* (Göttingen, 2001).

Gourdon, Vincent, *Histoire des grandparents* (Paris, 2001).

Grayzel, Susan R., *Women's identities at war: gender, motherhood and politics in Britain and France during the First World War* (Chapel Hill, 1999).

Green, S. J. D. and Whiting, R. C. (eds.), *The boundaries of the state in modern Britain* (Cambridge, 1996).

Greenblatt, Stephen, *Renaissance self-fashioning: from More to Shakespeare* (Chicago, 1980).

Greenhalgh, Paul, *Ephemeral vistas. The Expositions Universelles, Great Exhibitions and World's Fairs, 1851–1939* (Manchester, 1988).

Gregory, Adrian, *The silence of memory: Armistice Day 1919–1945* (Oxford and Providence, 1994).

'British "War Enthusiasm" in 1914: a reassessment', in G. Braybon, *Evidence, history and the Great War. Historians and the impact of 1914–18* (Oxford, 2003).

'Military service tribunals. Civil society in action, 1916–1918', in Jose Harris (ed.), *Civil Society in British History* (Oxford, 2003), pp. 177–90.

Grun, Berard, *Kulturgeschichte der Operette* (Berlin, 1967).

Grundmann, S., *Einsteins Akte. Einsteins Jahre in Deutschland aus der Sicht der deutschen Politik* (Berlin, 1998).

Grünefeld, V., *Heimgesucht* (Berlin, 1979).

Gullace, Nicoletta F., 'White feathers and wounded men: female patriotism and the memory of the Great War', *Journal of British Studies* 36, no. 2 (April 1997), pp. 178–206.

'The blood of our sons.' Men, women, and the renegotiation of British citizenship during the Great War (New York and Basingstoke, 2002).

Günther, Ernst, *Sarrasani wie er wirklich war* (Berlin, 1985).

Gutt, Barbara, *Frauen in Berlin, Mit Kopf und Herz und Hand und Fuß* (Berlin, 1991).

Gyáni, Gábor, *Identity and the urban experience: fin-de-siècle Budapest*, trans. Thomas J. DeKornfeld (New York, 2004).

Haber, F. L., *The poisonous cloud: chemical warfare in the First World War* (Oxford, 1986).

Habermas, Jürgen, *The social transformation of the public sphere: an inquiry into a category of bourgeois society* (Cambridge, 1989).

Halbwachs, Maurice, *On collective memory*, edited, translated, and with an introduction by Lewis A. Coser (Chicago, 1992).

Hall, Jacquelyn Dowd, 'Open secrets: memory, imagination, and the refashioning of Southern identity', *American Quarterly*, vol. 50, no. 1. (March, 1998), pp. 109–24.

Hamilton, Cicely and Baylis, Lilian, *The Old Vic* (London, 1926).

Hamilton, J. A. B., *Britain's railways in World War I* (London, 1967).

Hamilton, K. A., 'The pursuit of "Enlightened patriotism": the British Foreign Office during the Great War and its aftermath', *Historical Research*, 61, (1988), pp. 316–44.

Hämmerle, Christa, ' "Wir strickten und nähten Wäsche für Soldaten..." Von der Militarisierung des Handarbeitens im Ersten Weltkrieg', *L'Homme. Zeitschrift für Feministische Geschichtswissenschaft*, 3, 1 (1992), pp. 96–113.

' "Diese Schatten über unserer Kindheit gelegen..." –Historischen Anmerkungen zu einem unerforschten Thema', in Christa Hämmerle (ed.), *Kindheit im Ersten Weltkrieg* (Vienna, Cologne, and Weimar, 1993), pp. 275–94.

(ed.), *Kindheit im Ersten Weltkrieg* (Vienna, Cologne, and Weimar, 1993).

Hanak, Harry, 'The New Europe, 1916–1920', *The Slavonic and East European Review*, 39 (1961), pp. 369–99.

Hanley, Sarah, 'European history in text and film: community and identity in France, 1550–1945', *French Historical Studies*, vol. 25, no. 1 (Winter, 2002), pp. 3–19.

Hanna, M., *The mobilization of intellect. French scholars and writers during the Great War* (Cambridge, Mass., 1996).

Harel, Véronique (ed.), *Les affiches de la Grande Guerre* (Péronne, 1998).

Harries, Meirion and Susie, *The war artists. British official war art of the twentieth century* (London, 1983).

Harris, José, *William Beveridge. A biography* (Oxford, 1997).

(ed.), *Civil society in British history* (Oxford, 2003).

Harrison, Mark, 'Medicine and the management of modern warfare', *History of Science* 34, no. 4 (1996), 379–410.

'The medicalization of war — the militarization of medicine', *Social History of Medicine* (September 1996), 267–76.

Harrison, Royden, *Before the Socialists: studies in labour and politics, 1861–1881* (London, 1965).

Harte, Negley, *The University of London 1836–1986: an illustrated history* (London, 1986).

Harvie, Christopher, *The lights of liberalism: university liberals and the challenge of democracy, 1860–86* (London, 1976).

(ed.), *The making of modern tourism. The cultural history of the British experience, 1600–2000* (Basingstoke and New York, 2002).

Healy, Maureen, 'Exhibiting a war in progress. Entertainment and propaganda in Vienna, 1914–1918', *Austrian History Yearbook*, 31 (2000), pp. 56–85.

Henri, Sellier, Bruggeman, A., and Poëte, Marcel, *Paris pendant la guerre* (Paris, 1926).

Herzer, Manfred, *Magnus Hirschfeld* (Frankfurt, 1992).

Higonnet, Margaret (ed.), *Nurses at the Front: writing the wounds of the Great War* (Boston, 2001).

Higonnet, Margaret, et al. (eds.), *Behind the lines: gender and the two world wars* (New Haven and London, 1987).

Higonnet, Margaret and Higonnet, Patrice L.-R., 'The double helix', in Margaret Higonnet et al. (eds.), *Behind the lines: gender and the two world wars* (New Haven and London, 1987), pp. 31–47.

Higson, Andrew (ed.), *Young and innocent? The cinema in Britain 1896–1930* (Exeter, 2002).

Hiley, Nicholas, 'The British cinema auditorium', in Karel Dibbets and Bert Hogenkamp (eds.), *Film and the First World War* (Amsterdam, 1995), pp. 150–62.

Hirschfeld, Gerhard, Krumeich, Gerd, and Renz, Irina (eds.), *'Keiner fühlt sich hier mehr als Mensch...' Erlebnis und Wirkung des Ersten Weltkriegs* (Frankfurt am Main, 1996).

Hirschfeld, Gerhard, *et al.* (eds.), *Enzyklopädie Erster Weltkrieg* (Paderborn, 2003).

Hirschfeld, Magnus (ed.), *Sittengeschichte des Weltkrieges*, vol. I (Leipzig and Vienna, 1930).

Hoare, Philip, *Wilde's last stand. Decadence, conspiracy and the First World War* (London, 1997).

Hobsbawm, Eric and Ranger, Terence (eds.), *The invention of tradition* (Cambridge, 1980).

Hoffenberg, Peter H., *An empire on display. English, Indian, and Australian exhibitions from the Crystal Palace to the Great War* (Berkeley, Los Angeles, and London, 2001).

Hoffmann, C., 'The Jewish community in Germany 1914–1918', in John Horne (ed.) *State, society and mobilization* (Cambridge, 1999), pp. 80–93.

Hoffmann-Curtius, K., 'Das Kriegerdenkmal der Berliner Friedrich-Wilhelms-Universität, 1919–1926: Siegexegese der Niederlage', in *Jahrbuch für Universitätsgeschichte*, 5 (2002), pp. 87–116.

Holman, Valerie and Kelly, Debra (eds.), *France at war in the twentieth century: propaganda, myth and metaphor* (New York, 2000).

Holmes, Colin, *Anti-Semitism in British society, 1876–1939* (London, 1979).

Hölscher, Lucian, 'Öffentlichkeit', in Otto Brunner, Werner Conze, and Reinhard Koselleck (eds.), *Geschichtliche Grundbegriffe*, vol. IV (Stuttgart, 1978), pp. 413–33.

Homberger, Eric, 'The story of the Cenotaph', *The Times Literary Supplement*, 12 November 1976, pp. 1,429–30.

Hoover, Arlie J., *The Gospel of Nationalism: German patriotic preaching from Napoleon to Versailles* (Stuttgart, 1986).

God, Germany and Britain in the Great War: a study in clerical nationalism (New York, 1989).

Hope, Nicholas, *German and Scandinavian Protestantism* (Oxford, 1995).

Horne, John, *Labour at war: France and Britain, 1914–1918* (Oxford, 1991).

(ed.), *State, society and mobilization in Europe during the First World War* (Cambridge, 1997).

Horne, John and Kramer, Alan, 'German "atrocities" and Franco-German opinion 1914', *Journal of Modern History*, 66 (1994), pp. 1–33.

German atrocities, 1914. A history of denial (New Haven and London, 2001).

Horrall, Andrew, *Popular culture in London c. 1890–1918. The transformation of entertainment* (Manchester, 2001).

Huss, Marie-Monique, *Cartes postales et culture de guerre. Histoire de famille 1914–1918* (Noisy-le-Grand, 1998).

Inglis, K. S., 'A sacred place. The making of the Australian War Memorial', *War & Society*, 3, 2 (1985), pp. 99–126.

Inglis, Ken, 'Entombing unknown soldiers: from London and Paris to Baghdad', *History and Memory*, 5, 2 (Fall/Winter 1993), pp. 7–31.

Ingrao, Christian, 'Etudiants allemands, mémoire de guerre et militantisme nazi: étude de cas', in *14–18 Aujourd'hui-Today-Heute*, 5 (2002), pp. 55–71.

Jacobsen, Wolfgang, Kaes, Anton, and Prinzler, Hans Helmut (eds.), *Geschichte des deutschen Films* (Stuttgart, 1993).

Jagielski, Jean-François, *Le Soldat Inconnu. Invention et postérité d'un symbole* (Paris, 2005).

James, Pearl (ed.), *Picture this! Reading World War I posters* (Lincoln, Neb., 2006).

Japrisot, Sebastian, *Un long dimanche de fiancialles* (Paris, 1992).

Jarausch, Konrad, *Students, society and politics in Imperial Germany* (Princeton, 1982).

Jarausch, K. H. *Deutsche Studenten 1800–1970* (Frankfurt am Main, 1984).

Jelavich, Peter, *Berlin cabaret* (Cambridge, Mass., 1993).

'German culture in the Great War', in Roshwald and Stites (eds.), *European culture in the Great War* (Cambridge, 1999), pp. 36–42.

Jenkins, Roy, *Asquith* (London, 1964).

Jennings, J. (ed.), *Intellectuals in twentieth-century France. Mandarins and samurais* (London, 1993).

Jensen, Robert, *Marketing modernism in fin-de-siècle Europe* (Princeton, 1994).

Jessen, Ralph and Vogel, Jakob (eds.), *Wissenschaft und Nation in der europäische Geschichte* (Frankfurt and New York, 2002).

Joachimides, Alexis, *Die Museumsreformbewegung in Deutschland und die Entstehung des modernen Museums 1880–1940* (Dresden, 2001).

Johnson, Eric A. and Reuband, K-H., *What we knew. Terror, mass murder and everyday life in Nazi Germany: an oral history* (London, 2005).

Johnson, J. A., *The Kaiser's chemists: science and modernization in Imperial Germany* (Chapel Hill, 1990).

'Akademische Grabenkämpfe und industrielle Ressourcennutzung. Chemie im Spannungsfeld von "reiner" und "angewandter" Forschung', in J. Kocka *et al.* (eds.), *Die Königlich Preussische Akademie der Wissenschaften zu Berlin im Kaiserreich* (Berlin, 1999), pp. 355–80.

Joll, James, *1914: the unspoken assumptions; an inaugural lecture 25 April 1968* (London, 1968).

Jones, Barbara and Howell, Bill, *Popular arts of the First World War* (London, 1972).

Julian, Jenkins, *Christian pacifism confronts German nationalism – the Ecumenical Movement and the cause of peace in Germany, 1914–1933* (Lampeter, 2002).

Jüllig, Carola, ' "Ja, Frankreichs Geist, du bist verbannt für ewig…" Die erste Kriegsspielzeit der Berliner Theater', in Rainer Rother (ed.), *Die letzten Tage der Menschheit. Bilder des ersten Weltkrieges* (Berlin, 1994), pp. 137–48.

Kadish, S., *Bolsheviks and British Jews* (London, 1992).

Kansteiner, Wulf, 'Finding meaning in memory: a methodological critique of collective memory studies', *History and Theory*, 41 (2002), pp. 179–97.

Kaplan, Marion A., "Redefining Judaism in Imperial Germany: practices, mentality and community", in *Jewish Social Studies*, 9, 1 (Fall 2002), pp. 1–33.

Kavanagh, Gaynor, 'Museum as memorial. The origins of the Imperial War Museum', *Journal of Contemporary History*, 23 (1988), pp. 77–97.

Museums and the First World War. A social history (London and New York, 1994).

Keegan, John, *The face of battle* (New York, 1976).

Keene, J. D., *Doughboys: the Great War and the remaking of America*, (Baltimore, 2001).

Keller, K. and Schmidt, H. D. (eds.), *Vom Kult zur Kulisse. Das Völkerschlachtdenkmal als Gegenstand der Geschichtskultur* (Leipzig, 1995).

Kenyon, Frederic G., *The British Museum in war time. Being the fourth lecture on the David Murray Foundation in the University of Glasgow delivered on June 11th, 1934* (Glasgow, 1934).

Kern, Stephen, *The culture of time and space 1880–1918* (Cambridge, Mass., and London, 1983).

Kernot, Charles F., *British public schools' war memorials* (London, 1927).

Keylor, W. R., *Academy and community. The foundation of the French historical profession* (Cambridge, Mass., 1975).

Kienitz, Sabine, ' "Fleischgewordenes Elend". Kriegsinvalidität und Körperbilder als Teil einer Erfahrungsgeschichte des Ersten Weltkrieges', in Nikolaus Buschmann and Horst Carl (eds.), *Die Erfahrung des Krieges. Erfahrungsgeschichtliche Perspektiven von der Französischen Revolution bis zum Zweiten Weltkrieg* (Paderborn, 2001), pp. 220–34.

'Quelle place pour les héros mutilés? Les invalides de guerre entre intégration et exclusion', in *14–18. Aujourd'hui, Today, Heute*, no. 4 (2001), 'Marginaux, marginalité, marginalisation', pp. 151–65.

King, Alex, *Memorials of the Great War in Britain. The symbolism and politics of remembrance* (Oxford and New York, 1998).

Kloosterhuis, J., *'Friedliche Imperialisten'. Deutsche Auslandsvereine und auswärtige Kulturpolitik, 1906–1918* (Frankfurt am Main, 1994 [1981]).

Kocka, Jürgen, et al. (eds.), *Die Königlich Preußische Akademie der Wissenschaften zu Berlin im Kaiserreich* (Berlin, 1999).

Konvitz, Joseph W., 'Représentations urbaines et bombardements stratégiques 1914–1945', in *Annales* ESC (July–August 1989), pp. 812–47.

Koselleck, Reinhard and Michael Jeismann, *Der politische Totenkult, Kriegerdenkmäler in der Moderne* (Munich, 1994).

Kriegel, Annie, *La croissance des effectifs de la CGT, 1918–1921: essai statistique* (Paris and The Hague, 1966).

Krill, Karl-Heinz, *Die Ranke Renaissance: Max Lenz und Erich Marcks* (Berlin, 1962).

Krumeich, Gerd, ' "Gott mit uns", la Grande Guerre fut-elle une guerre de religion?', in Dumenil, Anne, Beaupré, Nicolas, and Ingrao, Christian (eds.), *1914–1945, L'ère de la Guerre, violence, mobilisation, deuil* (Paris, 2004, 2 vols.).

Kuhn, Annette, *Cinema, censorship and sexuality, 1909–1925* (London, 1988).

Kundrus, Birthe, *Kriegerfrauen: Familienpolitik und Geschlechterverhältnisse im Ersten und Zweiten Weltkrieg* (Hamburg, 1995).

Kushner, Tony, 'Local heroes. Belgian refugees in Britain during the First World War', *Immigrants and Minorities*, 18, 1 (1999), pp. 1–28.

Kushner, Tony and Lunn, Kenneth (eds.), *The politics of marginality: race, the radical Right and minorities in twentieth-century Britain* (London, 1990).

Lagarrigue, Louis, *Cent ans de transports en commun dans la région parisienne* (Paris, 1956).

Laitko, H., *Wissenschaft in Berlin. Von den Anfängen bis zum Neubeginn nach 1945* (Berlin, 1987).

Lambourne, Nicola, ' "Moral cathedrals". War damage and Franco-German cultural propaganda on the Western Front 1870–1938', doctoral thesis, University of London, 1997.

Lamprecht, Gerhard, *Deutsche Stummfilme 1913–1914* (Berlin, 1969).

Landau, Bernard, Monod, Claire, and Lohr, Evelyne (eds.), *Les grands boulevards: un parcours d'innovation et de modernité* (Paris, 2000).

Lange, Annemaria, *Das wilhelminische Berlin: zwischen Jahrhundertwende und Novemberrevolution* (Berlin, 1967).

Lange, Britta, *Einen Krieg ausstellen. Die 'Deutsche Kriegsausstellung' 1916 in Berlin* (Berlin, 2003).

Lawrence, Jon, *Speaking for the people: party, language and popular politics in England, 1867–1914* (Cambridge, 1998).

'Contesting the male polity: the suffragettes and the politics of disruption in Edwardian Britain', in Amanda Vickery (ed.), *Women, privilege and power: British politics, 1750 to the present* (Stanford, 2001), pp. 201–26.

Le bus dans la ville (Paris, 2000).

Leed, Eric J., *No man's land. Combat and identity in the First World War* (Cambridge, 1979).

Leese, Peter, Shell shock: traumatic neurosis and the British soldiers of the First World War (Houndmills: Palgrave, 2002).

Le Naour, Jean-Yves, *Misères et tourments de la chair durant la Grande Guerre. Les mœurs sexuelles des Français 1914–1918* (Paris, 2002).

Lepick, Olivier, *La Grande Guerre chimique 1914–1918* (Paris, 1998).

Lerner, Paul, *Hysterical men. War, psychiatry, and the politics of trauma in Germany, 1890–1930* (Ithaca, 2003).

Les enfants dans la Grande Guerre, ed. Historial de la Grande Guerre (Péronne, 2003).

Lesmanne, Serge, 'L'école et la guerre (1914–1918)', *Mémoires de la société d'histoire et d'archéologie de Pontoise* (1985–6), pp. 1–7.

Levitch, Mark, 'Young blood. Parisian schoolgirls' transformation of France's Great War poster aesthetic', in Pearl James (ed.), *Picture this! Reading World War I posters* (Lincoln, Neb., 2007).

Lindenberger, Thomas, *Straßenpolitik. Zur Sozialgeschichte der öffentlichen Ordnung in Berlin, 1900 bis 1914* (Bonn, 1995).

Lloyd, David William, *Battlefield tourism. Pilgrimage and the commemoration of the Great War in Britain, Australia and Canada, 1919–1939* (Oxford, 1998).

Loiperdinger, Martin 'Filmzensur und Selbstkontrolle', in Wolfgang Jacobsen, Anton Kaes, and Hans Helmut Prinzler (eds.), *Geschichte des deutschen Films* (Stuttgart, 1993), pp. 479–98.

Loubes, Olivier, *L'école de la patrie. Histoire d'un désenchantement, 1914–1940* (Paris and Berlin, 2001).

Lukes, Steven, *Emile Durkheim. His life and work, a historical study* (Stanford, 1973).

Lurz, Meinhold, *Kriegerdenkmäler in Deutschland*, vol. iv, *Weimarer Republik* (Heidelberg, 1985).

Maase, Kaspar, *Grenzenloses Vergnügen. Der Aufstieg der Massenkultur 1850–1970* (Frankfurt am Main, 1997).

MacIntyre, Alasdair, *Secularization and moral change*. The Riddell Memorial Lectures, 36th series, delivered at the University of Newcastle upon Tyne on 11, 12, and 13 November 1964 (Oxford, 1964).

Macleod, Jenny and Purseigle, Pierre (eds.), *Uncovered fields. Perspectives in First World War studies* (Leiden–Boston, 2004).

MacLeod, Roy, 'The chemists go to war: the mobilisation of civilian chemists and the British war effort, 1914–1918', *Annales of Science*, 50 (1993), pp. 455–81.

Macleod, Roy, 'L'entente chimique: l'échec de l'avenir à la fin de la guerre', 14–18, *Aujourd'hui, Today, Heute*, no. 6 (2003), pp. 135–51.

MacLeod, Roy and Andrews, E. Kay, 'The origins of the DSIR: reflections on ideas and men, 1915–1916', *Public Administration*, 48 (1970), pp. 23–48.

Malvern, Sue, 'War, memory and museums. Art and artefact in the Imperial War Museum', *Historical Workshop Journal*, 49 (2000), pp. 177–203.

Modern art, Britain, and the Great War. Witnessing, testimony and remembrance (New Haven, 2004).

Manela, Erez, *The Wilsonian moment* (New York, 2006).

Mangan, J. A., *Athleticism in the Victorian and Edwardian public school. The emergence and consolidation of an educational ideology* (Cambridge, 1981).

Marchand, Philippe, 'Les petits soldats de demain. Les bataillons scolaires dans le département du Nord, 1882–1892', *Revue du Nord*, 67 (1985), pp. 769–803.

Marchese, S., *La Francia ed il problema dei rapporti con la Santa Sede* (Naples, 1971).

Mares, A., 'Louis Léger et Ernest Denis. Profil de deux bohémisants français au XIXe siècle', in B. Ferencuhova, *La France et l'Europe centrale, special edition of Slovanski studii* (Bratislava, 1995), pp. 63–82.

Marin, Louis, *On representation*, trans. by Catherine Porter (Stanford, 2001).

Marquard, Odo and Stierle, Karlheinz (eds.), *Identität* (Munich, 1996).

Martin du Gard, Maurice, *Les Mémorables* (Paris, 1957).

Martin, M., 'Histoire et actualité. La *Revue historique* pendant la Première Guerre mondiale', *Revue historique*, 255 (1976), pp. 433–68.

Martin-Fugier, Anne, 'Les rites de la vie privée bourgeoise', in Michell Perrot (ed.), *Histoire de la vie privée*, vol. IV: *De la Révolution à la Grande Guerre* (Paris, 1986), pp. 175–241.

Martland, Peter, *Since records began: EMI, the first 100 years* (London, 1997).

Mason, Tony, *Association football and English society, 1863–1915* (Brighton, 1980).

Maurer, T., 'Der Krieg als Chance? Frauen im Streben nach Gleichberechtigung an deutschen Universitäten 1914–1918', in *Jahrbuch für Universitätsgeschichte*, 6 (2003), pp. 107–38.

McClelland, C. E., 'Berlin historians and German politics', in W. Laqueur and G. L. Mosse (eds.), *Historians in Politics* (London, 1974), pp. 191–221.

' "To live for science": ideals and realities at the University of Berlin', in T. Bender (ed.), *The University and the city*, (Oxford, 1988), pp. 162–85.

McDonald, Lyn, *The roses of No Man's Land* (New York, 1993).

McKibbin, Ross, *Classes and cultures; England 1918–1951* (Oxford, 1997).

McLeod, Hugh, *Piety and poverty: working-class religion in Berlin, London, and New York, 1870–1914* (New York, 1996).

Medd, Jodie, ' "The cult of the clitoris": anatomy of a national scandal', *Modernism/Modernity*, 9 (2002), pp. 21–49.

Mehnert, Gottfried, *Evangelische Kirche und Politik 1917–1919. Die politischen Strömungen im deutschen Protestantismus von der Julikrise 1917 bis zum Herbst 1919* (Düsseldorf, 1959).

Meinecke, S., *Friedrich Meinecke. Persönlichkeit und politisches Denken bis zum Ende des ersten Weltkrieges* (Berlin, 1995).

Meland, Bernard, *The secularization of modern cultures* (New York, 1966).

Merrington, W. R., *University College Hospital and its medical school: A history* (London, 1976).

Messinger, G. S., *British propaganda and the State in the First World War*, (Manchester, 1992).

Metzler, G., ' "Welch ein deutscher Sieg". Die Nobelpreise von 1919 im Spannungsfeld von Wissenschaft, Politik und Gesellschaft', *Vierteljahrheft für Zeitgeschichte*, 44 (1996), pp. 170–200.

Meuse, Jean-Jacques, *Paris-Palace ou le temps des cinémas 1894–1918* (Paris, 1995).

Meyer, Jacques, *Les soldats de la Grande Guerre* (Paris, 1966).

Meyer, K., *Theodor Schiemann als politischer Publizist* (Frankfurt am Main, 1956).

Meyer, Michael A. and Brenner, M. (eds.) *German-Jewish History in Modern Times* (New York, 1997).

Micale, Mark S. and Lerner, Paul (eds.), *Traumatic pasts: history, psychiatry, and trauma in the modern age, 1870–1930* (Cambridge, 2001).

Middell, Matthias, *Kulturtransfer und Vergleich* (Leipzig, 2000).

Milkovitch-Rioux, Catherine and Pickering, Robert (eds.), *Ecrire la guerre* (Paris, 2000).

Millman, Brock, *Managing domestic dissent in First World War Britain* (London, 2000).

Mommsen, Wolfgang J., 'Die Herausforderung der bürgerlichen Kultur durch die künstlerische Avantgarde. Zum Verhältnis von Kultur und Politik im Wilhelminischen Deutschland', *Geschichte und Gesellschaft*, 20 (1994), pp. 424–44.

Moriarty, Catherine, 'The absent dead and figurative First World War memorials', *Transactions of the Ancient Monuments Society*, 39 (1995), pp. 18–37.

' "Though in a picture only." Portrait photography and the commemoration of the First World War', in Gail Braybon (ed.), *Evidence, history and the Great War. Historians and the impact of 1914–18* (New York and Oxford, 2003), pp. 30–47.

Morris, J., *Religion and urban change: Croydon 1840–1914* (London, 1992).

Moses, John A., 'The mobilization of the intellectuals 1914–1915 and the continuity of German historical consciousness', *Australian Journal of Politics and History*, 48 (2002), pp. 336–52.

Mosse, George L., *Fallen soldiers. Reshaping the memory of the world wars* (Oxford, 1990).

Motherwell, Robert and Flam, Jack D. (eds.), *The Dada painters and poets* (Boston, 1981).

Müller, Heinrich, *Das Berliner Zeughaus. Vom Arsenal zum Museum* (Berlin, 1994).

Müller, Sven Oliver, 'Who is the enemy? The nationalist dilemma of inclusion and exclusion in Britain during the First World War', *European Review of History*, 9 (2002), pp. 63–83.

Murray, Williamson, *Les guerres aériennes, 1914–1945* (Paris, 2000).

Myers, Kevin, 'The hidden history of refugee schooling in Britain. The case of the Belgians, 1914–18', *History of Education*, 30 (2001), pp. 148–61.

Natter, Wolfgang G., *Literature at War 1914–1940. Representing the 'Time of Greatness' in Germany* (New Haven, 1999).

Nora, Pierre (ed.), *Les lieux de mémoire* (Paris, 1984–92, 7 vols.).

Nord, Deborah, *Walking the Victorian Streets* (Cornell, 1995).

Orlan, Pierre Mac, *Le bataillonnaire* (Paris, 1920; 1989 edn).

Otte, Marline, 'Sarrasani's theater of the world: Monumental circus entertainment in Dresden, from Kaiserreich to Third Reich', *German History*, 17 (1999), pp. 527–42.

Panayi, Panikos, 'Anti-German riots in London during the First World War' *German History* 7, 2 (1989), pp. 184–203.

'The British Empire Union in the First World War', in Tony Kushner and Kenneth Lunn (eds.), *The politics of marginality: race, the radical Right and minorities in twentieth-century Britain* (London, 1990).

The enemy in our midst. Germans in Britain during the First World War (Providence and Oxford, 1991).

Paret, Peter, *The Berlin secession. Modernism and its enemies in Imperial Germany* (Cambridge, Mass. and London, 1980).

Paris, Michael (ed.), *The First World War and popular cinema* (Edinburgh, 1999).

Parker, David H., ' "The talent at its command." The First World War and the vocational aspect of education, 1914–39', *History of Education Quarterly*, 35 (1995), pp. 233–47.

Parker, Peter, *The old lie. The Great War and the public-school ethos* (London, 1987).

Parsons, Deborah, *Streetwalking the Metropolis* (Oxford, 2000).

Pau-Hyries, Beatrix, 'Le transfert des corps des militaires de la Grande Guerre, 1914–1939. Etude comparée France-Italie/Belgique, Royaume-Uni, Etats-Unis'. Doctoral thesis, University of Montpellier, 2004.

Paul, H. W., *From knowledge to power: the rise of the science empire in France* (Cambridge, 1987).

Pedersen, Susan, 'Gender, welfare, and citizenship in Britain during the Great War', *American Historical Review*, 95 (1990), pp. 983–1006.

Penn, Alan, *Targeting schools. Drill, militarism and imperialism* (London and Portland, 1999).

Perreux, Gabriel, *La vie quotidienne des civils en France pendant la Grande Guerre* (Paris, 1966).

Perrot, Michelle (ed.), *Histoire de la vie privée*, vol. IV: *De la Révolution à la Grande Guerre* (Paris, 1986).

Peter, H. Rüdiger (ed.), *Schnorrer, Verschwörer, Bombenwerfer? Studenten aus dem Russischen Reich an deutschen Hochschulen vor dem 1. Weltkrieg* (Frankfurt am Main, 2001).

Pick, Daniel, *The war machine. The rationalisation of slaughter in the modern age* (New Haven, 1993).

Pierson, P., *100 ans d'histoire des jardins ouvriers 1896–1996* (Paris, 1996).

Pignot, Manon, *La guerre des crayons. Quand les petits Parisiens dessinaient la Grande Guerre* (Paris, 2004).

Poirier, J., *Les bombardements de Paris (1914–1918)* (Paris, 1930).

Porter, Patrick, 'Beyond comfort: German and English military chaplains and the memory of the Great War, 1919–1929', *Journal of Religious History* (2005).

Poser, Stefan, *Museum der Gefahren. Die gesellschaftliche Bedeutung der Sicherheitstechnik. Das Beispiel der Hygiene-Ausstellungen und Museen für*

Arbeitsschutz in Wien, Berlin und Dresden um die Jahrhundertwende (Münster, 1998).

Pourcher, Yves, 'La fouille de champs d'honneur', *Terrains*, 20 (March 1993), pp. 37–56.

Pratt, E. A., *British railways in the Great War* (London, 1921).

Pressel, B. W., *Die Kriegspredigt 1914–1918 in der evangelischen Kirche Deutschlands* (Göttingen, 1967).

Prévost, Cecile, *La mort, le deuil, le souvenir à Paris pendant la Première Guerre mondiale*, Master's thesis, University of Paris X, 2002.

Prevotat, J., 'La culture politique traditionaliste', in S. Berstein (ed.), *Les cultures politiques en France* (Paris, 1999).

Prochasson, Christophe, *Les intellectuels, le socialisme et la guerre, 1900–1938*, (Paris, 1993).

Prochasson, Christophe and Rasmussen, Anne, *Au nom de la patrie. Les intellectuels et la première guerre mondiale (1910–1919)* (Paris, 1996).

Prost, Antoine, *Histoire de l'enseignement en France 1800–1967* (Paris, 1968).

Les Anciens Combattants et la société française, 1914–1939 (Paris, 1977, 3 vols.).

'Verdun', in Pierre Nora (ed.), *Les lieux de mémoire*, La Nation, vol. III (Paris, 1992), pp. 111–42.

'Monuments to the dead', in Pierre Nora (ed.), *Realms of memory. The construction of the French past*, vol. II: *Traditions* (New York, 1997), pp. 307–30.

Republican identities in war and peace. Representations of France in the nineteenth and twentieth centuries (Oxford and New York, 2002).

'The contribution of the republican primary school to French national identity', in Antoine Prost, *Republican identities in war and peace. Representations of France in the nineteenth and twentieth centuries* (Oxford and New York, 2002), pp. 73–89.

Purseigle, Pierre (ed.), *Warfare and Belligerence. Perspectives in First World War Studies* (Leiden, Boston, 2005).

Rain, P., *Naissance de la science politique en France, 1870–1945* (Paris, 1963).

Rapp, Dean, 'Sex in the cinema. War, moral panic and the British film industry 1906–1918', *Albion*, 34 (2002), pp. 420–34.

Rappaport, Erika, *Shopping for pleasure: women in the making of London's West End* (Princeton, 2001).

Rasmussen, Anne, 'Mobiliser, remobiliser, démobiliser : les formes d'investissement scientifique en France dans la grande guerre', *14–18 Aujourd'hui-Today-Heute*, 6 (2003), pp. 49–59.

Reeves, Nicholas, 'Cinema, spectatorship and propaganda: "Battle of the Somme" (1916) and its contemporary audience', *Historical Journal of Film, Radio and Television*, 17 (1997), pp. 5–28.

'Official British film propaganda', in Michael Paris (ed.), *The First World War and popular cinema* (Edinburgh, 1999).

Reigl, Alois, 'The modern cult of monuments: its character and its origin', *Oppositions*, 25 (1982), pp. 21–51.

Reimann, Aribert, *Der grosse Krieg der Sprachen. Untersuchungen zur historischen Semantik in Deutschland und England zur Zeit des Ersten Weltkriegs* (Essen, 2000).

Reinhardt, Leslie Kaye, 'British and Indian identities in a picture by Benjamin West', *Eighteenth-Century Studies*, vol. 31, no. 3: 'Americas' (Spring, 1998), pp. 283–305.

Renken, Kathrin, ' "Die Kunst im Kriege". Eine Wanderausstellung des Deutschen Museums für Kunst in Handel und Gewerbe (Februar 1916–Juli 1917)', in Sabine Röder and Gerhard Storck (eds.), *Deutsches Museum für Kunst in Handel und Gewerbe. Moderne Formgebung 1900–1914* (Krefeld, 1997), pp. 400–8.

Reznick, Jeffrey S., *Healing the nation: soldiers and the culture of caregiving in Britain during the Great War* (Manchester, 2004).

Richter, Donald, *Riotous Victorians* (Athens, Ohio, 1981).

Rieger, Bernhard, 'Envisioning the future: British and German reactions to the Paris World Fair in 1900', in Martin Daunton and Bernhard Rieger (eds.), *Meanings of modernity. Britain from the late-Victorian era to World War II* (Oxford and New York, 2001), pp. 145–64.

' "Modern wonders". Technological innovation and public ambivalence in Britain and Germany, 1890s to 1933', *History Workshop Journal*, 55 (2003), pp. 152–76.

Rieger, Bernhard, *Technology and the culture of modernity in Britain and Germany, 1890–1945* (Cambridge, 2005).

Ringer, Fritz, *The decline of the German mandarins* (Cambridge, Mass., 1969).

Education and society in modern Europe (Bloomington and London, 1979).

Robert, Jean-Louis, 'Ouvriers et mouvement ouvrier parisien pendant la Grande Guerre et l'immédiat après-guerre: histoire et anthropologie', Doctorate, University of Paris – I, 1989.

Les ouvriers, la patrie et la Révolution, 1914–1919, Annales Littéraires de l'Université de Besançon (Besançon, 1995).

'Paris enchanté – le peuple en chansons (1870–1990)', in *Paris le peuple XVIIème–Xxème siècle* (Paris, 1999), pp. 195–206.

'La Parisienne aux Parisiens', Colloque 'Etre parisien', 26–28 September 2002, University of Paris – I.

'Les monuments aux morts de la Grande Guerre à Paris', in Charle, Christophe and Roche, Daniel (eds.), *Capitales culturelles, capitales symboliques: Paris et les expériences européennes, XVIIIe–XXe siècles* (Paris, 2002), pp. 130–55.

Röder, Sabine and Storck, Gerhard (eds.), *Deutsches Museum für Kunst in Handel und Gewerbe. Moderne Formgebung 1900–1914* (Krefeld, 1997).

Rolland, Romain, *Journal des années de la guerre 1914–1919: notes et documents pour server à l'histoire morale de l'Europe de ce temps* (Paris, 1952).

Rollet, Catherine, *La politique à l'égard de la petite enfance sous la Troisième République* (Paris, 1990).

Les enfants au XIXe siècle (Paris, 2001).

Rosenfield, Israel, 'Memory and identity', *New Literary History*, vol. 26, no. 1, Special Issue: 25th Anniversary. Narratives of Literature, the Arts, and Memory (Winter, 1995), pp. 197–203.

Rosenhaft, Eve, *Fighting the Fascists? The German Communists and political violence, 1929–1933* (Cambridge, 1983).

Roshwald, Aviel and Stites, Richard (eds.), *European culture in the Great War: the arts, entertainment, and propaganda, 1914–1918* (Cambridge, 1999).

Rossum, Gerhard Dohr van, *L'Histoire de l'heure. L'horlogerie et l'organisation moderne du temps* (Paris, 1997).

Rothblatt, Sheldon, 'London: a metropolitan university?', in Tom Bender (ed.), *The university and the city* (Oxford, 1988), pp. 119–49.

'State and market in British university history', in S. Collini, B. Young, and S. Whatmore, *British Intellectual History, 1750–1950. Economy, polity and society* (Cambridge, 2000), pp. 224–42.

The modern university and its discontents (Cambridge, 1997).

Rother, Rainer (ed.), *Die letzten Tage der Menschheit. Bilder des ersten Weltkrieges* (Berlin, 1994).

Roussel, Y., 'L'histoire d'une politique des inventions, 1887–1918', *Cahiers pour l'histoire du CNRS*, no. 3 (1989), pp. 19–57.

Roynette, Odile, *"Bons pour le service." L'expérience de la caserne en France à la fin du XIXe siècle* (Paris, 2000).

Rüger, Jan, 'Nation, empire and navy: identity politics in the United Kingdom, 1887–1918', *Past & Present*, no. 185 (2004), pp. 184–7.

Rüger, Jan, *The Great Naval Game: Britain and Germany in the Age of Empire* (Cambridge, 2007).

Rydell, Robert W., *World of fairs. The Century-of-Progress expositions* (Chicago and London, 1993).

Sanders, Lise Shapiro, ' "Indecent incentives to vice": regulating films and audience behaviour from the 1890s to the 1910s', in Andrew Higson (ed.), *Young and innocent? The cinema in Britain 1896–1930* (Exeter, 2002), pp. 97–110.

Sanders, M. L., 'Wellington House and British propaganda during the First World War', *Historical Journal*, 18 (1975), pp. 119–46.

Sanderson, Michael, *The universities and British industry, 1850–1970* (London, 1972).

Saul, Klaus, 'Jugend im Schatten des Krieges', *Militärgeschichtliche Mitteilungen*, 34 (1983), pp. 90–104.

Saunders, Nicholas, *Trench art. Materialities and memories of war* (Oxford and New York, 2003).

Schivelbusch, Wolfgang, *The Culture of defeat* (London, 2003).

Schlellenberg, Johanna, 'Probleme der Burgfriedenspolitik im ersten Weltkrieg. Zur innenpolitischen Strategie und Taktik der herrschenden Klassen von 1914 bis 1916', doctoral thesis, Humboldt University (East Berlin), 1967.

Schlör, Joachim, *Nights in the Big City. Paris, Berlin, London 1840–1930* (London, 1998).

Schmitz, Klaus, *Militärische Jugenderziehung. Preußische Kadettenhäuser und Nationalpolitische Erziehungsanstalten zwischen 1807 und 1936* (Cologne, Weimar and Vienna, 1997).

Schneider, Gerhard, 'Über hannoversche Nagelfiguren im Ersten Weltkrieg', *Hannoversche Geschichtsblätter*, 50 (1996), pp. 207–58.

'Zur Mobilisierung der "Heimatfront". Das Nageln sogenannter Kriegswahrzeichen im Ersten Weltkrieg', *Zeitschrift für Volkskunde*, 95 (1999), pp. 32–62.

Schneidereit, Otto, *Berlin wie es weint und lacht* (Berlin, 1968).

Scholder, Klaus, *The Churches and the Third Reich*, vol. I (Philadelphia, 1988).

Schor, R., *L'Opinion française et les étrangers. 1919–1939* (Paris, 1985).

Schroeder-Gudehus, Beatrice, *Les Scientifiques et la paix. La communauté scienti-fique internationale* (Montreal, 1978).

Schubert-Weller, Christoph, *'Kein schönrer Tod...'. Die Militarisierung der männ-lichen Jugend und ihr Einsatz im Ersten Weltkrieg 1890–1918* (Weinheim and Munich, 1998).

Schulte, Renata, 'Käthe Kollwitz's sacrifice', *History Workshop Journal* 41, (1996), pp. 193–221.

Schulte-Sasse, L., *Entertaining the Third Reich* (Raleigh, NC, 1996).

Schumann, Dirk, *Politische Gewalt in der Weimarer Republik, 1918–1933: Kampf um dir Straße und Furcht vor dem Bürgerkrieg* (Frankfurt am Main, 2001).

Schwartz, Vanessa R., *Spectacular realities: early mass culture in fin-de-siècle Paris* (Berkeley, 1998).

Seeberg, Reinhold, 'Invictis victi victuri', *Wir heissen Euch hoffen, vier akademische Reden* (Berlin, 1919).

Seeley, Robert and Rex Bunnett, *London musical shows on record: 1889–1989* (Harrow, Middlesex, 1989).

Sen, Amartya, *Poverty and famines: an essay on entitlement and deprivation* (Oxford, 1981).

Development as freedom (New York, 1999).

Sennett, Richard, *Flesh and stone. The body and the city in Western civilization* (New York and London, 1994).

Seton-Watson, H. and C., *The making of a new Europe: R. W. Seton-Watson and the last years of Austria-Hungary* (London, 1981).

Seton-Watson, R. W., 'The origins of the School of Slavonic Studies', *The Slavonic and East European Review* (January 1939), pp. 360–71.

Seymour, Lloyd, J., *Elections and how to fight them*, 2nd edn (London, 1909).

Sharp, A., 'Some relevant historians – the Political Intelligence Department of the Foreign Office, 1918–1920', *Australian Journal of Politics and History*, 34 (1989), pp. 359–68.

Shaw, Malcolm and Chase, Christopher (eds.), *The imagined past: history and nostalgia* (Manchester, 1989).

Shephard, Ben, *A War of Nerves* (London, 2000).

Sherington, Geoffrey, *English education, social change and war 1911–20* (Manchester, 1981).

Sherman, Daniel J., 'Objects of memory. History and narrative in French war museums', *French Historical Studies*, 19 (1995), pp. 44–57.

Sherman, Daniel J. and Rogoff, Irit (eds.), *Museum culture. Histories, discourses, spectacles* (London, 1994).

Shils, Edward, *Tradition* (Chicago, 1981).

Showalter, Elaine, *The female malady: women, madness, and English culture, 1830–1980* (New York, 1985).

Siegel, Mona, ' "History is the opposite of forgetting": the limits of memory and the lessons of history in interwar France', *Journal of Modern History*, 74 (2002), pp. 760–82.

Siegel, Mona L. *The moral disarmament of France. Education, pacifism, and patriotism, 1914–1940* (Cambridge, 2004).

Silver, Ken, *Esprit de corps. The art of the Parisian avant-garde and the First World War, 1914–1925* (Princeton, 1989).

Sirinelli, Jean-François, *Génération intellectuel, khâgneux et normaliens d'une guerre à l'autre* (Paris, 1988).

'Les intellectuals français et la guerre', in S. Audoin-Rouzeau and J.-J. Becker (eds.), *Les sociétés européennes et la guerre de 1914–1918* (Nanterre, 1990), pp. 130–47.

Smith, Leonard V., *Between mutiny and obedience: the case of the French Fifth Infantry Division during World War I* (Princeton, 1994).

Smither, Roger, ' "A wonderful idea of the fighting": the question of fakes in "The Battle of the Somme" ', *Historical Journal of Film, Radio and Television*, 13 (1993), pp. 149–69.

Snape, Michael F. and Parker, Stephen G., 'Keeping faith and coping: belief, popular religiosity and the British people,' in John Bourne, Peter Liddle, and Ian Whitehead (eds.), *The Great World War 1914–1945* (London, 2001), vol. II, pp. 400–18.

Soloway, Richard, 'Eugenics and pronatalism in wartime Britain' in J. M. Winter and R. Wall (eds.), *The upheaval of war* (Cambridge, 1988), pp. 369–88.

Sösemann, B., 'Politische Kommunikation im, "Reichsbelagerungszustand" – Programm, Struktur und Wirkungen des Klubs "Deutsche Gesellschaft 1914" ', in M. Bobrowsky and W. R. Langenbucher (eds.), *Wege zur Kommunikationsgeschichte* (Munich, 1987), pp. 630–49.

Soulez, Philippe, *Les Philosophes et la Guerre de 14* (Saint-Denis, 1988).

Stanca, L. M., *La chiesa italiana di San Pietro a Londra* (Rome, 2001).

Stark, Gary D. 'Cinema, society, and the state: policing the film industry in Imperial Germany', in Gary D. Stark and Bede Karl Lackner (eds.), *Essays on culture and society in modern Germany* (Arlington, Texas, 1982), pp. 122–66.

Stark, Gary D. and Lackner, Bede Karl (eds.), *Essays on culture and society in modern Germany* (Arlington, Texas, 1982).

Stauth, George and Turner, Brian (eds.), *Nietzsche's dance* (Oxford, 1988).

Stedman Jones, Gareth, 'The "Cockney" and the nation, 1780–1988', in David Feldman and Gareth Stedman Jones, *Metropolis: London, histories and representations since 1800* (London, 1989), pp. 272–324.

Steinberg, M., *Sabers and brown shirts. The German's path to National Socialism 1918–1945* (Chicago, 1977).

Stern, Fritz, *Einstein's German world* (Princeton, 1999).

Sternhell, Zeev, *La Droite révolutionnaire: les origines françaises du fascisme* (Paris, 1978).

Stevens, David (ed.), *The navy and the nation* (London, 2005).

Stewart, Susan, *On longing* (Baltimore, 1985).

Stierle, Karlheinz, *La capitale des signes. Paris et son discours* (Paris, 2001).

Stone, Lawrence, 'The size and composition of the Oxford student body, 1580–1909', in Stone (ed.), *Oxford and Cambridge from the 14th to the early 19th Century* (Princeton, 1974).

Stott, C., *Dick Sheppard: a biography* (London, 1977).

Strachan, Hew, *The First World War*, volume I: *To arms* (Oxford, 2002).

Strandmann, Hartmut Pogge von, 'British and German Historians in 1914', in C. Stray, *Classics transformed: schools, universities and society in England, 1830–1960* (Oxford, 1998).

Stromberg, Roland, *Redemption by war: the intellectuals and 1914* (Lawrence, Kansas, 1982).

Stuchtey and P. Wende (eds.), *British and German historiography*, (Oxford, 2000).

Stüttgen, Dieter, *Die Preußische Verwaltung des Regierungsbezirks Gumbinnen 1871–1920* (Cologne and Berlin, 1980).

Süchting-Hänger, Andrea, ' "Kindermörder". Die Luftangriffe auf Paris, London und Karlsruhe im Ersten Weltkrieg und ihre vergessenen Opfer', in Dittmar Dahlmann (ed.), *Kinder und Jugendliche in Krieg und Revolution. Vom Dreißigjährigen Krieg bis zu den Kindersoldaten Afrikas* (Paderborn, 2000), pp. 73–92.

Sussman, George D., 'The end of the wet-nursing business in France, 1874–1914', *Journal of Family History*, vol. IV, no. 3 (1977), pp. 220–48.

Sutherland, Gillian, 'Education', in F. M. L. Thompson (ed.), *The Cambridge social history of Britain 1750–1950*, vol. III, *Social agencies and institutions* (Cambridge, 1990), pp. 119–69.

Sweeney, Regina M., *Singing our way to victory. French cultural politics and music during the Great War* (Middletown, Conn., 2001).

Syon, Guillaume de, *Zeppelin! Germany and the airship, 1900–1939* (Baltimore, 2002).

Szöllösi-Janze, M., *Fritz Haber 1868–1934. Eine Biographie* (Munich, 1998).

Talbott, J., *The politics of educational reform* (Princeton, 1969).

Tartakowsky, Danielle, *Les manifestations de rue en France, 1918–1968*, (Paris, 1997).

'. . . Nous descendrons sur les boulevards', in Bernard Landau, Claire Monod, and Evelyne Lohr (eds.), *Les grands boulevards: un parcours d'innovation et de modernité* (Paris, 2000), pp. 197–201.

Tartakowsky, Danielle, *Nous irons chanter sur vos tombes. Le Père-Lachaise, XIXe–XXe siècle* (Paris, 1999).

Tate, Trudi, *Modernism, history and the First World War* (Manchester and New York, 1998).

Taylor, D., *The godless students of Gower Street* (London, 1968).

Thiers, E., 'Intellectuels et culture de guerre 1914–1918. L'Exemple du comité d'études et de documents sur la guerre', DEA, EHESS 1996.

Thom, Deborah, 'Making spectaculars. Museums and how we remember gender in wartime', in Gail Braybon (ed.), *Evidence, history and the Great War. Historians and the impact of 1914–18* (New York and Oxford, 2003), pp. 48–66.

Thompson, F. M. L. (ed.), *The Cambridge social history of Britain 1750–1950*, vol. III: *Social agencies and institutions* (Cambridge, 1990).

(ed.), *The University of London and the world of learning, 1836–1986* (London, 1990).

Thoss, B., 'Einjährig-Freiwillige' in G. Hirschfeld *et al.* (eds.), *Enzyklopädie Erster Weltkrieg* (Paderborn, 2003), p. 452.

Thuilier, Guy, *La vie quotidienne des professeurs de professeurs de 1870 à 1940* (Paris, 1982).

Tippett, Maria, *Art at service of war. Canada, art, and the Great War* (Toronto and London, 1984).

Toeplitz, Jerzy, *Geschichte des Films* (Munich, 1973).

Townshend, Charles, *Making the peace: public order and public security in modern Britain* (Oxford, 1993).

Trentmann, Frank (ed.), *Paradoxes of civil society. New perspectives on modern German and British history* (New York and Oxford, 2000).

Trevisan, Carine, 'Le silence du permissionnaire', in Catherine Milkovitch-Rioux, and Robert Pickering (eds.), *Ecrire la guerre* (Paris, 2000), pp. 201–9.

Les fables du deuil. La Grande Guerre: mort et écriture (Paris, 2001).

Uehlein, Georg (ed.), *Kreuz und Pickel haube: großstädtische Gesellschaft und Kirche zwischen 1850 und 1945 am Beispiel der Heilig-Kreuz-Gemeinde in Berlin* (Berlin, 1995).

Ulrich, Bernd, ' "... als wenn nichts geschehen wäre". Anmerkungen zur Behandlung der Kriegsopfer während des Ersten Weltkriegs', in Gerhard Hirschfeld, Gerd Krumeich, and Irina Renz (eds.), *'Keiner fühlt sich hier mehr als Mensch...' Erlebnis und Wirkung des Ersten Weltkriegs* (Frankfurt am Main, 1996), pp. 130–46.

Ulrich, Bernd, *Die Augenzeugen. Deutsche Feldpostbriefe in Kriegs- und Nachkriegszeit 1914–1933* (Essen, 1997).

Ungern-Sternberg, J. and W. von, *Der Anruf 'An die Kulturwelt': Das Manifest der 93 und die Anfänge der Kriegspropaganda im Ersten Weltkrieg,* (Stuttgart, 1996).

Van der Burgh, C. V. G. et al. (eds.), *Secularization in global perspective* (Amsterdam, c1981).

Veitch, Colin, ' "Play up! Play up! And win the war!" Football, the nation and the First World War', *Journal of Contemporary History*, 20 (1985), pp. 363–78.

Véray, Laurent, *Les films d'actualité de la Grande Guerre* (Paris, 1995).

Verhey, Jeffrey, 'Tönnies Begriff der "öffentlichen Meinung", oder: das Demokratieverständnis eines Vernunftrepublikaners', in Wolfgang Bialas and Georg Iggers (eds.), *Weimarer Intellektuelle: Neue Interpretationen* (Frankfurt am Main, 1996), pp. 159–76.

The spirit of 1914: militarism, myth and mobilization in Germany (Cambridge, 2000).

Vickery, Amanda (ed.), *Women, privilege and power: British politics, 1750 to the present*, The Making of Modern Freedom Series (Stanford, CA, 2001).

Vilain, Charles, *Le Soldat inconnu: histoire et culte* (Paris, 1933).

Villermet, B., 'Une grande école dans la tourmente: l'École Polytechnique pendant la Première Guerre mondiale, 1914–1920', *Bulletin de la société des amis de la Bibliothèque de l'École Polytechnique*, 10 (1993), pp. 5–62.

Vincent, G., *Sciences Po. Histoire d'une réussite* (Paris, 1987).

Voigt, G., *Otto Hoetzsch 1876–1946. Wissenschaft und Politik im Leben eines deutschen Historikers* (Berlin, 1978).

Voldman, Danièle, 'Les populations civiles, enjeux du bombardement des villes (1914–1945)', in Audoin-Rouzeau, Becker, Ingrao, and Rousso (eds.), *La violence de guerre 1914–1945* (Paris, 2002), pp. 151–73.

Walkowitz, Judith R., *City of dreadful delight: narratives of sexual danger in late-Victorian London* (London, 1992).

'The "vision of Salome": cosmopolitanism and erotic dancing in central London, 1908–1918', *American Historical Review*, 108 (2003), pp. 337–76.

Wall, Richard, 'English and German families and the First World War, 1914–18', in Richard Wall and Jay Winter (eds.), *The upheaval of war. Family, work and welfare in Europe, 1914–1918* (Cambridge, 1988), pp. 56–97.

Wall, Richard and Winter, Jay (eds.) *The upheaval of war. Family, work and welfare in Europe 1914–1918* (Cambridge, 1988).

Wallace, S., *War and the image of Germany, 1914–1918* (Edinburgh, 1988).

Waller, Philip, 'Altercation over civil society: the bitter cry of the Edwardian middle classes' in J. Harris (ed.), *Civil society in British history* (Oxford, 2003), pp. 115–34.

Walsh, Michael J. K., *C. R. W. Nevinson. This cult of violence* (New Haven and London, 2002).

Weber, Eugen, *The Action Française: royalism and reaction in twentieth-century France* (Stanford, 1962).

Weber, T., 'Studenten', in G. Hirschfeld *et al.* (eds.), *Enzyklopädie Erster Weltkrieg* (Paderborn, 2003), pp. 910–12.

Weindling, Paul (ed.), *The social history of occupational health* (London, 1985).

Weisz, George, 'Associations et manifestations: les étudiants français de la Belle Epoque', *Le Mouvement social* (July–September 1982), pp. 31–44.

The emergence of modern universities in France, 1863–1914, (Princeton, 1983).

Welch, David A., 'Cinema and society in Imperial Germany 1905–1918', *German History* 8 (1990), pp. 28–45.

Welch, David, *Germany, propaganda and total war, 1914–1918. The sins of omission* (London, 2000).

Weller, Ken, *Don't be a soldier! The radical anti-war movement in North London, 1914–1918* (London, 1985).

Wettmann, A., *Heimatfront Universität. Preußische Hochschulpolitik und die Universität Marburg im Ersten Weltkrieg* (Cologne, 2000).

Wetzel, Richard, *Inventing the criminal: A history of German criminology, 1880–1945* (Chapel Hill, 2000).

Whalen, Robert, *Bitter wounds. German victims of the Great War, 1914–1939*, (Ithaca, 1984).

Whitford, Frank (ed.), *The Berlin of George Grosz: drawings, watercolours and prints, 1912–1930* (New Haven, 1997).

Wilhelm, Jacques, *Les peintres du paysage parisien* (Paris, 1933).

Paris vu par les peintres (Paris, 1961).

Wilkinson, A., *The Church of England and the First World War* (London, 1978).

Williams, David, *Keeping the peace: the police and public order* (London, 1967).

Williams, S. C., *Religious belief and popular culture in Southwark, c. 1880–1939* (Oxford, 1999).

Willner, A. M. and Reichert, Heinz, *Das Dreimäderlhaus. Singspiel in drei Akten. Musik nach Franz Schubert. Für die Bühne bearbeitet von Heinrich Berté* (Leipzig and Vienna, n.d.).

Wils, L., *Flamenpolitik en aktivisme. Vlaanderen tegenover Belgie in de eerste wereldoorlog* (Louvain, 1974).

Wilson, Bryan R., *Religion in secular society: a sociological comment* (London, 1966).

Winkler, Henry R., *The League of Nations movement in Great Britain, 1914–1918* (New Brunswick, NJ, 1952).

Winter, Jay, 'Balliol's "Lost generation" of the First World War', *Balliol College Record*, 1975, pp. 1–11.

The experience of World War I (London and Basingstoke, 1988).

Sites of memory, sites of mourning. The Great War in European cultural history (Cambridge, 1995).

'British national identity and the First World War', in S. J. D. Green and R. C. Whiting (eds.), *The boundaries of the state in modern Britain* (Cambridge, 1996), pp. 261–77.

'Popular culture in wartime Britain', in Aviel Roshwald and Richard Stites (eds.), *European culture in the Great War: the arts, entertainment, and propaganda, 1914–1918* (Cambridge, 1999), pp. 339–40.

The Great War and the British people (London: 2nd edn., 2002).

Winter, Jay and Baggett, Blaine, *The Great War and the shaping of the twentieth century* (New York, 1996).

Winter, Jay and Prost, Antoine, *The Great War in history: debates and controversies 1914 to the present* (Cambridge, 2005).

Winter, Jay and Robert, Jean-Louis, *Capital cities at war. Paris, London, Berlin 1914–1919* (Cambridge, 1997).

Winter, Jay, Parker, Geoffrey, and Habeck, Mary R. (eds.), *The Great War and the twentieth century* (New Haven, 2000).

Wippermann, Klaus W., 'Die deutschen Wochenschauen im Ersten Weltkrieg', *Publizistik* 16 (1971), pp. 268–78.

Wirsching, Andreas, *Vom Weltkrieg zum Bürgerkrieg? Politischer Extremismus in Deutschland und Frankreich, 1918–1933/39. Berlin und Paris im Vergleich* (Munich, 1999).

Wittmer, Pierre, *Paul Landowski à Paris, une promenade de sculpture* (Paris, 2001).

Wohl, Robert, *The Generation of 1914* (Cambridge, Mass., 1979).

Wolff, T. *Tagebücher 1914–1919*, ed. B. Sosemann (Boppard am Rhein, 1984) (2 vols.).

Woodehouse, D. C., *Anti-German sentiment in Kingston upon Hull: The German community and the First World War* (Kingston upon Hull, 1990).

Woollacott, Angela, ' "Khaki Fever" and its control: gender, class, age and sexual morality on the British homefront in the First World War', *Journal of Contemporary History*, 29 (1994), pp. 325–47.

Wright, J., *'Above Parties'. The political attitudes of the German Protestant Church leadership 1918–1933* (London, 1974).

Wright, Patrick, *Tank. The progress of a monstrous war machine* (London, 2000).

Yankelévitch, Vladimir, *L'irriversible et la nostalgie* (Paris, 1974).

Yarrow, Stella, 'The impact of hostility on Germans in Britain, 1914–1918', in Tony Kushner and Kenneth Lunn (eds.), *The politics of marginality: race, the radical Right and minorities in twentieth-century Britain* (London, 1990), pp. 89–107.

Zahn-Harnack, A. von, *Adolf von Harnack* (Berlin, 1951).

Ziemann, Benjamin, *Front und Heimat. Ländliche Kriegserfahrungen im südlichen Bayern 1914–1923* (Essen, 1997).

Ziemann, Benjamin, 'Die deutsche Nation und ihr zentraler Erinnerungsort. Das "Nationaldenkmal fur die Gefallenen im Weltkriege" und die Idee des "Unbekannten Soldaten" 1914–1935', in Helmut Berding, Klaus Heller, and Winfried Speitkamp (ed.), *Krieg und Erinnerung, Fallstudien zum 19. und 20. Jahrhundert* (Göttingen, 2000), pp. 67–92.

Zippel, Martin, *Untersuchung zur Militärgeschichte der Reichshauptstadt Berlin von 1871 bis 1945* (Berlin, 1982).

Zuelzer, W., *The Nicolai case, a biography* (Detroit, 1982).

Zwach, Eva, *Deutsche und englische Militärmuseen im 20. Jahrhundert. Eine kulturgeschichtliche Analyse des gesellschaftlichen Umgangs mit Krieg* (Munster, 1999).

Index

Studies in the Social and Cultural History of Modern Warfare